Urban Life

Fifth Edition

D0710132

Urban Life

Readings in the Anthropology of the City   Fifth Edition

George Gmelch
University of San Francisco

Robert V. Kemper
Southern Methodist University

Walter P. Zenner
late of the State University of New York at Albany

WAVELAND
PRESS, INC.
Long Grove, Illinois

For information about this book, contact:
    Waveland Press, Inc.
    4180 IL Route 83, Suite 101
    Long Grove, IL 60047-9580
    (847) 634-0081
    info@waveland.com
    www.waveland.com

10-digit ISBN 1-57766-634-8
13-digit ISBN 978-1-57766-634-9

Printed in the United States of America

7 6 5

To our mentors—
Elvin Hatch and George M. Foster
—who set us on the path to urban anthropology

Contents

PART 4
Migration and Adaptation

PART 5
Globalization and Transnationalism

Preface

This volume provides students with access to research conducted by anthropologists and other social scientists on urban life and culture. We have sought broad coverage of the fieldwork strategies, theoretical issues, and global contexts for urban anthropology in the twenty-first century. The 29 chapters cover a wide geographic range, from North and South America to Europe and Africa, as well as the Middle East and Asia. This new edition of *Urban Life* offers a balance between classic studies and cutting-edge work, including 17 new chapters written exclusively for this volume.

When preparing the first edition of *Urban Life* (1980), the editors' emphasis was on finding clearly written accounts that would capture and hold the interest of our students. For each subsequent edition of the book (1988, 1996, 2002, and now 2010) we have continued that tradition. In planning this new edition, we surveyed our own students and queried our North American colleagues who had adopted earlier editions of *Urban Life* to determine which chapters were most widely used and should be retained. At professional meetings we queried other urban anthropologists in a search for scholars doing exciting new research and able to communicate with insight and clarity. As a result, over half the content of the Fifth Edition of *Urban Life* is new, and the collection has been reorganized to reflect the changing landscape of urban anthropology.

This edition of *Urban Life* is organized into five parts, each corresponding to a major focus in the field. Each part has an introduction, and each chapter begins with a headnote that highlights its significance. Part One deals with doing *fieldwork in the city*—the manner in which anthropologists have adapted their outlook and their research methods to the study of urban life. Part Two looks at *urban communities and places*, particularly the effects of urbanism on the social life and character of city dwellers. Part Three is concerned with *urban structures and institutions*, including poverty, social class, and family in the city. Part Four addresses *migration and adaptation*, a long-term interest of many anthropologists concerned with the city. Finally, Part Five considers urban anthropology's burgeoning interest in *globalization and transnationalism*.

Several themes underlie the selection of readings in *Urban Life*. The first is cross-cultural comparison, the testing of generalizations based on one culture with the experiences of other cultures. A second theme is the importance of small intimate groups among the masses of city inhabitants; such groups serve as a focus of urban life and help members maintain a meaningful pattern of expressive emotional relations. Most important is the familiar anthropological theme of adaptation—the strategies that individuals and groups use to cope with the demands of city life.

In the diverse urban settings where they carried out fieldwork, the contributors demonstrate their awareness of the demands posed by changing urban social environments and the ways in which people have learned to deal with them. Inherent in this ethnographic orientation is an understanding of the ideal-types of "the rural" and "the urban," and an awareness of how customs and institutions transcend such ideal-types in urban settings. Even when ethnographers focus on the urban adaptation of individuals and groups, we comprehend the city as a vital part of broader transnational and global systems.

The coeditor of earlier editions of *Urban Life*, Walter P. Zenner, passed away in 2003 at the age of 70, after a long fight with cancer. Robert V. Kemper, whose writings and assistance had been instrumental in preparing earlier editions of *Urban Life*, has taken over for Walter as coeditor. We thank Tom Curtin at Waveland Press, for his wise counsel and generous support, and Jeni Ogilvie, for corralling wayward grammar and superb editing. We are also grateful to Julie Adkins for special editorial assistance and to our student research assistants Sara Callahan and Diane Royal for vetting the dozens of readings considered for inclusion in this volume and for their critiques of the commissioned chapters. Thanks also to Rob Elias, Petra Kuppinger, and Kenji Tierney for sound advice. Above all, we are indebted to our colleagues who have contributed chapters prepared especially for this new edition of *Urban Life*—Julie Adkins, Danièle Bélanger, Caroline Brettell, Melissa Caldwell, Martin Cooke, Nell Gabiam, Sharon Gmelch, William Jankowiak, William Leggett, Karen Leonard, Setha Low, Ann Miles, Derek Pardue, Dianna Shandy, Jay Sokolovsky, Takeyuki Tsuda, James Diego Vigil, and Jeff Witsoe.

George Gmelch
Robert V. Kemper

PART 1

Urban Fieldwork
Anthropologists in Cities

In anthropology, "the field" refers to the place or cultural setting where anthropologists do their research. Until a few decades ago, most anthropologists did their "fieldwork" in non-Western societies, usually among tribal or peasant peoples. Ideally, this meant taking up residence in a village, learning the language, gaining rapport, and living as closely as possible to the way the "natives" did for a year or more. Many anthropologists still go to remote and unfamiliar places to do this kind of fieldwork, but, as the interests of anthropologists have broadened, so have the kinds of places where anthropologists do research. Today, the field can be just about anywhere—from a local neighborhood in the anthropologist's hometown to a faraway place, rarely visited by outsiders.

Regardless of geographic location or cultural group, the notion of *the field*—especially of being "in the field"—is for anthropologists symbolically and emotionally loaded. "Going to the field" means deep immersion and total absorption in the life of another culture. Doing fieldwork is a rite of passage and a crucible for turning graduate students into professional anthropologists (cf. Bernard 2011; Kemper and Royce 2002). Four of the chapters in Part 1 describe fieldwork that was first undertaken by the anthropologists (Bestor, S. Gmelch, Caldwell, and Leggett) when they were graduate students.

Part 1 opens with a chapter by George M. Foster and Robert V. Kemper that offers a historical overview of the fieldwork tradition in anthropology and the recent shift from rural to urban research. The next four chapters are all case studies in which anthropologists—Ted Bestor, Sharon Gmelch, Melissa Caldwell, and William Leggett—describe their urban fieldwork in four very different field settings: a neighborhood in Tokyo; a Traveller camp in Dublin, Ireland; a soup kitchen in Moscow; and a corporate office in Jakarta, Indonesia. The final chapter compares the fieldwork of students in Barbadian villages with the fieldwork of students in Hobart, the capital city of Tasmania.

In most field settings, anthropologists hope to reside among their research subjects, but this is not always possible in the city. For one, the mem-

1

bers of the group being studied in a city may not all live in the same neighborhood; instead, they may be dispersed across the city. Many of Melissa
Caldwell's and William Leggett's informants were scattered across Moscow
and Jakarta, respectively. Sharon Gmelch lived in a flat and commuted to the
distant camps of the Irish Travellers she wished to study for weeks before
finally being invited to move into a camp. Not surprisingly, nonresident fieldworkers often have more difficulty gaining the confidence of the people they
study than do fieldworkers who live in the neighborhood. Moreover, important activities often take place at times when the commuting anthropologist is
not present.

Even when urban anthropologists are able to live among their research
subjects, gaining access to informants is usually more difficult in cities than in
villages. With less outdoor space available, city dwellers tend to spend more
time inside their living quarters, making it more difficult for the fieldworker
to observe them or approach them. The nature of wage-paying jobs in the city
and the constraints of time are also important factors when it comes to interacting with informants. Most urbanites are employees: they work for someone else and keep regular hours at a workplace some distance from home.
Unlike rural anthropologists who may accompany their informants to their
gardens or fields, go on a hunt, or sit with them while they are making crafts
or repairing equipment, urban anthropologists often cannot observe or interview their informants in their workplace without interfering. Hence, in urban
societies, potential informants may be unavailable for much of each day. William Leggett actually took a job in the Indonesian corporate setting he wished
to study in order to gain access. The greater difficulty in finding people to
interview in the city is apparent in George and Sharon Gmelch's comparison
of the experiences of anthropology students in rural and urban field schools.

Offsetting some of the difficulties of urban field research are certain benefits absent in research among peasant and tribal societies. One resource
available to urban anthropologists is an enormous amount of data collected
in government censuses and surveys, which are available to researchers in
city and university archives. Sharon Gmelch relates the psychological boost
such easily accessed sources of information provided her during emotional
lows and slack periods in her fieldwork. In rural villages, fieldworkers often
must collect basic demographic information firsthand, through the time-con-
suming administration of household censuses.

Another benefit of urban fieldwork is the ease with which the anthropologist can escape the stresses of the field situation. Cities offer all sorts of
opportunities for recreation and entertainment—movies, fine restaurants,
museums, art galleries, etc.—that can provide a welcome relief from the fieldwork. In the city center, whether it is Bogotá or Kathmandu, anthropologists
may, if they need to, speak their own language, read *Time* or the *Herald Tri-
bune*, watch an American film, or buy a hamburger. As George M. Foster and
Robert V. Kemper note in their chapter, anthropologists may also make contact with local scholars who can offer sound advice and assurances that field

problems—real or imagined—are not as serious or intractable as they often appear. Anthropologists working in the countryside have very few of these outlets. When feeling lonely or alienated they must fall back on their own resources, such as writing in their journals, going for long walks, or escaping into the imaginary world of novels.

References

Bernard, H. Russell. 2011. *Research Methods in Anthropology: Qualitative and Quantitative Methods*, 5th ed. Walnut Creek, CA: AltaMira Press.

Kemper, Robert V., and Anya Peterson Royce, eds. 2002. *Chronicling Cultures: Long-Term Field Research in Anthropology.* Walnut Creek, CA: AltaMira Press.

Readings in Part 1

1. *Anthropological Fieldwork in Cities,* by George M. Foster and Robert V. Kemper

2. *Networks, Neighborhoods, and Markets: Fieldwork in Tokyo,* by Theodore C. Bestor

3. *Nomads in the City: Studying Irish Travellers,* by Sharon Bohn Gmelch

4. *Moscow Encounters: Ethnography in a Global Urban Village,* by Melissa L. Caldwell

5. *Fieldwork in the Corporate Offices of Jakarta, Indonesia,* by William Leggett

6. *Student Fieldworkers in Village and City,* by George Gmelch and Sharon Bohn Gmelch

1

Anthropological Fieldwork in Cities

George M. Foster and Robert V. Kemper

This chapter traces the development of the fieldwork tradition in anthropology, placing the field of urban anthropology in its historical context. The authors show how fieldwork in rural areas—first among tribes and later among peasants— shaped the interests and techniques of anthropologists who came to conduct research in contemporary cities. While exploring the problems and the advantages encountered in doing urban research, Foster and Kemper also reevaluate the ethical implications of shifting anthropologists' traditional role as neutral observer toward being collaborator with and advocate for the people we study.

Anthropologists are latecomers to urban research. By the 1920s sociologists were doing systematic research in American cities, especially through the efforts of the "Chicago School," and since that time most sociological research has dealt with urban phenomena. In contrast, the earliest anthropological research on city life took place only after World War II, and widespread interest in urbanization developed only in the 1960s and 1970s. Whereas urban sociology is a mature discipline, urban anthropology is still in its professional adolescence.[1] Only in the past two decades have we defined the parameters of the field, identified the topics to be studied, settled upon the most appropriate research strategies, and come to grips with new problems of ethics and relevance.

This recent interest in cities is the third—and probably the final—major revolution in anthropology's definition of its subject matter. When anthropology emerged as a formal science at the end of the nineteenth century it was concerned exclusively with "primitive" (i.e., nonliterate) peoples. Then, about 1940, interest began to shift to peasant societies, the rural dimension of traditional cultures. Now, as we turn to cities, we again face a major change.

Source: Adapted from the authors' previous work, Introduction: A Perspective on Anthropological Fieldwork in Cities. In *Anthropologists in Cities*, eds. George M. Foster and Robert V. Kemper, pp. 1–17. Boston: Little, Brown, 1974.

During these transformations the research goals, the definitions of problems, and the kinds of hypotheses that intrigued anthropologists have varied greatly. One principle, however, has remained constant: the anthropologists' dedication to fieldwork as a primary data-gathering strategy. Whether interested in tribal peoples, peasant villagers, or city dwellers, anthropologists believe that the richest, most complete information on how people live comes from direct, personal participation in gathering this information.

IN THE BEGINNING

Anthropologists have not always insisted that fieldwork is their basic data-gathering technique. With rare exceptions nineteenth-century anthropologists relied upon the descriptions of native life published by missionaries, colonial administrators, and travelers for the data on which they based their theories and hypotheses. Only when anthropology became a legitimate academic discipline at the turn of the century, with formal Ph.D. graduate programs, was field research accepted as essential to professional preparation and practice. In America, Franz Boas was the teacher most influential in standardizing this new approach to data gathering.

In some ways research methods have changed very little since those early days. Most anthropologists still draw the greater part of their data from first-hand contact with relatively small numbers of people. In other ways, though, the changes have been great. New research goals have been formulated, and field trips have grown longer. When Boas, Clark Wissler, A. L. Kroeber, Robert Lowie, and others of their generation began their research, anthropology was assumed to be a historical discipline rather than a social science. Faced with a bewildering array of languages, cultures, and physical types, anthropologists saw as their task the discovery of the origins and migrations of the world's people, especially "primitive" societies lacking written histories. In the United States, most indigenous cultures had already changed greatly as a consequence of white contact. Because even greater changes seemed inevitable, a related goal of field research here was to draw upon the memories of the oldest surviving Indians to reconstruct as completely as possible the "untouched" precontact situation.

Since most data gathering consisted of sitting with elderly Indians (who were usually paid for their help) and writing down what they remembered of earlier years, anthropologists needed little field equipment. As late as 1937, when Foster was preparing for his first research among the Yuki Indians of California, the only advice he received from his professor, A. L. Kroeber, was to "buy a pencil and a stenographer's notebook." In the United States prior to World War II, field trips were usually short, often limited to a summer's vacation. Even the largest departments of anthropology had only three or four staff members, and long leaves were difficult to arrange. Moreover, the research goals of ethnographers led them to see little advantage in spending twelve or more continuous months in the field; instead, they worked over several summers, beginning again each year where they had stopped the summer before. In the first quarter of the twentieth century, most American Indian tribes were disrupted and acculturated. This fact, plus the "memory culture" orientation of fieldworkers, combined to convince anthropologists that no single group needed or justified more than a few months' study. Because native peoples appeared to be dying out, anthropologists felt it their scientific responsibility to survey all groups, rather than to study intensively a few and neglect the rest.

Even in these relatively short, early field trips the distinctive methodological characteristic of anthropology was apparent. From the beginning anthropologists formed close personal ties with the people they studied, and almost all anthropologists of that period have written affectionately about their key informants, some of whom became lifelong friends. Anthropologists quickly realized that the best and most accurate data come from persons who like and trust them. Hence, "establishing rapport" came to be an anthropologist's first assignment upon arriving in the field: to search out the most knowledgeable individuals, present oneself to them in a plausible and empathetic role, and make friends. Without fully realizing it, these early anthropologists were inventing the "depth" interview—the ability to talk with, to probe, to "pump" informants, day after day, in order to extract maximum information about their history and culture. Today, in cities as in rural areas, most anthropologists retain this basic philosophy: good rapport with good friends, trust and confidence, and abundant conversation over long periods of time.

Fieldwork in the United States during the first third of the twentieth century was strongly conditioned by restrictions of time, distance, and money. Research in the West involved train trips of from three to six days in each direction, often followed by stagecoach, riverboat, or horseback rides to the final destination. Sources of financial support were limited, and long and costly trips of the type now routinely undertaken would have been difficult indeed. When, in the late 1920s and 1930s, American anthropologists began to embark on research in more distant areas, it was not unusual to spend six weeks in merely reaching the field site. Now that the most distant parts of the earth are rarely more than 24 hours away, young anthropologists often forget how huge the world was only a little over a generation ago.

As long as the emphasis of American anthropology was on the disappearing tribe, field research methods, including "scientific" equipment, changed very little. The first bulky portable typewriters, the Kodak camera, and primitive cylinder recording machines were occasionally carted to the reservation, but the pencil (or fountain pen) and the stenographer's notebook continued to be the only indispensable items of equipment.

THE BRITISH REVOLUTION

In England, meanwhile, a revolution in the concept of field research was occurring: long-term analysis of a viable community, emphasizing form and function in their synchronic rather than their diachronic dimensions. Tribal origins, it was assumed, were lost in dim antiquity; they could never be known. What *could* be known was the structure of the contemporary group, its form and content, and the way this system functioned. Anthropology was thus converted into a social science. Although he was not the first anthropologist to live for a long period with a single people, the Polish-born, British-naturalized Bronislaw Malinowski justly receives credit for introducing this new approach to fieldwork. Beginning in the early 1920s at the London School of Economics, he taught his students what he had discovered a few years earlier on the Trobriand Islands: live with the people, learn their language, observe their activities, question, speculate, theorize.

Malinowski and his students were favored in their revolutionary endeavors by conditions in the British Empire. Most of the Commonwealth's "native" peoples belonged to viable societies that functioned with much of their precontact vigor; they certainly were not disappearing. There was little need to press for "salvage" ethnography, to record while there was still time. Consequently, young anthropologists with enough financial support could afford to spend as much time as needed with a single group, untroubled by the nagging thought that they should turn their attention to disappearing groups elsewhere. Wherever they worked, field researchers were not foreigners; they were simply in parts of the Commonwealth where the societies were more exotic than at home. The British colonial service encouraged anthropological research, and the Union Jack flying at the District Officer's headquarters symbolized the special privileges that anthropologists could expect from government and native peoples alike. Under Malinowski's tutelage, and favored by the colonial setting—especially in Africa—a new generation of British social anthropologists produced superb monographs on a wide variety of topics which even today are required reading in most doctoral programs.

In the United States, research sophistication lagged behind that of England for a number of years; we lacked a Malinowski, and we were still committed to recording the ways of disappearing societies. The first American anthropologist to adopt the new approach, 10 years after Malinowski's pioneering efforts, was Margaret Mead, who in 1925 set out for nine months' research in American Samoa. She was soon followed by Robert Redfield, who spent eight months in Tepoztlán, Mexico, during 1926–1927, and by Hortense Powdermaker, who went to Lesu, in New Ireland, for 10 months during 1929–1930. (Although American-born, Powdermaker was a student of Malinowski, so she is perhaps best thought of as carrying on a British tradition in the United States rather than beginning an American style of fieldwork.)

In spite of the demonstrable advantages of long-term fieldwork, quickly brought to the attention of American anthropologists in *Coming of Age in Samoa* (Mead 1928), *Tepoztlán* (Redfield 1930), and *Life in Lesu* (Powdermaker 1933), extended field trips did not become commonplace until after World War II. Although a growing number of American anthropologists made long trips to India and Africa shortly before the war, most doctoral candidates (and their professors as well) continued the old tradition of short trips.

After the war, however, American researchers rapidly adopted the British research pattern, for several reasons. First, we had just about run out of Indians. The fairly exhaustive product of 50 years of North American research, coupled with the accelerating rate of acculturation of native North Americans, meant that these tribes looked much less attractive as research subjects than they had a generation earlier. Second, transportation to distant parts of the world had vastly improved; even in 300-mph piston planes, most places were no more than 48 hours from the United States. Research support, too, was becoming more abundant than in earlier years, and for the first time anthropologists could seriously contemplate prolonged research in foreign countries.

THE DISCOVERY OF PEASANTS

In growing numbers American anthropologists now traveled to Latin America, Europe, Africa, and Asia. Some—particularly in Africa—studied tribal peoples, but a majority chose to work in small rural communities in modern or developing nations, for it was soon discovered that these peasant villages made ideal research sites. During the 1950s and 1960s, half or more of American anthropological fieldwork was carried out in such communities.

With the study of peasants came greatly improved data-gathering techniques. Now fully aware of the importance of observing as much as possible, of being present when significant events occurred, anthropologists tried to be as close as we could to the people we studied. Under ideal circumstances we were able to live with village families, to sleep and work in a spare room, and to share meals with them. When this was not feasible, we rented a house near the center of the village, usually hiring local women to cook, clean, wash clothes, babysit—and simultaneously to serve as informants to explain the meaning of what we saw. Now we had opportunities to attend weddings, funerals, baptisms, and other family and community rites on a scale that had never before been possible. For the first time that familiar, but much abused, phrase "participant observation" really came alive. We did not simply ask informants how people behaved; we saw with our own eyes what happened, so that our notes took on a richness, a depth, a detail rarely if ever achieved by earlier researchers.

Because we were observing real people acting out real roles, we needed to know more about them as individuals than in the earlier days of salvage ethnography: where they lived, who their relatives were, their occupations, their incomes and socioeconomic statuses, and the like. To gather this data we adopted the census as a basic technique to provide a factual and statistical framework for our observations and interviews. We also buckled down and learned the local language. Prior to this time relatively few American anthropologists had mastered the language of the people they studied, preferring to use bilingual informants or interpreters. Now we realized that language competence was essential to good fieldwork, and intensive language training became a basic part of every well-planned field trip.

In the post-World War II era more elaborate recording and coding techniques to control and retrieve ever greater quantities of data came into common use. For many anthropologists, the five-by-eight-inch card or sheet, filed according to the Human Relations Area File code, replaced the stenographer's notebook (Murdock et al. 1961). Technological advances likewise vastly facilitated fieldwork: portable typewriters became truly lightweight, miniature cameras replaced the old Kodaks, and flash equipment was perfected. Transistors made possible small tape recorders, which greatly simplified recording linguistic texts, folklore, and other data such as dreams and projective tests (e.g., the Rorschach and Thematic Apperception Tests), where textual accuracy is essential. Antibiotics reduced the apprehension of serious illness in the field, and with radios and telephones, anthropologists were usually less isolated even in remote countries than their professional ancestors had been among Indian tribes in Canada and the western United States. For those who had known the conceptual limitations and technological handicaps of earlier field research, the fifties and sixties were a great time to be a practicing anthropologist.

URBAN ANTHROPOLOGY

After about a generation of intensive fieldwork in peasant communities, anthropologists realized that significant changes were occurring in the research situation. For one thing, we felt that we had defined rather completely the parameters of peasant societies and had constructed models to explain much of their cross-cultural variation. So, as with the Indians a generation earlier, we appeared to be approaching a point of diminishing returns. At the same time, many of our peasant friends were ceasing to be peasants. Influenced by radio and television, work experiences in foreign countries, and the modernity that follows new roads, many of them gave up their folk costumes and their fiestas; they adopted tractors, fertilizers, and insecticides in farming; and they sent their children to secondary schools and universities. Others simply packed up and moved to cities, where they found work in factories or service fields and after a few years became town dwellers themselves.

To a large extent the transformation of traditional peasant societies and the mass exodus to the city explain the new interest of anthropologists in urban research. Beyond this, many of us are genuinely concerned with the social, ethnic, and economic problems so clearly seen in cities; we believe that anthropology, along with the other social sciences, can help to ameliorate these problems. Together these events and convictions have created a new field, *urban anthropology*.

From the beginning, the urban research of anthropologists has differed significantly from that of other social scientists and historians. While they have been concerned primarily with the technologically developed countries of Europe and North America, we have been especially interested in the growing cities of Latin America, Africa, and Asia. Our theoretical orientation, too, is different. Because the first people we knew well in these countries were peasants and tribesmen, who today are moving to the cities in increasing numbers, we have been curious about what happens to them in urban environments. As a result, anthropological urban studies have dealt largely with *urbanization*, the process by which rural emigrants settle in and adjust to urban life, rather than with the way of life in cities, which is commonly referred to as *urbanism* (cf. Wirth 1938). In addition, because we have been interested primarily in how people adjust to urban life, we have paid much less attention than have other social scientists to broader issues involving the operation of the urban *system* (i.e., the network of cities within a nation, the ways in which these cities are interrelated, and how the lives of urbanites and rural residents are influenced by large-scale demographic, political, economic, and sociological processes). And finally, although anthropologists have occasionally utilized the results of comparative statistical studies, which have become so important in political science, economics, and sociology, we have continued to offer theories about urbanization on the basis of firsthand field research.

The anthropological urban studies that have appeared since World War II, and especially since the 1960s, make it possible for us to trace common patterns in the urbanization process and to discern fruitful directions for future work. But with few exceptions (e.g., Whyte 1943; Liebow 1967; Leeds 1968) these reports tell us little or nothing about the urban fieldwork experience. For anthropologists, how does this research compare with that undertaken in peasant villages and tribal groups? What research techniques are equally valuable in both settings? What new methodologies must be developed (or borrowed from other disciplines) to investigate urbanites? Are anthropologists working in a city a new breed of scientist, "urban anthropologists," or do we differ from our rural-based colleagues only by our choice of field site? That is, are urban anthropologists simply mirror images of rural sociologists?

In the second part of this chapter we discuss how the rural fieldwork tradition consciously and unconsciously shapes the anthropologist's definition of urban problems, what features of conventional methodology are useful in the city, what urban research topics arise that require new approaches, and how urban research may force a reevaluation of the profession's present dilemma regarding "relevance" and ethics.

URBANITES AS RURAL PEOPLE

Accustomed as we are to working in small, "bounded" rural communities, anthropologists are often disconcerted by the amorphous and heterogeneous populations of large cities. How are the boundaries of the urban sample to be determined, and how should the fieldworker proceed with his or her study? As Anthony Leeds has pointed out (1968:31), we often try to solve this problem by concentrating on slums, squatter settlements, or ethnic minorities, on the assumption that they are analogous to the small rural villages we know, and that they can be investigated in similar fashion. This tendency to see urban peoples in the light of our rural experiences may have serious consequences, as Peter Gutkind has pointed out for Africa:

> The methodological traditions brought to this [urban] field of research are mostly those acquired by social anthropologists working in rural areas. It is this background which for long fostered the view that we were studying tribesmen in town and not townsmen in town. (1967:136)

As a consequence, he continues, "Far less attention has been paid to those Africans who have been resident in urban areas for a considerable length of time than to migrants and those less committed to urban life" (1967:143–144). We believe that Gutkind is correct in noting that anthropologists have been shortsighted in ignoring long-settled urbanites.

In urban research anthropologists face one insurmountable problem: defining a population in the holistic context taken for granted in rural fieldwork. We may investigate a group of migrants from a single village, migrants from many regions, or a group composed of migrants and urban natives. The group may be dispersed throughout the metropolitan zone, clustered in a few neighborhoods, or restricted to a single spatial unit as small as an apartment house (as in Oscar Lewis's well-known studies of *vecindades* in Mexico City). Alternatively, the population may be defined in social terms, as members of a religious sect, a voluntary association, a professional or occupational category. Selecting and delineating the urban population segment to be investigated is *the* critical first step in urban anthropological research.

Once this decision is made, another issue emerges: should anthropologists concentrate on the internal structure of the group or on the relations of its members to the rest of the urban population? Most anthropologists, following the community study approach, have chosen the former. But, as Leeds argues, this "has led to a thorough failure to justify the units of study used and the failure to show mutual effects between the asserted 'units' of study and the city in which they are immersed" (1968:31–32).

GETTING SETTLED

Although fieldworkers face different problems in defining the group to be studied in rural and urban settings, the difficulties of settling in—of finding a place to live, experiencing culture shock, establishing a plausible role, and finding informants—remain much the same. As we have seen, in village fieldwork anthropologists usually live with a family or maintain quarters in the middle of town, in either case residing among the people studied and constantly observing their daily life. In cities, arrangements of this kind are more difficult; families studied by anthropologists almost always live in crowded quarters with barely enough room for themselves, much less for a researcher and family. Rented rooms, too, are usually less attractive in urban slums than in peasant villages. Moreover, unless anthropologists decide to study a compact population—a suburban neighborhood, an inner-city slum, or a peripheral squatter settlement—we almost literally cannot live "with" the informants. As a result, when anthropologists study a general social institution or a group of people spread throughout the city, we nearly always find an apartment or house in a convenient area, then commute to visit informants.

This arrangement has advantages and disadvantages. On the one hand, anthropologists gain privacy, a comfort often denied us in tribal or village areas where we are a constant object of curiosity. When tired and irritated, and on those days when we hope never to see another informant, we can retire to comfortable lodgings to rest and recuperate. On the other hand, many anthropologists who have lived like this feel both guilty and cheated. Conditioned by colleagues to expect a close emotional identification with the people studied, even the most conscientious researchers may come to question whether they are doing a good job and whether they are in fact true anthropologists, if fieldwork must be carried out in circumstances where the anthropologist is isolated much of the time from the target population.

MEETING INFORMANTS

When beginning research in a village, anthropologists sometimes have letters to a few people, who in turn can introduce us to others. More often, though, for the first few days we simply wander the streets, talk to as many people as possible, lean over fences to chat and make friends, give candy and balloons to children, and in other encounters try to explain why we are in the village and what we hope to accomplish. In this informal way, friendships develop. Often anthropologists "scout" several communities, then choose the most accepting one. All of the people met in these early contacts are potential informants.

In contrast, only a few of the people urban anthropologists meet in the course of a day are potential informants. Although casual encounters may offer insights into city life, researchers must work at building a network of informants. As intermediaries we may use members of the group itself (e.g., a migrant whom we already know), local officials, or other social scientists who are known to the people we have selected for study.

Just as rapport-building techniques vary from one fieldworker to another, finding a suitable role depends as much on circumstances as on planning. For doctoral candidates, the role of student preparing him- or herself for a teaching career and required by professors to learn about another way of life is usually satisfactory. For older anthropologists, the reverse role of professor seems to work best, at least outside of the United States. Sometimes it is as difficult to avoid a negative role as to establish a positive one; most anthropologists have at one time or another been accused of being a CIA agent, a Protestant missionary (if working in a Catholic community), a social worker, a tax collector, or even a misguided tourist.

Robert V. Kemper interviewing a Tzintzuntzan migrant in Mexico City (1974). [Photo by Rafael Campuzano]

OFFICIAL AND PROFESSIONAL TIES

Whether anthropologists undertake research in a foreign country or in the United States, it is considered proper—and usually it is essential—to notify the appropriate governmental and anthropological authorities of the research plan and to obtain their permission *before* beginning work. These formalities sometimes seem a nuisance, but for urban anthropologists they often provide an introduction to potential associates in the fieldwork setting. Precisely because cities are centers for universities and government agencies, urban fieldworkers need not be isolated from professional and official assistance.

Relationships with government officials are extremely important to all anthropologists, for an unsympathetic person in a position of power can make research impossible, while a helpful official can open otherwise closed doors. Ties with local anthropologists can be especially rewarding. As experts in residence, they can point out possible problems in the research design, suggest alternate groups for investigation, and introduce the newcomer to potential informants. Of course, local social scientists may not always be helpful, but taking them into our confidence at the outset may prevent subsequent misunderstandings and usually makes for good relationships in the future. This is especially important if an anthropologist plans to return later to continue the research project or wishes to carry out related fieldwork in other cities in the same country.

Urban anthropologists are more fortunate than rural anthropologists in that professional and social obligations to local colleagues can easily be repaid by attending their professional meetings, joining their societies, teaching part-time in their institutions, and (if a separate residence is maintained during fieldwork) bringing them into his or her home. In addition, local scholars and students may be included in the research project, an important advantage in equalizing anthropological skills and training throughout the world. Urban fieldwork also offers young anthropologists an opportunity to meet the community of scholars they will know and cooperate with throughout their careers.

RURAL RESEARCH MODELS IN THE CITY

We have already seen that anthropologists tend to view urban populations from a rural perspective, to look upon them as transplanted villagers. Not surprisingly, then, research design and problem definitions are often based on rural models, on the assumption that what works well in the country will also work well in the city. This "jack-of-all-trades" approach stands in sharp contrast to most other social science models for urban research, where team members are chosen to provide interdisciplinary and interethnic perspectives. Although rich data and valuable theoretical insights have emerged from these anthropological studies, the size and complexity of urban environments clearly place limits on what can be accomplished by a lone fieldworker, even when aided by a trained spouse. Paid assistants are a partial solution to this problem, especially in taking a census and conducting social surveys, but they are no substitute for a genuine team approach, whose advantages have been summarized by John Price:

> The team represents a wide variety of academic skills and personalities that together produce a wider variety of ethnography than an individual does over a long period of time. Through formal and informal discussions, the team is able to create a productive information exchange. It also accelerates the generation and testing of hypotheses much more rapidly than individuals working alone. (1972:27)

Although the lone researcher will continue to make important contributions to urban studies, we believe that anthropologists working in cities will increasingly do so as members of social science teams.

In still another way, urban anthropologists reflect a decidedly rural bias: often many of their best data come from the personal relationships rural fieldworkers have long cherished. Although it may not provide a full picture of city life, the ethnographic interview, with contact over a long period of time between anthropologist and respondent, continues to be a major research technique in the city. When combined with the statistical survey approaches favored in the other social sciences, it may well prove to be the single most important contribution anthropologists can make to urban studies.

But despite the benefits of such deep and continuing relationships, there is clearly a need for census and questionnaire data beyond the limits common in rural research. Chance contacts alone are insufficient to provide the balance that marks first-class research. The conclusion we draw is that anthropologists contemplating urban fieldwork will need to devote much more attention than they have in the past to sociological research techniques such as survey research and the design and pretesting of interview schedules. Familiarity with computers, too, is essential if anthropologists are to make the best use of census and questionnaire materials.

Whether urban anthropologists carry out fieldwork alone or as team members, we must strike a balance between "total immersion" and dependence on the more formal techniques of the other social sciences. Andrew Whiteford has described the dilemma we face:

> Such approaches as sampling techniques, the use of census data, and statistical analysis of masses of data would appear to be absolutely necessary for understanding [urban phenomena], but their use also tends to impersonalize the research and deprive the worker of his most satisfying experience, the personal identification with the people being studied. (1960:2)

Anthropologists become easily disenchanted when close friendships with informants are replaced by limited, impersonal contacts with "subjects" or "respondents." But, however we might wish it were not so, we must recognize that in cities we can neither observe our informants with the same ease as in villages, nor expect as many contact hours with factory workers as with craftsworkers who labor at home. Thus, unless we are content to limit ourselves to the "street corner" variety of urban research (e.g. Whyte 1943; Liebow 1967), we must learn to combine the most valuable features of traditional research models with the quantitative methods common in the other social sciences.

ETHICS AND RELEVANCE

Urban research introduces many new ethical problems to anthropology. We are not dealing with nameless faces in the crowd when describing and commenting on important people in cities. Their roles are distinctive enough to make them easily identifiable no matter how we try to disguise them in our reports. And when the attitudes and lifestyles of the urban elite strike anthropologists as unattractive, and when our analyses are constantly unflattering, what are we to do? Like tribesmen or peasants, these upper-class urbanites have great power over us, to the point of making our research impossible.

Even the least visible city dwellers we study are often literate. They are more interested than villagers in the end product of our research, and they are anxious to see what we say about them. Increasingly, anthropological publications are translated into the languages of the people studied, and they can read about themselves. As anthropologists, we must become more concerned about their privacy, and about the harm that careless revelations might cause them.

Although most anthropologists have carried into their urban research the traditional anthropological stance of objectivity—the desire to find out about what life was like in the community in question, without major concern for resolving social problems—it seems inevitable that future urban research will be more concerned with "relevance," that it will be more "applied" than earlier work. Already we see signs of this. During her two years of fieldwork in the Ciudad Guayana project in Venezuela, Lisa Peattie found herself becoming an advocate of the poor people she studied and lived among, defending them against the "system" represented by the project coordinators and their elite clientele. Her description of the role of "The Social Anthropologist in Planning" (1967) and her "Reflections on Advocacy Planning" (1968) make thought-provoking reading for urban anthropologists concerned with the relevancy of their work. In the same way, the Valentines have argued convincingly that urban fieldworkers owe a debt to the people we study, the people who make our job possible. This debt can best be repaid, they believe, when anthropologists become attentive to community needs and attempt to help our informants to cope with the urban system.

This combined emphasis on ethics and applied urban anthropology has led to a reevaluation of the anthropological "prime directive"—our commitment not to interfere with "native" life unless it is absolutely necessary. This in turn has raised an even more fundamental question: Is the best fieldwork performed by "outsiders" or "insiders"? For instance, can Anglo anthropologists understand the lifestyles of urban African Americans, Hispanic Americans, or Native Americans—or, for that matter, any group outside the white middle class—without falling prey to unconscious prejudices? Anthropologists have assumed that on many points insiders are less perceptive observers than outsiders, just as a fish is unaware of the water it lives in until the tank is drained. As the literate, predominantly urban, ethnic minorities in the United States strive to establish their identities, and similar forces are at work in developing nations, this fundamental bias of anthropological research is being put to the test. And more often than not, it is urban anthropologists rather than our rural colleagues who must withstand these pressures.

The net result of these transformations is still unclear, but it seems unlikely that future anthropologists will be allowed to carry out their research without some regard to contemporary social problems or to the needs and feelings of their informants. Just as peasant migrants to the metropolis face a new world, so anthropologists moving from the "bush" to the city must adapt their ideas regarding fieldwork to fit a new environment.

The future of anthropology, we believe, lies largely in urban research. Yet the available evidence indicates that urban fieldwork is more difficult than rural, and that it is often emotionally less satisfying, because of the problems of maintaining close affective ties with informants. At the same time urban research presents anthropology with challenges and opportunities that cannot be ignored if the profession is to increase its contributions to social science theory and to the resolution of society's problems.

And if, as Morris Freilich suggests, we ourselves are "the critical tool in anthropological research" (1970:33), then the ingenuity anthropologists have shown in working in tribal and peasant communities will serve in equal measure to master the problems of urban fieldwork. Just as in rural areas, urban anthropologists will find adequate housing, establish good rapport, define a suitable social role, overcome culture shock, deal successfully with government officials and anthropological colleagues, and ultimately combine the best in traditional research methods with the new techniques required for sound urban research.

Note

[1] For more information about the professional development of urban anthropology, see Kemper 1991a, 1991b, 1993a, 1993b; Kemper and Kracht 1991; Kemper, Kracht, and Campos 1991; and Kemper and Rollwagen 1995.

References

Freilich, Morris, ed. 1970. *Marginal Natives: Anthropologists at Work.* New York: Harper & Row.

Gutkind, Peter. 1967. The Energy of Despair: Social Organizations of the Unemployed in Two African Cities: Lagos & Nairobi. *Civilizations,* 17:186–211.

Kemper, Robert V. 1991a. Urban Anthropology in the 1990s: The State of Its Practice. *Urban Anthropology,* 20:211–223.

———. 1991b. Trends in Urban Anthropological Research: An Analysis of the Journal *Urban Anthropology,* 1972–1991. *Urban Anthropology,* 20:373–384.

———. 1993a. Urban Anthropology: An Analysis of Trends in U.S. and Canadian Dissertations. *Urban Anthropology,* 22:1–8.

———. 1993b. Urban Anthropology: A Guide to U.S. and Canadian Dissertations. *Urban Anthropology,* 22:9–229.

Kemper, Robert V., and Benjamin Kracht. 1991. Directory of Urban Anthropologists. *Urban Anthropology,* 20:225–360.

Kemper, Robert V., Benjamin Kracht, and Stuart Campos. 1991. The Journal *Urban Anthropology*: An Index of Its First Twenty Years. *Urban Anthropology,* 20:385–553.

Kemper, Robert V., and Jack Rollwagen. 1995. Urban Anthropology. In *Encyclopedia of Cultural Anthropology,* eds. Melvin Ember and David Levinson, vol. 4, pp. 1337–1344. Lakeville, CT: American Reference Publishing.

Leeds, Anthony. 1968. Brazilian Careers and Social Structure: An Evolutionary Model and Case History. *American Anthropologist,* 70:1321–1347.

Liebow, Elliot. 1967. *Tally's Corner.* Boston: Little, Brown.

Mead, Margaret. 1928. *Coming of Age in Samoa: A Psychological Study in Primitive Youth for Western Civilization.* New York: William Morrow.

Murdock, George P., Clellan S. Ford, Alfred E. Hudson, Raymond Kennedy, Leo W. Simmons, and John W. M. Whiting. 1961. Outline of Cultural Materials. *Behavior Science Outlines,* vol. 1. New Haven, CT: Human Relations Area Files, Inc.

Peattie, Lisa. 1967. *The View from the Barrio.* Ann Arbor: University of Michigan Press.

———. 1968. Reflections on Advocacy Planning. *Journal of the American Institute of Planners,* 34:80–88.

Powdermaker, Hortense. 1933. *Life in Lesu: The Study of Melanesian Society in New Ireland*. New York: W. W. Norton.

Price, John. 1972. Reno, Nevada: The City as a Unit of Study. *Urban Anthropology*, 1:14–28.

Redfield, Robert. 1930. *Tepoztlán: A Mexican Village*. Chicago: University of Chicago Press.

Whiteford, Andrew H. 1960. *Two Cities of Latin America*. Beloit, WI: Logan Museum.

Whyte, William Foote. 1943. *Street Corner Society*. Chicago: University of Chicago Press.

Wirth, Louis. 1938. Urbanism as a Way of Life. *American Journal of Sociology*, 44:3–24.

2

Networks, Neighborhoods, and Markets
Fieldwork in Tokyo

Theodore C. Bestor

Ted Bestor first went to Japan as a graduate student to study a Tokyo neighborhood. Years later he returned to do fieldwork in a large wholesale fish market. In this chapter, Bestor describes how he adapted traditional field techniques to these two Tokyo settings. His techniques proved to be well suited to the urban context in that they mimic characteristics of urban social life. He also discusses the importance of paying attention to little things, like styles of dress, company badges, signs, logos, and the spatial layout of ordinary activities. Urban fieldworkers must take advantage of chance encounters whenever possible, as they often lead to unexpected information and valuable insights. Bestor shows how urban fieldwork is often open-ended and multifaceted.

Tokyo is the core of a metropolitan region that includes about 25 million people, about 20 percent of the population of Japan. Tokyo prides itself on being the center of contemporary Japanese life, and in terms of politics, finance, mass media, arts, education, fashion, and most other dimensions of Japanese life, Tokyo is the unquestioned capital. But at first glance, the city itself is uninspiring: no broad vistas, few monuments, and even fewer visual clues about how the city is spatially and socially organized. Often, first-time foreign visitors find Tokyo overwhelming, an urban jumble that stretches for dozens of kilometers in all directions, a chaotic plain of low-rise buildings broken here and there by clusters of skyscrapers. But viewed through different lenses, Tokyo resolves into a manageable, comfortable urban environment.

Since the mid-1970s, I have been conducting ethnographic research in Tokyo. Some of my fieldwork has examined a single swatch of the urban fabric close-up, focusing on the microlevel of neighborhoods and the social ties

Source: Written expressly for *Urban Life*.

that sustain communities. I have also done research on a larger, less intimate scale, examining complex sets of social institutions that integrate urban society, such as wholesale markets. Both perspectives—on the ground or from a bird's eye view—help me see the real urban life of Tokyo beyond the trackless, featureless blur of urban sprawl. Like any urban place, Tokyo is a richly variegated city with a vibrant social life that is carried out in plain sight for those who take the time to look.

Over the years, my research has focused on an ordinary neighborhood that I call Miyamoto-chô (Bestor 1989, 1996), the lives and livelihoods of merchant families there and elsewhere (1990), and the politics of the neighborhood's annual festival (1992a). On a larger scale, I have looked at the distinctions of subculture and lifestyle by which Tokyoites distinguish themselves (1992b), food culture, consumption, and markets as expressions of social identity (1999, 2001), and the social structure of Tokyo's Tsukiji marketplace, the world's largest wholesale market for fresh and frozen seafood, where each year over $6 billion worth of food changes hands (1999, 2004).

The common focus in all my research has been on ordinary people's experiences of daily life; on ways in which urban life is organized by formal and informal institutions that frame politics, social ties, and economic life; and on the invention or reinvention of cultural traditions that give contemporary meaning and legitimacy to social institutions. Each of these projects has been based on intensive ethnographic fieldwork, including video fieldwork.[1]

Anthropological fieldwork is often explained as "participant observation," but the term is too vague to convey much insight into what actually takes place during ethnographic research. In reality, one cannot simply decide to participate and observe. It takes a long time to develop the access to be a "real" participant in local social life. Most fieldworkers cannot easily assume the social obligations or relationships required of "real" participants. Furthermore, "real" participants in most settings do not systematically compile information on the passing scene. And, finally, observation is too passive a term to describe the activity of constantly asking questions about what's going on. So, I prefer to think of this as "inquisitive observation" or "participant questioning." In this chapter I will try to illustrate some of the ways in which I use this technique in my own fieldwork. But whatever one calls this—participant observation, inquisitive observation, or hanging out—it is also important to note that this is only one aspect of doing ethnography. Inquisitive observation is the necessary prelude and cross-check for many other kinds of intensive research, including systematic formal interviewing, administering questionnaires, digging through public archives and statistical data, charting organizational structures, and carrying out detailed historical research (both oral and documentary).

FOLLOWING NETWORKS

When my wife and I arrived in Tokyo to begin research as graduate students in the spring of 1979, both of us had studied and worked in Japan before (in my case, several times, including a year and a half in Tokyo study-ing Japanese intensively), so I knew how to get around and spoke Japanese well. I knew (or thought I knew) what I wanted to study, but finding the field site was harder than I had anticipated and much more revealing about urban Japanese social life than I really understood until much later. My plan was to study local community life, to examine the ways in which local institutions created, for some people, a significant arena of local social, political, and eco-nomic opportunities. In particular, I wanted to examine how "old middle class" families, the proprietors of small, family-run businesses, participated in creating or maintaining local community life. In comparative terms, my inter-est was stimulated by anthropological questions about how face-to-face com-munities sustain themselves in a highly urbanized environment (in contrast to the conventional American sociological perspective that urban life causes an irreversible decline in community social life).

Japanese friends helpfully suggested neighborhoods for me to consider, and for several weeks my wife and I set out every day to explore different parts of the city that might be suitable research sites. In the midst of our search, we got together with a pair of American graduate students who were already in the field working on related topics, Christena Turner and Dorinne Kondo.[2] Over iced coffee, they commiserated about the difficulties of getting established in a field site. They offered many useful suggestions, and the one that stuck in my mind was Turner's comment: "choose a network, not a neighborhood." (See Kemper's chapter in this volume for another example of this point.)

This was excellent advice: determine where my contacts were strongest and where introductions from existing contacts could be most effective, and go there; don't search for an "ideal" place and then try to find a connection into it.

A day or two later, the Japanese friends with whom we were staying, the Machida family, asked again about the kind of community I wanted to study. I explained again about the sort of mixed residential neighborhood I hoped to find: not too rich nor too poor; not too peripheral nor too central; a place that had an active set of local organizations, like a neighborhood association (chôkai), a shopkeepers' guild, a PTA, a Shintô shrine parish, and so forth. Dr. and Mrs. Machida looked at one another and Dr. Machida said, "I never thought about it before, but you're looking for the kind of neighborhood where I grew up."

Dr. Machida's comment foreshadowed what I now recognize as a com-monplace problem in fieldwork. Ethnographic research so often focuses on mundane topics that even people who are trying very hard to provide useful suggestions frequently fail to recognize their own experiences as worth men-tioning. One of the essential keys to successful fieldwork is constantly cueing people to talk about their own lives.

The next day, my wife and I walked through Dr. Machida's childhood neighborhood, Miyamoto-chô, and liked what we saw. The neighborhood had most of the visible trappings of community life that I had catalogued in my mind. Moreover, a quick scan of some statistics at the municipal office showed me it had the demographic mix I was looking for. We went home and told our hosts we were very much interested. The next day, Mrs. Machida took us back to introduce us to a PTA friend of hers who was a local real estate agent. At the second apartment we visited, we met the landlord, Mr. Fukuda, who lived with his family in a house just behind his small apartment building; on the ground floor of this apartment building was his shop. Mr. Fukuda turned out to be a vice president of the local neighborhood association, a position he had held for 20 years. And he loved to talk!

We had hit pay dirt. We took the apartment, and began following the networks that our entry points into the neighborhood provided: gradually getting introduced to others in the neighborhood by our friends the Machidas, by the real estate agent, and by Mr. Fukuda and his family. Through Mr. Fukuda, I met other local leaders and activists and tagged along with him to many local events. Acting on Turner's advice, I followed where networks led me.

During the past 20 years, returning to Miyamoto-chô again and again, my networks have snowballed because I more or less put myself in the path of contacts. I simply tried to encounter people. A week or so after we moved into the Fukudas' apartment, the neighborhood association held its annual *Bon Odori* festival, a midsummer outdoor dance on the grounds of the local elementary school. The Fukuda family took us along and we were introduced to a number of people, but I really started to interact with some of the local leaders when I ventured up to the schoolyard early the next morning to take photos of the festival's lanterns (on which the names of local donors to the festival were written). While I was there, three of the younger neighborhood leaders arrived to take down the stage and lanterns. Feeling shy about my own presence taking pictures of an empty school yard, I went over and said hello. They started pulling the stage apart and I lent a hand. A couple of hours later we were done, and I had begun to get access into their circle, not from conscious planning but from being willing to pitch in unasked and stick out a morning of manual labor. (Twenty years later, two of the three have died—a sad reminder that fieldwork is real life, grief included—but I remain very close friends with this circle of families.)

Another major contact in the neighborhood developed with someone who didn't consider himself a leader, Mr. Kuroda, a shopkeeper who had married into a local family (as an adopted-son-in-law[3]). He was a friendly guy and always helped out with local events if asked, but he kept to himself and figured the business of the neighborhood association was really in the hands of local big shots, not him. We met because I was always taking pictures at local events, and he was a camera buff. At the elementary school's athletic field day in October of my first year of fieldwork, he came over to chat casually about my camera equipment (which didn't hold a candle to his own), and mentioned that his three kids were always talking about the young foreign couple in the neighborhood. At that point I didn't have a clue who his kids were, but he invited Vickey and me to share the picnic his wife had spread out for her family. When we saw his wife, we immediately recognized her and the three kids from many other neighborhood outings, even though we hadn't yet learned their names. Our ties with the Kuroda family grew from that picnic. Mrs. Kuroda frequently invited us over for casual family dinners in their tiny quarters above their shop, and Mr. Kuroda and I became regular drinking buddies. The Kurodas introduced us to local circles quite distinct from the neighborhood association, those centered on the elementary school and Mrs. Kuroda's networks of childhood friends.

As my networks of contacts grew through chance encounters as well as more intentional ones, my access to events—my social legitimacy as an involved quasi-member of the neighborhood—subtly began to shift. My initial sponsorship by the Machida family, and the role that my landlord and his family, the Fukudas, played in introducing us to our neighbors became less and less relevant. Never forgotten, of course, and even 20 years later people still recall vaguely that my wife and I arrived somehow through the Machida family (although exactly which of several related Machida households is now fuzzy in most people's memories). Increasingly, I meet people through introductions from people I know myself, through casual local interactions as well as through actively participating in any event to which I can legitimately get access.

ENTERING A MARKET

As I began my research in Miyamoto-chô, I had a topic in mind and found networks (and they found me). In my later research on the Tsukiji wholesale seafood market—the world's largest market for fresh seafood—networks led me to the site and only then to the realization that I had found an ideal project. People I met along the way helped me define the shape and viewpoint of my Tsukiji project, much more than was the case in my Miyamoto-chô research.

I started my research not by looking at the market *per se* but by looking at the commercial distribution system; by examining local shopping districts (based on my Miyamoto-chô experience) and the kinds of economic ties that integrate local merchants into larger economic and institutional frameworks. This proved to be too diffuse a topic, but as I was discovering this, I visited Tsukiji to interview a few wholesalers about their connections with retailers.

An official of the Tokyo Metropolitan Government whom I had met in New York introduced me to a colleague who was a senior administrator at the marketplace. Mr. Shimizu met me in his crowded office and began to outline a brief history of Tsukiji. Mr. Shimizu was a career bureaucrat who had rotated through several positions before landing in the marketplace only a year or so earlier. As a senior official, supervising a staff of dozens, he had the opportunity to exercise his curiosity and to read about current market activities as well as the historical background of the marketplace.

He turned out to be the perfect person to interview. He was a newcomer himself and was still fascinated by Tsukiji. He was happy to find me asking *him* to explain the market. He explained the basic patterns of transactions among the market's seven large auction houses and its hundreds of small-scale wholesalers, and among these small wholesalers and their clients, the fishmongers and *sushi* chefs who were typical of the shopkeepers I had been studying in neighborhoods scattered across the city.

Suddenly, Tsukiji came into sharp focus. What particularly struck me was the interplay Mr. Shimizu described between a complex economic system (in this case the market's auction system) and the market's small-scale wholesalers—*nakaoroshi gyôsha* or "intermediate wholesalers"—as well as the ways in which market institutions had affected and modified the balance of power over time between large corporations and family enterprises. Mr. Shimizu's explanations suddenly anchored my still unfocused ideas about the social embeddedness of the distribution system into a tangible social world that I could explore.

Excitedly, I accepted his offer of introductions, and within a week I met officials of a major trade federation in the marketplace, the organization that represented the 1,677 stalls occupied by intermediate wholesalers. Federation officials were polite and helpful, and showed me around the marketplace. I doubt they expected me to show up again and again, but when I did they rewarded my enthusiasm. They gave me access to documents, arranged interviews for me, and introduced me to many of their members. However, I was aware from the outset that the market was an enormously large and complex institution—market administrators estimate that some 60,000 people work or do business there each day—and I wanted to avoid being boxed in by reliance on a single source of introductions and access.

I had expanded my networks in Miyamoto-chô in part by playing the time-honored ethnographic role of inquisitive-observer (within the limitations I mentioned earlier). As a bona fide resident of the neighborhood I had both ample opportunities and a certain legitimate standing to do so. Guys in Miyamoto-chô had been happy to let me share in the drudgery of cleaning up after festivals or bundling up recycling. But here, in a busy marketplace, clearly there could be no legitimate inquisitive-observer role for a researcher. So my networks had to be created through more formal introductions. And though many of my networks at Tsukiji snowballed, just as in Miyamoto-chô, I self-consciously worked on a technique for gaining access to people at Tsukiji that I think of as "parachuting"—dropping in from multiple entry points.

In addition to my introductions from Mr. Shimizu to the wholesalers' federation, I went back to my connections from earlier research projects. I sought introductions from people in Miyamoto-chô. Mrs. Machida, my early guide to Miyamoto-chô, knew a woman (through the PTA for their daughters' exclusive private school) whose husband owned a Tsukiji stall that dealt in processed fish. The owner of the sushi bar where I went drinking with Miyamoto-chô's leaders introduced me to some of his suppliers. The greengrocer around the corner from my apartment took me through Tsukiji's vegetable auctions one morning. I sought out multiple entry points from as many angles as I could muster. Some led me only a short distance, others proved to be gold mines. And I could never predict ahead of time which would be which.

By way of example, the path of introductions that led me to one of my major, long-enduring sets of connections at Tsukiji started with one contact provided by a U.S. trade official who himself knew relatively little about Tsukiji. He introduced me to an American in the seafood business, who introduced me to his Japanese assistant. This woman's mother and sister worked at Tsukiji, and through them I met and gradually developed extremely close ties with half a dozen major tuna dealers. And these tuna dealers, in turn, have given me introductions and access to dozens of other people throughout the marketplace over the years, ranging from auctioneers to newspaper reporters, day laborers, and sushi chefs.

My entry into this network was based initially on introductions from outsiders who only knew intermediaries or one or two possible entry points into Tsukiji. At the outset, the people providing me with introductions really had no idea where those would lead, nor did I. But nonetheless I could follow these leads to a social space where the connections among people were overlapping, diffuse, multidirectional, and multistranded; in other words, a highly interconnected social world in which most of my contacts all knew each other in many different contexts. Because each was closely linked to others in the same tight social circles, once I was introduced to one person, I could easily get in touch with others. And, through this chain of connections I also gained access to several locations where I could hang out more or less on a daily basis—a Tsukiji social club and the stalls of a couple of tuna dealers—and engage in casual unstructured interviews with whomever showed up, thus extending my contacts more each day.

At Tsukiji, the kinds of social participation open to me in Miyamoto-chô were impossible, and my strategies for finding entry points had to be very different, hence my effort to pursue as many different networks as possible. In addition, at Tsukiji my research focus developed hand-in-hand with the elaboration of my contacts. I worked hard to expand my networks among intermediate wholesalers and discovered that the kind of face-to-face business they were in—strongly oriented toward introductions from others—made connections easy to establish. I cultivated these connections as my research led me to understand the position of intermediate wholesalers, and as these networks picked me up and passed me along, the centrality of the intermediate wholesalers became clearer to me. Thus, following a particular set of networks determined that my research would examine the marketplace from the perspective of intermediate wholesalers.

Ethnographic research such as mine puts a group of people and their daily lives on center stage, and usually the point of view of the social scene that I adopt reflects in some way the perspective of that group. Ethnography cannot achieve a balanced representation of all perspectives, and the challenge I face

The author standing in front of a portable shrine with friends from the wholesaler's association, at the Tsukiji market's festival. [From the collection of Ted Bestor]

instead is to recognize which of several contending points of view I have focused on and to understand the partiality that ethnographic networks inevitably create. At Tsukiji, my focus started—and continued—with the attempt to understand the market as it appears to those who show up each morning at the auctions with money to spend. In Miyamoto-chô, I started pursuing networks among local shopkeepers in order to understand the social significance of the community among residents for whom it was both home and workplace.

In both cases, if I had made other choices about the kinds of networks I wanted to pursue, about the kinds of social and cultural activity that I thought should be center stage, undoubtedly the ethnographies would have come out differently. But the network choices I had to make do not mean that my ethnographies are incomplete, in the sense of lacking perspectives that additional fieldwork could have provided. On the contrary, they are necessarily partial accounts—like any ethnography—because ethnographic research inevitably draws upon and creates a specific point of view.

READING THE SCENE

Finding and following networks is not an end in itself. Other techniques of "inquisitive observation" provide clues both about which networks and affiliations are significant in a field site, as well as about relevant questions to ask and issues to investigate.

Exploring a research setting—figuring out what its social dimensions and boundaries are—is always a challenge. I often begin with the feeling that I am standing on a tiny outcropping of known territory, containing just the few places and people I start with, surrounded by huge white spaces. Fortunately, I can take advantage of the fact that Japan is a well-labeled society. Signs are everywhere, and these enable me to collect rough-and-ready information on the local social environment and on the important categories of organizations, religious sects, and political parties with which people advertise their affiliations.

Walking slowly down a side street, for example, glancing at doorways and shop windows, I can pick up a lot about the character of local social life in many Tokyo neighborhoods. A family name on a house's nameplate gives me clues about multiple-generation families. If several households of the same surname live directly adjacent to one another, it's a reasonable assumption (to be checked in later interviews) that the land has been in the same family for some time, perhaps subdivided several times with the passing of generations. Some doorpost plaques announce that the occupants hold a local leadership position or belong to a political group. Others, draped in black, reveal that a death has occurred within the last year. Sometimes, amulets or charms decorate doorposts and demonstrate affinities for particular religious groups.

I try to pay attention to little things: styles of dress, uniforms, company badges, signs, logos, decorative motifs, even spatial orientations. At Tsukiji, I gradually learned that I can tell what people's jobs are and what organizations they belong to by the hats they wear. Literally, the colors and styles of baseball caps distinguish their wearers as auctioneers, buyers, or regulators, and also differentiate them by company and commodity specialization. In Miyamoto-chô, it is handy to be able to recognize at a glance which school children go to by the styles of their school uniforms. In other settings, I memorize company lapel pins on business suits in order to keep track of who's who in large meetings. And, almost without thinking about it anymore, I count the number of people in a meeting and try to figure out whether their seating arrangements indicate anything about relative social status.

Of course, learning to attach the proper significance to such indicators takes a long time. The labels of Japanese daily life are not always self-explanatory, and it took me a great deal of patient ethnographic research—lots of local inquisitive-observation followed up by informal and formal interviews—to be able to decode and then contextualize the signs, labels, and other visual cues I encountered. But once the significance became clear, I found that enormous amounts of social data were out there in the open. For example, at Miyamoto-chô's annual festival, the amounts that residents donate are recorded on large paper streamers in front of the neighborhood association hall, for all to inspect (and gossip about). Social status in the neighborhood is there for the note-taking: Mr. Kuroda gave ¥5,000, Mr. Fukuda gave ¥10,000, Bestor gave ¥3,000.

Looking for signs is a good way to gather material for later questions ("Are there many supporters of the so-and-so party in this neighborhood?" "How many different trade federations are there?" "Is that street a boundary between this neighborhood and the next?"). Once I started to pay attention to all the little signs, the knowledge made it possible to gather and map a lot of social data with quick visual inspections. Depending on what I was looking for, many data were available just by keeping my eyes open. Sometimes such data were useful because they reinforced information I had collected by other means; in other cases they prompted me to ask questions about things I had only just stumbled across. But in either case, the visual, written record of urban social life always provides lots of valuable information, there for the asking (or the looking).

SOCIAL MAPPING

Just as looking for labels has helped me to figure out the categories of actors, institutions, and experiences in various social settings, so too an understanding of the spatial layout of ordinary activities has helped me discern what the significant activities are, their organization, and their relationship to one another and to particular groups of actors.

At the start of my research in Miyamoto-chô, an important clue to the structure of neighborhood institutions and their boundaries came on the very first day my wife and I walked through the area, looking for an apartment. I was paying careful attention to street addresses and knew that we were walking around Yanagi 4-chôme, but within the space of three blocks, we came across two separate buildings labeled *chôkai kaikan* ("Neighborhood Association Hall"), one bearing the name "Yanagi 4-chôme Chôkai Kaikan," the other bearing the name "Yanagi Miyamoto Chôkai Kaikan." I was intrigued, and once we had settled into the Fukudas' apartment building, I set out to find out the significance of what appeared to be overlapping institutions. The answer to the question eventually led me to a significant line of argument about the conflict between government definitions of communities (the larger Yanagi 4-chôme being the creation of the government) and local residents' definitions of community, as expressed through the separate territories represented by the quite distinct Yanagi 4-chôme chôkai and the Miyamoto chôkai.

At Tsukiji, signs identifying shops and businesses as members of particular trade federations provided me with some of my first clues about the extent to which the marketplace was organized into dozens of trade communities, each with its own rules of business, its own specializations, and its own organizational infrastructure. During my first months of fieldwork at Tsukiji, I constantly looked for organizational names on signs, bulletin boards, doors, and posters. I ended up with an inventory of over 50 associational names that I used to frame interview questions to identify each group and its particular niche within the marketplace as a whole. And as this inventory became more detailed, I was able to identify the groups most crucial for understanding the auction system. From that I began to see how these groups coordinated the relationships of economic actors as they moved from place to place around the market. And finally, I was able to map the spatial layout of the dozens of auction pits around Tsukiji and connect each of them to different constellations of organizations. All of these were crucial steps in understanding the institutional structure of the market as a whole.

CUEING

Most people are pretty comfortable talking about their own lives, but they don't generally volunteer information about their own social environments if they don't have reason to think it is particularly interesting or significant. Successful fieldwork, therefore, requires me to explore that social environment on my own—through mapping, studying labels, and so forth—to become familiar with the features of the local scene that may turn out to be significant once I get people talking about them. My job as an ethnographic researcher is to get them talking by being interested, and, even more importantly, by asking questions that gently force people to think about (and to talk about) the mundane aspects of their lives. My own explorations help me pose better questions, convey to my informants what I think is significant or interesting, invite them to correct me, and prompt them to give me their own views.

Dr. Machida didn't think his own childhood neighborhood was worth my attention until I had explained several times that I was looking for a very ordinary urban place; I didn't understand until then how hard it would be to explain what kind of research setting I was looking for. I think this is a problem that all ethnographers have to face. By the time I started research at Tsukiji a decade later, I had learned that a constant flow of questions from me could usually elicit some interesting leads. The squid dealer who showed me around the market would never have mentioned the lottery system for stall locations—why would a foreigner want to know about that?—unless I had pressed him to explain the seemingly random arrangement of stalls.

Once I have cued someone to the fact that I am interested in mundane, day-to-day patterns of life, I've usually found that most people think their own lives are rather interesting and they're happy to talk about things they see as significant about themselves. One of the virtues of ethnographic inquisitive observation is that I can turn to the person next to me and ask, on the spot, "why are we doing this?" For example, I learned a lot about spatial and social community boundaries, the dynamics of leadership, and the sense of obligation to neighbors as a member of a pesticide-spraying crew in Miyamoto-chô during many smelly Sundays spread over several summers.

Since much of people's own experience of daily life, social activities, local institutions, and so forth is shared by many if not most of their family members, coworkers, or neighbors, there really aren't a lot of people with whom they talk who don't already understand the ins and outs of their lives. So, I often find that interviewees are almost eager to tell me about their lives, since everyone *else* they know either already knows the stories or doesn't care about them. Part of this, of course, is the time-tested advantage of being an ethnographer in a culture other than one's own. In Japan at least, as a foreigner, I can ask about the simplest things, things that even a six-year-old child ought to know. Very rarely does anyone think it odd that I ask.

Often, unlikely contacts turn out to have incredible amounts of information. At Tsukiji one morning, I stopped for a casual conversation with a sweeper who had simply greeted me as I passed by. A few days later, I ran into him again cutting up fish to load into a tiny open-sided van—a mobile fish store—that he drove around the Tokyo suburbs in the late afternoon, after finishing a full day's work at the marketplace. From our second conversation, I unexpectedly found out a great deal about Tokyo's food peddlers and Tsukiji's marginal workers.

I try to take advantage of such chance encounters whenever I can. But to do so requires that I create a framework in which it is both logical and legitimate that I ask questions. This seems like a simple point, but in most social settings "real" participants don't ask lots of questions. I think every ethnographer confronts the problems of figuring out how to present himself or herself in such a way that people don't mind questions. My solution (not always easy to achieve) is to create a persona as a researcher (which itself is not a typical social role in most people's experience) that is authentic in the eyes of those around me, while also overcoming my own shyness. Convincing myself that I can legitimately ask questions is always the first (and hardest) step. As my questions begin to flow more naturally, and as people see me interviewing, taking notes, taking photos, hanging around, and so forth, the social role of researcher gradually takes shape, and those around me start to accept my activities as an expected part of the social scenery.

The other closely related aspect of establishing myself as a bona fide researcher is to be able to explain what I am interested in and to offer some plausible reason why. Since my fieldwork *per se* rarely involves much discussion with other academics, I try to keep my explanations rather straightforward and nontechnical. Usually, the comment that whatever I'm asking about in Japan is different from what is familiar to most Americans is a sufficient rationale for most people, at least in a casual, observational context. I can watch auctions at Tsukiji for days on end with the simple explanation that we don't have such auctions in the United States. Few people need more explanation than that.

More intensive interaction, either through participation or focused interviews, requires more detailed explanation, but not always a lot more. In my Miyamoto-chô fieldwork, I generally explained I was interested in the local organizations that were active in neighborhood affairs, and the kinds of social networks that residents formed in, through, and around these organizations, because (1) they seemed to be important in daily life, and (2) in American urban society, neighborhoods did not often have such active and intense local activities and interpersonal ties. I rarely try to offer extended theoretical rationales for my research interests, since they are usually not interesting to the people among whom I am doing research. Since most people I was interviewing also believed that local groups and activities were important in their own lives, they accepted my interest as understandable, although perhaps a bit overblown. (In Miyamoto-chô, people often asked jokingly [?] if I was really writing a doctoral dissertation about such a mundane subject as their community; years later some of them take glee in introducing me as the "neighborhood association Ph.D.")

At Tsukiji, a fairly simple explanation that Tsukiji is—as everyone I talked with already knew—the world's largest fish market and that there were no markets like it in the United States was often sufficient rationale. The fact that the place has a long and colorful history, a complicated social structure that most outsiders do not fathom, a massive niche in Japan's economy, and a

The author getting a drumming lesson during the Tsukiji market's festival, September 1990. [From the collection of Ted Bestor]

product line—seafood—that is richly saturated with culinary folklore, made it simple to explain why the place was interesting to me and why it was worthy of study.

In the case of Tsukiji, however, misinterpretations of my role and motives caused occasional problems. It was hard to explain why an anthropologist would be doing research on a market, since most Japanese, like most Americans, think of anthropologists as studying isolated "primitive" societies. Many people at Tsukiji assume that I am an economist or a market researcher. This isn't usually a big problem, although one interviewee was rather irritated by some questions about institutional history and food culture since—as he chided me—it was not directly relevant to understanding contemporary supply and demand curves, which was the topic I had come to talk to him about. From then on, I learned to introduce my interests and topics of questioning at the outset with a somewhat broader—perhaps vaguer—definition.

In retrospect, I realized I had too narrowly defined my interests out of a misguided sense of insecurity. In setting up that interview, I was anxious not to appear too naïve about the topic and so had quickly focused on a very specific issue that was of interest to me (but wasn't my sole interest). This is a fundamental dilemma in conducting research, especially when my research brings me into contact with people I haven't met previously. Almost every day I have to explain myself to someone new, and with each person I start off as a blank slate. Even when I have been introduced by a mutual acquaintance, the person I am meeting won't know a lot about me, and may often fall back on the comfortable assumption that as a *gaijin* (a foreigner), I must not know anything.

This is tricky to play out in an interview. On the one hand, I am quite comfortable listening to interviewees explain something that I think I already understand quite well. Often, in fact, in the course of hearing something for the umpteenth time, I will pick up some new fragment of information, and will suddenly see it from the point of view of a different actor in the setting. So, it is valuable to travel over familiar terrain from time to time, and I sometimes play rather dumb while doing it, to draw out my interviewee further.

The other side of the coin, however, is that one does want to cut to the chase, and I am always anxious to cut through the inevitable framing of me as a gaijin. So I always try to establish a certain level of familiarity with the subject matter with some questions or comments, politely phrased, to help steer my host past the feeling that he or she should start at square one. But it is always a balancing act to know how much of my own knowledge I should display: too much knowledge can curtail the discussion or make the interviewee defensive, but too little knowledge may trap me at the starting point as a naïve gaijin visitor.

At Tsukiji other misinterpretations of my role came up as well. Because the international seafood industry is highly competitive and Tsukiji is a major world market, a few people assumed that I was working on behalf of trade negotiators. Others, seeing me as a bearded American college professor, assumed my interest in the market was motivated by sympathies for Greenpeace or other environmentalist groups that have attacked the Japanese fishing industry (most notably the whaling industry) for what these groups regard as unconscionable activities against the environment.[4]

In such cases, I have often been able to avoid misunderstandings by referring to the networks of introductions that have led me to the present interview, activity, or interaction. Throughout my research, the social sponsorship of people who have befriended me along the way has been essential—to get me started, to introduce me to others, and, occasionally, to vouch for me when questions arise.

CONCLUSIONS

Ethnographic research is inherently open-ended and multifaceted. Given its avowed goals of enabling a researcher to participate in, record, convey, and analyze something of the complexity and coherence of ongoing social and cultural life, how could it be otherwise? Any set of ethnographic research techniques is, therefore, necessarily partial. In this chapter, I have briefly outlined some of the methods and perspectives I have cultivated—sometimes by trial and error, sometimes by adapting techniques other anthropologists have relied on for generations—to enable me to make the most of informal interactions and casual opportunities to collect information about life in urban settings. In some ways, these techniques are ideally suited to specifically urban contexts in that they mimic (or use as protective coloration) some common characteristics of urban social life: fleeting, fragmentary, quasi-anonymous, fast-paced. It would be a mistake, however, to suggest that my research, or any other urban research, can rely solely on these techniques. These are means to get started and to keep going, to be deployed before and during other kinds of more formally structured research: survey questionnaires; analysis of government records; archival research; structured census-taking; or formal, in-depth interviews. Getting information on the move is, however, an essential first step. Without this, I cannot get my bearings, develop insights into local social contexts, or devise informed questions to subsequently pursue using more formally structured methods.

Notes

[1] I have collaborated with American and Japanese ethnographic filmmakers on a video documentary that focuses on my role as a researcher in Miyamoto-chô as I examine community rituals, neighborhood organizations, and residents' participation in local social and economic life. *Neighborhood Tokyo* (Media Production Group, 1992) runs 28 minutes, and it is available with a short viewers' guide from the Asian Educational Media Service at the University of Illinois, Urbana-Champaign (www.aems.uiuc.edu).

[2] See Kondo (1990) and Turner (1995) for their ethnographies of work and social identity in Tokyo, and their interesting discussions of the fluid interactions between researcher and the people among whom she is working.

³ In the traditional Japanese kinship system, a son-in-law may be adopted as the heir to a family, taking the name of the bride's family and becoming, for social and legal purposes, the son of his parents-in-law.
⁴ For the record, my research at Tsukiji is not connected with nor sponsored by trade negotiators or environmental activists.

References

Bestor, Theodore C. 1989. *Neighborhood Tokyo*. Stanford: Stanford University Press.
———. 1990. Tokyo Mom-and-Pop. *The Wilson Quarterly*, 14(4):27–33.
———. 1992a. Conflict, Tradition, and Legitimacy in a Tokyo Neighborhood. In *Japanese Social Organization*, ed. T. S. Lebra, pp. 23–47. Honolulu: University of Hawai'i Press.
———. 1992b. Rediscovering Shitamachi: Subculture, Class, and Tokyo's "Traditional" Urbanism. In *The Cultural Meaning of Urban Space*, eds. G. McDonogh and R. Rotenberg, pp. 47–60. North Hadley, MA: Bergen and Garvey.
———. 1996. Forging Tradition: Social Life and Identity in a Tokyo Neighborhood. In *Urban Life: Readings in Urban Anthropology*, 3rd ed., eds. G. Gmelch and W. P. Zenner, pp. 524–47. Long Grove, IL: Waveland Press.
———. 1999. Wholesale Sushi: Culture and Commodity in Tokyo's Tsukiji Market. In *Theorizing the City: The New Urban Anthropology Reader*, ed. S. M. Low, pp. 201–242. New Brunswick, NJ: Rutgers University Press.
———. 2001. Markets: Anthropological Aspects. In *International Encyclopedia of the Behavioral and Social Sciences*, eds. Neil J. Smelser and Paul B. Baltes, pp. 9227–9231. London: Elsevier Science.
———. 2004. *Tsukiji: The Fish Market at the Center of the World*. Berkeley: University of California Press.
Kondo, Dorinne K. 1990. *Crafting Selves: Power, Gender and Discourses of Identity in a Japanese Workplace*. Chicago: University of Chicago Press.
Media Production Group. 1992. *Neighborhood Tokyo*. Documentary video distributed by the Asian Educational Media Service, University of Illinois.
Turner, Christena. 1995. *Japanese Workers in Protest*. Berkeley: University of California Press.

3

Nomads in the City
Studying Irish Travellers

Sharon Bohn Gmelch

In this chapter, Sharon Gmelch discusses the personal experiences of an anthropologist studying another culture, in this case Irish Travellers—a poor, Gypsy-like population, living on the margins of Dublin, Ireland. We learn from her account that fieldwork in cities need not be less intimate or personal than that conducted in rural areas. We also learn some of the advantages and special requirements of urban field research and the dilemma anthropologists face in deciding whether to remain neutral observers or become advocates for the people with whom they do their fieldwork.

I first went to Ireland to participate in a cultural anthropology field school with a dozen other American graduate students.[1] It began with a two-week orientation in the capital city of Dublin, during which we took Irish language lessons and received lectures on Irish society and research techniques. The director then drove us to the countryside, placing each student in a different village where we would spend the rest of the summer learning firsthand what it was like to do fieldwork. The choice of rural Ireland was not surprising given anthropology's traditional focus on tribal and peasant societies. I was placed in the fishing village of Fenit (population 342) in county Kerry. I'll never forget nervously lugging my heavy suitcase to the small hotel that catered to summer visitors. (My suitcase contained, in addition to my clothes, a dozen books and an electric typewriter; this was before personal computers.) No room was available, but the staff took pity on me and let me sleep in a storage room. A couple of days later, I found a place to stay for the summer in a bed-and-breakfast house run by a *garda* (police officer) and his wife. Once ensconced there, I left the village only once to venture by bus into the nearby provincial town. To do so more often, I felt (and the program

Source: Written expressly for *Urban Life*.

director had strongly suggested) would diminish the experience of living in an "isolated" community and some of the hardship of this anthropological rite of passage.

In adopting this attitude, however, I was ignoring the crucial role played by urban centers in the lives of people everywhere. The village I lived in, although small, was hardly isolated. Despite its apparent economic self-suffi-ciency (its fishing fleet, farming, and occasional tourists), it served as a bed-room community for the provincial town of Tralee. Many residents took the bus or drove the seven miles to work there each morning; others commuted longer distances and returned home only at week's end. Many villagers also had sons or daughters living in Dublin or cities "across the water" like Lon-don, Birmingham, or New York. Most people also watched television, and everyone read newspapers or listened to the radio, which brought national and international news as well as urban values directly into their homes.

TRAVELLING PEOPLE

It was on the drive to Fenit that summer that I became aware of the Trav-elling People, Ireland's indigenous nomads who lived on the roadside in horse-drawn wagons, tents, and trailers. Commonly called "tinkers" by most people, they were a well-known group within Ireland yet little understood—the subject of folklore and fiction more than serious inquiry. I was struck by their "exotic" material culture and surprised by their very existence. How could such a small group of people (half a percent of the Irish population, I was later to learn), so fundamentally like the majority population (which was predominantly white, English speaking, Roman Catholic, and indigenous to Ireland), remain distinct?[2] Coincidentally, my husband George—also an anthropology graduate student—was to become involved with Travellers later that summer. While waiting in Dublin for my program to end, he was recruited to collect demographic information for a physical anthropologist conducting a genetic study of Travellers. He met many Dublin families then and photographed some. Before leaving Ireland, we bought a copy of a gov-ernment report about Travellers, detailing the "itinerant problem"—the hard-ships Travelling families faced living on the roadside and the problems their nomadic lifestyle created for the settled Irish community, especially in urban areas (*Report* 1963). Travellers were then moving into Irish cities and provin-cial towns at an increasing rate; the number in Dublin had grown almost ten-fold during the previous 20 years, from 158 to 1,435.

Back in graduate school that fall, we read—with the encouragement of faculty advisors—everything we could on Ireland and on itinerant artisan, trader, and entertainer minorities in other countries in order to develop research topics. George decided to examine the reasons Travellers were migrating to urban areas and the impact urbanization was having on their culture. I decided to study the issue that had originally fascinated me, namely, the Travellers' ability to maintain a unique identity. Strongly influenced by

Fredrik Barth's (1969) work on ethnicity and boundary maintenance, I planned to focus on the contexts in which Travellers and settled Irish met, the nature of their interactions, and each group's attitudes and beliefs about the other (Barth 1998 [1969]). Dublin, with its large population (then about 800,000) and growing number of Travellers, was the ideal place for both of us to base our research. Ironically, we were to study what in many respects was Ireland's most rural and culturally isolated population in the middle of a city. Without realizing it, I would be doing urban anthropology.

Even when conducted in cities, however, anthropological fieldwork is always an intensely personal experience. Unlike other social scientists, anthropologists usually live among the people they study for an extended period of time. It is their desire to know a culture through the eyes of its members and to observe actual behavior rather than rely solely on peoples' verbal responses to questions that separates anthropologists from other social scientists. Participant observation also means conducting research virtually around the clock, interacting with people in many different contexts and invariably developing close relationships. In the following account, I describe

A Traveller family negotiating Dublin traffic in their flat cart. [Photo by Pat Langan]

both my personal experience of doing fieldwork with Irish Travellers in Dublin and some of the issues and opportunities surrounding urban research.

BEGINNING FIELDWORK

We returned to Ireland in mid-July 1971 and checked into a bed-and-breakfast house on the south side of Dublin. Eager to get our fieldwork underway, the next day we made a list of what we needed to do: get a year's visa, contact local officials about our research, find an apartment, buy a car. George also called a social worker he had met the previous summer, and she invited us to attend a Traveller wedding the following day. At the time, I didn't question her right to do so, instead viewing it as a golden opportunity to meet Travellers. As it turned out, George had met some members of the wedding party the previous summer, and they had appreciated the photographs he sent back—so we were welcome. The marriage took place in a church on the south side of the city. I expected a large, gregarious crowd. Instead, only 13 people including the bride, groom, the social worker, George, and I witnessed the actual ceremony; an air of disinterest pervaded the gathering. Mag, the 15-year-old bride, appeared shy and somewhat woebegone in her wrinkled and ill-fitting dress. The groom wore a rumpled suit and an expression of detached resignation. The bride's father and the handful of women relatives inside the church shifted uncomfortably in the pews, murmuring among themselves. Then the priest arrived, took the bride and groom by their elbows, and jockeyed them into position in front of the altar. Perhaps unnecessarily, I felt acutely embarrassed for them, especially when he instructed them on what to say and when to say it in what seemed like a loud and impatient tone. A dozen or so neighborhood children filtered in during the ceremony and stood at the back of the church, gaping innocently at the spectacle before them. Suddenly it was over, the customary mass omitted. As the couple emerged from the church, a young garda leaned out of his patrol car window and called Johnny over, advising him to "start out right" and be "well behaved." Johnny, we were told later, was out on bail for the ceremony; larceny was a growing problem among Travellers in the city. We left soon after, our heads spinning with this glimpse of what was to come.

One of the first issues faced by any anthropologist working in a city is delineating the community he or she intends to study. My interest in Travellers defined in ethnic terms the group I was interested in, yet close to 1,500 Travellers lived in more than 50 camps scattered in the greater Dublin area. Some of these were temporary roadside encampments of one to three families; others were large government-sponsored "sites" for up to 40 families. Many were located on the fringes of the city, wherever Travellers could find an open field or unimpeded roadside verge wide enough to accommodate a wagon or trailer. Other families camped in the middle of the city amid the rubble of abandoned lots, often adjacent to industrial or building sites. As a lone researcher, I could not hope to study all of them.

The teenage couple following their wedding ceremony. [Photo by George Gmelch]

After visiting most of Dublin's larger sites and camps, we decided to focus on two government-sponsored sites. Both had large, somewhat stable populations. Labre Park was the first official site built for Travellers. It was located on the north side of the city in the working-class area of Ballymun, on land that once had been a city dump. It provided accommodation for 40 Travelling families in small prefabricated dwellings. Extra family members spilled over into trailers and wagons parked nearby. The second camp, Holylands, was an undeveloped site located on the edge of a suburban housing estate in Churchtown on the more affluent south side of the city. It was little more than a tree-ringed field with strips of blacktop on two sides that provided hard standing for wagons and trailers. A single water tap and a rarely used outhouse were the only amenities for a population of about 20 families. A shack containing a telephone stood at the entrance; it was manned during the day by a city employee, referred to by Travellers as the "watchman," who seemed to have no real responsibilities.

For several weeks we alternated visits between these two sites. Upon arriving in one, we would get out of our battered Volkswagen and walk off in separate directions, approaching people and attempting to engage them in conversation. At first, most of my conversations were with curious children, teenagers, and the elderly. I tried to clarify my role, as an American university student who would some day be a professor, and what I hoped to do—learn what it was like to be a Traveller. I explained about writing a doctoral dissertation, which they interpreted to mean a book. When they asked how long I was going to stay and I said a "year," they were understandably skeptical. Most of their previous contacts with outsiders anything like me had been with journalists. After repeated visits, however, people began to realize that I was serious. As I became more familiar, they became friendlier. Gradually I was developing rapport. No doubt, the fact that neither George nor I was Irish lessened their suspicions that we might be something other than what we claimed. Nevertheless, I learned later that a few people in Holylands had suspected that we were undercover police investigating the suspicious death that had occurred in camp not long before we arrived.

These early weeks of fieldwork were not easy. I remember vividly the sinking feeling I got whenever people acted distant or walked away. When in camp, I was always on guard, monitoring my behavior in an attempt to act appropriately, wanting to be friendly but not *too* friendly, to be interested but not *too* curious. I ate whatever food was offered me; casually negotiated my way around scrap piles, mangy dogs, and animal excreta; sat nonchalantly on mattresses I discovered too late on a couple of occasions were puddled with baby urine; and generally acted nonplussed by the unfamiliar sights and sounds around me. I was repeatedly asked the same questions, often during the course of single conversation: "Are you married? How long have you been married? Is he your husband? Do you have children? Don't you like children? Are you from America? Do you know Elvis?" Travellers were genuinely curious about these things, but I also came to view this questioning as a test of my truthfulness and consistency. Moreover, we had few common experiences on which to base a more wide-ranging conversation. Some days I thought I couldn't face driving into camp again. The thought of seeking out people to talk to, of risking rejection, of giving the same explanations over and over, was almost too much to bear.

Although we developed rapport quickly with some Travellers, commuting soon proved unsatisfactory. For one, there were logistical problems. Travellers lacked defined work and leisure hours; they made plans, even for major trips, on the spur of the moment. Some days I would arrive to find virtually everyone gone or to learn that the person I had most hoped to speak with had moved across the city or gone to England. Setting up an appointment to talk to a specific person at a specific time was nearly impossible. Travellers did not live by the clock, and in the 1970s many did not know how to tell time even if they had wanted to. My appointments were also far more important to me than to them.

I also felt that I was missing out on much of Traveller life. This feeling was reinforced each time I arrived in camp to be told something like, "You should have been here last night; the guards (police) came up and took Big John." Most importantly, I wanted to lose my outsider status and get "backstage," to use Erving Goffman's term, and blend into the background of camp life so that people would act naturally in front of me. Travellers were used to dealing with non-Travellers in a superficial and manipulative way. Most of their encounters with settled Irish people were brief and often required them to be skilled at impression management, as when begging, peddling goods, or interacting with the police (Gmelch, with Gmelch 1978). It was important for my research to get behind the scenes and learn what Travellers really thought. Moreover, because Travellers had never been studied in depth before, we felt an obligation to collect as wide a range of ethnographic data as possible (McCarthy 1972). Only living in a camp would enable us to do this.

FROM COMMUTER TO CAMP MEMBER

After seven weeks of commuting, we selected Holylands as our main research site. The layout of the camp, with families camped in wagons and trailers along two sides of a field, was better for social interaction and observation. At Labre Park, the small houses were lined up in a single long row with no commons. Holylands also had a better cross–section of the Traveller community. Some families came from the more prosperous East and Midlands, while others had arrived in Dublin from the poorer West. Travellers used two reputational categories when describing each other—"roughs" and "respectables"—which loosely correlated with a family's wealth, behavior (e.g., style of drinking and begging), and county of origin. Holylands contained both. Moreover, some families had been living in the city for a decade, while others were new arrivals and still quite mobile. Because Holylands was then an undeveloped site, families were free to move on and off and to change locations within camp at will. Thus, in addition to a stable core of families who remained the entire year of our research, I was also exposed to new families who were transient. Of equal importance, more families at Holylands than at Labre Park had been overtly receptive to us. In fact, several people had suggested that we move onto the site (something we had hoped to do). With the help of Red Mick Connors and Mike Donoghue, George bought a barrel-top wagon and a mare from a Traveller in another part of the city.

Our wagon, which was in need of paint and a few repairs, gave us something tangible to do when we arrived at Holylands each morning. As we worked on the wagon, people stopped by to give advice, lend a hand, or simply chat and ask about America, particularly about the west ("What are cowboys like? Are there still Indians?"). Some days we arrived to find that someone had worked on our wagon in our absence. Michael Donoghue painted its undercarriage and wheels a bright canary yellow (the correct color, we were told); his father Mick made a new window frame for the broken one on our front door. Paddy Maugham found replacement shafts. His wife, Nanny Nevin, gave me a lucky horseshoe to nail above the door and advised on flooring (red would be nice). Our transition from regular visitors and commuting anthropologists to camp residents was complete the first night we slept there.

Opposite page: A Traveller camp in Finglas, a Dublin suburb. In the foreground is scrap metal collected from homeowners. [Photo by George Gmelch]

I had spent most of the evening sitting in a neighbor's trailer quietly talking to the family and retired early. I was awakened about an hour later by the roar of vans and lorries racing into camp, the sound of doors slamming, and loud laughing and talking as people returned from the pubs. A half hour or so later, the camp settled down to sleep once more. But before long, an argument broke out in the trailer next door. Accusations, curses, and obscenities were hurled back and forth. As I peered cautiously through the front window of the wagon door, I heard screams, thuds, and then shattering glass. Seeing the woman next door stagger out from her trailer, a wave of paranoia washed over me as I envisaged being dragged from my own wagon and beaten. But things gradually quieted down, and the camp fell into a fitful third sleep. The next morning I acted as if nothing had happened. Everyone I saw, however, seemed subdued and somewhat sheepish. I was coyly asked by one woman if I'd slept well, but no direct reference to the fight was made. The eight-year-old son of the family involved came closest when he said, "You must have learned a lot last night." Indeed, I had. Many of the pretenses and polite fictions maintained for a visiting outsider had been broken. I learned that Thursdays, when Dublin Travellers then received the dole (unemployment payments), were invariably days of heavy drinking. Most fights began as arguments between husbands and wives that, fueled by alcohol, too often escalated into physical beatings. This domestic violence might draw in other family members, especially a woman's brothers or sons, but rarely anyone else. It was almost never reported to the police. As I later overheard one man chillingly warn his wife, "If I do prison, you do hospital."

Once living at Holylands, my research fell into a comfortable and quite enjoyable routine. Much of the Travellers' time was spent out of doors, which meant that people were more accessible to me than the house-dwelling urbanites or even the villagers in the west of Ireland had been. Each family lit a campfire in the morning and kept it burning until they went to bed at night. A blackened kettle of water was kept boiling, and pots of tea were brewed throughout the day. Much of my fieldwork in camp involved sitting next to a fire and having extended conversations with one or more people. At night, there were more conversations around the campfire or in people's trailers. Many Travellers were good storytellers and funny, so these evenings were often filled with laughter. After a few weeks living in camp, we were invited by Red Mick Connors to join a group of younger couples who were going to a pub; after that, we frequently went to pubs with Travellers in the evenings. At the time, Travellers were widely discriminated against, and few publicans would knowingly serve them. But a lot depended on how Travellers looked (i.e., how obvious it was that they were Travellers) and on their behavior or reputation. Most of the pubs they gained access to were in working-class areas of the city, often in rough neighborhoods.

Most mornings I jotted down a list of topics to explore and during the day steered conversations to them whenever an opportunity presented itself. I learned when (and when not) to ask direct questions, as well as what questions or topics I could talk about and in front of whom. Information is power, and Travellers transformed their conversations with the natural ease of chameleons changing color whenever the wrong person appeared on the scene. I raised what I hoped to be the least sensitive topics first, asking about the logistics of travel, the art of selecting a campsite, tinsmithing and other trades, what settled people were like in different parts of the country, and family stories and histories. As time passed, I raised more contemporary and potentially sensitive issues—begging, evictions, discrimination, relations with settled people, drinking behavior, family problems, and trouble with the law. Many of these topics also came up spontaneously and at the Travellers' instigation. It became common for some people to climb into our wagon, shut the door, and sit down to talk about their problems. Anthropologists, as neutral outsiders who have shown great interest in the people they live among, often become confidants. Information and feelings that Travellers could not share with each other for fear that it would not be held in confidence and might eventually be used against them, could be discussed with us. We also became sources of information—about foods, health, the meaning of words, and myriad other topics.

As with other anthropologists, I relied heavily on the friendship and assistance of several key "informants" or native teachers. One was Nan Donoghue, the woman who had been beaten that first night in camp and whose life story

A typical event at Holylands, the field research site. [Photo by Pat Langan]

I was later to write (Gmelch 1991 [1986]). I had met her on one of my earliest visits to Holylands when two of her youngest sons, Brendan and Sam, urged me to show her the kitten I had brought with me. Their mother was one of the few Travellers who kept a cat—a skilled "ratter" named Minnie. I remember walking to her campsite reluctantly, feeling rather foolish to be pulling her away from her work just to show her a kitten. When she first stepped out of the doorway of her battered trailer, I was startled. Unlike most other women in camp who were robust and matronly, Nan was frail and looked far older than her 52 years. A cluster of religious medals hung from a safety pin on her sweater; a pierced earring dangled from one ear—the other had been ripped. She walked over, wiping her hands on her apron, stroked the kitten and asked his name. Then smiling at me through three thin decaying teeth, she said, "He's going to be big. He looks like a very clever cat." And so my closest friendship began.

I rarely took field notes in front of Travellers. I felt it would be insensitive since few Travellers then could read. The proximity of my wagon made note taking immediately after an event or discussion relatively easy. If I had the time, I wrote down a conversation or described an event in detail; at the very least, I jotted down key information and reminders to myself, which I typed up later as complete field notes.[3] During the last few months of fieldwork, I taped numerous interviews to obtain detailed family histories and to record verbatim the Travellers' own descriptions and explanations of aspects of their culture. I did not use the tape recorder as often as I would have liked during this first research with Travellers, since it was a novelty and always attracted a crowd of children and young adults who wanted to sing into it.

Fieldwork is a process of adjustment. Just as the anthropologist must adjust to the people he or she is studying, so people must adjust to the presence of the anthropologist. I had numerous "unusual" habits. At first, small children gathered around me in the morning to watch me brush my teeth, talking and pointing: "Ah, would you look, Sharon's scrubbing her teeth." Travellers then had conservative and very patriarchal notions about the role of women. They were surprised that I knew how to drive a car, went places on my own, and that I wore trousers or jeans. They were curious about why we did not have children (I told them about birth-control pills), and several women commented to me with surprise on never hearing George yell at or hit me. One of the changes in Traveller culture that urban life was contributing to was a growth in the power and opportunities available to women. With so many Travellers camped around the city, the likelihood of a woman having relatives nearby who would support or defend her or with whom she could stay if necessary was greatly increased. This provided many women with a degree of security they lacked in the countryside. City buses also made getting to these relatives easier. Other factors in the urban environment, including the information and support provided by social workers and the women's begging patronesses—settled women whom they regularly visited— also played a role (Gmelch 1977).

My most difficult adjustment to fieldwork was the lack of privacy. Trailer and wagon walls are thin, and each family's campsite was located only a few yards away from the next. Moreover, Travellers are gregarious—the result of being raised in large families and crowded living conditions. They freely entered each other's dwellings without warning, sitting down to listen for a while, and then leaving, perhaps without uttering a word. As we became an accepted part of camp life, our wagon became a customary stop on people's visiting rounds. If someone wanted to talk, he or she simply pulled the wagon door open and came in. We could expect visitors at virtually any hour of the day or night. We put a latch on the door, which deterred some people, but most merely opened the double windows atop the half door and leaned in to talk or else tugged at the flimsy door until we opened it.

RESEARCH IN THE CITY

Not all my research was done within the confines of Holylands. To balance what I was learning by living there, I continued to make periodic visits to other Dublin camps. I also visited other towns and cities in Ireland to meet Travellers there and to talk to local people. I regularly attended the weekly meetings of a small group of social workers who worked with Dublin-area Travellers, and for six weeks I acted as a vacation substitute for one of them. These meetings were informative and informal, allowing for plenty of conversation and questions. They allowed me to cross-check impressions I was forming and provided me with an understanding of the issues facing Travellers in different parts of the city, especially in the areas of concern to social workers—the health or education needs of Traveller children, housing, welfare payments, and problems like alcohol abuse, domestic violence, and petty crime. My brief stint as a substitute provided me with direct experience of how Travellers interacted with social workers and the welfare system and the complaints and misunderstandings that arise between Travellers and neighboring settled Irish.

An important part of my research was observing Travellers outside the camp setting as they interacted with other urbanites. They had regular, highly patterned contact with non-Travellers. Most interactions were brief and instrumental, involving either economic exchanges (e.g., begging, collecting scrap metal or selling it to a metal merchant, picking up money at the labor exchange, buying groceries in a shop) or necessary dealings with institutional representatives (e.g., social workers, clergy, medical staff, police or court officials). In downtown Dublin, for example, I could observe the brief transactions that took place between the Travelling women and girls who begged on the street and the Dubliners who passed them. On a few occasions I accompanied Travelling women as they worked the suburbs knocking on doors to ask for charity; some of these women had regular "call backs" or "ladies" in the settled community with whom they had developed patroness–client relationships. These relationships sometimes approximated friendships and involved not only the exchange of food and clothing but also conversation over tea, advice, and the opportunity for the Travelling woman to take a bath. With George, I accompanied Travelling men as they collected scrap metal from private homes and business around the city and then sold it to metal merchants and foundries in the inner city. I also frequently accompanied Travellers to shops, cinemas, court appearances, the hospital, and the like and observed their behavior and how they were treated. Just riding the bus yielded data on many Dubliners' attitudes toward Travellers, as when a passenger remarked to me with disdain, "Don't get off here. That's the knackers' [Travellers] stop."[4]

To supplement the data I gained when in the company of Travellers and from my observations and informal conversations with settled Irish people, I undertook a series of formal interviews with people who had regular dealings with them: justices and local police, nuns and priests, settlement committee workers, teachers, social workers, doctors and nurses, scrap metal merchants, government housing officers, and the like. To more systematically learn about the general public's interactions with Travellers, I designed a questionnaire to elicit information on the frequency with which and the contexts in which settled people met Travellers and their attitudes towards them. This was answered by a little over 300 people in Dublin and three rural areas.

All cultural groups are part of larger political and economic systems. Moreover, Travellers were also transnational, making extended trips to the UK to find work and visit relatives.[5] The more I learned about this, the more important it seemed to make a trip there. My primary destination was Birmingham, where I visited relatives of families I knew in Holylands and interviewed social workers, police officers, and government employees who had regular contact or official responsibility for Travellers.

One advantage of urban research, especially in a capital city, over that conducted in most rural areas, is the anthropologist's access to diverse sources of information. These include government agencies and personnel, research institutes and their reports, university departments and faculty, and libraries and other archives. I spent many hours in the National Library ferreting out information relating to the early history of Travellers. I'll never forget the thrill of discovering references to "tinkers" in the verbatim testimony of the rural Irish interviewed by the Poor Law Commissioners in the 1850s. Their comments indicated that "tinkers" had traveled on the road in family units, intermarried, and formed a distinct group from other itinerant craftsmen and landless people for several generations at the minimum.[6] The clippings files then maintained in the library of the *Irish Times* (now most newspapers have searchable digitized archives) documented the emergence of the Itinerant Settlement Movement—the national campaign to settle Travellers on government sites and in conventional housing. They also documented the many clashes that had occurred throughout Ireland between Travellers and the settled Irish community over roadside camping and trespass, site construction and housing, and other issues like factional fighting and public disturbances. These articles revealed much about mainstream society's attitudes toward Travellers. The archives of the Folklore Department at University College, Dublin, contained the results of a questionnaire about Travellers that had been sent to schoolteachers across Ireland in the early 1950s. Their answers yielded a wealth of information on Travellers' lives—as viewed by these outsiders—and their relationship to the mainstream Irish population before their migration to urban areas. Whenever I felt depressed or anxious or sensed that my research among Travellers had reached a plateau, I went to one of these places. I always came back with a wealth of new information as well as new topics and questions to pursue.

When a complete rest from research was needed, the city provided shops, restaurants, plays, movies, museums, art galleries, and the zoo—a range of diversions unavailable to most anthropologists working in the countryside. The contacts we both developed during the year with settled people also meant that we were frequently invited to people's homes for dinner or tea. Good food in comfortable surroundings was always welcome, and conversations almost always yielded some new insight about Travellers or their relationship with the settled community.

NEUTRAL OBSERVER OR ADVOCATE?

Most research produces dilemmas. The people anthropologists work with, especially those in cities, such as ethnic minorities, migrants, refugees, and the disadvantaged, often face significant obstacles. This was true for Travellers, who, in the 1970s, were (and continue to be) discriminated against by the settled community and who were coping with frequent evictions, a new urban environment, and pressures to give up nomadism. During this first research, the national effort to settle Travellers on official sites and in houses—the Itinerant Settlement Movement—was just getting underway. (The logo of the movement was a winding road leading to a house.) It viewed integration with mainstream society as the solution to the "itinerant problem." The "itinerant problem" included both the problems Travellers faced (illiteracy, ill-health, frequent evictions, lack of basic services like water, electricity, and sanitation) and the problems their unregulated camping and lifestyle created for urban residents (the traffic hazards posed by wandering horses, the expense of cleaning up abandoned camps, the possible health risks, the general nuisance and threat to property values). The people who joined settlement committees were volunteers who wanted to "help" Travellers, and many wanted to know they were doing the right thing. Since we often attended settlement committee meetings, we were frequently asked our opinions. I resisted giving advice, however, believing that I should remain neutral and just carry out my research—the perspective we had acquired in graduate school. I also wanted to avoid making ill-informed pronouncements while I was still learning. What help I gave Travellers was given on a personal level: reading prescription labels, filling out medical cards and housing applications, interpreting legal notices, obtaining telephone numbers, occasionally reading or writing a personal letter, and giving people necessary rides. Yet, the pressure to give advice to settlement workers continued and was reinforced by my natural desire to help Travellers if I could.

Traveller girl and a younger sister begging on O'Connell Bridge in Dublin in the 1970s. [Photo by Pat Langan]

By the end of our research, we decided that we were sufficiently knowledgeable to make what we regarded as a few commonsense suggestions to settlement workers. We also felt we owed it to Travellers. To be truly dispassionate when working with people, particularly a stigmatized group like Irish Travellers, is in some ways inhuman. Moreover, anthropologists are often in a far better position than other outsiders to speak for the people among whom they have lived. At the urging of a prominent settlement worker, George and I wrote an open letter to Ireland's settlement committees, assessing their work from the Traveller point of view. Later, we wrote a critique of the Itinerant Settlement Movement for an Irish journal (Gmelch, with Gmelch 1974b). We urged providing serviced campsites for Travellers who wished to continue traveling rather than focusing all efforts on permanent settlement, whether on sites like Labre Park or in housing. In other words, Travellers needed to be given a choice, and had the right to retain some degree of nomadism. We also strongly recommended that Travellers be directly involved in the work of settlement committees—a novel suggestion at the time—particularly that they be given a voice in planning. These suggestions were endorsed by some settlement workers, but resented by others for a variety of reasons including a deeply ingrained charity model of social welfare and, for some, that we were American outsiders.

EPILOGUE

I continued to conduct research with the Travelling People through the 1970s until the mid-1980s, returning to Dublin many times for periods of three months to a year. This work resulted in academic articles, a photo-essay book published in Ireland for the general public and Travellers, and later, a biography of Nan Donoghue, who had been one of my closest friends at Holylands.[7] In 1981–1982, George and I conducted a year-long study of Irish Travellers and British Gypsies in the UK for the British Department of the Environment. It focused on travel patterns and accommodation needs, and involved contact with families all over England and in Ireland. Since then, I have kept in contact with several Travellers and some of their offspring through letters, phone calls, and now e-mail. My most recent trip to Holylands occurred in 2001 when I returned to Ireland for six months on a Fulbright Fellowship.

Today, the number of Travellers living in Dublin has tripled from the time of my first research, while the size of the greater Dublin area has doubled.[8] Holylands has changed dramatically. Since we left in 1972, it was developed into a permanent Traveller site with small houses similar to those at Labre Park. These were replaced in the mid-1980s by more substantial homes. In 2001, the old site was closed and a brand new housing estate for Travellers was opened adjacent to it. Now eight families live there in solidly built, four- and five-bedroom bungalows that are indistinguishable from those of the settled community. The offspring of other Holylands families live in roadside camps, on official sites in other parts of the city, and in housing estates. Still others have left Dublin for other parts of the country and England. One of the most difficult aspects of my long relationship with Travellers is returning to find so many people I had known gone. Travellers lead a hard life and many die early; less than 3 percent of Travellers are 65 and older compared to 11 percent of the general population.[9] Most of the adults I knew at Holylands, including Nan, are now gone and so are many of their children. Travellers also have been affected by the negative changes occurring in Irish society at large, namely, drugs and violent crime.

Ireland has changed since my first fieldwork. It joined the European Union in 1973, which spurred economic growth. EU membership also introduced new social and environmental legislation that has had an impact even on Travellers' lives. It is virtually impossible today, for example, for Travellers to make a living collecting and recycling scrap metal as they had when I lived among them. They simply cannot afford to comply with the costly environmental protections the new legislation now requires of the industry. New anti-discrimination legislation means that Travellers now have greater legal recourse than before.[10] Some Travellers have taken publicans, stores, and other businesses to court over denial of service, false accusations of theft, and other forms of targeted discrimination. In the 1970s such cases were nonexistent.

As Ireland's prosperity grew during the mid-1990s (the "Celtic Tiger" years), new immigrants and asylum seekers arrived, mainly from Asia, Africa, and Eastern Europe, including Roma (Gypsies) from Romania and Bulgaria. The expansion in the number of EU member states, whose citizens can move freely between countries, has also contributed to a more ethnically diverse Ireland. After 2004, for example, more than 100,000 Polish immigrants entered Ireland. Today, 11 percent of Ireland's population is foreign-born. There are now four times as many Asians and Blacks (mainly Africans) as there are Travelling People, once Ireland's only visible minority.[11] Nevertheless, Travellers are still the focus of much discrimination.

Travellers are better off financially today; some told me in 2001 that there are "no more poor Travellers." Indeed, it is rare to see an Irish Traveller begging on the streets. Continuing the trend promoted by the Settlement Movement, about 70 percent of Traveller households now live in houses. But after nearly 40 years of government efforts to settle Travellers, 30 percent continue to live in trailers, and an unknown number of Travellers living in houses return to the road during the summer months. These families are as subject to eviction as Travellers had been in the early 1970s. More Travelling children attend school today than in the 1970s, although very few yet complete secondary school or go on to higher education.[12] In the 1970s Travellers lacked any organizations of their own, but today they have several including the Irish Traveller Movement, the National Traveller Women's Forum, and Pavee Point, which provide social and educational services, give information to the media, and at times act as political lobbies.

Doing fieldwork with Irish Travellers had a profound effect on my life, professionally and personally. The information I acquired resulted in a doctoral dissertation, articles, and books, which in turn helped me secure an academic job and tenure. Living with them also taught me valuable life lessons: the insignificance of material things, the capacity to make do with little, the importance of recycling, the rewards of living for the moment, and the value of finding humor in even unpleasant situations. Living with Travellers also exposed me in a direct way to some of life's harsher realities: the destructive impact of alcoholism on families and individual health, the many limitations posed by illiteracy, and the insidiousness of discrimination. More than anything, living with Travellers gave me an appreciation for human resilience. Travellers are masters of survival. Anthropological fieldwork, even when conducted in the large and relatively anonymous setting of the city, is a profoundly rewarding experience. The friendships I made with Travellers and the experiences I shared with them have remained among the most meaningful of my life.

Notes

[1] It was funded by the National Science Foundation and run through the Department of Anthropology at the University of Pittsburgh. Professor Eileen Kane was the director the year I participated.

[2] At the time of my first research, Travellers were the primary "ethnic" group in Ireland, although the mainstream Irish population did not at the time use that label. Today, there are many more immigrants from diverse backgrounds in Ireland. (Contemporary figures come from Central Statistics Office 2007:22.)

[3] We kept a rented room throughout our research so that we had a safe place to store our field notes, electricity for our typewriters, and a place to take much needed baths. We usually visited it a couple times a week.

[4] Some Travellers "knackered" horses, that is, took them to the slaughterhouse.

[5] Still other Irish Travellers emigrated to the United States, some as early as the mid-1800s. Well-known communities of Irish Travellers can be found in the southern United States; other families live throughout the country.

[6] Of course there are much earlier references to "tynklers" in British statutes and even in Shakespeare. See, Sharon Gmelch, with George Gmelch 1974a.

[7] The photo-essay, titled *Tinkers and Travellers,* published in Ireland, combined my text with photographs taken by George Gmelch and by Pat Langan, an *Irish Times* photographer. It won Ireland's book publishers' "Book of the Year" award in 1975. The biography, *Nan: The Life of an Irish Travelling Woman,* was published in 1986 by W.W. Norton in the U.S. and by Souvenir Press and Pan Books in the UK. It is still in print in the U.S., published by Waveland Press. Both received considerable public and media attention in Ireland and for some time helped heighten the general population's understanding of Traveller life.

[8] The 2006 census recorded 4,235 Travellers in Dublin; another 2,578 lived in the cities of Cork, Limerick, Galway, and Waterford (a total of 31% of the Traveller population). The number living in "aggregate town areas" (cities and towns over 1,500 in population) equaled 64%, while 36% lived in "aggregate rural areas" (countryside and towns under 1,499 in population) (Central Statistics Office 2007:21–22).

[9] *Census 2006: Ethnic or Cultural Background* reveals that this is still true. Travellers aged 65 and older account for just 2.6% of the total Traveller population compared with 11% for the general population (Central Statistics Office 2007).

[10] Some of this legislation (such as the Equal Status Act of 2000) emerged internally; other legislation (such as the Equality Act of 2004) was prompted by EU directives.

[11] According to *Census 2006: Ethnic or Cultural Background,* there were 21,935 Travellers in Ireland (about .5% of the total population) versus 43,435 "Blacks" (1%), and 41,415 Asians (1%)

(Central Statistics Office 2007:22). Figures cited elsewhere in the census give the number of Travellers in Ireland as 22,435.

[12] According to *Census 2006: Ethnic or Cultural Background*, 69% of Travellers aged 15 and over who were no longer in school either had no formal education or had only completed primary school. Of the remainder no longer attending school, 16% had finished lower secondary, 3% had completed upper secondary, and less than 1% had received any third-level education (Central Statistics Office 2007:45).

References

Barth, Fredrik, ed. 1998 [1969]. *Ethnic Groups and Boundaries: The Social Organization of Cultural Difference.* Long Grove, IL: Waveland Press.

Central Statistics Office. 2007, July. *Census 2006: Ethnic or Cultural Background,* vol. 5. Dublin: Government Stationery Office.

Gmelch, Sharon Bohn. 1977. Economic and Power Relations among Urban Tinkers: The Role of Women. *Urban Anthropology,* 6(3):237–247.

———. 1991 [1986]. *Nan: The Life of an Irish Travelling Woman.* Long Grove, IL: Waveland Press.

———, with George Gmelch. 1974a. The Emergence of an Ethnic Group: The Irish Travellers. *Anthropological Quarterly,* 49:225–238.

———. 1974b. The Itinerant Settlement Movement: Its Policies and Effects on Irish Travellers. *Studies: An Irish Quarterly Review,* 63:1–16.

———. 1978. Begging in Dublin: The Strategies of a Marginal Urban Occupation. *Urban Life,* 6(4):439–454.

McCarthy, Patricia. 1972. Itinerancy and Poverty: A Study in the Sub-culture of Poverty. Unpublished Masters Thesis, Department of Sociology, University College, Dublin.

Report of the Commission on Itinerancy. 1963. Dublin: Government Stationery Office.

4

Moscow Encounters
Ethnography in a Global Urban Village

Melissa L. Caldwell

Since the mid-1990s, Melissa Caldwell has been conducting fieldwork in Moscow, a megacity of more than 12 million people. The communities at the center of her research are groups of people brought together by cultures of food sharing and shared eating. By following her informants out of these food settings and into the other dimensions of their lives in Moscow's urban spaces, Caldwell describes ways in which Moscow's residents experience the metropolis as a small, intimate setting. She suggests that urban spaces are more similar to rural spaces than might be expected. Finally, Caldwell offers advice for conducting fieldwork in urban spaces in ways that make them manageable and knowable.

Since 1995 I have been conducting fieldwork in Moscow, Russia, a hypermodern, global city that is home to more than 12 million residents. My work examines how Russians have responded to processes of globalization and the economic transition to market capitalism that were sparked by the collapse of the Soviet Union in 1991. Food has become a central theme in my research, not only because the effects of these changes have been especially evident in Russians' food practices, but also because Russians love food and, perhaps more importantly, love to talk about food. In my research I have used food to understand a diversity of issues ranging from the emergence of a new culture of deliberately conspicuous consumption focused on the abundance of food to the stunning impoverishment of many citizens and the persistence of massive food shortages. Topics that I have written about include the impact of McDonald's and other transnational food companies on local culinary cultures and grocery shopping practices, the emergence of explicitly "nationalist" and patriotic food cultures; the significance of garden foods and wild foods like mushrooms; and the persistent problems of food shortages and the

Source: Written expressly for *Urban Life*.

role of churches and other charities to feed poor Russians. Each of these topics has been intimately connected to the experiences of urban life, as this is the setting where new forms of food production, distribution, acquisition, and consumption have typically emerged first, before traveling elsewhere in the country. Moreover, changes in Russians' food habits have perhaps been most visible in urban settings like Moscow, as the local landscape has changed dramatically to accommodate new restaurants, fast-food chains, grocery stores, sidewalk kiosks, food markets, and public feeding programs.

In very real and profound ways, food became my way into Russia—not just into people's kitchens and dining rooms, but into the rhythms, spaces, and encounters of their daily lives. Eating, shopping, and gardening with people transformed the otherwise large, anonymous city of Moscow into a place where I have many dear friends and acquaintances and where I feel completely at home. In the next sections, I will draw on my Moscow research to address the following issues: How did I get started with my fieldwork in such a place? How did I find a "local community" in the middle of a global city? How did I meet people? What did I find to study? Above all, I hope to demystify some of the mythologies of urban fieldwork and urban spaces.

Moscow: The Urban Village

It can be difficult to orient oneself within the social world of Moscow, not only because of the geographic size and population density of this city, but also because of the incredibly diverse and oftentimes peculiar cultural sensibilities that exist here. Moscow is a space of breathtaking contrasts and paradoxes, where the strange and the familiar, the old and the new, the global and the local constantly bump up against one another. Despite its appearance as a modern, capitalist mecca, Moscow has often been affectionately described by Russians as an urban village, a representation that evokes nostalgic sensibilities about a traditional culture rooted in a peasant heritage and an intimate community.

As a city founded almost 900 years ago, Moscow is a quirky, surreal place where the unexpected is always somehow expected and not particularly noteworthy. Circus workers regularly exercise their camels on city streets, and farmers lead their goats and wagons loaded with pails of fresh milk for sale down the sidewalks near the Kremlin. At the same time, it is a setting where the ordinary takes on qualities of extraordinariness, as discreet plaques on modest, nondescript buildings mark those spaces as sites of world-changing events. Moscow is a mythic space, inhabited by larger-than-life figures, past and present, from the country's colorful political, national, and literary history. These ghostly figures roam the city, sometimes quite literally as both impersonators and statues of public figures move from place to place (Boym 2001). It is also a city of constant change, as street names, roadways, and the appearances of buildings can change overnight. Finally, Moscow is a city marked by intense speed. Streets are always busy with cars, buses, and trucks whizzing through the center of the city down eight- and ten-lane highways and often up along sidewalks and through courtyards behind and between buildings. Pedestrians hustle along at a similarly rapid pace, trying to dodge traffic and one another. In Moscow's subway system, escalators transport passengers to the underground stations at a terrifyingly rapid pace. Passengers never wait more than a few moments for an arriving train to whisk them away at an equally rapid clip to the next station.

Russians engage Moscow, their capital city, with a mixture of awe and exasperation. Historic sites such as the Kremlin, St. Basil's Cathedral, Lenin's Tomb, and Red Square provide enticing subject matter for photographs, not just for foreign tourists but also for local residents. At the same time, the dramatically different architectural styles and commercial advertising introduced by global capitalism compete with more traditional styles such as the gingerbread-style carvings on wooden cottages and the brightly colored onion-shaped domes that top Orthodox churches. Local residents fear that Moscow's aesthetic sensibility as a uniquely Russian cultural space is compromised by the proliferation of Western fast-food chains, hypermarkets, and English-language billboards. City residents pride themselves on their cosmopolitan attitudes and the city's history as an international hub, even as they lament the arrival of foreigners and foreign cultural trends. And Muscovites claim that they love their city and would never live anywhere else, even as

Russian tourists to the capital take pictures of one another in front of Lenin's Tomb and the Kremlin. [Photo by Melissa L. Caldwell]

they make plans to escape the hustle, bustle, and pollution on weekend trips to their summer cottages outside the city.

Urban spaces present their own sets of unique challenges for ethnographers. Some of these challenges are ethnographic, such as trying to determine which elements of a large city are unique to that city and which are representative of the larger society in that country. Others are methodological, such as trying to identify and become integrated into a community of manageable size when one is living in the midst of millions of people. Yet another set of issues concerns scale, particularly when trying to identify a local community and then situate that local community within its larger national, and even global, contexts.

The possibilities these settings offer for reconsidering and resolving these challenges are what make fieldwork in Russian cities like Moscow so intriguing. Russia's unique history of urbanization and modernization has reconfigured differences between rural and urban, and between small-scale and large-scale. Despite its rural peasant heritage, today's Russia is a country of cities. The industrialization push that began in the late nineteenth century encouraged a mass migration from the countryside to the cities, a trajectory that continued throughout the twentieth century and into the present. Approximately 75 percent of Russia's population is estimated to live in cities, a figure that may be growing as rising poverty rates in the countryside propel even more young people to the cities in search of opportunities. At the same time, throughout the twentieth century, state planners implemented homogeneous architectural designs, so that all apartment buildings erected throughout the country resembled one another. These two trends came together in the Russian countryside, as rural villages were redesigned with the same generic styles of apartment blocks, public buildings, and transportation systems. Thus, the features that are conventionally presumed by anthropologists to distinguish urban from rural settings do not always hold up in Russia.

I think it is important to introduce my own research with this description of Moscow not just to provide readers with a sense of the city itself but also to engage with the issue of how to do fieldwork in an urban setting like Moscow. It is important to distinguish between doing fieldwork "on the city" and doing fieldwork "in the city." The two approaches require different methodologies and different modes of analysis. People behave very differently than do buildings, and how we describe and engage with human informants is very different from how we describe and engage with inanimate objects like streets, statues, and traffic.

Yet we should not lose sight of the fact that to do fieldwork "in the city" also requires that we acknowledge and incorporate that city into our analyses. For informants like my Muscovite acquaintances, their activities, beliefs, and experiences are very much shaped by how they live in, move through, and respond to the city. Muscovites describe direct links between the city they inhabit and their health, sleeping patterns, and ability to socialize with friends and relatives. Muscovites who report suffering from medical issues and insomnia blame the city's noise, air pollution, constant dust, and frenetic pace. The design of apartment buildings, especially the cramped quarters that many families share, shapes how people understand such fundamental concepts as privacy. Many apartment buildings still lack telephone service, a fact that until the recent proliferation of cell phones (*mobilniki*) forced residents to travel across the city in order to make their calls from the post office or from the homes of friends who did have telephones. The layout of the city even affects how and where Muscovites shop for groceries—at outdoor markets located far outside the city center, at tiny kiosks and temporary stands set up on busy sidewalks, in overcrowded supermarkets that are taking over residential areas, or in small storefronts tucked away in the basements or upper floors of office buildings in the city center. These spatial arrangements in turn influence how Muscovites determine the healthfulness and tastiness of the foods they buy in these settings. Thus, as such examples reveal, the city matters to Muscovites in terms of how they live their lives and the values they hold. Consequently, to do research in a place like Moscow, one must acknowledge and incorporate the influences that come from the city from the very beginning of one's research.

WHERE IS THE LOCAL IN A GLOBAL CITY LIKE MOSCOW? OR, FINDING THE TREES IN THE URBAN FOREST

One assumption often made about cities, particularly global cities like Moscow, Tokyo, or Mexico City, is that the sheer size and density of the population create a monolithic, impersonal setting inhabited by an anonymous, homogeneous mass of people. In such settings, it can be difficult for any one person to stand out and for any sense of a distinctive "local" community to emerge (Ritzer 2004). For anthropologists, the challenge is finding an actual "local" community and then an entry point into that community. Where do you start when there are millions of potential informants? How do you access informants if they work in large office buildings (a question that William Leggett addresses in his chapter) and live in large apartment buildings or housing complexes? Can the experiences of urbanites be distilled into discrete "local" communities? Villages, towns, and rural communities, by contrast, are typically depicted as more manageable spaces where local communities are more evident and accessible. Rural residents are presumed to have more time and inclination to visit with the anthropologist who has dropped unannounced into their midst than are urbanites who are constantly "on the go." Spontaneously meeting neighbors at the village well, over the back fence, or in the village rum (or vodka) shop seems easier and more comfortable than waiting around at the neighborhood announcement board where residents post "lost dog" and "for sale" notices.

At first glance, these qualities of density, anonymity, and impersonality certainly seem to describe Moscow. Simply arriving in Moscow and getting settled is a daunting task that immediately throws one into the crowd. Three international airports serve Moscow; each is a massive, impersonal maze of

Moscow's downtown Arbat Street district is a busy area filled with pedestrians, cars, shops, businesses, and apartment buildings. [Photo by Melissa L. Caldwell]

unmarked corridors lined by unsmiling armed guards and stern-faced airport personnel who ensure that arriving passengers stay within these secure spaces and arrive in the immigrations hall to have their travel documents processed. The arrival halls in Moscow's airports provide an early taste of being anonymous within a heaving mass of people. Typically, passengers from multiple jumbo planes that have arrived at the same time are herded into the same tiny arrivals hall, where they must jostle each other in a chaotic scrum to reach the tiny cubicle where immigrations officers carefully and wordlessly scrutinize passengers' passports and visas. Nervous passengers are further unsettled by the stares of immigrations officers who must match the photographs in the documents to the individuals standing in front of them. After what seems to be an eternity, the officials finally stamp the documents and return them, thereby allowing one to move through the gates and into the baggage delivery area. Inside the baggage area, the luggage from these multiple flights has been off-loaded onto the same two carousels, forcing hundreds of passengers from around the globe to fight with one another to find and claim their luggage. The experience is repeated as passengers who have successfully collected their bags push their way through the customs lines, only to arrive in the main reception hall where hundreds of family members and taxi drivers press against the flimsy rope dividers to wait for their charges. Once one has successfully been packed into a car, the sense of being swallowed up continues as drivers struggle to extricate their vehicles from an overflowing parking lot and somehow merge into a never-ending stream of traffic onto the freeway. While the drive between the airports and downtown Moscow can theoretically be made in less than 45 minutes (especially during the late evening and early morning hours), the trip can more often take two to three hours as drivers inch along the freeway.

For the arriving anthropologist, this feeling of being swallowed up by the city and its populace can be personally disconcerting and methodologically taxing. When I arrived in Moscow in 1997 for my first year of fieldwork, my driver dropped me at the apartment I was renting on the western side of the city. My landlady, who was waiting for me at the apartment, quickly gave me the keys, accepted my payment for two months' rent, told me that there was a bus stop outside the apartment building, and then scurried out. I was alone, and I didn't know where the nearest metro station was, never mind a grocery store or a bank where I could change money. My first few days were spent trying to learn my neighborhood, find the elusive bus stop and even more elusive metro station, and locate the office buildings in the center of the city where I would need to drop off and collect my visa and other legal documents. Because it was late autumn, there were only a few hours of daylight every day, which gave the city a strange appearance, and I discovered how difficult it is to get one's bearings in the dark. The cold temperature and frequent snows also meant that few Muscovites remained out-of-doors. Thus, the city felt perpetually empty, and I felt completely alone in a city of millions.

These feelings of aloneness, emptiness, and disorientation were terrifying, and I anxiously worried if I would ever feel settled or ever meet people. Of course, my fears did not last long. Within two weeks I was fully immersed in a community that has become my permanent "home away from home."

HOW DOES ONE FIND A COMMUNITY?

In my case, I started with two sites—a restaurant chain and a church. Because my initial research interests focused on how Russians' food practices were changing after the collapse of the Soviet Union, I decided that I needed to get a feel for the experiences of both those who could consume in the new economy and those who could not. To pursue the first theme, I began visiting McDonald's restaurants. One advantage of this choice was that I could sit in McDonald's for several hours and feel as if I were part of a larger community, thus alleviating some of the initial loneliness in my first days in Moscow. As I lingered at my table, developing my skills at stretching my meal out for several hours (unlike in the United States, Russian McDonald's employees do not enforce time limits on customers), I observed how customers moved through the restaurant, navigated the lines at the counter, interacted with their companions and employees, and occupied themselves at their tables.

Over time, I realized that many other customers were doing the same thing as I was and lingering in the restaurant for hours at a time. I also discovered that McDonald's was occupied by individuals who never bought a single item from the menu. Some people, like construction workers and elderly visitors, brought their own lunches into the restaurant, while homeless adults and street children scavenged meals from the leftovers on other customers' trays. By sitting inside McDonald's restaurants for hours at a time, I became aware of an entire community of people who came together in these spaces. Managers and store employees knew some of their visitors, including managers at one McDonald's who acted as surrogate aunts and uncles for the homeless teenagers who gathered in the store. These small communities were all the more intriguing because the McDonald's restaurants in Russia are among the largest and busiest in the world.

Although I myself never became a "local" in Russia's McDonald's society, I was sufficiently integrated that I could document and analyze the ways in which McDonald's had become a "local" community with its own distinct cultural values, practices, and participants. This research (Caldwell 2004a) has informed my subsequent research on other types of consumer communities in Russia, including a recent study of how public dining spaces like those in restaurants and coffeehouses disrupt Russians' distinctions between private and public spaces, because private activities of eating and socializing take place in public settings (Caldwell in press).

To pursue my second research topic concerning Muscovites whose personal financial and social circumstances prevented them from participating in this new consumer economy, I needed to find a community where I could find these types of people. Although I could have approached a public welfare agency to see if social workers could introduce me to poor people, I accidentally stumbled into a much better opportunity. During my second week in Moscow, I met an American student who was living and working in Moscow. When I described my interests to him, he mentioned that his church sponsored a soup kitchen program for elderly and disabled Russians. He was an active volunteer with the program, and he suggested that I attend church on Sunday and learn more about the program. That invitation was a key moment in the evolution of my research. Before the church service had concluded, I had been welcomed by a diverse community of Moscow residents and received clearance to visit the soup kitchens. Early the next morning found me at the soup kitchen, serving food, clearing tables, and meeting volunteers and recipients for almost four hours. I volunteered every day that week. By Friday I realized that the soup kitchen program was in itself a vibrant community of recipients, volunteers, cafeteria employees, and church congregants.

During that year of fieldwork, I became completely enmeshed in this community. I volunteered at the soup kitchens on a daily basis, becoming friends and colleagues with the African students who staffed the programs, the elderly Russians who came for meals, the Russian social workers who referred clients, the Russian cafeteria employees who prepared the meals, and the North American and European expatriates who served as volunteers and provided donations. I also attended church services every week, as well as the many fel-

Through the soup kitchen, Russian recipients, volunteers, and church members have formed a vibrant community of friendship and support that extends far beyond the walls of this cafeteria and across the globe. [Photo by Melissa L. Caldwell]

lowship activities that the church's congregation enjoyed. The church's membership represented a diverse community of Russians, North Americans, Europeans, and Africans, and services were an eclectic mixture of the many cultural, religious, and linguistic traditions represented by its members.

The longer that I worked within the communities formed by the church and its soup kitchens, the more deeply I was drawn into the lives, dramas, and networks of my informants. In addition to the more usual fieldwork methods of interviewing informants, observing their interactions, following them on their daily activities, celebrating holidays and special occasions with them, and analyzing public documents relating to religion, food aid, and public welfare policies, I have also been fortunate to participate in many more intimate, unique, and revealing aspects of their lives. I have celebrated raucous vodka-filled birthdays for 80-year-old Russian grandmothers, debated social theorists like Foucault and Habermas with high-ranking religious leaders while sitting in their living rooms, visited friends at their rural summer cottages and picked mushrooms and berries with them during our strolls through the forest, and mediated feuds between elderly recipients at the soup kitchen.

More importantly, these connections drew me outside the institutional settings of the church, its food programs, and the local welfare bureaucracy and into the larger social worlds of my informants. Personal relationships and chance encounters provided opportunities to follow my informants into the other domains of their lives: family, work, school, the doctor's office, their neighborhoods, and their social clubs. Through all of these interactions I came to know what life was really like for Moscow's residents, the multiple social and economic groups and subgroups that Muscovites move into and out of, the types of relationships that exist between people, and how a community like this one may seem unique but is, in fact, a microcosm of Russian society (Caldwell 2004b).

This church, its soup kitchen program, and the larger communities in which they are situated, have become my "home base." I return almost every year for up to several months of research in this community, and I have been fortunate to follow members of this community as they grow older, grapple with new challenges, and move on to new phases of their lives, sometimes out of Moscow or even out of Russia altogether. We keep in touch through a mixture of conventional communication such as letter writing and passing on messages through mutual acquaintances, and more modern forms of communication such as e-mail, text messaging, and Internet social networking sites. What was surprising to me was how multigenerational these connections are. Although, children, young adults, and middle-aged Russians were early adopters of Web and cellular technology, my elderly friends are also increasingly linked into these networks and use them to maintain contacts with one another and me. Thus, in the midst of such a massive city and a global web of constant mobility, this community has remained constant, local, and accessible. At the same time, the welcoming, inclusive, and accessible qualities of this community raise important questions about the extent to which cities can ever be spaces of true intimacy.

ARE CITIES IMPERSONAL SPACES?

Issues of intimacy and familiarity emerged repeatedly during my research and evolved into both theoretical questions and methodological strategies that have guided my research. One of the issues that I have had to resolve over the years is how to identify the boundaries of the communities I am studying and how to determine who belongs to this community and who does not. This is particularly important in Moscow, where people are mobile and routinely move into, across, and out of the city. When I first arrived in Moscow, one of my dissertation advisors suggested that I employ the standard ethnographic method of network mapping. My task was to try to diagram the social networks of my informants and determine the parameters of their social groups. I did so by paying attention to conversations among informants (who spoke with whom; were these encounters brief and businesslike or were they more personal; did people give each other things, and if so, what did they exchange; did people ever complain about others; who sat together; who traveled together; who knew someone else's telephone number; and so on). Because many of my informants formally belonged to the church and soup kitchen program, it was relatively easy to observe and trace their connections with one another and document the ever expanding and multiple overlapping connections that brought them together.

It was when I began expanding these network diagrams outward that I found intriguing details that became significant for reconsidering intimacy in urban spaces. During interviews and casual conversations with informants, I paid careful attention to the people they described to me or greeted in my presence—relatives, neighbors, friends, acquaintances, work colleagues, and welfare and aid workers. When I was out in public with my informants, I observed how they interacted with other people. How my informants greeted other people revealed different degrees of closeness, familiarity, respect, and social status, as Russians use different names (first and middle name, nickname, formal "you," or informal "you") to indicate these social differences. Similarly, I observed whether my informants demonstrated a preexisting relationship with salesclerks, bus drivers, social workers at the local welfare office, local officials, public maintenance workers, and other individuals who might at first glance appear to be unknown to them. Looking through personal photo albums with my informants was another way to identify the people who were meaningful enough to appear in such personal spaces.

Through these methods, I learned that my informants' social networks were flexible, extended far outside their immediate neighborhoods and socio-economic groups, and included both ordinary people and famous public figures. For instance, the social networks of one woman, a retired historian and regular recipient at the soup kitchen, were revealing. The woman was the granddaughter of a famous icon painter before the 1917 Russian Revolution, and her networks included a KGB agent, a journalist, and a top-ranking diplomat from one of the former Soviet Central Asian republics. This particular individual also knew most of the regional politicians on a first-name basis, through her participation in neighborhood programs for the elderly, as well as many state-level politicians and intelligence officials, through her neighbors in her apartment building.

Another informant was related through different networks of family and friends to vendors in an outdoor souvenir market, professors at the local university, and an internationally known media personality. Through yet another informant, a staff person at one of the organizations connected to the soup kitchen program, the networks included retired middle-class Russians, members of one of Russia's minority populations, immigrants, and a former minister in the federal government.

Thus by exploring the extended networks of my informants, I encountered a much more diverse and complex social world than would have otherwise been revealed in the more bounded structures of apartment buildings, workplaces, or assistance organizations such as soup kitchens.

Serendipity, a theme that George Foster emphasized as an essential yet often under-recognized element in field research (2002), also played an important role in my ability to track these expanded networks. On several occasions

I stepped into a crowded subway car far outside the neighborhoods where my informants lived, only to discover people I knew sitting nearby. On several other occasions, I visited public offices where I did not have any previous contacts, only to discover that employees were people I knew from other contexts.

By connecting people through these network mapping tactics and seemingly chance encounters, I was able to see how the physical and demographic distances implied by the sheer size and density of Moscow were not, in fact, that great when measured in social terms. People move across the city and belong to multiple social groups that transcend any one place. It is this reality of flexible and expansive social networks that shrink a city the size of Moscow into a much smaller social space. These networks also transform urban spaces into intimate spaces filled with familiar faces.

In the next section, I would like to draw from my fieldwork experiences a few tips for doing ethnography in large, global cities in ways that will make those spaces knowable, familiar, and comfortable and will offer insight into how local residents—informants—make intimate and meaningful lives in those spaces.

TIPS FOR DOING ETHNOGRAPHY IN GLOBAL CITIES

1. Equip yourself with several good maps that present the city in different ways. When I first arrived in Moscow, maps were difficult to find. Part of the reason for this was that during the socialist period, maps were protected documents. The state limited the production of maps and their accessibility to the general public, because they could potentially fall into the wrong hands (i.e., Western hands) and reveal state secrets. Hence, during the first few years of the postsocialist period, there were limited maps available, and those that were available were often based on Soviet-era details rather than post-Soviet realities. Although I had an excellent tourist map (one that I still use today, albeit for different purposes as a historical reference document), I quickly discovered that many of the street names listed on the map were the names used during the Soviet period and did not reflect the name changes that had been made in the post-Soviet period. I spent several weeks trying to find one office building that was located on a renamed street whose new name was not on any map, before accidentally stumbling upon the street during a walk.

In the past decade, maps have become more commonplace and are geared toward diverse audiences with different needs. Maps for pedestrians identify major streets, side streets, alleys, courtyards, numbered buildings, and public transit lines with their numbers and stops. Maps for drivers indicate roadways, petrol and repair stations, traffic-police inspection stations, and areas where left turns are possible. Maps for tourists, meanwhile, show important attractions, restaurants, hotels, and other cultural, political, and historical sites of interest to visitors. I carry at least one map with me at all times, so that I can easily meet informants and find office buildings. These maps are also useful for meeting and helping passersby, as one of the universal features of Moscow life is that no one—including local residents—ever seems to know where they are going.

2. Spend time learning the city by walking it. Although public transportation is beneficial for saving time and energy, it also gives one a skewed orientation to the city as one becomes familiar with particular routes that bypass side streets. A city, then, is condensed into its public transit lines. Whenever I first arrive in a new city, I immediately begin walking in order to map the space through my own bodily knowledge. By walking, I can experience the city in different ways: I learn how it smells (some sections of Moscow smell like car exhaust, others like green forests, and still others like the herbs used in nearby restaurants), how it sounds (the chiming bells of neighborhood churches, the gurgles of rivers and streams running through neighborhoods, the relative quiet of suburban neighborhoods), how it changes colors (from the brightly lit neon signs of the city center to the leafy green of the neighborhoods by the city parks to the drab-colored apartment complexes in the industrial neighborhoods), and even how it feels (hot and humid in the city center, cool and dry in the suburbs).

Walking also allows you to learn where the more mundane, but no less meaningful, spaces of our informants' lives are located: schools, stores, banks, public offices, company offices, theaters, dry cleaners, pet food shops, and so on. Do not be afraid to wander off the beaten path, because you might discover something fascinating and completely unexpected. In Moscow, like many Russian cities, apartment buildings have interior courtyards, which can be put to a variety of uses: parking areas, children's playgrounds, tiny private gardens, ping-pong tables, chess tables, shops, museums, and even business offices. Neighbors often sit and visit with one another in these courtyards, thus making them prime locations for a visiting ethnographer to meet people and get a feel for daily life in the neighborhood. Russians' deep compassion for animals is often on display in these tucked-away spaces, as neighbors leave out bowls of water and food for stray dogs and cats.

3. Travel the city with informants. Although I have come to know Moscow intimately through my own travels, it is through my travels with my informants that I have discovered the existence of alternative Moscows. More importantly, these excursions have allowed my informants to reveal details from their lives that are only meaningful in relationship to the spaces in which these events occurred. On one occasion when I was staying at a hotel in downtown Moscow near the parliament building, a close friend, a woman in her 80s, introduced me to the small alleys tucked away in the neighborhood, including the buildings that had once been a children's hospital and orphanage. More significantly, by narrating the neighborhood as we walked through it, my friend revealed that she had been a temporary resident in the orphanage during World War II, a detail that she had never told me despite our frequent conversations about her childhood during the many years we had known one another. Another informant, a man in his 60s, led me on a tour of a different part of Moscow, a district home to many embassies and art

galleries. While we walked he told me about his mother, who had walked with him through the neighborhood many years before.

At the same time that accompanying informants as they travel through the city is a productive methodological strategy for the anthropologist, it is also an activity that Muscovites, like many post-Soviet citizens, share with their friends, relatives, and neighbors (Lemon 2000). During the Soviet

From the 15th-story balcony of a friend's apartment it is possible to see the larger neighborhood of massive apartment blocks and the network of courtyards that connect them. During the day these courtyards are busy places where children play, mothers and grandparents push baby carriages, and retirees sit and talk. [Photo by Melissa L. Caldwell]

On summer nights, Muscovites enjoy leaving their apartments and relaxing in city parks. In this neighborhood park, local residents are visiting with one another while enjoying accordion music. [Photo by Melissa L. Caldwell]

period, strolling slowly along city sidewalks or through city parks and department stores was relaxing, not simply as a form of leisure, but also as a form of socializing and transmitting information beyond the prying eyes and ears of neighbors or police informants.

Today, post-Soviet citizens continue to enjoy walking as a social activity. In some places in the former Soviet Union, local residents have organized formal walking or running groups as social clubs, such as in the Ukrainian city of Odessa, another large and historically important post-Soviet city, as described by anthropologist Tanya Richardson (2008) in her ethnography about how members of a walking club revive and relive the multiple histories that coexist in this city. Walking through a city with local residents, then, reveals the existence of complex social worlds and meaningful stories that may otherwise go unnoticed by the anthropologist.

4. Practice the art of appearing to daydream. It is possible to spend multiple hours of the day traveling across Moscow by public transportation, usually on the metro. The social world of public transportation provides important and fascinating opportunities for understanding the place of movement in everyday life (a point that Derek Pardue raises in his chapter) and for observing what fellow passengers do and the information that is available inside these public spaces (advertisements, public service announcements,

posters for upcoming events, graffiti). Yet, accessing what people do when they are in motion presents its own challenges. Travel times are intimately personal moments for Russians, and passengers typically refrain from overtly observing one another, although exceptions are made for the amusing, such as small children and pets, and the outrageous, such as teenagers experimenting with alternative fashions. Otherwise, overt watching immediately marks one as a foreigner, an outsider. Even so, Russians are keenly aware of what is taking place around them, and passengers have mastered the art of pretending to ignore their surroundings through such activities as reading, feigning sleep, and daydreaming.

Pretending to read a newspaper or stare at nothing allows one the freedom to see what else is taking place in these spaces, which can provide an important glimpse into larger concerns in society. While I was studying poverty and social assistance, for instance, my informants repeatedly told me that Russians only provide assistance to relatives and friends—in other words, to people they know. Assistance to strangers was relatively rare. Yet, again and again in metro cars, I witnessed strangers helping one another with tiny gestures such as sharing a bit of food or pressing a few rubles into someone's hands. Most acts were very discreet and might otherwise have gone unnoticed, or even been curtailed, had I not been able to watch them while appearing to have my attention focused elsewhere.

(RE)SIZING UP CITIES

While conducting research in cities can require different tactics and approaches than does research in smaller settings, urban spaces can be accessed just as effectively and deeply as rural spaces. Because so many ordinary people throughout the world do live in cities, or at least spend time in cities, even if it is just in transit to another destination, it is essential that we understand their experiences in those contexts. Because anthropologists are interested in real life as it is experienced by real people, it would be analytically disingenuous to pretend that real people do not live in cities. At the same time, attention to urban spaces helps us reconsider what, if anything, makes rural spaces different. Are differences between rural and urban spaces related to differences in the nature of everyday life in those two realms, or are they related to different qualities of life in those two realms? Or are those differences in fact differences of perception, either by residents or by outside observers?

For places like Russia, it can be difficult to pinpoint precise differences between the nature and quality of life in rural and urban settings. Russia's long history of urbanization, coupled with the more recent spread of modern technologies such as cell phones, the Internet, and a thriving car culture, has done much to minimize both physical and social distances between urban and rural spaces. Russia is also a place where people regularly move between urban and rural spaces, and sometimes where features of urban and rural life coexist adjacent to, or even within, one another. Because of the categorical confusions of urban and rural in Russia, as well as the persistent sense of physical and social disorientation that Russians invoke to describe contemporary life in a world of constant motion, it is necessary for anthropologists to take on these issues explicitly as analytical questions and methodological challenges.

Even as a sprawling, global metropolis like Moscow may seem to be at odds with more conventional, anthropological field sites, it is, in fact, just as ordinary, meaningful, and manageable as smaller, more rural settings. More importantly, conducting fieldwork in a city like Moscow offers unique opportunities for anthropologists to rediscover and rethink some of the most enduring issues that have shaped our discipline. In particular, urban anthropology challenges us to consider carefully how people organize their lives to include other people, many of whom may not be immediately at hand. Degrees of social proximity—intimacy, in other words—are critical aspects of daily life for people no matter where they live in Russia, or elsewhere in the world for that matter. It is essential that anthropologists get a handle on what intimacy feels like and means within a local society so that we can understand and represent how our informants create and live meaningful lives and relationships in that society. In other words, we must get to the inside of our informants' lives and understand their lives and relationships as they experience them, whether that is in a small village or a megacity. Intimacy thus is a universal anthropological quest that transcends the geographic or demographic size of any particular community. No matter the location, intimacy is a matter of how well we know our informants and the dimensions of their everyday lives.

References

Boym, Svetlana. 2001. *The Future of Nostalgia*. New York: Basic Books.

Caldwell, Melissa L. 2004a. Domesticating the French Fry: McDonald's and Consumerism in Moscow. *Journal of Consumer Culture*, 4(1):5–26.

———. 2004b. *Not By Bread Alone: Social Support in the New Russia*. Berkeley: University of California Press.

———. In Press. Tempest in a Coffee Pot: Brewing Incivility in Russia's Public Sphere. In *Food and Everyday Life in the Postsocialist World*, ed. Melissa L. Caldwell. Bloomington: Indiana University Press.

Foster, George M. 2002. A Half Century of Field Research in Tzintzuntzan, Mexico: A Personal View. In *Chronicling Cultures: Long-Term Field Research in Anthropology*, eds. Robert V. Kemper and Anya Peterson Royce, pp. 252–283. Walnut Creek, CA: AltaMira Press.

Lemon, Alaina. 2000. Talking Transit and Spectating Transition: The Moscow Metro. In *Altering States: Ethnographies of Transition in Eastern Europe and the Former Soviet Union*, eds. Daphne Berdahl, Matti Bunzl, and Martha Lampland, pp. 14–39. Ann Arbor: University of Michigan Press.

Richardson, Tanya. 2008. *Kaleidoscopic Odessa: History and Place in Contemporary Ukraine*. Toronto: University of Toronto Press.

Ritzer, George. 2004. *The Globalization of Nothing*. Thousand Oaks, CA: Pine Forge Press.

5

Fieldwork in the Corporate Offices of Jakarta, Indonesia

William Leggett

William Leggett first went to Indonesia as a graduate student to study cross-cultural encounters in transnational corporations. He soon found that urban fieldwork in a corporate setting posed unanticipated obstacles. He learned that getting on the inside, particularly gaining access to corporate elites, required being employed by the very corporations he wished to study. Getting a company job did make it possible for him to study those holding positions of power, but unexpectedly also made it difficult to conduct interviews with employees whose job status was lower than his. Ultimately, Leggett discovers that doing fieldwork in a corporate office requires a rethinking of some time-honored notions of anthropological fieldwork. His chapter also raises some questions about utilizing ethnographic methods in spaces not normally associated with traditional anthropology.

INTRODUCTION

In the summer of 1996, while stumbling through the early phases of a graduate degree in anthropology, I was in Jakarta, Indonesia, searching for a space to conduct ethnographic research. My project, as initially constructed, revolved vaguely around global economic processes and their role in bringing together disparate populations. On this morning in early June, however, my quest for sites of cultural encounter took a backseat to my stomach. As I walked away from an abruptly canceled meeting with an American banker (meetings with anthropologists, I came to understand, are rarely the top priority of working professionals), I found myself heading toward the smell of fried chilies wafting up from the food canteen downstairs. Sitting with a plate of *nasi goreng* (fried rice), mulling over my next move and my dwindling

Source: Written expressly for *Urban Life*.

funds, I overheard a group of women discussing the *aneh* (strangeness) of seeing a *bulé* (white foreigner) sitting in their midst (I later learned expatriate employees rarely ate lunch at the local canteens and food stalls, preferring instead the familiarity of Western-style restaurants.) Unable to contain their curiosity one of the women shouted in English, "Hey! What is your name?"

After some rather awkward bilingual introductions, I learned these women worked together in the Jakarta office of a transnational company that provided sales and management training to corporate employees. Over a shared plate of *goreng-gorengan* (literally, "fried-fried," a popular snack of heavily battered fried vegetables, yams, tofu, and tempé [made from soybeans]), I began to realize these women worked in just the kind of space I was searching for. Here was an office that employed individuals from throughout the world as salespeople and consultants, whose day-to-day operations took them into offices, factories, and laboratories throughout Indonesia. The more I learned the more excited I got—to the point that my new acquaintances were visibly wary with the idea of escorting me to their workspace. Again, identifying oneself as an anthropologist does not always open doors. There was a growing sense of suspicion as their questions became increasingly pointed: What would I be doing in their office? Why would I want to study *them*? Shouldn't I go to Irian Jaya, Aceh, or Bali if I wanted to learn about Indonesian "culture"? I could not be sure, but I thought I heard the letters "CIA" whispered during one awkward silence.

THE "PLACE" OF TRANSNATIONAL FIELDWORK

This chapter is about doing ethnographic fieldwork in transnational corporate offices, urban spaces that do not easily fit into our popular imagination of cultural anthropology. We tend to imagine our anthropologists, if we imagine them at all, as travelers, explorers on foot in the most isolated corners of our world. Our photographic legacy even depicts us as such—a lone white male (rarely female) surrounded by tribal populations sitting before thatched huts in remote jungle clearings. While these romantic images of the anthropologist in the field are problematic at best—certainly rural populations have never been as stable or as isolated from global processes as depicted in our early ethnographies—urban anthropology in a transnational setting does much to upset popular conceptions of the anthropologist at work

Doing anthropology in a corporate office disturbs the mythical image of anthropological work in a number of ways; at the same time, it raises important questions about the efficacy of our ethnographic methods. What do we do when our population of study is not a small isolated community, accessible 24 hours a day, and instead consists of hundreds of dispersed workers continually jetting off to offices and factories across the globe? How do we conceive a field site not so easily defined as the rural village scraped out of a surrounding rainforest? How do we provide an opportunity for both critique *and* expansion of our research theories and methods when conducting fieldwork in spaces not normally associated with the "exotic" history of anthropology?

The sheer scope of my field site (or perhaps, better stated, the absence of a single self-contained field site) became clear to me one day as I sat in the back of one of Jakarta's ubiquitous Bluebird taxis. Stuck in one of Jakarta's equally ubiquitous traffic jams, I decided to take advantage of this forced "down time" to telephone my wife. Ida, coincidentally also an anthropologist, was busy conducting research in a rural farming village in northern Thailand. She was fortunate to be staying with a family that possessed the only telephone available for miles. Cell phone technology had not yet reached this region of northern Thailand, nor could the people of this impoverished village afford what was still considered by most in Southeast Asia a luxury. From the back of my taxi I called and in the only Thai I could muster asked if *Khun* Ida was "there"? From what I could gather through the static, the answer was "yes" (*krup*), though the 15 minutes of silence that followed encouraged a rethinking of this assumption. Eventually Ida came to the phone, her stilted speech unable to conceal her attempts to catch her breath. It turns out Ida was not at the house but about a half-mile away at the local school. Yet, indeed, Ida was "there." She was in the community and everyone knew where she was (at all times!). She was clearly "in" her field site, her place of research and temporary home. Needless to say, my desire for a casual "chat" was not well received, as I had inadvertently created the most impressive point of village gossip for the foreseeable future. Still, my technologically based intrusion into the lives of a northern Thai village, and into Ida's field site, forced me to examine some basic ethnographic assumptions. Was I also, sitting in the back of a taxi stuck in rush hour traffic, *in* my field site? Or, was I outside, away from my work? The answer is not an easy one, and indeed, some conceptual work had to be done if I were to establish the "place" of my research.

THE URBAN SETTING: JAKARTA

Jakarta is a city richly layered with the strata of classical, colonial, national, and transnational encounter. A city of migrants, domestic and international, Jakarta is coherent in the way of a Robert Rauschenberg "combine": a style of three-dimensional art that brings together painting, sculpture, collage, and found objects in the making of something entirely new and strange, but somehow, simultaneously, familiar. Much like the best of Rauschenberg's work, the fragments of architectural and social difference abutting one another along Jakarta's busy and overcrowded streets provoke in the city traveler a simultaneous sense of tension and harmony as one stumbles across a terrain both foreign and familiar.

The usual visual juxtaposition evoked in the travel literature for Jakarta (and most other primate[1] cities of the so-called "Third World," for that matter), illustrated with the requisite photographic trope of glass-and-steel skyscrapers bearing down on dilapidated, tin-roofed shanties, does little justice to a landscape constructed through the centuries by the hands of numerous, often migratory, sometimes imperial, self-interested actors. Jakarta's streets are colored as much by the aesthetics of ethnic identity, colonial nostalgia, and a national desire for the public displays of modernity as they are by the dramatic class divisions evoked through the photographic trope of skyscraper and shanty. The popular divisions in the landscape are tangible in rooflines and road signs, in the names on storefronts, in the aromas of cooking, and in the wary or welcoming looks on people's faces—so much so that even the uninitiated city traveler is quickly aware of boundaries being crossed.

Jakarta's multi-ethnic, multi-cultural landscape promotes a constant sense of dislocation—for both resident and visitor alike. When, for example, a newly arrived American traveler enters one of Jakarta's many shopping malls or Western-style restaurants, he or she might feel, if only for a moment, a sense of transportation from the strange to the familiar. But the sensation is temporary. The juxtaposition of an American-style steakhouse next to a Starbucks and across the street from a Hard Rock Café presents something of a Disney "imagineering" of home for our imagined traveler; a space familiar yet somehow artificial and out of place.

Jakarta is a place of layers and juxtapositions that speak to the longevity of global projects at work on its terrain. These layers do much to confound the modern-day resident, as choices must be made on a daily basis about language, dialect, clothing style, food consumption, and many other arenas of life while traveling on a fairly small body of land (more than 10 million people live within the approximately 411 miles of Jakarta). As such, Jakarta proves an inviting (if challenging) space for ethnographic investigation into the creative processes through which people negotiate identity and construct meaningful places out of the spaces in which they work and live.

The Corporate Setting: The Office as a Space of Dislocation, Disruption, and Difference

In the end, I never did visit the offices of the women I met over gorenggorengan. I did, however, note this encounter in my journal and returned to it often as I contemplated various research strategies. I realized, based on my earlier futile attempts to interview corporate executives, that for these people to let me into their lives I needed a reason to be there. Ethnographic research was of little interest to people busy negotiating constant shifts in the global economy. On the other hand, an anthropologist familiar with the local culture, who could also speak the local language, might be of some use.

I realized that to do my work I must also work with/for those whom I wished to engage ethnographically. To my surprise, in 1997 I found employment within the Jakarta office of a U.S.-based training company much like the one I was introduced to on that fateful day one year earlier. I was hired, despite the fact I had never conducted one training session, did not fully understand what the company actually did, had no experience in the corporate economy, and was naively unguarded with my anthropological skepticism toward the management concepts that peppered my initial interview. My assets, it quickly became clear, lay in that fortunate combination of nature and nurture: I was an American who also possessed a working, if deeply porous, command of *bahasa Indonesia*, the national language of Indonesia. I was just what was needed to expand Consulting Alliance's (a fictional name) presence in the U.S.-based transnational corporate offices of Jakarta, Indonesia.

My business cards identified me simply, if somewhat ambiguously, as a "Consultant." It was through this occupational position—with business card in hand—that I gained entrée into the offices of multiple Fortune 500 companies operating out of Southeast Asia. Consulting Alliance was a corporate service company that catered to the management and personnel needs of an exploding transnational corporate presence in Jakarta. The company's primary service, and its main source of income, was designing and conducting management and cross-cultural training programs for companies either new to the region or working to expand their operations.

Consulting Alliance leased a small office on the eighth floor of a shabby cement high-rise colored charcoal grey through years spent up against the traffic of Jalan Gatot Subroto, one of three streets that make up Jakarta's corporate district known as the Golden Triangle.[2] Taking the glass elevator up the side of the building, one could hope, if often in vain, to emerge from the dense smog of the street into a panorama of steel girders climbing their way up a blue sky, already cluttered with the monumental architecture of big business. Inside, stepping off the elevator, one feels that the smog seemed to have followed, but it was instead wafts of *kretek* cigarette smoke roiling from beneath the men's room door. Inside the office, fluorescent lights shone down on low-walled cubicles crammed into an 800-square-foot space. To the right was a small meeting room with a conference table, easels loaded with newsprint pads, and walls lined with whiteboards filled with the numbers of monthly sales goals. Next door was a spacious office with tinted glass walls and mahogany desks and bookcases. This was the office of Consulting Alliance's Director. Michael Gibson had first come to Indonesia from the University of Michigan as a Peace Corps volunteer. Eighteen years later, he was somewhat hesitant to call Jakarta home. "My wife [who is Indonesian] says I still live like a college student." Michael's house in Menteng, a prestigious neighborhood in the heart of Jakarta, remained surprisingly stark with unpacked boxes lining the white plaster walls and serving as footstools and side tables in the living room. Michael's attitude, I later learned, was not unusual for a member of an expatriate community that considered life in Jakarta a temporary hardship. Yet, Michael's position is complicated by the fact that, through marriage, he is tied into local kinship and social networks that operate outside of his work environment. One might thus read these unpacked boxes as a sign that Michael is still negotiating the complicated space he occupies between two cultural worlds.

In the office I was part of a small staff of around 15 Americans and Indonesians that turned over frequently due to a common practice among competing corporations of aggressively "poaching" skilled personnel from one's competition. The practice of poaching was an unexpected complication to ethnographic research. No sooner had I begun to develop rapport(?), become friendly(?), become acquainted(?)—any of these is perhaps more evocative than "make progress"—with a set of employees, getting a feel for their inter-actions within a particular office context, than they disappeared, only to show up in another corporate office. Through all the comings and goings, however, there remained a few employees who were integral in assisting me through my initial treks into the unfamiliar landscapes of corporate Jakarta.

Lina, one steadfast employee who was helpful to me, worked as the Assistant to the Director of Consulting Alliance. Her father was a well-posi-tioned man in the military. Lina had benefited from her father's position and income, receiving an education that had taken her from Java to Italy and England. Lina, who had an outgoing personality, was not shy in pointing out my almost daily mistakes in office protocol. She enjoyed ridiculing my rudi-mentary Indonesian skills as well, usually loudly enough to ensure the plea-sure of everyone around. But she was also the first to take pity on me within the office. Throughout our friendship Lina went to great lengths to introduce me to her Jakarta and showed great patience while I learned the basics of sur-vival within a global city. Richard, a fellow consultant with several years of experience at Consulting Alliance, directed me through a somewhat different map of Jakarta's spaces than Lina's, all the while blessing me with an extended and highly quotable monologue on life for an American in the city.

It is worth noting one particular benefit to ethnography with those savvy to the workings and technology of transnationalism: relationships do not end with the inevitable departure of either the anthropologist or the subjects of his or her research. I have been fortunate to maintain electronic communica-tion with Lina until the present (the virtual communities of Web sites like MySpace and Facebook have proved an exciting if not yet fully explored boon to transnational fieldwork). This ongoing communication allows for long-term follow-up, the filling of gaps in knowledge, the raising of new ques-tions one never thought to ask in the first place. In a sense, one never quite *leaves* the field in this new interconnected world.

As an employee of Consulting Alliance I was part of an expanding tran-snational network intent on governing the flow of people and ideas, raw materials, monies, technologies, and finished commodities to and from vari-ous and dispersed spaces of design, production, distribution, marketing, and retail. I clung tightly to a single strand in this network concerned with "knowledge transfer"—broadly speaking, the dissemination of technological, economic, and cultural information about corporations and corporate citi-zens (Martin 1994). My own responsibilities were primarily ideological in that I trained those working as (or aspiring to become) managers and execu-tives in Western-owned transnational corporations.

In this capacity, I traveled throughout Jakarta teaching prepackaged courses on successful management practices appropriate for the transcul-tural/transnational terrain of the global economy. My field experience was thus one of continuous movement and engagement with people in different office settings. One day I would be in the company of engineers searching for oil in the waters that surround the Indonesian archipelago. The next, I was in the office of a major sporting-goods manufacturer. Needless to say, continuities were difficult to find. Relationships in one office, with its own peculiar hierarchy, corporate culture, and personnel issues, had little to do with those in another. My research ultimately came to rest on the exploration of discontinuities and disruptions more than the development of any particular set of transnational corporate cultural practices and beliefs that might be emerging in reaction to our globalized economy. My primary concern came to be how people coped with the highly "flexible" world of transnational corporations. While not part of this chapter, I found that people relied on the history of Indonesia in "imagining" a coherent structure (one populated by colonizers and colonized) in order to make sense of and "order" a world that lacked stability and coherence (see, for example, Leggett 2007, 2008).

THE POSITIONED ANTHROPOLOGIST

As a "consultant" and ethnographer, I was both an anthropologist of *and* an agent for capital—observing while simultaneously producing anthropological knowledge (re)packaged for the sake of corporate profit. My time within the offices of Western-owned transnational corporations was spent somewhat schizophrenically toggling between these two social positions: observing the negotiations of different employees, from different backgrounds, with different employment positions in a complicated cultural terrain, on the one hand, and teaching a somewhat simplistic, sometimes useful, often coercive package of corporate cultural knowledge on the other. Tensions, spawned from the intellectual and ethical contradictions inherent in these two personas, were never, nor could they ever have been, fully resolved. The ethics of ethnography are deeply enmeshed in an ideology of providing a voice for the world's most marginal populations. Yet, here I was, an anthropologist working for the most powerful corporations in the world, making recommendations that affected the economic futures of many of those for whom I wished to "speak." Clearly, my complicated social position as employee and ethnographer held consequences for my research.

At first, these tensions were not clear to me. I felt I was making progress. Each day I set aside some time to interview employees at whichever corporation I might be working with that day. We met in the offices of executives, in meeting rooms, or over lunch, usually at a hotel restaurant. Afterward, I would return to the office to conduct a training session for the corporation's Indonesian employees: how to be a better manager; how to talk to your superiors/subordinates; how to make decisions; how to be more efficient; how to be a leader.

As I began to compile the data from my interviews, it became clear that my most productive interviews were with the executives and managers at the top of the corporate ladder. These interviews, due to the implicit glass ceiling imposed on local employees within Jakarta's transnational corporations, also happened to be with the American or European employees of the corporations. Transnational corporations operating out of Indonesia are required by national law to train local employees for a future as executives within the corporation (a key reason for the flourishing of companies like Consulting Alliance), but this promise was rarely fulfilled. Instead, the most skilled Indonesian national employees tended to rise to and then hover within mid-level management, while executives from outside the country came and went at a fairly rapid pace (most assignments were for 2–3 years before being relocated to another office within the global network).

Still, I garnered a lot of information from these rather formal interview sessions during office hours and lunch breaks. However, my interviews with Indonesian employees who inevitably occupied organizational positions several rungs lower on the hierarchy were, to put it bluntly, ethnographic failures. Questions remained unanswered, or responded to with evasion and deception as their primary goal. On one occasion, I was sent on a "wild goose chase" after an employee who would be a "perfect" subject for my interviews. The ruse was complex: this individual had worked for a number of different corporations, had been promoted up the corporate ladder through a distant office, only to be fired once the other executives had come to see him as a threat to their own jobs. I could find him on the outskirts of Jakarta, now occupying the relatively lower position of factory supervisor. He would certainly talk to me. Needless to say, this person did not exist.

Nevertheless, I pressed on. The whole situation was uncomfortable for everyone involved. It was not until I returned to Jakarta in 1999 and revisited many of my acquaintances that I fully understood the situation. As an employee of Consulting Alliance working under contract for these corporations, I was viewed by the Indonesian employees—correctly, I must say—as an authority figure with decision-making power over their future in the company. As a corporate trainer, my recommendations for retention and promotion held weight. My own discomfort with this decision-making power did not diminish the fact that it was present in all conversations and observations. Why would I expect someone to be honest and open with me about his or her perceptions of working in a transnational corporation when I was very much a cog in the corporate machine?

I was only able to overcome the one-sidedness of my ethnographic interactions on return to Jakarta in 1999 when I was no longer under the employ of Consulting Alliance. Friendship replaced (at least for most) the suspicion of the previous year. It did not hurt that I, like so many others, fell victim to the cost cutting and downsizing of the Asian economic crisis. Our shared terminations—with their inherent frustrations, uncertainties, and anxieties—became a point of departure for reflection on experiences of work, cross-cultural engagement, conflict, and communication. Still, these relationships that proved so valuable to my research would never have existed had I not been employed within the transnational corporate environment. At the same time, the compromises in intimacy this positioning entailed could not be ignored and instead became a central component of my research. In the end, the various publications that came from this experience were all much attuned to the tensions and conflicts of the transnational corporate office. To borrow a phrase from a preeminent anthropologist on globalization, Arjun Appadurai (1996), "disjunctures and differences" dominated my research agenda more so than any coherent corporate culture yet to emerge in our transnational world.

CONCLUSION

Ethnographic studies are founded on a notion of long-term engagement in a particular community. In this chapter I have tried to highlight some difficulties in carrying this premise into a transnational corporate context that (a) is not centrally located, (b) is defined at least in part by the mobility of its employees, and (c) is not necessarily receptive to the time requirements or intrusive nature of ethnographic research. To speak of a "field site" under these circumstances requires a rethinking of the term—one that unhinges the idea of fieldwork from research conducted within a settled geographic place. The "place" of urban research shifts as people shift. Moreover, any notion of community must come to terms with the fact that the network of relations that make up a corporate "community" is highly flexible, global, and perhaps suspicious of anthropological query.

To overcome these obstacles to conducting fieldwork in an urban, transnational setting I chose to take a professional position within the corporate world that was, at times, at odds with my desired research agenda and the ethics of my discipline. Because of this decision, I occupied a position that was simultaneously above *and* below the people with whom I wished to do research. On the one hand, this provided opportunities for "studying up," a term coined by the anthropologist Laura Nader (1972) for the study of those with more status, power, authority, and/or money than the anthropologist. On the other hand, due to my occupational position, I was constrained in my attempts to gain intimacy and trust from those "below" me in the corporate hierarchy. Furthermore, for some working individuals I was doubly positioned as someone to be wary of: an anthropologist with corporate authority. While all anthropologists must come to terms with the way they are positioned in the field, as well as with some distrust toward the anthropological enterprise, working within a transnational corporate office involves a unique set of issues for the urban anthropologist. One must weigh the risks and rewards of gaining entrée into this economically driven social arena and, perhaps most importantly, make the reading audience aware of the effects this positioning has on one's research project.

Notes

[1] "Primate" is a term used to refer to those cities that draw populations out of the countryside and into the city, thereby causing the city to become immense, disproportionately larger than

any other city in the region, and in many ways unmanageable. In addition to Jakarta, Mexico City, Sao Paulo, Mumbai, and Bangkok are just a few that fit into this category.

2 *Jalan* means street. Gatot Subroto is named after an Indonesian colonel remembered in the nation's history due to his role in driving the colonial Dutch military from Indonesia. Gatot Subroto is also important in the history of military coups, successful and failed, that color the Indonesian government's formative political years.

References

Appadurai, Arjun. 1996. *Modernity at Large: Cultural Dimensions of Globalization.* Minneapolis: University of Minnesota Press.

Leggett, William. 2007. Expatriate Ethnoscapes: Transnational Masculinity and Sexual Transgressions. In *Ethnic Landscapes in an Urban World,* eds. Ray Hutchison and Jerome Krase, pp. 223–246. Boston: Elsevier.

———. 2008. Making Distance through a Violent Imagination. In *Ruminations on Violence,* ed. Derek Pardue, pp. 41–53. Long Grove, IL: Waveland Press.

Martin, Emily. 1994. *Flexible Bodies: The Role of Immunity in American Culture from the Days of Polio to the Age of AIDS.* Boston: Beacon Press.

Nader, Laura. 1972. Up the Anthropologist: Perspectives Gained from Studying Up. In *Reinventing Anthropology,* ed. Dell H. Hymes, pp. 284–311. New York: Pantheon.

6

Student Fieldworkers
in Village and City

George Gmelch and Sharon Bohn Gmelch

This chapter compares the research and field experiences of students studying in rural villages with those of students studying in a city. The student subjects are participants in two anthropology field-training programs (rural Barbados and urban Tasmania) designed to give them a hands-on experience of anthropological fieldwork. The comparison of rural and urban field schools reveals some effects of place—village versus city—on the conduct of field research and on the students' experiences. Students doing fieldwork in the city, for example, have greater difficulty identifying a "community" and locating informants, and they gather far more of their data through interviewing. On the other hand, the village fieldworkers did more participant-observation and had a more difficult time adjusting to the culture. This chapter builds upon some of the points George M. Foster and Robert V. Kemper made in their chapter.

For the past 30 years, we have been taking undergraduates abroad to give them a hands-on experience of anthropological fieldwork.[1] For the first two decades, our "field schools" were based in rural areas—first in Ireland and then throughout the 1980s and 1990s in Barbados. In both countries, students were placed with local families, one student to a community.[2] In 2001, we moved the program to Kilkenny town, Ireland, for one term before moving it to the Australian state of Tasmania and its capital city Hobart (pop. 205,000), where it is based today. What does this change in venue—from rural to urban environment—mean for student ethnographers?

Before answering this question, some background is needed on the reasons we moved the field school from rural Barbados to urban Australia. The shift from village to city was in some senses a natural one, reflecting both our changing world and changes within anthropology. Half of the world's popula-

Source: Written expressly for *Urban Life*.

tion now lives in urban areas; about 70 percent will be city dwellers by 2050 according to United Nations projections. The days when cultural anthropologists primarily studied small-scale, "isolated" societies are also gone. As George M. Foster and Robert V. Kemper (see chapter 1 in this volume) have noted, anthropologists had so thoroughly described peasant and tribal societies and "constructed models to explain much of their cross-cultural variation" that their study had reached the point of diminishing returns. At the same time, the pace of globalization is accelerating, with capital, ideas, people, goods, technology, and culture flowing between what had previously been regarded as bounded entities. Anthropologists now study diverse topics in diverse places, from urban street corners and sweatshops to corporate boardrooms and cyberspace. The American Anthropological Association now has 35 special interest sections or "societies" representing different and often fairly new fields of scholarship, including the "Anthropology of Consciousness" and the "Society for Urban, National and Transnational/Global Anthropology."

We also moved the field school for practical reasons.[3] Over the years more and more residents of the Barbadian villages in which our students lived had begun commuting to jobs in the capital city and a nearby provincial town and were no longer around during the day. Consequently, there were fewer people available to our students as cultural mentors and potential research subjects. With wage-paying jobs, fewer residents had time for the subsistence activities—fishing, raising animals, farming, and cultivating "kitchen gardens"—which made rural life especially interesting and distinctive for our students. And, personally, after spending 10 semesters or nearly three years living in and supervising students in Barbadian villages, we were ready for a change.

So, while our field school students once did traditional "people and places" village ethnography, today they practice urban anthropology—although less anthropology *of* the city than anthropology *in* the city. That is, they are not studying urbanism per se, but rather are doing fieldwork on a variety of topics in the city. Moving our field school to the city has revealed a number of contrasts between rural and urban fieldwork, especially for beginning fieldworkers. It is these differences, the adjustments students face in both settings, and the changes we have had to make to the program, that are the focus of this paper. But first, a brief word about our data.

METHOD

In 1990, we administered a survey to our students in Barbados in order to better understand their research experience and the personal impact that living and studying in a Caribbean village was having on them. The survey elicited information on their research experience (e.g., the number and demographic characteristics of their key informants, what data-gathering techniques they had most relied on), how they felt they were being changed by the experience, and also what they were learning about their own culture as a result of studying another. After this study was completed and the results written up (G. Gmelch 1992, 1999), we continued to survey students at the end of subsequent field programs and discussed how their experiences compared with those of previous groups. In addition to the surveys, the students kept field notes and at the end of each week wrote a two-page assessment of their fieldwork—a sort of progress report in which they also discussed any difficulties they might be having. Finally, one of us (George) regularly recorded his impressions of the students' adjustment and fieldwork in a personal journal. All of these data have to varying degrees informed this paper.

THE FIELD SCHOOL SETTINGS

Both Barbados and Tasmania are islands. The former is located in the eastern Caribbean and the latter in the Southern Ocean off the coast of mainland Australia. Both are also former British colonies and remained under British rule from their initial colonization to independence: Barbados in 1966 and Tasmania, as part of Australia, in 1901. In other respects they are quite different. While Barbados is a small island (166 sq. miles), Tasmania is large (24,411 sq. miles); in fact, it is 147 times larger than Barbados. Barbados is densely populated (1,692 people per sq. mile), while Tasmania has only 20 people per square mile.

The composition of their populations is also different. Within a few decades of colonization in 1627, the British established sugarcane plantations across Barbados and imported African slaves to work them. Most Barbadians today are descendants of those slaves. Tasmania was colonized much later, in 1803, and began as a penal colony. Initially named Van Diemen's Land, its earliest settlers were "transported" convicts from Britain and their military guards, followed by free settlers who, together with freed convicts, had the task of developing agriculture and other industries. Many present-day Tasmanians are their descendants. Both islands' indigenous populations—Amerindians in Barbados and Aboriginals in Tasmania—were eliminated by a combination of European diseases and violence.[4] The absence of a visible Aboriginal population in Tasmania today causes many people, who do not understand how much cultural anthropology has changed, to ask our students what they could possibly have come to study.[5] "Weren't the Aboriginals wiped out years ago?" they ask, as though nothing else in Tasmania would be of interest to anthropologists.

Today both Barbados and Tasmania are major tourist destinations. Barbados is best known for its white sand beaches, tropical climate, and world-class resorts; Tasmania features unspoiled nature—20 percent of the island is World Heritage Wilderness—and exotic marsupials including the Tasmanian Devil. Tasmania attracts eco-tourists, some of whom come to hike the famous Overland Track, while Barbados attracts the more conventional "sand, sun, and sea" visitor. Both islands rank near the top of the world's most desirable tourist destinations and draw close to one million visitors per year. Both also rank high on the human development Index (HDI)—a com-

Hobart, with 4,000 foot Mount Wellington in the background. [Photo by George Gmelch]

parative measure of life expectancy, literacy, education, standard of living, and GDP per capita for countries worldwide.

THE STUDENT EXPERIENCE

In Barbados, our students lived in villages located in the northernmost parish of St. Lucy, the least developed part of the island and furthest removed from the capital city of Bridgetown. The villages range in size from 200 to 800 people; most began as tenantries, marginal plantation lands given to the newly emancipated (1833) but landless slaves. In Tasmania, our students live in the neighborhoods and suburbs of Hobart, the state's capital city. In Barbados, most of our students lived with working-class, village families; in Tasmania most live with middle-class Australian families.

The city and suburbs of Hobart are much more familiar settings to our students than were Barbadian villages. In Barbados, when they conducted their household census, students were usually surprised to discover that the people they approached knew most everyone in the village. The students had never encountered such communal intimacy before. Villagers not only knew each other as neighbors but often in other contexts as well—work, church, and play. Most also shared a common history and had relationships that extended back generations. In the city of Hobart, there is nothing comparable to this intimacy.

In their field notes, our students often favorably compared the warmth, friendliness, and frequent sharing of food and other resources that took place in the village with the impersonality, individualism, and detachment of life in the suburb or city in which they had grown up. But they also learned about the drawbacks of living in a small community where there is no anonymity, and many people seemed nosy and unduly interested in the affairs of their neighbors. Students also discovered to their dismay that they were sometimes the object of local gossip, as when some of our female students learned that stories were circulating that they were sleeping with their host father or brother. Such gossip hurt, for the students worked hard to gain local acceptance and develop rapport, and they worried about the damage such rumors might do to their reputations and fieldwork.

In all field research, no matter where it takes place, anthropologists must draw on their social and interpersonal skills to gain the cooperation of the local people.[6] We must find people who are willing to converse with us and answer our questions. Here, a major contrast between doing fieldwork in villages and in the city emerged. When students in Barbados left their homestay households in the morning, they nearly always encountered someone who was a potential informant. In Hobart, when our fieldworkers go out the doors of their mostly suburban homes in the morning, they seldom encounter anyone. Furthermore, in the villages, nearly every resident was aware of our students' presence—they were the American girl living with Miss Valenza or the "white boy" living down the road with the Griffiths. Many residents learned the students' names and greeted them on the street. Not so in the city and suburbs of Hobart. Even by the end of the semester, few of our students know

Student and her home stay family sitting in their "gallery," or porch, in the village of Josey Hill, St. Lucy. [Photo by George Gmelch]

their host family's immediate neighbors, and many of these people were probably unaware of their presence. At the end of her second week in Hobart, Nancy wrote, "I'm still not sure how to find informants." No student in Barbados ever reported that problem. Another difficulty for students in the city is that it is not socially acceptable to approach strangers and start talking to them. Our students do, of course, make friends with local Tasmanians, but they are usually people they meet when out at night in clubs and bars, at their internship, or as a result of a formal, pre-arranged interview.

Students in the city expend a lot of effort tracking down potential research subjects and repeatedly have to explain who they are and what they are doing in Hobart. It gets tiresome. Most of the time interviews are arranged by telephone or e-mail, since research subjects are typically dispersed across the city. A lot of time is spent confirming interview times and meeting places and then walking or traveling by bus to get there. Our village fieldworkers in Barbados only needed to stroll through the village or stop by the rum shop or sports ground to find people willing to talk. They also had many more opportunities to participate in village life—helping out in a local shop or someone's kitchen garden, attending church services, playing soccer or netball, or simply "liming" or hanging out with locals. Because most, if not all, of their subjects lived in close proximity, students in Barbados spent more time each day actually doing fieldwork than do our students in Tasmania.

In end-of-term-surveys, we ask students how many local people they had gotten to know by name. Those doing village fieldwork averaged twice the 15

Village rum shop, a favorite gathering place for men, and a setting where some students have done fieldwork. [Photo by Ellen Frankenstein]

reported by our urban fieldworkers. In the same survey, we also ask students to give the age and gender of their three best informants. Here, too, there is a significant difference. In village Barbados, these people were usually elders; in Hobart, students relied much more on younger people. The major reason for this difference is that more elderly villagers are outside and available to students during the day than is true in the city. Students in both places of course also heavily rely on members of their homestay families for information.

Urban fieldwork turns out to be quite different from what our students expect before they arrive in Tasmania. Their notion of fieldwork has been shaped by what they have read or listened to in their classes on campus; many of the most memorable accounts of fieldwork have been written by anthropologists working in tribal settings such as the Bushmen studied by Richard Lee, the Trobriand Islanders studied by Bronislaw Malinowski and Annette Weiner, or the Yanomamö studied by Napoleon Chagnon. This, combined with the similarity of urban Hobart to their own backgrounds, means that many students at first feel like they are not doing "real" anthropology in Tasmania. As Katie wrote at the end of her first week in the field, "I'm desperately trying to feel like an anthropologist, but I don't at all. This is very different from what I had imagined anthropologists do." We now better prepare students by making sure they read some urban anthropology and by reminding them of the range of research that anthropologists do today.

For students in Barbados, there is never any confusion about the "unit of analysis." It is the village in which they live, that nucleated cluster of houses, rum shops, churches, and other buildings whose outer boundaries are clearly demarcated by the surrounding fields of sugarcane. In Hobart, in contrast, students have a difficult time locating a "community" or even grasping what might constitute one. The sheer size of the place, the social diversity of its residents, and their neighbors' unfamiliarity with one another, makes for a different kind of social entity, and one that is too complex for a novice fieldworker to make sense of, especially in a single semester. The somewhat holistic "community study" that we required our students to write in Barbados—one of their two major writing projects—had to be dropped as a requirement in the urban field program. In Hobart, students focus their research either on a subculture (e.g., refugees, market vendors, cricket fans, fishing crews, environmentalists) or on an issue (e.g., the controversy over building a new pulp mill).

RURAL VS. URBAN RESEARCH METHODS

Student fieldworkers in village Barbados did more participant-observation than do students in Hobart. Conversely, students in the city conduct more formal interviews. We first sensed this difference when reading students' field notes, and confirmed it in the survey by asking them about their dependence on different data-gathering techniques. The differences between the fieldwork conducted by Steve in rural Barbados and Elizabeth in urban Tasmania on the same topic are illustrative. Both researched the role cricket played in everyday life (a legacy of British colonialism, cricket is the national pastime in both societies). Steve conducted his study in the village of Rock Dundo, while Elizabeth did her work in Bellerive, a suburb of Hobart. Steve collected most of his data by hanging around the local cricket pitch and the rum shop, and occasionally by playing the game. He knew his informants well and had multiple conversations with them over the course of the semester about their involvement in the sport. He also had the opportunity to overhear conversations and to observe the role sport played in local life. Elizabeth was forced to collect most of her data through arranged interviews, although she had an internship with the Tasmanian Cricket Association and developed some deeper relationships there. Most of her data, however, came from single interviews with people she had never met before and would never see again. Both projects were well executed and produced some interesting findings, but Steve's deep immersion as a resident in his research setting yielded a more nuanced understanding of the place of cricket in local culture.

To offset some of the difficulties in locating a community in the city and in relying so heavily on formal interviewing as a data-collecting technique, we added internships to the Hobart field school; each student now volunteers and conducts research for an organization.[7]

The heavy reliance on formal interviews by students in the city means they do not often see their subjects in natural social settings. This can be a considerable disadvantage, as Nashab discovered in her study of African refugees who live scattered across Hobart and never seem to come together in one place. Nashab described her frustration:

> Because I'm never able to observe them outside of the interviews, I can't tell if what my informants tell me is actually how they live their lives. I didn't think this was a problem until I observed an African man on Australia Day [a national holiday] sitting by himself on a bench by the sea watching the boat race. There were people standing around him also watching the race but none sat down next to him. Another bench just two meters from him was filled with five people who could barely fit on. This got me thinking about segregation in Hobart and I wondered what else I was missing out on because of my inability to observe them in daily life.

Because students in the city do less participant-observation than their village counterparts, they also take far fewer field notes. This was not something that we anticipated. In fact we were quite surprised by students' lower productivity during our first urban field seasons in Kilkenny and Hobart. The students were just as good, but they did not produce nearly as many pages of field notes. Students in Barbados had each turned in about a dozen single-spaced, typed pages of field notes per week—double that of the students in Kilkenny and Hobart. Students in Barbados produced so many combined pages of field notes, journal entries, field exercises, in addition to two research papers, that some students called it "the writing term abroad."

In Barbadian villages—like small, rural places everywhere—entertainment options are limited. Indeed, one of the challenges our students faced was finding ways to stave off boredom. The attractiveness of rural Barbados lies in its open spaces, tranquility and an unhurried pace of life, people's connection to the land, and strong community (Gmelch and Gmelch 2001[1997]). These are not qualities that most young Americans from urban and suburban backgrounds value or would trade for the excitement of the city. Students in the villages filled their considerable downtime just hanging out with local people and, as a result, learned more about the culture. They learned to treat this downtime as an opportunity to do fieldwork—for example, to steer conversations onto the topics they were researching. As Dan wrote:

> I'm exposed to learning about this culture 24 hours a day. At Union [College] you can always put down the book and walk away, and when you leave a class, the lecture is over. But here the information keeps coming at you, even when you are at the dinner table I'm learning new stuff.

And the absence of distractions and familiar forms of entertainment resulted in students doing even more fieldwork and writing more field notes.

Although most of the massive shift in the world's population from rural areas to towns and cities since World War II is the result of the search for better economic opportunity, the city is also a magnet in other ways. Hobart, for example, offers movie theaters, nightclubs, two museums, a university, a symphony orchestra, a large botanical garden, an open-air craft and food market with live music, a pedestrian shopping precinct with many boutiques, and a lively waterfront with outdoor cafés and bars. There is also professional cricket to watch, and just a few miles away are beaches and hiking and biking trails. None of our students have admitted to being bored in Hobart. In fact there are so many entertainment possibilities that some struggle to keep up with their fieldwork. Because these activities are so familiar to them, they also have trouble viewing them as fieldwork opportunities—as ways to learn about Tasmanian culture and society.

When we asked the Hobart students to read an essay one of us had written about student fieldworkers in Barbados and to comment on how their urban field experiences were different from the village, Katie wrote:

> Hobart is nothing like being part of a community or village. You can walk around town and only see a few people you recognize . . . you never really get absorbed into the culture like the students do in Barbados. Also, it's so easy to get off track from the research because there are so many temptations, there's always something else to see and do in the city.

In the village, fieldwork had no limits; our students were surrounded at all times by the subjects of their study. They also were separated from other students most of the week and forced to rely on local people for companionship. Consequently, fieldwork became the focus of their lives and occupied much of their daily thoughts. In the city, in contrast, it is easier for students to get together. Sometimes they bump into each other accidentally, but more often, they arrange to meet. Being together, especially in groups of three or more,

Hobart's Salamanca Market, a crafts and food market and a setting for field-work. [Photo by George Gmelch]

usually makes it difficult to meet local people. Moreover, from our point of view, it also results in too much conversation centering on people, places, and events back home rather than the society they are in.

ADJUSTING TO FIELDWORK

How much does the setting—rural or urban—influence how student fieldworkers adjust to living abroad? Is one setting more likely than the other to produce culture shock? In both rural Barbados and urban Tasmania, our students initially are intimidated by the requirements of doing fieldwork: living with a local family, coping with an unfamiliar environment, having to go out each day and start conversations with strangers. No matter how gregarious and socially skilled they are back on campus, most students find these to be daunting tasks. They feel anxious and doubt their ability to make friends in this new and alien setting. Here is Andrew writing about his feelings after parting from the other students to move in with his homestay family:

> I feel the real world of Hobart starting to crack through and it's scary. It's not the city itself, but what the city is asking of me, and what I am asking of myself. Walking into town on the very first day with my homestay, my legs shook so fiercely I could barely keep a straight line and my mind was flying with nervous gusts so that every detail of the town around me was lost. I was paralyzed with fear.

Students' anxieties were heightened in Barbados because as the only student in their community (and with a strict rule against visiting their fellow American students), they were more completely on their own. Some students in Barbados were also hypersensitive about their identity the first few weeks.[8] When they took the bus into town, they were usually the only white person onboard. Some noted that people stared at them and that as the bus filled up, the seat next to them was the last to be taken. As Robin wrote about one of her early bus experiences, "I felt very alone and very unwanted, like the mere presence of my color was making a lot of people very uneasy." Fortunately, the students' sensitivity to being different and concerns about race diminished rapidly as they settled into village life.

The most common reaction of newly arrived fieldworkers in both rural and urban settings is to stay indoors—taking long naps, listening to music, reading novels, and writing or e-mailing home—in order to avoid having to start their fieldwork and meet local people. At the end of her first week in Tasmania, Jenny admitted, "I have been reading a 600-page book, I guess as a way to postpone having to deal with the real world." Amanda likewise finished two novels before venturing outside her Hobart neighborhood. Liana "found comfort in reading local newspapers like *The Mercury* and *The Australian*. I felt as though I was learning about the culture without putting myself out there too much since I was still frightened by the whole experience." Having had the same experiences when we were students in anthropology field schools (George in Mexico in 1969 and Sharon in Ireland in 1970), we are aware of what our students are experiencing and encourage them to get outside as soon as possible in order to get over their fear. In Barbados, we required students during the first week to draw a map of their community showing all roads, footpaths, structures, and major landmarks. This forced them to get out and walk around. In doing so, they were seen by locals, some of whom came up to them and started conversations; a few even assisted them with their mapping. Unfortunately, we have not yet found a comparable exercise for Hobart and its suburbs.

In rural Barbados, most villagers knew our students' host families; the families were also good at introducing them around. This helped smooth students' entry into the community. Host families in Hobart also introduce students to family members and friends, but these people rarely live in the local neighborhood and therefore are less likely to become informants.

In both rural and urban settings, students struggle with the unstructured nature of fieldwork. Accustomed to the regimentation of college life—having to be in class at set times, complete assignments by a certain date, write term papers on prescribed topics, take scheduled exams, and so forth—students feel lost at first. They have never had so much "free" time or so much liberty to determine what, when, and where they will do their work. Susie wrote in her first-week assessment, "Many days I am not sure exactly what I should be doing, where I should be going, and what I should be seeing." To help the students get started we assign several "field exercises." In Hobart, these include making observations at a weekly market; deconstructing the text of a guided brewery tour; interviewing tourists; and comparing their homestay household's architecture, layout, décor, landscaping, and the like to that of their parents' home in the U.S. Once they develop a daily routine, it does not take most students long to value the independence and creativity of field-work. "The freedom to have my own schedule and go out and explore on my own has been incredibly useful for my life skills," wrote Emma at the end of the program. "I feel like I've learned more from this field experience than in my entire college education up to this point because of being forced to go out and learn on my own, outside the classroom."

While some aspects of doing fieldwork are more difficult for students in the city—such as having to work harder to find informants and develop a net-work of contacts—the personal adjustment required of students was greater for students in rural Barbados. The major reason is unrelated to rural–urban differences. Afro-Caribbean culture simply differs more from our students' own backgrounds than mainstream Australian culture does. We have taken students abroad to a half dozen countries (Japan, Vietnam, Ireland, Austria and, of course, Barbados and Australia) on both field schools and conventional terms abroad, and the greater the difference between their own culture and that of the host society, not surprisingly, the greater the personal adjust-ment required. (Language also plays an important role, which is why we have run our field schools in English-speaking countries.) However, since this chapter is primarily about the contrast between urban and rural settings, let us focus on this rather than on cultural differences between Barbados and Australia when examining the students' adjustment to fieldwork.

Privacy is an issue for many anthropologists doing fieldwork. For stu-dents, this was especially true in rural Barbados because village housing was often cramped and the walls between rooms thin, sometimes little more than a partition. While most students had their own bedrooms, they all had to adjust to the inevitable noise created when families share small spaces—radio, television, stereos, and conversations. "It seems like the TV hasn't been turned off since I arrived here five weeks ago," complained Sarah in a journal entry. Families also tended to be larger, so there were always people around. For students in Hobart, privacy and noise are rarely a problem since they live with small, middle-class families in fairly spacious accommodations.

The much slower pace of life in the countryside also takes some getting used to. Country people, especially in a hot climate like that of Barbados, are not in a hurry to get things done. At the shop, students, like all customers, must wait to be served until the clerk finishes chatting with others. Locals think little of being late for appointments. Accustomed to the punctuality and time-centeredness of North American life, our students are often impatient and frustrated. As the weeks pass, however, they adjust to the slow pace, and by the end of the term, most talk about wanting to maintain their new, more relaxed lifestyle when they return home.

Having the emotional support of other people who are going through the same experience can be very helpful when adjusting to a new culture. Here, too, students in rural Barbados were at a disadvantage in that they did not have access to other students in the field school except on our weekly seminar day. In Hobart, it is easy for students to meet whenever they feel the need. Public transportation is good and the distances are not great. Some students can walk to each other's homestay household. (Over the years, our students' capacity to get together has been greatly facilitated by technology—e-mail, cell phones, and text messaging.) Students claim that getting together with each other is immensely helpful because they are able to counsel and offer emotional support to one another when dealing with homesickness and culture shock. In Susie's words, "Talking to the other girls, who were going through the same thing, having the same problems, helped me see that it wasn't just me and my circumstances, but that this was part of the experience of living abroad. It would be a lot tougher for me without their help."

One measure of adjustment in the field is culture shock—the anxiety and feelings of disorientation and confusion that people experience when they are forced to operate in a new cultural environment. It is an especially common affliction among students studying abroad. For our purposes, it is also a pretty good measure of the difference in the challenges student ethnographers face in rural versus urban settings. Since 1990, we have routinely collected data on culture shock through a questionnaire in which students are asked to describe their symptoms, how long they lasted, and whether they believed they were truly experiencing "culture shock." "I knew in coming to Tasmania that I would have culture shock because everyone says that when you go aboard you will have it," wrote Anne. "But I didn't know what it was going to be like or what was going to trigger it." Meredith wrote:

> At first the simple Tasmania life seemed everything I've always wanted and I was seriously contemplating selling my ticket home and staying. Then, a week later, I decided that I hated the place and everything to do with it. It was all driving me insane and all I wanted to do was to go home to New York; all I wanted was to be in my own familiar surroundings with all of my things. I wanted my own room, my own everything!!! But after a few days I got out of that funk or that stage, and became calm and just mellowed out.

Anne's and Meredith's responses are representative of the comments made by students in both settings. However, while only half of the students in urban Hobart feel that they have experienced culture shock, fully 95 percent of those in village Barbados had. Not only did our urban fieldworkers experience less culture shock, but the duration and symptoms (e.g., physical ailments) they describe also tend to be less severe.

CONCLUSION

In conclusion, the field school setting—village versus city—does influence the conduct of fieldwork and the character of student ethnographers' experiences. Students who do fieldwork in the city have greater difficulty than those in villages identifying a "community" and locating "informants." They gather much more of their data through formal interviews than through participant-observation, write fewer field notes as a result, and are not as immersed in the subject of their research on a daily basis as were rural fieldworkers in Barbados. To compensate for this we have introduced research-centered internships into the Tasmania program to provide students with a "community" (e.g., the workplaces of a nonprofit organization or a government agency), "informants," and more opportunities to do participant-observation.

Our students' personal adjustment, however, is easier in the city. It is a known environment, which provides many familiar activities and forms of entertainment. Students also have greater access to one another in the city and experience less culture shock than did students in rural Barbados. Other factors, notably the cultural and class similarity between students and the host community in urban Tasmania, also play a role in the relative ease of their personal adjustment.

Whether in village or city, however, all students benefit immensely from living in and conducting independent research in another culture. Ethnographic field schools provide them with their first real understanding of what anthropological research is like, especially its around-the-clock and opportunistic nature. Many students have told us that they never fully grasped the meaning of basic concepts like culture, community, and values until they had experienced and grappled with them firsthand in the field. Students also acquire a more in-depth knowledge of the host culture than they could ever gain on a conventional term abroad that merely replicates in a foreign setting the kind of education students are accustomed to at home (e.g., dorm life, classroom instruction, university setting). This knowledge later becomes a referent when learning new anthropological concepts and theory in the classroom. The hands-on, experiential nature of doing fieldwork is also personally transformative. We believe that student fieldworkers—in village and city—experience a much greater degree of personal development—maturity, independence, and self-reliance—than do students on conventional study-abroad programs.

Notes

[1] We would like to thank the following individuals for their comments on earlier drafts of this paper: Karen Brison, Sara Callahan, Tom Curtin, Jerry Handler, Richard K. Nelson, Katie Newingham, Jeni Ogilvie, Petra Kuppinger, Diane Royal, Robert V. Kemper, and Tim Wallace. A version of this article appeared in *City and Society* under the title "Moving a Field School to the City: What It Means for Student Ethnographers."

[2] We take 10 students on each field program. Usually about 25 apply for the program; applicants are then interviewed by a committee comprised of the two field directors and several students from the previous program. We have found the student interviewers to be more adept at

weeding out applicants who are ill-suited to fieldwork. Over the years, we have taken a total of 100 students to Barbados and so far 30 to Tasmania.

[3] Excellent discussions of field schools in cultural anthropology can be found in Diamente and Wallace (2004), Hawkins and Adams (2005) and Wallace (1999, 2004).

[4] The Indians vanished sometime after the Portuguese had first landed in Barbados (1536) and before the English arrived a century later. No one knows for sure what happened to them, but according to early Spanish documents, many Indians were abducted from small Caribbean islands like Barbados and taken to work in the fields and mines of the larger Spanish colonial islands. Famine or disease may also have been responsible.

[5] Tasmanian Aboriginals were not exterminated but nearly so. Today the descendants of Aboriginal mothers and European men, mainly whalers who operated on offshore islands, live throughout Tasmania although they are not visibly identifiable.

[6] The students are not required to have any formal training in research methods before arriving in the field; however, anywhere from one-quarter to one-half will have taken the on-campus anthropology research methods course. During the first week in the field, the students are given field exercises that introduce them to different data-gathering techniques. Research methods and the students' field experiences are part of the discussion at weekly seminars. Students are required to turn in their field notes each week, and about once per week the field directors meet with them individually.

[7] So far, these have included Tasmania Parks and Wildlife, where several students have conducted research in natural parks with trekkers and "discovery rangers," the Wilderness Society, Volunteering Tasmania, and Lifeline Hobart.

[8] Only two of the students we have taken to Barbados over the years have been nonwhite. One was African American and the other was a Japanese exchange student.

References

Diamente, Daniela N., and Tim Wallace. 2004. Apprenticing Ethnographers in Ethnographic Field Schools and Community Service Learning. In *Passages: The Ethnographic Field School and First Fieldwork Experiences,* ed. Madelyn Iris. Washington DC: American Anthropological Association, *NAPA Bulletin,* 22(1):147–158.

Gmelch, George. 1992. Learning Culture: The Education of American Students in Caribbean Villages. *Human Organization,* 51(3):245–252.

———. 1999. Lessons from the Field. In *Conformity and Conflict,* 12th ed., eds. J. Spradley and D. McCurdy, pp. 45–55. Boston: Allyn & Bacon.

Gmelch, George, and Sharon Bohn Gmelch. 2001[1997]. *The Parish Behind God's Back: The Changing Culture of Rural Barbados.* Long Grove, IL: Waveland Press.

Hawkins, John P., and W. P. Adams. 2005. *Roads to Change in Maya Guatemala.* Norman, OK: University of Oklahoma Press.

Wallace, Tim. 1999. Mentoring Apprentice Ethnographers Through Field Schools. *Anthropology and Education Quarterly,* 30(2):210–250.

———. 2004. Mentorship and the Field School Experience. In *Passages: The Ethnographic Field School and First Fieldwork Experiences,* ed. Madelyn Iris. Washington, DC: American Anthropological Association, *NAPA Bulletin,* 22(1):142–146.

PART 2

Urban Communities

Urban anthropologists carry out research in communities. But what is a *community*? And what makes a community *urban*? For generations, these simple questions have been at the top of the research agenda for social scientists interested in cities and city life. In his famous essay on "Urbanism as a Way of Life," first published in 1938, Louis Wirth suggested that "a city may be defined as a relatively large, dense, and permanent settlement of socially heterogeneous individuals." Wirth's definition is still widely used, but it also has been challenged because its emphasis on size, density, and heterogeneity is often inadequate to understand the distinctive forms of communities that urban anthropologists encounter in their fieldwork around the world.

Clearly, we need to agree on the meanings for basic terms such as *city*, *urban*, *urbanism*, and *urbanization*. What kinds and sizes of settlements count as urban? Where do we draw the line between town and city; between rural, suburban, and urban? Answer these questions for yourself. In what kinds and sizes of places have *you* lived? Is *your* background urban, suburban, or rural, or some combination of these broad categories? Now add the experiences of your friends, their friends, and their friends' friends—and you will begin to see the challenges of making sense of the complexities of contemporary urban life.

In answering these basic questions, it is useful to distinguish "urbanism"—the *patterns* of city life, whether present in a particular place or found in a wide range of places—from "urbanization"—the *processes* of urban transformation over time. For example, a hundred years ago in Chicago, working-class European immigrant populations resided in neighborhoods where today working-class Latin American immigrants live. Those Europeans had a certain way of life; today's Hispanics have another. The changes in the way of life of those who populate the city illustrate the urbanization process and permit us to witness broad structural differences and similarities in urban life across the generations.

Cities are places in which people can and do create communities, and these urban communities may take on distinctive features in different societies. Islamic cities, for example, can be quite different from Western ones.

Unlike American cities, Islamic cities in the Middle East were subdivided into small residential neighborhoods (known as "quarters") that persisted for decades or even centuries. These quarters in Islamic cities represent defensible spaces, even when they do not involve ethnic or sectarian segregation. This is unlike the more fluid boundaries of the neighborhoods in Los Angeles or the *barrios* in Mexico City. Middle Eastern Islamic cities also emphasize the segregation of men and women to an extent not found in Europe, North America, or Latin America. To accomplish their goals, Islamic urban planners created building codes to prevent males who do not belong to a household from seeing the women belonging to that household. The layout of houses, courtyards, and neighborhoods, as well as the screening of windows, made it possible for women to see men, but not vice versa. In this way, not only are neighborhoods made into defensible spaces, so are individual households designed in defensive terms (Abu-Lughod 1987).

Official definitions of terms such as *rural, urban, city*, and *metropolitan* often vary widely from those used by the people living in these places. Census bureaus in most countries define rural and urban according to population, with 2,500 being the magic number separating the two domains, although few people are aware of such governmental definitions. Moreover, few of us can draw a rough sketch (much less an accurate map) of the zip-code demarcations, the census tracts, or the census-block groups within which we and our friends reside. Such official identifiers rarely match what the urban planner Kevin Lynch (1960) has called our "mental maps" of urban spaces. Nor do official maps indicate the special features of urban life, which Lynch characterizes as paths, edges, nodes, districts, and landmarks, all of which may be known only to community insiders. Your grandfather tells you to "turn right at the corner where the Standard Oil service station used to be"; you tell a friend to "cut through an alley and come through the only back gate painted red"; you spot certain symbols spray painted on buildings on one side of a street and quite different (but equally unknown to you) symbols on those across the street. In every case, your experiences affirm Lynch's critical observation that local people live in urban communities whose real dimensions can be rather different from what may be known by outsiders.

Consider another example: in our urban anthropology classes, we have found that students define the community where they attend college in light of the characteristics of their home communities. Thus, students from smaller communities are more likely to declare a mid-sized college town to be "urban" or "a city" than are students from large metropolitan areas, whether they live in the U.S. or in foreign countries. No wonder it is so difficult to arrive at a cross-culturally acceptable definition of urban community!

Part 2 opens with a chapter by Louis Wirth in which he defines the elements of urban communities as these differ from rural communities. "Urbanism as a Way of Life" has stood for more than 70 years as the core text representing the ecological approach of the "Chicago School of Sociology." Whereas Wirth emphasized a general theoretical perspective, and thus gave few concrete examples to support his arguments, Sally Engle Merry's "Urban Danger" looks at numerous cases of the social relations between strangers in a high-crime neighborhood as a way to appreciate how people in urban communities manage their fears. Merry's case study is followed by Setha Low's comparative analysis of two gated communities, one in San Antonio, Texas, and the other in the Borough of Queens, New York. In these seemingly quite different urban settings, Low sheds light on the fears of city dwellers who seek refuge for themselves and their children behind the walls of communities marked more by exclusion than by inclusion. Segregation in the face of urban danger is also a highlight of Nell Gabiam's study of the Palestinian refugee camps in Damascus, Syria. Definitions of urban life take on new meaning in Derek Pardue's ethnography of São Paulo, Brazil, where transportation systems and hip-hop music seem to blend into a vibrant urban culture that, to a large extent, turns Wirth's concept of urbanism on its head. Rather than adopt the static ecological approach to the patterns of urban life espoused by Wirth, Pardue emphasizes the flows of events and activities that keep Brazilian urban life "in motion."

When taken together, the findings by Merry, Low, Gabiam, and Pardue confront Wirth's familiar notions about urban communities in numerous ways, thereby challenging us to reconsider and transform our twentieth-century views of cities as we move forward in the twenty-first century.

References

Abu-Lughod, Janet. 1987. The Islamic City: Historic Myth, Islamic Essence, and Contemporary Relevance. *International Journal of Middle Eastern Studies*, 19:155–176.

Lynch, Kevin. 1960. *The Image of the City.* Cambridge, MA: MIT Press.

Readings in Part 2

7

Urbanism As a Way of Life

Louis Wirth

In this chapter, Louis Wirth speculates on how cities influence the social organization, attitudes, and personality of their inhabitants. Wirth begins his analysis by defining the city sociologically as a type of community that is large, dense, and comprised of socially heterogeneous individuals. He then deduces the essential properties of urban existence—anonymity, transitory and impersonal relationships, secularization of thought, and so on. In this ideal-type approach to urban life, Wirth contrasts "the urban" with "the rural" and, as a consequence, gives relatively little attention to the important internal variations among populations in urban places and those in urban spaces.

THE CITY AND CONTEMPORARY CIVILIZATION

Just as the beginning of Western civilization is marked by the permanent settlement of formerly nomadic peoples in the Mediterranean basin, so the beginning of what is distinctively modern in our civilization is best signalized by the growth of great cities. Nowhere has humankind been farther removed from organic nature than under the conditions of life characteristic of great cities. The contemporary world no longer presents a picture of small isolated groups of human beings scattered over a vast territory, as Sumner (1906:12) described primitive society. The distinctive feature of the mode of living of human beings in the modern age is their concentration into gigantic aggregations around which cluster lesser centers and from which radiate the ideas and practices that we call civilization.

The degree to which the contemporary world may be said to be "urban" is not fully or accurately measured by the proportion of the total population living in cities. The influences which cities exert upon the social life of individuals are greater than the ratio of the urban population would indicate, for the city is

Source: *American Journal of Sociology*, XLIV (1938):1–24. © 1938 by University of Chicago. Reprinted by permission of the University of Chicago Press.

not only in ever larger degrees the dwelling place and the workshop of modern human society, but it is the initiating and controlling center of economic, political, and cultural life that has drawn the most remote parts of the world into its orbit and woven diverse areas, peoples, and activities into a cosmos.

The growth of cities and the urbanization of the world is one of the most impressive facts of modern times. Although it is impossible to state precisely what proportion of the estimated total world population of approximately 1.8 billion is urban, 69.2 percent of the total population of those countries that do distinguish between urban and rural areas is urban (Pearson 1935:211). Considering the fact, moreover, that the world's population is very unevenly distributed and that the growth of cities is not very far advanced in some of the countries that have only recently been touched by industrialism, this average understates the extent to which urban concentration has proceeded in those countries where the impact of the industrial revolution has been more forceful and of less recent date. This shift from a rural to a predominantly urban society, which has taken place within the span of a single generation in such industrialized areas as the United States and Japan, has been accompanied by profound changes in virtually every phase of social life. It is these changes and their ramifications that invite the attention of the sociologist to the study of the differences between the rural and the urban mode of living. The pursuit of this interest is an indispensable prerequisite for the comprehension and possible mastery of some of the most crucial contemporary problems of social life since it is likely to furnish one of the most revealing perspectives for the understanding of the ongoing changes in human nature and the social order.[1]

Since the city is the product of growth rather than of instantaneous creation, it is to be expected that the influences which it exerts upon the modes of life should not be able to wipe out completely the previously dominant modes of human association. To a greater or lesser degree, therefore, our social life bears the imprint of an earlier folk society, the characteristic modes of settlement of which were the farm, the manor, and the village. This historic influence is reinforced by the circumstance that the population of the city itself is in large measure recruited from the countryside, where a mode of life reminiscent of this earlier form of existence persists. Hence we should not expect to find abrupt and discontinuous variation between urban and rural types of personality. The city and the country may be regarded as two poles in reference to one or the other of which all human settlements tend to arrange themselves. In viewing urban-industrial and rural-folk society as ideal types of communities, we may obtain a perspective for the analysis of the basic models of human association as they appear in contemporary civilization.

A SOCIOLOGICAL DEFINITION OF THE CITY

Despite the preponderant significance of the city in our civilization, however, our knowledge of the nature of urbanism and the process of urbanization is meager. Many attempts have indeed been made to isolate the distinguishing characteristics of urban life. Geographers, historians, economists, and political scientists have incorporated the points of view of their respective disciplines into diverse definitions of the city. While in no sense intended to supersede these, the formulation of a sociological approach to the city may incidentally serve to call attention to the interrelations between them by emphasizing the peculiar characteristics of the city as a particular form of human association. A sociologically significant definition of the city seeks to select those elements of urbanism which mark it as a distinctive mode of human group life.

The characterization of a community as urban on the basis of size alone is obviously arbitrary. It is difficult to defend the present census definition which designates a community of twenty-five hundred and above as urban and all others as rural. The situation would be the same if the criterion were four thousand, eight thousand, ten thousand, twenty-five thousand, or one hundred thousand population, for although in the latter case we might feel that we were more nearly dealing with an urban aggregate than would be the case in communities of lesser size, no definition of urbanism can hope to be completely satisfying as long as numbers are regarded as the sole criterion. Moreover, it is not difficult to demonstrate that communities of less than the arbitrarily set number of inhabitants lying within the range of influence of metropolitan centers have greater claim to recognition as urban communities than do larger ones leading a more isolated existence in a predominantly rural area. Finally, it should be recognized that census definitions are unduly influenced by the fact that the city, statistically speaking, is always an administrative concept in that the corporate limits play a decisive role in delineating the urban area. Nowhere is this more clearly apparent than in the concentrations of population on the peripheries of great metropolitan centers which cross arbitrary administrative boundaries of city, county, state, and nation.

As long as we identify urbanism with the physical entity of the city, viewing it merely as rigidly delimited in space, and proceed as if urban attributes abruptly ceased to be manifested beyond an arbitrary boundary line, we are not likely to arrive at any adequate conception of urbanism as a mode of life. The technological developments in transportation and communication which virtually mark a new epoch in human history have accentuated the role of cities as dominant elements in our civilization and have enormously extended the urban mode of living beyond the confines of the city itself. The dominance of the city, especially of the great city, may be regarded as a consequence of the concentration in cities of industrial and commercial, financial and administrative facilities and activities, transportation and communication lines, and cultural and recreational equipment such as the press, radio stations, theaters, libraries, museums, concert halls, operas, hospitals, higher educational institutions, research and publishing centers, professional organizations, and religious and welfare institutions. Were it not for the attraction and suggestions that the city exerts through these instrumentalities upon the rural population, the differences between the rural and the urban modes of life would be even greater than they are. Urbanization no longer denotes merely the process by which persons are attracted to a place called the city and incorporated into its system of life. It refers also to that cumulative accentuation of the characteristics distinctive of the mode of life which is associated with the growth of cities, and finally to the changes in the direction of modes of life recognized as urban which are apparent among people, wherever they may be, who have come under the spell of the influences which the city exerts by virtue of the power of its institutions and personalities operating through the means of communication and transportation.

The shortcomings which attach to number of inhabitants as a criterion of urbanism apply for the most part to density of population as well. Whether we accept the density of ten thousand persons per square mile as Mark Jefferson (1909:537–566) proposed, or one thousand, which Willcox (1926:119) preferred to regard as the criterion of urban settlements, it is clear that unless density is correlated with significant social characteristics it can furnish only an arbitrary basis for differentiating urban from rural communities. Since our census enumerates the night rather than the day population of an area, the locale of the most intensive urban life—the city center—generally has low population density, and the industrial and commercial areas of the city, which contain the most characteristic economic activities underlying urban society, would scarcely anywhere be truly urban if density were literally interpreted as a mark of urbanism. Nevertheless, the fact that the urban community is distinguished by a large aggregation and relatively dense concentration of population can scarcely be left out of account in a definition of the city. But these criteria must be seen as relative to the general cultural context in which cities arise and exist and are sociologically relevant only insofar as they operate as conditioning factors in social life.

The same criticisms apply to such criteria as the occupation of the inhabitants, the existence of certain physical facilities, institutions, and forms of political organization. The question is not whether cities in our civilization or in others do exhibit these distinctive traits, but how potent they are in molding the character of social life into its specifically urban form. Nor in formulating a fertile definition can we afford to overlook the great variations between cities. By means of a typology of cities based upon size, location, age, and function, such as we have undertaken to establish in our report to the National Resources Committee (1937:8), we have found it feasible to array and classify urban communities ranging from struggling small towns to thriving world metropolitan centers; from isolated trading centers in the midst of agricultural regions to thriving world ports and commercial and industrial conurbations. Such differences as these appear crucial because the social characteristics and influences of these different "cities" vary widely.

A serviceable definition of urbanism should not only denote the essential characteristics which all cities—at least those in our culture—have in common, but should lend itself to the discovery of their variations. An industrial city will differ significantly in social respects from a commercial, mining, fishing, resort, university, and capital city. A one-industry city will present different sets of social characteristics from a multi-industry city, as will an industrially balanced from an imbalanced city, a suburb from a satellite, a residential suburb from an industrial suburb, a city within a metropolitan region from one lying outside, an old city from a new one, a southern city from a New England, a middle-western from a Pacific Coast city, a growing from a stable and from a dying city.

A sociological definition must obviously be inclusive enough to comprise whatever essential characteristics these different types of cities have in common as social entities, but it obviously cannot be so detailed as to take account of all the variations implicit in the manifold classes sketched above. Presumably some of the characteristics of cities are more significant in conditioning the nature of urban life than others, and we may expect the outstanding features of the urban-social scene to vary in accordance with size, density, and differences in the functional type of cities. Moreover, we may infer that rural life will bear the imprint of urbanism in the measure that through contact and communication it comes under the influence of cities. It may contribute to the clarity of the statements that follow to repeat that while the locus of urbanism as a mode of life is, of course, to be found characteristically in places that fulfill the requirements we shall set up as a definition of the city, urbanism is not confined to such localities but is manifest in varying degrees wherever the influences of the city reach.

While urbanism, or that complex of traits that makes up the characteristic mode of life in cities, and urbanization, which denotes the development and extensions of these factors, are thus not exclusively found in settlements that are cities in the physical and demographic sense, they do, nevertheless, find their most pronounced expression in such areas, especially in metropolitan cities. In formulating a definition of the city it is necessary to exercise caution in order to avoid identifying urbanism as a way of life with any specific locally or historically conditioned cultural influences that, while they may significantly affect the specific character of the community, are not the essential determinants of its character as a city.

It is particularly important to call attention to the danger of confusing urbanism with industrialism and modern capitalism. The rise of cities in the modern world is undoubtedly not independent of the emergence of modern power-driven machine technology, mass production, and capitalistic enterprise. But different as the cities of earlier epochs may have been by virtue of their development in a preindustrial and precapitalistic order from the great cities of today, they were, nevertheless, cities.

For sociological purposes a city may be defined as a relatively large, dense, and permanent settlement of socially heterogeneous individuals. On the basis of the postulates which this minimal definition suggests, a theory of urbanism may be formulated in the light of existing knowledge concerning social groups.

A THEORY OF URBANISM

In the rich literature on the city we look in vain for a theory of urbanism presenting in a systematic fashion the available knowledge concerning the city as a social entity. We do indeed have excellent formulations of theories on such special problems as the growth of the city viewed as a historical trend and as a recurrent process (Park et al. 1925; Sombart 1931), and we have a wealth of literature presenting insights of sociological relevance and empirical studies offering detailed information on a variety of particular aspects of urban life. But despite the multiplication of research and textbooks on the city, we do not as yet have a comprehensive body of compendent hypotheses that may be derived from a set of postulates implicitly contained in a sociological definition of the city and from our general sociological knowledge which may be substantiated through empirical research. The closest approximations to a systematic theory of urbanism that we have are to be found in a penetrating essay, "Die Stadt," by Max Weber (1925:514–601), and a memorable paper by Robert E. Park (1925, chapter 1) on "The City: Suggestions for the Investigation of Human Behavior in the Urban Environment." But even these excellent contributions are far from constituting an ordered and coherent framework of theory upon which research might profitably proceed.

In the pages that follow we shall seek to set forth a limited number of identifying characteristics of the city. Given these characteristics we shall then indicate what consequences or further characteristics follow from them in the light of general sociological theory and empirical research. We hope in this manner to arrive at the essential propositions comprising a theory of urbanism. Some of these propositions can be supported by a considerable body of already available research materials; others may be accepted as hypotheses for which a certain amount of presumptive evidence exists but for which more ample and exact verification would be required. At least such a procedure will, it is hoped, show what in the way of systematic knowledge of the city we now have and what are the crucial and fruitful hypotheses for future research.

The central problem of the sociologist of the city is to discover the forms of social action and organization that typically emerge in relatively permanent, compact settlements of large numbers of heterogeneous individuals. We must also infer that urbanism will assume its most characteristic and extreme form in the measure in which the conditions with which it is congruent are present. Thus the larger, the more densely populated, and the more heterogeneous a community, the more accentuated the characteristics associated with urbanism will be. It should be recognized, however, that in the social world institutions and practices may be accepted and continued for reasons other than those that originally brought them into existence, and that accordingly the urban mode of life may be perpetuated under conditions quite foreign to those necessary for its origin.

Some justification may be in order for the choice of the principal terms comprising our definition of the city. The attempt has been made to make it as inclusive and at the same time as denotative as possible without loading it with unnecessary assumptions. To say that large numbers are necessary to constitute a city means, of course, large numbers in relation to a restricted area or high density of settlement. There are, nevertheless, good reasons for treating large numbers and density as separate factors, since each may be connected with significantly different social consequences. Similarly, the need for adding heterogeneity to numbers of population as a necessary and distinct criterion of urbanism might be questioned, since we should expect the range of differences to increase with numbers. In defense, it may be said that the city shows a kind and degree of heterogeneity of population which cannot be wholly accounted for by the law of large numbers or adequately represented by means of a normal distribution curve. Since the population of the city does not reproduce itself, it must recruit its migrants from other cities, the countryside, and—in this country until recently—from other countries. The city has thus historically been the melting pot of races, peoples, and cultures, and a most favorable breeding ground of new biological and cultural hybrids. It has not only tolerated but rewarded individual differences. It has brought together people from the ends of the earth because they are different and thus useful to one another, rather than because they are homogeneous and like-minded.[2]

There are a number of sociological propositions concerning the relationship between (a) numbers of population, (b) density of settlement, (c) heterogeneity of inhabitants and group life, which can be formulated on the basis of observation and research.

Size of the Population Aggregate

Ever since Aristotle's *Politics*, it has been recognized that increasing the number of inhabitants in a settlement beyond a certain limit will affect the relationships between them and the character of the city. Large numbers involve, as has been pointed out, a greater range of individual variation. Furthermore, the greater the number of individuals participating in a process of interaction, the greater is the *potential* differentiation between them. The personal traits, the occupations, the cultural life, and the ideas of the members of an urban community may, therefore, be expected to range between more widely separated poles than those of rural inhabitants.

That such variations should give rise to the spatial segregation of individuals according to color, ethnic heritage, economic and social status, tastes and preferences, may readily be inferred. The bonds of kinship, of neighborliness, and the sentiments arising out of living together for generations under a common folk tradition are likely to be absent or, at best, relatively weak in an aggregate the members of which have such diverse origins and backgrounds. Under such circumstances competition and formal control mechanisms furnish the substitutes for the bonds of solidarity that are relied upon to hold a folk society together.

Increase in the number of inhabitants of a community beyond a few hundred is bound to limit the possibility of each member of the community knowing all the others personally. Max Weber, in recognizing the social significance of this fact, pointed out that from a sociological point of view large numbers of inhabitants and density of settlement mean that the personal mutual acquaintanceship between the inhabitants which ordinarily inheres in a neighborhood is lacking (1925:514). The increase in numbers thus involves a changed character of the social relationships. As Simmel points out:

> [If] the unceasing external contact of numbers of persons in the city should be met by the same number of inner reactions as in the small town, in which one knows almost every person he meets and to each of whom he has a positive relationship, one would be completely atomized internally and would fall into an unthinkable mental condition. (1903:187–206)

The multiplication of persons in a state of interaction under conditions which make their contact as full personalities impossible produces that segmentalization of human relationships which has sometimes been seized upon by students of the mental life of the cities as an explanation for the "schizoid" character of urban personality. This is not to say that the urban inhabitants have fewer acquaintances than rural inhabitants, for the reverse may actually be true; it means rather that in relation to the number of people whom they see and with whom they rub elbows in the course of daily life, they know a smaller proportion, and of these they have less intensive knowledge.

Characteristically, urbanites meet one another in highly segmental roles. They are, to be sure, dependent upon more people for the satisfactions of their life-needs than are rural people and thus are associated with a greater number of organized groups, but they are less dependent upon particular persons, and their dependence upon others is confined to a highly fractionalized aspect of the other's round of activity. This is essentially what is meant by saying that the city is characterized by secondary rather than primary contacts. The contacts of the city may indeed be face-to-face, but they are nevertheless impersonal, superficial, transitory, and segmental. The reserve, the indifference, and the blasé outlook which urbanites manifest in their relationships may thus be regarded as devices for immunizing themselves against the personal claims and expectations of others.

The superficiality, the anonymity, and the transitory character of urban-social relations make intelligible, also, the sophistication and the rationality generally ascribed to city dwellers. Our acquaintances tend to stand in a relationship of utility to us in the sense that the role which each one plays in our life is overwhelmingly regarded as a means for the achievement of our own ends. Whereas, therefore, the individual gains, on the one hand, a certain degree of emancipation or freedom from the personal and emotional controls of intimate groups, he or she loses, on the other hand, the spontaneous self-expression, the morale, and the sense of participation that comes with living in an integrated society. This constitutes essentially the state of *anomie* or the social void to which Durkheim alludes in attempting to account for the various forms of social disorganization in technological society.

The segmental character and utilitarian accent of interpersonal relations in the city find their institutional expression in the proliferation of specialized tasks that we see in their most developed form in the professions. The operations of the pecuniary nexus lead to predatory relationships, which tend to obstruct the efficient functioning of the social order unless checked by professional codes and occupational etiquette. The premium put upon utility and efficiency suggests the adaptability of the corporate device for the organization of enterprises in which individuals can engage only in groups. The advantage that the corporation has over the individual entrepreneur and the partnership in the urban-industrial world derives not only from the possibility it affords of centralizing the resources of thousands of individuals or from the legal privilege of limited liability and perpetual succession, but also from the fact that the corporation has no soul.

The specialization of individuals, particularly in their occupations, can proceed only, as Adam Smith pointed out, upon the basis of an enlarged market, which in turn accentuates the division of labor. This enlarged market is only in part supplied by the city's hinterland; in large measure it is found among the large numbers that the city itself contains. The dominance of the city over the surrounding hinterland becomes explicable in terms of the division of labor which urban life occasions and promotes. The extreme degree of interdependence and the unstable equilibrium of urban life are closely associated with the division of labor and the specialization of occupations. This interdependence and instability is increased by the tendency of each city to specialize in those functions in which it has the greatest advantage.

In a community composed of a larger number of individuals than can know one another intimately and can be assembled in one spot, it becomes necessary to communicate through indirect mediums and to articulate individual interests by a process of delegation. Typically in the city, interests are made effective through representation. The individual counts for little, but the voice of the representative is heard with a deference roughly proportional to the numbers for whom he or she speaks.

While this characterization of urbanism, insofar as it derives from large numbers, does not by any means exhaust the sociological inferences that might be drawn from our knowledge of the relationship of the size of a group to the characteristic behavior of the members, for the sake of brevity the assertions made may serve to exemplify the sort of propositions that might be developed.

Density

As in the case of numbers, so in the case of concentration in limited space, certain consequences of relevance in sociological analysis of the city emerge. Of these only a few can be indicated.

As Darwin pointed out for flora and fauna and as Durkheim (1932:248) noted in the case of human societies, an increase in numbers when area is held constant (i.e., an increase in density) tends to produce differentiation and specialization since only in this way can the area support increased numbers. Density thus reinforces the effect of numbers in diversifying people and their activities and in increasing the complexity of the social structure.

On the subjective side, as Simmel (1903:187–206) has suggested, the close physical contact of numerous individuals necessarily produces a shift in the mediums through which we orient ourselves to the urban milieu, especially to other people. Typically, our physical contacts are close but our social contacts are distant. The urban world puts a premium on visual recognition. We see the uniform which denotes the role of the functionaries and are oblivious to the personal eccentricities that are hidden behind the uniform. We tend to acquire and develop a sensitivity to a world of artifacts and become progressively farther removed from the world of nature. We are exposed to glaring contrasts between splendor and squalor, between riches and poverty, intelligence and ignorance, order and chaos. The competition for space is great, so that each area generally tends to be put to the use which yields the greatest economic return. Place of work tends to become dissociated from place of residence, for the proximity of industrial and commercial establishments makes an area both economically and socially undesirable for residential purposes.

Density, land values, rentals, accessibility, healthfulness, prestige, aesthetic consideration, absence of nuisances such as noise, smoke, and dirt determine the desirability of various areas of the city as places of settlement for different sections of the population. Place and nature of work, income, racial and ethnic characteristics, social status, custom, habit, taste, preference, and prejudice are among the significant factors in accordance with which the urban population is selected and distributed into more or less distinct settlements. Diverse population elements inhabiting a compact settlement thus tend to become segregated from one another in the degree in which their requirements and modes of life are incompatible with one another and in the measure in which they are antagonistic to one another. Similarly, persons of homogeneous status and needs unwittingly drift into, consciously select, or are forced by circumstances into, the same area. The different parts of the city thus acquire specialized functions. The city consequently tends to resemble a mosaic of social worlds in which the transition from one to the other is abrupt. The juxtaposition of divergent personalities and modes of life tends to produce a relativistic perspective and a sense of toleration of differences that may be regarded as prerequisites for rationality and that lead toward the secularization of life.[3]

The close living together and working together of individuals who have no sentimental and emotional ties foster a spirit of competition, aggrandizement, and mutual exploitation. To counteract irresponsibility and potential disorder, formal controls tend to be resorted to. Without rigid adherence to predictable routines a large compact society would scarcely be able to maintain itself. The clock and the traffic signal are symbolic of the basis of our social order in the urban world. Frequent close physical contact, coupled with great social distance, accentuates the reserve of unattached individuals toward one another and, unless compensated for by other opportunities for response, gives rise to loneliness. The necessary frequent movement of great numbers of individuals in a congested habitat gives occasion to friction and irritation. Nervous tensions which derive from such personal frustrations are accentuated by the rapid tempo and the complicated technology under which life in dense areas must be lived.

Heterogeneity

The social interaction among such a variety of personality types in the urban milieu tends to break down the rigidity of caste lines and to complicate the class structure, and thus induces a more ramified and differentiated framework of social stratification than is found in more integrated societies. The heightened mobility of individuals, which brings them within the range of stimulation by a great number of diverse individuals and subjects them to fluctuating status in the differentiated social groups that compose the social structure of the city, tends toward the acceptance of instability and insecurity in the world at large as a norm. This fact helps to account, too, for the sophistication and cosmopolitanism of urbanites. No single group has the undivided allegiance of individuals. The groups with which they are affiliated do not lend themselves readily to a simple hierarchical arrangement. By virtue of their different interests arising out of different aspects of social life, individuals acquire membership in widely divergent groups, each of which functions only with reference to a single segment of their personalities. Nor do these groups easily permit a concentric arrangement so that the narrower ones fall within the circumference of the more inclusive ones, as is more likely to be the case in the rural community or in primitive societies. Rather the groups with which persons typically are affiliated are tangential to each other or intersect in a highly variable fashion.

Partly as a result of the physical footlooseness of the population and partly as a result of their social mobility, the turnover in group membership generally is rapid. Place of residence, place and character of employment, income, and interests fluctuate, and the task of holding organizations together and maintaining and promoting intimate and lasting acquaintanceship between the members is difficult. This applies strikingly to the local areas within the city into which persons become segregated more by virtue of differences in race, language, income, and social status, than through choice or positive attraction to people like themselves. Overwhelmingly city dwellers are not home owners, and since a transitory habitat does not generate binding traditions and sentiments, only rarely are they truly neighbors. There is little opportunity for individuals to obtain a conception of the city as a whole or to survey their place in the total scheme. Consequently, they find it difficult to determine what is to their own "best interests" and to decide between the issues and leaders presented to them by the agencies of mass suggestion. Individuals who are thus detached from the organized bodies which integrate society comprise the fluid masses that make collective behavior in the urban community so unpredictable and hence so problematical.

Although the city, through the recruitment of variant types to perform its diverse tasks and the accentuation of their uniqueness through competition and the premium upon eccentricity, novelty, efficient performance, and inventiveness, produces a highly differentiated population, it also exercises a leveling influence. Wherever large numbers of differently constituted individuals congregate, the process of depersonalization also enters. This leveling tendency inheres in part in the economic basis of the city. The development of large cities, at least in the modern age, was largely dependent upon the concentrative force of steam. The rise of the factory made possible mass production for an impersonal market. The fullest exploitation of the possibilities of the division of labor and mass production, however, is possible only with standardization of processes and products. A money economy goes hand in hand with such a system of production. Progressively as cities have developed upon a background of this system of production, the pecuniary nexus which implies the purchasability of services and things has displaced personal relations as the basis of association. Individuality under these circumstances must be replaced by categories. When large numbers have to make common use of facilities and institutions, an arrangement must be made to adjust the facilities and institutions to the needs of the average person rather than to those of particular individuals. The services of the public utilities, of the recreational, educational, and cultural institutions must be adjusted to mass requirements. Similarly, the cultural institutions, such as the schools, the movies, the radio, and the newspapers, by virtue of their mass clientele, must necessarily operate as leveling influences. The political process as it appears in urban life could not be understood without taking account of the mass appeals made through modern propaganda techniques. If individuals would participate at all in the social, political, and economic life of the city, they must subordinate some of their individuality to the demands of the larger community and in that measure immerse themselves in mass movements.

THE RELATION BETWEEN A THEORY OF URBANISM AND SOCIOLOGICAL RESEARCH

By means of a body of theory such as that illustratively sketched above, the complicated and many-sided phenomena of urbanism may be analyzed in terms of a limited number of basic categories. The sociological approach to the city thus acquires an essential unity and coherence enabling empirical investigators not merely to focus more distinctly upon the problems and processes that properly fall in their province but also to treat their subject matter in a more integrated and systematic fashion. A few typical findings of empirical research in the field of urbanism, with special reference to the United States, may be indicated to substantiate the theoretical propositions set forth in the preceding pages, and some of the crucial problems for further study may be outlined.

On the basis of the three variables—number, density of settlement, and degree of heterogeneity—of the urban population, it appears possible to explain the characteristics of urban life and to account for the differences between cities of various sizes and types.

Urbanism as a characteristic mode of life may be approached empirically from three interrelated perspectives: (1) as a physical structure comprising a population base, a technology, and an ecological order; (2) as a system of social organization involving a characteristic social structure, a series of social institutions, and a typical pattern of social relationships; and (3) as a set of attitudes and ideas, and a constellation of personalities engaging in typical forms of collective behavior and subject to characteristic mechanisms of social control.

Urbanism in Ecological Perspective

Since in the case of physical structure and ecological processes we are able to operate with fairly objective indices, it becomes possible to arrive at quite precise and generally quantitative results. The dominance of the city over its hinterland becomes explicable through the functional characteristics of the city which derive in large measure from the effect of numbers and density. Many of the technical facilities and the skills and organizations to which urban life gives rise can grow and prosper only in cities where the demand is sufficiently great. The nature and scope of the services rendered by these organizations and institutions and the advantage which they enjoy over the less developed facilities of smaller towns enhance the dominance of the city and the dependence of ever wider regions upon the central metropolis.

The urban-population composition shows the operation of selective and differentiating factors. Cities contain a larger proportion of persons in the prime of life than rural areas, which contain more old and very young people. In this, as in so many other respects, the larger the city the more this specific characteristic of urbanism is apparent. With the exception of the largest cities, which have attracted the bulk of the foreign-born males, and a few other special types of cities, women predominate numerically over men. The heterogeneity of the urban population is further indicated along racial and ethnic lines. The foreign born and their children constitute nearly two-thirds of all the inhabitants of cities of one million and over. Their proportion in the urban population declines as the size of the city decreases, until in the rural areas they comprise only about one-sixth of the total population. The larger cities similarly have attracted more African Americans and other racial groups than have the smaller communities. Considering that age, sex, race, and ethnic origin are associated with other factors such as occupation and interest, it becomes clear that one major characteristic of urban dwellers is their dissimilarity from their neighbors. Never before have such large masses of people of diverse traits as we find in our cities been thrown together into such close physical contact as in the great cities of America. Cities generally, and American cities in particular, comprise a motley of peoples and cultures, of highly differentiated modes of life between which there often is only the faintest communication, the greatest indifference and the broadest tolerance, occasionally bitter strife, but always the sharpest contrast.

The failure of the urban population to reproduce itself appears to be a biological consequence of a combination of factors in the complex of urban life, and the decline in the birth rate generally may be regarded as one of the most significant signs of the urbanization of the Western world. While the proportion of deaths in cities is slightly greater than in the country, the outstanding difference between the failure of present-day cities to maintain their population and that of cities of the past is that in former times it was due to the exceedingly high death rates in cities, whereas today, since cities have become more livable from a health standpoint, it is due to low birth rates. These biological characteristics of the urban population are significant sociologically, not merely because they reflect the urban mode of existence but also because they condition the growth and future dominance of cities and their basic social organization. Since cities are the consumers rather than the producers of the population, the value of human life and the social estimation of the personality will not be unaffected by the balance between births and deaths. The pattern of land use, of land values, rentals, and ownership, the nature and functioning of the physical structures, of housing, of transportation and communication facilities, of public utilities—these and many other phases of the physical mechanism of the city are not isolated phenomena unrelated to the city as a social entity, but are affected by and affect the urban mode of life.

Urbanism as a Form of Social Organization

The distinctive features of the urban mode of life have often been described sociologically as consisting of the substitution of secondary for primary contacts, the weakening of bonds of kinship and the declining social significance of the family, the disappearance of the neighborhood, and the undermining of the traditional basis of social solidarity. All these phenomena can be substantially verified through objective indices. Thus, for instance, the low and declining urban-reproduction rates suggest that the city is not conducive to the traditional type of family life, including the rearing of children and the maintenance of the home as the locus of a whole round of vital activities. The transfer of industrial, educational, and recreational activities to specialized institutions outside the home has deprived the family of some of its most characteristic historical functions. In cities, mothers are more likely to be employed, lodgers are more frequently part of the household, marriage tends to be postponed, and the proportion of single and unattached people is greater. Families are smaller and more frequently without children than in the country. The family as a unit of social life is emancipated from the larger kinship group characteristic of the country, and the individual members pursue their own diverging interests in their vocational, educational, religious, recreational, and political life.

Such functions as the maintenance of health, the methods of alleviating the hardships associated with personal and social insecurity, the provisions for education, recreation, and cultural advancement have given rise to highly specialized institutions on a community-wide, statewide, or even national basis. The same factors which have brought about greater personal insecurity also underlie the wider contrasts between individuals to be found in the urban world. While the city has broken down the rigid caste lines of preindustrial society, it has sharpened and differentiated income and status groups. Generally, a larger proportion of the adult-urban population is gainfully employed than is the case with the adult-rural population. The white-collar class, comprising those employed in trade, in clerical, and in professional work, are proportionately more numerous in large cities and in metropolitan centers and in smaller towns than in the country.

On the whole, the city discourages an economic life in which the individual in time of crisis has a basis of subsistence to fall back upon, and it discourages self-employment. While incomes of city people are on the average higher than those of country people, the cost of living seems to be higher in the larger cities. Home ownership involves greater burdens and is rarer. Rents are higher and absorb a larger proportion of the income. Although urban dwellers have the benefit of many communal services, they spend a large proportion of their income for such items as recreation and advancement and a smaller proportion for food. What the communal services do not furnish the urbanite must purchase, and there is virtually no human need that has remained unexploited by commercialism. Catering to thrills and furnishing means of escape from drudgery, monotony, and routine thus becomes one of the major functions of urban recreation, which at its best furnishes means for creative self-expression and spontaneous group association, but which more typically in the urban world results in passive spectatorism on the one hand, or sensational record-smashing feats on the other.

Being reduced to a state of virtual impotence as an individual, urbanites are bound to exert themselves by joining with others of similar interest into organized groups to obtain their ends. This results in the enormous multiplication of voluntary organizations directed toward as great a variety of objectives as there are human needs and interests. While on the one hand the traditional ties of human association are weakened, urban existence involves a much greater degree of interdependence between people and a more complicated, fragile, and volatile form of mutual interrelations over many phases of which individuals as such can exert scarcely any control. Frequently there is only the most tenuous relationship between the economic position or other basic factors that determine individuals' existence in the urban world and the voluntary groups with which they are affiliated. While in a primitive and in a rural society it is generally possible to predict on the basis of a few known factors who will belong to what and who will associate with whom in almost every relationship of life, in the city we can only project the general pattern of group formation and affiliation, and this pattern will display many incongruities and contradictions.

Urban Personality and Collective Behavior

It is largely through the activities of the voluntary groups, be their objectives economic, political, educational, religious, recreational, or cultural, that urbanites express and develop their personalities, acquire status, and are able to carry on the round of activities that constitute their life-careers. It may easily be inferred, however, that the organizational framework that these highly differentiated functions call into being does not of itself ensure the consistency and integrity of the personalities whose interests it enlists. Personal disorganization, mental breakdown, suicide, delinquency, crime, corruption, and disorder might be expected under these circumstances to be more prevalent in the urban than in the rural community. This has been confirmed insofar as comparable indices are available; but the mechanisms underlying these phenomena require further analysis.

Since for most group purposes it is impossible in the city to appeal individually to the large number of discrete and differentiated individuals, and since it is only through the organizations to which people belong that their interests and resources can be enlisted for a collective cause, it may be inferred that social control in the city should typically proceed through formally organized groups. It follows, too, that the masses of people in the city are subject to manipulation by symbols and stereotypes managed by individuals working from afar or operating invisibly behind the scenes through their control of the instruments of communication. Self-government either in the economic, the political, or the cultural realm is under these circumstances reduced to a mere figure of speech or, at best, is subject to the unstable equilibrium of pressure groups. In view of the ineffectiveness of actual kinship ties we create fictional kinship groups. In the face of the disappearance of the territorial unit as a basis of social solidarity we create interest units. Meanwhile the city as a community resolves itself into a series of tenuous segmental relationships superimposed upon a territorial base with a definite center but without a definite periphery and upon a division of labor which far transcends the immediate locality and is worldwide in scope. The larger the number of persons in a state of interaction with one another the lower is the level of communication and the greater is the tendency for communication to proceed on an elementary level, i.e., on the basis of those things which are assumed to be common or to be of interest to all.

It is obviously, therefore, to the emerging trends in the communication system and to the production and distribution technology that has come into existence with modern civilization that we must look for the symptoms which will indicate the probable future development of urbanism as a mode of social life. The direction of the ongoing changes in urbanism will for good or ill transform not only the city but the world. Some of the more basic of these factors and processes and the possibilities of their direction and control invite further detailed study.

It is only insofar as sociologists have a clear conception of the city as a social entity and a workable theory of urbanism that they can hope to develop a unified body of reliable knowledge, which what passes as "urban sociology" is certainly not at the present time. By taking our point of departure from a theory of urbanism such as that sketched in the foregoing pages to be elaborated, tested, and revised in the light of further analysis and empirical research, it is to be hoped that the criteria of relevance and validity of factual data can be determined. The miscellaneous assortment of disconnected information which has hitherto found its way into sociological treatises on the city may thus be sifted and incorporated into a coherent body of knowledge. Incidentally, only by means of some such theory will sociologists escape the futile practice of voicing in the name of sociological science a variety of often insupportable judgments concerning such problems as poverty, housing, city planning, sanitation, municipal administration, policing, marketing, transportation, and other technical issues. While sociologists cannot solve any of these practical problems—at least not by themselves—they may, if they discover their proper function, have an important contribution to make to their comprehension and solution. The prospects for doing this are brightest through a general, theoretical, rather than through an ad hoc approach.

Notes

[1] Whereas rural life in the United States has for a long time been a subject of considerable interest on the part of governmental bureaus, the most notable case of a comprehensive report being that submitted by the Country Life Commission to President Theodore Roosevelt in 1909, it is worthy of note that no equally comprehensive official inquiry into urban life was undertaken until the establishment of a Research Committee on Urbanism of the National Resources Committee. (Cf. *Our Cities: Their Role in the National Economy*, Washington: Government Printing Office, 1937).

[2] The justification for including the term *permanent* in the definition may appear necessary. Our failure to give an extensive justification for this qualifying mark of the urban rests on the obvious fact that unless human settlements take a fairly permanent root in a locality the characteristics of urban life cannot arise, and conversely the living together of large numbers of heterogeneous individuals under dense conditions is not possible without the development of a more or less technological structure.

[3] The extent to which the segregation of the population into distinct ecological and cultural areas and the resulting social attitude of tolerance, rationality, and secular mentality are functions of density as distinguished from heterogeneity is difficult to determine. Most likely we are dealing here with phenomena which are consequences of the simultaneous operation of both factors.

References

Durkheim, Émile. 1932. *The Division of Labor in Society*. New York: Free Press.

Jefferson, Mark. 1909. The Anthropogeography of Some Great Cities. *Bulletin of the American Geographical Society*, 41:537–66.

Park, Robert E., Ernest W. Burgess, and Roderick D. McKenzie. 1925. *The City*. Chicago: University of Chicago Press.

Pearson, S. V. 1935. *The Growth and Distribution of Population*. New York: G. Allen & Unwin Ltd.

Research Committee on Urbanism of the National Resources Committee. 1937. *Our Cities: Their Role in the National Economy*. Washington, DC: Government Printing Office.

Simmel, Georg. 1903. Die Grossstädte und das Geistesleben. In *Die Grossstadt*, ed. T. Petermann, pp. 187–206. Dresden: Jansch.

Sombart, Werner. 1931. Städtische Siedlung, Stadt. In *Handwörterbuch der Soziologie,* ed. Alfred Vierkandt. Stuttgart.

Sumner, William Graham. 1906. *Folkways.* Boston: Ginn.

Weber, Max. 1925. *Wirtschaft und Gesellschaft.* Tübingen: J. C. B. Mohr.

Willcox, Walter F. 1926. A Definition of "City" in Terms of Density. In *The Urban Community,* ed. Ernest W. Burgess, pp. 115–121. Chicago: University of Chicago Press.

8

Urban Danger
Life in a Neighborhood of Strangers

Sally Engle Merry

In a landmark study, Louis Wirth argued that the urban way of life is character-ized by relations between strangers. Despite considerable research that shows that urbanites' social lives include intimate and enduring social ties, relations between strangers continue to define an essential and problematic quality of urban social life. Sally Engle Merry's ethnographic study of a multiethnic housing project in a high-crime neighborhood shows how the boundaries between social groups contrib-ute to the sense that the city is dangerous. The existence of social boundaries makes the project a fertile place for crime, while the residents' awareness of danger comes from their belief that they live in a world of dangerous and unpredictable strangers. These strangers are people in other social networks, known across the social bound-aries which divide the intimate worlds of the project.

In "Urbanism As a Way of Life," Louis Wirth describes cities as places of anonymity and disorder, as settlements in which people treat each other with indifference, competition, and exploitation. A city is a place of strangers. The web of gossip, social pressure, and concern about the opinions of others is unable to hold in check the criminal, the prostitute, and the social deviant, or to prevent the personal breakdown of the increasingly isolated individual. Wirth's famous article, written in 1938, distills the ideas of two decades of urban research done by sociologists and anthropologists at the University of Chicago during the early twentieth century. He argues that the ecological conditions of size, density, permanency, and heterogeneity create a social world of impersonal, superficial, transitory relationships in which individuals are detached from close ties to social groups, such as communities and fami-lies, and are freed from the constraints of social control. Intimate ties of fam-ily and neighborhood become less important, while more impersonal and

Source: Written expressly for *Urban Life*.

instrumental relationships come to predominate. Cities are characterized by anomie: by a sense of normlessness, both in the sense of the individual's lack of attachment to a moral code and of a collective loss of moral consensus.

In the years since Wirth's article was published, numerous studies of the social life of cities have challenged his theory. Many researchers have described neighborhoods, workplaces, religious communities, and other urban settings in which people know one another and treat each other in terms of intimacy and interdependence (e.g., Lewis 1952; Whyte 1955; Young and Willmott 1957; Gans 1962; Hannerz 1969; Stack 1974; Hannerz 1980). In these places, the close community life which Wirth saw as characteristic of villages flourished. Other critics argued that Wirth was really describing the impact of industrialization, not urbanism. Preindustrial cities lacked the anonymity and disorder of large industrial cities (Sjoberg 1955; Krapf-Askari 1969; Fox 1977). Still others claimed that, despite the apparent disorder of the city, particularly its lack of cohesive neighborhood communities, new forms of community have emerged in modern industrial cities based on social networks, voluntary associations, and other more ephemeral, yet important, *quasi-groups* that stretch across neighborhoods and regions (Mitchell 1969; Boissevain 1974).

Despite these serious and legitimate criticisms of Wirth's vision of the city, however, sociologists and anthropologists still return to his article because they have a lingering sense that he has special insight into the issues; that there are some features of the city life he describes that do resonate with the experience of living in the modern industrial city. Such cities do have many strangers, and strangers are particularly taxing and troubling for urbanites. They lie behind the problems of urban crime, the fear of crime, and even the fear of immigrants and newcomers, of people who are culturally strange and different.

Although Wirth's theory of urbanism does not describe the totality of urban social life, it does apply to particular aspects of city life. It describes the boundaries between separate social worlds. Neither Wirth nor Park, an early and influential sociologist at the University of Chicago, thought that the city lacked close-knit urban villages, but saw the city as a collection of these small communities. Park described the city as "a mosaic of little worlds which touch but do not interpenetrate" (1952:47). It is at these boundaries that the characteristic features of urban social life, as Wirth described them, appear. Such social boundaries within a single housing project—Dover Square—and how they generate both crime and a sense of danger will be explored in this chapter.

LIFE IN A HIGH-CRIME NEIGHBORHOOD

Inspired by Wirth's vision of urban social life, I decided to conduct a cultural study of urban danger. I wanted to learn how people who live in high-crime urban areas think about danger, how they deal with it on a daily basis, and how anonymity fosters crime. After perusing crime statistics and neighborhood descriptions, I selected a subsidized housing project located deep in a neighborhood with one of the highest crime rates in a major northeastern city. Since the intent was also to investigate the impact of several ethnic groups living side-by-side, a neighborhood that had a broad mixture of residents was chosen. After locating an ideal small development housing 300 white, black, Chinese, and Hispanic families, I moved into an apartment three blocks from the project and spent a year and a half carrying out anthropological field research. The residents were questioned regarding how they thought about danger and about how they handled the high rate of crime surrounding them. Project residents who committed crimes against their neighbors were also interviewed concerning their views of crime and danger.

In the mid-1970s   the study was conducted, the neighborhood was slowly changing fro   ·ed area populated by homeless alcoholics and characterized by   nusing projects to a trendy neighborhood attractive to ·   More daring members of this group bought the   ˙ich had a tarnished elegance about them, ar   townhouses. In the 10 years since the cr   ·entrification in the surrounding nei   ˙.ıas remained much the same. ·   ιo describe the project.
                  .oject are 55 percent Chinese, 14 per-
cent bι.   .ent Hispanic, by population, although the numb.   .venly distributed. The Chinese residents, most of whc.   .ıgrants from Hong Kong, speak little or no English, althouℓ   .ren are typically fluent in English. They plan to stay in the United ╷   Many of the blacks arrived in the city in the 1950s during the massive black migration from the South and have lived in less attractive parts of the city for 10 years or more. A substantial number of the whites are connected to an established Syrian-Lebanese community nearby dating from the early 1900s. Some of this community was razed to build the project. The Hispanics are recent arrivals from Puerto Rico and many do not speak fluent English. Many plan to return to their homeland and consider their stay in the city temporary.

The project is federally subsidized, designed to house both low- and moderate-income families. It opened in the mid-1960s and, 10 years later, had a remarkably stable population for a housing project: well over half the families had lived in the development since it opened, and the rate of turnover was under 5 percent per year. Yet, despite this stability, the neighborhood has not become a community. It is not a cohesive, integrated social system, but rather a series of distinct, unconnected social networks occupying the same geographical space. Each ethnic group is scattered throughout the development, yet residents maintain virtually all of their close social relationships with neighbors of the same ethnicity. Consequently, neighbors who belong to different ethnic groups often remain strangers, despite years of sharing the same stairwells, porches, and walkways.

A social network is a way of conceptualizing those parts of social life that do not form bounded, enduring social groups (see Barnes 1954; Bott 1957; Epstein 1969; Mitchell 1969; Boissevain 1974). Each person is the center of a group of friends and relatives, the central point from which radiates a series of links to other people. This constellation forms an egocentric social network. Members of this network also know others, some of whom the first person does not. These are second-order links, friends of friends. By extension, each second-order link also has social contacts, so that one can imagine a network of social relationships extending outward from any individual to first, second, and further orders of contact. Since these networks of relationship are also potential communication channels, mapping their structure and boundaries provides important clues to the flow of gossip and information through a social system (Merry 1984). Boundaries in social networks tend to be gaps in the flow of information.

In Dover Square, intimate networks—links to close friends and relatives—are almost always restricted to a single ethnic group. An extended network of acquaintances crosscuts ethnic lines at a few points, but also tends to remain within a single ethnic group. A few individuals have social networks consisting almost entirely of a different ethnic group, such as the white youths who regularly hang out with a gang of young black men and women. Since each ethnic group is scattered throughout the area, the social organization of the project consists of a series of discrete, overarching social networks. One can imagine this social composition as several layers of fishnet strung over the same space with a few threads running between the layers.

The social boundaries between ethnic groups persist because each group is encapsulated within a network of social relationships and a set of institutions that stretches to nearby black, white, Chinese, and Hispanic communities. The majority of families in the project regularly visit relatives, friends, religious groups, and social organizations in their nearby ethnic communities. Chinatown lies on one side of the project, an established Syrian-Lebanese community on another, the black community is close by on another side, and a substantial Hispanic settlement is in the middle of the slowly gentrifying neighborhood nearby. Jobs, friends, marriage partners, churches, social services, and recreational opportunities are all primarily available within these communities. Consequently, relations with members of the same ethnic group carry an expectation of continuity that is not characteristic of relations with neighbors in Dover Square. Neighbors are only temporary associates, here today but gone whenever they move away, while people in the same ethnic group are connected by enduring ties. The denser mesh of personal ties and group affiliations within ethnic groups means that Dover Square residents are far more accountable to their fellow ethnics than they are to their neighbors of different ethnicity.

Because of the boundaries between ethnic groups, neighbors are often anonymous. This anonymity provides opportunities for crime, since criminals can rob their neighbors with little fear of apprehension. Many project residents observed that, in general, criminals prefer not to work close to home where they can too easily be identified by their neighbors, but here, where neighbors are often strangers, a resident can rob or burglarize people close to home without fear of identification. This means that a project resident can commit crimes on his home territory, which is relatively safe, predictable, and familiar, while appearing to victims as a stranger from a distant area. The same people can be robbed whose daily habits and material possessions are easily visible.

At the same time, the widespread fear and distrust of neighbors undermines community efforts at controlling crime. As one of the leaders of the youth group active in committing crimes in the area put it:

> The people who are being affected by crime don't understand that they are the cause of crime. I think a lot of people around here don't want other people's houses to be safe. People are beginning to be cold-hearted, not caring enough, because, if people cared enough about other people, they would care about theirs. In order to protect your house, you have to protect your neighbor's.

Social control is undermined by this structure of social networks since the implementation of sanctions, of punishments for rule-breaking, is unlikely across the social boundaries. For sanctions to be effective in discouraging rule-breaking, they must be both powerful and certain of implementation. A sanction that is severe will have little deterrent effect if the offender feels that there is little chance that he or she will feel its weight. When the offender is anonymous to his victim, it is obviously difficult to catch him or to impose any penalty on him. If the person who observes a crime knows who the perpetrator is or even where he lives or who his friends are, she might be able to impose some kind of pressure on him. When the perpetrator is a stranger, however, even observing the crime act leaves the observer powerless. The strategies Dover Square residents develop to cope with living in a hazardous environment reveal the critical role played by this knowledge of who the dangerous people are, both in protecting the individual from victimization and in reducing the sense of danger.

CONCEPTIONS OF DANGER

As I became further acquainted with the residents who lived in the project, I discovered that they differed greatly in their perceptions of and approaches to the dangers in their environment. One young Chinese woman, for example, never returned home alone on foot after dark. When she arrived by car, she honked the horn to alert her parents and then dashed the 20 feet to her door. A white man cautiously packed his suitcases into his car under cover of darkness before leaving for a trip to escape being noticed by potential burglars. A middle-aged black woman sneaked surreptitiously from her home at 6:00 AM to do her laundry before the neighborhood youths gathered in the laundromat to visit and smoke. She was anxious not to leave her home vacant, even for a few minutes, lest the burglars she constantly feared notice that her house was unguarded.

Yet, in the same neighborhood, a young black woman moved freely, visiting neighbors late at night with no thought of danger. Young men would rendezvous in dark secluded hallways even though they were aware that they risked being mugged. A Chinese man, reputed to possess marvelous skill in the martial arts, was studiously avoided by youths seeking safe and profitable robbery victims. He walked through the project without fear. Lastly, an adult black man declared that his neighborhood was very safe because he knows everyone, and everyone knows him.

All of these people face the same hazards, yet their attitudes, fears, and modes of coping vary enormously. Why do they respond so differently to the same risks? Urbanites, in general, continually make decisions about which situations and persons they consider dangerous, but these judgments are rarely based on detailed statistics about where and when crimes occur. Nor are such people's attitudes proportional to the statistical risks of victimization, either in this project or nationwide. A survey of the victimization experiences of two-thirds of the 300 households suggested that the rates of victimization of black and Chinese households are roughly the same: about half of each had experienced a robbery, burglary, or assault since moving into the development 10 years earlier. Yet, when asked how dangerous they found their environment, the Chinese residents reported much higher levels of fear: 30 percent of those interviewed said the project was dangerous in contrast to only 13 percent of the black respondents, and 18 percent said it was not at all dangerous, while 65 percent of the blacks interviewed felt this way. National statistics show a similar discrepancy between fear and the chance of victimization: although fear focuses on the random, unpredictable attack of the stranger, the risk of assault and murder by friends is far greater.

Clearly, danger cannot be equated with the statistical probability of being the victim of a crime. Instead, it is the individual's interpretation of the surrounding environment. The process of forming attitudes about which kinds of people, places, and times of day and night are safe or dangerous, and the cues which identify them, is one facet of the elaborate process by which an individual comes to know her world. Information from the mass media, from friends and neighbors, and from the urbanite's own experience is constructed into a mental map of the city which guides behavior and creates a sense of safety in the midst of danger. What the individual considers harmful is itself a cultural product. For some, danger is the risk of losing property; for others, it is name calling and personal humiliation; and for others, the degradation of abusive police and social service workers.

The term *risk* is used to refer to the likelihood of experiencing a crime or some other harm. It is thus a concept that refers to the external world and to the hazards it contains. Danger is a cultural construct that describes the way an individual conceptualizes the hazards and risks in his or her world and assesses what they mean to him or her. Fear refers to the inner emotional state an individual experiences as he or she contemplates the danger he or she believes to exist. Thus, both danger and fear are subjective in a way in which risk is not. On the other hand, they are not inevitably connected. Some may see a situation as dangerous but not regard it with fear, while others may see the same situation as dangerous and feel fearful about it. Ideas about danger are a component of culture: they are learned, shared within groups, and influence the way the world is interpreted and understood. Fear is more individualized, depending on each person's experience with harm, sense of competence and control, sense of vulnerability in general, and other psychological characteristics.

Other cultures similarly define danger in terms of more general belief systems about their world. For example, a group of Indians living in remote forest settlements in Canada, the Salteaux, do not fear wolves or bears but consider snakes, toads, and frogs dangerous (Hallowell 1938). Although these are among the most harmless of the inhabitants of the forest, they are believed to be emanations of powerful supernatural forces, capable of acting as emissaries for sorcerers, of exuding malevolent magic, and of serving as omens of ill fortune. Monster toads and frogs roam the forest. On the other hand, the Azande farmers of East Africa consider dangerous the man who is quarrelsome, spiteful, and dirty, as well as the person who defecates in others' gardens and eats house rats, since he is believed to possess witchcraft, the power to inflict misfortune, wasting disease, and death on others (Evans-Pritchard 1937).

Notions of danger in American cities, as in other cultural settings, draw on more general social understandings of who and what is dangerous, the kinds of persons who are believed to be violent and immoral, and the characteristics of people who are believed likely to commit crimes. In both simple and complex societies, those who suffer misfortune do not always know exactly where the final responsibility lies. In small-scale societies, the witch or supernatural forces are blamed; whereas in American cities, the faceless criminal receives the blame. Yet, in both, it is the outsider, the stranger, who is held responsible. Such persons are not full members of the observer's social and cultural world, but are people whose behavior appears strange and irrational.

The attitudes of the project residents I talked to vividly illustrate these images of danger. Danger has a variety of meanings for project residents. It means encounters with muggers on deserted streets, invasion by culturally alien neighbors, or the nuisance of disheveled drunks asleep on the sidewalk. Essentially, danger is fear of the stranger, the person who is potentially harmful and whose behavior seems unpredictable and beyond control. Those residents who are the most convinced that their environment is dangerous tend not to be those most victimized, but rather those who lack any social connection to street youths. Such people see themselves awash in a sea of dangerous strangers.

To Chinese residents, the blacks, all of whom seem to look alike and are thought to be robbers whose favorite victims are Chinese, appear most dangerous. Whites seem dangerous because they are members of a dominant group which has long excluded the Chinese from full membership in its social institutions and has treated them with disdain and indifference. Yet, to blacks, who recognize that only a small proportion of the project youths are actually involved in crime (only 10 percent of the black families have children who commit crimes), the project appears as a safe place in which they know almost everyone and can anticipate which few youths might be inclined to rob them. As one young black woman said to a young Chinese woman, also a resident of the project:

> To you, all the blacks are dangerous because you can't tell them apart,
> but to me they are George, Johnny, and Jamesy, and I know who to look
> out for and who will not bother me.

Black adults who endeavor to guide their children into a life of steady jobs and stable family ties find the project youths who pursue a glamorous life of hustling, easy money, and the *fast lane* dangerous in that they threaten to tempt their children away from their values. Some whites find the blacks dangerous, but those who know the black families and have watched their children grow up know which youths are active in crime and hustling and which are not and take comfort in the belief that, because they know them, they will not bother them.

Places that seem dangerous are not those where crimes occur most often, but are those that are unfamiliar or are favorite hangouts of tough-looking youths. Nor are places thought to be safe free from crime. A playground in the center of the project, a favorite hangout for a group of youths blamed for local crime, was generally seen as very dangerous, although few crimes actually took place there. On the other hand, the area seen most often as safe was the street in front of each person's house. Yet this was also one of the most common places for robberies. Most people said that their side of the project was safe, but they feared to venture to the other, more dangerous side. Those who lived in the center of the project avoided the edges and those who lived on the periphery regarded the center of the project as a dangerous place to be carefully avoided. The victimization survey revealed no differences in the rate of robberies on any one side of the project. Thus, notions of safe and dangerous places do not simply reflect crime rates, but take into account ideas about territory, ethnic hostilities and conflicts, the presence of hostile strangers, familiarity, the availability of allies, and the design of spaces.

Not all crimes are dangerous, nor are all dangerous events crimes. Some crimes that are technically serious are not so perceived by their victims, while others that are not considered serious by the police loom large as dangerous experiences. For example, crimes of violence or threatened violence committed by strangers seem dangerous even if little or no property is taken, such as unsuccessful robbery attempts or attempted burglaries. These incidents are reported when residents are asked if they have been the victims of crimes but rarely elicit a phone call to the police. On the other hand, assaults by people who know each other are not perceived as crimes, even though they are technically defined as crimes by the police. Those who were assaulted in vicious, interpersonal battles never mentioned these incidents when queried about their experiences with victimization. Assaults by strangers, on the other hand, are regarded as crimes and engender fear, not knife fights between rivals for a woman's affection or punches between neighbors over barking dogs or damaging gossip.

Residents of this high-crime environment respond to the dangers that surround them by constructing mental maps of the kinds of people and locations that are dangerous and safe. These maps are subjective representations imposed on the physical realities of space and time, constructions of reality that reflect the individual's past experience and knowledge. They guide movements through the project and channel behavior toward strangers. Yet not all mental maps are equally accurate or helpful. The process of constructing these maps involves drawing distinctions and making generalizations. Maps of areas that are well known are more finely differentiated, while maps of unfamiliar areas are blank or vague. Those with greater knowledge of the potentially hazardous people around them and of the particular uses of the surrounding spaces develop more accurate and differentiated mental maps. Such people also find their environment far less dangerous.

Chinese residents, for example, were generally unable to tell the black residents apart, lumping them all into a criminal and predatory population, despite the fact that 90 percent of the families had no connection to crime. They also failed to make fine distinctions between the relative danger of different parts of the development. On the other hand, the blacks were far more sophisticated in drawing distinctions between black residents and were equipped with highly differentiated locational maps of the project. Yet, they lumped all Chinese together into the category of rich restaurant owners, despite the fact that the vast majority were poor cooks and waiters in Chinese restaurants. The use of these unsophisticated mental maps thus exacerbates residents' feelings that they are surrounded by a faceless mass of dangerous strangers.

How do these people cope with their dangerous environment? Some residents adopt a defensive strategy, turning their homes into fortresses barricaded with expensive locks and elaborate window bars, stockpiling guns, learning to live with large guard dogs in small apartments, and calling the police to report every incident. They are always cautious, staying at home at night and avoiding social contact with anyone but close friends and relatives. These are the people whose lives are most constricted by the fear of crime: the elderly, residents who speak only Chinese, and social isolates. Their mode of defense is escape and retreat, but, if the fragile shell of safety around their homes is violated by a crowbar mark on the door or an attempted purse snatching on the porch, the loss of a sense of security is devastating.

Others adopt offensive strategies, developing reputations as dangerous, tough people who are willing to fight back if abused, either by violence, by calling the police, or by going to court. These people are still vulnerable to victimization by outsiders who do not know their reputations or by insiders who are angry at them, but they do not feel the same sense of helplessness in the face of anonymous dangers. Unlike the defensive residents, who are vulnerable every time they leave their homes, those who adopt offensive strategies carry their protective armor around with them. Thus, the residents of this project range from those who cower in fear in a barred haven of safety to those who traverse the city at any time of day or night with a sense of confidence and ease springing from their mastery of the urban environment and their extensive knowledge of its locations, its residents, and its cultural patterns.

A THEORY OF DANGER

This analysis suggests a more general theory: that the sense of danger is rooted in feelings of uncertainty, helplessness, and vulnerability triggered by encounters with strangers who belong to unfamiliar, hostile, and potentially harmful groups. A stranger is not perceived as a unique individual having a personal history, reputation, and location in social space. Instead, visible cues such as age, sex, dress, demeanor, ethnicity, location, and mode of speaking are used to place a stranger in a social category associated with certain expected behaviors. Mitchell terms this a categorical relationship, one that arises in situations in which interactions are superficial and perfunctory (1966:52). Such categories codify and order social interaction in otherwise uncertain, unstructured urban situations. These categories are constructed through experience and shared cultural conceptions, but the process of construction is rarely conscious or deliberate; rather, it proceeds through the creation of implicit categories that feel like instinctive descriptions of the world.

Categorical identities inevitably ignore individual variation and are likely to lump very different individuals together. Because finely honed categories develop through familiarity and contact, socially distant and unfamiliar strangers will be assigned to grosser and less refined categories than those who inhabit more familiar social worlds. The less contact an individual has with members of other groups, the less accurately will she categorize these groups. Entire ethnic or age groups can be lumped into the dangerous, immoral or threatening camp. The dangerous group generally differs in ethnic background, but suspicions may also arise due to differences in class and lifestyle.

Predictions of behavior based on categorical identities are far less certain than predictions based on knowledge of the particular habits and propensities of a specific person. The stranger's behavior is likely to appear unexpected and unprovoked, leaving the observer with the feeling that there is little she can do to avoid attack. Psychological research suggests that fear comes from the experience of helplessness in the face of harm, the sense that there is no place or time of safety nor any course of action that will guarantee safety (Seligman 1975).

In Dover Square, the coexistence of separate social worlds divided by sharp social boundaries creates conditions under which residents are likely to experience their environment as dangerous. Those who make contacts across the boundaries, who come to know those in other social networks, see the project as much less dangerous than those who do not, who consequently function with far less differentiated and accurate categorical identities and who lack the sense of certainty and control provided by knowing who the potentially harmful people are. Knowing their identities does not protect one from harm, but it does diminish the sense of living in a world of unpredictable and uncontrollable strangers.

Wirth argued that individuals who are detached from organizations and groups pose the greatest threat to social order because they are not controlled by any social group or moral code (1928:76). However, it is not those who are detached, but those who appear detached, who are responsible for crime, disorder, and fear. These individuals are least susceptible to social control. Although they are firmly anchored in existing social groups, their social moorings are unknown to the observer, who sees them as *detached* persons. Criminals in Dover Square actively fostered their appearance of anonymity, of detachment, in order to escape punishment from their victims. Thus, it is the separation between social worlds, as much as the detachment of individuals, that produces anomie and social disorder.

URBAN SOCIAL THEORY AND SOCIAL BOUNDARIES

This description of life in a multiethnic neighborhood suggests that Wirth's vision of urbanism as a way of life was not wrong, but only a partial view. Primary and intimate relationships exist within urban villages and social networks, but the problematic interactions are those that lurk in the gaps between these worlds. Wirth and the Chicago sociologists hinted at the problem of the relationship between the pieces of the urban social mosaic, but it was generally ignored. These pieces may be geographically based communities or nonlocalized social networks (Jacobson 1971). Several nonlocalized networks can occupy the same space, as they do in Dover Square. Whatever their configuration, the question of how these networks articulate with one another is a critical problem for urban anthropology. It is here that the breakdown of social control is the greatest and the freedom to be different the greatest challenge. Anthropologists tend to focus on enduring ties, yet it is these fleeting relationships and social boundaries between enduring groups which are most problematic for urban social life.

References

Barnes, J. A. 1954. Class and Committees in a Norwegian Island Parish. *Human Relations*, 7:39–58.

Boissevain, Jeremy. 1974. *Friends of Friends: Networks, Manipulators, and Coalitions.* New York: St. Martin's Press.

Bott, Elizabeth. 1957. *Family and Social Network: Roles, Norms, and External Relationships in Ordinary Urban Families.* London: Tavistock.

Epstein, A. L. 1969. The Network and Urban Social Organization. In *Social Networks in Urban Situations: Analysis of Personal Relationships in Central African Towns*, ed. J. Clyde Mitchell. Manchester: Manchester University Press.

Evans-Pritchard, E. E. 1937. *Witchcraft, Oracles, and Magic among the Azande.* Oxford: Clarendon Press.

Fox, Richard. 1977. *Urban Anthropology: Cities in Their Cultural Settings.* Englewood Cliffs, NJ: Prentice-Hall.

Gans, Herbert. 1962. Urbanism and Suburbanism as Ways of Life: A Reevaluation of Definitions. In *Human Behavior and Social Processes*, ed. A. M. Rose, pp. 625– 648. Boston: Houghton Mifflin.

Hallowell, A. Irving. 1938. Fear and Anxiety as Cultural and Individual Variables in a Primitive Society. *Journal of Social Psychology*, 9:25–47.

Hannerz, Ulf. 1969. *Soulside: Inquiries into Ghetto Culture and Community.* New York: Columbia University Press.

———. 1980. *Exploring the City.* New York: Columbia University Press.

Jacobson, David. 1971. Mobility, Continuity, and Urban Social Organization. *Man*, 6:630–645.

Krapf-Askari, Eva. 1969. *Yoruba Towns and Cities: An Enquiry into the Nature of Urban Social Phenomena.* London: Oxford University Press.

Lewis, Oscar. 1952. Urbanization without Breakdown. *Scientific Monthly*, 75:31–41.

Merry, Sally Engle. 1984. Rethinking Gossip and Scandal. In *Toward a General Theory of Social Control*, ed. Donald Black, Vol. 11. New York: Academic Press.

Mitchell, J. Clyde. 1966. Theoretical Orientations in African Urban Studies. In *The Social Anthropology of Complex Societies*, ed. Michael Banton, Association of Social Anthropologists Monograph no. 4. London: Tavistock.

———. ed. 1969. *Social Networks in Urban Situations: Analysis of Personal Relationships in Central African Towns.* Manchester: Manchester University Press.

Park, Robert E. 1952. *Human Communities.* Glencoe, IL: The Free Press.

Seligman, Martin E. P. 1975. *Helplessness: On Depression, Development and Death.* San Francisco: W. H. Freeman and Co.

Sjoberg, Gideon. 1955. The Preindustrial City. *American Journal of Sociology*, 60:438–445.

Stack, Carol. 1974. *All Our Kin.* New York: Harper & Row.

Whyte, William F. 1955. *Street Corner Society.* Chicago: University of Chicago Press.

Wirth, L. 1928 (1956). *The Ghetto.* Chicago: University of Chicago Press.

Young, Michael, and P. Willmott. 1957. *Family and Kinship in East London.* London: Routledge & Kegan Paul.

9

The Edge and the Center
Gated Communities and
the Discourse of Urban Fear

Setha M. Low

*By comparing gated residential communities in San Antonio, Texas, and the Bor-
ough of Queens in New York City, Setha Low uncovers the discourses of fear that
cause people to move ever farther from urban centers. Those who live in gated communities have come to reject life in intimate downtown neighborhoods and in
"open" suburbs. They are especially afraid that their children are at risk playing
outdoors without constant supervision and are wary of the proximity of ethnic and
socioeconomic "Others." While residents living in gated communities may feel
more secure behind their walls, this sense of safety at home often increases their
fears of the city that remains beyond their gates.*

Contemporary anthropological studies of the city focus predominantly
on the center, producing ethnographies of culturally significant places such as
markets, housing projects, gardens, plazas, convention centers, waterfront
developments, and homeless shelters that articulate macro- and micro-urban
processes (Low 1999). These studies illuminate both the material and meta-
phorical power of spatial analysis for theorizing the city. One problem, however, is the perpetuation of an uneasy relationship between suburban and
urban studies. The historical division between "rural" and "urban" exacerbates this tendency by sorting researchers into separate disciplinary and
methodological camps.

The shift to a spatial analysis of the city requires reconsidering this separation in that contradictions and conflicts at the center are often drawn more
vividly at the edge. So we find that the suburban "malling of America" is a
spatial counterpart of economic restructuring and the deindustrialization of

Source: Adapted from the author's earlier work (with the same title) that appeared in *American
Anthropologist* 103(1) (March 2001):45–58.

central cities (Zukin 1991), and the cultural diversity and racial tension of the center are reflected in the segregation and social homogeneity of the suburbs (Massey and Denton 1988). The gated residential development is particularly intriguing, mirroring changes in social values that accompany rapid globalization. Understanding this spatial form, its historical and cultural context, and why residents choose to live there provides an important perspective on the central city that is often overlooked.

UNLOCKING THE GATED COMMUNITY

Estimates of the number of people who live in gated communities within the United States vary from four million to eight million (Architectural Record 1997). One-third of all new homes built in the United States in recent years are in gated residential developments (Blakely and Snyder 1997), and in areas such as Tampa, Florida, where crime is a high-profile problem, gated communities account for four out of five home sales of $300,000 or more (Fischler 1998).

Sally Merry found that middle-class and upper-middle-class urban and suburban neighborhoods exhibit an increasing pattern of building fences, cutting off relationships with neighbors, and moving out in response to problems and conflicts. At the same time: "Government has expanded its regulatory role. . . . Zoning laws, local police departments, ordinances about dogs, quiet laws, laws against domestic and interpersonal violence, all provide new forms of regulation of family and neighborhood life" (1993:87).

The suburb as an exclusionary enclave where upper-class followed by middle-class residents search for sameness, status, and security in an ideal "new town" or "green oasis" reinforces these patterns (Langdon 1994; McKenzie 1994). Land speculation beginning with the streetcar suburbs of Philadelphia accelerated the growth of new middle-class enclaves (Jackson 1985). The expanding suburbs of the 1950s, 1960s, and 1970s generated "white flight" from densely populated, heterogeneous cities (Sibley 1995; Skogan 1995).

The development of common interest developments (CIDs) provides the legal framework for the consolidation of this form of residential segregation (Judd 1995). CID describes "a community in which the residents own or control common areas or shared amenities," and that "carries with it reciprocal rights and obligations enforced by a private governing body" (Louv 1985:85 as cited in Judd 1995:155). Specialized covenants, contracts, and deed restrictions (CC&Rs) create new forms of collective private land tenure and new forms of private government called "homeowner associations" (McKenzie 1994).

Upon completing a national survey of gated community residents, Edward Blakely and Mary Gail Snyder come to a similar conclusion:

> In this era of dramatic demographic, economic and social change, there is a growing fear about the future of America. Many feel vulnerable, unsure of their place and the stability of their neighborhoods. . . . This is

reflected in an increasing fear of crime that is unrelated to actual crime trends or locations, and in the growing numbers of methods used to control the physical environment for physical and economic security. The phenomenon of walled cities and gated communities is a dramatic manifestation of a new fortress mentality growing in America. (1997:1–2)

METHODOLOGY

This study[1] is based on two gated communities, each located at the edge of a culturally diverse city with publicized incidents of urban crime. San Antonio and New York City are known for their multiculturalism and cultural inclusiveness, as well as for interethnic conflicts resulting from rapid changes in neighborhood composition. Both cities have increasing socioeconomic disparities, a history of residential segregation, and a documented movement of middle-class residents to an ever-widening outer ring of suburbs. They also provide excellent comparative cases because of differences between them in (1) population size and density, (2) history of gated community development, (3) scale and design of the gated communities, (4) legal and governmental structure, (5) crime rates for the region, and (6) cultural context and norms of behavior. Because of the complexity and size of New York City, I use Queens, the outer borough adjacent to the study site, to describe the cultural context, population size, and crime statistics relevant to this analysis. Many of the residents cited in this chapter moved from Queens to their gated community.

San Antonio is a medium-size city with an estimated population of 1,464,356 inhabitants in 1995. The city began in the eighteenth century as a cohesion of different Spanish missions and has retained much of its Mexican-Spanish heritage. Since 1990, Texas has accounted for 14 percent of all new jobs created in the United States, including rapid growth in high-tech manufacturing causing labor shortages of highly trained workers. Population in the Metropolitan Statistical Area (MSA) grew 21.5 percent from 1980 to 1990 and an additional 10.1 percent from 1990 to 1994 (America's Top-Rated Cities 1997). This increase in skilled jobs and number of residents stimulated construction of new middle-class suburbs and continuing growth in the downtown area (related to the Paseo del Rio [Riverwalk] flood control projects begun in the 1920s). It was in San Antonio that I first gained entrance to a number of homes located within a locked, gated, and walled community on the outskirts of the city and found young, white, middle-class teenagers discussing their fear of "Mexicans" who live nearby.

New York City, in comparison to San Antonio, is a global city of more than seven million inhabitants. Located on the eastern seaboard, New York City has been a major entryway for immigrants from Europe, via Ellis Island, and more recently from Africa, parts of Asia, and the Middle East. Queens, the easternmost borough, is known for its cultural diversity and ethnic neighborhoods where over 138 languages are spoken (Sanjek 1998). Queens became incorporated into New York City in 1897, linked by both the Long Island Railroad and electric trolleys to Brooklyn, and to Manhattan-bound ferries from Long Island City (Gregory 1998). With a population of 1,966,685 in 1997, it provides a better comparison to San Antonio because of its scale and proximity to Long Island suburbs.

Even though Seagate in Brooklyn is an example of a gated community built more than 100 years ago, and doorman buildings of Manhattan have guarded entrances, there are only a few gated residential developments in New York City. In Queens, there are only three gated condominium complexes comprised of townhouses and apartments. The loss of manufacturing jobs—10 million square feet of industrial space has been converted to retail, residential, or office space—as well as lower salaries and lack of available land for development may account for this slow growth. Although Queens is the most economically diverse of the New York City boroughs, with manufacturing, transportation, trade, and services each accounting for at least 10 percent of private sector jobs in 1998, it has not experienced the same accelerated growth in the service sector as the rest of New York City. Further, in the early 1990s, higher-paying jobs were being replaced with lower-paying ones as growth occurred in areas offering lower average salaries (McCall 2000).

Nassau County, Long Island, on the other hand, experienced a resurgence of residential development, some of it gated, following the decline of the real estate market in the early 1990s. With a population of 1,298,842 in 1997, Nassau County abuts the eastern boundary of Queens and provides a suburban comparison for the analysis of crime statistics.

New suburban housing developments with surrounding walls and restrictive gates located approximately a 30-minute drive from their respective downtown city halls were selected at the edge of each city. Single-family house prices ranged from $650,000 to $880,000 in New York and $350,000 to $650,000 in San Antonio in 1995. Each gated community has its own regional style and distinctive design features, but all are enclosed by a five- to six-foot masonry wall broken only by the entry gates and monitored in person by a guard (New York) or by video camera from a central guardhouse (San Antonio).

The New York development is situated on an old estate with the original manor house retained as a community center. The individual houses are large (approximately 3,500 to 4,500 square feet), mostly two-story structures, built in a variety of traditional styles: Hampton Cottage, Nantucket Village, Mid-Atlantic Colonial, and Western Ranch. Houses are organized along a winding thoroughfare with dead-end streets branching off, leading to groups of houses clustered quite close together on small lots of less than a third of an acre. The remaining property is landscaped to create a park-like atmosphere. Since the community was developed as a community interest development, all of the common grounds are maintained by the homeowners association. The final community will contain 141 houses, tennis courts, a swimming pool, and a clubhouse. At the time of this writing, not all the lots have been purchased, and houses are still being built.

The San Antonio gated community is part of a much larger northern suburban development centered on a private golf and tennis club with swimming pools, a restaurant, and a clubhouse. The subdivision includes 120 lots, a few fronting one section of the golf course, surrounded by a six-foot masonry wall. The main entrance is controlled by a grid-design gate that swings opens electronically by a hand transmitter or by a guard who is contacted by an intercom and video camera connection. The broad entrance road divides into two sections leading to a series of short streets ending in cul-de-sacs. The houses are mostly large (3,500-5,500 square feet), two-story brick colonial or stucco Scottsdale designs with a few one-story brick ranch-style houses. More than two-thirds of the houses have been built and occupied, while the remaining lots are currently under construction at the time of this writing.

RESEARCH DESIGN AND SPECIFIC METHODS

Field methods included open-ended interviews with residents, participant-observation within and around the communities, interviews with key informants such as the developers and real estate agents, and the collection of marketing, sales, and advertising documents. An unstructured interview guide was developed to elicit residents' decision-making processes concerning their move to the gated community. The research team collected field notes and interviews in the New York area, while I worked alone in San Antonio. The interviews lasted between one and two hours, depending on whether the interviewer was taken on a tour of the house. We did not ask to be taken on a tour, but many times interviewees offered, and we used the tour to learn more about the person's tastes, interests, and preferences.

It was difficult to obtain entry into these communities and to contact residents. A sales manager in the gated community outside of New York City helped by contacting two residents she thought would be willing to speak with us. We then used introductions either from the sales manager or from other interviewees to complete the first 10 interviews. In San Antonio, a local resident provided entrée by contacting two residents; those residents referred four others, and I met three interviewees strolling on the golf path on the weekends.

Opportunities for participant-observation were limited, but it was possible to talk with people while they were exercising or walking their dogs, attending homeowner and club meetings, and participating in neighborhood celebrations. Further, spending time in the local commercial areas—shopping, going to restaurants, and visiting real estate agents—provided other contexts for learning about everyday life.

Open-ended, unstructured interviews were conducted in the home with the wife, husband, or husband and wife together over a three-year period from 1995 to 1998. The majority of the interviewees were European Americans and native born, however, three interviews were in households where one spouse was born in Latin America, one interviewee was born in the

South Pacific, and one interviewee's spouse was born in the Middle East. Interviewees were aged 27 through 75; all husbands were either professionals such as doctors or lawyers, businessmen, or retired from these same pursuits. In most cases, the wives remained at home, while the husband commuted to his place of work. A few women worked part-time.

THE SEARCH FOR SAFETY AND SECURITY

A majority of interviewees perceived an increase of crime in their urban neighborhoods before moving to a gated community. Eighteen of the 20 interviews include discussions of residents' search for a sense of safety and security in their choice of a gated community, and their relief that they did feel safer and more secure with the addition of gates, walls, and guards. Many interviewees mention changes in social composition of the surrounding areas as a primary motivation for moving, and the loss of local amenities, particularly in the New York area. Interviewees also talk about the investment value of the house, the status implications of their move, and their need for more space and privacy, but these concerns are not examined in this analysis.

One noteworthy finding is that once people live in a gated community, they say that they would always choose a gated community again, even if safety was not the basis of their initial decision. Three of the 20 interviewees had lived previously in gated developments: one family lived in Latin America where they enjoyed the security of a gated and guarded compound; one family retired first in Florida where most retirement communities are gated; and one newly married woman had lived in a gated condominium complex. These couples did not even consider a nongated community when looking for a new home.

New York

Nine of the 10 interviewees in New York mention urban crime as a major reason for selecting a gated community. The tenth interviewee, although she says that crime and safety had no bearing on why they moved, mentions that in her old neighborhood her car had been stolen from outside her door.

Nine of the 10 interviewees are from the local area and moved from New York City or a nearby Long Island urban center. Many are quite vocal about the changes that they experienced in their original neighborhoods. For instance, Sharon is willing to "give up community convenience for safety." She says that increased local political corruption and neighborhood deterioration left her feeling uncomfortable in the house where she had lived for more than 25 years. Even though she knew everyone in her old neighborhood and enjoyed walking to the corner store,

> when Bloomingdale's moved out and Kmart moved in, it just brought in a different group of people . . . and it wasn't the safe place that it was. . . .

I think it's safer having a gated community. . . . They are not going to steal my car in the garage. . . . [In the old neighborhood] every time we heard an alarm we were looking out the window. My daughter and son-in-law lived next door and their car was stolen twice.

Barbara and her husband Alvin express it differently:

Alvin: [Our old neighborhood was] a very, very educated community. You know so every one goes on to college, and it stressed the role of family, and you know, it's just a wonderful community. But it *is* changing. It's undergoing internal transformations.

Barbara: It's ethnic changes.

Alvin: Yeah, ethnic changes, that's a very good way of putting it.

Interviewer: And *is* this something that started to happen more recently?

Barbara: In the last, probably, seven to eight years.

Cynthia also is concerned about staying in her old neighborhood. At first she did not want to live in a house at all since she would feel afraid being alone. She had grown up in Queens and would never live in a house there, because they had been robbed. Her childhood home had been in a nice neighborhood where thieves knew they could find valuable things to steal:

Cynthia: And then I have a lot of friends who live in a neighborhood in Queens, and there's been more than 48 robberies there in the last year and a half. And I said to myself, those are homes with security and dogs and this and that. . . .

Interviewer: And are they gated?

Cynthia: No, they're not gated. They had alarms, and they were getting robbed because they were cutting the alarms, the phone wires outside. So I'm saying to myself, all this is in my mind, and I'm saying . . . I can get robbed. That's why I moved. . . .

Sally also feels that the neighborhood where she lived was changing: she was having problems finding a place to park, and people were going through her trash at night. Her bicycle was stolen off her terrace, and her friend's car was stolen. Her husband began to travel a lot, and she could not accompany her husband on his trips because she was worried about being robbed. They loved their old neighborhood, but it no longer offered safety and comfort. So they decided to move to a gated community that would provide the security that she felt they now needed. Once having made the decision and completed the move, she said that she loved her newly found freedom from house responsibilities and parking problems. As she put it:

I got to feel like I was a prisoner in the house. . . . You didn't park on the street too long because you are afraid your car is going to be missing something when you get out, or the whole car is missing. . . . So there's a lot of things we have the freedom here to do that we didn't do before. . . .

Helen comments that it was "very nice at night to come in . . . and to have a gate and there's only one entrance to the property, so I think that makes for possibly less robberies. . . ." For her, safety is:

> not a main concern, but a concern. Otherwise, if I bought something . . . on two acres of land, I would have been very uncomfortable there . . . no children around . . . just being alone now in the dark . . . and my husband would get home later. I just didn't want to be surrounded by two acres of land.

She has friends (in the old neighborhood) who were burglarized and had become more distressed. She feels the guards at the entrance are not careful, but it is still difficult for thieves to escape. Her mother and her children also live in gated communities.

San Antonio

Nine of the interviewees in San Antonio mention crime and a fear of "others" as a reason for moving. Stay-at-home mothers like Felicia and Donna worry about threats to their children. Felicia states her feelings about her fear of crime and other people very clearly:

Setha: . . . has it changed how you feel about being in the gated community?

Felicia: Yes. It allows a lot more freedom for my daughter to go outside and play. We're in San Antonio, and I believe the whole country knows how many child kidnappings we've had. . . . And I believe that my husband would not ever allow her outside to play without direct adult supervision unless we were gated. It allows us freedom to walk at night, if we choose to. It has, you know, it does have a flip side.

Setha: What flip side?

Felicia: Several things. First of all, it's a false sense of safety if you think about it, because our security people are not "Johnny-on-the-spot," so to speak, and anybody who wants to jump the gate could jump the gate. . . . There's a perception of safety that may not be real, that could potentially leave one more vulnerable if there was ever an attack.

* * *

Setha: Who lives in your community?

Felicia: People who are retired and don't want to maintain large yards. . . . People who want to raise families in a more protected environment [long pause].

Setha: What do you mean by that?

Felicia: There are a lot of families who have, in the last couple of years, after we built, as the crime rate, or the reporting of that crime rate, has become such a prominent part of the news of the community, there's been a lot of "fear flight." I've mentioned that people who were building or going to build based on wanting to get out of the very exclusive subdivisions without a gate, solely for the gate.

Setha: Really. There has been?

Felicia: Oh, yeah. I was telling you about a family that was shopping [for a house in Felicia's gated community] because they had been randomly robbed many times.

* * *

Felicia: When I leave the area entirely and go downtown [little laugh], I feel quite threatened, just being out in normal urban areas, unrestricted urban areas. . . . Please let me explain. The north central part of this city, by and large, is middle class to upper middle class. Period. There are very few pockets of poverty. Very few. And therefore if you go to any store, you will look around and most of the clientele will be middle class as you are yourself. So you are somewhat insulated. But if you go downtown, which *is* much more mixed, where everybody goes, I feel much more threatened.

Setha: Okay.

Felicia: My daughter feels very threatened when she sees poor people.

Setha: How do you explain that?

Felicia: She hasn't had enough exposure. We were driving next to a truck with some day laborers and equipment in the back, and we were parked beside them at the light. She wanted to move because she was afraid those people were going to come and get her. They looked scary to her. I explained that they were workmen, they're the "backbone of our country," they're coming from work, you know, but. . . .

Donna's concerns with safety also focus on her child and his reactions to the city. She, like Felicia, is aware that a false sense of security develops living inside the gates putting her and her children in greater danger:

Donna: You know, he's always so scared. . . . It has made a world of difference in him since we've been out here.

Setha: Really?

Donna: A world of difference. And it is that sense of security that they don't think people are roaming the neighborhoods and the streets and that there's people out there that can hurt him.

Setha: Ah . . . that's incredible.

Donna: . . . That's what's been most important to my husband, to get the children out here where they can feel safe, and we feel safe if they could go out in the streets and not worry that someone is going to grab them. . . . We feel so secure and maybe that's wrong too.

Setha: In what sense?

Donna: You know, we've got workers out here, and we still think "oh, they're safe out here." . . . In the other neighborhood I never let him get out of my sight for a minute. Of course they were a little bit younger too, but I just, would never, you know, think of letting them go to the next street over. It would have scared me to death, because you didn't know. There was so much traffic coming in and out, you never knew who was cruising the street and how fast they can grab a child. And I don't feel that way in our area at all . . . ever.

Other San Antonio interviewees are less dramatic in expressing their concerns with safety and concentrate more on taxation and the quality of the security system and guards. Harry and his wife feel that the biggest difference with gating is "not just anyone can come by." They are more upset about the way that the government treats private gated communities in terms of taxation. Karen was not even looking for a place in a secured area:

Karen: It was just by accident that it was [gated]. . . . But after living here, if we moved it would be different.

Setha: And why is that?

Karen: Because after seeing . . . this is a very nice neighborhood and after seeing that there are so many beautiful neighborhoods here and in other parts of the country that are not in a secure area, that's where burglary and murders take place, not here, because it's an open door [there] . . . come on [in]. Why should they try to do anything here when they can go somewhere else first? It's a strong deterrent, needless to say.

Other residents are not so sure that the gates are an adequate deterrent. Edith talks about her problems with the security guards who supposedly patrol at night and monitor the gates with security cameras. She feels the guards do not do their job. Another interviewee points out that with any gate monitored by a security camera and a guard in a remote station, two cars can enter at the same time creating an unsafe situation.

There seems to be no end to residents' concern with safety and security. In both New York and San Antonio, most residents have burglar alarms they keep armed even when home during the day.

DISCUSSION

In New York, residents are fleeing deteriorating urban neighborhoods with increased ethnic diversity and petty crimes, concluding that the neighborhood is "just not what it used to be." New Yorkers cite changes in the local stores, problems with parking and securing a car, and frequent robberies of bicycles and cars. In San Antonio, there is a similar pattern, but here the emphasis is on a fear of kidnapping and illegal Mexican workers. Residents cite newspaper stories of children being kidnapped, drive-by shootings, neighbors being burglarized, and talk about the large number of "break-ins."

The intensity of the language and underlying social discourse seems more intense in San Antonio. As a younger, sprawling, Southern city, it has much greater horizontal spatial segregation than the older boroughs and Long Island suburbs of New York City. As Felicia explains, residents of the northern outskirts of San Antonio are physically insulated from the poorer sections of the city. In New York City, this kind of spatial and social insulation is much harder to achieve. Nonetheless, in both cities, residents move to gated communities based on what Felicia calls "fear flight," the desire to protect oneself, family, and property from dangers perceived as overwhelming them. Yet gating offers a kind of incomplete boundedness, in that workers from feared groups enter to work for residents and residents themselves need to leave to shop.

Whether it is kidnapping or bike snatching, Mexican laborers or "ethnic changes," the message is the same: residents are using the walls, entry gates, and guards in an effort to keep the perceived dangers outside of their homes, neighborhoods, and social world. The physical distance between them and the "others" is so close that contact incites fear and concern, and in response, they are constructing exclusive, private, residential developments where they can keep other people out with guards and gates. The walls are making visible the systems of exclusion that are already there, now constructed in concrete.

CONCLUSIONS

From these interviews there appears to be a wealth of data about fear of crime, increased social diversity, and neighborhood change. Residents talk about their fear of the poor, the workers, the "Mexicans," and the "newcomers," as well as their retreat behind walls where they think they will be safe. But there is fear even behind the walls. As the two mothers from San Antonio point out, there are workers who enter the community every day, and they must go out in order to buy groceries, shop, or see a movie. The gates provide some protection, but they would still like more. I wonder what "more" would be. Even though the gates and guards exclude the feared "others" from living with them, "they" can slip by the gate, follow your car in, crawl over the wall, or worse, the guard can fall asleep or be a criminal her- or himself. Informal conversations about the screening of guards and how they are hired, as well as discussions about increasing the height and length of the protective walls as new threats appear, are frequent in the locker room of the health club, on the tennis court, and during strolls in the community in the evening. What would be the next step in this progression?

In this chapter, I have not considered why developers are building gated communities, yet even without an analysis of marketing strategies, the allure of the gated community is clear. Even residents who did not select the community for its gates now would only live behind protective walls. Further, during the day residents are primarily women who do not work. Is the gated community creating new patterns of gendering in these spaces? What about the men who go outside the community each day to work? Are they the ones who primarily find a refuge from diversity when coming home? And gates and walls also have an impact on children and their relationship to other people and environments. Will the children who grow up in these new communities depend on walls for their sense of security and safety? What does it mean that 17 teenage heroin overdoses occurred in the suburban gated communities of Plano, Texas, in 1998 (Durrington 1999)? Will the walls and gates become standard for any middle-class home? And with what consequence for the future?

This chapter suggests that the discourse of urban fear encodes other social concerns including class, race, and ethnic exclusivity as well as gender. It provides a verbal component that complements, even reinforces, the visual landscape of fear created by the walls, gates, and guards. By matching the discourse of the inhabitants with the ideological thrust of the material setting, we enrich our understanding of the social construction and social production of places where the well-to-do live (Low 2000; Tuan 1979).

Urban fear, and its relationship to new forms of social ordering, needs to be better understood in the context of the entire metropolis. The spatial ordering of the edge responds to the social dialectic of the center, played out in an ever-changing suburban landscape.

Note

[1] Funding from the Wenner-Gren Foundation for Anthropological Research and from the Research Foundation of the City University of New York made this research project possible. I would like to thank Joel Lefkowitz, Laurel Wilson, Stephane Tonnelat, Kristin Koptiuch, Kevin Birth, Carole Browner, Sally Merry, Ivelisse Rivera-Bonilla, and Gary McDonogh for their contributions to this project. I also would like to thank my co-researchers Elena Danaila, Suzanne Scheld, and Mariana Diaz-Wionczek. Elena Danaila and Mariana Diaz-Wionczek worked on the analysis of these interviews, adding their understanding to my formulation of the problem. Melissa Waitzman, Cindi Katz, and the members of the Social Theory seminar contributed insightful comments on the theoretical ideas presented here. I, however, am solely responsible for the conclusions.

References

America's Top-Rated Cities. 1997. *A Statistical Handbook. Volume: Southern Region*, 5th ed. Boca Raton, FL: Universal References Publications.

Architectural Record. 1997. To Gate or Not to Gate. Record News. *Architectural Press Roundup*, (April 24):45.

Blakely, Edward J., and Mary Gail Snyder. 1997. *Fortress America*. Washington, DC: Brookings Institute.

Durrington, Matthew. 1999. Unpredictable Spaces: The Discourses of Drugs in Suburban Dallas. Paper presented at the Annual Meeting of the American Anthropological Association, Chicago, IL.

Fischler, M. S. 1998. Security the Draw at Gated Communities. *New York Times* (August 16): sec. 14LI, p. 6.

Gregory, Steve. 1998. *Black Corona*. Princeton, NJ: Princeton University Press.

Jackson, Kenneth T. 1985. *Crabgrass Frontier.* Oxford: Oxford University Press.

Judd, D. 1995. The Rise of New Walled Cities. In *Spatial Practices,* eds. H. Ligget and D. C. Perry, pp. 144–165. Thousand Oaks, CA: Sage.

Langdon, Philip. 1994. *A Better Place to Live.* Amherst: University of Massachusetts Press.

Low, Setha M., ed. 1999. *Theorizing the City: The New Urban Anthropology Reader.* New Brunswick, NJ: Rutgers University Press.

———. 2000. *On the Plaza: The Politics of Public Space and Culture.* Austin: University of Texas Press.

Massey, D. S., and Nancy Denton. 1988. Suburbanization and Segregation. *American Journal of Sociology,* 94(3):592–626.

McCall, C. 2000. *Queens: An Economic Review.* New York: Office of the State Deputy Comptroller.

McKenzie, Evan. 1994. *Privatopia.* New Haven, CT: Yale University Press.

Merry, Sally. 1993. Mending Walls and Building Fences: Constructing the Private Neighborhood. *Journal of Legal Pluralism,* 33:71–90.

Sanjek, Roger. 1998. *The Future of Us All.* Ithaca, NY: Cornell University Press.

Sibley, D. 1995. *Geographies of Exclusion.* London: Routledge.

Skogan, W. G. 1995. Crime and the Racial Fears of White Americans. *Annals of the American Academy of Political and Social Sciences,* 539(1):59–72.

Tuan, Y. 1979. *Landscapes of Fear.* New York: Pantheon Books.

Zukin, Sharon. 1991. *Landscapes of Power.* Berkeley: University of California Press.

10

Rethinking Camps
Palestinian Refugees in Damascus, Syria

Nell Gabiam

Using her fieldwork experience in Yarmouk, a long-established Palestinian refugee camp within Damascus, the capital city of Syria, Nell Gabiam seeks to refine Wirth's theories of urbanism. Despite being surrounded by the city, despite some camp residents having lived there for more than 50 years, and despite generally good relations with Syrians, the residents of Yarmouk still feel like a community of outsiders. Many urban Syrians consider the camp to be a zone of danger, while Palestinian camp residents, though grateful for their welcome within Syria, await the day when they can return to their real homes in Palestine.

INTRODUCTION

From 1947 to 1949—a period that saw the creation of the state of Israel and the resulting clashes between Palestine's Arab population and Jewish supporters of the newly formed Israeli state—approximately 750,000[1] Palestinian Arabs became refugees. These refugees ended up in parts of Palestine that had been awarded to the Arab population under the United Nations partition plan[2] (West Bank and Gaza) and the neighboring Arab countries of Jordan, Lebanon, and Syria; a small number of them made their way to Egypt and Iraq (Takkenberg 1998). Among the refugees, approximately 82,200 were located in Syria by the end of 1950 (Schiff 1995). Probably due to their urban origins, the first Palestinian refugees settled in and around Damascus, where 70 percent of all Palestinian refugees in Syria still live (Kodmani-Darwish 1997). One of the areas where these refugees settled became known as Yarmouk Camp, or *mukhayyam el-Yarmouk* in Arabic.

In this chapter, I demonstrate the importance of going beyond an understanding of refugee camps as physically isolated or sealed spaces character-

Source: Written expressly for *Urban Life*.

ized by destitution. I argue that "refugeehood" has emotional and political dimensions that—in the case of Yarmouk—take the form of a sense of identity and set of practices that transcend the limits imposed by a stereotypical understanding of life in a refugee camp. Urbanization and the passing of time have given Yarmouk Camp the feel of a vibrant working/middle-class neighborhood in Damascus, but these transformations have not changed Yarmouk's identity as a refugee camp or its inhabitants' identity as Palestinian refugees. While Yarmouk has become physically integrated within Damascus's urban landscape, it continues to exist as a separate space of Palestinian refugee identity through its inhabitants' sociopolitical activism as well as the sense of danger that it connotes to outsiders who are unfamiliar with it.

Yarmouk, with a population of a little over 100,000 inhabitants, represents the largest grouping of Palestinian refugees in Syria.[3] UNRWA, the United Nations Relief and Works Agency for Palestine Refugees in the Near East—which was created in December 1949 to assist the hundreds of thousands of dispossessed Palestinian refugees who had fled hostilities or been expelled from their homes by Israeli forces—refers to Yarmouk as an "unofficial" camp. This distinction results from Yarmouk not having been officially set aside by the United Nations—in cooperation with the Syrian government—to serve as a refugee camp in the aftermath of the 1948 Israeli–Palestinian war and the Palestinian refugee situation that ensued. Yarmouk, situated on the outskirts of the Syrian capital, Damascus, was "established as a camp" in 1957 to accommodate refugees who had been squatting in the area.[4]

UNRWA's distinction between "official" and "unofficial" camps is somewhat blurry and confusing, resulting in a different tally of the number of refugee camps in Syria depending on the source consulted. For instance, some sources only count "official" camps as genuine Palestinian refugee camps. This distinction begs the question of what exactly constitutes a Palestinian refugee camp. UNRWA provides services to both "official" and "unofficial" camps, with the difference being that it is not responsible for the collection of waste in unofficial camps (which task falls to the Syrian government). Thus, UNRWA runs 28 schools and a health center, and sponsors two community-run "Women's Program Centers" in Yarmouk.[5] Regardless of the formal definition of a refugee camp, UNRWA, the Syrian government and people, and the Palestinians themselves recognize, in practice, that areas homogeneously populated by large numbers of Palestinian refugees are camps. This state of affairs helps explain why Palestinian refugees have staunchly held on to their refugee identity for six decades now and continue to advocate their right of return to towns and villages in pre-1948 Palestine.

An analysis of Yarmouk's gradual transformation into a neighborhood within the city of Damascus, all the while retaining its identity as a "refugee camp," will help illuminate the relationship between urbanization and identity as well as provide some insight into the lives of Palestinian refugees within an urban setting.

SYRIA AND PALESTINIAN REFUGEES

The Syrian government and people have had a welcoming approach toward Palestinian refugees (Kodmani-Darwish 1997). First, Palestinian refugees share similarities with the Syrian population in their religious (both groups are primarily Sunni Muslim) and cultural background. Second, Palestine was historically part of the area known as Greater Syria or *Bilad al-Sham* (which translates into English as "the lands of Damascus"), an area that also encompassed the present-day states of Syria, Lebanon, and Jordan. Palestine became a separately administered entity after the defeat of the Ottoman Empire during World War I, which resulted in the Franco-British Sykes-Picot agreement on May 16, 1916. According to this agreement, Jordan and Palestine were carved out as separate territories to be administered by the British while the rest of Greater Syria—which encapsulated the present-day states of Syria and Lebanon—was to be administered by the French. In the 1950s, the Syrian government adopted the pan-Arab ideology of Ba'thism, which viewed all Arabs as members of a single nation and, until recently, continued to hold on to the idea of a unified Greater Syria (Talhami 2001). In 1956, the Syrian government adopted a law declaring that Palestinians residing in Syria had the same rights as native Syrians with regard to work, trade, and national duty, while retaining their "nationality" of origin (Kodmani-Darwish 1997:96). In legal terms, this means that the main difference between Palestinian refugees and Syrian citizens is that only the latter have the right to vote in national elections.

Yarmouk is often touted as a symbol of "successful integration" of refugees into their host country (Kodmani-Darwish 1997; FAFO Report 2007). While Yarmouk was established outside of Damascus, it has gone through a process of incorporation into the city. Aside from an arch that signals the entrance to *Sharea el-Yarmouk* (Yarmouk Street), the main street that cuts across the camp and that has become a commercial hub, lined with clothing and shoe stores, bakeries, grocery stores, and other businesses, the camp blends into the surrounding areas that make up the outer limits of Damascus. The camp's dense landscape, consisting of three- to four-story apartment buildings separated by narrow streets, is similar to that of other working/middle-class neighborhoods in Damascus. Yarmouk is connected to Damascus's transportation network, which serves the Syrian capital through the *Yarmouk* and *Falasteen* (Palestine) "micro" buses.[6] While a recent survey conducted by FAFO (the Norwegian Institute for Applied Social Science) notes that 20 percent of Yarmouk's inhabitants live below the poverty level (FAFO Report 2006:200), a number of Yarmouk's Palestinian refugees are teachers, doctors, lawyers, engineers, and university professors.

Yarmouk's history helps explain the rather high economic status of its refugees. The first and biggest wave of Palestinian refugees who settled in Yarmouk came mostly from cities inside present-day Israel (Kodmani-Darwish 1997). In addition, because Yarmouk Camp was erected at the outskirts of Damascus, it was able to take part in the area's rapid urbanization in the 1950s. Yarmouk also benefited from social and economic services provided by the PLO (Palestine Liberation Organization) throughout the 1960s, when the camp was considered the political capital of the Palestinian refugee struggle for the right of return and for Palestinian self-determination. In addition, remittances from family members working abroad have sheltered Yarmouk's population from a series of economic crises affecting Syria (Kodmani-Darwish 1997). According to political scientist Kodmani-Darwish, Yarmouk has become "an indistinguishable part of the capital, and one of its most vibrant commercial centers" (1997:98, translation mine).

As argued by Wirth (this volume), urbanism in the case of Yarmouk is not simply a physical process of integration but a question of lifestyle as well. Wirth identifies the loosening of kinship ties and face-to-face interaction as salient characteristics of an urban lifestyle. Unlike other camps in Syria, which are smaller and more isolated, everyone does not know everyone else in Yarmouk, and it is easy for outsiders to come and go unnoticed or without attracting much attention. In fact, Yarmouk's commercial areas are popular with Syrians who are attracted to the cheaper prices and wider range of products. There are even a number of Syrians who live in Yarmouk. In contrast, in the Palestinian refugee camps of Neirab and Ein al Tal, located in the vicinity of Aleppo, Syria's second largest city, all one needs to find a camp resident is a name.

Neirab and Ein el Tal camps are small (their populations are 18,000 and 4,000 respectively) and isolated, and are considered by UNRWA to be two of the poorest Palestinian refugee camps in Syria (Gabiam 2008). The face-to-face relations that characterize life in Neirab and Ein el Tal make it easier for the Syrian government to keep track of what is going on inside these camps. Although no official rules ban foreigners or outsiders from entering the camps, foreigners are discouraged from visiting. When they do, they and their Palestinian hosts may be subjected to intimidating questions by Syrian security forces. I became familiar with Neirab and Ein el Tal camps during my second year of fieldwork when I was working as a UNRWA volunteer on a development project in these camps. Because I was working under UNRWA sponsorship, I was able to circulate more or less freely in the camps. However, I had to go through the bureaucratic process of getting official permission from Syrian authorities to be in the camps as a UNRWA volunteer on the project. In addition, Syrian authorities forbade me to live in the camps or spend the night there. Because of their relatively small population, their isolated location, and the intimate nature of their social interactions, it is very difficult if not impossible to break these rules without being noticed.

When I first arrived in northern Syria, I was only working in Ein el Tal Camp and thus did not have permission from Syrian authorities to be in the neighboring Neirab Camp. A Palestinian volunteer on the project who lived in Ein el Tal offered to take me to Neirab, but we limited ourselves to the camp's outer limits so as not to get into trouble. Even though we had not really gone *inside* the camp, the next day the volunteer was summoned by Neirab's security office and questioned because someone had apparently seen and reported us. The volunteer denied the allegations that we had been any-where near the camp and, to my relief, there were no repercussions. Some months later, the UNRWA project assistant who oversaw the foreign volun-teers involved with the project was summoned to the Aleppo offices of the Syrian branch of the government that oversees Palestinian refugee camps. She recounted that she was summoned because a foreign UNRWA volunteer had been caught spending time in Neirab Camp even though she only had permission to be in Ein el Tal Camp where she was working. The volunteer had assumed that, entering the camp dressed in an *abaya* (a long black cloak worn by some women in the Muslim world) with her head covered and face veiled, she would escape the scrutiny of Neirab's security office and its net-work of informants.

Foreigners do not have to deal with these issues in Yarmouk Camp. I lived in Yarmouk for the last three months of my fieldwork, sharing a nice two-bedroom apartment with a New Zealand-born woman of Lebanese ori-gin. Other foreigners, including Westerners, also live in Yarmouk. The pro-cess of renting a place in Yarmouk turned out to be no different from renting housing in other parts of Damascus. The building I lived in belonged to an extended Palestinian family whose members lived in some of its apartments and rented others. The family also operated a fashionable clothing store on the first floor of the building. Being within Yarmouk's commercial district, which attracts crowds of outsiders on a daily basis, I led a relatively anony-mous existence.

Since the publication of Wirth's influential essay on urbanism, many scholars have advocated a more nuanced understanding of social relations within the realm of the city (Merry, this volume). They have shown that com-munity and social networks do not necessarily disappear in an urban setting even if such a setting, taken as a whole, offers a certain degree of anonymity and social independence. Those living in cities can be members of subgroups of ethnic or cultural character, or belong to social networks from which they derive a sense of community. While no significant physical barriers separate Yarmouk from the rest of the Syrian capital, several factors coalesce in per-petuating its identity as a refugee camp. In her work on the projects area of a major U.S. city, Sally Engle Merry (this volume) shows how notions of dan-ger—with regard to specific spaces and people within the projects—on the part of residents contribute to forming boundaries around the different ethnic groups living in these projects.

One of the factors that contributes to Yarmouk's continued identification as a separate entity and as a "camp" is the notion of danger associated with it, as is the case with other Palestinian refugee camps in Syria. When I arrived in Damascus in the spring of 2004 to conduct fieldwork, I was originally inter-ested in focusing on Yarmouk's socioeconomic integration into Damascus and the consequences in terms of Palestinian refugee identity. I was therefore looking into the possibility of living in Yarmouk. At the time, I had some apprehensions about living there mostly because of my American nationality and because the subject of Palestinian refugees is a politically charged one. As a Fulbright fellow, I had to get official permission from the Syrian government to carry out my research, permission that had been denied to others in the past.[7] Even though I did get permission from Syrian authorities to carry out my research, I was worried that moving to the camps might draw unwanted scrutiny from Syrian authorities or might even result in limitations on my ability to carry out my project. My concerns over my American nationality were linked to U.S. foreign policy in the Middle East at the time.

I arrived in Damascus about a year after the American invasion of Iraq, a widely unpopular action in the Middle East, including Syria and its Palestinian refugee camps. Some Palestinians were quick to link the American occupation of Iraq and the Israeli occupation of Palestinian territories, and I would hear reports of Palestinians leaving their camps to fight with the Iraqi insurgency. There was also talk in 2004 that Syria might be the next country to be invaded by the United States. I was worried that, within the prevailing political climate and the strong reaction that the U.S. invasion of Iraq elicited among Palestinians, I might be greeted in Yarmouk with a certain amount of distrust or resentment.

Syrian acquaintances who knew of my interest in Yarmouk had very different concerns. Through my conversations with them, I realized that refugee camps are perceived by many Syrians as spaces of poverty and danger that are to be avoided, regardless of the actual conditions in the camps. Merry (this volume) points out, with regard to her research on notions of danger in an urban housing project, that those who expressed the most fear about neighboring areas were usually those most unfamiliar with them. I found the same to be true in the case of Yarmouk. Shereen, the daughter of my first Syrian landlord in Damascus, where I lived during most of my first year of fieldwork, was very emphatic about not liking Palestinians. Aside from asserting that Palestinians were "not good people" and that she just didn't like them, she complained that Palestinians were taking away jobs and opportunities from Syrians who needed them. When I announced to her that I was thinking about moving to Yarmouk, Shereen advised me to be very careful because Yarmouk was a poor, and therefore dangerous, area. When I inquired whether she had ever been to Yarmouk, she acknowledged that the closest she had come to the camp was once driving through it.

Other Syrian acquaintances were equally alarmed when they learned that I was spending time in Yarmouk or thinking about moving there. During a conversation with some Syrian friends living in Damascus, Bassam, a graphic designer, was shocked to learn that I was spending time in Yarmouk (I had not moved there at that point). He then asked a question I would never have anticipated: "Do people wear shoes there?" I gave him an incredulous look, so he continued, "or do they wear those plastic sandals?" As he mentioned the plastic sandals, I understood what he meant. He was talking about plastic slippers that a middle-class Damascene like him might wear inside his home, but that a person of lower social status and minimal education might wear in the streets of Damascus.

The Syrians I met who were actually familiar with Yarmouk had a very different view. One young Syrian woman casually told me that she liked to shop in Yarmouk after I complimented her on the pair of jeans she was wearing. I met another young Syrian woman who had fond memories of living in Yarmouk during the few years when her father owned a business there. Thus, when I explained to Bassam that Yarmouk was actually not so different from other neighborhoods in Damascus and was even a popular shopping area, he looked at our other friend, Louai, with a questioning look. "Yes, that is true," said Louai. "People like to go shopping there because the products are cheaper." Still, Bassam was not convinced that Yarmouk was up to his standards. He concluded that his view of Yarmouk as a dangerous place probably was due to his unfamiliarity with it. He then observed that, as an American, I probably thought that the place was like being in "Chicago." I believe he said this because he associated Chicago with poverty, crime, and racialized ghettos.

The connection between Palestinian refugee camps and racialized ghettos was further elaborated during an incident involving Saleem, a Palestinian friend and sometime "research assistant." Saleem, an economics student at the University of Damascus, helped me with translating documents in Arabic and with improving my spoken Arabic when I first arrived in Syria and was living in Damascus. In the beginning, I met with him in Yarmouk, where he lived in a nice three-bedroom apartment with his parents, his younger brother, and his two teenage sisters. Because Saleem's house was somewhat far from where I lived, we ultimately decided that we would take turns going to each other's house for our weekly lessons. At the time, I was renting a room in the house of an elderly Christian Syrian woman in the Old City of Damascus. I obtained permission from her to have Saleem come over once a week and help me with my Arabic. However, Saleem had asked me not to tell my landlady that he was Palestinian. "Why?" I inquired. "Because she's old and she might get scared. She might think I'm uneducated and dangerous because I live in the camp," he answered.

The first time Saleem came over, my landlady was seated in the house's internal courtyard under an orange tree at the foot of the stairs that led to my room. After introductions, we sat down at a table in the courtyard and proceeded to work. Later on, as I went into the kitchen across the courtyard to make us some tea, Saleem followed me, frantically asking, "What if she asks me where I'm from? What should I say? She's old; she might get scared if I tell her the truth." "Tell her the truth," I responded. "It's the best thing to do." My landlady never did ask Saleem where he was from as they sat alone while I was making tea. However, as our lesson was ending, her oldest son, according to his mother the only Christian to have risen to the rank of general in the Syrian army, walked in. He greeted us, and my landlady explained to him that Saleem was helping me with Arabic. As I went back into the kitchen to wash the tea dishes, I could hear my landlady's son questioning Saleem, although I could not make out all the words of the conversation. I was feeling very uncomfortable at this point. I was starting to think it had been a bad idea to have Saleem come over.

By the time I came out of the kitchen, the questioning had stopped. Saleem got up to leave, and, as I walked him out the door, my landlady's son invited him to stay for coffee, which he politely declined. Being invited for coffee meant that the session had gone well and that he was welcome in the house. Saleem added that he was happy he had told the truth about himself but maintained that the encounter could have gone either way. I asked him why he thought some Syrians might be suspicious about Palestinians. He answered that it was because some Palestinians are "bad" (sayyi'). The educated ones like him were good people, and in Yarmouk there was a mixture of educated Palestinians and some uneducated ones of rural background. According to him, the uneducated ones had given the camp a bad reputation. In neighboring Geramana Camp, outside of Damascus, they were all "bad" because they were mostly of poor and rural background. I asked him what he meant by "bad." He meant aggressive in the sense that if someone annoyed you, you would be quick to settle it though blows. He then went on to compare the situation in Geramana camp to that of African Americans in the United States.

The imagery of camps as dangerous or violent ghettos is one that I encountered a few times. For example, much later in my fieldwork, a Syrian acquaintance who learned I was going to be working in Neirab Camp told me to be careful. He had met some Palestinians from Neirab Camp while in military service and they were, in his words, hotheaded. This imagery demonstrates that, in addition to being national spaces of Palestinian identity, Palestinian refugee camps often are associated with poverty and perceived through the lens of class/ethnic differences.

Comparisons between African Americans and Palestinians did not always draw on negative stereotypes. A Palestinian writer and researcher who lives in Yarmouk once told me during a conversation that he enjoyed African American literature. He liked to go to the library of the American cultural center in Damascus to check out books by African American authors. He was interested in "how people who are discriminated against identify themselves in the face of this discrimination, which attempts to impose a certain identity on them." From a different perspective, he felt that the experience of African Americans in the United States provided a useful parallel to understanding Palestinian identity.

A CAMP IS A FEELING INSIDE

Part of what contributes to the assumption that Yarmouk is a space of danger as well as a specifically Palestinian space is the political activism of its refugees. In the 1960s, Yarmouk became a center of Palestinian political activism as major Palestinian political parties installed their headquarters there.

The PLO (Palestine Liberation Organization), which serves as an umbrella for most Palestinian political parties, exerted major influence in the camp and pumped economic resources into it. When PLO leader Yasser Arafat fell out of favor with the Syrian government in the 1970s and his political party Fatah was banned, Yarmouk continued to be, at least on a local level, a center of Palestinian refugee political activism. I witnessed a huge parade commemorating Arafat's death in November of 2004 and one celebrating the Israeli withdrawal from Gaza in September of 2005. Posters and banners expressing opinions regarding events relating to the Israeli–Palestinian conflict or featuring the picture of the latest martyrs fallen for the Palestinian cause adorn the walls of the camp. Most streets in Yarmouk are named after villages or towns in historical Palestine. The camp has a great number of associations involved in social programs to benefit the Palestinian community. These associations are usually tied to the many political parties present on Yarmouk's landscape and often frame their activities within the larger political goal of returning to the areas they inhabited in pre-1948 Palestine or within the language of Palestinian resistance to Israeli domination. During the summer of 2005, several of the youth centers in Yarmouk organized an activity during which the young children enrolled in the centers gathered at one of Yarmouk's roundabouts to paint a gigantic banner that was then displayed at the roundabout. The banner's title was "Dreaming of the Homeland."

Children painting a banner entitled "Dreaming of the Homeland" to be displayed at the Palestine roundabout (Dowra Falasteen). [Photo by Nell Gabiam]

The Palestine roundabout (Dowra Falasteen) in Yarmouk Camp. [Photo by Nell Gabiam]

One could say that when I arrived in Syria, I subscribed to the notion of Yarmouk as a space of "danger" in the sense that I felt I needed to be cautious about moving there. I was hesitant about moving to Yarmouk at a time when American foreign policy was extremely unpopular in the Middle East. As I came to know people in Yarmouk, I found that people in Syria, whether Syrian or Palestinian, distinguish foreign nationals—the "people"—from their "government." Thus, I never experienced resentment or aggressive behavior in Yarmouk from anyone who discovered or was aware of my American nationality.

Saleem had been one of the Palestinians from Yarmouk whom I met in the early stages of my fieldwork. A German acquaintance had given me Saleem's home phone number. My acquaintance warned me that, should Saleem's parents answer the phone, I must not tell them my nationality because they would react negatively. My acquaintance told me this, although he himself had never met Saleem's parents. When I recounted this to Saleem months later, after we had become good friends, he was hurt by the words of my German acquaintance—whom he considered a friend—and the way his parents had been stereotyped as hotheaded radicals. When I did meet Saleem's family, they proved to be gracious and welcoming. They even took me along on a seaside vacation in a coastal village close to the Syrian border with Turkey.

Saleem's father is an engineer who works for the Syrian government, and his mother is a homemaker. As a government employee, Saleem's father makes the equivalent of about US$300 a month, which is about average by Syrian standards. One of the first actions Saleem took when I visited him at his house was to show me pictures of Safad, the Palestinian town from which his paternal family fled in 1948. Safad is now within the boundaries of the state of Israel and has been completely depopulated of its Palestinian inhabitants. Yet, Safad is what Saleem considers home. He has a map of the town, which lists all of the Palestinian families who used to live there. While Saleem and his family have been able to improve their lives in Syria, acquiring advanced education and living a relatively comfortable and secure existence, they—like most of the refugees in Yarmouk—are deeply attached to their Palestinian origins and to the idea of one day returning to their homes in historical Palestine.

Although some Palestinians believe that because Yarmouk is looking less like a camp than it used to, refugees there may forget their origins; others discount these concerns. For instance, Saleem is not worried about Yarmouk's landscape or its incorporation within Damascus. When I asked him what Yarmouk symbolizes, he replied:

> I consider Yarmouk a part of me. We were born in the camp and our family members were born in the camp and raised us in here [Yarmouk]. Today, the landscape of the camp has improved to the point where there no longer are traces of suffering and we now have houses instead of tents and we have businesses and jobs and are not dependent on [outside] help like we used to be in the past. This is why we like the camp a lot. And even if I one day have enough money to buy a house outside of the camp in a better neighborhood, maybe I'll buy the house, but I won't give up my house in Yarmouk, inside the camp, because I was born here and I want to stay here in the camp and I will stay until I return to my country, Palestine.

For Saleem, Yarmouk is a camp for the simple reason that it is populated by Palestinian refugees. In this sense, the camp is a part of him but he is also a part of the camp.

Saleem's uncle moved to Yarmouk in 1960 when he was still a child, after having lived in a refugee camp inside *Bab Touma*, part of the older section of Damascus. According to Saleem's uncle, Syrian authorities encouraged his family to leave the camp in Bab Touma and move to Yarmouk because Syrian authorities did not like the idea of a camp inside the city. Like Saleem, his uncle is not perturbed by the changes that have occurred in Yarmouk and continues to feel strongly about his Palestinian identity and desire to return to Palestine someday:

> A camp is not only buildings. It's a social state—it's a feeling you have inside. We live in Syria; we have good relations [with Syrians], but we feel a sense of exile [*ightirab*]. Even if I lived in a castle I would still feel like a refugee and that my homeland is Palestine. I prefer to live in a dirty area in Palestine rather than in a castle outside Palestine. Our situation in

Syria [having the same social rights as Syrians] does not cancel [*yulghī*] our relationship with the land. It is rare for people to give up their sense of national belonging.

CONCLUSION

In making the argument that urbanism is not just a question of incorporation into the realm of the city but a question of lifestyle as well, Wirth implicitly recognizes that boundaries do not operate only within the context of clearly delimited and physically separate spaces. Other scholars have refined Wirth's theories on urbanism by pointing out the persistence of community in urban settings despite the large number of people and the social heterogeneity that characterize these settings. In this tradition, we can say that a camp is not simply a bounded and isolated place; the notion of camp exceeds its geographical understanding and, in the case of the Palestinian refugees of Yarmouk, is tied to identity as well as well as lifestyle.

Yarmouk has become part of the mosaic of people who live and work in Damascus, and it lacks the intimate, close-knit, face-to-face interactions that characterize smaller and more isolated camps in Syria. However, Yarmouk continues to exist as a community of refugees. This community is held together by a similar history and strong attachment to Palestinian identity expressed through its network of sociopolitical activism. As such, geographical location alone does not explain what happens in a particular space.

We must understand the ways social relations not only create but also dismantle boundaries. In the end, if most of the people in Syria continue to consider Yarmouk a camp and refer to it as such, it is because, as noted by Saleem's uncle, a camp is not just a "place; it is a *feeling inside.*" Among those living in the camp, this feeling takes the form of collective pride in one's Palestinian origins and a sense of injustice with regard to forced exile from one's homeland. Among non-Palestinians this feeling can take the form of fear of refugee spaces as arenas of danger, as no-entry zones. Yarmouk also shows that camp and city are not in opposition to each other. While Yarmouk's Palestinian refugees have subscribed in many ways to a Damascene urban lifestyle, they actively re-create their separate refugee status on a daily basis.

Notes

[1] This number has been debated by Israeli sources, which argue that the number of Palestinian refugees was closer to 500,000, and Arab sources, which put it at around 1,000,000. I chose to rely on UNRWA's (United Nations Relief and Works Agency for Palestine Refugees in the Near East) figures; www.unrwa.org (accessed August 2, 2008).

[2] On November 2, 1917, Lord Balfour wrote a letter on behalf of the British government that expressed support for the establishment of a homeland for the Jews in Palestine. The declaration led the League of Nations, the precursor to the United Nations, to endorse the creation of a Jewish state in Palestine. On November 29, 1947, the UN General Assembly passed a resolution endorsing the partition of Palestine and the creation of the state of Israel on part of its territory.

[3] According to UNRWA figures, there were 112,550 registered refugees in Yarmouk as of June 30, 2002; www.unrwa.org (accessed August 2, 2008).

⁴ Information gathered from UNRWA's official Web site: www.unrwa.org (accessed August 2, 2008).

⁵ Information gathered from UNRWA's official Web site: www.unrwa.org (accessed August 2, 2008).

⁶ Microbuses, often referred to as *meecro*s in Syria, are van-like buses that are more ubiquitous in Damascus than the typical larger buses.

⁷ For example, Benjamin Schiff (1995) explains that he was not able to gather data on Palestinians living in Syria because he was not granted permission by the Syrian government to carry out research there.

References

FAFO Report. 2006. Palestinian Refugees in Syria: Human Capital, Economic Resources and Living Conditions. Fafo-report 514, http://almashriq.hiof.no/general/300/320/327/fafo/reports/index.html (accessed July 5, 2008).

———. 2007. Keeping Up: A Brief on the Living Conditions of Palestinian Refugees in Syria. Fafo Report-2007:13, http://almashriq.hiof.no/general/300/320/327/fafo/reports/index.html (accessed July 5, 2008).

Gabiam, Nell. 2008. In Order Not to Forget: Dignity and Development in Syria's Palestinian Refugee Camps. Doctoral Dissertation. University of California, Berkeley.

Kodmani-Darwish, Bassma. 1997. *La Diaspora Palestinienne*. Paris: Presse Universitaire de France.

Schiff, Benjamin. 1995. *Refugees unto the Third Generation: UN Aid to Palestinians*. Syracuse: Syracuse University Press.

Takkenberg, Lex. 1998. *The Status of Palestinian Refugees in International Law.* Oxford: Clarendon Press.

Talhami, Ghada Hashem. 2001. *Syria and the Palestinians: The Clash of Nationalisms*. Gainesville: University Press of Florida.

11

In Motion
Transportation and Knowledge in São Paulo

Derek Pardue

In recent years, urban anthropologists have sought to understand cities by analyzing their spaces. In the process, we have learned that people live in different city spaces depending on their social class and access to wealth. Public and private spaces are often clearly separated, with the affluent able to retreat to their own "space" while the less fortunate are afforded fewer options and less privacy. In this chapter, Derek Pardue explores space and social difference in São Paulo, Brazil, through the lens of its transportation system. He argues that not only can we discover certain truths about social class by understanding the types of transportation—bus, train, private automobile—utilized by various citizens, especially those involved in the hip-hop music scene, but also that their very different mental maps of the city correlate with their modes of transportation.

> It's in the space between things that I exist
> It's in the space between things that I exist
> —Rapper Parteum in "Do Espaço"

One of the most palpable ideologies of social difference and power is space. Urban anthropologists, drawing from geographers, philosophers, and, of course, local community actors, have contributed significantly to debates about the structures and meanings of cities in terms of social space. One method of inquiry into city spaces is to investigate movement around the city, that is, transportation. As any sound expression of knowledge, methodology should link to one's theory. How we know something is inevitably connected to what one might potentially conclude or understand about an event or phenomenon. This chapter reflects on the theory that social difference is spatialized and that we can approach this difference and its social dynamics by focusing on the meaning of transportation.

Source: Written expressly for *Urban Life*.

You are part of the city even when you ignore it.

We don't realize how connected we are to the space we occupy.

I just try to bring elements that call attention to this puzzle in my music.

It doesn't always make sense at first, but it is a true register and, you know, it has to be complex in order to represent what the city is. A city, any street, any hotel room, any library, any subway car, any bus stop inspires, and I have to believe that there exists a reciprocity between a person and that object. . . .

These statements were part of one response to a recent, informal survey I conducted with hip-hoppers about their relationship to São Paulo, the largest city in Brazil and South America overall. More specifically, the insightful comments above were uttered by Parteum, a Brazilian rapper who represents a relatively new voice in local hip-hop and a provocative perspective on the city. Parteum, an artistic name based loosely on the Latin word for "birth," is actually one of several personae the impressive Fábio (Parteum's given name) embodies. His ventures in skateboarding, modernist literature, science fiction, opera, world beat, and information technology locate Parteum as a mix between Fernando Pessoa, the famous early twentieth-century Portuguese writer with several alter egos, and the popular, crossover New Jersey-based hip-hop collective, the Wu-Tang Clan. His recent projects with Mzuri Sana, a hip-hop collective based on the ubiquitous Swahili phrase for "very good," include a provocative recording entitled the "Oblique Opera" (Ópera Oblíqua) (2006). While Parteum and others of various "underground" hip-hop alternative groups claim an "obliqueness" and "off-centered" approach to representation, they continue to stick to concrete subject matter—the city and its hard surfaces of streets, walls, turnstiles, and mudslide alleys.

Parteum has emerged from a long line of Brazilian hip-hoppers, particularly *paulistano* (from São Paulo city), who have tried to transform descriptions of city life into programmatic recipes for social change. They have done so by deploying terms of "conquest" (*conquista*) and territory (*espaço*) as they call out certain neighborhoods and urban locales. During most of the 1990s, São Paulo hip-hoppers found the greatest level of recognition and social effect by emphasizing a particular idea of locality, an extremely literal and empirical notion of *periferia* (periphery). "Periferia" refers to the outlying, "suburban," areas of Brazilian city sprawl. It is composed of the working-class millions, who have for the most part created their own residential homes and neighborhood structure.

As more and more urban youth honed their hip-hop skills and access to information technology gradually increased, divergences emerged not only in aesthetics but also in the role and the very meaning of periferia for the hip-hop community. As I have argued elsewhere (Pardue 2004, 2008), creativity in Brazilian hip-hop derives, in part, from a difference in opinion regarding the value of "concrete" or transparent versus the "oblique" or abstract in the representation of reality. Parteum and the like claim that urban reality necessitates a mix and is not a question of either/or.

Similar to Parteum's trajectory, I as an urban anthropologist find myself between strong traditions of representation. Is the city best characterized as a set of institutions and patterns of demographic shifts, or is it best captured as experience and metaphoric allusions? Over the years, urban scholars have held differing opinions on this issue. For my part, I take a cue from Parteum, and in the following pages I hope to provide a feeling for São Paulo through reflection, not in an overall, ethereal manner, but rather vis-à-vis the grounded infrastructure of transportation.

São Paulo is a megacity, a chaotic area with roughly 20 million inhabitants. One out of every 10 Brazilians lives in the São Paulo metro area. Over 50 percent of these dwellers live in something called the periferia, and a variable portion of this area can be defined as some sort of slum.[1] My experience in São Paulo has been dominated by fieldwork with local hip-hoppers (rappers, DJs, graffiti artists, street dancers, and various other kinds of participants).[2] While this text is not about hip-hoppers per se, my thoughts on this matter come from lessons they taught me about being in, knowing, and potentially "conquering" the various city spaces within this place called São Paulo.

View of São Paulo from atop the Edifício Itália showing the modernist Copan building designed by Oscar Niemeyer. [Photo by Derek Pardue]

More panoramic view of the extent of São Paulo's skyscrapers. [Photo by Derek Pardue]

IN MOTION

The argument of this chapter is not a discovery; rather, it is a call to give attention to the mundane. Most people are struck by their first visit to a big city, in particular during the initial days of "orientation." Literally and figuratively, we need time to find ourselves and achieve a level of familiarity with our new surroundings and circuits of daily activity. As one spends more time, paths may change; yet, in general, one begins to settle into a routine of everyday motion. And in this process of routinization one realizes, usually at a level of implicit knowledge, certain differences within the city. One begins to produce mental maps with imagined borders bolstered by judgmental language—the "good" and "bad" areas of town, the "rough" side, and so forth. Sometimes our maps are more specific and sociological—the "theater" district, "little Italy," the "projects," or the "black" part of town. As the latter "maps" indicate, the process of popular cartography is a social one. We trade stories about "cool" or "risky" events in our lives located in a particular coordinate and thus give ethnographic weight to our "maps." We debate borders; real estate agents articulate such borders to create markets and produce their own discursive terms such as "pioneer" or "transition" neighborhoods.

Furthermore, and more to the point of this chapter, such map areas are not meaningful in and of themselves. Their value depends on their relationship to modes of transportation. In the case of São Paulo, while there have been a number of urbanization models implemented (Sachs 1999[1990]; Caldeira 2000), including British, French, and U.S. plans of "garden cities," "the promenade," and the "gated community" enclave, respectively, the most pertinent frame with which to understand São Paulo continues to be center-periphery. This model dictates that there is a historic and commercially vibrant downtown. As one moves further and further away from the center, basic services and social status significantly diminish. In fact, it is more accurate to discuss São Paulo as a complex network of *centers* and *peripheries*, because as the elite classes—who, in the case of São Paulo, are families of coffee barons and financial entrepreneurs organized in spatialized conglomerates—fragment away from their traditional locations, new "centers" are established. Concurrently, peripheries are variegated; they differ in history, racial makeup, employment concentration, and urban locale. The one cohesive mark of periferia is that these places and their residents are disenfranchised from varying levels of state support, including water, electricity, roads, education, libraries, health services, and information technology.

Similar to many contemporary hip-hoppers, I move in between various peripheries and various centers as part of my fieldwork. In the following sections, I present a number of narrative pieces that focus on cognitive maps related to the social geography of São Paulo.

TRAINS, SUBWAYS, BUSES, AND OTHER *CONDUÇÃO*

Upon consideration of the multiple "centers" and "peripheries" within the São Paulo metro area, it is important to remember that the two main determining forces of the modern São Paulo landscape are industry and real estate capitalism. Although the city was founded in 1554, São Paulo only began to exert any significant urban presence in the early decades of the twentieth century. Modern industries of textiles, electrical power, automobiles (and, later, airplanes), and urban construction itself provoked local government officials to make a series of spatial decisions. Namely, there would be business and financial "centers" with management housing nearby—for example, Paulista Avenue with adjacent Jardins ("garden" district) and Higienópolis ("hygiene city") and, later, Luis Carlos Berrini Avenue with adjacent Morumbi luxurious neighborhoods. Workers would be displaced literally, in relatively far-flung makeshift areas, to ensure an "order" (the slogan of the Brazilian flag is "order and progress") of space and society. Over decades, these work camps would become stable middle-class districts such as Barra Funda, Santana, Jabaquara, Penha, and Itaquera. What was left in between was both literally and socially empty, a wasteland, conduit space for the new, imposed system of transportation—the British-sponsored train.[3] The complex notion of periferia was born and with it a stigma of both place and personhood. As time went on, the geographical gaps in between were filled by increasing numbers of "centers" and "peripheries," but the terms themselves have held relatively firm as markers of class, race, culture, intelligence, and general status. This brief background helps contextualize the following stories of Robson, Edilaine, and my fieldwork experiences.

In fieldwork, cultural anthropologists employ strategies of elicitation. In cities, one successful tactic is to talk about commutes. This is particularly effective with working-class people, because their trajectories are often longer, more varied, and more complex than those of middle-class laborers. I found this approach helpful with Robson. Robson, 18, works in an entry-level data-processing position in a hospital accounting office on the famous Paulista Avenue, a hub of primarily financial institutions. This is his first "serious" job, and he likes to talk about the technical specificities of the computer software he uses. Robson comes from a family of little means. His father, Gerson Oliveira, the sole "breadwinner" of the household, has had various odd jobs ranging from truck driver to a customer representative for a water cooler company. Mister Oliveira prides himself on having creative ideas but an unfortunate lack of capital. Dona Maria Aparecida, Robson's mother, hated school and was relieved to find a husband early on, as she never was interested in wage labor. For Mister Oliveira, providing for his family was a matter of pride and masculine honor. He and his wife are a fine match. The family has an intimate knowledge of the train, but always preferred to arrive at family and group functions by bus. Robson explained, "It was a more decent way of getting around than train. The train is a sardine can; the bus affords some view on life, some perspective on things."

Robson had a point. Although the cost is basically the same, the bus signifies a higher rank than the train. As Robson describes,

> I like being up high; I enjoy the view of the traffic. I look down at some poor soul in his car. In some ways, I can forget the dozens of people around me sweating or stinking or sick or ugly or whatever. I can sometimes use this height and dream about another life scenario.

As Robson goes on, it becomes apparent that the value of the bus is not simply about literal height but also a feeling of urban engagement.

> There's another thing. You see, in a bus you are on the street. You see stuff happening; you move through some nice neighborhoods. You see fancy cars; you pass by various parts of the city. In a train you pass by forgotten places, removed tracks, somewhere without people. At least during the day. . . . At night, you can see random people about, but it's weird . . . I don't know, I prefer the bus.

Robson's discursive retreat into the vague category of "weird" (*esquisito*) is understandable. It is a commonsense way to deal with the discomfort of what the train represents—displacement. The "out of place" nature of the train in contemporary São Paulo makes it the most undesirable and lowest form of public transportation, even with respect to illegal forms of transportation such as the *kombi*.[4]

Robson grew up on the extreme east side of São Paulo, and for most of his life the sights of "fancy cars" and "nice neighborhoods" would only occur after at least half an hour of bus travel. Robson admits that "during the week my father would usually take the train downtown to the small office space where he worked [off and on]. It was simply faster than the winding bus route." After a particularly rough period of economic woes, the family moved to a small city in the interior of the state of Paraná, a neighboring state south of São Paulo. Robson's father missed the big city, and after three years, the family moved back, this time to the neighborhood of Parque Novo Mundo (New World Park).

For Robson, this place was perfectly named; it was, indeed, a "new world" and a new time of his life. Eager to work, Robson studied the transportation maps and was excited that New World Park was relatively close to Tatuapé, a "center" of *nouveau riche* affluence on the East Side of São Paulo since the late 1980s. Despite his family living in housing comparable to that of his childhood in the extreme East Side, Robson quickly identified himself as part of Tatuapé.

> Now, I live in Tatuapé. I take a short bus ride [15 minutes if there's no traffic] and I'm there at the subway station. I'm there at the big shopping mall with the movie theaters, everything is there. I'm ready to go to work on Paulista Avenue. I know these areas well now and invite my friends to places I see basically everyday on my way to and from work.

During our conversation, Robson and I debated about the exact whereabouts of Parque Novo Mundo. I questioned his choice of bus routes, maintaining that perhaps he might be better served taking a bus to Santana, a well-established middle-class neighborhood on the North side of town and home to a subway station on a different line, thus requiring only one line-change to arrive at Paulista Avenue. In fact, Robson's mother had impressed on me earlier in the visit that Parque Novo Mundo was, in fact, part of the "North Side" in terms of schooling and that she was happy to get away from the destitute East Side. For Robson, though, it was all about Tatuapé. "Derek, you don't understand the bus routes around here. It's a straight shot to Tatuapé. It's great and it's Tatuapé, not the run-down Santana. That place is old style."

Robson, his mother, and I were operating on slightly, but significantly, different models of social geography. We had different notions of value related to city spaces, and we evaluated modes of transportation (train, subway, and bus) in slightly different terms. In part, these discrepancies revealed useful information regarding sociological categories such as age, class, and nationality. In short, we learn that as interest and identifications shift, one's cartography of the city changes accordingly.

UNPACKING *CONDUÇÃO*

The English cognate of *condução* (conduct) is a complex puzzle. As an introduction to Edilaine's story, I'd like to bring together families of meaning and assert that within the idea of condução, we can discern connotations of transportation and behavior. The direct English cognate is "conduct"—in the sense of motion, such as a train conductor, or in the sense of direction within the realm of physics, such as certain metals that conduct heat. Certainly, a condução is a form of transportation and movement from one place to another. Yet, it is another set of connotations within "condução/conduct," both in contemporary English and in older Brazilian Portuguese, which I would like to explore. Of course, "conduct" also refers to demeanor and behavior and thus an index of class. In Brazilian Portuguese, the term condução is often one of employment contract, an agreement between worker and employer about wages. As I mentioned above, for millions of Brazilians in São Paulo, a single mode of transportation does not suffice; it is a complex matrix of trains, buses, kombis, subways, walking, etc. Frequently, employers negotiate some sort of compensation for this matrix—the category of condução. The term is deeply inflected with class, specifically the relations between patron and client, manager and laborer.

Part of this history directly relates to behavior, as there was a particular demeanor of respect, humility, and discipline associated with labor relations. While this is a transcultural phenomenon, Brazil articulated this relationship as a national hallmark. The so-called "cordial man" became one of the hallmark figures of Brazilian modernity. The famous Brazilian historian Sérgio Buarque de Hollanda theorized that this characterization of the Brazilian attitude by European visitors during the nineteenth and early twentieth centuries (and then echoed by elite Brazilians themselves) is not so much about "good manners" as it is related to a "sentimental capitalism," an attractive technique of doing business (Hollanda 1979 [1936]:106–107). A behavior of cordiality and apparent inclusion across stark racial and class lines thus became the Brazilian *jeitinho* (little way) of circumventing social differences and articulating a nascent spirit of nationalism by the 1930s.

This thumbnail sketch of Brazilian historical socioeconomic relations helps contextualize the narrative of Edilaine, a soft-spoken but increasingly opinionated woman, as she remembers moving from the working-class neighborhood of Freguesia do Ó to the upper-class district of Higienópolis. As mentioned above, Higienópolis is a neighborhood of extreme wealth, a place with its own mall designed with faux Greek columns and water fountains for the poodles of strolling madams.

Edilaine grew up during the military dictatorship in the late 1960s and throughout the 1970s in the working-class periphery neighborhood of Freguesia do Ó. Her smooth, dark brown skin and equally dark hair were certainly common enough at home. Then, as she worked her way through the world of journalism and later as an editor of a professional news release for medical doctors, Edilaine was addressed in "cordial" terms, such as "little Indian girl." At times, people assumed she was part of a circulating group of dark-skinned nannies who periodically strolled with light-skinned babies around neighborhoods such as her current place of residence, Higienópolis.

When asked about changes between her time in Freguesia do Ó and the present, Edilaine focuses on "attitude."

> I am very different now. I mean, I look basically the same, but I feel and act differently. I remember taking all sorts of complicated transportation [condução] to get to work and to journalism school. I remember talking to my first boss and accepting what was half of the transportation costs because I was afraid to explain to him the current costs. I remember feeling embarrassed; I just wanted to work and get out of there. I remember I used to pass by part of this neighborhood, Higienópolis, on my way to that first job downtown and thinking what it might be like to live here. Of course, I met my current husband, Nero, a medical doctor and leader of the physicians' union, and we years later were able to buy an apartment in this very neighborhood. I learned to forget about condução and all those annoying, trivial parts of periphery life. Of course, I now have my own condução of sorts [laughter], a private driver to take me or my daughters to their school and so on.

Edilaine turns linguistically on condução, a word that had haunted her younger years, as now she has control and can confidently take a position on the other side of the negotiating table with private chauffeurs and the like. Edilaine did admit that before the hiring of the private driver, she enjoyed taking the subway for reasons of "modernity." "I used to like the line that goes along Paulista Avenue. It was so new then [early 1990s] and was frequented by mostly business people, people who were modern and who read interesting looking newspapers and magazines. I loved going to the art theaters on Augusta Street right off the Consolação subway stop. That was different; the subway in this way is not a condução; it was almost a pleasure."

TRAVELS AND HISTORIES

In 2001, I made contact with Força Ativa, a legendary hip-hop organization founded in 1988 in the neighborhood cluster of Cidade Tiradentes. The district name is revealing in itself. "Tiradentes" (literally "pull teeth") refers to the nationalist martyr and dentist, Joaquim José da Silva, who, due primarily to his relatively lower-class standing, was the one sacrificed after the failed independence revolt against the Portuguese colonial regime in 1792. When traveling to Cidade Tiradentes it seems as though one has left São Paulo. By way of avenues named after industries, such as Textile and Metallurgy Avenues, one traverses long stretches of roads lined with occasional residential shacks and substantial forests. After going over a hill or two, one passes Negreiros, a supermarket chain located solely in the borderland regions of São Paulo's East Side. Take a right, and suddenly one faces an immense network of housing projects. Interestingly, the name "Negreiros" refers to the Portuguese slave ships. Part of the store's logo contains a longboat icon. I felt very odd when I first saw this emerging from the "nowhere" just prior. In fact, "negreiros" is an occasional, pejorative nickname for the buses that make the trek out to the extreme neighborhoods of the *periferia.* Conflating racism and class prejudice, *negreiros* is one more example of how Brazilians frequently invoke colonial metaphors of segregation and difference as part of contemporary imaginations. However, the above association is not the official one. "Negreiros" is also the title of one of the most famous poems by Castro Alves, an abolitionist of the late nineteenth century. Further investigation confirms this logic, as a cross-street is indeed called Castro Alves Lane.

City construction under the agency of COHAB (Metropolitan Company of Residence) began in the late 1970s, and in 1980, Cidade Tiradentes had 10,000 residents. Today, the population stands at over 500,000. In population, the district of Cidade Tiradentes is a city (*cidade*), a separate community boasting over 200 four-story residential buildings. The center plaza features a statue of Tiradentes, the historical martyr of Brazilian Independence. The purpose of my trip was to discuss the hip-hop organization's involvement in the opening of the community library. The library was part of a larger project called "Let's Read a Book: Center of Documentation and Youth Group for Human Rights" and was the result of over six years of negotiation between Força Ativa and COHAB.

While the stories of Robson and Edilaine represent individual relationships with urban transportation that reflect race, social class, age, and family, the case of the Cidade Tiradentes library is a collective statement of "occupa-

COHAB 1 on Eastside São Paulo. Cidade Tiradentes looks similar with a larger and more dense layout. [Photo by Derek Pardue]

tion." Hip-hoppers use the phrase *"conquistar espaço"* not only to refer to liter-ally "spatial occupation" but also as a value judgment related to a specific hip-hop event. If an artist or a group had a great, positive impact, they are said to have "occupied space" that particular day. Since the protagonists in virtually all of Brazilian hip-hop are periphery dwellers, there is a collective sense by extension that the result of a "good" show is that "we" in the periph-ery have, indeed, "occupied space" today.

It is not purely coincidental that the first hip-hop get-togethers in the early 1980s took place in the public space surrounding a downtown subway stop called São Bento. Similar to Edilaine's depiction of her "attitude," hip-hoppers have historically targeted public spaces to express a self and collec-tive confidence that they *are* somebody. Whereas Edilaine experienced "atti-tude" through socioeconomic upward mobility, hip-hoppers emphasize that their confidence and rights to public spaces are based on a morally deserved recognition. Perhaps better stated, hip-hoppers seek to control how they, and by extension periphery dwellers, are viewed—not as criminals or "marginals" (*marginais*) but as legitimate and knowledgeable citizens. This crusade toward a more "real" visibility began in the temporary city spaces, such as transpor-tation hubs, but has since moved on to more concrete institutions such as the Cidade Tiradentes library and the Casa de Cultura Hip-hop or Hip-hop House, recognized in 2007 by the Brazilian Federal Government as a "cul-tural point" within the national network of state subsidized projects of popu-lar culture.

For hip-hoppers, public transportation represents a stepping-stone to greater accomplishments in gaining recognition from society. In my case, traveling to Cidade Tiradentes and other far-flung periferia areas has served as a kind of "social capital" in my ongoing relationships with hip-hoppers. I have developed a certain extent of local knowledge, which affords me some authority and discursive grounds to participate in conversations. I do not claim comparison on any systematic level. Of course, I do not live in the per-iferia, knowing full well that I could and would leave relatively soon. For me, the anthropologist, the use of condução, the psychological sentiment and pragmatic knowledge of transportation systems and spaces, is an ethical tool to elicit meaningful stories.

DOING RESEARCH

The above narratives are three of many I have collected since 1995 when I first arrived in São Paulo. It would not be until years later that I would begin to reflect on my own circuits of urban motion and how they related to Brazil-ians from the periferia as well as to middle- and upper-class Brazilians. Cur-rently, there is an ever-looming crisis of transportation in São Paulo due to the increasing number of automobiles on the roadways. The infrastructure is crumbling, and government agencies have been unwilling and at times unable to invest in more extensive road networks and, even more important, a more cohesive public transportation matrix. What is missing from this chapter, but is certainly deserving of interpretation, are the narratives of middle-class Brazilians who, similar to their U.S. counterparts, find solace in being in their car. They are able to escape the madness of public transportation and create their own environment and deal more comfortably with the traffic outside the door. Furthermore, there are the narratives of the hundreds of thousands of São Paulo *motoqueiros,* the motorcycle deliverymen (almost all I have ever seen are men). They zoom by the "corridors" located in between the cars "like flies," so the colloquial description goes, and routinely come to a deadly end. Finally, there are the missing narratives of a growing number of elite São Paulo residents who travel by helicopter. São Paulo presently boasts the largest fleet of urban transportation helicopters in the world. Of course, as these numbers grow arithmetically, the number of periphery dwellers grows geometrically.

The "order and progress" manifested in São Paulo's transportation system and social geography is multifaceted. There are always "remainders" of modernity, and it is in their relationships that we, as scholars and engaged citizens, can glean knowledge about social difference and the power embedded in it. It is this sort of "reciprocity" that rapper Parteum rhymes about, and what I attempt to interpret when I write scholarly texts and give pedagogic presentations.

Notes

[1] See Davis (2006) and Packer (2006) for more about global slums, in particular regarding the microeconomic connections between urban districts and the larger impact of slums on the world as a whole.

[2] In his collection of essays, longtime hip-hop activist Walter Limonada makes the point that to be "of hip-hop" goes beyond the conventional forums of performance. One must consider the community leaders who open up spaces for hip-hoppers, hip-hop consumers, sympathetic and critical media, family members and scholars whose interests dovetail with the core themes of hip-hop (Limonada 2008:44–45).

[3] For a discussion of the similar historical processes in Rio de Janeiro, see Meade 1997.

[4] The *kombi* is a term for an old Volkswagen bus transformed into an informal bus. Until recently, there were thousands of kombis providing alternative routes for periferia residents. These routes were usually more effective although at times more dangerous. After 2004, the municipal government implemented a successful campaign to regulate the kombis and thus the "unofficial" status/stigma has been eliminated.

References

Caldeira, Teresa P. R. 2000. *City of Walls: Crime, Segregation, and Citizenship in São Paulo.* Berkeley: University of California Press.

Davis, Mike. 2006. *Planet of Slums.* New York: Verso.

Hollanda, Sérgio Buarque de. 1979 [1936]. *Raízes do Brasil,* 13th ed. Rio de Janeiro: Livraria José Olympio Editora.

Limonada, Walter. 2008. *Trokando umas idéias e rimando outras.* São Paulo: Gráfica Maxprint.

Meade, Teresa. 1997. *"Civilizing" Rio: Reform and Resistance in a Brazilian City, 1889-1930.* University Park: Pennsylvania State University Press.

Packer, George. 2006 The Megacity: Decoding the Chaos of Lagos. *The New Yorker,* November 13, 61–75.

Pardue, Derek. 2004. Putting *Mano* to Music: The Mediation of Race in Brazilian Rap. *Ethnomusicology Forum*, 13 (November):253–286.

———. 2008. *Ideologies of Marginality in Brazilian Hip Hop.* London: Palgrave Macmillan.

Sachs, Céline. 1999[1990]. *São Paulo: Políticas Públicas e Habitação Popular.* Translated into Portuguese by Cristina Murachco. São Paulo: Editora USP.

Discography

Mzuri Sana. 2006. *Ópera Oblíqua.* Trama.

PART 3

Urban Structures
and Institutions

The ecological approach to urban places, epitomized by Wirth's "Urbanism As a Way of Life," was soon challenged by anthropologists carrying out research in cities beyond the United States. We often did not encounter the social disorganization and individual alienation predicted by the theories of the Chicago School of Sociology. Instead, we found that living in cities—whether in Latin America, Africa, India, or the Middle East—could be a positive process for individuals, their families, and their extensive social networks. Indeed, we learned through our fieldwork that even recent migrants could become connected to other individuals of similar backgrounds and interests. How did such adaptations occur? And why did the experiences of urban dwellers in non-Western countries seem to be different from those reported in places like Chicago?

Extensive research in cities large and small around the world has shown that the urban structures and institutions in these far-flung places are critical to the successes—and failures—that people encounter in cities. One of the first, and most influential, studies to reveal the powerful impact of urban structures and institutions was that of Oscar Lewis (1952). In the late 1940s and early 1950s he conducted research in Mexico City on migrants from the peasant community of Tepoztlán, where the anthropologist Robert Redfield (1930) had done pioneering fieldwork a generation earlier. Describing what he called "urbanization without breakdown," Lewis demonstrated how social structures and institutions—especially family and social networks—help people adapt to urban life.

Continuing his research during the 1950s in Mexico City (and later in New York City, Puerto Rico, and Cuba), Lewis developed his controversial concept of the "culture of poverty." Scholarly and public reactions to his ideas launched a generation of research in Mexico, the U.S., and elsewhere. Not unlike what had occurred in the wake of Wirth's earlier work, Lewis's ideas provided the framework for a new anthropological focus on issues of urban poverty that coincided with the U.S. government's "War on Poverty" of the 1960s and 1970s.

These studies of urban poverty have demonstrated that poverty rarely is the "fault" of those who lack sufficient economic resources to meet their daily needs and those of their families. Far more frequently their poverty reflects the structural features of contemporary capitalist societies. Year after year, we hear reports about U.S. unemployment rates—with lows around 5 percent and highs above 10 percent—but these rates hide the challenges faced by residents in many urban communities where as many as half of the adults are without jobs. Lack of work opportunities has much to do with where you live, your education, your skills, and even who is in your social network—as many recent college graduates soon discover.

While social structures such as families and networks can help, urban institutions often make the difference in people's lives. Governments at all levels, from local to national, are key players in the urban systems in which people are embedded. In developing nations, international agencies and NGOs (nongovernmental organizations) can be critical to the survival of millions of people. Governments and NGOs can provide direct social welfare support to those in need; they can serve as mediators for local populations seeking external resources and opportunities for improving their lives; and they can act as consultants to provide support, information, and expertise in collaborative enterprises for local urban development. NGOs working among urban populations tend to focus their programs on specific targets, such as education for children or adults, gender equity issues, health and wellness, housing and homelessness, or the creation of jobs. In some urban communities, however, literally dozens of governmental agencies and NGOs tackle different pieces of the poverty problem, sometimes with too little coordination among their efforts.

Despite programs sponsored by governments and NGOs, urban residents often turn to alternative ways of supporting themselves and their families. Instead of typical nine-to-five jobs, men and women may be forced to pursue "opportunities" that others would define as illegal or even immoral. Yet, from a legal standpoint, at least, many of these "entrepreneurial schemes" and "petty crimes" might be deemed less unacceptable when compared with governmental corruption, corporate malfeasance, and high-level Ponzi schemes perpetrated by elites across the globe. Drug dealers, hustlers, prostitutes, panhandlers, and the homeless "work" each day to survive to the next. As a result, they are wise in the ways of the city.

To get a better idea of what it takes to survive in a city, whether in the United States or anywhere in the world, just imagine that this coming Friday evening, you will be unceremoniously deposited on the main street of a large city. To make your adventure a bit more challenging, your credit cards have been taken away and you have been given $25—and told that you will be picked up on Sunday evening. Soon, you discover that surviving for 48 hours on the funds in your pocket will not be easy. After a while, you will start looking for a bite to eat and a place to spend the night. Based on this information, we invite you to fill in the rest of the story—your plunge into the center of a large city.

Millions of people around the world endure similar challenges every day of their lives. They learn to use the available structures and institutions to survive from day to day, week to week, month to month, and year to year. The poor operate in urban spaces unknown to members of the middle class and the elite, while being aware of the affluent city all around them. This is the fundamental truth of the anthropological research reported in Part 3.

Following Lewis's vivid portrayal of the consequences of "The Culture of Poverty," Judith Goode provides evidence from the United States to counter the myths about the urban poor. She argues that people living in poverty are generally realistic about their situations and strive to find coping strategies that go beyond the welfare state to embrace an activist stance vis-à-vis their poverty. Philippe Bourgois shows how some urban residents go beyond the legitimate sector of the economy in seeking to overcome their situations. He describes the lives of Puerto Rican drug dealers, in the impoverished area of East Harlem in New York City, who have developed effective strategies for doing business in the underground economy. Another challenge of living in American cities involves the lack of affordable housing. Julie Adkins examines the role of The Stewpot, a faith-based homeless assistance center in downtown Dallas, Texas, in the lives of the 6,000 homeless persons struggling to make it from day to day and night to night in a city where some of America's wealthiest families make their homes.

Based on his long-term studies in Southern California, James Diego Vigil looks at the role of street gangs in the urban area. He shows how they provide a sense of community where other social structures and institutions fail to include young persons, especially Hispanic males. At the other end of the spectrum, Jay Sokolovsky shows that community gardens in New York City create important spaces where the wisdom of the elderly can be shared with the vigor of younger generations. These gardens become points of urban renewal, as overgrown, trash-filled lots are converted into spaces shared by community members committed to growing food and increasing social interaction. The challenge of sustaining social connections provides the framework within which William Jankowiak examines the lives of migrants to the provincial Chinese city of Hohhot. He reports that traditional neighborhood obligations tend to be discarded in favor of other forms of connectivity, especially those based on friendships established in school and the workplace and in the emerging bilateral multigenerational family. Finally, Jeffrey Witsoe examines caste, politics, and criminality in urban India. His chapter brings together the wide spectrum of anthropological concerns with urban structures and institutions, as he explores life in the city of Patna. Specifically, he shows that the political realignments that have taken place in India since the early 1990s have also transformed urban life, especially in mid-sized provincial cities like Patna, where the traditional power of upper-caste elites has been greatly weakened. Entering into the twenty-first century, the people of Patna find themselves facing fundamental changes in the city's social fabric, a breakdown of its public institutions, and a surge in criminal activities.

Part 3 offers case studies that challenge conventional wisdom about urban life. From Mexico City to Patna, with stops in a provincial Chinese city and in several American metropolitan areas, anthropologists use their field experiences to show how people in diverse cities work through political, religious, and social structures and institutions to make their way through the economic maze of urban life.

References

Lewis, Oscar. 1952. Urbanization without Breakdown. *The Scientific Monthly*, 75:31–41.
Redfield, Robert. 1930. *Tepoztlán: A Mexican Village*. Chicago: University of Chicago Press.

Readings in Part 3

12

The Culture of Poverty

Oscar Lewis

This chapter by Oscar Lewis is probably the most widely cited article ever written on poverty. Lewis first mentioned the "subculture of poverty" (later shortened to "culture") in his book Five Families *(1959), describing the daily lives of five Mexico City households. The concept appears again in his* Children of Sanchez *(1961), and later in its fully developed form in the introduction to* La Vida: A Puerto Rican Family in the Culture of Poverty *(1966a), and in an article in the journal* Scientific American *(1966b). Through the "culture of poverty" Lewis attempts to show that poverty is not just a matter of economic deprivation but that it also involves behavioral and personality traits. Once people adapt to poverty, attitudes and behaviors that initially developed in response to economic deprivation are passed on to subsequent generations through socialization. The implication that poverty is cultural has been severely criticized, as in the following chapter by Judith Goode, "How Urban Ethnography Counters Myths about the Poor."*

Although a great deal has been written about poverty and the poor, the concept of a culture of poverty is relatively new. I first suggested it in 1959 in my book *Five Families: Mexican Case Studies in the Culture of Poverty.* The phrase is a catchy one and has become widely used and misused. Michael Harrington used it extensively in his book *The Other America*, which played an important role in sparking the national antipoverty program in the United States. However, he used it in a somewhat broader and less technical sense than I had intended. I shall try to define it more precisely as a conceptual model, with special emphasis upon the distinction between poverty and the culture of poverty. The absence of intensive anthropological studies of poor families from a wide variety of national and cultural contexts, and especially from the socialist countries, is a serious handicap in formulating valid cross-cultural regularities. The model presented here is therefore provisional and subject to modification as new studies become available.

Throughout recorded history, in literature, in proverbs, and in popular sayings, we find two opposite evaluations of the nature of the poor. Some characterize the poor as blessed, virtuous, upright, serene, independent, honest, kind, and happy. Others characterize them as evil, mean, violent, sordid, and criminal. These contradictory and confusing evaluations are also reflected in the infighting that is going on in the current war against poverty. Some stress the great potential of the poor for self-help, leadership, and community organization, while others point to the sometimes irreversible, destructive effect of poverty upon individual character, and therefore emphasize the need for guidance and control to remain in the hands of the middle class, which presumably has better mental health.

These opposing views reflect a political power struggle between competing groups. However, some of the confusion results from the failure to distinguish between poverty per se and the culture of poverty and the tendency to focus upon the individual personality rather than upon the group—that is, the family and the slum community.

As an anthropologist I have tried to understand poverty and its associated traits as a culture or, more accurately, as a subculture with its own structure and rationale, as a way of life which is passed down from generation to generation along family lines. This view directs attention to the fact that the culture of poverty in modern nations is not only a matter of economic deprivation, of disorganization, or of the absence of something. It is also something positive and provides some rewards without which the poor could hardly carry on.

Elsewhere I have suggested that the culture of poverty transcends regional, rural-urban, and national differences and shows remarkable similarities in family structure, interpersonal relations, time orientation, value systems, and spending patterns. These cross-national similarities are examples of independent invention and convergence. They are common adaptations to common problems.

The culture of poverty can come into being in a variety of historical contexts. However, it tends to grow and flourish in societies with the following set of conditions: (1) a cash economy, wage labor, and production for profit; (2) a persistently high rate of unemployment and underemployment for unskilled labor; (3) low wages; (4) the failure to provide social, political, and economic organization, either on a voluntary basis or by government imposition, for the low-income population; (5) the existence of a bilateral kinship system rather than a unilateral one; and finally, (6) the existence of a set of values in the dominant class that stresses the accumulation of wealth and property, the possibility of upward mobility and thrift, and explains low economic status as the result of personal inadequacy or inferiority.

The way of life which develops among some of the poor under these conditions is the culture of poverty. It can best be studied in urban or rural slums and can be described in terms of some seventy interrelated social, economic, and psychological traits. However, the number of traits and the relationships between them may vary from society to society and from family to family. For example, in a highly literate society, illiteracy may be more diagnostic of the culture of poverty than in a society where illiteracy is widespread and where even the well-to-do may be illiterate, as in some Mexican peasant villages before the revolution.

The culture of poverty is both an adaptation and a reaction of the poor to their marginal position in a class-stratified, highly individuated, capitalistic society. It represents an effort to cope with feelings of hopelessness and despair which develop from the realization of the improbability of achieving success in terms of the values and goals of the larger society. Indeed, many of the traits of the culture of poverty can be viewed as attempts at local solutions for problems not met by existing institutions and agencies because the people are not eligible for them, cannot afford them, or are ignorant or suspicious of them. For example, unable to obtain credit from banks, they are thrown upon their own resources and organize informal credit devices without interest.

The culture of poverty, however, is not only an adaptation to a set of objective conditions of the larger society. Once it comes into existence it tends to perpetuate itself from generation to generation because of its effect on the children. By the time slum children are age six or seven they have usually absorbed the basic values and attitudes of their subculture and are not psychologically geared to take full advantage of changing conditions or increased opportunities which may occur in their lifetime.

Most frequently the culture of poverty develops when a stratified social and economic system is breaking down or is being replaced by another, as in the case of the transition from feudalism to capitalism or during periods of rapid technological change. Often it results from imperial conquest in which the native social and economic structure is smashed and the natives are maintained in a servile colonial status, sometimes for many generations. It can also occur in the process of detribalization, such as that now going on in Africa.

The most likely candidates for the culture of poverty are the people who come from the lower strata of a rapidly changing society and are already partially alienated from it. Thus landless rural workers who migrate to the cities can be expected to develop a culture of poverty much more readily than migrants from stable peasant villages with a well-organized traditional culture. In this connection there is a striking contrast between Latin America, where the rural population long ago made the transition from a tribal to a peasant society, and Africa, which is still close to its tribal heritage. . . .

The culture of poverty can be studied from various points of view: the relationship between the subculture and the larger society; the nature of the slum community; the nature of the family; and the attitudes, values, and character structure of the individual.

1. The lack of effective participation and integration of the poor in the major institutions of the larger society is one of the crucial characteristics of the culture of poverty. This is a complex matter and results from a variety of factors which may include lack of economic resources, segregation and dis-

crimination, fear, suspicion or apathy, and the development of local solutions for problems. However, "participation" in some of the institutions of the larger society—for example, in the jails, the army, and the public relief system—does not per se eliminate the traits of the culture of poverty. In the case of a relief system which barely keeps people alive, both the basic poverty and the sense of hopelessness are perpetuated rather than eliminated.

Low wages, chronic unemployment, and underemployment lead to low income, lack of property ownership, absence of savings, absence of food reserves in the home, and a chronic shortage of cash. These conditions reduce the possibility of effective participation in the larger economic system. And as a response to these conditions we find in the culture of poverty a high incidence of pawning of personal goods, borrowing from local moneylenders at usurious rates of interest, spontaneous informal credit devices organized by neighbors, the use of second-hand clothing and furniture, and the pattern of frequent buying of small quantities of food many times a day as the need arises.

People with a culture of poverty produce very little wealth and receive very little in return. They have a low level of literacy and education, usually do not belong to labor unions, are not members of political parties, generally do not participate in the national welfare agencies, and make very little use of banks, hospitals, department stores, museums, or art galleries. They have a critical attitude toward some of the basic institutions of the dominant classes, hatred of the police, mistrust of government and those in high position, and a cynicism which extends even to the church. This gives the culture of poverty a high potential for protest and for being used in political movements aimed against the existing social order.

People with a culture of poverty are aware of middle-class values, talk about them and even claim some of them as their own, but on the whole they do not live by them. Thus it is important to distinguish between what they say and what they do. For example, many will tell you that marriage by law, by the church, or by both, is the ideal form of marriage, but few will marry. To men who have no steady jobs or other sources of income, who do not own property and have no wealth to pass on to their children, who are present-time oriented and who want to avoid the expense and legal difficulties involved in formal marriage and divorce, free union or consensual marriage makes a lot of sense. Women will often turn down offers of marriage because they feel it ties them down to men who are immature, punishing, and generally unreliable. Women feel that consensual union gives them a better break; it gives them some of the freedom and flexibility that men have. By not giving the fathers of their children legal status as husbands, the women have a stronger claim on their children if they decide to leave their men. It also gives women exclusive rights to a house or any other property they may own.

2. When we look at the culture of poverty on the local community level, we find poor housing conditions, crowding, gregariousness, but above all a minimum of organization beyond the level of the nuclear and extended family. Occasionally there are informal, temporary groupings or voluntary asso-

ciations within slums. The existence of neighborhood gangs which cut across slum settlements represents a considerable advance beyond the zero point of the continuum that I have in mind. Indeed, it is the low level of organization that gives the culture of poverty its marginal and anachronistic quality in our highly complex, specialized, organized society. Most primitive peoples have achieved a higher level of sociocultural organization than our modern urban slum dwellers.

In spite of the generally low level of organization, there may be a sense of community and esprit de corps in urban slums and in slum neighborhoods. This can vary within a single city, or from region to region or country to country. The major factors influencing this variation are the size of the slum, its location and physical characteristics, length of residence, incidence of home and land-ownership (versus squatter rights), rentals, ethnicity, kinship ties, and freedom or lack of freedom of movement. When slums are separated from the surrounding area by enclosing walls or other physical barriers, when rents are low and fixed and stability of residence is great (twenty or thirty years), when the population constitutes a distinct ethnic, racial, or language group, is bound by ties of kinship or *compadrazgo*, and when there are some internal voluntary associations, then the sense of local community approaches that of a village community. In many cases this combination of favorable conditions does not exist. However, even where internal organization and esprit de corps are at a bare minimum and people move around a great deal, a sense of territoriality develops which sets off the slum neighborhoods from the rest of the city. In Mexico City and San Juan this sense of territoriality results from the unavailability of low-income housing outside the slum areas. . . .

3. On the family level the major traits of the culture of poverty are the absence of childhood as a specially prolonged and protected stage in the life cycle, early initiation into sex, free unions or consensual marriages, a relatively high incidence of the abandonment of wives and children, a trend toward female- or mother-centered families and consequently a much greater knowledge of maternal relatives, a strong predisposition to authoritarianism, lack of privacy, verbal emphasis upon family solidarity which is only rarely achieved because of sibling rivalry, and competition for limited goods and maternal affection.

4. On the level of the individual the major characteristics are a strong feeling of marginality, of helplessness, of dependence, and of inferiority. I found this to be true of slum dwellers in Mexico City and San Juan among families who do not constitute a distinct ethnic or racial group and who do not suffer from racial discrimination. In the United States, of course, the culture of poverty among African Americans has the additional disadvantage of racial discrimination, but as I have already suggested, this additional disadvantage contains a great potential for revolutionary protest and organization which seems to be absent in the slums of Mexico City or among the poor whites in the South.

Other traits include a high incidence of maternal deprivation, of orality, of weak ego structure, confusion of sexual identification, a lack of impulse control, a strong present-time orientation with relatively little ability to defer gratification and to plan for the future, a sense of resignation and fatalism, a widespread belief in male superiority, and a high tolerance for psychological pathology of all sorts.

People with a culture of poverty are provincial and locally oriented and have very little sense of history. They know only their own troubles, their own local conditions, their own neighborhood, their own way of life. Usually they do not have the knowledge, the vision, or the ideology to see the similarities between their problems and those of their counterparts elsewhere in the world. They are not class-conscious, although they are very sensitive indeed to status distinctions.

When the poor become class-conscious or active members of trade-union organizations, or when they adopt an internationalist outlook on the world, they are no longer part of the culture of poverty, although they may still be desperately poor. Any movement, be it religious, pacifist, or revolutionary, that organizes and gives hope to the poor and effectively promotes solidarity and a sense of identification with larger groups destroys the psychological and social core of the culture of poverty. In this connection, I suspect that the civil rights movement among African Americans in the United States has done more to improve their self-image and self-respect than have their economic advances, although, without doubt, the two are mutually reinforcing.

The distinction between poverty and the culture of poverty is basic to the model described here. There are degrees of poverty and many kinds of poor people. The culture of poverty refers to one way of life shared by poor people in given historical and social contexts. The economic traits which I have listed for the culture of poverty are necessary but not sufficient to define the phenomena I have in mind. There are a number of historical examples of very poor segments of the population that do not have a way of life that I would describe as a subculture of poverty. Here I should like to give four examples:

1. Many of the primitive or preliterate peoples studied by anthropologists suffer from dire poverty which is the result of poor technology and/or poor natural resources, or of both, but they do not have the traits of the subculture of poverty. Indeed, they do not constitute a subculture because their societies are not highly stratified. In spite of their poverty they have a relatively integrated, satisfying, and self-sufficient culture. Even the simplest food-gathering and hunting tribes have a considerable amount of organization, bands and band chiefs, tribal councils, and local self-government—traits which are not found in the culture of poverty.

2. In India the lower castes (the Chamars, the leather workers, and the Bhangis, the sweepers) may be desperately poor, both in the villages and in the cities, but most of them are integrated into the larger society and have their own *panchayat* organizations (a formal organization designed to provide caste leadership) which cut across village lines and give them a considerable

amount of power. (It may be that in the slums of Calcutta and Mumbai an incipient culture of poverty is developing. It would be highly desirable to do family studies there as a crucial test of the culture-of-poverty hypothesis.) In addition to the caste system, which gives individuals a sense of identity and belonging, there is still another factor, the clan system. Wherever there are unilateral kinship systems or clans one would not expect to find the culture of poverty, because a clan system gives people a sense of belonging to a corporate body with a history and a life of its own, thereby providing a sense of continuity, a sense of a past and of a future.

3. The Jews of eastern Europe were very poor, but they did not have many of the traits of the culture of poverty because of their tradition of literacy, the great value placed upon learning, the organization of the community around the rabbi, the proliferation of local voluntary associations, and their religion, which taught that they were the chosen people.

4. My fourth example is speculative and relates to socialism. On the basis of my limited experience in one socialist country—Cuba—and on the basis of my reading, I am inclined to believe that the culture of poverty does not exist in the socialist countries. I first went to Cuba in 1947 as a visiting professor for the State Department. At that time I began a study of a sugar plantation in Melena del Sur and of a slum in Havana. After the Castro Revolution I made my second trip to Cuba as a correspondent for a major magazine, and I revisited the same slum and some of the same families. The physical aspect of the slum had changed very little, except for a beautiful new nursery school. It was clear that the people were still desperately poor, but I found much less of the despair, apathy, and hopelessness that are so diagnostic of urban slums in the culture of poverty. [The slum dwellers] expressed great confidence in their leaders and hope for a better life in the future. The slum itself was now highly organized, with block committees, educational committees, party committees. The people had a new sense of power and importance. They were armed and were given a doctrine which glorified the lower class as the hope of humanity. (I was told by one Cuban official that they had practically eliminated delinquency by giving arms to the delinquents!)

It is my impression that the Castro regime—unlike Marx and Engels—did not write off the so-called lumpen proletariat as an inherently reactionary and anti-revolutionary force, but rather saw its revolutionary potential and tried to utilize it. In this connection, Frantz Fanon makes a similar evaluation of the role of the lumpen proletariat based upon his experience in the Algerian struggle for independence. He wrote:

> It is within this mass of humanity, this people of the shanty towns, at the core of the lumpen proletariat, that the rebellion will find its urban spearhead. For the lumpen proletariat, that horde of starving men, uprooted from their tribe and from their clan, constitutes one of the most spontaneous and most radically revolutionary forces of a colonized people. (1968:129)

My own studies of the urban poor in the slums of San Juan do not support the generalizations of Fanon. I have found very little revolutionary spirit or radical ideology among low-income Puerto Ricans. On the contrary, most of the families I studied were quite conservative politically, and about half of them were in favor of the Republican Statehood Party. It seems to me that the revolutionary potential of people with a culture of poverty will vary considerably according to the national context and the particular historical circumstances. In a country like Algeria which was fighting for its independence, the lumpen proletariat was drawn into the struggle and became a vital force. However, in countries like Puerto Rico, in which the movement for independence has very little mass support, and in countries like Mexico which achieved their independence a long time ago and are now in their postrevolutionary period, the lumpen proletariat is not a leading source of rebellion or of revolutionary spirit.

In effect, we find that in primitive societies and in caste societies, the culture of poverty does not develop. In socialist, fascist, and in highly developed capitalist societies with a welfare state, the culture of poverty flourishes in, and is generic to, the early free-enterprise stage of capitalism and . . . is also endemic in colonialism.

It is important to distinguish between different profiles in the subculture of poverty depending upon the national context in which these subcultures are found. If we think of the culture of poverty primarily in terms of the factor of integration in the larger society and a sense of identification with the great tradition of that society, or with a new emerging revolutionary tradition, then we will not be surprised that some slum dwellers with a lower per capita income may have moved farther away from the core characteristics of the culture of poverty than others with a higher per capita income. For example, Puerto Rico has a much higher per capita income than Mexico, yet Mexicans have a deeper sense of identity.

I have listed fatalism and a low level of aspiration as one of the key traits for the subculture of poverty. Here too, however, the national context makes a big difference. Certainly the level of aspiration of even the poorest sector of the population in a country like the United States with its traditional ideology of upward mobility and democracy is much higher than in more backward countries like Ecuador and Peru, where both the ideology and the actual possibilities of upward mobility are extremely limited and where authoritarian values still persist in both the urban and rural milieus.

Because of the advanced technology, high level of literacy, the development of mass media, and the relatively high aspiration level of all sectors of the population, especially when compared with underdeveloped nations, I believe that although there is still a great deal of poverty in the United States (estimates range from thirty to fifty million people), there is relatively little of what I would call the culture of poverty. My rough guess would be that only about 20 percent of the population below the poverty line (between six and ten million people) in the United States have characteristics which would justify classifying their way of life as that of a culture of poverty. Probably the largest sector within this group would consist of very low-income African Americans, Mexican Americans, Puerto Ricans, Native Americans, and Southern poor whites. The relatively small number of people in the United States with a culture of poverty is a positive factor because it is much more difficult to eliminate the culture of poverty than to eliminate poverty per se.

Middle-class people, and this would certainly include most social scientists, tend to concentrate on the negative aspects of the culture of poverty. They tend to associate negative valences [with] such traits as present-time orientation and concrete versus abstract orientation. I do not intend to idealize or romanticize the culture of poverty. As someone has said, "It is easier to praise poverty than to live in it"; yet some of the positive aspects which may flow from these traits must not be overlooked. Living in the present may develop a capacity for spontaneity and adventure, for the enjoyment of the sensual, the indulgence of impulse, which is often blunted in the middle-class, future-oriented man. Perhaps it is this reality of the moment which the existentialist writers are so desperately trying to recapture but which the culture of poverty experiences as natural, everyday phenomena. The frequent use of violence certainly provides a ready outlet for hostility so that people in the culture of poverty suffer less from repression than does the middle class.

In the traditional view, anthropologists have said that culture provides human beings with a design for living, with a ready-made set of solutions for human problems so that individuals don't have to begin all over again each generation. That is, the core of culture is its positive adaptive function. I, too, have called attention to some of the adaptive mechanisms in the culture of poverty—for example, the low aspiration level helps to reduce frustration, the legitimization of short-range hedonism makes possible spontaneity and enjoyment. However, on the whole it seems to me that it is a relatively thin culture. There is a great deal of pathos, suffering, and emptiness among those who live in the culture of poverty. It does not provide much support or long-range satisfaction and its encouragement of mistrust tends to magnify helplessness and isolation. Indeed, the poverty of culture is one of the crucial aspects of the culture of poverty.

The concept of the culture of poverty provides a high level of generalization, which, hopefully, will unify and explain a number of phenomena viewed as distinctive characteristics of racial, national, or regional groups. For example, matrifocality, a high incidence of consensual unions, and a high percentage of households headed by women, which have been thought to be distinctive of Caribbean family organization or of African American family life in the U.S.A., turn out to be traits of the culture of poverty and are found among diverse peoples in many parts of the world and among peoples who have had no history of slavery.

The concept of a cross-societal subculture of poverty enables us to see that many of the problems we think of as distinctively those of special racial or ethnic groups also exist in countries where there are no distinct ethnic minority groups. This suggests that the elimination of physical poverty per se may not be enough to eliminate the culture of poverty which is a whole way of life.

What is the future of the culture of poverty? In considering this question, one must distinguish between those countries in which it represents a relatively small segment of the population and those in which it constitutes a very large one. Obviously the solutions will differ in these two situations. In the United States, the major solution proposed by planners and social workers in dealing with multiple-problem families and the so-called hard core of poverty has been to attempt slowly to raise their level of living and to incorporate them into the middle class. Wherever possible, there has been some reliance upon psychiatric treatment.

In the underdeveloped countries, however, where great masses of people live in the culture of poverty, a social-work solution does not seem feasible. Because of the magnitude of the problem, psychiatrists can hardly begin to cope with it. They have all they can do to care for their own growing middle class. In these countries the people with a culture of poverty may seek a more revolutionary solution. By creating basic structural changes in society, by redistributing wealth, by organizing the poor and giving them a sense of belonging, of power, and of leadership, revolutions frequently succeed in abolishing some of the basic characteristics of the culture of poverty even when they do not succeed in abolishing poverty itself.

References

Fanon, Frantz. 1968. *The Wretched of the Earth*. New York: Grove Press.
Lewis, Oscar. 1959. *Five Families: Mexican Case Studies in the Culture of Poverty*. New York: Basic Books.
———. 1961. *The Children of Sanchez*. New York: Random House.
———. 1966a. *La Vida: A Puerto Rican Family in the Culture of Poverty*. New York: Random House.
———. 1966b. The Culture of Poverty. *Scientific American*, 215: 19–25.

13

How Urban Ethnography
Counters Myths about the Poor

Judith Goode

In this chapter, Judith Goode seeks to refute stereotypes of poor people as irrational human beings who must be retaught and regimented by governmental actions. She argues that the insights provided by urban ethnography have shown that poor people, given their limited choices, are just as rational in finding solutions to their problems as are people in other social strata. They are realistic about their own circumstances and are not any more self-destructive than are those who are affluent. Goode is critical of attempts to justify an unequal social order by blaming the poor for their circumstances while ignoring inequities in the political-economic structure. In particular, she criticizes Oscar Lewis's "Culture of Poverty" as legitimizing explanations of persistent poverty that lay the blame on pathological individual behavior and the culture of the poor.

Myths that justify an unequal social order by blaming those at the bottom for their own lowly position have been widespread throughout human history. Blaming the persistence of poverty in capitalist societies on the individual moral flaws and the deviant cultures of poor people is a belief that has developed along with industrial capitalism itself (H. Lewis 1971; Katz 1989). These ideas dehumanize poor people and make them into the "Other": people who are socially different, isolated from normal citizens, and threatening to society through crime, violence, and other moral lapses.[1]

Urban ethnography has been involved in both the generation and critique of myths about the behavior of the poor. In this chapter I will explore the contributions of such ethnography toward humanizing poor people in the face of sensationalized accounts of pathological personalities and dysfunctional family structures. Ethnography involves long-term, close-up, personal observation

Source: Written expressly for *Urban Life.*

and listening to people in the context of their everyday lives. Urban ethnography leads to new understandings of urban poverty in two ways. First, poor people are rehumanized as competent and moral social actors. Second, such descriptions of lived experience, especially when they are related to the context of larger political and economic constraints, helps to make sense out of seemingly irrational behaviors. This new understanding reveals the subtle ways in which public and private institutions such as government agencies or housing and labor markets sometimes exacerbate poverty and limit the possibility of choice for poor people. Recently, in order to respond to the popular view that the poor represent a major threat of violence to society, some analysts have begun to refer instead to these institutional pressures themselves as a form of *structural violence* against the poor (Sharff 1998).

The belief that poor people are culturally removed from the mainstream found in allusions to a "culture of poverty" or "underclass culture" is itself an aspect of the culture or ideology of industrial capitalism. Ideas such as these justify the existing social order with its significant inequality in resources. These justifications "blame the victim" (Ryan 1983). They encourage policies that focus on reforming flawed individuals rather than building on the ingenuity they demonstrate in strategies for survival. Such ideas also imply that since poverty is an intractable problem produced by inadequate individuals, there is nothing problematic about the political-economic structure itself. The following discussion will look at how the insights provided by ethnography refute several concepts that try to scientifically legitimize the moral and cultural explanations of the persistence of poverty.

During the Great Depression of the 1930s, significant attention was paid to how the nature of industrial capitalism itself—with its boom-and-bust cycles and continuously transforming structures—created poverty. As firms responded to the worldwide depression with massive layoffs, the shared vulnerability of so many produced a shift from blaming the poor to emphasis on the destructive structural uncertainties of the economy, and generated public acceptance of government's responsibility for public welfare through New Deal social programs.[2] At the same time, the right of labor to bargain collectively was legally enabled and, for a brief time, support for a living family wage became standard.

Nonetheless, in the second half of the twentieth century, beginning with the end of World War II and the start of the Cold War era, we have seen the growth of explanations of poverty that ignore the political-economic structure and lay blame on pathological individual behavior and the culture of the poor. Social scientists have legitimized these ideas as "scientific" in three formulations: the "culture of poverty" of Oscar Lewis, the notion of "welfare dependency" promulgated by Murray (1984), Gilder (1981) and Mead (1992), and the model of an "isolated underclass" by William Julius Wilson (1987). These ideas have been widely disseminated to middle-class Americans through books and popular journals.[3]

Oscar Lewis recognized that the "culture of poverty" was a response to both economic structures and concentrated social stigma for those at the bottom in capitalist societies. He states:

> The culture of poverty is both an adaptation and a reaction of the poor to their marginal position in a class stratified, highly individuated, capitalistic society. (see Lewis, this volume)

While Lewis provided a mass of information about the ingenuity of poor people's strategies in coping with a lack of jobs and income, their social lives are described in terms of pathologies that keep them in poverty: broken families, a lack of male presence, social isolation, flawed personalities, weak egos, and passivity. They are described as lacking future-time orientation and political awareness.

Lewis was mostly concerned with widespread poverty in the Third World, which he thought required revolutionary political mobilization to overcome. He was not specifically interested in poverty in the United States, which he saw as a minor "leftover" problem amenable to a "social work" solution that would work on individuals to change their flawed culture and behavior.

Lewis's ideas fitted well with American ideas of the time. In the postwar United States, "policy science" was emerging within social science. There was considerable optimism about the way that social problems could be solved through applying social scientific knowledge. Poverty was thus seen as a limited problem, easily eliminated in our affluent society. Lewis's ideas were used in War on Poverty programs in the 1960s to uplift the "leftover" poor.[4] This optimism about the ease with which poverty could be eradicated ignored the extremely uneven economic development in different regions in this country resulting from different levels of investment. For example, the South, until the advent of cheap air conditioning, and Appalachia were sites of underdevelopment. Some sectors of the economy were more advantaged than others depending on changes in technology and world market dynamics. Where you lived and the nature of the local industries had more to do with your success than your character. Lewis also ignored the persistence of institutional racism in the labor market that excluded people of color from family-wage jobs. Furthermore, he did not anticipate the economic crisis that would develop from expanding economic globalization in the 1970s.

ETHNOGRAPHIC INSIGHTS ABOUT COPING STRATEGIES

Before we look ahead, let us examine some of the insights about living in poverty generated by both Lewis and other urban anthropologists. Lewis's own ethnographic data often contradicted his negative formula for the culture of poverty (Valentine 1968; Eames and Goode 1973). In fact, we are indebted to Lewis for demonstrating many of the ingenious material coping practices among the Mexican and Puerto Rican poor. Other ethnographic work has built on Lewis's findings that many seemingly irrational economic and social behaviors are really survival skills that make perfect sense for the poor, who work on the margins of the labor market in high-turnover, low-wage jobs.

Rather than illustrating laziness and work avoidance, ethnographers have discovered that making ends meet involves hard work and management skills. Household strategies develop in which adults and children all combine irregular formal low-wage jobs, informal work, and income from government programs. Valentine (1978), Edin and Lein (1997), and Sharff (1998) provide data from poor communities and households that demonstrate the complex orchestration of work across the household by all members of a family.

Sharff (1987) describes the opportunity structure of one low-income neighborhood through the work experience of 133 families over a period of one year. In one case, a menial but steady job in the formal economy required a five-hour daily commute, but was short-lived because the employer did not tolerate lateness or absence. Informal work included not only drug dealing but also working as a street mechanic—fixing cars on sidewalks or in empty lots—or in the home-based production and sale of food and items for celebrations. Looking at household budgets, Sharff saw that many households actually depended on the work of their children in government funded summer jobs programs to tide them over the year.

Liebow (1967) and Valentine (1978) illustrate the ways in which the peripheral labor market limited people's choices and the cultural practices that emerged in response. Liebow (1967) and Bourgois (this volume) show why some kinds of work, especially in the high-risk, high-turnover, low-paying, dead-end segment of the labor market, are often rationally rejected. These jobs are all physically difficult, dangerous, and dirty. Liebow demonstrates that low-end construction labor is so physically demanding that only those in extraordinary shape with job continuity to maintain new musculature can last more than a short time. Bourgois examines how the demeaning experiences of young drug dealers who sought office work in the mainstream economy encouraged them to return to high-risk, violent work as the only way to achieve what they saw as mainstream success.

Informal credit pools that collect regular small contributions and distribute them through rotation or auction have developed throughout the world to help the urban poor cope with emergencies. Lewis demonstrates that informal savings can be achieved by storing wealth in expensive goods like furniture or appliances that can then be pawned. Sharff (1998) provides an example of how long-term layaway payments often work as a form of goal-oriented disciplined saving, leading to the acquisition of major desired commodities in spite of small incomes. Thus the kind of purchases viewed by the middle class as irrational and leading to undeserved spendthrift consumption is actually a form of savings.

Ethnographers have provided many insights about alternative (informal or underground) forms of production and consumption that poor people use. For example, self-built, makeshift housing; second-hand markets for clothing;

home-based production of cooked food and other commodities; and unlicensed transportation systems emerge and flourish in poor communities (Uzzell 1975). While viewed as illegal and substandard by bureaucrats and the middle class, these activities provide both sources of income and cheap commodities for the poor. Unfortunately, they also make it possible for the substandard wage system to persist without massive social protest, thereby subsidizing a system of inequality with a wide gap between the rich and poor. In a comparative analysis, Eames and Goode (1973) found these income-production and consumption practices as well as the sharing mechanisms discussed below to extend to the urban poor all over the world. The very complexity of these cultural adaptations rebuts the culture of poverty notion that the poor cannot plan for the future.

FAMILY STRUCTURE AND SHARING NETWORKS

Central to the survival of the poor are the informal sharing networks for mutual aid that develop between households in the face of deteriorating living conditions. These networks are based on kinship or *fictive* kinship, in which friends act like kin. In this way, one family that currently has housing or income in a social network can help out the struggling households to which it is linked. Peattie (1968) in Venezuela and Roberts (1973) in Guatemala both found that in the poor communities they studied, only a small fraction of the households had a steady income at a given time and that their steady jobs were short-lived. Nonetheless, by helping out their unemployed kin or friends, they insured that they would be supported when they lost their jobs.

In the 1970s, many anthropologists studied these sharing networks to rebut Lewis's view that the poor had no social relations outside the family. They were also concerned with debating the infamous Moynihan report, *The State of the Negro Family*, which, along with Lewis's ideas, had informed War on Poverty policy. The classic works of Stack (1974) about African Americans in a Midwest city, Lomnitz (1977) in a squatter settlement in Mexico City, and Safa (1974) in San Juan, Puerto Rico, revealed the cultural logic and practice of large extended family support networks. Carol Stack (1974) demonstrated that the multigenerational core networks of African American women in a midwestern urban community were adapted from preexisting forms developed earlier in the rural South and readapted to the precarious economic circumstances of deindustrializing northern cities. Eames and Goode (1973) surveyed similar women-centered networks among the poor in urban Africa and Asia. More recently, studies of how homeless families in the United States respond by "doubling up" or moving into the small apartments of kin or fictive kin provide still other examples of the strategic use of social ties (DeHavenon 1996).

When we look at households and their sharing networks, we see a preponderance of female-centered structures. Women head many households and develop and maintain network relationships. Even when people's traditional kinship systems were patrilineal, giving rights to children to the father's family, a move to the city and entry into the wage-labor market put the major burden for children on women for reasons discussed below.

In cross-cultural studies of the family, residential composition and child-care arrangements have long been seen as patterns that are very responsive to economic constraints. As Marvin Harris (1971:367) pointed out, when the job market for male labor is limited and unstable, and women have equal opportunities to earn income, the conjugal bond between men and women is weakened. The frequency of male unemployment and underemployment, coupled with the need to migrate long distances to look for work, makes the presence of husbands inconsistent and makes an unemployed male a drain on limited resources. Formal marriage is displaced by consensual unions that do not involve the costs of marriage and divorce and permit greater flexibility.

Consider the following facts for the case of African Americans in the United States. There is a long historical relationship between high rates of unemployment among black males resulting from labor market discrimination and consequently high labor force participation among black females, yielding more black women as primary wage earners and more black single motherhood (Mullings 1995). While this is the outcome of women not being able to count on consistent male economic assistance, it has also been exacerbated by biases against married couples in government programs (a problem discussed in more detail in a later section).

Yet, this by no means eliminates the presence of males from the household. First, fathers often retain a presence in the life of their children (Liebow 1967; Sharff 1998). In addition, a mother may rely on her own male relatives to help raise her children. Furthermore, the parents and siblings of the father often participate in the child's life even if the father is not around. In other words, even in the absence of formal marriage, a woman, by having a child, often extends her sharing network to include her nonformal "in-laws." Finally, new relationships with men may be developed to bring in extended support networks through the men's families. Sharff looks at why so many women continue to develop relationships with new men in the poor community that she studied ethnographically over more than a decade. She found that women who had no male kin to protect them in the increasingly dangerous neighborhood felt safer with males in the household and often found relationships with their new "in-laws" to be helpful as well.[5] Of course, social relationships are based on much more than mere calculated economic advantages. However, mating and reproduction decisions that look irresponsible from the outside often make good sense in the context of poverty.

Mullings (1995) shows that having children and making sacrifices for and investments in their future provide a major incentive for most of the black women whom she studied. Her ethnographic information rebuts the popular view that having children is a sign of immaturity or irresponsibility, or springs from the desire for more government support.

Ethnographic data that look at multihousehold mutual aid networks from the perspective of poor women turn all the underclass stereotypes about the dysfunction of female-headed households upside down. In depicting the underclass, a correlation between poverty and female-headed households is used to imply that such households are pathological and responsible for producing the moral pathologies of laziness, dependency, and hypersexuality. They are thus seen as the mechanism that perpetuates poverty. Ethnographic studies reveal these behaviors to be major coping structures to ameliorate the instability and uncertainty of living in poverty.

THE UNDERCLASS DEBATE

The idea of an "underclass" culture emerged in the 1980s in a period that witnessed new global economic integration and competition, which in turn led to deindustrialization as manufacturing was moved to cheaper labor markets—often outside the United States—while the U.S. economy was restructured as a service economy. The desire for a flexible labor force meant that jobs were less secure (downsizing) and the obligation to provide a family wage and job security was no longer acknowledged. Companies increasingly relied on contingent labor, that is, part-time or temporary work that offered few benefits. Unions, which had protected the living wage, were weakened. These trends were exacerbated as both people (predominantly middle-class whites) and new jobs moved to the post-war suburbs, leaving poor and minority populations in declining urban neighborhoods.[6]

In spite of the continued attacks on labor costs and the demand for flexible pools of labor, with few exceptions (for example Jencks and Peterson 1991; Katz 1993; Axinn and Stern 1988; Sassen 1992), discussions about the structural production of poverty played little role in antipoverty policy making at this time. Instead, cultural explanations were revived and strengthened (Goode and Maskovsky 2001). In fact, a massive political campaign for the withdrawal of funding from many programs in the War on Poverty occurred at the same time as wage rates declined and jobs became more insecure (Morgen and Weigt 2001).

At the same time, rising housing prices accompanied job instability to produce a rise in homelessness. In the 1980s, increased drug use and importation in the United States led to an increase in crime and violence that was felt predominantly in poor, increasingly minority neighborhoods where the retail drug distribution networks were located. Drug use itself was widespread in white suburbs. However, as drug distribution became the best paying, albeit most dangerous, underground job in the inner city, mandatory sentencing targeted minority youth from poor neighborhoods and led to unprecedented rates of incarceration (Buck 1992).

As the poor were increasingly represented in the media as black single mothers, they became stereotyped as hypersexualized, lazy, and immoral welfare cheats (Katz 1989), and were denied the virtues of motherhood accorded to middle-class women. Journalists often provided images of the poor through sensationalized glimpses of exotic deviant "cultures": remorseless, violent teenagers; clever, entrepreneurial drug dealers; and welfare mothers as passive victims. This further reinforced stereotypes and social distance between the middle class and the poor.

In a book entitled *The Underclass* (1983), journalist Kenneth Auletta described women on welfare as incomprehensibly bewildered and passive. His narrow and shallow descriptions of these women came from brief glimpses and snippets of conversation in the context of welfare offices. He did not examine why their actions made sense within the context of their everyday lives—a context that offered extremely limited choices. He coined the term "underclass," and it became widely used to describe a dehumanized, incomprehensible population, either predatory or bewildered and incompetent and greatly removed from the mainstream.

Other discussions of the underclass relied heavily on statistical data rather than close-up, long-term ethnographies by anthropologists. If you connected the statistical correlations between poverty and measures of deviant behavior with the media's brief snapshots of incomprehensible behavior, a picture of a depraved, dysfunctional underclass developed. This was a new version of the persistent pathological culture of poverty, in which people were "infected" by "epidemics" of crime, violence, and sexual irresponsibility.

The complex, nuanced understandings of these families receded from view in the face of these depraved images. Ethnographic explanations of how living in poverty encouraged female-headed households; why women-centered sharing networks made sense; how women invested in their children's futures; and the managerial skills required to weave together sources of income from formal work, the underground economy, and public programs were once again invisible. Such ideas could not compete with the sensationalized and dehumanizing accounts that implied that nothing could or should be done about the growing inequality—short of fixing flawed individuals. In fact, the very flexible household structures and sharing networks that allowed poor people to survive now became viewed as the main cause of persistent poverty.

During the Reagan years in the 1980s, cultural explanations of poverty were rampant as the War on Poverty was replaced by a war against the poor (Gans 1992). A new argument asserted that antipoverty programs themselves had created dependency and reinforced an underclass mentality. Writers like Gilder (1981), Murray (1984), and Mead (1992) argued that it was dependency on the state rather than poverty that destroyed people's lives. In his book *Losing Ground* (1984), Murray ignored the recent economic restructuring and argued that War on Poverty programs had destroyed the ethic of family and work among the poor. Such programs, he said, created "welfare dependency," which threatened the family by encouraging promiscuity and out-of-wedlock births as a way to increase cash assistance.

In contrast, William Julius Wilson's notion of the underclass recognized the importance of recent structural economic transformations. He traced the persistence of poverty fundamentally to the loss of good jobs during the processes of deindustrialization and restructuring. Furthermore, he argued for the importance of job creation in social policy. However, his work—like that of Lewis, Murray, and Mead—left the causal link between behavioral pathology and poverty intact. In *The Truly Disadvantaged* (1987), Wilson viewed poverty as perpetuated by "cultural" factors produced by the isolation of the ghetto and the spatial concentration of what he saw as behavioral pathologies and cultural deficits: unwed teenage motherhood, absent male role models, reliance on the underground economy, crime, drugs, and violence. Thus, Wilson also did not seem to realize that many of these practices—when seen within the context of people's limited choices—made sense for survival. Most significantly, he seemed unaware that these adaptive practices had long been characteristic of the urban poor within industrial capitalism in all times and places.

Wilson further attributed these pathologies to the flight of middle-class African Americans from the ghetto after affirmative action. This flight, he believed, removed positive cultural role models from communities and led to an increase in social pathology. As Brett Williams (1992) and Katherine Newman (1992) have pointed out, Wilson's picture of pathology is not substantiated by the grounded ethnographic analyses of the lives of the poor.

For Wilson, the best solution to poverty was to provide work for men so they could marry the mothers of their children and live in stable nuclear families (Di Leonardo 1998). This emphasis on the threat to family values especially resonated with the public at a time when Americans across classes were being affected by women's new roles as workers and by high rates of divorce. The growing awareness that we were experiencing a change to alternative forms of viable family structures led to a fear of "moral decline" brought on by the "contagion" of poor people's immorality.

Naples (1997) analyzed the congressional debates leading up to the rollback on welfare and characterized them as focusing almost entirely on family values and morality. So pervasive was this belief that even when massive research showed that women did not have children to add a few dollars to their welfare benefits, one congressman stated:

> Statistical evidence does not prove those suppositions [that welfare benefits are an incentive to bear children]; and yet even the most casual observer of public assistance programs understands there is indeed some relationship between the availability of welfare and the inclination of many young women to bear fatherless children. (Quoted in Watts and Astone 1997:415)

In other words, in spite of tangible evidence, everyone just "knows" that a causal relationship exists. This preoccupation with morality displaces any concern about growing economic inequality in the United States.

ETHNOGRAPHY AND THE CONTRADICTIONS OF WELFARE

Ethnographic studies show that welfare programs can indeed be criticized for their effects on the poor, but not in the ways that dependency theorists assert. In recent years, ethnographic research has explored the way poor people navigate the social service system. These studies demonstrate over and over that poor people want to work, and that the average length of time on welfare is short. Moreover, as Kingfisher (1996) demonstrates through her ethnographic analysis of welfare workers and clients, the bureaucratic nature of welfare applications and periodic face-to-face evaluation meetings with social workers mean that being on welfare is hard and demeaning work. It is also rife with contradictory rules arbitrarily applied. Furthermore, the most costly kinds of fraud or dishonesty in the system come from welfare landlords, health professionals, and other providers (Axinn and Stern 1988). For example, a whole sector of welfare housing has developed in response to welfare rent payments. Landlords are able to charge more for substandard housing. Because most of the housing market rejects welfare families, they are a captive population for welfare housing (Susser and Kreniske 1987).

The welfare dependency theorists ignored the fact that welfare benefits themselves were inadequate to support a family at the poverty line. Since the initial War on Poverty programs, reduction in benefits and/or failure to upgrade benefits in response to inflation have made it impossible for single mothers on welfare to make ends meet. The ethnographic work of Susser and Kreniske (1987) and Edin and Lein (1997) demonstrates how the practices of the welfare bureaucracy force subversion by those who must depend on it. People are increasingly forced to depend on banned work in the underground economy, which leaves them vulnerable to both sanctions and an image as welfare cheats. When the only rational response of recipients in many situations is to hide information, they become vulnerable to charges of fraud. This opens them up to exploitation by such service providers as landlords, who can threaten to inform on them, sometimes using false information.

Ethnographic work has long uncovered the ironic fact that state policy itself separates men from women and children. Stack (1974) first noted the effects that the oldest cash assistance program, Aid to Families with Dependent Children, had on removing men from families since it supported only single women and denied benefits to those who were discovered living with males. Through recent ethnographic work in homeless shelters and transitional housing in New York, Susser (1999) has found that state policies actually work to break up families by developing separate shelters for men and women, and removing teenage boys from shelters for women and children.

THE ACTIVIST POOR

In both the popular stereotype of those in poverty and the "scientized" formulations of the "culture of poverty" and "underclass," poor people are assumed to lack organization beyond the (broken) family (Lewis) or to be "isolated" in ghettos without competent political actors as role models. Both visions see the poor as politically incompetent, disengaged, and passive in regard to larger societal structures.

Here again, long-term ethnographic work contradicts this image. Poverty does not create crushing passivity but can produce active resistance and political activism. Lewis, whose ethnographic work largely took place through tape-recorded interviews of people away from their communities, was not in a position to observe much community organizing. He based his conclusions on a handful of households viewed as bounded entities. This was not a good vantage point for locating the significant informal and formal political organizing that so many other ethnographers have found in poor communities.

The first examples of the activism of the poor came from studies of Latin American squatter settlements (Leeds 1971; Lomnitz 1977; Roberts 1973; Peattie 1968; Uzzell 1975; and Safa 1974). In fact, Leeds used this work to specifically rebut Lewis's "culture of poverty" thesis. Much of the work demonstrated that communities who squatted on public land and invested money and labor in self-built housing developed links with the political system and were able to mobilize politically because they were vulnerable to state eradication and were interested in making their communities legal and/or gaining access to schools, electricity, and water.

Piven and Cloward (1971, 1979) have written much about the ways in which poor people in the United States participated in both the welfare rights and civil rights activism of the 1960s and 1970s, and have continued their activism within the War on Poverty program called Community Action Program (CAP). For example, Naples (1991, 1998) has described how poor women employed through CAP retained their earlier activist ideas and practices developed around issues of child safety and education.

Moreover, Bookman and Morgen (1988) argue that a meaningful definition of politics should include those everyday practices undertaken to change power relations. Recent in-depth analyses of poor women's lives have demonstrated that such women engage in politics in response to their concerns for their children. They do this by mobilizing their expanded informal networks to participate in broader coalitions and collective action. They participate as community builders and political activists making demands for resources in an era when the government has withdrawn services from poor communities. Many had learned political organizing skills as participants in the earlier movements noted above.

Poor white women, African American women, Latino women, and multiracial alliances of women and families have moved beyond the family to participate in a variety of collective social movements: seeking better schools (Goode 2001; Pardo 1998), preventing the removal of a local firehouse (Susser 1982), strengthening the role of activist community organizations (Naples 1998; Pardo 1998; Stack 1996; Goode 2001), and reinforcing tenant management in public housing (Hyatt 2001). Wagner (1993) has ethnographically analyzed a mobilization of homeless people in one New England city while Lyon-Callo (2001) has discussed the constraints on mobilizing the homeless in another city. Maskovsky (2000) analyzes the predicament of one group of poor, minority AIDS activists in Philadelphia. Each of these studies, like the squatter studies before them, attempts to understand the conditions under which political activities have the potential for success as well as to identify the strategies and tactics which account for success or failure.

VICTIMS OF STRUCTURAL VIOLENCE

It is important not to overemphasize the success of poor people's coping strategies. Recent trends toward a greater gap between rich and poor occurring in global cities (Sassen 1992; *Newsweek* 1993), coupled with the crises of homelessness, the increased impact of drug use in cities, the withdrawal of cash assistance to the poor, and the related prison expansion have only increased the misery of the poor and decreased their options for coping and the strength and capacity of their sharing networks (Goode and Maskovsky 2001).

In seeking to explain structural violence, ethnographers have written about poor people living in homeless shelters and other institutions, making their predicaments understandable in ways that do not blame them as individuals. Both Elliot Liebow in *Tell Them Who I Am* (1993) and Alisse Waterston in *Love, Sorrow and Rage* (1999) provide portraits of destitute women in residential institutions which allow us to see them as persons with dignity and resourcefulness, and as victims of the structural violence resulting from inequities in the labor and housing markets and contradictory bureaucratic rules in the criminal justice and welfare systems.

Structural violence leads to intolerable, deplorable living conditions that often produce culturally constructed beliefs that allow people to cope with intolerable circumstances in ways that are ultimately self-destructive but meaningful. Philippe Bourgois (1996) graphically describes violent self-destructive behavior among Puerto Rican drug dealers in New York. He sees these practices as a search for meaning and respect, which parodies the ideology of the larger society and its values: competition, advancement, and excessive material consumption. Unfortunately, by looking at the community from the vantage point of only those deeply involved in drug distribution, he does not put enough emphasis on the fact that this alternative drug culture is not the dominant pattern in poor neighborhoods. In contrast, the ethnographic work of Sharff (1998) shows that many boys may participate in the lower rungs of the trade for brief periods of time to provide income for their household, but few actually become permanently enmeshed. In other words, many boys are never involved in the drug trade, others use drug trading sporadically as a partial source of income in difficult times, and only a few become the violent predatory characters depicted by Bourgois.

CONCLUSIONS

Explaining poverty by blaming poor people's behavior has a long history in Western capitalism. During the expansion of industrial capitalism in the nineteenth century—as slums became more visible in Europe and America—

Social Darwinist ideas based on incipient scientific racism even argued that it was "natural" for the obviously inferior poor to be left alone so that the "survival of the fittest" could run its course. Looking at poor people's behavior instead of the political-economic system suggests that no change in the structure is necessary because some people are just unfit.

One step removed from this "biological" argument is the assumption that the poor are flawed individuals who need to be reformed by letting experts repair their damaged psyches and values. These ideas underlie the concepts of the "culture of poverty," "welfare dependency," and "the underclass." All of these ideas argue for a massive remaking, from the ground up, of individuals stereotyped as either violent and depraved, or passive, bewildered and lacking self-esteem. These drastic reform programs often take on aspects of punishment and control and operate in arbitrary and contradictory ways. One irony is that in trying to rebuild self-esteem into "faulty" individuals, a great deal of paternalism and disrespect is manifested by individuals and bureaucratic organizations.

The ethnography of the urban poor enables us to see up close how people struggle to make the best choices under dreadful conditions. The poor create strategies to cope and find meaning in their lives. These strategies include ways to stretch and save income as well as to make ends meet by managing a household labor pool that works in a complex set of unstable formal jobs, underground activities, and the "work" of dealing with social service bureaucracies. Critical to survival are the sharing networks that develop between female-headed households. In turn, these networks of females and often their male relatives, working hard to increase their children's life prospects, frequently engage in local community building and political activism.

Nonetheless, as the gap between the rich and poor keeps getting wider, as homelessness increases, as skewed rates of incarceration remove many young males from the community, and as the social safety net is loosened, support networks are weakened and individuals are more vulnerable. They do not have the resources of the middle class to deal with such problems as substance abuse and mental illness, which they share with the middle class.

The depiction of the life experiences of the poor illuminates the ways in which many societal structures, especially the wage-labor market and many of the social service bureaucracies, unintentionally work to perpetrate structural violence against the poor. Instead of working to reform the poor, ethnographic work argues for reforming these structures and building on the personal and social strengths of poor people themselves.

Notes

[1] The notion that poor people have moral flaws that cause and perpetuate their poverty has become firmly embedded in modern European, American, and increasingly international thought as industrial capitalism expanded in the last two centuries. In one form or another, it has been expressed since the seventeenth-century Elizabethan Poor Laws (Piven and Cloward 1971; Eames and Goode 1973).

[2] Social welfare programs soon followed in other industrial countries, where they surpassed the United States in protecting populations from social risk.

[3] Oscar Lewis's definition of the "culture of poverty" was first published in his best-selling monograph *La Vida* (1966) and then in the popular journal *Scientific American*. It was adopted by Michael Harrington and incorporated in his best-selling work, *The Other America*. Journalist Ken Auletta publicized this concept in a series of articles in the *New Yorker* which later formed the basis of his best-selling book, *The Underclass* (1983).

[4] Lewis's work influenced several War on Poverty programs in the 1960s. Ironically, since this was not his intent, the concept had more impact on United States policy than elsewhere. His work was influential in shaping and reinforcing the work of others, such as the Moynihan report on the black family (1965) and psychological research "proving" that the poor could not defer gratification (Miller, Reissman, and Seagull 1965), which served to justify an emphasis on programs that worked on the "culture" of the poor and deflected attention from issues of redistribution.

[5] Women's particular circumstances, such as whether they had adult sons or helpful brothers, made a big difference in how they dealt with the dangers of local street violence that accompanied the expanding drug trade.

[6] Brodkin (1998) demonstrates how postwar policies such as the GI Bill and FHA mortgages acted as a major affirmative action program to create a new, white, suburban middle class. Minorities were formally and informally excluded from these advantages. Later in the 1980s, Reagan tax policy created an economic redistribution that shifted more wealth to the top and widened the gap between top and bottom (Phillips 1990; Barlett and Steele 1992).

Acknowledgments

I would like to thank Edwin Eames for his collaboration in earlier versions of this work. Thanks also go to Jeff Maskovsky, whose insights about poverty have been profoundly important in my thinking. I also am indebted to my colleague and fellow poverty researcher, Susan Hyatt, for her insights about women's networks. Richard J. Malloy provided crucial insights about the reiterations of the culture of poverty debate.

References

Auletta, Ken. 1983. *The Underclass*. New York: Vintage.

Axinn, June, and Mark Stern. 1988. *Dependency and Poverty: Old Problems in a New World*. Lexington, MA: Lexington.

Barlett, Donald L., and James B. Steele. 1992. *America: What Went Wrong?* Kansas City, MO: Andrews and McMeel.

Bookman, Ann, and Sandra Morgen, eds. 1988. *Women and the Politics of Empowerment*. Philadelphia: Temple University Press.

Bourgois, Philippe. 1996. *In Search of Respect: Selling Crack in El Barrio*. Cambridge: Cambridge University Press.

Brodkin, Karen. 1998. *How Jews Became White Folks and What This Says About Race in America*. New Brunswick: Rutgers University Press.

Buck, Pem. 1992. With Our Heads in the Sand: The Racist Right, Concentration Camps and the Incarceration of People of Color. *Transforming Anthropology*, 3: 13–18.

DeHavenon, Anna Lou. 1996. Doubling-Up and New York City's Policies for Sheltering Homeless Families. In *There's No Place Like Home: Anthropological Perspectives on Housing and Homelessness in the United States*, ed. Anna Lou DeHavenon, pp. 51–66. Westport, CT: Bergin and Garvey.

Di Leonardo, Micaela. 1998. *Exotics at Home: Anthropologies, Others and American Modernity*. Chicago: University of Chicago Press.

Eames, Edwin, and Judith Granich Goode. 1973. *Urban Poverty in a Cross-Cultural Context*. New York: The Free Press.

Edin, Kathryn, and Laura Lein. 1997. *Making Ends Meet: How Single Mothers Survive Welfare and Low-Wage Work.* New York: Russell Sage Foundation.

Gans, Herbert. 1992. The War Against the Poor Instead of Programs to End Poverty. In *Dissent*, Fall: 461–65.

Gilder, George. 1981. *Wealth and Poverty.* New York: Bantam Books.

Goode, Judith. 2001. Let's Get Our Act Together: How Racial Discourses Disrupt Neighborhood Activism. In *The New Poverty Studies: The Ethnography of Power, Politics, and Impoverished People in the United States*, eds. Judith Goode and Jeff Maskovsky, pp. 364–398. New York: New York University Press.

Goode, Judith, and Jeff Maskovsky, eds. 2001. *The New Poverty Studies: The Ethnography of Power, Politics, and Impoverished People in the United States.* New York: New York University Press.

Harris, Marvin. 1971. *Culture, Nature and Man.* New York: Crowell.

Hyatt, Susan Brin. 2001. From Citizen to Volunteer: Neoliberal Governance and the Erasure of Poverty. In *The New Poverty Studies: The Ethnography of Power, Politics, and Impoverished People in the United States*, eds. Judith Goode and Jeff Maskovsky, pp. 201–235. New York: New York University Press.

Jencks, Christopher, and Paul E. Peterson, eds. 1991. *The Urban Underclass.* Washington, DC: The Brookings Institution.

Katz, Michael. 1986. *In the Shadow of the Poorhouse: A Social History of Welfare in America.* New York: Basic Books.

———. 1989. *The Undeserving Poor: From the War on Poverty to the War on Welfare.* New York: Pantheon Books.

———. 1993. *The "Underclass" Debate: Views From History.* Princeton, NJ: Princeton University Press.

Kingfisher, Catherine. 1996. *Women in the American Welfare Trap.* Philadelphia: University of Pennsylvania Press.

Leeds, Anthony. 1971. The Concept of the "Culture of Poverty": Conceptual, Logical and Empirical Problems with Perspectives from Brazil and Peru. In *The Culture of Poverty: A Critique*, ed. E. Leacock, pp. 226–284. New York: Simon and Schuster.

Lewis, Hylan. 1971. Culture of Poverty? What Does it Matter? In *The Culture of Poverty: A Critique*, ed. E. Leacock, pp. 345–363. New York: Simon and Schuster.

Lewis, Oscar. 1966. *La Vida: A Puerto Rican Family in the Culture of Poverty.* New York: Random House.

Liebow, Elliot. 1967. *Tally's Corner.* Boston: Little, Brown.

———. 1993. *Tell Them Who I Am: The Lives of Homeless Women.* New York: Free Press.

Lomnitz, Larissa. 1977. *Networks and Marginality: Life in a Mexican Shanty Town.* New York: Academic Press.

Lyon-Callo, Vincent. 2001. Homelessness, Employment, and Structural Violence: Exploring Constraints on Collective Mobilizations Against Systemic Inequality. In *The New Poverty Studies: The Ethnography of Power, Politics, and Impoverished People in the United States*, eds. Judith Goode and Jeff Maskovsky, pp. 293–318. New York: New York University Press.

Marks, Carol. 1991. The Urban Underclass. *Annual Review of Sociology*, 17: 445–66.

Maskovsky, Jeff. 2000. Fighting for Our Lives: Poverty and AIDS Activism in Neoliberal Philadelphia. Unpublished Ph.D. dissertation, Temple University, Philadelphia, PA.

Mead, Lawrence M. 1992. *The New Politics of Poverty: The Non-Working Poor in America.* New York: Basic Books.

Miller, S. M., Frank Reissman, and Arthur A. Seagull. 1965. Poverty and Self-Indulgence: A Critique of the Non-Deferred Gratification Pattern. In *Poverty in America*, ed. Louis A. Ferman, Joyce L. Kornbluh, and A. Haber, pp. 285–302. Ann Arbor: University of Michigan Press.

Morgen, Sandra, and Jill Weigt. 2001. Poor Women, "Fair Work," and Welfare-To-Work That Works. In *The New Poverty Studies: The Ethnography of Power, Politics, and Impoverished People in the United States*, eds. Judith Goode and Jeff Maskovsky, pp. 152–178. New York: New York University Press.

Moynihan, Daniel. 1965. *The Negro Family: The Case for National Action.* Washington, DC: Department of Labor.

Mullings, Leith. 1995. Households Headed by Women: The Politics of Race, Class and Gender. In *Conceiving the New World Order: The Global Politics of Reproduction*, eds. Faye Ginsburg and Rayna Rapp, pp. 122–139. Berkeley: University of California Press.

Murray, Charles. 1984. *Losing Ground: American Social Policy 1950–1980.* New York: Basic Books.

Naples, Nancy A. 1991. Contradictions in the Gender Subtext of the War on Poverty: The Community Work and Resistance of Women from Low Income Communities. *Social Problems,* 38(3):316–332.

———. 1997. The "New Consensus on the Gendered Social Contract": The 1987–1988 U.S. Congressional Hearings on Welfare Reform. *Signs: The Journal of Women in Culture and Society,* 22(4):907–945.

———. 1998. *Grassroots Warriors: Activist Mothering, Community Work and the War on Poverty.* New York: Routledge.

Newman, Katherine. 1992. Culture and Structure in "The Truly Disadvantaged." *City and Society,* 6: 3–25.

Newsweek. 1993. America's Poor Showing. October 18: 44.

Pardo, Mary S. 1998. *Mexican American Women Activists: Identity and Resistance in Two Los Angeles Communities.* Philadelphia: Temple University Press.

Peattie, Lisa. 1968. *The View from the Barrio.* Ann Arbor: University of Michigan Press.

Phillips, Kevin. 1990. *The Politics of Rich and Poor: Wealth and the Electorate in the Reagan Aftermath.* New York: Random House.

Piven, Francis Fox, and Richard Cloward. 1971. *Regulating the Poor: The Functions of Public Welfare.* New York: Pantheon Books.

———. 1979. *Poor People's Movements: Why They Succeed and How They Fail.* New York: Vintage Books.

Roberts, Bryan. 1973. *Organizing Strangers.* Austin: University of Texas Press.

Ryan, William. 1983. *Blaming the Victim.* New York: Vantage Books.

Safa, Helen. 1974. *The Urban Poor of Puerto Rico: A Study of Development and Inequality.* New York: Holt, Rinehart and Winston.

Sassen, Saskia. 1992. *The Global City: New York, London and Tokyo.* Princeton, NJ: Princeton University Press.

Sharff, Jagna. 1987. The Underground Economy of a Poor Neighborhood. In *Cities of the United States: Studies in Urban Anthropology*, ed. Leith Mullings, pp. 19–50. New York: Columbia University Press.

———. 1998. *King Kong on 4th Street: Families and the Violence of Poverty on the Lower East Side.* Boulder, CO: Westview Press.

Stack, Carol. 1974. *All Our Kin.* New York: Harper and Row.

———. 1996. *Call to Home: African Americans Reclaim the Rural South.* New York: Basic Books.

Susser, Ida. 1982. *Norman Street*. New York: Columbia University Press.

————. 1999. Creating Family Forms: The Exclusion of Men and Teenage Boys from Families in the New York City Shelter System, 1987–1991. In *Theorizing the City*, ed. Setha Low, pp. 67–82. New Brunswick: Rutgers University Press.

Susser, Ida, and John Kreniske. 1987. The Welfare Trap. In *Cities of the United States: Studies in Urban Anthropology*, ed. Leith Mullings, pp. 51–70. New York: Columbia University Press.

Uzzell, Douglas. 1975. The Interaction of Population and Locality in the Development of Squatter Settlements in Lima. In *Latin American Urban Research*, vol. 4, eds. Wayne A. Cornelius and Felicity Trueblood, pp. 113–134. Beverly Hills: Sage Publications.

Valentine, Bettylou. 1978. *Hustling and Other Hard Work*. New York: Free Press.

Valentine, Charles. 1968. *Culture and Poverty: A Critique and Counterproposal*. Chicago: University of Chicago Press.

Wagner, David. 1993. *Checkerboard Square: Culture and Resistance in a Homeless Community*. Boulder, CO: Westview Press.

Waterston, Alisse. 1999. *Love, Sorrow and Rage: Destitute Women in a Manhattan Residence*. Philadelphia: Temple University Press.

Watts, Jerry, and Nan Marie Astone. 1997. The Personal Responsibility and Work Opportunity Reconciliation Act of 1996. *Contemporary Sociology*, 26: 409–415.

Williams, Brett. 1992. Poverty among African Americans in the Urban United States. *Human Organization*, 51(2):164–174.

Wilson, William J. 1987. *The Truly Disadvantaged: The Inner City, The Underclass and Public Policy*. Chicago: University of Chicago Press.

14

Office Work and the Crack Alternative among Puerto Rican Drug Dealers in East Harlem

Philippe Bourgois

In this chapter, Philippe Bourgois shows that those who become drug dealers do so for a variety of reasons. One has to do with the quality of work which they find in the legitimate sector of the economy. Drug dealers, as he shows, have had legal jobs, but they find their relationships with their superiors in these jobs unsatisfactory. In the incidents described here, the young Puerto Ricans felt unable to use the ways of behaving that they had learned in El Barrio in mainstream jobs, both because of their Latino heritage and because of the differences between the street culture and that of the office and factory. Gender, class, and ethnic and racial identity all play a role in the antagonism felt by Caesar and Primo toward their immediate superiors. Both the office and the street are arenas for these conflicts, and Bourgois emphasizes that the structure of power and conflict can lead to self-destruction.

For approximately three and a half years during the late 1980s and early 1990s, I lived with my wife and young son in an irregularly heated, rat-filled tenement in East Harlem, New York. This two-hundred-square-block neighborhood—better known locally as *El Barrio* or Spanish Harlem—is visibly impoverished yet it is located in the heart of New York, one of the richest cities in the Western Hemisphere. It is just a stone's throw from multimillion-dollar condominiums, and in the 2000s was undergoing rapid gentrification. Although one in three families survived on some form of public assistance in

Source: This chapter draws from Bourgois, Philippe. 1995. *In Search of Respect: Selling Crack in El Barrio* (New York: Cambridge University Press).

East Harlem child biking through a block of abandoned buildings. [Photo by Philippe Bourgois]

1990, the majority of El Barrio's 110,600 Puerto Rican and African American residents fell into the ranks of the working poor.[1] They eked out an uneasy subsistence in entry-level service and manufacturing jobs in one of the most expensive cities in the world.

The public sector (e.g., the police, social welfare agencies, the Sanitation Department) had broken down in El Barrio and was not functioning effectively. This caused the legally employed residents of the neighborhood to lose control of their streets and public spaces to the drug economy. My tenement's block was not atypical, and within a few hundred yards' radius I could obtain heroin, crack, powder cocaine, hypodermic needles, methadone, Valium, angel dust,[2] marijuana, mescaline, bootleg alcohol, and tobacco. Within 200 feet of my stoop there were three competing crack houses selling vials at two, three, and five dollars. Several doctors operated "pill mills" on the blocks around me, writing prescriptions for opiates and barbiturates upon demand. Within view of my living-room window, the Housing Authority police arrested a 55-year-old mother and her 22-year-old daughter while they were "bagging" 22 pounds of cocaine into $10 quarter-gram "Jumbo" vials of adulterated product worth over a million dollars on the streets. The police found $25,000 in cash in small-denomination bills in that same apartment. In other words, millions of dollars' worth of business was going on directly in front of the youths growing up in East Harlem tenements and housing projects. Why should these young men and women take the subway downtown to work poorly paid, entry-level jobs in downtown offices when they can usu-ally earn more, at least in the short run, by selling drugs on the street corner in front of their apartment or schoolyard?

The dynamic underground economy is predicated on violence and sub-stance abuse. It has spawned what I call a "street culture" of resistance and self-destruction. The central concern of my study is the relationship of street culture to the worlds of work accessible to street dealers—that is, the legal and illegal labor markets that employ them and give meaning to their lives. I hope to show the local-level implications of the global-level restructuring of the U.S. economy away from factory production and toward services. In the process, I have recorded the words and experiences of some unrepentant vic-tims who are part of a network of some 25 street-level crack dealers operating on and around the block where I lived. To summarize, I am arguing that the transformation from manufacturing to service employment—especially in the professional office work setting—is much more culturally disruptive than the already revealing statistics on reductions in income, employment, union-ization, and workers' benefits would indicate. Low-level service sector employment engenders a humiliating ideological—or cultural—confronta-tion between a powerful corps of white office executives and their assistants versus a younger generation of poorly educated, alienated, "colored" work-ers. It also often takes the form of a sharply polarized confrontation over gen-der roles.

SHATTERED WORKING-CLASS DREAMS

All the crack dealers and addicts I interviewed had worked at one or more legal jobs in their early youth. In fact, most entered the labor market at a younger age than the typical American. Before they were 12 years old they were bagging groceries at the supermarket for tips, stocking beers off-the-books in local *bodegas*, or shining shoes. For example, Primo, the night manager at a video game arcade that sells five-dollar vials of crack on the block where I lived, pur-sued a traditional working-class dream in his early adolescence. With the sup-port of his extended kin who were all immersed in a working-class "common sense," he dropped out of junior high school to work in a local garment factory:

> I was like 14 or 15 playing hooky and pressing dresses and whatever they were making on the steamer. They was cheap, cheap clothes.
>
> My mother's sister was working there first and then her son, my cousin Willie—the one who's in jail now—was the one they hired first, because his mother agreed: "If you don't want to go to school, you gotta work."
>
> So I started hanging out with him. I wasn't planning on working in the factory. I was supposed to be in school; but it just sort of happened.

Ironically, young Primo actually became the agent who physically moved the factory out of the inner city. In the process, he became merely one more of the 445,900 manufacturing workers in New York City who lost their jobs as factory employment dropped 50 percent from 1963 to 1983 (Romo and Schwartz 1993).

Almost all the crack dealers had similar tales of former factory jobs. For poor adolescents, the decision to drop out of school and become a marginal factory worker is attractive. It provides the employed youth with access to the childhood "necessities"—sneakers, basketballs, store-bought snacks—that 16-year-olds who stay in school cannot afford. In the descriptions of their first forays into legal factory-based employment, one hears clearly the extent to which they, and their families, subscribed to mainstream working-class ideologies about the dignity of engaging in "hard work" rather than education.

Had these enterprising, early-adolescent workers from El Barrio not been confined to the weakest sector of manufacturing in a period of rapid job loss, their teenage working-class dreams might have stabilized. Instead, upon reaching their mid-20s, they discovered themselves to be unemployable high school dropouts. This painful realization of social marginalization expresses itself across a generational divide. The parents and grandparents of the street-sellers often continued to maintain working-class values of honesty and hard work, which conflicted violently with the reality of their children's immersion in street culture. Street-sellers are often accused of slothfulness by their mothers and even by friends who have managed to maintain legal jobs. They do not have a regional perspective on the dearth of adequate entry-level jobs available to "functional illiterates" in New York, and they begin to suspect that they might indeed be *vago bons* (lazy bums) who do not *want* to work hard and cannot help themselves. Confused, they take refuge in an alternative search for career, meaning, and ecstasy in substance abuse.

Formerly, when most entry-level jobs were found in factories, the contradiction between an oppositional street culture and traditional working-class, masculine, shop-floor culture was less pronounced—especially when the work site was protected by a union. Factories are inevitably rife with confrontational hierarchies. Nevertheless, on the shop-floor, surrounded by older union workers, high school dropouts who are well versed in the latest and toughest street culture styles function effectively. In the factory, being tough and violently macho has high cultural value; a certain degree of opposition to the foreman and the "bossman" is expected and is considered appropriate.

In contrast, this same oppositional street-identity is nonfunctional in the professional office worker service sector that has burgeoned in New York's high-finance-driven economy. It does not allow for the humble, obedient, social interaction—often across gender lines—that professional office workers routinely impose on their subordinates. A qualitative change has occurred, therefore, in the tenor of social interaction in office-based employment. Workers in a mail room or behind a photocopy machine cannot publicly maintain their cultural autonomy. Most concretely, they have no union; more subtly, there are few fellow workers surrounding them to insulate them and to provide them with a culturally based sense of class solidarity.[3] Instead they are besieged by supervisors and bosses from an alien, hostile, and obviously dominant culture who ridicule street culture. Workers like Primo appear inarticulate to their professional supervisors when they try to imitate the language of power in the workplace and instead stumble pathetically over the enunciation of unfamiliar words. They cannot decipher the hastily scribbled instructions—rife with mysterious abbreviations—that are left for them by harried office managers. The "common sense" of white-collar work is foreign to them; they do not know how to write memos or set up filing systems. When they attempt to show initiative and improvise they often fail miserably and instead appear inefficient, or even hostile, for failing to follow "clearly specified" instructions.

Their "social skills" are even more inadequate than their limited professional capacities. They do not know how to look at their fellow co-service workers, let alone their supervisors, without intimidating them. They cannot walk down the hallway to the water fountain without unconsciously swaying their shoulders aggressively as if patrolling their home turf. Gender barriers are an even more culturally charged realm. They are reprimanded for harassing female coworkers.

The cultural clash between white "yuppie" power and inner-city street-smarts in the service sector is much more than a superficial question of style. It is about access to "cultural and symbolic capital" and power (see Bourdieu 2000; Bourdieu and Wacquant 1992). Service workers who are incapable of obeying the rules of interpersonal interaction dictated by professional office culture will never be upwardly mobile. Their supervisors will think they are dumb or have a "bad attitude." Once again, a gender dynamic exacerbates the confusion and sense of insult experienced by young, male inner-city employees because most supervisors in the lowest reaches of the service sector are women. Street culture makes it difficult for males to maintain their sense of self-respect when they are subordinated across gender lines.

"GETTIN' DISSED"

On the street, the trauma of experiencing a threat to one's personal dignity has been frozen linguistically in the commonly used phrase "to diss," which is short for "to disrespect." Significantly, one generation ago ethnographers working in rural Puerto Rico specifically noted the importance of the traditional Puerto Rican concept of *respeto* in mediating labor relations:

> The good owner "respects" (*respeta*) the laborer . . . It is probably to the interest of the landowner to make concessions to his best workers, to deal with them on a respect basis, and to enmesh them in a network of mutual obligations. (Wolf 1956:235; see also Lauria 1964; Totti 1986)

Puerto Rican street-dealers do not find respect in the entry-level service sector jobs that have increased twofold in New York's economy since the 1950s. On the contrary, they "get dissed" in the new jobs that are available to them. Primo, for example, remembers the humiliation of his former work experiences as an "office boy," and he speaks of them in a race- and gender-charged idiom:

I had a prejudiced boss. She was a fucking "ho'," Gloria. She was white. Her name was Christian. No, not Christian, Kirschman. I don't know if she was Jewish or not. When she was talking to people she would say, "He's illiterate."

So what I did one day was, I just looked up the word, "illiterate," in the dictionary and I saw that she's saying to her associates that I'm stupid or something!

Well, I am illiterate anyway.

The most profound dimension of Primo's humiliation was being obliged to look up in the dictionary the word used to insult him. In contrast, in the underground economy, he is sheltered from this kind of threat:

Rocky [the crack house franchise owner] he would never disrespect me that way. He wouldn't tell me that because he's illiterate too. Plus I've got more education than him. I got a GED.

Reflecting on the period he spent as a knife-wielding mugger on the street, Primo could not contrast more dramatically with his vulnerabilities to humiliation in a low-level service-sector job.

I was with Rico and his girl, Daisy. We saw this Mexican . . . He was just probably drunk. I grabbed him by the back of the neck, and put my 007 [knife] in his back [grabbing me in a half-nelson from behind]. Right here [jabbing my lower back]. And I was jigging him *HARD* [grinning for emphasis at his girlfriend, who was listening, rapt with attention]!

I said: "*No te mueve cabrón o te voy a picar como un pernil* [Don't move mother-fucker or I'll stick you like a roast pork]" [Chuckling with his girlfriend]. Yeah, yeah, like how you stab a pork shoulder when you want to put all the flavoring in the holes.

I wasn't playing, either, I was serious. I would have jigged him. And I'd regret it later, but I was looking at that gold ring he had [more chuckling].

The Mexican panicked. So I put him to the floor, poking him hard, and Daisy started searching him.

I said, "Yo, take that asshole's fucking ring too!"

After she took the ring we broke out. We sold the ring and then we cut out on Daisy. We left her in the park, she didn't get even a cent. She helped for nothing [more chuckling].

Primo excels in the street's underground economy. His very persona inspires fear and respect. In contrast, in order to succeed in his former office job, Primo would have had to self-consciously alter his street identity and mimic the professional cultural style that office managers require of their subordinates and colleagues. Primo refused to accept his boss's insults and he was unable to imitate her interactional styles. He was doomed, consequently, to a marginal position behind a photocopy machine or at the mail meter. Behavior considered appropriate in street culture is considered dysfunctional in office settings. In other words, access to upward mobility in the service sector requires familiarity with specific types of cultural style that conjugate powerfully with racism.

> I wouldn't have mind that she said I was illiterate. What bothered me
> was that when she called on the telephone, she wouldn't want me to
> answer even if my supervisor who was the receptionist was not there.
> [Note how Primo is so low in the office hierarchy that his immediate
> supervisor is a receptionist.]
>
> When she hears my voice it sounds like she's going to get a heart
> attack. She'd go, "Why are you answering the phones?"
>
> That bitch just didn't like my Puerto Rican accent.

Primo's manner of resisting this insult to his cultural dignity exacerbated his
marginal position in the labor hierarchy:

> And then, when I did pick up the phone, I used to just sound *Porta'rrrican*
> on purpose.

In contrast to the old factory sweatshop positions, these just-above-minimum-
wage office jobs require intense interpersonal contact with the middle and
upper-middle classes. Close contact across class lines and the absence of a
working-class autonomous space for eight hours a day in the office can be a
claustrophobic experience for an otherwise ambitious, energetic, young,
inner-city worker.

Caesar, who worked for Primo as lookout and bodyguard at the crack
house, interpreted this requirement to obey white, middle-class norms as an
affront to his dignity that specifically challenged his definition of masculinity:

> I had a few jobs like that [referring to Primo's "telephone diss"] where
> you gotta take a lot of shit from bitches and be a wimp.
>
> I didn't like it but I kept on working, because "Fuck it!" you don't
> want to fuck up the relationship. So you just be a punk [shrugging his
> shoulders dejectedly].

One alternative for surviving at a workplace that does not tolerate a street-
based cultural identity is to become bicultural: to play politely by "the white
woman's" rules downtown only to come home and revert to street culture
within the safety of one's tenement or housing project at night. Tens of thousands of East Harlem residents manage this tightrope, but it often engenders
accusations of betrayal and internalized racism on the part of neighbors and
childhood friends who do not have—or do not want—these bicultural skills.

This is the case, for example, of Ray, a rival crack dealer whose tough
street demeanor conflates with his black skin to "disqualify" him from legal
office work. He quit a "nickel-and-dime messenger job downtown" in order
to sell crack full time in his project stairway shortly after a white woman fled
from him shrieking down the hallway of a high-rise office building. Ray and
the terrified woman had ridden the elevator together, and, coincidentally, Ray
had stepped off on the same floor as her to make a delivery. Worse yet, Ray
had been trying to act like a "debonair male" and suspected the contradiction
between his inadequate appearance and his chivalric intentions was responsible for the woman's terror:

You know how you let a woman go off the elevator first? Well that's what I did to her but I may have looked a little shabby on the ends. Sometime my hair not combed. You know. So I could look a little sloppy to her maybe when I let her off first.

What Ray did not quite admit until I probed further is that he too had been intimidated by the lone white woman. He had been so disoriented by her taboo, unsupervised proximity that he had forgotten to press the elevator button when he originally stepped on after her:

> She went in the elevator first but then she just waits there to see what floor I press. She's playing like she don't know what floor she wants to go to because she wants to wait for me to press my floor. And I'm standing there and I forgot to press the button. I'm thinking about something else—I don't know what was the matter with me. And she's thinking like, "He's not pressing the button; I guess he's following me!"

Self-portrait spray painted by an East Harlem crack dealer to mark his sales point. [Photo by Philippe Bourgois]

As a crack dealer, Ray no longer had to confront this kind of confusing humiliation. Instead, he could righteously condemn his "successful" neighbors who worked downtown for being ashamed of who they were born to be:

> When you see someone go downtown and get a good job, if they be Puerto Rican, you see them fix up their hair and put some contact lens in their eyes. Then they fit in. And they do it! I seen it.
>
> They turn-overs. They people who want to be white. Man, if you call them in Spanish, it wind up a problem.
>
> When they get nice jobs like that, all of a sudden, you know, they start talking proper.

SELF-DESTRUCTIVE RESISTANCE

During the 1980s, the real value of the minimum wage for legally employed workers declined by one-third. At the same time, social services were cut. The federal government, for example, decreased the proportion of its contribution to New York City's budget by over 50 percent (Berlin 1991:10; Rosenbaum 1989:A1) and cuts to welfare and services for the poor increased during the 1990s and 2000s. The breakdown of the inner city's public sector is no longer an economic threat to the expansion of New York's economy because the native-born labor force it shelters is increasingly irrelevant to the globalized U.S. economy (see Bourgois and Schonberg 2009, Wacquant 2009).

New immigrants arrive every day, and they are fully prepared to work hard for low wages under unsavory conditions. Like the parents and grandparents of Primo and Caesar, many of New York's newest immigrants are from isolated rural communities or squalid shanty towns where meat is a luxury and access to running water or electricity is limited. Half a century ago Primo's mother fled living conditions similar to the ones these new immigrants are only just struggling to escape. Her reminiscences about childhood in her natal village reveal the time warp of improved material conditions, cultural dislocation, and crushed working-class dreams that is propelling her second-generation son into a destructive street culture:

> I loved that life in Puerto Rico, because it was a healthy, healthy, healthy life.
>
> We always ate because my father always had work, and in those days the custom was to have a garden in your patio to grow food and everything that you ate.
>
> We only ate meat on Sundays because everything was cultivated on the same little parcel of land. We didn't have a refrigerator, so we ate *bacalao* [salted codfish], which can stay outside and a meat that they call *carne de vieja* [shredded beef], and sardines from a can. But thanks to God, we never felt hunger. My mother made a lot of corn flour.
>
> Some people have done better by coming here, but many people haven't. Even people from my barrio, who came trying to find a better life [*buen ambiente*] just found disaster. Married couples right from my neighborhood came only to have the husband run off with another woman.

> In those days in Puerto Rico, when we were in poverty, life was better. Everyone will tell you life was healthier and you could trust people. Now you can't trust anybody.
>
> What I like best was that we kept all our traditions . . . our feasts. In my village, everyone was either an Uncle or an Aunt. And when you walked by someone older, you had to ask for their blessing. It was respect. There was a lot of respect in those days [original quote in Spanish].

The Jewish and Italian-American white workers that Primo's mother replaced a generation ago when she came to New York City in hope of building a better future for her children were largely absorbed into an expanding economy that allowed them to be upwardly mobile. New York's economy always suffered periodic fluctuations, such as during the Great Depression, but those difficult periods were always temporary. The overall trend was one of economic growth. Primo's generation has not been so lucky, and the generation following him has fared worse. The contemporary economy does not particularly need them, and ethnic discrimination and cultural barriers overwhelm them whenever they attempt to work legally and seek service-sector jobs. Worse yet, an extraordinarily dynamic underground drug economy beckons them.

Rather than bemoaning the structural adjustment that is destroying their capacity to survive on legal wages, street-bound Puerto Rican youths celebrate their "decision" to bank on the underground economy and to cultivate their street identities. Caesar and Primo repeatedly assert their pride in their street careers. For example, one Saturday night after they finished their midnight shift at the crack house, I accompanied them on their way to purchase *El Sapo Verde* (The Green Toad), a $20 bag of powder cocaine sold by a new company three blocks away. While waiting for Primo and Caesar to be "served" by the coke seller a few yards away, I engaged three undocumented Mexican men drinking beer on a neighboring stoop in a conversation about finding work in New York. One of the new immigrants was already earning $500 a week fixing deep-fat-fry machines. He had a straightforward racist explanation for why Caesar—who was standing next to me—was "unemployed":

> OK, OK, I'll explain it to you in one word: Because the Puerto Ricans are brutes! [Pointing at Caesar] Brutes! Do you understand?
>
> Puerto Ricans like to make easy money. They like to leech off of other people. But not us Mexicans! No way! We like to work for our money. We don't steal. We came here to work and that's all [original quote in Spanish].

Instead of physically assaulting the employed immigrant for insulting him, Caesar embraced the racist tirade, ironically turning it into the basis for a new, generational-based, "American-born," urban cultural pride. In fact, in his response, he ridicules what he interprets to be the hillbilly naiveté of the Mexicans who still believe in the "American Dream." He spoke slowly in street-English as if to mark sarcastically the contrast between his "savvy" Nuyorican (New York-born Puerto Rican) identity versus the limited English proficiency of his detractor:

212   Office Work and the Crack Alternative in East Harlem

That's right, m'a man! We is real vermin lunatics that sell drugs. We don't want no part of society. "Fight the Power!"[4]

What do we wanna be working for? We rather live off the system. Gain weight, lay women.

When we was younger, we used to break our asses too [Gesturing towards the Mexican men who were straining to understand his English]. I had all kinds of stupid jobs too . . . advertising agencies . . . computers.

But not no more! Now we're in a rebellious stage. We rather evade taxes, make quick money, and just survive. But we're not satisfied with that either. Ha!

CONCLUSION: ETHNOGRAPHY AND OPPRESSION

The underground economy and the social relations thriving off of it are best understood as logical products of U.S. political and economic policies toward the poor. Street culture provides an illusion of resistance to subordination in the service sector of the high finance-dominated U.S. economy. This resistance, however, results in individual self-destruction and wider community devastation through substance abuse and violence. This complex and contradictory dynamic whereby resistance leads to self-destruction in the inner city is difficult to convey to readers in a clear and responsible manner. Mainstream society's "common sense" understanding of social stratification around ethnicity and class assumes the existence of racial hierarchies and blames individual victims for their failures. This makes it difficult to present ethnographic data from inner-city streets without falling prey to a "pornography of violence" or a racist voyeurism.

Most of the general public is not persuaded by a structural economic understanding of Caesar and Primo's "self-destruction." Even the victims themselves psychologize their unsatisfactory lives. Similarly, politicians and, more broadly, public policy ignore the fundamental structural economic facts of marginalization in America. Instead, the first priority of federal and local social "welfare" agencies is to change the psychological—or at best the "cultural"—orientations of misguided individuals (Katz 1989). U.S. politicians furiously debate family values while multinational corporations establish global free-trade zones, and unionized factory employment in the U.S. continues to disappear as overseas sweatshops multiply. Social science researchers, meanwhile, have remained silent for the most part. They politely ignore the urgent social problems engulfing the urban United States. The few marginal academic publications that do address issues of poverty and racism are easily ignored by the media and mainstream society.

There is a theoretical and methodological basis for anthropology's reticence to confront devastating social misery in its front yard. Qualitative researchers prefer to avoid tackling taboo subjects such as personal violence, sexual abuse, addiction, alienation, self-destruction, etc., for fear of violating the tenets of cultural relativism and of contributing to popular racist stereotypes. Anthropology's cautious and often self-censored approaches to social marginalization have obfuscated an ethnographic understanding of the multi-faceted dynamics of the experience of oppression, and, ironically, sometimes even serve to minimize the depths of human suffering involved. It is safer and easier to retreat into documenting the "poetics" of exotic "others." It remains to be seen whether anthropology is prepared to face the twenty-first century's challenges as poverty is increasingly concentrated into segregated metropolises, and larger proportions of the world's population are incarcerated or recruited into armies and paramilitary forces.

EPILOGUE

In the years since this chapter was first published, five major dynamics have altered the tenor of daily life on the streets of East Harlem and have deeply affected the lives of the crack dealers and their families depicted in these pages: (1) the U.S. and the global economies have become even more stratified between very rich and very poor, (2) the size of the Mexican immigrant population in New York City, and especially in East Harlem, has increased dramatically, (3) East Harlem has undergone considerable gentrification, and apartment rents have risen dramatically, (4) the War on Drugs escalated into a quasi-official public policy of criminalizing and incarcerating the poor and the socially marginal, and (5) drug fashion trends among inner-city youth rendered marijuana even more popular and crack and heroin less popular among Latinos and African Americans.

Crack, cocaine, and heroin can still be bought on the block where I lived, but they are delivered more discreetly. It is still easy to purchase narcotics throughout East Harlem, but much of the drug dealing has moved indoors, out of sight. Street-sellers no longer shout out the brand names of their drugs. Deliveries are generally arranged over cell phone. Most importantly, heroin, crack and injection drug use continue to be spurned by Latino and African American youth who have seen the ravages those drugs committed on the older generations in their community. In the U.S. inner city there remains an aging cohort of long-term addicts. In most large cities crack is most visibly ensconced in predominantly African American neighborhoods on the poorest blocks, often surrounding large public housing projects. In New York City, Puerto Rican households also continue to be at the epicenter of this ongoing, but now more self-contained, stationary cyclone of crack consumption.

In contrast to crack, heroin consumption has increased. Throughout most of the United States, heroin is cheaper and purer than in the early 1990s, belying any claims that the War on Drugs is winnable. Heroin's new appeal, however, is primarily among younger whites outside the ghetto for whom crack was never a drug of choice. It is not a drug of choice among Latino and African American youth, although on the Island of Puerto Rico, disproportionately large numbers of youth continue to initiate heroin and cocaine injection.

To summarize, both heroin and crack continue to be part of a multi-billion-dollar business that ravages inner-city families with special virulence. The younger generations of East Harlem residents, however, are more involved as sellers rather than consumers. Those Latino and African American youth who do use crack or heroin generally try to hide the fact from their friends.

Some of the crack dealers and their families (especially the women) have benefited at least fleetingly from the cycles of economic growth that intermittently reduced unemployment levels in the mid-1990s and early 2000s. For example, during the summer of 2000, one dealer managed to become a unionized doorman, another worked intermittently as a home health care attendant, another was a plumber's assistant, three others were construction workers for small-time unlicensed contractors, one was a cashier in a discount tourist souvenir store, and Primo's new girlfriend worked steadily as a bank teller. A few were still selling drugs—including Primo who was discreetly brokering small amounts of heroin via a cell phone and offered home delivery for 10 packets or more. Most of the other street sellers whom I befriended in the late 1980s and early 1990s were either dead or incarcerated on long-term sentences in the first decade of the twenty-first century. Even when the U.S. economy was booming in the early 2000s, a growing number of street youth found themselves excluded from the legal labor market. These marginalized men and women have become virtually superfluous to the legal economy; they remain painfully embroiled in a still-lucrative drug economy, a burgeoning prison system, and in a quagmire of chronic substance abuse and interpersonal violence. Consistent with this dynamic of long-term exclusion even from the lowest paid sectors of the legal economy (referred to as "lumpenization" by Marxist scholars, see Bourgois and Schonberg 2009), increasing proportions of the inner-city poor are being certified by doctors and educators as mentally ill or emotionally/behaviorally disabled with "personality disorders." This has swollen the size of special education classes in schools and routinized the use of psychiatric terms such as "bipolar," "borderline," and "attention-deficit disorder (ADD)" as markers of self-identification among inner-city adults.

From a long-term political and economic perspective, current conditions do not bode well for the future of the inner-city poor of New York or the United States more broadly. The United States has consistently had the highest levels of income inequality of any wealthy nation, and the gap between rich and poor increased through most of the first decade of the 2000s because of the consolidation of neoliberal political and economic policies (Porter 2006). In a nutshell, the U.S. version of neoliberalism dismantles services for vulnerable populations in favor of punitive interventions that have dramatically expanded public spending on prisons, police forces, and the military. Simultaneously, government subsidies have been provided to multinational corporations and restrictions on finance capital have been eased (Harvey 2005), prompting the prolonged global recession of 2008–2009. The United States rates poorly in international comparisons of the quality-of-life statistics that measure life expectancy, health, homicide, income inequality, incarceration, ethnic segregation, literacy, and homelessness (United Nations Development Programme 2006:295–296). Most alarming has been the quadrupling of the size of the imprisoned population from the early 1980s through the early 2000s due to the war on drugs (with African American men incarcerated at six times the rate of whites). In 2008 the United States was the country with the highest proportion of its citizens held in captivity of any nation in the world (Human Rights Watch 2008; Public Safety Performance Project 2008). More subtle, but equally disturbing, has been the way the wars against drugs and communism from the late twentieth century have bled into the war on terrorism in the twenty-first century to create a popular common sense that legitimizes punitive solutions to rising social inequality.[5]

Notes

[1] According to the 1990 Census, 39.8% of East Harlem residents were below the poverty line, compared to 28.3% in 2006. In 1990, 60% of all households reported legally earned incomes compared to 69.5% in 2006 (New York City Department of City Planning 2009). Twenty-six percent in 1990 received Public Assistance, and 6.3 percent received Supplemental Security Income (New York City Department of City Planning 1993) compared to only 8.5% receiving Public Assistance and 14% receiving Supplemental Security Income in 2006. Between 1990 and 2000, the white non-Hispanic population increased by 20%, jumping a further 67% by 2006 with a total of 11.2% of East Harlem residents identifying themselves as "white non-Hispanic" (Sharman 2006; U.S. Census Bureau 2009).

[2] Angel dust, known as PCP or "Zootie," is an animal tranquilizer that is sprinkled on mint leaves which are then smoked in joints. It was the national drug scourge of the mid-1970s and continues to be popular among the younger generation in El Barrio, New York, and in Philadelphia, where, in the early 2000s, it was referred to as "wet."

[3] Significantly, there are subsectors of the service industry that are relatively unionized—such as hospital and custodial work—where there is a limited autonomous space for street culture and working-class resistance.

[4] "Fight the Power" is a rap song composed in 1990 by the African American group, Public Enemy.

[5] For further information, see Bourgois 1989, 1995a, 1995b, 1995c.

Acknowledgments

The author would like to thank the following institutions for their support: The Harry Frank Guggenheim Foundation, The Russell Sage Foundation, The Social Science Research Council, The National Institute on Drug Abuse R03-DA06413, The Wenner-Gren Foundation for Anthropological Research, the United States Bureau of the Census, the San Francisco Urban Institute, and San Francisco State University. Updated data was made possible by NIH grant DA10164 with background data from DA021627, MH078743 and CHRP ID08-SF-049. Finally, this could not have been written without the typing of Harold Otto, Henry Ostendorf, Charles Pearson, and Kathryn Coneybear.

References

Berlin, Gordon. 1991. *The Poverty among Families: A Service Decategorization Response.* New York: Manpower Demonstration Research Corporation. Photocopied Report.

Bourdieu, Pierre. 2000. *Pascalian Meditations.* Translated by Richard Nice. Stanford, CA: Stanford University Press.

Bourdieu, Pierre, and Loïc Wacquant. 1992. *An Invitation to Reflexive Sociology.* Chicago: University of Chicago Press.

Bourgois, Philippe. 1989. In Search of Horatio Alger: Culture and Ideology in the Crack Economy. *Contemporary Drug Problems,* 16:619–649.

———. 1995a. *In Search of Respect: Selling Crack in El Barrio.* New York: Cambridge University Press.

———. 1995b. From Jíbaro to Crack Dealer: Confronting Capitalism in Spanish Harlem. In *Articulating Hidden Histories: Anthropology, History, and the Influence of Eric*

R. Wolf, eds. Jane Schneider and Rayna Rapp, pp. 125–141. Berkeley: University of California Press.

———. 1995c. The Political Economy of Resistance and Self-Destruction in the Crack Economy: An Ethnographic Perspective. *Annals of the New York Academy of Sciences,* 749:23–44.

Bourgois, Philippe, and Jeff Schonberg. 2009. *Righteous Dopefiend.* Berkeley: University of California Press.

Harvey, David. 2005. *A Brief History of Neoliberalism.* Oxford: Oxford University Press.

Human Rights Watch. 2008. US: Prison Numbers Hit New High. Available at: http://www.hrw.org/en/2008/06/05/us-prison-numbers-hit-new-high (accessed August 10, 2009).

Katz, Michael. 1989. *The Undeserving Poor: From the War on Poverty to the War on Welfare.* New York: Pantheon Books.

Lauria, Anthony, Jr. 1964. *"Respeto," "Relajo,"* and Interpersonal Relations in Puerto Rico. *Anthropological Quarterly,* 37(2):53–67.

New York City Department of City Planning. 1993 (March). Socioeconomic Profiles: A Portrait of New York City's Community Districts from the 1980 & 1990 Censuses of Population and Housing. New York: Department of City Planning.

———. 2009. Manhattan Community District 11 Demographic and Housing Estimates: 2005–2007, American Community Survey US Census Bureau. New York: Department of City Planning.

Porter, Eduardo. 2006. After Years of Growth, What about Workers' Share? *New York Times,* October 15, p. B3.

Public Safety Performance Project. 2008. One in 100: Behind Bars in America 2008. Washington DC: Pew Center on the States. Available at: http://www.pewcenteronthestates.org/report_detail.aspx?id=35904

Romo, Frank, and Michael Schwartz. 1993. The Coming of Post-Industrial Society Revisited: Manufacturing and the Prospects for a Service-Based Economy. In *Explorations in Economic Sociology,* ed. Richard Swedburg, pp. 335–373. New York: Russell Sage Foundation.

Rosenbaum, David E. 1989. Bush and Congress Reach Accord Raising Minimum Wage to $4.25. *New York Times,* November 1, p. A1.

Sharman, Russell Leigh. 2006. *The Tenants of East Harlem.* Berkeley: University of California Press.

Totti, Xavier F. 1986. A Face-Threatening Act: Ideology, Language, and Power in the Caribbean. Paper presented at the 85th annual meeting of the American Anthropological Association, December 3–7.

United Nations Development Programme. 2006. *Human Development Report.* New York: Palgrave Macmillan.

U.S. Census Bureau. 2009. Manhattan Community District 11 Selected Economic Characteristics 2005–2007, American Community Survey: New York City Department of Planning. Available at http://www.nyc.gov/html/dcp/pdf/census/nyc_econo_all_05_06_07_pumas.pdf#mn11

Wacquant, Loïc. 2009. *Punishing the Poor: The Neoliberal Government of Social Insecurity.* Durham, NC: Duke University Press.

Wolf, Eric. 1956. San Jose: Subcultures of a "Traditional" Coffee Municipality. In *The People of Puerto Rico,* ed. Julian Steward, pp. 171–264. Chicago: University of Illinois Press.

15

The View from the Front Desk
Addressing Homelessness and
the Homeless in Dallas

Julie Adkins

In this chapter, Julie Adkins describes the encounters between homeless persons and the staff and volunteers who operate The Stewpot, a faith-based daytime shelter and social-service agency in Dallas, Texas. Her poignant account of the diverse characteristics of the homeless who come to The Stewpot provides insights into the questions "Who are the homeless?", "How many are homeless?", and "Why are they homeless?" She then examines the responses of governmental agencies and nongovernmental organizations to their plight. Adkins concludes her analysis by contemplating the evolving strategies being deployed by national and local agencies to solve the persistent homelessness "problem" in the United States.

The police officer for the day unlocks the door at 8:00 AM, and, depending on the weather, a crowd of anywhere from 100 to 300 people push their way in, aiming in several different directions. Some rapidly make their way to the restroom, their first chance at a clean facility since closing time the previous afternoon. Forty or more head directly for the coffee pot and the morning's wake-up brew. If you want coffee, it's important to get there first, because once the pot is empty, there will be no more made until tomorrow. A few folks are just looking for a comfortable place to sit—particularly when the weather is extremely cold, hot, or wet—and they quickly settle in at one of the round tables or in a favorite spot on the floor. Most, however, have needs that are a little more complicated. These people form a line along the wall heading west, then turning all the way down the length of the south wall, and halfway across the far wall heading back to the east. In my role as "intake volunteer," it will take me the better part of two hours just to speak briefly with each of the 100-plus people in this line, to hear what it is that they need, and to begin to process their requests.

Source: Written expressly for *Urban Life*.

This is The Stewpot, a daytime shelter and social-service agency that is a ministry of First Presbyterian Church, located in the heart of downtown Dallas, Texas. Begun in 1975 as a response to hungry people sitting literally on the church's doorstep—spearheaded by an assistant pastor who had just handed two cans of food to one individual and then observed the man trying to open the cans with a key, the only "tool" he had—The Stewpot has evolved from a soup kitchen serving a midday meal to an agency with full-time and part-time casework staff, medical and dental clinics, job training, and a myriad of other services for Dallas's homeless and at-risk populations.

WHO ARE THE HOMELESS?

Denise[1] is in her early 30s, slender, with graying hair. She comes in nearly every day: for Denise, The Stewpot is almost like Cheers, "where everybody knows your name." Her caseworker is also her representative payee, meaning that Denise's Social Security Disability (SSDI) check is sent directly to The Stewpot and the funds are disbursed on her behalf, as she is not capable of handling her own finances. The caseworker pays her rent and other fixed expenses and parcels out the remaining funds as spending money to Denise on a weekly basis. Denise has no family, but she will carry their legacy as long as she lives: permanent brain damage from her mother's alcohol abuse while pregnant. Rarely in a hurry for anything, Denise normally waits until the line at the front desk has diminished before she makes her approach, which enables her to get away with sneaking behind the desk to give everyone a hug. Unlike with many of their guests[2] who struggle with mental illness, no one at The Stewpot is afraid of Denise. If anything, they are afraid *for* her.

Marcus is another matter altogether. Unlike Denise, his mental illness is controllable with medication. Unfortunately, he often chooses not to take it. Some days, The Stewpot's only contact with Marcus is when he comes through the line gruffly demanding a toothbrush, razor, or other hygiene item. (The gruffness is a sure sign that he's off his meds.) Marcus also has a caseworker/payee, but his recent behavior has been so erratic that she has had to give him an ultimatum: either Marcus starts taking his meds again or The Stewpot will no longer provide him with services. Some days, the staff *are* afraid of him.

Juanita is in her late 60s. A widow for many years, she never held a job outside the home. After her husband's death, she gradually slid into poverty, and, when her home began falling down due to lack of maintenance, she found herself having to seek out a shelter. Juanita has enrolled in The Stewpot's employment program and is looking for work, but few employers are interested in talking to a senior citizen with no work experience. In one sense, Juanita is fortunate: there are many more social services available for senior adults than for those of working age—but one has to know where to go, whom to ask, and how to engage the system. At present, Juanita has few skills to be able to help herself.

Trish aroused suspicions in all of the staff who saw her pull into The Stewpot's parking garage in a brand-new Chevy Suburban that had to have cost more than a caseworker's annual salary. Her bruised face and referral letter told the story: the Suburban was *all* that she and her children had left after fleeing from an abusive husband/father. Luckily, the domestic violence shelter had had space for them, and staff there were caring for her children while Trish went about the tedious tasks of getting new copies of their birth certificates and other necessary documents, finding a safe place for them to live permanently, and pursuing legal matters such as a restraining order and, ultimately, a divorce.

Carl tries everyone's patience. His physical and mental-health issues are overwhelming, far more than he is capable of addressing. Some would blame Carl for his own troubles: years of alcohol abuse have destroyed his memory and thought processes and have ravaged his body, leading to ongoing problems with incontinence and other unpleasantness. He is alternately argumentative and flirtatious, his voice always several decibels louder than necessary. It is not certain whether Carl is still drinking or not; it doesn't much matter, as the damage has already been done. Carl has tried to live in permanent supportive housing,[3] but has been kicked out more than once. The on-site caseworker from his most recent apartment complex frequently comes to The Stewpot to fetch Carl when he has become so confused that he cannot make his way home. He spends some nights in a shelter for the same reason. Carl *needs* to be in a nursing home-type of facility, preferably in a memory-care unit from which he cannot stray. The chance of this ever happening for a "difficult" homeless man is approximately zero.

There are as many different stories as there are people in the line. Contrary to the "skid row" stereotype, there is no "typical" homeless person. Many are veterans, but more are not. Some have been homeless for only a month or two; others have lived on the streets for more than 20 years. Some stay with friends as a last resort after losing their own place; some stay regularly in a shelter; some prefer the anonymity of the street. Some do abuse drugs and/or alcohol; some have been "clean" for extended periods of time; some have never used at all. Some are highly educated and skilled; in fact, some are working full-time but cannot afford a place to live. Others desperately need job training and placement assistance. A few are so impaired that holding onto a job is out of the question. Some have known nothing but poverty since childhood; others have "fallen" a long way from a middle-class lifestyle. Part of the reason that there are so many agencies and organizations helping the homeless is that there are so many different "kinds" of homeless. Juanita has good prospects for leaving homelessness; Carl has few. Trish needs different services than Denise; Marcus needs more oversight and supervision than either of them.

In general, single homeless adults are more likely to be male (67.5 percent), whereas, among homeless households, a majority of the homeless are female (65 percent). Nationwide, the ethnic background of the homeless population is 42 percent African American, 39 percent Anglo, 13 percent Hispanic, 4 percent Native American, and 2 percent Asian (NCH 2008). In contrast, Dallas's homeless population is approximately 81 percent male and 19 percent female, and the ethnic mix is 65 percent African American, 27 percent Anglo, 4 percent Hispanic, and 4 percent "Other."[4]

HOW MANY ARE HOMELESS?

No one knows how many are homeless in the U.S. at any particular point in time. It is difficult to obtain an accurate count of a population that is highly mobile. One never knows, for example, where Carl may be found: on any given night he might be sleeping in his apartment, in a shelter, or on the street. Will he be counted more than once, or will he be overlooked as he moves from one place to the other? In addition, it is even more difficult to count homeless persons who do not wish to be found. Among the long-term homeless in particular, there are those termed "shelter resistant," who choose to set up camp in out-of-the-way places in the hope of being left alone by everyone except perhaps other homeless persons. Many of these suffer from schizophrenia and other forms of mental illness. They are fearful of shelters—some are afraid of enclosed spaces of any kind—and rarely, if ever, seek help or services from agencies like The Stewpot. Some have given up hope that any shelter or other helping agency has anything useful to offer them. How do we count people who do not want to be found?

In the United States, the federal agency with the largest share of responsibility for providing funds and programs for addressing homelessness is the Department of Housing and Urban Development (HUD). Cities that receive HUD funding are required to conduct a point-in-time census of their homeless populations in the last week of January, at least once every two years.[5] As in most cities, the Dallas census is conducted on a single night, thus minimizing the risk of double-counting persons.[6] Shelters are asked to provide their total head count for the night; in addition, dozens of volunteers assist in locating and conducting surveys of both sheltered and unsheltered homeless persons in order to obtain more detailed information about their histories and their needs. Once these data have been gathered from all the participating cities, HUD can construct an estimate of the number of people who are homeless on any given night. It is, of course, a *minimum* number, since there are undoubtedly thousands of unsheltered homeless who are *not* located and surveyed. For 2007, the most recent year for which there is complete data, the point-in-time count revealed (no fewer than) 671,859 homeless persons in the United States. Dallas's homeless count for January 2009, according to the point-in-time count, was 5,675, a number that has not changed appreciably (variation of ±5 percent) over the past five years.

HUD also mandates that the homeless be tracked through a database that it calls the Homeless Management Information System (HMIS), which is able to track people across time. Through observing this count across a period of several months, we are able to see that there is a substantial turnover rate in the population of the homeless.[7] On the one hand, this is good news of a sort: for many, homelessness appears to be a short-term phenomenon. They seek out shelter, they receive assistance, and they are able to get back on their feet fairly quickly, vacating shelter beds for the next individuals in need. On the other hand, it is also bad news: no sooner is a shelter bed relinquished than it is needed again for another who has become homeless in the meantime. That is, there appears to be a continual risk of homelessness for many in the U.S. Indeed, the National Law Center on Homelessness and Poverty suggests that, in any one calendar year, anywhere from 2.3 to 3.5 million people in the U.S. will experience an episode of homelessness (NLCHP 2007).[8]

At the other end of the spectrum from those who are able to transition in and out of homelessness rapidly are those whom HUD calls the "chronically homeless." These individuals either have been continuously homeless for a year or more or have had at least four episodes of homelessness within the past three years. In addition, they must be staying either in a shelter or on the street and must have some kind of disabling condition that limits their ability to work and to perform the activities of daily living. The chronically homeless represent 15–25 percent of the homeless population, but because of their increased needs and limited ability to care for those needs, they utilize more than 50 percent of the total resources of programs in place to serve the homeless. (Some estimates run as high as 80 percent.)

In addition, there are some homeless persons who, by definition, do not get counted. The McKinney-Vento Homeless Assistance Act defines homelessness fairly narrowly; in general, one must be staying either in a shelter or on the street (or in one's car, in an abandoned building, at the bus station). Thus, there are quite a few people in need who are not included: An otherwise homeless individual who is serving a 30-day jail term for public intoxication is not counted among the homeless. A family that has been evicted, but is temporarily (and illegally) sharing a friend's apartment, is not considered homeless. A couple whose home went into foreclosure, and who are staying in a cheap motel because they have no other place to go, are not defined as homeless. Thus, these "invisible" homeless are missed when a census is conducted.

WHY ARE THEY HOMELESS?

All too often, the "commonsense" explanations given for homelessness blame the homeless themselves for their predicament. "People are homeless because they are mentally ill." "They're homeless because they abuse drugs and/or alcohol." "Some people are lazy and just don't want to work." "Some people just prefer to live on the street and have the freedom to do what they want." Examining the partial truths in each of these statements will enable us to gain a better idea of the broader societal forces at work that cause and perpetuate homelessness. This process also leads to a better understanding of what will be required in order to end the problem.

"People are homeless because they are mentally ill." Numerous analyses have shown that anywhere from one-fourth to one-third of the homeless—in particular the chronically homeless—suffer from mental illness in one form or another, from major depressive disorder to bipolar disorder to schizophrenia. In the 1980s, tens of thousands of patients were released from psychiatric hospitals in the belief that they no longer needed to be institutionalized. The rationale was that, with new antipsychotic medications available and appropriate social services provided, most could live happily and productively within the community rather than in institutions. This assumption was never tested, however, and deinstitutionalization took place *without* any subsequent increase in funding for community-based support and services. As a result, a significant portion of the increase in homelessness in the 1980s was a direct result of deinstitutionalization.

Today, few of the patients who were deinstitutionalized in the 1980s remain; they have mostly not survived the loss of their safety net. However, the system of available care remains radically diminished. In general, persons may not be institutionalized against their wishes unless it can be demonstrated that they present a clear danger either to themselves or to someone else. "Danger" has been narrowly defined as the risk that an individual may commit suicide or homicide. Thus, the "choice" to stop taking antipsychotic drugs and to sleep outdoors in subfreezing weather is not construed as "presenting a danger" to oneself. Today, there is a *new* cohort of homeless mentally-ill persons for whom there is too little supportive housing available, too few psychiatric social workers to oversee their care, and inadequate medical insurance to cover the medications that many will need to take for the rest of their lives.

In addition, it is not always clear which comes first: the mental illness, or the state of being homeless. Clearly, there are cases in which untreated mental illness leads an individual into a downward spiral that results in the loss of job, family, and home. But there are also documented cases in which persons have become mentally ill only after several months of living on the streets or in shelters. The coping skills required to survive as a homeless person— heightened awareness of threat, hypersensitivity to one's surroundings and safety, remaining awake and vigilant all night to ensure that belongings are not stolen—are so disturbing that some suffer a breakdown as a result.

Even granting that a substantial number of the homeless are mentally ill, it does not follow logically that this has caused their homelessness. There are far more U.S. citizens with mental illness who are *not* homeless than who *are* homeless. To be sure, such disorders place people at higher risk. But some have families who can care for them, while others do not. Some have medical insurance that provides a high level of care and covers the medications and therapy they need; others do not. Mental illness alone cannot explain why even a certain percentage of people find themselves without shelter. Even if it did, are we as citizens prepared to argue that those persons are somehow deserving of their predicament? And that their being homeless is somehow, therefore, "appropriate"?

"People are homeless because they abuse alcohol and/or drugs." It is clear that a high percentage of the homeless, perhaps even a majority, use alcohol and/or drugs to numb the pain of their lives. Carl, described above, is just one example. But as with mental illness, it is not always clear which came first: the homelessness, or the substance abuse. Certainly, there are documented cases of drug use leading to the loss of job, housing, and even family. But perhaps just as often, occasional substance use turns to abuse in the face of repeated disappointments, inability to find work, disrespectful treatment by social workers, assault by other homeless persons.

As with mental illness, there are many more substance abusers who are housed than homeless. Addicted students live on college campuses in residence halls and "Greek" houses with everyone else; they are not homeless. Celebrities have their struggles with substance abuse paraded through the gossip columns, but they go into treatment, not into a homeless shelter. Drug and alcohol abuse certainly exacerbate the problems of homelessness; they do not *cause* it.

"Some people are lazy and just don't want to work." Taken by itself, this is undoubtedly a true statement; however, it is hardly restricted to the homeless. Anyone who has sufficient money can be as lazy as she or he chooses without suffering ill consequences. No one suggests that the jet-setting "idle rich" should be forced into homeless shelters because they are living on inherited wealth rather than working to earn an income of their own.

Furthermore, many of the homeless actually have jobs, or are seeking employment. Dallas's census figures show that 25–30 percent of the homeless surveyed are working at least part-time, while another 20–25 percent list "job placement" as being among their five greatest needs. Even so, a minimum-wage job does not provide sufficient income to rent an apartment at fair market value. Being employed is no guarantee that a person will not become homeless.

"Some people just prefer to live on the street and have the freedom to do what they want." On rare occasions, I have actually heard this from the lips of homeless persons themselves. However, the real meaning becomes clear when one digs a little deeper to find out what they are contrasting "living on the street" with. Many have made occasional stays in shelters and found them to be unfriendly places. In some, clothing and other personal items are frequently stolen. In others, there is a strict nighttime curfew and residents are kicked out early in the morning. Some shelters require that their guests attend a worship service if they are going to remain overnight; most shelters forbid drinking alcohol and smoking on the premises. While at one level these seem logical enough restrictions, how many of us who are "housed" would tolerate having items stolen out of our homes, being told we must stay away from 6:00 AM until 6:00 PM, or being required to listen to a sermon every night before we could go to bed? In many respects, what the homeless are seeking is the same freedom that the rest of us take for granted. And if those freedoms are too restricted by the available shelters, many homeless people make the choice—except perhaps in the worst weather—to stay outdoors. The experience of Dallas's new "homeless assis-

tance center" (The Bridge), which within a week after opening was filled to more than double its capacity, suggests that many who remain on the streets are eager for the opportunity to "come in" if an appropriate setting is provided.

Why, then, are people homeless? Two related factors seem to offer the best explanation for how homelessness is created and sustained. First, people are homeless because they are poor. Second, people are homeless because there is not enough affordable housing. Let's look at these factors more closely.

People are homeless because they are poor. At first this seems redundant. Yet the statistical correlation is clear between increases in national, state, and local poverty rates and increases in the number of homeless individuals and families. Several factors are involved: wages for the lowest tier of the workforce, those earning minimum wage, have fallen (in real value) by more than 25 percent in the last 20 years. In addition, the offshoring of unskilled manufacturing jobs has often left people unable to find work at all. When jobs *are* available, they tend to provide fewer benefits than in the past. This combination of factors, together with a decline in public assistance, has left many families and individuals with few to no options for providing for themselves.

Hopper (2003) argues that poverty is an unfortunate but inevitable result of an unregulated capitalist economic system. In order for profits to increase for the owners of the means of production (company owners, shareholders), wages must be kept as low as possible. The way to keep wages low is always to have a certain percentage of the workforce "in abeyance": out of work and in a position to be called on immediately if demand increases and workers are needed. While they are not working, those "in abeyance" remain available as a quiet threat to those who are currently employed: anyone unwilling to work for the pay being offered by an employer is "free" to leave and be replaced by someone who *is* willing to work for a substandard wage rather than no wage at all. In short, some people are homeless because the majority of us benefit from an economic system that depends on keeping a certain percentage of the population out of the workforce.

There is not enough affordable housing available. This is, of course, related to the question of poverty. As noted above, everywhere in the United States there is a significant gap between wages and fair market value rent. This has resulted not only from the stagnation of income at the minimum-wage level but also from a decrease in inexpensive housing options. Cities engaging in "urban renewal" have torn down older apartment complexes and single-room-occupancy facilities, leaving thousands of residents with no place to go. Of course, it is preferable to have families and individuals living in clean and safe places rather than in run-down rooms and apartments. However, most of those displaced by urban renewal projects and gentrification have not been provided with an affordable living option, much less a clean and safe one.

For most among the homeless, a combination of factors has led them to their present situation. Clearly, not everyone living below the poverty line is homeless; some have family or other sources of assistance; a few have been able to access affordable housing and/or Section 8 vouchers that subsidize them in market-rate apartment rentals. Rosenthal (1994) suggests that perhaps the best analogy for understanding homelessness is to think of it as being like the game of musical chairs, in which jobs and/or housing are the "chairs" for which players are competing. The longer the game continues, the fewer the seats that remain available for players to sit on. Some players inevitably have characteristics that make them less likely to get a chair; someone who is slow-moving, or small and easily pushed aside, does not last long in the battle for chairs. Likewise, a person who is disabled, mentally compromised, or poorly educated is less likely to find employment that pays a living wage. Instead, someone more "able" will get the job/"chair." Similarly, housing is limited for those who are poor, who need colocated support services, or who lack transportation and are limited in where they can live. The more "able" a person is, the more "chairs" there are available to choose among. So, yes, there are personal characteristics that make it more or less likely that certain persons will end up homeless, "without a chair." However, it is even more important to recognize that the system, like the game, *is set up so that* there are not enough "chairs" for everyone who needs one.

WHAT IS ANYONE IN DALLAS DOING ABOUT IT?

Historically, Dallas has done very little *as a city* to address the needs of the homeless persons in its midst. As long ago as 1915, newly elected Dallas mayor Henry Lindsley stated that one of his top priorities as mayor would be "an overnight shelter for the homeless" (Payne 1994:54). This, among other progressive ideas, got him voted out of office at the earliest opportunity. Dallas has a long history of opposition to public spending on social welfare programs, preferring instead to rely on private charity to provide for any who are truly needy. Hill notes that the Dallas elite have preferred to give donations to local organizations—which they often do quite generously—rather than to pay higher taxes to support the same causes, commenting that private giving "did not jeopardize one's commitment to capitalism" (Hill 1996:99).

In 1994 the topic of a "homeless assistance center" was again on the table for city leaders. As Dallas prepared to host the World Cup soccer matches, city leaders were also making plans to raze an encampment of more than 200 homeless persons who had been living for years under one of the bridges of Interstate 45. Apparently oblivious to the reality that every major city in the world struggles with how to shelter and care for its impoverished populations, Dallas's leaders could not conceive that a "world class city"—as Dallas is fond of thinking of itself (Kemper 2002:106)—would have homeless people visible in its midst. While one former city council member had suggested that the simplest solution would be to put all the homeless on a bus and send them to Fort Worth (30 miles west), city leaders did appoint a task force to study the problem and took its recommendations seriously—up to a point. The mayor and the city council agreed in principle that an "assistance center" was needed—and that it needed to be located centrally—but they then, under pressure from downtown business owners, proceeded to place so many restrictions on the plan that it became clear that the center would never be built. In the meantime, however, soccer fans were coming to Dallas, and so the encampment was bulldozed and the area quickly encircled by a fence to prevent re-entry. Not only were the "dwellings" of the homeless completely destroyed, but their few possessions were also either crushed by the bulldozers or thrown into dumpsters. While city leaders *claimed* that the purpose behind razing the encampment was to encourage those who were homeless to seek out shelters and services, they were very much aware that Dallas had far too few shelter beds and far from adequate mental-health services to address the needs of this longtime homeless population.

For the most part, Dallas city leaders have not so much understood *homelessness* as the problem; rather, they perceive *the homeless* as being the problem. Thus, proposed "solutions" have not, until quite recently, involved provision of shelter, increased spending on social services, or encouraging the development of affordable housing. Instead, the city council has attempted to address homelessness by criminalizing certain behaviors that are, for the most part, *only* engaged in by homeless persons, thus earning Dallas the dubious distinction of being one of the top 10 "Meanest Cities" in its treatment of the homeless (NCH/NLCHP 2006).[9]

In addition, in 2000 the City found itself in serious trouble with HUD for the misuse of federal monies intended for services to the homeless. While no deliberate misconduct was ever alleged, a HUD audit found that the City had not provided all the services it had promised, had not expended HUD funds in a timely manner, and had not properly documented the funds it *did* spend. As a result of these findings, HUD auditors recommended that the City of Dallas receive *no* further funding until it had addressed the problems. By the following year, an audit found far fewer problems, in part because the job of administering the grants had been taken over by a nonprofit coalition of public entities, service providers, business groups, private nonprofit organizations, and formerly homeless individuals.

During these years, the only facility resembling a shelter that the city provided was a daytime-only location called the Day Resource Center, where restrooms and showers were available, and where numerous social-service providers kept weekday office hours to meet with and assist the homeless (e.g., the Veterans Administration, county mental-health providers, etc.). In addition, in recent years the City has fielded a Crisis Intervention Team, consisting of both trained social workers and formerly homeless persons. Team members make contact with the homeless in places where they like to congregate, to encourage them to begin the process of getting into treatment for their mental illness and/or addiction challenges and to offer referrals to shelters and other helping agencies. Nevertheless, despite some individual success stories, there are still not enough resources to meet the needs.

Given these challenges, where *do* homeless persons in Dallas find help? The answer lies in a broad range of agencies and care providers, each addressing a few pieces of the puzzle. For those who are seriously ill, the county hospital (Parkland) offers care, at least until a crisis has passed. Veterans are eligible for assistance from the Veterans Administration, but many of them have difficulty accessing the medical care to which they are entitled because they cannot afford to ride the bus to southern Dallas where the VA hospital is located. For the most part, though, the needs of Dallas's homeless have been addressed, when they have been addressed at all, by faith-based agencies. Until The Bridge opened in May 2008, the only emergency overnight shelters in Dallas (a total of six) were ministries of faith-based groups. The first transitional housing[10] facility and program in Dallas was begun by a Presbyterian congregation. Genesis Woman's Shelter, for victims of domestic violence, was formed by a partnership of faith communities. The agency that provides daily child care for homeless children, along with family counseling and other services, is a project of the Dallas Jewish Coalition. The Stewpot was the first agency to provide meals to the hungry and homeless in downtown Dallas. If it were not for churches and synagogues, congregational partnerships and other religious organizations, there would until recently have been few to no services for the city's homeless.

The sheer number of agencies is a function of at least two different issues. First, *because* the agencies are separate nonprofits, their resources are limited. Even those that receive significant federal funding—and many faith-based programs receive none—must carve out a niche and do a few things well rather than trying to serve all needs for all clients. Second, the needs of the homeless are so varied—and at times mutually contradictory—that for a single agency to try to meet them all is not even practical. If we think back to the homeless persons introduced at the beginning of this chapter: Trish and her children cannot and should not be asked to share shelter space with Marcus when he is off his meds. Nor, in finding housing, do they have the same long-term support needs as Carl. Denise would not benefit from the same job-skills training that will help Juanita find employment. Just as each story is different, each set of needs requires different programs. The Stewpot, in contrast to many nonprofits, attempts to provide a wide range of services: medical and dental clinics, clothing, help obtaining identification, weekend activities for children, job training and readiness, Bible study, art classes . . . the list would cover more than a page. Even so, they still cannot meet all needs. There is no provision for overnight shelter. Except for serving meals, no food is offered. In-town transportation assistance is not available. Front-desk staff and volunteers are expected to know where to refer clients who have needs The Stewpot cannot meet; even so, it is a frustrating experience for all concerned.

In many respects, being homeless is a full-time job. Few of us who are housed realize the lengths to which the homeless must go in order to survive. Even those who have given up on leaving the streets have to move around in search of food: until recently, there was no one place in Dallas where a homeless person could get a meal three times a day. Most night shelters require their residents to leave during the day, so people without a home spend much of the day on their feet, wandering. The Dallas police will not let them sit and rest in public spaces, even on benches in public parks. (It is unclear how City leaders have reached the conclusion that homeless people are not part of "the public," though this is not unique to Dallas.) Finding a restroom is a challenge in a city where "public" restrooms are nonexistent. Even those who panhandle as their only source of income must keep at it for long hours if they hope to earn anything at all (urban legends to the contrary notwithstanding). Many homeless gather aluminum cans and scrap metal to turn in for cash—it is not surprising that one of the City's major metal-recycling businesses is less than a block from the Austin Street Centre, an overnight shelter. Beyond these, those homeless who *are* trying to become housed once again often have an even more difficult time. Imagine having to go to one agency in the morning for a bite of breakfast; another to get a decent change of clothes for a job interview; a third to get a bus pass to take you to that interview—and still manage to get to the interview on time. Some shelters impose curfews that inadvertently cause residents to miss skills classes or interviews. Homeless persons are understandably reluctant to ask potential employers to adjust the time of an interview to meet the schedule of a shelter; as a result, they run the risk of losing even their temporary housing for the sake of a job interview that is no guarantee of something better.

In a city the size of Dallas, the "system" is immensely complicated. There is no one person or agency that has a complete grasp or understanding of everything that is available, everything that goes on, every potential service provider. While HUD requires that all agencies receiving federal funding cooperate with one another—and defines a "continuum of care" that tries to ensure that services are available for homeless persons with all different levels of need—the "universe" of available services is huge and constantly changing. Dallas's coordinating agency, the Metro Dallas Homeless Alliance, is made up of representatives from nonprofit agencies, interested members of the public, homeless and formerly homeless persons, and representatives from public entities as well, such as the police department, the public library, the Dallas School District, the County hospital, and so forth. Even these experts, many of whom work full-time with the homeless, struggle to keep themselves informed and up-to-date with their information.

Nevertheless, as the relatively unchanging number of homeless in Dallas suggests, even dozens of agencies, which together spend millions of dollars, cannot make significant headway against the problem of homelessness in the city. As City leaders have gradually—and reluctantly—become aware, until the City itself takes the homeless and their needs seriously, rather than simply legislating against them, the situation is not going to change. There are a couple of key reasons that City involvement is crucial.

As in any city, NIMBY ("not in my back yard") issues are a problem in Dallas. Whenever proposals are made for building a shelter, building apartments to provide permanent supportive housing, or creating transitional housing there will always be an outcry from neighboring property owners claiming that such a facility will negatively affect the value of their property.[11] Dallas, in particular, has historically given neighborhood associations virtual veto power over anything within their boundaries; as a result, most Dallas neighborhoods have created such associations to lobby on their behalf with the City Council and other leaders. Associations in Dallas are so powerful that, in order to bring a more equal voice to the table, the homeless have organized to form their own "Homeless Neighborhood Association." Without a commitment among the highest level of City leaders to finding permanent solutions to homelessness, the competing interests of these associations will simply shut the process down— as, indeed, they did in 1994 and have done at numerous other times in the past.

Furthermore, the City has resources at its disposal that no nonprofit agency can hope to access. In 2003, voters passed a bond issue allocating $3 million for the construction of a new, City-owned, 24-hour "homeless assistance center." The same bond election also approved *$11 million* for a new *animal* shelter; even so, this was a historic moment in Dallas's history. For the first time, the City was going to assume some responsibility for sheltering its most vulnerable citizens. With its leverage, the City has been able to pry funds out of County budgets as well, arguing that providing shelter for the homeless means that fewer of them would be spending time in the County jail and fewer of them would need the services of Parkland Hospital. The City is also working in concert with other big-city mayors across the state of Texas to gain access to state-level funds for various services provided at the shelter. Only a political entity such as the City has the authority and the clout to make such claims against other political entities.

At last, and to much fanfare, the City's new homeless shelter, now called "The Bridge," was opened in May 2008. Built to house just over 300 people per night, within the first week The Bridge was struggling to accommodate more than 700 every night, thus giving the lie to the oft-repeated statement that "the homeless don't *want* to come in off the streets."

WHAT HAPPENS NEXT?

The number of homeless nationwide appears to have been dropping, but the most recent numbers have not taken into account the "Great Recession" which began in 2008. A survey of member agencies in the Metro Dallas Homeless Alliance (conducted in May 2009) suggests that the demand for their services increased hugely in 2009, without an accompanying rise in donations or other funding. Dallas's housing market has not been hit as hard as in other parts of the United States, but foreclosure rates are such that it seems probable that the number of homeless is again on the increase.

Nationwide, a strategy called "Housing First" is gaining momentum and showing a great deal of promise. Its premise is simply this: until people have a place of their own that is stable and where they feel safe, they cannot make significant progress toward solving their problems, whatever those may be. Thus, an apartment is provided *before* requiring a person to attend job-skills classes. A client is permitted to live in permanent supportive housing *before* she or he is stabilized on antipsychotic medication. In contrast to "tough love" policies of the past, which demanded that homeless persons first show some "effort" toward recovery, Housing First operates on the premise that recovery is unlikely as long as people feel unsafe and must spend entire days getting basic needs met (as discussed above). In addition, the track record thus far in a number of different cities suggests that providing housing for the homeless is actually *less* expensive than allowing people to remain homeless. Once people are housed, they are no longer being jailed periodically for sleeping on the street; they require far fewer emergency health services; and (obviously) they no longer need a bed in a shelter.

Dallas's City Council has committed itself to the development of several hundred units of permanent supportive housing, with the required mental-health services already promised by two different agencies. Nevertheless, as of this writing (June 2009), the council has turned down two potential sites and proposals on the basis of neighborhood NIMBY complaints. The homeless and their advocates are waiting to see whether the council intends to honor its commitment to Dallas's most vulnerable citizens.

Notes

[1] Some characters are based on real clients/guests of The Stewpot; others are composites of the stories of several people. Names have been changed in all cases.

[2] There is much debate, among both scholars and care providers, about what terms(s) should be used to refer to the people who come for services. "Clients" is accurate in some regards, but it emphasizes the inequality between giver and receiver. The Metro Dallas Homeless Alliance tends to use the term "customers," which reminds providers that they are there to *serve* the population, but (to me) implies a certain level of free choice among multiple options that most of those receiving services do not in fact have. "Guests" is often heard as well, especially for shelter residents but also in other contexts. In this chapter, I will use both "guests" and "clients" to refer to the homeless in their relationship with service providers.

[3] Permanent supportive housing combines affordable and/or subsidized rental housing with supportive services such as case management, mental-health and substance-abuse services, health care, and employment—either on-site or within an easily accessible distance.

[4] Except to note that the Hispanic count may be lower than the national percentages due to Dallas's relative proximity to Mexico, which allows immigrants to return to their home country in extended periods of joblessness, I cannot account for the differences between Dallas's percentages and the national ones.

[5] The rationale for January is this: Homeless persons are more likely to seek indoor shelter when the weather is cold. It is easier to count persons indoors, in a shelter, than to try to locate hundreds if not thousands of people sleeping on the streets or in homeless encampments. Thus, a count done in winter is more likely to come close to the true number of homeless in a given location than is one performed when the weather is conducive to outdoor living.

[6] Los Angeles, for example, with more than twice as many homeless as Dallas, requires three nights in order to complete its census—but this is the exception rather than the rule.

[7] For example, for late January 2005 the point-in-time homeless census reported 415,000 *sheltered* homeless people counted in the U.S. Using HMIS, researchers were able to discover that between the end of January and the end of April 2005, there were 704,000 individual homeless people who were sheltered at some time in that three-month period (HUD 2007). Thus, there is a substantial turnover rate in the population of sheltered homeless—something that could not have been discovered only through use of a point-in-time count.

[8] NLCHP has cited these figures for a number of years. I am unable to locate the original source for the estimate or the research on which it was based; in more recent documents they simply cite themselves.

[9] In Dallas's case, the designation was based on the following criteria: (1) passage of an ordinance making it illegal to take shopping carts off store property; (2) "sweeps" in December 2004 in which all personal property of homeless persons was confiscated and destroyed, including blankets, identification, and prescription medication; (3) a "sweep" by the Texas Department of Transportation, chasing homeless persons out from under highway overpasses, on *the day after* the point-in-time census; (4) bulldozing of a large homeless encampment in May 2005 (again, with too few shelter beds for all the people displaced); (5) an ordinance prohibiting panhandling at street corners and in any locations where presumably nonhomeless people are having to use cash (e.g., at an ATM, a parking meter, a gas station); (6) in September 2005, the passage of a new ordinance penalizing any group that serves food to the needy outside of city-designated areas; and (7) a proposal by the mayor to begin ticketing anyone who gives money to a panhandler, as the ordinance prohibiting panhandling was not proving effective.

[10] Transitional housing is an intermediate step for persons or families who are ready to leave an emergency shelter but who cannot yet afford market-rate housing. During a one- to two-year stay in a transitional housing program, participants receive reduced rent and are expected to participate in programs such as job training, budgeting, and other life skills. Many are waiting for Section 8 (federally subsidized) housing to become available. The story of Oasis Housing Corporation is recounted in Adkins and Kemper (2006).

[11] In fact, evidence shows that just the opposite occurs, particularly in the case of transitional and permanent supportive housing. Over time, these facilities have proven to be "good neighbors" in a variety of cities.

References

Adkins, Julie, and Robert V. Kemper. 2006. Oasis Housing Corporation: From Solutions to Dissolution in a Faith-Based Organization. *Urban Anthropology*, 35(2-3):237–264.

Hill, Patricia Evridge. 1996. *Dallas: The Making of a Modern City*. Austin: University of Texas Press.

Hopper, Kim. 2003. *Reckoning with Homelessness*. Ithaca, NY: Cornell University Press.

Kemper, Robert V. 2002. Dallas-Fort Worth. In *Encyclopedia of Urban Cultures*, eds. Melvin Ember and Carol R. Ember, pp. 94–107. Danbury, CT: Grolier.

National Coalition for the Homeless. 2008. How Many People Experience Homelessness? NCH Fact Sheet #2. Available online at http://www.national homeless.org/factsheets/How_Many.html (last accessed June 3, 2009).

National Coalition for the Homeless and National Law Center on Homelessness and Poverty. 2006. A Dream Denied: The Criminalization of Homelessness in U.S. Cities. Available online at http://www.nationalhomeless.org/publications/crimreport/report.pdf (last accessed June 1, 2009).

National Law Center on Homelessness and Poverty. 2007. 2007 Annual Report. Available online at http://www.nlchp.org/content/pubs/2007_Annual_Report2.pdf (last accessed May 29, 2009).

Payne, Darwin. 1994. *Big D: Triumphs and Troubles of an American Supercity in the 20th Century*. Dallas: Three Forks Press.

Rosenthal, Rob. 1994. *Homeless in Paradise: A Map of the Terrain*. Philadelphia: Temple University Press.

U.S. Department of Housing and Urban Development Office of Community Planning and Development. 2007. The Annual Homeless Assessment Report to Congress. Available online at http://www.huduser.org/Publications/pdf/ahar.pdf (last accessed May 28, 2009).

16

Gangs, Poverty, and the Future

James Diego Vigil

In this chapter, James Diego Vigil examines urban street gangs in the context of the impoverished barrios (neighborhoods) where Chicanos and other ethnic groups are concentrated in Los Angeles, California. Calling upon more than 30 years of field-work in the barrios, the author demonstrates how street gangs have emerged as a consequence of marginalization, destabilization, and fragmentation of people's lives—what Vigil calls their circumstance of "multiple marginality." Recognizing that current law enforcement tactics are having uneven success in addressing the violence and other criminal activities associated with urban street gangs, Vigil suggests that early intervention and prevention tactics are likely to be more beneficial and less costly.

Poverty is the central reason for the rise of street gangs throughout the contemporary world. The children of the poor are put at risk by factors over which they have no control: their family's living conditions, work situations, health problems, and educational limitations. Especially damaging are the social structural breakdowns that occur when family resources are strained, school systems overwhelmed, and law enforcement agencies overburdened in their attempts to solve the problems of troubled youth. The effects of poverty in children's lives are clear, and what children learn in the streets shapes and molds them in powerful ways. This chapter will examine the linkages between poverty and urban gangs in light of the experiences of Chicanos and other ethnic groups in Los Angeles, California.

Based on over 30 years of street-level ethnographic investigations, I have learned that street gangs are the offspring of marginalization. In hierarchical societies, certain groups become relegated to the fringes, where social and economic conditions result in the destabilization and fragmentation of people's lives. A sense of powerlessness can develop when these conditions continue over a long period of time. Some of the gang members that I have known have

Source: Written expressly for *Urban Life*.

come from such stressed and unstable circumstances that one wonders how they have survived at all. In this chapter, I will use the phrase "multiple marginality" (Vigil 2002) to reflect these strains and their persistence over time.

MULTIPLE MARGINALITY

In its simplest trajectory, multiple marginality can be modeled thus: place/status → street socialization → street subculture → street identity. Many factors are intertwined, and the actions and reactions among them spawn gangs and gang members. With respect to place/status, *barrios* (neighborhoods) or ethnic enclaves derive from the external barriers imposed on a people and, from that, people's choice to live together in their own community. Living in spatially separate and socially distanced neighborhoods makes for a marginal existence that closes rather than opens doors to social mobility. Race and cultural differences also serve as a rationale for the isolation and mistreatment of each ethnic group.

The model of multiple marginality helps us to dissect and analyze the ways in which marginal place/status undermines and exacerbates social, cultural, and psychological problems in ethnic minority communities. These forces contribute to the breakdown of social control and the emergence of gangs and gang members. Social dysfunctions especially affect family life, educational trajectories, and interactions with law enforcement. In the absence of these influences, the gang replaces parenting, schooling, and policing to regulate the lives of many youth. Ultimately, a gang subculture arises to set rules and regulations for its members.

STREET GANGS

Early in the history of social science research on urban gangs, anthropologists and other scholars built strong arguments about economic inequality in urban areas as the best explanation for gang delinquency (Cartwright, Tomson, and Schwartz 1975), especially among immigrant populations. One of the best known was Merton's (1949) "strain theory," which focused on the mismatch between the status goals established by the dominant society and the inadequate means available for low-income people to reach those goals. A sense of marginality results when poor people recognize their "place" on the socioeconomic fringes. With such structural barriers firmly in place, some young persons learn to pursue alternative opportunity paths, many of which are illicit or illegal.

Large-scale societal forces lead to economic instability and employment barriers, the fragmentation of social control, material impoverishment, and psychological strains among large segments of ethnic communities in Los Angeles. Within these communities, people face inferior housing conditions, strains and changes in personal and family relationships, and cultural repression and racism in schools. Although most members of these communities

234 Gangs, Poverty, and the Future

cope well enough with these adverse circumstances to lead productive, conventional ways of life, some youth in such communities join gangs.

Most gangs are composed of male adolescents and youth who have been together since childhood in specific low-income neighborhoods. Today, close to 1,000 gangs and almost 200,000 gang members operate in the Los Angeles area. Among the youth in impoverished enclaves, only about 10 to 15 percent join gangs (Esbensen and Winfree 1998; Short 1996; Vigil 1988); and despite the conventional wisdom offered by many officials ("once a gang member, always a gang member"), about 70 percent eventually "mature out" of their gangs (Short 1996; Vigil 2007). Gang participants combine both conventional and antisocial behavior in their daily activities. It is the antisocial behavior, however, that attracts the attention of authorities as well as the general public.

As many anthropologists have long noted, social control is an important function in all societies. Institutions such as the family, schools, and police are expected to provide this control; however, where these institutions have broken down, the situation is ripe for the rise and perpetuation of street-level gangs. Operating without conventional influences or secure tethers, gang members do not know how to behave in acceptable ways; nor are proper sanctions applied for unacceptable behavior. When poor people live in crowded homes with large families, they often seek privacy outside the home. For the street-socialized gang member, the rooftops, alleyways, and empty sections of parks serve this purpose.

Los Angeles has had Mexican barrios since the nineteenth century. Those located just east of the town center are collectively referred to as East Los Angeles (Romo 1983). In an ecological sense, "East Los" (as shortened by young native speakers) can be seen as a macro-barrio that serves as an overlay for dozens of meso- (encompassing several street blocks) and micro- (just two or three blocks) barrios. These enclaves have their own place names and spatial markers. Within the vast ecosystem of East Los Angeles exist barrios like El Hoyo Maravilla, White Fence, Cuatro Flats, Little Valley, and numerous others.

The power of place cannot be overemphasized. The barrios have provided generations of Mexican Americans with deep memories and lasting impressions. Immigrants who worked on the railroads, in brickyards, inside garment districts, and at hotel and business establishments often had to live in marginal areas near their workplaces. As immigrants continued to be forced into inferior locations and worn-out residences, this workplace and residential linkage became embedded in the minds of the residents, especially the youth. For example, the 38th Street gang is located in the middle of Vernon, near meatpacking factories. Such homes and apartments became part of the stigma associated with poor people, especially among those living in public housing developments (the "projects"). Living in such places—and the associated isolation, rejection, and alienation—often leads individuals to think of themselves as "outsiders." Responses to these challenging circumstances can lead to a continuing spiral of disaffection and inner turmoil.

Living in poverty in such spatially distinctive neighborhoods—the hollows, ravines, "across the tracks"—has not eased the adjustment of Mexican immigrants to American society. In the decades following the U.S. takeover of Texas, California, and the Southwest in the 1840s, Mexicans who found themselves residing in the United States felt unwanted and suffered discrimination. During the past century and a half, large-scale immigration to densely populated areas has created the conditions for major social problems. Throughout this period street children have formed "boy gangs" that, according to numerous commentators, warranted careful observation and perhaps intervention. Even as we move through the twenty-first century, a "street gang subculture" represents a dangerous underside of life in Los Angeles, with the result that violence and drug trafficking have generated problems far beyond the barrios to affect people across the entire Los Angeles region. Children in gang neighborhoods continue to be subjected to the challenges inherent in marginal places that contribute to the lower status fueled by racial and ethnic discrimination.

In contrast to the Mexican American population, the African American population began to develop street gangs during the Depression, and their growth accelerated in the aftermath of World War II with high rates of migration from the U.S. South to South Central Los Angeles. As a result, the problem of ghettos—of poverty and neighborhood deterioration—soon worsened in that section of the city. Children in this overcrowded environment had no place to play safely, as recreational facilities were insufficient. Outlets for youth were few and far between. Furthermore, economic opportunities and avenues for social mobility remained blocked and, in large part, were responsible for the emergence of gang activity and its persistence today.

Yet, most youth living in these situations avoided getting involved in gang activities. For other individuals, casual, episodic, almost reluctant participation in the gang acts became the norm, while others were continually committed to delinquent or even sociopathic actions.

To understand how gang members become violence-prone individuals, we need to be aware that gang members spend most of their time in social activities common to most adolescent and youth groups: casual repartee and joking, drinking beer and wine, playing sports, meeting at the local hangout, and catching up with the news of peer groups. The media, police, and public care little about such normal, conventional patterns but focus more on the gangs' unacceptable activities: the drive-bys, random shootings, and criminal lifestyles. Often unnoticed by gang observers and authorities are the values (i.e., ought-tos) and norms (i.e., blueprints for action) that guide gang members' thinking and behavior. The following cases give some indication of how this works for older, traditional East Los Angeles gangs.

Case #1
Street life, with its crime, drugs, and predators of all stripes and persuasions, necessitates that one acquire protection against dangerous situations and people. One 13-year-old from Cuatro Flats (4th Street Flats

barrio) explained this to me in very succinct terms. "I used to come home from Hollenbeck Junior High every day and even though it was only about three or four blocks away, I had to watch my back all the time. The guys from White Fence, King Kobras, Primera (First Street) were always around the area. One time, the King Kobras got me and pushed me around and said they would kick my ass if they saw me again. At school the next day, I told the guys from my neighborhood what had happened and they went over to where the King Kobras hung out on the school yard and told them to leave me alone as I was from their barrio, Cuatro Flats. Soon after I was 'jumped into' [initiated into] Cuatro Flats. Since then I never had to watch my back as it was always covered." Thus, much of the camaraderie and "homeboy" and "homegirl" bonding involves a practical consideration—help when one's life is at stake or potential risks are at hand.

Case #2

After initiation into the gang, young members have to show their allegiance and loyalty. One 14-year-old had just been inducted into VNE (Varrio Nuevo Estrada) and was walking around the periphery of the barrio turf, where encounters with outsiders from rival gangs often materialize, and was stopped in his tracks when a car going in the same direction approached the curb and stopped. There were three older "cholos" in the '62 Chevy Malibu, all looking at the youngster in the "mad dog" style of gang members. "*¿De dónde eres?*" ("Where are you from? What gang?"), yelled one guy from the car. Freezing up right on the spot, the kid bought time by being deliberate. He knew this could be a test since not all the gang members from VNE knew each other, especially the older guys unfamiliar with the younger novitiates. So, he decided to throw caution to the wind and uttered "VNE" with confidence and a proud, defiant look. All the guys in the '62 started laughing and one said, "We were just testing you, but you were scared, huh?" A test of loyalty under fire is expected of a gang member.

Case #3

In addition to fulfilling basic human needs of friendship and emotional support—that is, creating a sense of fictive family—street gangs also aid persons under duress to survive. A 15-year-old from El Hoyo Maravilla had to learn how to act *loco* (crazy) in order to gain the recognition and respect of his fellow gang members. He would go out of his way to show that he wasn't afraid of anything. One time there was a drive-by where the White Fence gang members sprayed bullets at him and two other homeboys standing on the corner of their barrio. They all ducked when the shots were fired; while the other guys stayed put, the "loco" jumped up right away and starting chasing on foot the car that was racing away. Along the way he picked up anything he could find on the ground—rocks, bottles, sticks—and threw it at the car. The car was soon too far away, but his actions left an impression on the two onlookers, who later recited the story to the other members of their gang. Whatever respect he had before was doubled by this act of fearlessness and spontaneity.

These case studies show that young people learn how to navigate their way through the aggressiveness and violence that pervade certain places within their neighborhoods. All youth in these neighborhoods are affected, whether or not they are involved in local gangs. Gang families can be distinguished from nongang families along a number of dimensions (see Thornberry 2001 for the association between family dynamics and delinquency). In the end, it seems that some families are more vulnerable to gang membership. Gang households, for example, are poorer, significantly larger, and more likely to be headed by single females. There are also indications of greater economic stress in the gang families, including a smaller proportion of those households having access to a car, in a region such as Los Angeles where automobiles are often the only reliable means of transportation. Previous research in similar neighborhoods (Moore 1978, 1991; Moore and Vigil 1987; Vigil 1993) has shown differences in family dynamics, variations that account for why some children within a neighborhood undergo street socialization early and become gang members and why others are able to pursue a more conventional lifestyle.

Generally, institutions of social control (families, schools, and law enforcement) have broken down in the communities where gangs are found. Chronic unemployment, lack of adequate employment skills, a high incidence of drug use and sales, and a pervasive street gang presence affect nearly all residents.

One issue to focus on is how the streets generate—through the process of street socialization—a need to seek out the gang in order to survive, especially when families falter and schooling comes up short. These are certainly precursors to street socialization, and reflect the broader "multiple marginality" and poverty that shape Latino, as well as other ethnic minority, neighborhoods. Human developmental trajectories are thwarted under such situations and conditions. Group/gang activities are sought for approval and praise. Participation in gang life provides a sense of worthiness not found anywhere else. All of this occurs at a time in young people's lives when they are expending high energy and enjoying practicing new skills to function in the streets. Guidance and supervision in other outlets for these children in highly stressed families and overburdened schools are practically nonexistent.

It is, as previously noted, primarily in the most stressed households that children find themselves bereft of supervision and thus seek attention and adventure in the streets. Poor immigrant families and their second-generation offspring are more likely than affluent families to experience such adaptation problems. When immigrant parents adjust to a new place and source of livelihood, their children also are acculturating, and for many it is a problematic experience. In gang-ridden neighborhoods, street gangs compete with other sources of identity formation, often replacing family, school, and other conventional influences. Among Mexican Americans, gang members are often called *cholos* from the Spanish word *solo* (alone, abandoned)—as a reflection of their marginal identity.

Among members of the African American community of Los Angeles, the situation was no better than it was among Mexican Americans. During the 1980s, the unemployment rate for African American youth was a staggering 45 percent. The dramatic rise of African American gangs between 1978 and 1982 was most evident in Los Angeles, Compton, and Inglewood and was due in part to deindustrialization, which led to some 70,000 layoffs during this period. As Davis (1992:88) writes, "This deterioration in the labor-market position of young Black men is a major reason why the counter-economy of drug dealing and youth crime has burgeoned." Another reason has been the growing poverty in Los Angeles County. During the 1980s, 40 percent of African American children lived below or just above the poverty line.

For many young persons, joining a gang is the beginning of a life of aggression and violence. It is a violent lifestyle: violence against others in the form of rampant gang conflicts and killings, and against oneself through the abuse of drugs and other chemical substances. These represent the destructive, debilitating habits that separate gangs from other adolescent peer networks. Such public and private destructive acts, including *locura*, reflect the "crazy" orientation that is a feature of Chicano gang members' behavior style. For some, this street style is an available *persona* to use when warranted, while for a smaller number it becomes an expression of their more unthinking violent personalities.

The violence brought about by youth gangs is not insignificant. An examination of gang-related homicides in Los Angeles County over two decades confirms the long-term impact of gang violence on their communities. Gang-related killings reached all-time highs during the 1990s, when Latino immigration into Southern California was peaking (see the figure below).

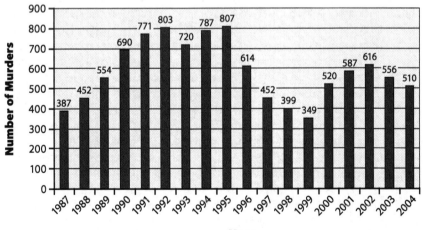

Source: Adapted from data provided by Sgt. Wes McBride, retired, Los Angeles Sheriff Department.

Gang-Related Homicides

Such violence represents a form of "storm and stress" during adolescence, when daring, excitement, courage, and adventure are valued by peers. Indeed, doing "gang" work earns respect and recognition as a dependable gang member with *huevos* (balls). Notwithstanding their attempts to conform to such expectations, however, most youth remain conscious of, and concerned with, the detrimental effects of such behavior. Oftentimes, the negative results of this behavior accelerate the "maturing out" process, which hastens one's exit from a gang. These human sentiments show, as Edgerton (1978:444) has noted in his study of deviance generally, that such individual and group behavior must be viewed not as that of "freaks in a side show," but rather as "principal performers in the everyday dramas of life."

Research in communities where gangs maintain a significant presence suggests that such "neighborhoods are female-based in the home and youth-dominated on the streets" (Cartwright, Tomson, and Schwartz 1975:65). In such spaces, the behavioral adaptation of many young males becomes focused on the streets around them, where they learn very quickly that one must become or act "like a man" in order to survive in the street-gang world. Enculturation to street values and customs proceeds apace in their social interactions and networks. Fear is omnipresent in street life, especially if one is unprotected. Being and acting "tough" has become a focal street value and a salient aspect of gang members' behavior, as Miller (1958) discovered in studying East Coast youth. A youth's sense of self is affected by his concern for being tough, especially insofar as outsiders label him as such, and how he responds.

The more isolated and poverty stricken a barrio, the more its "boundedness" results in its children having severe problems that lead to prolonged street-gang socialization. These spatial features of communities generate the toughest, most active, and most violent of the street gangs. Barrio youth, whether part of a gang or not, know that their self-identities are shaped by the boundedness of barrio life; they recognize that both spatial and social distance separate them from their more affluent neighbors. This ecological distinctiveness affects their quality of life in terms of job opportunities, education, and the like. Poverty, discrimination, and group choice helped create Mexican barrios, but the effects of urbanization—along with poor city planning and uncaring authorities—have made the barrios an ecologically inferior place for raising a family.

Efforts during the 1970s to ameliorate difficult community conditions led to the creation of such programs as the Job Corps, the Neighborhood Youth Corps, and the Comprehensive Employment and Training Act (CETA). The dismantling of these programs by Ronald Reagan (first as governor, then as president) left Latino and African American youth with nowhere to turn. For gang members, especially, there were virtually no legitimate job opportunities in or near their home communities. As one youth counselor commented, "You could pull 80 percent of gang members, seventeen years old or younger, out of gangs, if you had jobs, job training and social alternatives" (Davis 1992:101).

Schools also have long been a serious problem for impoverished ethnic minority communities in the Los Angeles area. California now ranks 42nd nationwide in per capita spending on students, and the Los Angeles Unified School District (the nation's second largest district, with over 700,000 students) has a dropout rate of 30 to 59 percent in inner-city neighborhoods. In 1995, the California state budget for 150,000 *prisoners* stood at $4 billion, the same amount as was budgeted for all of the children enrolled in the Los Angeles Unified School District. Further, there is de facto racial segregation and tracking of students based on biased test scores, with the result that African American males from South Central Los Angeles are three times more likely to end up in prison than at a University of California campus.

If ethnic minority students manage to graduate under such challenging conditions, they find few opportunities open to them after high school. Because good jobs are practically nonexistent, "Young street people enlist in the . . . youth employment program operated by the cocaine cartels" (Davis 1992:257).

Connecting, engaging, involving, and grounding youth in a socially acceptable belief system is nearly impossible if social control is broken or absent. Poverty situations and conditions regularly undermine social control foundations, especially those taught in the home and at school. In this void it is difficult to shape conformity to a dominant society that otherwise shows little interest in assisting large numbers of children living in marginalized conditions. Thus, the alternative street socialization process is strongly influenced by the breakdown of family life and the tendency to drop out of school. From a structural perspective, the streets become a replacement for the schools. Involvement with street gangs starts in the elementary school years, typically between the ages of seven and nine years, and continues beyond the (often aborted) high school years into young adulthood.

CONCLUSION: TOWARD THE FUTURE

Law enforcement and suppression tactics, already overtaxed as a solution to a problem they did not start, are having only moderate and uneven success in addressing the gang problem. It does not make any difference how many jails we build or how many cells are set aside for each new gang cohort; the current strategy has failed. It has failed because it is *not* based on the facts of human development or common sense. We need to be honest in recognizing this reality, and be willing to take bold and courageous steps in charting a new course. A focus on the roots, not the buds, of the problem will generate logical solutions and aim not merely to stem the worst violence but to begin the long hard march to regain social control in urban areas. While the stick of punishment will have its role, emphasis will shift to introducing carrots—rewards—early in a person's life to balance the present formula to include prevention and intervention.

Such a balanced approach is sensible and workable and reflects human developmental principles. Programs step in and phase out, each one a separate, age-specific entity, but each involves working with the same common coordinated goal of winning the hearts and minds of youth. Would matters turn out differently for gang members if their family lives were more structured and if their parents provided more direction and guidance? How can we address the absence of parenting and the early voids in the development of connections that are so necessary for leading children to positive engagements, involvements, and beliefs? We must not forget that families and other household members do not exist in a vacuum.

Instead of a vacuum, a long history of racism and poverty has generated lingering effects throughout urban areas, including where people live and what types of jobs are available to them. This in turn is related to how family life is structured so that young people can participate effectively in society. Moreover, to the extent that poor people often receive short shrift from all types of authorities, especially law enforcement officials, it is hardly surprising that family life has been negatively affected and that a sentiment of distrust and fear of the police persists among Latinos and Blacks. Any new program that can present the police in a favorable light will be a "win-win" situation because it not only will be creating a new future but also will help to wipe out the memories of the past.

What is needed today to address gang problems and related social problems is a balance of prevention, intervention, and law enforcement—the carrots and sticks that enable parents to help their children conform to society's standards of behavior. We must begin to think of our society's children, particularly those who are less fortunate, as our responsibility to care for at an early age. Detractors will claim that this strategy is unworkable, impractical, and—if it were implemented—just another expensive form of welfare. Failing to realize that the present criminal justice apparatus is also a form of welfare—what we might label "criminal justice welfare"—these naysayers forget that hundreds of billions of dollars are spent every year to warehouse hundreds of thousands of largely poor, ethnic minority peoples and to support the middle-class bureaucrats who handle their cases, even though many studies (cf. Sherman et al. 2002; Walker et al. 1996) have shown that the benefits of early intervention and prevention tactics, especially through schools and community organizing efforts, would be far less expensive than the current failed strategy.

References

Cartwright, Desmond, Barbara Tomson, and Hershey Schwartz. 1975. *Gang Delinquency.* Monterey, CA: Brooks/Cole.
Davis, Mike. 1992. *City of Quartz: Excavating the Future in Los Angeles.* New York: Vintage.
Edgerton, Robert. 1978. *Deviant Behavior and Cultural Theory.* Addison-Wesley Module in Anthropology, #37. Reading, MA: Addison-Wesley Pub. Co.
Esbensen, Finn-Aage, and Thomas Winfree. 1998. Race and Gender Differences between Gang and Non-Gang Youth: Results from a Multisite Survey. *Justice Quarterly,* 15(3):505–526.
Merton, Robert K. 1949. *Social Theory and Social Structure.* Glencoe, IL: Free Press.

Miller, Walter. B. 1958. Lower class culture as a generating milieu of gang delinquency. *Journal of Social Issues,* 14(3):419–435.

Moore, Joan W. 1978. *Homeboys: Gangs, Drugs, and Prison in the Barrios of Los Angeles.*
Philadelphia: Temple University Press.

———. 1991. *Going Down to the Barrio: Homeboys and Homegirls in Change.* Philadelphia: Temple University Press.

Moore, Joan W., and James Diego Vigil. 1987. Chicano Gangs: Group Norms and
Individual Factors Related to Adult Criminality. *Aztlan,* 18(2):27–44.

Romo, Ricardo. 1983. *East Los Angeles: History of a Barrio, 1900–1930.* Austin: University of Texas Press.

Sherman, Lawrence W., David P. Farrington, Brandon C. Welsh, and Doris Layton
MacKenzie. 2002. *Evidence-Based Crime Prevention.* New York: Routledge.

Short, James F., Jr. 1996. Personal, Gang, and Community Careers. In *Gangs in America,* 2nd ed., ed. C. R. Huff, pp. 3–11. Thousand Oaks, CA: Sage.

Thornberry, Terence P. 2001. Risk Factors for Gang Membership. In *The Modern Gang
Researcher,* 2nd ed., eds. Jody Miller, Cheryl L. Maxson, and Malcolm W. Klein,
pp. 32–43. Los Angeles: Roxbury.

Vigil, James Diego. 1988. *Barrio Gangs: Street Life and Identity in Southern California.*
Austin: University of Texas Press.

———. 1993. Gangs, Social Control, and Ethnicity: Ways to Redirect Youth. In *Identity and Inner City Youth: Beyond Ethnicity and Gender,* eds. Shirley Brice Heath and
Milbrey W. McLaughlin, pp. 94–119. New York: Columbia University Press.

———. 2002. *A Rainbow of Gangs: Street Cultures in the Mega-City.* Austin: University of
Texas Press.

———. 2007. *The Projects: Gang and Non-Gang Families in East Los Angeles.* Austin: University of Texas Press.

Walker, Hill M., Robert H. Horner, George Sugai, Michael Bullis, Jeffrey R. Sprague,
Diane Bricker, and Martin J. Kaufman. 1996. Integrated Approaches to Preventing Antisocial Behavior Patterns Among School-Age Children and Youth. *Journal of Emotional and Behavioral Disorders,* 4:194–209.

17

Civic Ecology, Urban Elders, and New York City's Community Garden Movement

Jay Sokolovsky

"Community" and "garden" would seem to be unlikely urban partners, and even less likely to be the subject of anthropological fieldwork. For Jay Sokolovsky, however, community gardens in cities like New York become focal points for residents to join forces not only to grow food but also to reclaim the landscape. In New York's 500+ community gardens, older adults create spaces where they can share their knowledge and spend free time, where young people can learn not only about food but also about their heritage, and where members of different ethnic groups can work together to produce more than mere foodstuffs. In this sense, urban community gardens constitute acts of "civic ecology," as the undesirable activities that used to plague such sites are transformed into spaces of social action benefiting entire communities.

> East 125th St., Harlem, New York, Jackie Robinson Garden: "It was a vision from God . . . he spoke to me, one day I was walking down the street and I look over there and saw all this garbage and stuff . . . and I saw they were using it for prostitution and they were shooting up over there, and I said to myself, Lord I sure would like to make a big garden over there. And the voice said, 'You can do that, just step out on my word.' But today if you see it you wouldn't believe it. We got peach trees, grape trees . . . apple trees . . . , you wouldn't believe it to see this dump come to paradise!" (Field notes, June 14, 2002)

As I sat with 72-year-old Betty Gaither, munching on one of the apples from this garden in Harlem, I indeed felt like I was in a certain version of paradise. This uptown green space is wedged between elevated subway tracks, apart-

Source: Adapted from "Elders, Urban Community Greening and the Rise of Civic Ecology," in *The Cultural Context of Aging*, 3rd ed., J. Sokolovsky, ed. (Westport, CT: Praeger, 2009).

ment buildings, and a lot with junked cars. Yet, spending an afternoon there with its garden members might lead even a stranger to believe that urban community gardens, in the hands of energetic urban elders working with those of younger generations, might just save the world.

Betty is just one among many elders who have been part of an international movement to create green spaces and community gardens in what once were abandoned urban sites eroding neighborhood well-being (Linn 2007). What I heard from Betty was repeated many times during the period (1998–2007) when I sought to document the history of New York City's community garden movement (Sokolovsky 2008). It is a powerful story of how people living in the city's poorest neighborhoods transformed otherwise barren and often criminally hazardous zones with plants, trees, simple structures, locally inspired art, performance, and political activism.

Through documenting the creation of these green oases, I began to see a pattern in the role of active urban elders. In working to sustain community gardens, they were creating alliances across generational, economic, and ethnic lines during one of the most troubled times in the city's history. When community elders could not obtain adequate city help, or the situation required instant action, they either started projects on their own or strong-armed a small cadre of younger kin and immediate neighbors to get things started or to protect what they had done from those who had other ideas for the space. Such urban community greening activities can be seen as acts of "civic ecology," whereby local citizens use collective action to reorder a physical space into a more enabling environment (Tidball and Krasny 2007). Such actions frequently promote and enhance community involvement and social inclusion. Their impact is especially powerful when undertaken in the face of great socioeconomic inequities and rapid environmental degradation.

In this chapter, I will examine the rise of the community gardening movement in New York City, focusing on the involvement of seniors who use the creation of such places to enhance their neighborhood's ability to act collectively for the benefit of others. I also will discuss the connection of civic greening to creating therapeutic landscapes in public venues and care settings where the aged may one day reside. In effect, green spaces can enhance the social lives of even the frailest of older adults.

URBAN DECLINE AND THE FLOWERING OF CIVIC GREENING AND COMMUNITY GARDENS

Few people would associate twenty-first-century New York City with gardening and urban agriculture, yet this archetypical world city is home to one of the largest such urban community greening efforts in North America. Its five boroughs contain over 500 locally developed and maintained community gardens and even a few small farms. This figure does not include the 300–400 gardens being maintained, often by seniors, in the city's extensive public housing system, where some 125,000 seniors lived in 2008. From

Coney Island, Brooklyn, to Manhattan's Lower East Side and the once-dev-astated South Bronx, poor and minority elders such as "Miss Betty" and their neighbors have created miracles that have been a major but unheralded part of New York City's renaissance during the past 30 years.

Creating urban gardens on vacant public land has a long history in the United States. Many people know about the "victory gardens" of the two World Wars, but most have forgotten about the attempts of cities to help poor citizens grow food on vacant urban land during bad economic times. For example, during the 1893–1897 depression, "potato patch farms" enabled masses of the unemployed in cities like Detroit to survive by growing food in vacant lots. Other cities, such as Chicago, Buffalo, Boston, and Providence, quickly developed similar programs, but as better economic times reemerged, these gardens faded away and the spaces reverted to real estate development.

During the Great Depression of the 1930s, New York City's welfare department, in conjunction with the federal Works Project Administration, sponsored almost 5,000 "relief" gardens on vacant public land. This program ended in 1937, when the U.S. Department of Agriculture began to distribute surplus farm production through the food stamp program. Since that time, multitudes of short-lived efforts have arisen in hard times or during the two World Wars. For example, during World War II, all available New York City-owned land became available for "Victory Gardens," a pattern replicated around the country. These fruit and vegetable plots were established in back-yards, on rooftops, and even at the White House—producing an estimated 40 percent of U.S. food production during World War II. Such efforts came to a halt after the war, when food rationing ended and a corporate-based frozen foods industry was launched.

In Europe, a less community-oriented effort called the "allotment sys-tem," based on individual plots of land, was developed in the eighteenth and nineteenth centuries. Allotments were usually located on city outskirts, where poor families could grow food as millions of rural peasants rushed to cities where they toiled for an "unliving" wage. In contrast to the early emphasis of Europeans on food production, over the past two decades some countries, especially England, have refocused the traditional system of allotment gar-dens toward the community inclusive ideals of civic ecology (Hancock 2001).

NEW YORK CITY AND ITS COMMUNITY GARDEN MOVEMENT

When most people think of green space in New York City, they conjure up "manicured" landscapes such as monumental public parks like Central Park or the magnificent botanical gardens in Brooklyn and the Bronx. In 1859 when the city government opened Central Park, it was thought of as a green oasis intended to "civilize" the newly arrived masses of immigrants and to ease the stress of urban life. Today's community gardens represent a totally different relation to place, space, and power. Across contemporary New York City, citizens from poor and neglected neighborhoods have reversed this process by reclaiming abandoned public lands to civilize city-owned spaces that they saw as being dangerously out of control. What were once "open sores" on the urban landscape have been transformed into places of transcendent beauty, cultural meaning, and often social and political activism. In this regard, this latest civic greening movement appears more long lasting than prior incarnations. It is connected to an emerging new vision of urban possibilities, whereby citizens can create more livable, more sustainable, and healthier communities (Smit and Bailkey 2006).

In New York City, if there were not such good documentation on community gardens, they might have been written off as pure urban myth. During the 1970s, the city's housing stock and infrastructure were crumbling, violent crime had skyrocketed, and the treasury was bare. As banks redlined entire neighborhoods and landlords abandoned their properties, the city acquired upwards of 20,000 lots. In the Lower East Side of Manhattan, 70 percent of the population was displaced as 3,400 living units were demolished, fires occurred almost daily, and a lively drug trade moved in (von Hassell 2002). Uptown in Community District 3, the heart of the South Bronx, almost two-thirds (64.4 percent) of its population was lost from 1970 to 1980 (Chait et al. 2000). In this broader area, 500 acres of former housing were burned down and reverted to the city for back taxes. Many such spaces came to be used as illegal garbage dumps, drug-shooting galleries, and places to abandon cars.

GREEN DREAMS AND THE COMMUNITY-BASED STRUGGLE TO CREATE COMMUNITY GARDENS

In 1973, an artist named Liz Christie got some friends together and began to reclaim as garden space a small abandoned lot bordering Manhattan's Lower East Side and Skid Row. In a dream, she envisioned repeating this, even in fenced lots, by tossing over balloons armed with water and seeds. Her dream also revealed a name, "Green Guerillas" (spelled incorrectly in her vision), which would become a group to teach others how to repeat this success.

Two years later, she developed the Open Space Greening Program for the city's Council on the Environment. These acts of grassroots activism were but some of the sparks that ignited New York City's current community garden movement. By the late 1970s, there were so many gardens created on abandoned public lands that the city established "Operation Green Thumb," which initially leased plots for $1 a year and provided technical support to sustain greening activities (see www.greenthumbnyc.org). Over the ensuing three decades, additional support from the Trust for Public Land and the New York Restoration Project (see www.nyrp.org) has facilitated the purchase of more than 100 garden properties to prevent them from being sold to developers. City governments throughout North America have seen the benefits of supporting community garden creation and have instituted their own governmental support units, such as Seattle's P-Patch, Boston's Urban Gardeners, and Philadelphia Green.

This is *not* a story about rich kids or bored elders in white gloves who form garden clubs to indulge their passion for hybrid roses or organic tomatoes. Here is a gut-wrenching, often lonely and continuing struggle for community control of neighborhoods, public space, and the very lives and well-being of neighborhood children (von Hassell 2002). As the late greening activist Adam Honigman frequently reminded people, "Land Use is a Blood Sport!" On the Lower East Side during the 1970s, this sometimes involved violent struggles against drug addicts, street gangs, and anarchists who refused to have others in the neighborhood transform "their" space for public use. Since the mid-1990s, the biggest conflicts have been with real estate developers and city government, especially the administration of former Mayor Rudy Giuliani, who sought to auction off over 100 garden lands for housing and refused to consider plans to incorporate some of the garden spaces into proposed construction plans. Despite substantial community protests, some of the oldest and most socially important gardens were uprooted in the late 1990s, until the state's attorney general obtained an injunction against such actions in 1998. In interviews with a State attorney involved with the case, I was told that despite studies showing the feasibility of including part of established gardens into the planned housing, the Giuliani administration was unwilling to compromise, and thus forced the hand of the state to prevent further destruction of many of the gardens.

The importance of community voices and initiatives in creating and sustaining common green space is illustrated by an early misguided effort of New York's city government, which in 1976 spent 3.6 million dollars to design and build gardens throughout the city, with little or no community input on vacant land awaiting housing development. Neighborhood residents, who were expected to maintain them, were not given proper tools or technical assistance; as a result, these gardens soon were vandalized and abandoned. The residents knew that they had no real say in the construction and use of these sites, which eventually would be sold to developers to build whatever they wished.

ELDERS AND THE COMMUNITY GARDEN MOVEMENT

Wherever strong civic greening movements emerged as part of the process of community reclamation in the late 1960s and 1970s, persons of all ages were involved in initiating and continuing these projects. In New York City, I seldom have encountered a well-functioning community garden where older adults were not active participants and leaders. At the Clinton Gardens, not far from Times Square, a retired teacher tends to and educates visitors about the bee hives in this space; on almost any summer day, in Harlem's Harmony Garden, Cynthia and Haja participate in a children's environmental learning program that this elder, husband-wife team has developed; and in almost any Casita garden, expert older adult hands are playing and listening to Puerto Rican "Plena" music after work hours. What I saw in these spaces stands in dramatic contrast to some studies of elders in "World Cities" like New York or Paris where the concern is combating isolation and barriers to engagement with the local environment (Gusmano 2009).

Older adults can choose to become active in civic greening projects because they have free time to devote to such activities, or because it reminds them of gardening while they were growing up. Often, elders who become active in community gardens come from rural regions, where growing food, medicinal plants, and even gourds for musical instruments was part of their early lives. The experiences of these elders have been crucial in providing the knowledge base to show their neighbors that it is possible to grow tomatoes or collard greens in the middle of Manhattan.

From another perspective, in previously devastated zones such as Manhattan's Lower East Side or the South Bronx, only the older long-term residents had experienced intact, functioning communities in these areas during the 1950s and 1960s. Persons of this older generation were the ones most likely to hope that this might again be possible. This was vividly brought home to me when I showed my documentary *Urban Garden* in a university class in Florida. As it was ending with an upbeat message, I heard a 30-year-old male student softly sobbing in the back of the room. I asked him what was wrong, and he told the class that he had lived the first eight years of his life in the Bronx, close to one of the beautiful gardens shown in the video— the Garden of Happiness. He said:

> Much of the area was a pile of rubble and burned-out buildings, full of violent crime and junkies. I never imagined that in my lifetime, the residents themselves could create such a thing of beauty and live across from such a garden in nice town houses; this is beyond my comprehension.

As I spent time in a wide variety of gardens, I came to realize that, while nurturing organic beauty via neighborhood hands was one of the functions of such places, it usually became secondary to the *social* plantings and harvests occurring within. What I began to see were community-created public spaces beckoning those who entered to transcend the traditional barriers of wealth, ethnicity, and age. I have seldom encountered other urban spaces in New York City where people of differing ages and backgrounds so readily mingle for common efforts. In the mid-1970s, when the gardens were being established, elderly blacks from the rural South could be seen teaching life-long Anglo urbanites how to plant tomatoes and greens; or Caribbean elders would grow huge squash plants and teach local kids how to turn their dried husks into musical instruments. In 2003, I observed a 12-year-old boy who sought refuge in a well-established garden from a difficult foster-care setting. There, a small group of older garden members nurtured him, and a retired 78-year-old teacher tutored him in math.

Studies of community gardens have produced an impressive list of benefits: increasing the sense of community ownership and stewardship; providing a neutral space for neighborhood activities; providing inexpensive access to nutri-

A former resident of the rural south (on the right) helps a life-long urban dweller get the most from his planting in a garden on Manhattan's Upper West Side, being developed in the early 1980s. [Photo by Lynn Law]

tious fruits and vegetables; exposing inner-city youth to nature; connecting people across boundaries of cultures, class, and generations; and even reducing crime (Malakoff 1995). In addition, community gardening promotes what Robert Putnam calls "social capital," that is, features of social organization such as networks, norms, and trust that facilitate coordination and cooperation for mutual benefit (2000). Under the proper circumstances, social capital helps to create trusting, reciprocal relationships that can empower individuals to act collectively to create stronger, economically healthier, and safer communities.

Some of the best-documented impacts of community gardening projects have shown reductions in neighborhood crime. For example, large-scale studies in Chicago found a strong association between safer environments and promoting civic ecology (Kuo and Sullivan 2001). Green common spaces reduced mental fatigue and served as a resource for coping with poverty. In fact, the largest study of crime and community ever completed in that city found that the best indicator of impending neighborhood crime reduction was an area's ability to create and sustain a community garden (Sampson, Raudenbush, and Earls 1997). Such actions, if they were successful, invariably increased the level of what the authors call "collective efficacy," a measure of residents' ability to act together, especially for the interest of local children. In developing community gardens, residents build stronger relationships among themselves and create a neighborhood support system that provides alternatives to violence.

HEALTH, HEALING, AND THERAPEUTIC URBAN GREEN SPACES

I am spending the day in the Bronx at a small farm and community garden with a man of Afro-Caribbean heritage in his late 60s. He was one of several key older residents who worked to reclaim this space about a decade ago with the help of their grandkids, some neighbors, and the city's support organization "Green Thumb." After I had helped him dig out an old bed of some spiny plants, he noticed a quickly developing rash on the back of my hand, which began to itch intensely. He led me into another part of the garden and bent down to show me a plant with green shiny leaves. Pointing to the bright red on my skin he tells me, "My grandson sometimes gets that," and winking his eye, he says, "I just tell the little one to crush those leaves in his palm and put the juice on the rash." Catching on, I follow these indirect instructions and almost immediately feel relief. Over the course of the next several hours, he proceeds to describe in detail the use of dozens of medicinal herbs interspersed with the food crops of corn, several varieties of tomatoes and squashes, eggplants, greens, peaches, apples, and plums.

> You see, I was brought up in the Caribbean by my grandfather who was a roots medicine healer and I know everything about these plants for making people better . . . but I have to be careful about claiming to be a doctor, so when people ask, I just say well, I don't know about that, but when my wife or cousin has a problem like that I just pick the so and so plant and put it in a tea for them. (Field notes July 15, 2002)

Having such an elder with this level of folk health knowledge is not common, but most gardens in ethnic minority communities maintain an assortment of medicinal plants that are used regularly for minor bodily complaints. It is the older members upon whom people rely for learning their proper uses. In thinking of gardens as healing places, we should remember that the current community garden movement arose in marginalized, minority neighborhoods that typically had the lowest access to both public green space and health care services in the city.

As large congested cities—like New York, London, and Tokyo—have come to serve as the homes of millions of older citizens in the twenty-first century, the impact of local urban environments on healthy aging has become a major concern (Milligan, Gatrell, and Bingley 2004; Gusmano 2009). Studies have consistently shown the ameliorative effects of civic greening in mitigating chronic urban stress among poor communities and moderating its link to negative health conditions such as hypertension, diabetes, asthma, or heart problems (Thwaites, Helleur, and Simkins 2005; Bell et al. 2008).

The most frequent and spontaneous statements about people's experiences in community gardens refer to enhanced psychological moods and their perceptions of stress relief. Many of their narratives contrast the harsh, concrete-dominated city landscape with the softer, earth-based, peaceful, and healing environment of the gardens. In 1998, barely 15 minutes into my first

Children's Education Day at "Belmont Little Farmers Garden" in the Bronx, 2002. [Photo by Pedro Diez]

encounter with a community garden, I learned of the personal impact that these spaces can have:

> I came to this garden in the late 1970s, I had just gotten a divorce and did not realize I was bipolar and very depressed. This garden saved me, it healed me. (Field notes, sixty-four-year-old female, April 28, 1998)

The idea of healing gardens is an old one, dating at least to the Middle Ages. In the United States, horticultural therapy was introduced early in the 1800s at the Friends Hospital in Philadelphia and is still being employed in many kinds of formal rehabilitative settings, including hospitals, hospices, domestic violence shelters, and prisons (Winterbottom 2005).[1] For example, at Manhattan's famous Bellevue Hospital, a psychiatrist has established an art-focused "sobriety garden" where patients in addictive services can interact with and help construct a "participatory landscape" as part of their treatment.

Especially during the past decade, the notion of therapeutic landscapes has come to be applied to the most frail among the elderly, with the premises of bringing civic greening into highly restrictive long-term care environments (Predny and Relf 2004). In fact, the notion of "elder gardens" has been at the center of revolutionizing and humanizing such spaces in developing the "Eden Alternative" and "Green House" models of care (McLean 2009). As Silverman and McAllister (1995:207) found in their study of a specialized Alzheimer's unit:

While activities such as gardening may be important in maintaining or reactivating certain practical skills, they are equally important in the maintenance or reactivation of a sense of self and self-worth. Such activities and the practice of specialized skills also provide a context for remembering and recounting important aspects of residents' personal history.

CONCLUSION: COMMUNITY GARDENING AND CIVIC ECOLOGY

While today's urban community gardens began under the kinds of dire economic circumstances that sparked greening efforts in earlier eras, they have not only persisted much longer but also have morphed into vital community-building nodes of social inclusion.[2] This stands in sharp contrast to the exclusionary impact of all too many "urban renewal" projects that end up destroying the only kinds of housing that elder long-term residents and their interconnected kin and friends can afford. Margaret Bjornson suggests that the conjunction of community garden development and the surprising bottom-up renewal of low-income urban neighborhoods occurred by "greenlining" communities that were "formerly 'redlined'—barricaded by socioeconomic, cultural and political and agendas that separate those in place by those in power" (2002:33).

Using grassroots civic ecology to develop sustainable communities or care environments often requires specialized knowledge about the environment and the means of making it accessible, usable, and meaningful to persons of varied ages, backgrounds, and physical competence. In North America the most thriving and longest-lasting civic greening endeavors are actively supported by experts from urban governments. They also forge partnerships with universities, nongovernmental organizations, and socially responsible corporations (see especially www.communitygarden.org).

As a key element in applying civic ecology to the situations of marginalized citizens, community gardens can reach across generations or repair communities blown asunder by natural disasters or unnatural wars. Programs such as Seattle's "Youth Garden Works" (see www.sygw.org) or Brooklyn's "Added Value" programs (see www.added-value.org) are attempting to stabilize the lives of "at risk" children. These efforts seek to empower homeless and disadvantaged youth through creating their own urban community organic gardens and farms and, eventually, in the case of "Added Value," building leadership skills directed at community improvement. As part of a broader effort in developing urban school gardens, in Berkeley, California, "The Edible School Yard" project at Martin Luther King Middle School was conceived in 1995 with the help of world-renowned chef Alice Waters. She funded the building of a substantial organic garden and a state-of-the-art kitchen where children cook and eat the plants they grow (see www.edibleschoolyard.org).[3]

However, using such spaces to forge strong intergenerational community ties is harder to achieve (Larson and Meyer 2006). One of the most promising models for such a goal is "Garden Mosaics," a project that connects youth and elders through understanding the interdependence of plants, people, and culture in gardens. These programs combine science learning with intergenerational mentoring, multicultural understanding, and community action (www.gardenmosaics.cornell.edu). A number of pilot projects using this model are operating throughout the United States and in other countries (Liddicoat et al. 2007).

Internationally, the idea of civic ecology and community gardens has even emerged in the tragic crucible of civil wars and globalization, when national food distribution and local systems of support have been disrupted. For example, following recent horrific warfare, community gardens in the city of Sarajevo and in a Bosnian refugee community in Toronto were developed with the aid of the American Friends Service Committee to help begin the postconflict healing process. In a broader sense, civic ecology has become a powerful contributor to a growing movement in Europe and the United States to construct urban spaces to meet criteria as "life span communities." In such spaces, elders and youth not only feel an attachment to place but also have access to vital inclusionary landscapes where all feel compelled to contribute to the well-being of their neighborhood (see especially Harding 2007; Stafford 2009, 2010).

Over the past decade, often related to concerns of food safety, a new organically oriented "Victory" garden movement is emerging alongside Community Supported Agriculture (CSAs) and multiple variants of urban community gardens. For example, "Victory Gardens 2008+" is a pilot project funded by the City of San Francisco to support the transition of backyard, front yard, window boxes, rooftops, and unused land into organic food production areas (www.sfvictorygardens.org). In Boston, the youth-centered "Food Project" grows nearly a quarter of a million pounds of food without chemical pesticides, donating half to local shelters and selling the remainder at farmers' markets in disadvantaged neighborhoods or through shares in Community Supported Agriculture.

Not to be outdone, in 2009, shortly after a new presidential administration took office, Agriculture Secretary Tom Vilsack transformed a patch of cement at the USDA building into a green space by planting "The People's Garden." With the help of local schoolchildren, First Lady Michele Obama also began an organic garden on White House grounds (see http://www.thewhofarm.org/). The food produced from the White House garden will be cooked in the White House kitchen and some of it given to Miriam's Kitchen, which serves the homeless in Washington, D.C.

In the end, the case of New York City and others like it shows that, no matter how beautiful, peaceful, and productive any urban community garden may be, what really matters are the connections established between the people caring for it and the caring community created by their actions.

Notes

[1] For a general discussion of health and urban greening, see "Health Benefits of Urban Agriculture," by Anne Bellows at: www.foodsecurity.org/UAHealthArticle.pdf.

2 However, some of the intensely ethnic gardens can sometimes act counter to the notion of social inclusion and discourage persons from other backgrounds in taking advantage of the space.

3 One aspect of such urban projects applicable across the life span is minimizing what Richard Louv calls "nature-deficit disorder," caused by being shut out from the psychological benefits of unstructured engagement with the natural world (Louv 2005).

Acknowledgments

There are many people to thank for helping me in my research on community gardens, especially for the materials discussed in this chapter. These persons include: Edie Stone, Adam Honigman, Sid Glasser, Annie Chadwick, Betty Gaither, Gerard Lordahl, Dee Parisi, Jane Grundy, Donald Loggins, Abu Talib, Carolyn Radcliffe, Jackie Beach, Jane Weisman, Kate Chura, Lynn Law, Haja Worley, Cynthia Niebbelink-Worley, Len Librizzi, and Daniel Winterbottom.

References

Bell, Simon, Val Hamilton, Alicia Montarzino, Helen Rothnie, Penny Travlou, and Susana Alves. 2008. *Greenspace and Quality of Life: A Critical Literature Review.* Stirling, Scotland: Greenspace Scotland (http://www.greenspacescotland.org.uk/upload/File/greenspace_and_quality_of_life_literature_review_aug2008.pdf).

Bjornson, Margaret Ross. 2002. Greenlining: An Invitation to Cross the Bridges to Urban Greenspace and Understanding. In *Interaction by Design: Bringing People and Plants Together for Health and Well-Being*, ed. C. Shoemaker, pp. 33–40. New York: Wiley.

Chait, Jocelyne, Margaret Seip, Petr Stand, and Kira Gould. 2000. Achieving a Balance: Housing and Open Space in Bronx Community District 3. New York: Trust for Public Land and Bronx Community Board 3.

Gusmano, Michael. 2009. Growing Older in World Cities: Benefits and Burdens. In *The Cultural Context of Aging*, 3rd ed., ed. J. Sokolovsky, pp. 395–417. Westport, CT: Praeger.

Hancock, Trevor. 2001. People, Partnerships and Human Progress: Building Community Capital. *Health Promotion International*, 16(3):275–280.

Harding, Ed. 2007. Towards Lifetime Neighbourhoods: Designing Sustainable Communities for All: A Discussion Paper. International Longevity Centre UK, Department for Communities and Local Government. Available at: www.agingsociety.org/agingsociety/publications/public_policy/ilclifetime.pdf

Kuo, Francis, and William Sullivan. 2001. Environment and Crime in the Inner City: Does Vegetation Reduce Crime? *Environment and Behavior*, 33(3):343–367.

Larson, Jean, and Mary Meyer. 2006. *Generations Gardening Together—A Sourcebook for Intergenerational Therapeutic Horticulture.* Binghamton, NY: Haworth

Liddicoat, Kendra, Jamila Simon, Marianne Krasny, and Keith Tidball. 2007. Sharing programs across cultures: Lessons learned from Garden Mosaics in South Africa. *Children, Youth and Environments*, 17(4):237–254. Also at www.colorado.edu/journals/cye/17_4/17_4_12_GardenMosaics.pdf

Linn, Karl. 2007. *Building Commons and Community.* Oakland, CA: New Village Press.

Louv, Richard. 2005. *Last Child in the Woods: Saving Our Children from Nature-Deficit Disorder.* Chapel Hill, NC: Algonquin Books.

Malakoff, David 1995. What Good is Community Greening? http://communitygarden.org/docs/whatgoodiscommunitygreening.pdf (accessed March 23, 2008).

McLean, Athena. 2009. Beyond the Institution: Dementia Care and the Promise of the Green House Project. In *The Cultural Context of Aging*, 3rd ed., ed. J. Sokolovsky, pp. 589–605. Westport, CT: Praeger.

Milligan, Christine, Anthony Gatrell, and Amanda Bingley. 2004. Cultivating Health: Therapeutic Landscapes and Older People in Northern England. *Social Science & Medicine*, 58(9):1781–1793.

Predny, Mary Lorraine, and Diane Relf. 2004. Horticulture Therapy Activities for Preschool Children, Elderly Adults and Intergenerational Groups. *Activities, Adaptation & Aging*, 28(3):1–18.

Putnam, Robert. 2000. *Bowling Alone: The Collapse and Revival of American Community*. New York: Simon & Schuster.

Sampson, Robert, Stephen Raudenbush, and Felton Earls. 1997. Neighborhoods and Violent Crime: A Multilevel Study of Collective Efficacy. *Science*, 277:918–924.

Silverman, Myrna, and Carol McAllister. 1995. Continuities and Discontinuities in the Life Course: Experiences of Demented Persons in a Residential Alzheimer's Facility. In *The Culture of Long Term Care: Nursing Home Ethnography*, eds. J. N. Henderson and M. D. Vesperi, pp. 197–220. Westport, CT: Bergin and Garvey.

Smit, Jac, and Martin Bailkey. 2006. Urban Agriculture and the Building of Communities. In *City Farming for the Future*, ed. R. van Veenhuizen, pp. 145–170. Ottawa: IDRC Publications. Also available at: www.idrc.ca/en/ev-103777-201-1-DO_TOPIC.html

Sokolovsky, Jay. 2008. *Urban Garden: Fighting for Life and Beauty*. Video Documentary, St. Petersburg, FL: Ljudost Productions, jsoko@earthlink.net

Stafford, Phil. 2009. Aging in the Hood: Creating and Sustaining Elder-Friendly Environments. In *The Cultural Context of Aging*, 3rd ed., ed. J. Sokolovsky, pp. 441–452. Westport, CT: Praeger.

———. 2010. *Elderburbia: Aging and a Sense of Place in America*. Westport, CT: Praeger.

Thwaites, Kevin, Elizabeth Helleur, and Ian Simkins. 2005. Restorative Urban Open Space: Exploring the Spatial Configuration of Human Emotional Fulfillment in Urban Open Space. *Landscape Research*, 30(4):525–547.

Tidball, Keith, and Marianne Krasny. 2007. From Risk to Resilience: What Role for Community Greening and Civic Ecology in Cities? In *Social Learning Towards a more Sustainable World*, ed. A. Wals, pp. 149–164. Wageningen, Netherlands: Academic Publishers. Also available at http://krasny.dnr.cornell.edu/file/Tidball_Krasny_Urban_Resilience.pdf

von Hassell, Malve. 2002. *The Struggle for Eden: Community Gardens in New York City*. Westport, CT: Bergin & Garvey.

Winterbottom, Daniel. 2005. The Healing Nature of Landscapes, *Northwest Public Health*, Spring/Summer: 18–20.

18

Neighbors and Kin in Chinese Cities

William Jankowiak

In this chapter, William Jankowiak examines social transformations in Hohhot, capital of the Inner Mongolia Autonomous Region in northern China. The residents of this provincial city are caught up in the impact of global economic restructuring on the traditional Chinese rural-urban social system. The author finds that Hohhotians have begun to discard old-fashioned neighborhood obligations in favor of other forms of social connectivity, especially those based on friendships established in school and in the workplace. Among the current generation of China's young single adults, allegiance to the traditional patrilineal ideology has been weakened to the point of irrelevancy. In this social vacuum, the bilateral multigenerational family is emerging as a primary reference for the construction of kinship obligations.

INTRODUCTION

Throughout the 1980s, there were two Chinas: one rural and the other urban, and whatever was said about one would not apply to the other. The social distinction arose from the Communist Party's decision to institutionalize a household registration (or passport) system that linked an individual's fate to his or her place of birth. The registration system transformed small farmers into peasants who, much like European serfs, were bound to the land. In time, China's urban population, which was given better food rationing, housing, and medical facilities, forgot that there had once been constant movement between the countryside and the city. The gross disparity in living standards made most urbanites ashamed of the countryside and everything associated with it. Its peasants were now considered second-class citizens.

Source: Written expressly for *Urban Life*.

By the mid 1980s China's top-down command economy had begun to unravel. New leadership wanted to transform Chinese society away from Mao Zedong's earlier policy of regionally balanced growth to a strategy of unbalanced regional growth. The leadership adopted a "trickle down" hypothesis whereby economic development would diffuse from the center to the periphery. In the case of China, this meant from the economic powerhouse coastal region to the underdeveloped interior. Today, scholars continue to discuss the "two Chinas." However, the distinction no longer refers to the rural/urban divide but to the new economic and social cleavages that separate the coastal regions from the interior.

The new policy of rapid industrialization and technological modernization has required fewer subsistence farmers and more urbanized workers. To speed the transformation, the party encouraged the creation of industrialized townships. This was accomplished in two ways: first, farmers were allowed to move to the city to work on a temporary basis for longer periods, and second, more townships were built in China's hinterland. The new policy was successful; between 1978 and 2003 it resulted in the number of small Chinese towns exploding from 2,176 to 20,312, while the number of cities increased from 190 to 663. While in 1981 only 20 percent of China's population lived in cities, by 1993 this number had grown to 43 percent and by 2000 to nearly 48 percent. It is estimated that by 2010 the majority of Chinese will live in some kind of urbanized community.

The husband and wife are laid-off state workers who opened a successful restaurant. [Photo by William Jankowiak]

THE METAPHOR AND THE CITY

Cities are the by-product of regional and global interconnections that need to be explored in order to highlight the "new topographical features" of urban China. This need would be puzzling, however, to the earlier twentieth-century Chinese literati, who, much like their Western counterparts, entertained conflicting images of the city. One view, often referred to as the *Beijing perspective*, did not consider the city worthy of study at all. This perspective glorified rural life as an idyllic setting where people reflect simplicity and a purity of heart. Much like Simmel's perception of the twentieth-century European city, the city was regarded as a bleak settlement and the source of social alienation and personal disillusionment. In contrast, the *Shanghai perspective* regarded the city as the embodiment of novelty, exuberance, reform, stylistic experimentation, and thus ongoing modernity (Zhang 1999). Initially, the Communist party endorsed the Beijing perspective and with it the idealization of the farmer (Guldin 1998). It would not be until the 1990s that the party-state would embrace the Shanghai perspective and its idealization of the consumer (Logan 2002).

MIGRATION AND FORMS OF COMMUNICATION

An immediate impact of the government's relaxation of its household registration policies was a massive rural-to-urban movement of over 100 million people. It is has been the largest internal migration in human history (Solinger 1999). At the beginning, most migrants, or sojourners, did not develop a localized or urban identity. Instead, their primary frame of reference continued to be their home village or native place. However, by the 1990s migrants were once again forming native place associations in the larger cities. By 2000, it was common for rural migrants to want to settle down in the city. Many young peasants insisted that, with the exception of education costs (schools charged higher fees for nonurban youth), there was no substantial downside in not having an urban resident permit.

URBAN KINSHIP: THE NEIGHBORHOOD AS A SOURCE OF SOCIAL CONNECTION

In the early 1980s, urban China was organized around a *danwei* (work unit or place of employment) system that strove to re-create an idealized version of rural village life, with its emphasis on fellowship, support, and insularity in life orientation. Such work units were expected to nurture their members by promoting a cooperative spirit that would transcend the need to maintain a patrilineal descent ideology and its male-centered lineage organization. The Party leadership hoped to foster an expansion of kinship ties to include coresidents, work associates, and the work unit itself. Elderly citizens recalled the 1950s as a time when the Communist Party insisted that it should be loved more than a person's own kin. The institutionalization of a nationwide danwei organization resulted in a more homogenized urban landscape (Gaubatz 1995).

In contrast to pre-1949 Chinese village life, the socialist-inspired work unit was highly restrictive of individual, social, and geographical mobility. Its opportunity structures were quasi-feudal, emphasizing political position and bureaucratic rank. The danwei—the local embodiment of the communist state—stressed social values similar to those emphasized in Soviet-dominated Eastern Europe. It also produced an insular orientation that resulted in the construction of compounds protected by high walls and guarded gates, and the development of a cautious mind-set. The Party effort to expand people's sense of relatedness to include workmates reshaped the way Chinese perceived and valued neighborhood interaction.

THE URBAN "NEIGHBORHOOD": PROXIMITY, FRIENDSHIP, AND RELATEDNESS

In China's urban neighborhoods, physical proximity does not obligate a person to perform ritualistic exchanges; more is required to construct and sustain friendship ties. This pattern is evident in the way individuals discuss the meaning of neighborhood. There is no Chinese word for "neighborhood." Although the word *linjiu* (neighbor) and *jie* (street) have been translated as "neighborhood" (Schipper 1977), these involve less of a relationship with physical space than a relationship with specific individuals who occupy that space. This restriction may account for an urban Chinese perception of neighborhood that is less expansive than it is in the United States. For example, when I asked informants to draw a map of their "neighborhood," in every case the map contained only those dwellings that could readily be seen from the steps of the informant's front door. If a person lived in a U-shaped courtyard, the drawing depicted only that courtyard. If s/he lived in a lane of seven houses, only that lane was drawn, with an occasional alleyway to the main street. If the informant lived in a multistory apartment complex, only those units adjacent to the informant's own apartment were drawn.

Does this mean that Chinese refuse to recognize or enter into neighborly relationships with others living on different floors or in nearby lanes? Clearly not. In the 1980s and again in the 2000s, when I directly asked my informants, they readily agreed that people living in the general area (i.e., within a two- or three-minute walk from one another), if they had established personal ties, would also be neighbors. Here, the emphasis is on "the establishment of personal ties," which individuals must construct through their own efforts. Being urban neighbors differs from the customary obligations found in some northern Chinese villages (Stafford 2000; Yan 1996), where residency or physical proximity automatically makes one related and thus obligated to engage in ritualistic exchanges within the "neighborhood." In this way, the Chinese conception of a neighborhood was anchored in, and structured by, the ties that a person maintained within a personal network, and not with an object or imagined social border. In short, bonds of relatedness are individualistic and thus highly personalized creations.

The issue of neighborly relations is a sensitive one in Hohhot, a northern Chinese city in which I have been conducting long-term field research since the 1980s.[1] I have found that the composition of neighborhoods is changing and that different groups and classes of people are interacting on a scale previously unknown. Massive internal migration in recent years has transformed the ways in which Hohhotians understand and relate to one another in their neighborhoods. Instead of polite, albeit reserved, formalistic interactions, there is a noticeable posture of complete indifference. Those who leave their work unit for a new residence soon discover there is no basis for commonality, or a desire to establish one. The news media are filled with stories of the decline in trust and neighborly cooperation. For the majority of Chinese urbanites, physical proximity no longer serves as the base for developing a sense of relatedness. Most people prefer this. A 49-year-old man, for example, informed me that "we are happier moving and starting a new life. We do not have close relationships with our neighbors but that is okay, as we do not want them. We are very connected to other people in the city, however."

In 2000, I saw another example of Hohhotians' disinterest in becoming too familiar with their neighbors when I tried to locate a friend's new apartment. Not certain whether he lived on the third or fourth floor, I knocked and inquired if anyone knew my friend's apartment. A man told me: "No, I do not recognize his surname." I was then shooed away. I suspect that the man—who did not open the door—thought, based on hearing my Chinese accent, that I was a southern migrant and thus, from his perspective, up to no good. His behavior stood in stark contrast to the 1980s, when people readily opened their doors to talk to a stranger. The next day I returned with my friend to his apartment and found that he lived in the apartment immediately adjacent to the one from which I had been turned away the previous evening. Clearly, he and his neighbor had never interacted.

The decline in neighborly relations does *not* mean that urban China has become a place of disconnection and psychological anomie. On the contrary, people continue to favor rich webs of connections based on former school ties, newly formed work contacts, association with places of origin, friendship bonds, and close family relationships. China remains a society in which people continue to define personal satisfaction less through the development of personal careers than through their social relationships. Individuals who have achieved fame while losing social bonds are regarded with pity.

An individual's web of connections can be readily observed in the ubiquitous use of cell phones, often involving no more than brief exchanges for determining when and where people will come together for conversation. The desire to maintain contacts applies less and less within the world of the urban neighborhood, as coresidential bonds have been replaced by selective friendships based more in particularistic ties than in any expectation that close proximity automatically reclassifies someone into a type of kin. Relat-

Urban neighborhoods are safe places for kids to play or just hang out. [Photo by William Jankowiak]

edness is no longer anchored in residential proximity. Today, the tacit obligations that linked villagers together have effectively vanished from much of China's urban landscape (Yan 1996).

SOCIAL RELATIONS: ETHNICITY, NATIVE PLACE, AND RELIGION

The decline in neighborhood relationships as a source of fellowship does not mean that Chinese cities have become centers of homeless souls adrift in asocial space. Socially supportive relationships based in proximity are giving way to a new array of connections used as a basis for establishing emotionally salient bonds equal to and even surpassing those found between villagers and former danwei neighbors. City dwellers draw their friends from a wide arena of possible associations, including secret societies, guilds, school ties, classmates, teacher–student bonds, and common ethnic and/or religious affiliation.

Cities are often arenas of ethnic solidarity. In Hohhot, I am repeatedly struck by the persistence and strength of ethnic/religious solidarity in ordinary life. The city's Mongol and Hui (Chinese Muslim) residents tend to confine their most intimate interpersonal contacts to members of their own ethnic groups. In the 1980s and again in 2006, I found that fewer than 40 percent of Mongols regularly associated with a Han in a socially intimate, nonwork setting. The high frequency of association based on ethnicity reflects a conscious preference for the company of people who share a similar ethnic/ religious heritage. The emphasis on intentionality is aptly summarized by a 39-year-old Mongolian woman who, in 2006, told me "when I was a child I actively played with Han children, but when I started to attend high school I made a conscious decision to pull back and associate only with Mongols." For most Mongols and Hui, social life continues to be defined by their commitment to an ideal of ethnic and religious exclusivity. In this way, friendship bonds wear a cultural face.

As part of China's massive internal migration, native place associations have become ubiquitous in every major city. This is not new. During the nineteenth and early twentieth centuries, people also preferred to associate with others from a similar native place. In many ways, such native-place associations are similar to those founded on ethnic or religious affiliation; they emphasize a strong emotional identification with a territory, ancestors, and cultural or linguistic fellowship. Taken together, ethnicity, religion, and native place associations serve as essential bases for the formation of social connections or kinship ties.

GUANXI: FRIENDSHIP AND SOCIAL CAPITAL

In urban China, individuals who are outside the formal (e.g., bilateral or patrilineal) genealogical systems are frequently transformed from casual friends into close quasi-kin through the idiom of kinship. It is conventional practice for parents to instruct their child to call a visiting acquaintance or a true close friend *shushu* (uncle) or *aiyi* (aunt). Further, in Hohhot's countryside (but not in the city proper) it is common for children to address strangers as shushu or aiyi. Susanne Brandtstader (personal communication) observed a similar pattern in southern China, where it was customary to address younger people unknown to an individual as *didi* or *meimei*. Both terms are associated with membership in a patrilineal descent system, and thus attest to the lingering symbolic efficacy of that system. It is also common for friends to use fictional kin terms to refer to one another as older/younger brother (*gege/didi*), or elder/younger sister (*jiejie/meimei*). For example, I often found myself with an old friend at late nightclubs; whenever his friends happened to meet him they would hug him and say "he is my older brother" or "he is my younger brother." Upon learning that I was a longtime friend, they immediately said to me, "if you are my older brother's friend then you are my friend." In this way, an individual's close friends are transformed into the equivalent of conjugal family. Hohhotians, like most people, continue to reserve their strongest bonds for their more immediate blood relatives from either side of the family.

URBAN KINSHIP: THE DOMESTIC ARENA AND DESCENT

Kinship among contemporary Hohhotians has come to have two features: (1) a network of mutual help established bilaterally between households, and (2) the remnant of a patrilineal descent ideology enforced through symbolic arrangements (as in family photographs), social orderings, and material gifts at ritual events such as funerals and marriages. Elements of the patrilineal system's survival can be found in the centering of elderly persons in family photographs, in the preference for using certain patrilineal kin terms of address (brother, sister, aunt, and uncle), and especially in the custom of the groom's family paying for the wedding (if it is their son's first marriage). Aside from these habits, other aspects of the patrilineal system have been abandoned in favor of individuals' situational needs. There is no rule to define where a bride and groom should live after their wedding. Most will find their own apartment, while others may live with the groom's or the bride's family, depending upon the spouses' needs and desires. Unlike in Imperial China, there are no inheritance laws favoring patrilineal kin or sons over married daughters. Today, neither gender nor marital status serves as a legal basis for paternal inheritance. The decline in the importance of patrilineal descent extends to naming practices as well. In the past, it was common to take names only from the father's side of the family. Naming practices now include both paternal and maternal relations.

The expansion of the market economy requires Hohhotians to pursue a broad-based strategy of social interaction that includes forming relationships with kin and nonkin. One insightful informant, when asked to make a distinction between kin and friends, acknowledged, "Friends are for mundane matters, family is for ritual affairs." A 28-year-old female informant poignantly observed, "We hide from our cousins but not from our friends." In this way, genealogical kin are in competition with "friends." In general, the "big family" (*da jia*) no longer exists in urban China as a form of social organization or, if it does, it exists only in small numbers. Only in times of major family occasions (e.g., marriage, death, or serious illness) will all siblings and their children congregate.

There is a worldwide pattern in the way intergenerational bonds have been reorganized as economic and noneconomic resources have shifted: from offspring giving to parents, to a growing tendency for parents to give to children. This pattern, with only a few modifications, is typical of intergenerational relations in urban China. This does not mean that children do not feel a deep-seated responsibility for their parents' well-being. Most do. Robert Marsh's longitudinal research on Taiwan revealed that the intergenerational flow of help and resources from offspring to their parents was greater in 1991 than in 1963 (Marsh 1996:305). In Hohhot, the intergenerational resource exchange is somewhat mixed. For example, a 22-year-old Hohhotian young man told me that he never gave money to his parents since he himself "needs money to buy things and improve my life." He also knew that his parents did not need money. His response is representative of more well-off youth. The two exceptions to this general pattern were found among youth whose parents had been laid off from their jobs, or among those who wished to demonstrate with a small gift their affection and appreciation for their parents.

Although the range of kinship bonds is shrinking, the value extended to marriage and family life has never waned. People continue to think of the family (*jia*) as the dominant lens through which to assist and evaluate another's progress through life. Marriage and the establishment of a family remain critical, yet truncated, markers that urban Chinese use to sort each other out into relative degrees of social maturity and psychological stability. The increase in geographical mobility has resulted in visiting kin less frequently than in the past. In this new social universe, it is easy to forget an uncle or an aunt, to say nothing of a distant cousin, but paternal and maternal grandparents still are *not* to be forgotten. In Chinese cities, patrilineal descent systems have been transformed into networks of bilateral bonds based on affection and personal preference.

RECONFIGURING THE BILATERAL MULTIGENERATIONAL FAMILY

The strength of these emotional bonds is especially evident in the way parents are coming to embrace their roles as grandparents. Grandparent-child relationships have always occupied an esteemed position in Chinese society, especially those between grandfathers and grandsons. Funerals for deceased males who had one or more grandsons were called "red happiness"—a time of grief for the death and celebration for the continuity of the lineage. It was common for fathers who had assumed an aloof posture toward their own offspring to demonstrate greater public affection toward their grandsons. This behavioral pattern is consistent with the logic of patrilineal descent. Since only males remained in their home village to work the family farm, sons were celebrated and honored as the more "worthy" gender. This historical sex bias faced a serious challenge when the government imposed a single-child policy a generation ago. As the years have passed, most city dwellers have come to value their daughters as much as their sons. Less appreciated is how the single-child policy has reshaped the ways in which maternal and paternal grandparents relate to each other.

Because the patrilineal ideal is no longer critical to achieve material gain or social success, urban Chinese have come to live in a *de facto* bilateral universe organized around sentiment and ongoing negotiation of ethical obligations. Both paternal and maternal grandparents now claim rights of access to what is usually a solitary grandchild. This new social context has led the Chinese to respond by creating a new institution, so recent that it does not yet have a formal name, organized around the sharing of responsibilities in rearing the one grandchild. Without well-established, formal norms, parents and grandparents must now negotiate their rights, responsibilities, and future obligations. Taken together, these negotiations are reshaping historically patrilineal extended families into a kinship system that blends both paternal *and* maternal families of origin into bilateral multigenerational families. Such multigenerational families are based not on kinship rules, but on sentiment and personal commitment.

China's one-child policy has resulted in urban families loving daughters as much as sons. [Photo by William Jankowiak]

Grandparent–grandchild relationships have become increasingly signifi-cant in contemporary urban China. In 1989 and 1993, Susan Short and her colleagues (2001) carried out a survey of 3,800 households in eight provinces and autonomous regions, resulting in the discovery that one-third of the chil-dren were raised by their grandparent(s). In my 2000 survey in Hohhot, the results were even more dramatic: 82 percent of the 261 people interviewed had lived for a time with a grandparent. There was little evidence of a patri-lateral bias; 45 percent of the respondents lived for a period of time with their paternal grandparents, while 39 percent lived with their maternal grandpar-ents. The length of time living with a grandparent ranged from one to 16 years, with the average being 8.2 years. Length of time spent, however, does not tell the entire story. When asked with which grandparent a single adult person felt closest, the majority acknowledged their mother's mother (*laolao*). This is, effectively, a rejection of the long-standing patrilineal system.

The urban Chinese bilateral multigenerational family is a fragile institu-tion. The relationship between paternal and maternal grandparents is seldom strong, especially when they migrated to the city from different rural communi-ties. An uneasy alliance is sustained between these parties, all of whom under-stand that they are potential rivals in their efforts to gain access to a scarce resource, their only grandchild. Through my survey, I found that 80 percent of my respondents felt closer emotionally to their grandmothers than to their grandfathers. Moreover, more than 60 percent felt closest to their mother's mother. In grandparents' efforts for greater access to their only grandchild, the maternal side appears to have the edge. The Chinese pattern is now consistent with studies of grandparent–grandchild interaction carried out in highly urbanized, capitalist nations such as Germany and the United States (Buss 2007; Lawton, Silverstein, and Bengston 1994). The continuing strength of the grandparent–grandchild bond represents a modification of William Goode's (1963) "conjugal loyalty thesis," which asserted a close relationship between the level of urbanization and an increase in conjugal exclusivity. It is clear that urban Chinese grandparents now devote a large amount of time to interacting with their grandchild. This emerging trend constitutes the essence of China's newest social institution, what I call "the bilateral multigenerational family."

Although common in other parts of the world, the bilateral multigenerational family had no official existence in a Chinese society where the patrilineal descent system legally elevated the rights of the father's kin over those of the mother's kin. In this milieu, intergenerational ties were primarily but not entirely unilineal (Watson 1985). All this changed under socialist China's policies designed to create a new society. Party polices that required younger women to work outside the home meant that child care, especially infant care, became a pressing national concern. As had occurred earlier in some Eastern European countries—e.g., the Czech Republic and Hungary—both paternal and maternal grandparents stepped into the void and performed necessary child care in Chinese cities. As the years passed, this growing involvement of grandparents with the grandchild established a stronger, more vibrant relationship and undermined the principle of patrilineal descent as it used to be imagined and practiced in urban China.

Chinese grandparents understand the importance of staying connected to their child's child. For most, grandchild care represents fulfillment, not an onerous duty. For example, a 66-year-old grandmother said the following about spending so much time with her granddaughter: "I enjoy taking care of her [granddaughter]." Another 64-year-old grandmother added, "She is me." And a 72-year-old grandfather acknowledged, while simultaneously hugging his three-year-old grandson, that "he is my life."

Grandparental involvement did not depend on the sex of the grandchild; a granddaughter was cared for and fussed over just as readily and happily as a grandson. Grandparents' role in rearing their grandchild has reshaped many urban Chinese families into a blend of conjugal loyalties and bilateral multigenerational emotional linkages. This recent transformation in child care duties sometimes has the unintended effect of undermining the affective bonds of children toward their parents, especially the mother. For example, a 34-year-old woman confided, "I feel more comfortable with my grandmother than I do with my mother. I did not listen to her [i.e., her grandmother], as I know what she had to tell me about the contemporary world was nonsense. Her ideas were old. But I simply enjoyed being around her." Another 29-year-old woman acknowledged, "My mother [who did not raise her] is always ordering me to do this or that. She makes lists. I still resist her. We are *not* close." However, she added, "This is not the case when I am with my grandmother. I just want to sit next to her."

CONCLUSION

The social transformation of the urban Chinese family is also intertwined with a reconfiguration of parenting style. Neighborhood obligations have been discarded in favor of other forms of connectivity, especially those based on friendships established in school and the workplace, and in the emerging bilateral multigenerational family. In those areas that have been only mildly impacted by contemporary urban development, the sense of relatedness among neighbors continues to mirror those found in the earlier "work unit" era. In more fluid locations, where rural–urban migration has increased dramatically, physical proximity as a basis for establishing and sustaining close relations has disappeared. In Hohhot, relatedness based in shared ethnicity and religion remains vibrant among Mongols, as it does among the Hui, and even among the city's small Protestant and Catholic communities. Finally, bonds between parents and child(ren) remain strong, with emotional involvement and obligations flowing both ways. Although a remnant of patrilineal descent ideology continues to be a force in the symbolic arrangements of ritual events (e.g., funerals and marriages), it has lost much of its significance and power in structuring individuals' life strategies. This is especially so among the current generation of China's young single adults, for whom the patrilineal ideology has been weakened to the point of irrelevancy.

In Chinese urban settings like Hohhot, maternal and paternal interests are creating a more complex family system. The bilateral multigenerational family has emerged as a primary reference for the construction of kinship obligations. The conjugal family's emotional monopoly over a child's affection has been diluted by the continuing involvement of the senior (or grandparental) generation. The persistence with which Hohhotian grandparents participate in what has become an intergenerational enterprise dedicated to raising their only grandchild is transforming our ethnographic understanding of contemporary Chinese urban life.

Note

[1] Hohhot is the capital of the Inner Mongolia Autonomous Region in northern China. The city has grown from a 1981 population of fewer than 500,000 to its present size of over one million inhabitants. Although primarily an ethnically Han Chinese city, Hohhot also is home to around 100,000 Mongols (most born in the city) and 20,000 Chinese Muslims (or Hui).

References

Buss, David. 2007. *Evolutionary Psychology: The New Science of the Mind,* 3rd ed. Boston: Allyn & Bacon.

Gaubatz, Piper. 1995. *Beyond the Great Wall: Urban Form and Transformation on the Chinese Frontiers.* Stanford, CA: Stanford University Press.

Goode, William J. 1963. *World Revolution and Family Patterns.* New York: The Free Press.

Guldin, Gregory E. 1998. Farewell to Peasant China. *China Information,* 13(1):165–170.

Lawton, Leora, Merril Silverstein, and Vern Bengtson. 1994. Solidarity Between Generations in Families. In *Intergenerational Linkages: Hidden Connections in American Society,* eds. Vern Bengtson and Robert Hasrootyan, pp. 19–42. New York: Springer Publishing Co.

Logan, John. 2002. The Three Challenges for the Chinese City: Globalization, Migration and Market Reform. In *The New Chinese City,* ed. John Logan, pp. 3–21. New York: Blackwell Publishers.

Marsh, Robert Mortimer. 1996. *The Great Transformation: Social Change in Taipei, Taiwan Since the 1960s.* Armonk, NY: M. E. Sharpe.

Schipper, Kristofer M. 1977. Neighborhood Cult Associations in Traditional Tainan. In *The City in Late Imperial China,* ed. G. William Skinner, pp. 651–678. Stanford, CA: Stanford University Press.

Short, Susan E., Zhai Fengying, Zu Siyuan, and Yang Mingliang. 2001. China's One-Child Policy and the Care of Children: An Analysis of Qualitative and Quantitative Data. *Social Forces,* 79(3):913–943.

Solinger, Dorothy J. 1999. *Contesting Citizenship in Urban China: Peasant Migrants, the State, and the Logic of the Market.* Berkeley: University of California Press.

Stafford, Charles. 2000. Chinese Patriliny and the Cycles of Yang and Laiwang. In *Cultures of Relatedness: New Approaches to the Study of Kinship,* ed. Janet Carsten, pp. 37–55. Cambridge: Cambridge University Press.

Watson, Rubie. 1985. *Inequality among Brothers: Class and Kinship in South China.* Cambridge: Cambridge University Press.

Yan, Yunxiang. 1996. *The Flow of Gifts: Reciprocity and Social Networks in a Chinese Village.* Stanford, CA: Stanford University Press.

Zhang, Yingjin, ed. 1999. *Cinema and Urban Culture in Shanghai, 1922–1943.* Stanford, CA: Stanford University Press.

19

Caste, Politics, and Criminality in Urban India

Jeffrey Witsoe

This chapter examines the ways that democratic politics impacts everyday life in India through an examination of the relationships between politics, caste, and criminality in Patna, a midsize city in North India. The situation in Patna reflected the changes brought about by a politics of lower caste empowerment, including a transformation of the social fabric of the city, a breakdown of public institutions, and a surge of criminality, providing a very different perspective on life in contemporary urban India.

Urban India is often portrayed in the international press as the economic engine of an emerging superpower, a rapidly modernizing place with its booming high-tech sector, where traditional ties such as caste are rapidly dissolving in the wake of globalization. This, however, is only a small part of the story of urban India. Industries related to the much hyped "outsourcing," such as business process outsourcing and call centers, for example, account for fewer than one million jobs in a country of over a billion people. The other side of urban India can be seen in the massive slums of megacities like Mumbai, and also in the dozens of smaller but still substantial provincial cities, where a large percentage of India's urban population resides. Provincial cities are much more connected to rural India, serving as the gateway to India's myriad villages where 70 percent of Indians continue to live. Many, if not most, residents in these cities continue to keep strong ties with their native villages, visiting for festivals and weddings, sending money, or even residing in the village while working in the city. It is therefore not surprising that provincial cities are enmeshed in regional and state-level politics and are influenced by the prevalence of caste, violence, and social antagonisms that

Source: Written expressly for *Urban Life*.

are so much a part of the democratic experience in India. This chapter will explore life in one such city, Patna, in order to provide an alternate view of life in contemporary urban India.

Patna, with a population of 1.8 million, is the capital of Bihar, a large state with a population of more than 90 million in the "Hindi belt" of North India. Bihar is India's poorest state, known for endemic caste conflict, political violence, and criminality. At the same time, since the early 1990s a dramatic democratic empowerment of lower castes has occurred in Bihar and other parts of North India. While displacing upper castes from power, this political change was accompanied by considerable violence and instability. The conflicts and destabilizations that swept rural North India also transformed urban life, especially in midsize provincial cities like Patna where the power of upper-caste elites—who had long dominated the city—was weakened. Life in Patna reflected the changes brought about by the politics of lower-caste empowerment, including a transformation of the social fabric of the city, a breakdown of public institutions, and a surge of criminality.

CRIME IN THE CITY

While I was living in Patna between 2000 and 2003, there was always a palpable sense of unease as the sun began to descend in the evening, with most people making sure that they were indoors before nightfall. There were good reasons for these fears. An ineffective, fund-starved, and corrupt police force was unable to contain the spread of criminal networks patronized by politicians and sometimes by the police themselves. According to government statistics, Bihar accounted for 26 percent of India's total murders with the use of firearms in 2000, and the relatively small city of Patna accounted for 40 percent of all murders with the use of firearms in Indian cities. Between 1992 and 2005 criminal groups carried out a reported 30,000 kidnappings in Bihar, many in Patna, as kidnapping for ransom became a growth industry. While many kidnapping rings were patronized by politicians who received a cut of the proceeds as "donations," some of the larger kidnapping rings were actually headed by Bihar's infamous "mafia" politicians. With elected members of the state legislature and the national parliament involved in Bihar's kidnapping industry (some of whom even served as ministers in the state and national governments), and with the police either involved themselves or powerless to act because of the political patronage received by the kidnapping rings, it is little wonder that most people felt that law and order had completely collapsed in the state.

The apartment that I kept in the city—where I stayed when I was not engaged in fieldwork in rural Bihar—was in one of the more upscale neighborhoods where many professionals and higher-level civil servants lived. Although Patna is a spread-out city of largely single-story housing, taller apartment buildings had become popular for those who could afford them because they were perceived as safer than houses. My apartment building had two guards who followed what I found to be a somewhat disconcerting practice every night of locking not only the large front gate leading into the complex by road but also securing all of the entrances into the building with chains—essentially locking us in for the night (after which the guards invariably fell asleep). But even these precautions did not prevent incidents. One person riding a motorcycle at night was abducted just in front of the apartment building—which gave me great pause considering that this was also my mode of transport and that I was often at the same location at the same time trying to wake up the guards so that they could unlock the front gate.

In another incident, a neighbor living in my building was leaving the complex by car with his two children and wife in the middle of the afternoon when two motorcycle-riding assailants peppered his car with machine-gun fire (although he was injured, fortunately his family was not). Another car then pulled up, and some men put the wounded victim into their vehicle where they reportedly shot him many times before dumping his body in front of the city zoo. This all occurred in broad daylight, and my apartment building was only a few hundred yards from a police station. Everyone in the building was shocked, and nobody could understand why this quiet, seemingly family-oriented man was killed in this manner. It was later discovered that he had been a member of a kidnapping ring and had apparently double-crossed his coconspirators.

In Patna, kidnapping rings targeted mostly affluent, largely upper-caste neighborhoods. The first victims were wealthy business families. Eventually, however, these families either left the state or paid off powerful politicians to gain protection. The next victims were engineers of the state-owned electricity board who had access to illicit sources of income: people in Patna are often forced to pay bribes to have electricity lines connected or repaired, and businesses pay much larger bribes to avoid paying their bills. The problem was that once an engineer or his son was kidnapped, his coworkers would shut off electricity to entire areas of the state in protest. This would lead to pressure on politicians from their constituents to resolve the issue, and often the kidnapped victim would be spontaneously released after political pressure was applied (since the kidnappers were linked to the politicians). After engineers turned out to be such a hassle, successful doctors were targeted. The doctors, in addition to working in government hospitals, also ran private practices. To express solidarity with their kidnapped colleagues, doctors across the city went on strike after abductions, even closing down emergency rooms. This strategy resulted in deaths as people were denied medical attention, which of course, also created political pressure and complications for the kidnappers. Finally, professors were found to be relatively defenseless targets. Many were making considerable earnings engaging in private tutoring—since the public colleges and universities in the state had more or less stopped functioning—but even the abduction of professors would frequently result in noisy student protests after a favorite professor was abducted.

Although there were pressures to end the mafia-instigated kidnappings, as described in the above examples, most people tolerated mafia figures in

Bihar and routinely elected many of them to office. In the 2005 state assembly elections, for example, a reported 34 percent of candidates fielded by the major parties had criminal cases pending against them. Elections are often contested from jail, and the most important mafia figures are elected representatives of the state assembly or, in the case of the biggest players, the national parliament. While shadowy backroom relationships between politicians and criminal figures are not uncommon in many countries, in Bihar elected office and the domain of criminality—referred to in Bihar with the America term "mafia"—are embodied in the same individuals. While spending time with imprisoned mafia politicians at hospital jail cells in Patna, I always observed two or three of their attendants answering mobile phones. Activities related to electoral politics, the official work of the legislature, and criminal actions were all being conducted simultaneously.

Why did people support and vote for corrupt politicians known to be involved in the kidnapping industry and other criminal activities? In order to answer this question, we must explore the relationship between caste, politics, and state institutions. The progression of the kidnapping industry in Bihar reveals the extent to which public institutions had broken down in the state. Perhaps the most detrimental impact was the deteriorating law and order situation. Kidnappings targeted individuals who received illicit income generated from corruption in government departments, as well as the health and education systems. Most of the bureaucrats, police, engineers, doctors, and teachers who benefited from this corruption were from upper-caste backgrounds. Most of the kidnapping and other criminal activities, in contrast, were being carried out by new entrants on the scene: lower-caste criminals connected to a rising class of lower-caste politicians. In response, upper-caste mafia politicians also emerged to protect the interests of their upper-caste supporters against the increasing challenge from lower-caste politics. People supported politicians who were seen to protect their caste effectively, regardless of the methods used to achieve this end. Within this context, many people supported politicians not only despite perceptions that they were corrupt but precisely because they were perceived as corrupt—capable of using their positions for the benefit of their supporters. Mafia politicians were clear about their political role: when a journalist whom I was accompanying asked a prominent mafia politician about his political ideology during an interview that I had arranged, he answered emphatically, "I am the protector of my caste" (*aapna jaat kaa raksha kaarte hai*).

CASTE IN THE CITY

As the phenomenon of mafia politicians makes clear, criminality in Bihar is connected not only with politics but also with caste—it is on the basis of protecting their caste that people not only tolerate but even support criminal politicians. I often heard it remarked in Bihar that "in other countries people cast their vote but in India people vote their caste." As one person put it, "My neighbor is Yadav. He votes RJD [the ruling party]. I am Rajput. I vote for Vajpayjee [former Prime Minister of the BJP]. This is Bihar's politics, *jatisangartan* [association through caste]." This is not a new phenomenon. There is a long history of the relationship between caste and politics in Bihar and other parts of India (Jaffrelot 2003). Still, almost all people with whom I interacted in Bihar—professional politicians and citizens alike—expressed what they felt to be the increasing importance of caste in political life, especially since the early 1990s. People often conceded that caste always has been a factor but believe that it has become much more salient in recent years. For example, when I asked a long-serving official at the state assembly about the influence of caste in assembly politics, he replied, "Before it was there but silent. Now it is openly displayed. I think everyone knows this." I sometimes heard politics referred to as a *nanga naach,* a "naked dance," emphasizing this explicit exposure of what was previously present but concealed. People said that in the past politicians had at least spoken the rhetoric of development and national unity, even if their actions may have been directed by other considerations. By the time of my fieldwork, however, many felt that explicit appeals to caste identities and the "naked" exercise of power had become ends in themselves. This reality is in stark contrast to the assertion of many middle-class Indians that caste is disappearing in urban India.

The scriptural representation of caste was derived from the fourfold *varna* system of Brahmins (priests), Ksatriyas (warriors/rulers), Vaishnas (merchants/farmers), and Shudras (servants) found in the Vedas, the "Laws of Manu," and other ancient texts. The Rig Veda presents a classic representation of the "cosmic man" (*puram purush*) composed of these four varnas: "His mouth was the Brahman [caste], his arms were the Rajanaya [Ksatriya caste], his thighs the Vaisya [caste]; from his feet the Sudra [caste] was born."

As numerous village-level ethnographies have documented, however, this overarching fourfold schema was quite different from actual social life, at least as it was observed in the mid-twentieth century. Numerous anthropological "village studies" (for example, Marriott 1986, Srinivas 1980) described dozens of caste groups (known as *jatis*) within a given village, ranked in complex, overarching hierarchies based on perceived gradations of purity and pollution—although the ranking differed depending on the perspective of various caste groups. This representation of hierarchy was expressed in seating arrangements during village feasts and through transactional taboos, especially relating to the transfer of water and cooked food. The most oppressive face of caste was experienced by so-called "untouchable" castes (now referred to as "Dalits," meaning "the oppressed"), who were viewed as so polluting that they were denied access to temples, were banned from using village wells, and were generally relegated to the economic position of landless laborers.

Democracy has had a progressive and profound impact on the experience of caste in India. While notions of hierarchy are still present in many contexts, and while some castes continue to dominate others and caste discrimination remains, democratic representation has become the central medium through which caste is now expressed in public life. In the wake of the penetration of democracy, representations of hierarchy have been confronted with concepts such as the justice, equality, and fundamental rights affirmed in the Indian constitution, and with an electoral practice that privileges numbers. Within this changed context, caste dominance lost its scriptural legitimacy; now, it is viewed both implicitly and explicitly as a product of power, not divine right. This has meant that the power of upper castes could be challenged through democratic politics. Since all caste groups are not represented equally within a democratic practice based on numbers—with more populous and well-organized castes enjoying a rather distinct advantage (such as Yadavs in Bihar)—this democratic shift in caste representation has profoundly altered the ways in which caste relations are popularly imagined, replacing representations of hierarchy with castes perceived more as discrete groups in competition (Gupta 2000).

While in most Indian villages caste remains a central part of everyday life, caste also remains important in many cities, such as Patna. One reason for the continued salience of caste in urban India can be traced to what I refer to as "caste networks." In the early twentieth century, upper-caste landowners in Bihar and other parts of North India formed caste associations in order to lobby the colonial government to privilege their respective castes, which were then imagined as much larger groups than the village jatis described above. Caste organizations founded universities and patronized caste-based educational scholarships. In this way, agricultural surplus and rural power were channeled into urban pursuits, educational capital, and access to government, on the basis of caste networks. Thus, caste identities became crucial for accessing state resources and public employment in the city. Privileged access to administrative jobs, in turn, allowed patronage networks that disproportionately transferred public resources to already dominant castes.

I first realized the practical importance of caste networks by observing Akhilesh, my research assistant in Patna, use his Rajput caste connections in order to locate a contact—often a distant relative or friend of a relative—in virtually every government department to which we needed access. The pervasive influence of caste networks explains why in getting a job or a loan, interacting with the police, dealing with mafia figures, interacting with or negotiating a bribe with a government official, and even renting an apartment or commercial space, caste matters. It is no coincidence that government offices, apartment complexes, universities, shopping complexes, and criminal networks in Patna are often populated with people sharing similar caste backgrounds. These caste networks have long served to privilege upper castes, providing access to resources and employment that lower-caste people were denied. Since bureaucrats and police, particularly at higher levels of government, are overwhelmingly from upper-caste backgrounds, the social networks in which they participate tend to perpetuate upper-caste dominance. The politicians who have emerged since the 1990s in Bihar, however, are mostly drawn from lower castes. The democratic empowerment of lower castes challenged these upper-caste networks and allowed many lower-caste people access to government resources for the first time.

THE POLITICS OF LOWER-CASTE EMPOWERMENT

Popular participation in the electoral process has surged in North India since the late 1980s, especially among people from lower-caste and rural backgrounds, a phenomenon that Yadav (1997) has termed the "second democratic upsurge." This upsurge in voting turnout by people from lower castes coincided with a progressive increase in the number of members of state legislative assemblies and members of the national parliament from lower-caste backgrounds. A political watershed occurred in 1989 when V. P. Singh, then prime minister of India, decided to implement the recommendations of the Mandal Commission (headed by B. P. Mandal, former chief minister of Bihar) to reserve a large portion of central government jobs for what is known as the "Other Backward Classes" (OBCs), a governmental category that excludes upper castes but includes lower castes that did not suffer a history of untouchability. This affirmative action policy had an explosive political impact marked by violent protests, including a number of self-immolations by upper-caste students, as well as an ensuing upsurge of lower-caste political mobilization.

Although politicians from upper-caste backgrounds dominated political life in Bihar for most of the post-Independence period, it is difficult now to imagine a future chief minister in Bihar from an upper-caste background. Jaffrelot (2003) has gone so far as to refer to these changes—following V. P. Singh's apt expression—as a "silent revolution" in North India. For example, in the space of the 10 years between 1985 and 1995 the number of OBC candidates elected to the assembly in Bihar more than doubled to 50 percent, while the number of upper-caste candidates was reduced by more than half to 17 percent—a profound transformation of political representation in the state.

The politics of lower-caste empowerment, as well as the many failures of the Bihar government, became embodied for most people in the political figure of Lalu Prasad Yadav, a charismatic lower-caste leader. Yadav challenged the hegemony of Bihar's upper-caste elite and consistently dominated politics in Bihar from the time when he became chief minister in 1990 until the electoral victory of the rival NDA in 2005. Lalu's militant campaigning for caste empowerment earned him a reputation as the foremost leader of a lower-caste state government fighting against upper-caste dominance. Lalu built a mass base of support for himself in villages across Bihar, using a helicopter (which he called his "flying machine") to access remote areas of the state, many of which had never before been visited by a prominent politician. Instead of visiting the upper-caste sections of villages or urban areas, where politicians in the past had inevitably been received, Lalu made a point of visiting lower-caste areas.

Lalu's politics of caste empowerment consciously marginalized development-related issues. A popular RJD slogan was *"vikaas nahiñ, samaan cha-hiye"* (we need dignity, not development). In fact, he explicitly put issues related to honor and voice above development. As Lalu famously commented, "I may not have given them heaven, but I have given them voice [*swarg nehi, swar diya*]." Instead of development, Lalu Yadav's core political project was an all-out effort to displace the upper castes from the center of Bihar's political, social, and economic life. He described the fruits of this project to me toward the end of his rule; "The forward castes [upper castes] used to rule Bihar. I have finished them off."

Lalu's government significantly changed the face of Patna. Soon after coming to power, he closed the city golf course, which he believed to be an unnecessary luxury for wealthy upper castes, and turned it into grazing land, benefiting his pastoralist Yadav caste. Cowsheds were built in the heart of the city for hundreds of rural Yadavs who moved in along with their cows and buffalos, selling milk door to door (although protests over the traffic jams and health hazards caused by the animals eventually ended this practice). In a blatant attack on caste discrimination and upper-caste conceptions of purity, Lalu appointed a Dalit as high priest of the government-run Hanuman temple that occupies a central place next to the city train station. Many lower-caste people who had lived in the city and adopted ambiguous surnames to conceal their caste now changed their names to proudly reflect their caste identity—the surname "Yadav," in particular, was suddenly visible everywhere. Most dramatically, Lalu held huge rallies with tens of thousands of lower caste villagers descending on the capital, paralyzing city life and essentially taking over the capital, and symbolically inverting the city's historical dominance over the countryside.

A CONFLICT IN RAJIV NAGAR

The neighborhood of Rajiv Nagar in Patna had been farmland before being acquired by the state government 30 years ago in order to build housing for government employees. Since the government offered to pay significantly less than market value for the land, landowners filed lawsuits and the courts ordered a freeze on government construction—a freeze that lasted for decades as the litigation stalled in India's tortuously slow legal system. During this time, land was bought and sold at a discount by a "land mafia" that obtained legal documents outside the state, and a thriving neighborhood emerged. Partly because of its ambiguous legal status, mafia politicians were central figures in the neighborhood. Even the cable television business in Rajiv Nagar needed mafia connections in order to compel people to pay their bills and prevent widespread illegal connections. My friend Ajay ran a lower-end restaurant in the market area of Rajiv Nagar, where we would sit, drink tea, and discuss local politics with his customers (Ajay once had been a kidnapping victim but was released). Residents of Rajiv Nagar were overwhelmingly from two upper-caste groups, Rajputs and Bhumihars, although other castes also lived there. Bantu Gope, a Bhumihar, became the dominant politician and mafia figure in the neighborhood after he was elected as the local city council representative and his Rajput rival was imprisoned.

Ajay and I had a mutual friend, Mitilesh, who ran two small grocery stalls in the market with his son. Mitilesh had a business dispute with another merchant that escalated into a fight in which Mitilesh and his son beat the merchant unconscious (an unfortunately common way to resolve disputes in Patna). The problem was that this merchant was a Bhumihar, and Mitilesh and his son are Rajputs. Knowing that his actions would create a backlash from Bantu Gope, who would seek to protect his Bhumihar caste-mate and seek revenge, Mitilesh shuttered his grocery stalls and fled the neighborhood. Since our friend Ajay also happens to be a Bhumihar, Mitilesh enlisted his help and asked him to approach Bantu Gope in order to settle the dispute. After returning from his meeting with the mafia politician, however, Ajay reported that Bantu Gope had declared, "I will not allow Mitilesh to open his stalls until he comes to see me in person, and when I see him, I am going to kill him!"

This obviously put Mitilesh in an impossible position. He was forced to keep his grocery stalls closed for weeks while his family slept at friends' houses outside the neighborhood. Without income from his business, he was beginning to run out of money, and he needed a resolution quickly. He once again approached his friend Ajay for help. Ajay decided to go "above" Bantu Gope and met with Dinesh Yadav, a Yadav mafia politician whose enormous house is near Rajiv Nagar and whom people consider much more powerful than Bantu Gope. The influence of Dinesh Yadav reflected the dominance that lower castes, and particularly Yadavs, had achieved in Patna. Although Bantu Gope was a member of the city council, he was one of only a handful of upper castes. Out of 57 elected councilors, 27, including the mayor, were Yadavs. Dinesh was the elected chairman of the Patna district council, a high-level post, and his nephew was the mayor of Patna. The first time that I ran into Dinesh was while I was purchasing groceries at a stall in front of my apartment. Dinesh Yadav had rented an apartment in the adjacent building for "business" purposes. He and his entourage arrived in two black SUVs filled with around 15 gunmen armed with AK-47 assault rifles, apparently returning from some "business." Dinesh Yadav was someone who could definitely settle Mitilesh's dispute.

This time, Ajay was able to broker a deal. Dinesh Yadav demanded that Mitilesh donate 10,000 rupees (around $200) to the Shiva temple in Rajiv Nagar, issue an apology to the merchant whom he beat up, and, in return, Dinesh Yadav forced Bantu Gope to forgive and forget. This episode illustrates the role of caste and informal sources of power in structuring life in Rajiv Nagar. It is significant that neither party went to the police or the courts to settle the dispute—they both accepted the authority of the local mafia politicians. Although the dispute began as an altercation between two merchants, it was interpreted as a conflict between two castes, reflecting the political alliances of the neighborhood. Had Mitilesh been a Bhumihar, for example, this conflict would have played out very differently. Mafia politicians like Dinesh Yadav and Bantu Gope maintained order and resolved conflicts in the neighborhood. Mitilesh's punishment was being forced to give a substantial donation to the neighborhood temple, an act that reaffirmed community spirit, even as it resolved the conflict in a way that reinforced the local political order. Dinesh Yadav's authority over Bantu Gope (and, by extension, Yadav dominance over Bhumihars), and Bantu Gope's authority over Mitilesh (and, by extension, Bhumihar dominance over Rajputs) was publicly demonstrated. This incident, therefore, reflects the importance of caste and mafia politicians within the life of the neighborhood. It also explains why people vote for mafia politicians—they provide a type of order and protect the interests of their supporters.

POLITICAL CHANGE

Since politics was central to both caste relations and criminal activities in Patna, political change had the potential to alter the experience of caste and criminality in the city. In the state assembly elections in Bihar in 2005, the opposition National Democratic Alliance (NDA) succeeded in mobilizing a coalition of discontented lower castes who felt that Yadavs had captured too much of the benefits of the RJD's "lower-caste" rule, and upper castes, particularly Bhumihars, who sought to return to power a decade and a half after being displaced. The first election resulted in a hung assembly, meaning that no party or coalition was able to put together a majority to form the state government. The result was the imposition of president's rule, whereby the central government takes over the state administration until new elections can be held. After the imposition of president's rule a reported 12,000 criminals were arrested within a 12-day period. Bihar's then director general of police, Narain Mishra, commented, "Now criminals know that nobody can save them. Under president's rule they have lost their patrons."

In the second round of elections, which followed eight months later, the opposition NDA won a decisive victory, capturing 143 seats in the 243-seat assembly. This ended the long period of RJD rule and profoundly altered Bihar's political geography. The election led to the fall of the RJD government after 15 years and the election of Nitish Kumar (a lower-caste Kurmi) as chief minister. This new political alliance between many lower castes and upper castes led to significant change in Patna. When I returned to Patna for three months in 2007, the atmosphere of the city was markedly different. Bihar's largely upper-caste bureaucracy and police force supported the new government, and government institutions in the state were strengthened. Many mafia politicians were imprisoned and politically weakened, including Bantu Gope (although others were still active). Kidnappings were still occurring, but people were no longer afraid to be on the streets after dark. The most dramatic example of this was during the Hindu festival of Durga Puja, where I was surprised to see entire families celebrating on the streets of the city until late in the night, something that would have been unthinkable during the preceding decade.

The political changes that transformed Patna, first with the coming to power of Lalu Yadav in 1990 and then his fall from power in 2005, demonstrate the ways that politics impacts everyday life in urban India. As we have seen, the importance of politics is based on the pervasive relationships between politics, caste, and criminality. While political and social alignments have shifted in recent years, and will likely shift again in the future, caste and politics will undoubtedly continue to impact life in Patna and other Indian cities.

References

Gupta, Dipankar. 2000. *Interrogating Caste: Understanding Hierarchy and Difference in Indian Society.* New York: Penguin Books.

Jaffrelot, Christophe. 2003. *India's Silent Revolution: The Rise of the Low Castes in North Indian Politics.* Delhi: Permanent Black.

Marriott, McKim, ed. 1986. *Village India: Studies in the Little Community.* Chicago: University of Chicago Press.

Srinivas, M. N. 1980. *The Remembered Village.* Berkeley: University of California Press.

Yadav, Yogendra. 1997. Understanding the Second Democratic Upsurge: Trends of Bahujan Participation in Electoral Politics in the 1990s. In *Transforming India: Social and Political Dynamics of Democracy,* eds. Francine Frankel, Zoya Hasan, Rajeev Bhargava, and Balveer Arora, pp. 120–145. Oxford: Oxford University Press.

PART 4

Migration and Adaptation

Early studies of migration focused on mass movements, particularly the transatlantic movement of people from Europe to the New World in the late nineteenth and early twentieth centuries (Jackson 1969; Kasdan 1970). It was this migration that brought to America the ancestors of many of today's students. In analyzing the causes of migration, early research focused on large economic and social forces such as land shortages. Less attention was given to the characteristics and motives of individual migrants themselves or to why in the same circumstances some individuals choose to leave while others remain at home.

Once the migrants were in the city, researchers focused on *problems* of adjustment rather than the successful ways in which most migrants adapted. This emphasis was largely the result of the prevailing views about the differences between rural and urban society. The pioneering writings of Louis Wirth and Robert Redfield, for example, described urban society as disorganized, secular, and individualistic. This led observers to expect that cityward migration by rural peoples would be disruptive and would cause social disorganization, culture conflict, and even *anomie* (the breakdown of norms), as well as alienation. Oscar Lewis's landmark study, "Urbanization without Breakdown" (1952), was the first study to question this view. Among his Tepoztecan migrants in Mexico City, urbanization did not result in weakened kinship bonds, social disorganization, change in religious beliefs, or alienation. Lewis's findings were later corroborated by others such as Janet Abu-Lughod's (1962) study of Egyptian migrants in Cairo, who had adapted to the city with little disruption of their traditional ways.

In the 1960s anthropologists began to pay more attention to individual migrants and their decision-making and coping strategies. Today, migrants are less likely to be viewed as pawns automatically responding to large structural forces than as active agents who understand their situation and the alternatives open to them. Poor Mexican peasants, for example, whose lands are neither large enough nor fertile enough to make a satisfactory living, do not blindly migrate to the nearest large city or north to the United States. Rather, they have a number of alternatives to consider: (1) continue working their

281

land as best they can, (2) remain at home while commuting to a nearby town to work, (3) move to a large city, leaving some family members at home but returning on weekends, (4) move their family to the city and give up their village home, or (5) leave the country altogether and go to the United States or Canada, either alone or with family members. Hence, migration must be viewed as a process in which individuals consciously change their own situations in search of a more rewarding life. Only in extreme cases of hardship such as famine and war (e.g., genocide in Darfur, civil war in Afghanistan and Iraq, natural disasters in New Orleans and along the Gulf Coast) is migration motivated by a single factor.

Once in cities, migrants must find a place to live, get a job, and develop a network of friends to satisfy their many needs. Of concern to urban anthropologists are the strategies migrants adopt to accomplish these goals. These strategies may be *individualistic*, in that migrants may depend primarily on their own resources and initiative, or their strategies may be more *group-oriented*, with migrants relying upon others—usually kin or fellow villagers—for assistance. Migrants seeking housing, for example, may find accommodation on their own or through their kin networks. Often migrants reside with their kin for several months until more suitable accommodations can be obtained. Similarly, in establishing friendships migrants may seek contacts with other members of the wider urban society or may choose relationships primarily among their own kind—especially kin and fellow villagers.

The individualistic strategy is also characteristic of the adjustment of students who go away to college, and again after they graduate and move to a new location where they do not have family or friends who can assist them in getting settled and acclimated to the new place and people. Of course, some graduates move to new places where former classmates provide contacts at their new destination. Once in their new locations, graduates may bond with fellow workers or college alumni, or seek out others who have similar backgrounds and interests. In short, the strategies they employ may not be all that different from some rural-urban migrants. Overall, the group-oriented approach in which the migrant relies on kin and community members for help in getting established in the city is most common among tribal and peasant migrants in the cities of developing countries/nations. Most of the chapters in this section describe, at least in part, the adaptations of migrants in their new urban environments; these include Robert V. Kemper's study of Tzintzuntzeño villagers in Mexico City, George Gmelch's narrative of a West Indian migrant in London, and Martin Cooke and Danièle Bélanger's research on Native Americans in Canadian cities. While these studies emphasize individual or family-level strategies, Kemper also describes how Mexican migrants organize "voluntary associations" to satisfy their needs. Such associations are usually comprised of members of the same ethnic groups or sometimes just individuals from the same rural villages. They assume many of the functions that were performed by kinship groups in the migrants' home villages. In some respects, they operate much like the guilds of preindustrial cities, by giving migrants a sense of belonging, providing financial aid in times of need, and organizing recreational activities. In short, such associations provide a strong support group that eases the migrant into the urban world.

Unless they have taken a course on globalization or transnationalism, most college students tend to think of migration as a one-way (usually rural to urban) process, since this has been the historical trend and often the pattern of their own ancestors. It has also been the migration pattern that elicits the greatest concern since it is linked to the explosive growth of Third World cities. Nevertheless, a closer look reveals that not all migrants who arrive in the city remain permanently. Some return home, some move on to other locales, and some even immigrate to a new country. Two of the chapters in this section—Takeyuki Tsuda's on Japanese Brazilians and George Gmelch's on West Indians—deal with "returnees," that is, migrants who eventually move back home. In most cases this was their original intention, as many migrants plan to be away only long enough to accomplish a specific objective, such as saving a set amount of money before returning home.

In some societies the dominant migration pattern is circular, in which individuals move back and forth periodically between their rural homes and urban centers—between two economic systems—with the migrants leaving the rural area and its limited prospects for a wage-earning job in the city. While the migrants may spend more time in the city and develop social networks there, their primary identification remains with the home village or country. This is a common pattern among the Canadian Aboriginals or "First Nation" peoples who move between the "reserve" (equivalent to "reservation" in the U.S.) and the city, described in the chapter by Cooke and Bélanger. Kemper reports a similar pattern among the Tzintzuntzan migrants who maintain a strong connection with their natal community, even when they are living far away. He employs the concept of "extended community" in addressing this phenomenon.

By 2005, half of the world's population was living in cities. In 1900 that figure had been just 13 percent, rising to 29 percent in 1950. Much of the increase in urban population, especially in developing countries, is comprised of migrants leaving farms and villages in search of a better life in cities. Consider greater Mexico City, where migrants from the Mexican countryside helped swell the population from five million in 1960 to over 22 million in 2008. An estimated half of that increase was made up of migrants, which equals an average of 15,000 new migrants arriving each month or about 500 new residents each day, all in need of food and water, shelter, and employment—and, if they have children, schooling. Although not on the same scale, many American cities are also swollen by new migrants. Today about 12 percent of the U.S. population (and 28 percent of Californians) were born in another country and immigrated to the United States, with most having settled in cities. This massive *urbanization* (i.e., shift in population from rural to urban places) has drawn the attention of many social scientists, not only in anthropology but also in sociology, demography, and economics. In fact, there is such a large amount of literature on the subject that migration has nearly become an independent field of study. There are dozens of periodicals devoted to migration scholarship, including *Asian and Pacific Migration Journal, Finnish Journal of Ethnicity and Migration, International Migration, International Migration Review, İrìnkèrindò: A Journal of African Migration, Journal of Ethnicity and Migration, Law and Migration, Migration, Migration and Health, Migration Letters, Studies in Forced Migration, Women and Migration in Asia,* and *World Migration.* It is likely that more urban anthropologists have conducted research on rural-urban migration than on any other topic.

In the last chapter of this section, Caroline Brettell and Robert Kemper discuss the types of adaptations migrants make, how research on rural-urban migration has been redirected to include a broader range of groups and issues than previously examined, and what is in store for the future. They discuss how the concept of "transnationalism" is used to describe the interconnectivity and the movements of migrants between their homelands and host societies. This type of ongoing international movement of migrants between two or more social spaces will be treated in more depth along with globalization in Part 5.

References

Abu-Lughod, Janet. 1962. Migrant Adjustment to City Life: The Egyptian Case. *American Journal of Sociology,* 47:22–32.

Jackson, J. A., ed. 1969. *Migration.* London: Cambridge University Press.

Kasdan, Leonard. 1970. Introduction. In *Migration and Anthropology,* ed. Robert F. Spencer, pp. 1–8. Seattle: University of Washington Press.

Lewis, Oscar. 1952. Urbanization without Breakdown. *Scientific Monthly,* 75:31–41.

Readings in Part 4

20

The Extended Community
Migration and Transformation in Tzintzuntzan, Mexico

Robert V. Kemper

For more than 40 years, Robert V. Kemper has followed the migrations of people from the Mexican village of Tzintzuntzan. A study that began among Tzintzuntzeño migrants in Mexico City has evolved into a long-term, lifelong study of the village and its people, wherever they may be. Tzintzuntzeños are able to spend decades at a distance without losing their sense of membership in their culturally and histori-cally distinctive community. Kemper gives special attention to their adaptive strate-gies, including their residential choices, group organization, employment, and psychological adjustment to urban life in Mexican and U.S. cities. In the process, Tzintzuntzeños—and the anthropologists who work among them—have come to redefine the spatial boundaries of the village as an "extended community."

On February 16, 2001, the front page of *The Washington Post* featured a story by Mary Jordan about the town of Tzintzuntzan, Michoacán, and its migrants. This story provided millions of readers and Internet users with back-ground for the first meeting between U.S. President George W. Bush and Mex-ican President Vicente Fox, both greatly concerned with the "problem" of Mexican migrants flowing into the United States without proper documenta-tion and without adequate protections for their human rights. In preparation, Jordan called me in Dallas from Mexico City and then went to Tzintzuntzan where she interviewed several migrants, finally settling on Remigio Morales as the central figure for her article. More than 40 years ago, when I began my involvement with the migrants of Tzintzuntzan (located about 350 km west of Mexico City), I never would have expected to see such a newspaper story pub-lished or to be quoted in the story as an anthropologist "who has been study-ing the migration and demographic patterns of this town since 1969."

Source: Written expressly for *Urban Life*.

BACKGROUND

When I began my dissertation fieldwork among Tzintzuntzan migrants in Mexico City, most anthropological thinking about Mexican peasant villages included critical assumptions about their "closed corporate" and "limited" characteristics (see Potter, Diaz, and Foster 1967). My theoretical and methodological frameworks were modeled after earlier studies done in Mexico City among rural–urban migrants from Tepoztlán (Lewis 1952) and from Tilantongo (Butterworth 1962). Thus, from the outset, my objectives in studying migrant adaptation were framed first within the then prevailing paradigms of acculturation and modernization (Kemper 1977), and more recently in terms of broader political-economic relationships between city and countryside (cf. Kemper and Rollwagen 1996).

This could have been just another one-shot field study leading to a dissertation, a monograph, and some articles. Instead, it became the basis for a continuing 40-year-long investigation of the "extended community" of Tzintzuntzan, a place famous among tourists as the capital of the Tarascan (the indigenous term "Purépecha" now is preferred) Empire and among students of anthropology for the pioneering, long-term fieldwork carried out there by George M. Foster (1948, 1967).

In retrospect, it is clear that I entered the field at a critical moment. The late 1960s were not only tumultuous times in Mexico City (e.g., the October 2, 1968, massacre of students at the Plaza de las Tres Culturas took place only six months before I entered the field), but they also marked the transition out of the long-standing (1942–1964) bilateral agreement known as the Bracero Program, through which a generation of Mexican laborers had been contracted to work in the United States.

The impact of the Bracero Program on towns in Mexico, and especially in Michoacán, was not lost on ethnographers of that era. In fact, in concluding his monograph on the Sierra Tarascan community of Cherán, Ralph Beals had remarked:

> Cherán, like many Indian communities of Mexico, is increasingly influenced by the town and the city. . . . Cherán is probably more influenced by Gary (Indiana, U.S.A.), Mexico City, and Morelia (possibly in diminishing order) than it is by Uruapan and Pátzcuaro. (1946:211)

Foster also had noted the positive experiences of Tzintzuntzeños—almost 50 percent of the village's adult males—who had traveled north to work in the United States: "Most are very anxious to get back to the United States, either to live permanently or to work for an extended period" (1948:149). During the 1950s, from 50 to 150 men went to the U.S. each year—at a time when few Tzintzuntzeños ventured to work and live in Mexico City.

Because I approached the migration problem from a singular perspective—that of a community already well-known ethnographically through Foster's work—I could define broadly the people and places relevant for questions such as, "Who is migrating?" "Where are they going?" and "From where are they returning?" Thus, although my first fieldwork was concentrated in Mexico City, for my dissertation I also analyzed Foster's master data file of all individuals censused in 1945, 1960, and 1970 to determine the destinations of *all* Tzintzuntzan migrants throughout Mexico and the United States. In this way, I got a sense of the broader picture within which cityward migration took place—and I opened a Pandora's box in terms of dealing with the broader migration *system* in which the community of Tzintzuntzan was participating.

THE TZINTZUNTZAN MIGRATION PROJECT[1]

When I first arrived (with my wife) in Mexico City, I had a list of about 20 migrants' names and just two addresses; when I departed the field 16 months later in summer 1970, I had gathered information on nearly 500 persons involved with Tzintzuntzan migrant households in Mexico City. Subsequently, in 1974, I conducted an ethnographic survey of the Tzintzuntzan migrants in the capital and, using a key informant in each village neighborhood, collected individual and family-level data on migrants' destinations—to Mexico City and elsewhere. During this first phase of fieldwork, I used the standard array of anthropological data-gathering procedures: participant observation, censuses, household budget surveys, in-depth interviews, questionnaires, projective tests (Thematic Apperception Test), and life histories.

In 1979–80, my wife and I spent nearly 15 months in Mexico City among the migrants as well as with the people of Tzintzuntzan in their hometown. We gathered data on some 200 households dispersed around the Mexico City metropolitan area. In addition, I obtained information on Tzintzuntzeños in several other Mexican provincial cities. I also extended my own fieldwork to the United States in effort to locate migrants known to be living and working in the states of California and Illinois. This additional fieldwork yielded data on about 150 households beyond what we had found in Mexico City. Back in Tzintzuntzan, I co-directed, with my former mentor George M. Foster, the fieldwork for the 1980 village census and took charge of the data analysis and archival work that followed.

As we worked on the census, it became clear that the simple division of the population into residents and migrants was inadequate to represent a continually changing social and economic reality. A significant increase in four socioeconomic categories—i.e., high school and university students attending schools at campuses in the state capital or even outside the state, workers commuting daily to other localities, persons working full-time outside of Tzintzuntzan who returned from time to time to be with their families, and illegal immigrants laboring in the United States—all combined to complicate the definition of who should be counted as "present" in the community.

Our solution to this ethnographic problem was to create an intermediate category that we called the "extended population." These people share one important characteristic: they are beyond the village much more than in it, and their eventual ties to the community are uncertain. Thus, for 1980, we counted a "core" population of 2,506 persons in Tzintzuntzan and an "extended" population of another 143.

The villagers of Tzintzuntzan provided us with a dramatic example of how they themselves could "extend" their community when, in 1979, some 45 families invaded a strip of land belonging collectively to their own *comunidad indígena* (indigenous community) about two km south of the village along the road to Pátzcuaro. Since this new settlement was composed entirely of people from Tzintzuntzan, we chose to count its residents as continuing members of Tzintzuntzan proper.

Throughout the 1980s, I continued what had become our routine biennial village-based survey of population changes in Tzintzuntzan. Thus, by the time we carried out the comprehensive 1990 census of the village and migrants, I had come to conceive of this population as a spatial and temporal social field focused on Tzintzuntzan, but with extensions in Mexico City, other urban and rural places in Mexico, and sites across the border in the United States. As time passed, my research was transformed from a study of migrants in Mexico City into a multilocation, long-term study of the people of Tzintzuntzan, wherever and whenever they might be.

Our 1990 ethnographic census revealed that Tzintzuntzan had a "core" residential population of 2,999 persons, plus 350 individuals classified as members of the "extended" population. As in 1980, we counted the 200 resi-

A founding family of Colonia Lázaro Cárdenas in front of their temporary house in 1980. Soon thereafter, they were able to replace it with a permanent structure with painted adobe-stucco walls, a traditional tile roof, and a front-room store where they could sell their crafts to passing tourists. [Photo by Robert V. Kemper]

dents of Colonia Lázaro Cárdenas as a component part of Tzintzuntzan. In 1991, another invasion occurred—across the road from the colonia—involving perhaps another 20 families (some of whom were the married children of colonia residents). By adding a second colonia, this one called Tzintzuntzita (little Tzintzuntzan), the villagers themselves continued to redefine the spatial boundaries of their community.

Throughout the 1990s, we saw the flow of emigrants shift dramatically— away from Mexico City and northward toward Tacoma, Washington, and nearby farming communities. This change in the migration stream reflected the serious economic crisis that had begun in the 1980s and eventually brought Mexico, the United States, and Canada to create the economic partnership known as the North American Free Trade Agreement (NAFTA), which began on January 1, 1994.

In January 2000, I assembled a team of 30 local residents to carry out the census. The team visited more than 700 households, and another 264 "extended" individuals for Tzintzuntzan proper and its colonias (Lázaro Cárdenas, Tzintzuntzita, and the newest one, called San Juan). We also gathered data on migrants throughout Mexico and in the United States, especially in the state of Washington, which now claims the largest enclave outside of Mexico City. In sum, about half of the people of Tzintzuntzan were living in and around the village and the other half were living temporarily or permanently removed from their natal community. This is a dramatic transformation from the situation in 1970, and even more striking when compared with the circumstances in 1945, when Foster first did fieldwork in Tzintzuntzan, then a community of only 1,231 residents.

MIGRATION AND URBAN ADAPTATION

Although the experiences of migrants from Tzintzuntzan are diverse, certain patterns emerge through the decades. The first issue faced by Tzintzuntzeños involves their decision to stay at home or to leave the community. Once they decide to emigrate, they face important choices and systemic constraints regarding survival issues, especially those related to where they live and work. Finally, the emigrants confront new ways of thinking about the world and understanding their place in it, particularly if they are successful enough to see their children and grandchildren move a few more rungs up the socioeconomic ladder from the place they had reached by leaving Tzintzuntzan.

Buscar La Vida: **The Decision to Emigrate**

In the period since World War II, the forces of technology, economic modernization, and improved health and sanitation have combined to transform life in thousands of Mexican villages, and Tzintzuntzan is no exception. The once stable population of Tzintzuntzan has tripled since 1945. Penetration of the community by highway, rail, radio, television networks, and, most recently, by the Internet has greatly increased its participation in national and international affairs. The growing tourist market for the locally produced pottery and crafts and the active involvement of villagers in the Bracero Program of the 1950s and early 1960s (and continuing involvement in legal and undocumented labor migration to the United States) have combined to raise the standard of living for nearly all Tzintzuntzan residents. The construction of a secondary school in the village (in conjunction with the remodeling of the old primary school) in the mid-1970s has been followed in recent years by the construction of a high school, which has greatly reduced the cost of commuting to nearby cities.

In this context, migration has become a routine, even expected, matter for the people of Tzintzuntzan. Between 1930 and 1940, when nearly one of every nine Mexicans was moving across state boundaries, only a handful of Tzintzuntzeños ventured outside of the state of Michoacán. Now it seems that "everybody" has a family member outside the community. In their words, they emigrate to *buscar la vida*, to "search for life."

Tzintzuntzan migrants offer many reasons for having left the village to pursue the "good life," whether in Mexico City or in Tacoma. For example, Emiliano Guzmán, a 29-year-old factory worker, lamented the lack of progress in Tzintzuntzan while reciting his opportunities for steady, albeit low-paying, employment in Mexico City. José Zavala, a middle-aged teacher, recalled the tranquility and pleasant pace of village life in contrast to the overcrowded, smoggy, and hectic metropolis but confessed that there was no job for him in the village. Raúl Silva disliked being separated from friends and relatives in the city but, at the same time, admitted that he has no wish to go back to Tzintzuntzan to become a potter like his father. Many others made similar comments when asked why they emigrated. Taken as a whole, they weigh the good and bad of village and destination, whether close at hand or across the northern border, and pursue what promises to be a better life.

As these examples show, for many people in Tzintzuntzan migration has become the default option, with remaining in the village a distant second choice. The decision to migrate is rarely simple, nor is it always related to visible economic conditions. Tzintzuntzeños select destinations based on their perceptions of available opportunities, which they learn about through friends and relatives who already live beyond the local scene. In this regard, we may speak of migration *strategies* by which villagers manipulate (although not always maximize) available contacts to improve their situations.

Tzintzuntzeños survive their initial encounters with life away from their hometown because, when they arrive at their destination, they can stay *arrimado* (up close to, i.e., as a guest) with relatives or friends already established there. The arrimado network, with its promise of assistance in finding housing and work, is certainly responsible for much of the growth in the migrant group, whether in Mexico City or in Tacoma. Complex social networks now bridge the gap between origin and destination, transforming what once were individual migration itineraries into a continuing and expanding social process. The set of actors is constantly changing, with new migrants profiting from the experiences—pleasant and unpleasant—of friends and relatives who preceded them along the migrant path.

The limitations on affordable urban housing stock have a significant impact on migrants. One serious consequence is a restructuring of their traditional family and household arrangements. Although the conjugal family remains important, enclaves of extended families have appeared in several neighborhoods. For example, in Mexico City, I found several migrants renting adjacent rooms in a *vecindad* (a building containing low-income apartment units) while others purchased lots with kinfolk and shared the burden of house building. In a similar fashion, I found several families of Tzintzuntzeños living in the same apartment complexes in the small farm towns of Fife and Sumner near Tacoma. These migrant residential strategies conserve limited financial and social resources in unfamiliar environments. One common practice involves sharing child care responsibilities among women—and men, too— during their different work shifts at nearby fields and factories.

Palancas: The Struggle for Economic Success

Most Tzintzuntzan migrants arrive at their destinations without a job assured; instead, they hope to find work through the assistance of relatives and friends already working there. Thus, in addition to providing temporary lodging, the more experienced migrants often serve as *palancas* (levers) in finding jobs for new arrivals. The length of time needed to find a "good" job depends on the migrants' personal attributes (especially, their previous work experience and educational background), on the sequence and quality of their earlier experiences outside of Tzintzuntzan, and on their own definition of what constitutes adequate employment. Generally, the migrants find some work immediately upon arrival, but a satisfying job seldom comes quickly. After some initial job instability, most migrants settle into relatively permanent niches. This does not mean that they retain the same job year after year; on the contrary, they continually search for better opportunities, with the final decision to change careers or company affiliations determined by their perception of the best available combination of wages, tenure, and social security benefits.

Few migrants expect to get wealthy, but some do make the critical shift from manual to "professional" jobs, and most believe (or hope) that their children will enter the ranks of white-collar workers. The Tzintzuntzeños are well aware that it is difficult to get ahead without adequate educational and job training. For this reason, children are encouraged to stay in school as long as possible and to obtain the best "credentials" possible. Indeed, in recent years, one of the main reasons for the emigration of young people from Tzintzuntzan is to get an advanced education, which will then open doors to professional employment opportunities in Mexico City and in other urban centers.

A shift from traditional to modern concepts of "success" is an integral part of the process of economic adaptation to urban life. When the migrants compare their positions with those of their parents or siblings still in Tzintzuntzan, nearly all conclude that the city offers the better prospects for themselves and for their children. Moreover, very few would consider returning to the village as an alternative to seeking other urban employment if they were to lose their current positions. The most important shift, however, occurs when the migrants realize that a dependence on their fellow migrants poses severe limitations on their own prospects, since their opportunities are unlikely to be superior to those available to their fellows.

Tzintzuntzeños eventually recognize that, while fellow migrants are keys to the initial job, long-term economic success is the result of individual initiative, hard work, and a good network of migrant and nonmigrant palancas. As one migrant remarked, "What are my dreams? Well, with hard work a person begins to think about his future, in having his own home, in helping his children and in seeing them achieve a social and economic level that he himself doesn't enjoy."

The experiences of the earlier migrants in Mexico City are also seen in the lives of those who more recently have traveled great distances to work in the United States. They begin with their connections to other Tzintzuntzeños, but soon look for others who can help them find stable, well-paying jobs. Even undocumented migrants to the United States depend on their palancas for obtaining jobs and housing. The steady increase in the number of villagers who have experiences outside Tzintzuntzan has made an awareness of the importance of these social and economic ties a standard part of the "migrant culture" of Tzintzuntzeños.

A Tzintzuntzeño and his coworker in a nut orchard near Modesto, CA, 1990. [Photo by Robert V. Kemper]

Imagen del Mundo: **Psychological Adaptations to Migrant Life**

Migrating from Tzintzuntzan not only involves people in new residential and occupational strategies, it also may require modification of their *imagen del mundo* (worldview). The psychological dimensions of urban adaptation must be understood not merely in terms of a rural–urban continuum but also in terms of the relative socioeconomic positions occupied by migrants before and after they leave the village. A migrant may hold values inappropriate for city life; these may not necessarily be *rural* values but instead attitudes acquired in the process of interacting in situations where the migrants have been defined as inferior.

Tzintzuntzeños near the bottom of the socioeconomic scale in their urban destinations face pressures and frustrations that parallel those of the poorest peasants in the village. For both groups, their concern is day-to-day survival, not upward mobility. Of course, since most migrants come from the better educated, more affluent, and more ambitious village families, their economic success beyond the village is not surprising. Those migrants with steady urban jobs tend to have an optimistic worldview in which a pragmatic balance is struck between present needs and future hopes. The ideal of most working-class Tzintzuntzeños is to provide a base upon which their children can build even better lives.

The small but growing numbers of professional-level migrants often face a frustration common to middle sectors of many urban societies. They may earn quite respectable wages, but they can rarely hope to belong to the elite groups whom they emulate. The psychological dangers of excessive "social climbing" haunt long-term as well as recent migrants. For example, when they lived in Mexico City, the Zavala family was eager to send their daughter to a private academy—preferably, a French-speaking school—because they wanted her to receive a "proper" education (which to them meant an upper-class, foreign-oriented curriculum). Ultimately, however, the financial drain outweighed the benefits, and they enrolled her in the inexpensive public high school near their apartment. Subsequently, she entered a professional school where she received training—and learned English rather than French—for work in the growing field of international tourism.

This concern for education as the means to upward social and economic mobility is a key indicator that a "modern" worldview has become dominant among most migrants—as well as among the village families who are now sending their children to the secondary school and high school in Tzintzuntzan and then onward to the colleges and universities in the state capital. This emphasis on education implies a strong achievement motivation and a healthy future orientation. These values are especially strong among young professionals. For example, Martín Calva worked as a well-paid government employee in the computer analysis division of the Treasury Department. He moved steadily up the job ladder so that he was able to acquire a nice home in which his wife, child, and younger siblings reside. Just as his relatives helped him through the university in years past, so he has assisted a chain of his own brothers and sisters to get an education and move ahead in the urban system. Martín Calva and other migrants reason that, if a primary school certificate was enough to lift an earlier generation of migrants out of the village and into a working-class job in Mexico City, then a secondary or university diploma would be needed to assure that their children attain professional positions.

Unfortunately, the gap between the working class and the middle class is too wide for many people to bridge in a single generation. Furthermore, the competition for civil service jobs and professional (e.g., doctor, lawyer, engineer) positions through Mexican society has become increasingly arduous since the economic "crisis" of the 1980s. To fulfill their dreams of upward mobility, young migrants have had to reevaluate Mexico City as a destination. Often, they opt to go north to the United States, even if it means trading professional status for manual work. For instance, one man with a university engineering degree left the capital in the late 1980s and took his family to live near Tacoma, where he labors in the fields. He earns more money and feels better about the future for his children in the north than if he had remained in Mexico City.

TZINTZUNTZAN AS EXTENDED COMMUNITY

There are certainly hundreds, if not thousands, of community studies in the anthropological literature. Most of these works, especially those from earlier times, are focused tightly on a single place in time and space. Our continuing long-term fieldwork among the people of Tzintzuntzan suggests that we need to rethink our notion of community (cf. Foster 2002).

First, I am struck particularly by how hard it has become to define who is and who is not a resident of Tzintzuntzan. As we have seen, a growing proportion—perhaps now almost 50 percent—of the local households have one or more "extended" members away from the village at any given moment, yet the families tend not to think of these persons as being migrants. In addition, given the flow of individuals and families from and back to the village in accord with academic schedules, vacations, and the planting–harvesting cycles in U.S. fields, the population is always in flux.

Second, distance is no longer the significant factor that it used to be. The transportation infrastructure permits relatively inexpensive travel by bus, private car, or even airlines to all parts of Mexico and to the United States. In recent years, local church records show that an increasing number of children born outside Tzintzuntzan—even in the United States—are being registered in the village for their baptisms, first communions, and confirmations. These rituals in the Roman Catholic Church usually coincide with major community fiestas. These positive connections across the distances that separate the emigrants from the village are offset, to a lesser degree, by the return to Tzintzuntzan of the bodies of persons who have died—most often from car accidents, violence, or drugs—and whose bodies have been sent back by air to Guadalajara and thence by bus or family-owned truck to Tzintzuntzan for funeral and wake services.

Third, outside forces have transformed the basic communications infrastructure. The traditionally limited access to telephone service has been upgraded to fully automatic service (now that Teléfonos de México has been privatized) for the 100 or so households with landlines. More significant is that virtually every young adult carries a cell phone and has a service plan with a certain number of pre-paid minutes per month. Within the past year or so, several persons have set up Internet places in town. Earlier efforts were limited because they only offered dial-up services. The most recent Internet service centers offer high-speed Internet access—for less than $1 per hour.

Fourth, the increased participation of the young people of Tzintzuntzan in the higher educational system of Mexico means that many of them are away from the village for several years, except for vacation periods or weekends. Yet, they continue to return to the community even after settling in urban areas where their hard-won job skills can be applied. For instance, one medical doctor has his practice in Morelia but insists (even over his non-Tzintzuntzan wife's objections) on maintaining a weekend practice in Tzintzuntzan. More than 150 persons from the village have become school teachers, which is remarkable enough, but more interesting is that many desire to practice their profession while living in the village and commuting daily to other localities, even when this requires coming back just on weekends.

Fifth, earnings and remittances from persons beyond the immediate community have become vital to the continuing economic survival of Tzintzuntzan and hundreds of similar Mexican villages. During the 40 years of the Tzintzuntzan migrant project, the Mexican peso declined from a fixed value of 12.5 to the dollar to about 3,000 to the dollar by 1990, then despite a 1,000 to 1 "adjustment," continued to decline to about 15 pesos to the dollar as of mid-2009. As a result, the shift of the extended community toward the United States—and away from Mexico City—has become more marked. When men fail to send money or do not return after the fall harvest season in the United States, their spouses and children suffer serious deprivations. In recent years, the "closing" of the U.S.–Mexico border has made frequent short-term travel very difficult. Even for those with proper documents, it is hardly worth the hassle to cross the border except for such important events as baptisms, weddings, and funerals. One of the unintended consequences of U.S. border policies since the events of 9/11 has been the social disorganization brought about by the long-term forced separation of family members.

Sixth, inheritance is an important issue for residents and their relatives living away from Tzintzuntzan. A number of older migrants—some away from the village for more than 40 years—still own houses or land there. Will they leave this property to their children, some of whom have rarely traveled to Tzintzuntzan, or will they pass it on to family members still living in the village? On the other side of the equation, many younger migrants want to establish their claims to a share of the family lands by continuing to visit

Tzintzuntzan on a regular basis. This appears to be one of the reasons that so many children are brought back to the local church for their life-course rituals—that is, to establish their claims for being "members" of the local community as well as of its extended community.

Finally, Tzintzuntzan long has been famous for its annual cycle of fiestas and religious celebrations (Brandes 1988; Cahn 2003). Many migrants—as well as thousands of other tourists—come to the community to participate in these festivals. Especially at the February festival, held in honor of the *Señor del Rescate* (Lord of Rescue), many migrants return to baptize or confirm their children in the parish church. Often, they select compadres (co-godparents) from among village residents or other returned migrants, thus emphasizing their solidarity with their natal community. This sense of membership and affiliation also applies to the people of the hamlets surrounding the village proper. Conveniently, the main elements of the annual fiesta cycle occur at times when Tzintzuntzeños living away from the village can return as participants or observers. Consider the case of two recent fiestas for the Señor del Rescate—in 2004 and 2009:

In the first instance, at the 2004 celebration a large *"Bienvenidos Peregrinos"* ("Welcome Pilgrims") banner was sponsored by Luigi's Pizza of Gary, Indiana. This seems bizarre, unless one knows that Luigi's is owned by Patricio Delgado Alba, a man from Tzintzuntzan whose family members long have lived in and around South Chicago, just across the state line from Gary. The thousands of tourists and visitors who attend the February festival will have no clue about this connection, but locals (and their anthropologist) certainly appreciate this sponsorship from a distance.

In the second case, the 2009 fiesta showed the growing importance of the migrant community in the Tacoma region. For the first time, the fiesta's Organizing Commission had two sides: the traditional village Commission with 11 members and a new Commission of seven members in Tacoma. The local Commission raised almost $15,000 from some 540 individual contributors. In Tacoma, the migrant Commission raised almost $7,000 from about 150 donors. About half of the funds were spent on hiring two musical groups to perform consecutively during the first two and last two days of the four-day fiesta.

For about 10 years, the emigrants in Tacoma have been celebrating a replicate fiesta in honor of the Señor del Rescate at a Roman Catholic church attended by most of the Tzintzuntzeños in the area. They are joined in this celebration by thousands of others, not associated with Tzintzuntzan, who come just to have a good time. This replicate fiesta has taken on extra significance in recent years as U.S. immigration policies have unintentionally encouraged many emigrants (especially those who are undocumented) to stay in the U.S. once they have made it safely past the border zone. The celebration of the Señor del Rescate fiesta in Tacoma thus owes its existence not only to emigrants' desire to sustain their role in the Tzintzuntzan "extended community" but also to prevailing U.S.–Mexico border politics.

"Welcome Pilgrims" banner, sponsored by a Tzintzuntzan migrant in the United States, 2004. [Photo by Robert V. Kemper]

CONCLUSION

The popularity of the Tacoma-based fiesta has brought Tzintzuntzan emigrants to the attention of the media in Washington State. For example, in February 2008, Liz Jones, a reporter for a Seattle-based Public Radio station, presented a weeklong series about the many thousands of Michoacán emigrants living in the Seattle-Tacoma region. As part of her preparation for this story, she traveled to Michoacán in early January and met me in Tzintzuntzan, where we spent two days discussing the importance of emigration and the "extended community" for communities like Tzintzuntzan.

The people of Tzintzuntzan, like those of many other Mexican communities, have learned that they can sustain substantial levels of migration without losing their sense of local community and cultural distinctiveness. Migrants who live in Mexico City, in Guadalajara, in the border city of Tijuana, as well as those as far away as Tacoma, Washington, or Gary, Indiana, do find their way back to Tzintzuntzan nearly every year to participate in the local fiestas and other special occasions—and thus to reconfirm their membership in this "extended community."

If Tzintzuntzan continues to develop as it has during the past 40 years, the challenge to our theories and methodologies will be significant. What once was treated—by villagers and anthropologists alike—as if it were a "closed" system (cf. Foster 1967) will become an even more spatially and temporally "extended community." Indeed, for the migrants and their children returning to what some of them have jokingly identified as "Tzintzunlandia" (a play on "Disneyland"), the community is both "home" and a "re-creation" site where they, like other tourists, can encounter ancient Purépecha and Spanish colonial culture in twenty-first century dress. Even more important, they encounter their own cultural and social circumstances being transformed before their very eyes. This is a community still tied to pre-Conquest legends and more than 400 years of colonial and post-colonial history. It is caught up in government-sponsored tourist campaigns to retain its traditional facade, but it is also striving to cope with modern life in a global system represented by cell phones, the Internet, satellite television, border crossings, and transnationalism—a world in which the historic community of Tzintzuntzan finds itself featured on a Seattle-based Public Radio station and on the front page of *The Washington Post*.

Note

1 The initial fieldwork in Mexico City during 1969–1970 was funded through NIGMS Training Grant GM-1224. The Wenner-Gren Foundation for Anthropological Research provided a Grant-in-Aid (No. 3027) for the summers of 1974 and 1976 and for preparation of the Spanish- and English-language monographs based on that fieldwork. In the periods July 1979–June 1980 and July–December 1991, fieldwork was supported by Fulbright-Hays Advanced Research Awards (American Republics Program). The Ford Foundation (Office for Mexico and Central America) provided a small grant to support two Mexican graduate students on the project in 1980. I also have received continuing support from Southern Methodist University through Faculty Research Fellowships and Awards for the periods August–December 1979, June 1986–July 1987, January–June 1990, August 1999–May 2000, and August–December 2008, with additional time to be provided in January–May 2010 for carrying out the seventh ethnographic census. Many other trips to the field as well as ongoing data analysis and archival work have been funded by the Foster family and matched by my own contributions.

References

Beals, Ralph L. 1946. *Cherán: A Sierra Tarascan Village*. Smithsonian Institution, Institute of Social Anthropology, Publication No. 2. Washington, D.C.: U. S. Government Printing Office.

Brandes, Stanley. 1988. *Power and Persuasion: Fiestas and Social Control in Rural Mexico*. Philadelphia: University of Pennsylvania Press.

Butterworth, Douglas. 1962. A Study of the Urbanization Process among Mixtec Migrants from Tilantongo in Mexico City. *América Indígena*, 22(3):257–274.

Cahn, Peter. 2003. *All Religions Are Good in Tzintzuntzan*. Austin: University of Texas Press.

Foster, George M. 1948. *Empire's Children: The People of Tzintzuntzan*. Smithsonian Institution, Institute of Social Anthropology, Publication No. 6. México, D.F.: Imprenta Nuevo Mundo.

———. 1967. *Tzintzuntzan: Mexican Peasants in a Changing World*. Boston: Little, Brown.

———. 2002. A Half Century of Field Research in Tzintzuntzan, Mexico: A Personal View. In *Chronicling Cultures: Long-Term Field Research in Anthropology*, eds. Robert V. Kemper and Anya Peterson Royce, pp. 252–283. Walnut Creek, CA: AltaMira Press.

Kemper, Robert V. 1977. *Migration and Adaptation: Tzintzuntzan Peasants in Mexico City.* Beverly Hills, CA: Sage.

Kemper, Robert V., and Jack Rollwagen. 1996. Urban Anthropology. In *Encyclopedia of Cultural Anthropology, vol. 4 (S-Z)*, eds. David Levinson and Melvin Ember, pp. 1337–1344. New York: Henry Holt and Company.

Lewis, Oscar. 1952. Urbanization without Breakdown. *Scientific Monthly*, 75:31–41.

Potter, Jack M., May N. Diaz, and George M. Foster. 1967. *Peasant Society: A Reader.* Boston: Little, Brown.

21

A West Indian Life in Britain

George Gmelch

In this chapter, George Gmelch examines the migration of West Indians to Britain and their return to the Caribbean. The oral history of a single migrant, Roy Campbell, is used to give the reader an inside view of the challenges faced by people who try to go home again. The author points out that most migrants from the Caribbean are interested in remaining abroad only long enough to satisfy certain economic or educational goals that cannot be met by staying home. In this case study of transnational migration and the adaptation of migrants to a new culture, Gmelch shows that urban anthropologists should not abandon our traditional emphasis on the motives and experiences of individual migrants caught up in global processes.

About one of every 10 residents of the island of Barbados has emigrated at one time or another. High rates of outmigration are common throughout the small, overpopulated, and resource-poor islands of the Caribbean. It is so pervasive that nearly every village household has a relative or close friend in Britain or North America. Migration is of such fundamental importance to the islanders' economic adaptation that some scholars refer to it as "livelihood migration."[1]

At the time of their departure, most migrants do not intend to settle abroad permanently; rather, they expect to be away only long enough to save sufficient money to build a respectable house at home, complete a college education, or learn a trade. In 2008 there were over 750,000 Afro-Caribbean people living in Britain, particularly in the cities of London, Birmingham, Nottingham, Slough, and Manchester. An even greater number live in the United States and Canada, with 82 percent living in the U.S. northeast, particularly New York. In New York and Miami, Florida, the West Indian population is concentrated in just a few neighborhoods, for example, Bedford-Stuyvesant in Brooklyn.

Source: Written expressly for *Urban Life*.

Through the story of one Barbadian individual, in his own voice, this chapter looks at one migration and what it is like to be a black immigrant in a predominantly white society. But first, some background.

BARBADOS

Barbados lies in the eastern Caribbean, about 200 miles north of the South American continent, and east of the great arc of volcanic islands that sweeps a thousand miles from the Virgin Islands in the north to Trinidad in the south. With a gentle terrain ideal for agriculture, Barbados was the archetypal "sugar island," producing sugar, molasses, and rum for its colonial master, Great Britain, for over 300 years.[2] Most Barbadians are descendants of Africans who were transported to the island to work as slaves on the sugar plantations. Barbados is the only Caribbean island to have had a single colonial master. In fact, Barbados is often referred to as "Little England" by its inhabitants as well as its neighbors, though more recently it has become a hackneyed phrase of the tourist trade. In the realm of sport, British colonial rule introduced cricket, now the island's popular national pastime. The long history and close bond between the two nations made Britain the obvious and most popular destination for Barbadian emigrants in search of wage labor and new opportunities. Independent from Britain since 1966, today Barbados is better known to the outside world for its white sand beaches and sunny, tropical climate, which make it a popular tourist destination. Its reputation is far larger than its size, just 21 miles from north to south.

WEST INDIAN MIGRATION

The patterns of Barbadian migration are typical of the other islands in the region. Prior to the abolition of slavery in the 1830s, of course, there was no migration since the majority of West Indians were not free to move. In the first 50 years after emancipation, many moved away from the plantations on which they had been enslaved to small holdings and towns on their home islands. Some managed to go to other islands, largely in response to the availability of work in the newer colonies of British Guiana and Trinidad, which were expanding sugarcane cultivation.

After the 1880s, the migrants went further afield, to Cuba and the Dominican Republic to work on large sugar estates, to Central America to work on banana plantations, to Bermuda to construct a dry dock, and, notably, to Panama to excavate and build the Panama Canal. During the Great Depression of the 1930s, migration subsided, and many earlier migrants returned home. It was considered better to scratch out a living on a small parcel of land at home than to be unemployed abroad.

With the outbreak of World War II, a new wave of migration began as workers moved to Britain, the United States, and Canada to fill the jobs of citizens who were away in the armed forces. The war was only a prelude to the mass migration to Britain that followed. The war itself provided the conditions that promoted such extensive migration—namely, the enormous loss of life and the devastation of many British cities, which created a high demand for labor. Hence, in the 1950s, West Indians migrated in large numbers to Britain, *the mother country*. In just a six-year period (1955 to 1961), Barbados saw nearly 8 percent of its citizens board ships and depart for England.[3]

Most migrated alone, not as couples or families. In most households, the male emigrated first, followed by his wife or girlfriend and by some, but seldom all, of their children. Why men first? Are they more ambitious, adventurous, or independent than West Indian women? Definitely not, according to Nancy Foner (1978) in a study of Jamaican migrants. Rather, in most households, there simply was not enough money for the entire family to emigrate together, and, as men were the principal breadwinners, it was natural that they would go first. If employment and housing conditions abroad were favorable and enough money could be saved for additional fares, women and children followed.

Most West Indian governments made no effort to prevent their citizens from leaving. In fact, emigration was often seen as a safety valve for excess population and high unemployment. The Barbadian government assisted British companies in recruiting workers. London Transport and the Lyons Hotel and Restaurant Association, for example, were allowed to set up offices in Bridgetown to interview Barbadians. A Barbadian from a tiny village in the north of the island could make his way to Bridgetown and apply for a job 3,000 miles away as a bus conductor, a ticket taker on the platform at Euston Station, or a dishwasher in a Piccadilly restaurant.

What was it like to leave the familiarity and security of home for an uncertain future in white London or Birmingham? How well did the Barbadians, many barely out of school, adjust? The following pages focus on the experiences of Roy Campbell, one of 10 Barbadian migrants whose life histories I recorded in the late 1980s. I use Roy's account here because, in many respects, he comes closest to being typical of the postwar Barbadian migrants in terms of education, jobs, housing, and social adjustment.

ROY CAMPBELL: AN IMMIGRANT LIFE

Roy grew up in the small, quiet village of Rockfield on the remote northeastern coast of Barbados. Tourists who visit the area today are struck by the rugged coastal scenery, which some guidebooks claim is the best in Barbados. Like many Barbadian villages, Rockfield consists of small, brightly colored, wooden houses stretched single file along a narrow main road, with other houses connected by a footpath or dirt track. Scattered among them are larger "wall" or cement-block houses owned by better-off families, often emigrants who have returned from abroad. Surrounding the village are sugarcane fields, which cover much of Barbados, and bordering the fields are lines of casuarina trees imported from Australia by the early British planters.

A chattel house—traditional village housing near Rockfield, where Roy Campbell grew up.

Roy remained in school until age 15, earning his *leaving certificate* (high school diploma). He then obtained a job as an apprentice automobile mechanic in a garage in Bridgetown, the capital and Barbados's only city. Four years later, he was still earning apprentice wages of seven dollars per week when British army recruiters came to Barbados. Roy volunteered, took the physical exam, and was accepted into the British army, but his father, fearing another war, refused to let his only son enlist. Instead, he gave Roy money to pay for a new suit of clothes, a suitcase, and his passage to England.

> I wanted to go [to England], because I wasn't getting anywhere here in Barbados, and because I wanted to see what England was like after hearing so much in school about the mother country. I was nineteen, and many of my friends had gone over already. I left on the boat the 16th of June, 1962, with my suitcase full of warm underclothing and food: rice, sugar, rum, peppers, pepper sauce, flour, yams, and potatoes. I thought it would be hard to get West Indian food there.[4]
>
> I went on the *Serrienta*, an Italian ship. I was seasick for about three days, but after I recovered, the days started going too quickly. I wanted to stay on a bit longer—the food was so good, and, at night, you could go down to the cinema. And they had a lounge where you could listen to the news, and they had comics so you could sit down and read if you wanted. And they had a bar where you could have a drink. The ship had an Italian band, but they played samba music so that both the Italians and the West Indians could dance to it. I'll tell you, I didn't want to come off the ship.

After seven days at sea, we stopped at Tenerife in the Canary Islands, then Barcelona, then Naples and then finally we got off in Genoa, Italy. I was seeing places I'd never seen, places I'd never heard of. In Tenerife, I saw policemen walking the streets with guns. I said to myself, "These people are not as free as our people back home." I'd never seen a policeman with a gun. At first, I was terrified. I was afraid if I said anything bad I'd be shot.

In Tenerife and Barcelona, I saw white people begging. I never knew of such things. Then I saw white people working as refuse collectors, and I thought to myself that I'd never do that job and here are whites doing it. Then I saw white taxi drivers. I said to myself, "Is it going to be like this in England?" My whole attitude began to change. I was going to England thinking of only picking the jobs that I wanted, but seeing white people doing those bad jobs made me think that I might have to do bad jobs too.

From Italy, we took the train across the continent to France and the English Channel, where we got the ferry over to the English side and then the train to Waterloo Station in London. There my sister met me.

West Indian immigrants arriving at the docks in Southhampton, England, in 1956. [Courtesy of the Hulton Picture Library]

West Indian immigrants waiting at Victoria Station in London after having disembarked from a ship at Southhampton, gone through customs, and traveled by train to London (1956). [Photo by Haywood Magee, the Hulton Deutsch Collection]

More than half the arriving West Indians settled in London; the others gravitated to cities in the Midlands and the north of England. Where an immigrant settled was determined largely by where his relatives and friends had settled before him. They provided temporary accommodation, helped the new arrival find a job, and assisted in acclimating him to English life—how to ride the bus, where to shop, and so forth. As each new immigrant, in turn, assisted others, colonies of transplanted West Indians developed in particular neighborhoods of most major cities. Anthropologist Douglas Midgett (1975) found half of the 290 migrant households from the village he had studied on the island of St. Lucia in the same London neighborhood of Paddington. Roy remembers:

> The first week, I stayed with my sister, her husband and their boy. Then she got me another room in the same house. I shared it with a Barbadian who worked for London Transport, on the buses. He did his own cooking and sometimes he'd cook for me, but mostly I'd only sleep there, because I'd go up to my sister's to eat and watch television. When the landlord sold the house, we all had to move. My sister and her husband got a flat with three rooms, and she rented one of the rooms to me.
>
> It was hard to find a place to stay in England. Rooms were available, but you'd see signs—"No Blacks," "No Coloured," "No Irish." Or you

might see "English Only." And when you did get a room, the landlord would put restrictions on you, like telling you all visitors must be out of your place by ten o'clock.

England was rough in the beginning; it wasn't what I expected. The first morning my sister and I walked down to the bus stop, and she didn't say "good morning" or "hello" to the people there, and I am thinking, "This is strange." Anywhere in Barbados, you say "good morning" and "hello" to people. The next morning, I go to fetch the milk off the stoop, and, when I get there, the lady next door was there to pick up her milk as well. I said, "Good morning." She just looked surprised and didn't answer. When I got upstairs, I told my sister; then she told me that was the custom in England. Nobody says "good morning" or "hello," at least not to black people.

When I first saw all the houses joined together with all their chimneys up in the air and smoke coming out the top, I wondered where the people lived. I thought the houses were factories. I had never heard of people making fires in their houses, and they all looked the same, every building, every street, all the same way. I said to a man, "How do you know which is your house?" He said, "By the numbers." That alone put me off.

When I got to England my thinking was that I'd be away no more than five years. I wanted to save enough money to get a little home in Barbados. At that time, the pound was worth $4.80, and I thought that if I could save $10,000, I would be able to buy enough building materials to build a home. Building material was pretty cheap then; you'd get a [cement] block for thirty-six cents, a board for about forty cents, and labor was cheap. I wasn't thinking about getting married, settling down, or anything like that. I only wanted to make some quick money, see the country, and come back home.

The first winter, I really wanted to go back home. It was so cold, the worst winter they'd had in many years. But my father told me before I left Barbados that it was the last money he was going to spend on me and that I was on my own from now on. So I wouldn't write him and ask for my fare. After that winter, I wanted to get back to Barbados as fast as I could, but it took a long time to save any money. And by the time I saved enough for my passage, I was starting to get settled down.

My first job in England was working at a bakery as a porter. It was a Jewish bakery in East London. The pay was 8 pounds, 10 shillings per week. I had to load the van with the cakes, then I'd clean the bread trays, pack the fridge with the cakes for the next day, and sometimes I'd sweep up. In Barbados, I wouldn't have done that kind of work, but, as I said, seeing white people doing those jobs, I knew I'd have to do them too. They didn't pay me enough for the work I was doing, but the bakery was walking distance from home, plus they let me have rolls and buns for lunch. I'd bring a piece of ham to work, and I'd eat their rolls. Plus they gave me free milk to put in my tea. So I saved an extra ten shillings a week that I would've spent on lunch somewhere else. I guess that's why I didn't leave the bakery.

In the bakery, there were a half dozen Barbadians, a couple of Jamaicans, and a half dozen Montserratians. The foreman, assistant foreman, oven man and storekeeper were all Jewish. Only the cake maker was English. You had more West Indians there than anybody else. That was because we were cheap labor and did all the hard work. All the West Indians became very friendly. We used to go to each other's house to have a drink and party. There was a lot of mickey taking [poking fun] at each other, especially about the country you came from. Jamaicans would call us "Small Island" because Jamaica was so much bigger than our islands. Then we'd say that the cricket players from Montserrat can't bowl very fast because, if they take a long run, they'll land in the sea. Or we'd say,

A West Indian immigrant on the streets of Birmingham, England in the late 1950s. [Photo by Thurston Hopkins, the Hulton Deutsch Collection]

they can't even grow pumpkins in Montserrat because the vines have to run and land is so scarce they haven't got anywhere to go. We'd make fun of each other's speech, too. We used to laugh at the way Jamaicans talk, because they talk back to front. Bajans would say the "top of my head" is hurting me, where Jamaicans would say "my head top" is hurting me. I would say, "Bring me the bottle," but Jamaicans would say, "Go carry come the bottle." We laughed at them, but they'd just say all small islanders are "fou fou" [foolish].

About this time, I met the woman, Wendy, that became my wife. I met her when I went to visit a friend of mine, and she was there. I got talking to her and her girlfriend, and I spent the whole day there. I told Wendy about my work, and she told me about her work at the Lyons Restaurant at the corner of Oxford Street and Tottenham Court Road. She had come to England on a contract with Lyons Hotel and Restaurant when they were recruiting girls in Barbados.

The following day, my friend's girlfriend called me at work to tell me that Wendy wanted to see me again and that she was off from work that day. So I told my boss I had to go home. I caught the bus and went straight there. She made me a cup of tea and something to eat. After that, I'd meet her every night after work and take her home. After two or three months courting I said, "It is not profitable for you paying rent and me paying rent—why not live together?" So we moved in together, and she got pregnant. She lost the first baby, but got pregnant again and, in November 1966, had the baby.

When she was pregnant, she said, "You know, this is not Barbados. Here, if you have children and you are not married, they look down on you." I said I would try to get a different job to make more money so that we could get married. There were a lot of colored immigrants working for London Transport, so I decided to give them a try. At the driving test [for bus driver] there were a half dozen of us, five white guys and me. We got in this old Routemaster double-decker bus. We all sat upstairs except for the guy who was being tested on driving. Each guy drove for fifteen minutes. Well, I drove pretty well, and the guy said, "You drive damn good." When all of us completed the driving, he took us back to the depot. The inspector said, "You all let me down; this black boy here drove better than any of you." So then I figured that everything was going to be okay, that I was going to get the job. But he called me to one side. "What I advise you to do," he says, "is take a conductor's job, and maybe later you'll get to drive the bus." Back in the room I talked to the five white guys, and they told me that they all got through, that they were all going to be bus drivers. When I told them about me, they said, "Blimey, you drive better than us." That really put me off. I didn't bother with the conductor's job then, I just started for home.

On the train on the way back home, I got the *Midday Standard*, and I saw a position for a postman. So I sent in the form. Two days later, I got a reply asking me to come in for a test. Two dozen of us took the test, and after we finished, we all went out in the room and waited. They called out eight of us. I heard them tell the others that they would have to try another time—that they hadn't made it. I really felt good then. I'd made it!

They sent me to postman's school to learn the towns and cities in England, Scotland, Ireland, and Wales. And I had to learn the London districts, learn the whole of London.

At the school we'd test each other:

"Where is Southeast 3?"

"Greenwich."

"Where is Tottenham?"

"North 15."

We had three days to learn London and nine days to learn all the towns and cities. They gave us a pack of cards to take home at night so that we could study. I gave my girlfriend the cards, and she would test me, even when we were eating:

"Where is Wellingborough?"

"Northhampton."

"Yeah, you know that one. Okay, where is Limerick?"

"Ireland."

And so on.

I learned them all with two days to spare. There were three of us colored fellows in a class of eighteen, and we all passed the exam early. Some of the white guys said they couldn't understand how these black people come here and learn these places faster than they who were born here. I'd think to myself, "Hey, I am doing great in this white man's country." We wanted to do well, so we really put our minds to it.

I started in the north London post office. There were about eight West Indians and a dozen Africans. At first, they gave us, the black fellows, the dirty jobs, like sorting parcels. Whatever they told us to do, we'd always try to do it to our best so that the governor [supervisor] couldn't come in and say that you, a black person, wasn't doing a good job. My boss used to call me Sam. I asked why he called me Sam and not my real name, Roy. He said that in his school days, they used to call all little black boys Sam, "You know, Sambo. So if I call you Sam," he says, "don't be annoyed." Another English guy at the post office told me that when he was in school, he thought black boys had tails. He and his friend had followed a black man into a public lavatory to see if it was true. When the black man went into the toilet stall, they got up on the next toilet and looked over the top at him. The black guy pretended he didn't see them peeping on him, but then, when he was done, he rushed for them and banged their two heads together.

But West Indians got on better with the whites than with the Africans. The white workers usually wouldn't show their prejudice. The Africans thought we were inferior to them. They would say that all West Indians are descended from slaves, and the slave masters were white people who had sex with our great grandmothers and their mothers, and that is why we were much fairer in color than the Africans.

Roy's primary leisure activity in England was playing cricket. After several years playing with other West Indians in the London Post Office League, Roy was invited to play for a white English club.

> My friend Winston introduced me to the fellows from Trinity. They were all white except Winston, his brother, and me. The first match, I did very badly. I made naught [didn't score any runs]. I felt bad for Winston because he had told them what a good bat I was. But the second match, I did a little better, and the third match I was still better. Eventually I was opening the batting [batting first in the order].[5] Playing on an English team was different from playing in the West Indies. If you did well, say you scored a century [100 runs in one match], you'd have to buy drinks. In the West Indies, they'd buy you the drinks. Playing with the English fellows, you always wanted to do well, but you also knew that if you did well it was going to cost you money.
>
> After Wendy had the baby, I said to her that we had to be careful, because we want to go back to Barbados, and if we have more children we won't ever be able to afford to go back. I said, "Let's quit having kids for awhile." But we had a second kid in 1969. I said, "That's it, no more kids." I was eight years in England then, and it was time to start preparing to go home.
>
> After we got married, Wendy's mom wrote from Barbados to tell us that there was some land being sold, that it would be a good spot. We withdrew what money we had and sent it home to buy the spot. The price was $3,300.
>
> When I went back to Barbados on a visit for the first time in 1968, you could see great improvement: there were many more cars, the roads were much better, and the people were doing better. In the stores, you'd see many of the same things that you'd see in England. In 1973, Wendy and I came back together and had a plan drawn up for a house, and then we went back to England to save more money.

When Roy and Wendy returned to England in 1973, they left their two children behind in Barbados with Wendy's parents. They did so in order to save money and hasten their permanent return to Barbados. Although their children were in good hands, the separation was traumatic for the parents. Roy had difficulty even talking about it years afterward. A few years later, they returned to Barbados again, but they still did not have enough money to build a house. Nevertheless, they contracted with a relative to begin construction.

> We went to my wife's uncle and asked him to start the house. We told him to build until our money was gone. When we left Barbados that time, I said to Wendy that the next time we came back it must be for good. There were the kids to think about, and I really wanted to be back in Barbados to enjoy my own country. Barbados looked so good to me, all the sunshine and the friendliness of the people. In England, you only get three or four months of what they call sunshine, in what they call summer. You always seem to be loaded down with lots of clothes—shoes, socks, T-shirt, shirt, vest, cardigan, coat, and what not. The weight on you made you feel old. In Barbados, you can just put on a pair of shorts and walk outside barefoot.

In 1979, six years after leaving their children, Roy and Wendy returned to Barbados for good, having finally saved enough to finish the construction of their house. Roy, who had injured his back while working at the post office, was given a medical disability and a pension, which would help support them in Barbados.

> We arrived home on the 30th of November, 1979, which was Independence Day. We stayed at my mother-in-law's until our things arrived by boat, and then, just before Christmas, we moved into our own house. Coming home made me a bit nervous. I wondered if I could get a job. My first job was as a security guard but the pay was small. I didn't have much choice, I had to make some money because the kids were in school, Wendy didn't have a job, and the house wasn't finished.
>
> Then I met a friend from England who had come back to Barbados, and after a lot of trying, he got me a job at the Transport Board. They made me an inspector. Being able to travel all around the island, riding on all the different bus routes, I was able to meet a lot of people. People on the buses or at the bus stops saying, "Good morning, Mr. Campbell," or "Hello, Roy," people knowing your name and wanting to speak to you and you just being back from England—well, that made me feel pretty good. It made me feel glad to be home.
>
> Coming back to Barbados wasn't very hard on me, mostly because I'd come home a few times to visit. I knew what to expect.

Roy Campbell in front of his Bridgetown, Barbados home, after his return from England. [Photo by George Gmelch]

Some things, however, do bother me. One thing is that people here are not good at timekeeping. If someone agrees to meet you at eight o'clock they don't turn up until eight-thirty or nine, and they don't say they are sorry for being late. If the English say they will get here at eight o'clock, they will be here at eight o'clock. And people here aren't as mannerly. The English always say "please" and "thank you," but you don't hear that said much here.

I wasn't able to adjust myself to the West Indian type of cricket either. I was thirty-five when I came home and the boys here were young and really fast [bowlers], and the pitches were hard. I decided that I had played enough, so I packed it in. I still watch a lot of cricket; when a touring team comes to Barbados, I go out to Kensington Oval to see the match. I meet a lot of the blokes who played for the post office teams in England there, and we talk about what we used to do in England and how we used to play over there, and remember the old times.

RETURNING HOME

About a fourth of the Barbadians who emigrated to Britain during the 1950s and 1960s have since returned home. Many more have visited Barbados and considered returning home, but for various reasons, have never managed it. Those who have fared poorly overseas are disinclined to return because they will lose face, since all emigrants are expected to come home with at least enough money to buy a home of their own. Many remained abroad far longer than they had intended, yet all the while they clung to the hope that someday, if only at retirement, they would be able to return. Hanging onto an "ideology of return" is important, for it gives the migrants a psychological safety valve, an idea and a place to fall back on when life abroad becomes too difficult. The very successful also seldom returned, because it would mean giving up well-salaried positions and a standard of living that could not be equaled in Barbados. It can also mean costly obligations to share their wealth with less well-off kinfolk at home.

Not all returning migrants adjust as easily as Roy and Wendy. Of the 135 returnees that I surveyed in an earlier study, 53 percent were so dissatisfied during their first year at home that they wished they had remained abroad. Friendships did not always materialize as hoped. Sometimes the old friends that the migrants looked forward to seeing and with whom they hoped to recapture the lost memories of their youth were themselves gone. Disappointed to find that most of their former friends had emigrated, many did not know the younger crowd at the rum shop or any of the children. Neighbors, who had appeared affable or chummy during return holiday visits when presents were distributed, now seemed distant or disinterested once the migrants returned for good. One woman made an observation about the people in her village:

The people say that I don't want friends, they say I don't want to share. Them that do the talking are the same ones that I brought goods for. I give them rice; I give them coffee; I give them dinner plates. I give all around and I try to keep friendship with them. They took my things, but then they cut me up.

In their interactions with fellow villagers, the returnees often conclude that Barbadians who have never lived abroad are provincial and narrow-minded. One woman whispered to me, as though she were afraid of being overheard:

> I have no good friends who have never been away. There are very few here I would want to call friends . . . their outlook on life is so small, so tiny, it's like they have blinkers on, like they're always going down a one-way street.

Some returnees feel they no longer share the same interests as their neighbors. They say their own interests are now more cosmopolitan and transcend the local community and the island. A man who had spent 23 years in London complained that the village women he met were boring and that he could not make conversation with them. "They sit there like great lumps of pudding with nothing at all to say." Moreover, many sense that the villagers who stayed behind are jealous of their prosperity—their large houses, their new cars, and their children's higher education. Some villagers diminish the migrants' accomplishments and elevated status by saying that money is easy to earn abroad and that anyone who goes away can come back rich. One prosperous family I know well, rather than being credited with having worked hard, was falsely rumored to have won a lottery.

A common irritation to all migrants returning from the industrialized world is the slow pace of life at home. It is difficult to get things done.[6] Returnees are easily frustrated at the delays in getting servicemen to make repairs, in getting a telephone installed, in clearing an overseas parcel at the local post office, and in having to wait in line while salesclerks chat with other customers. Having grown accustomed to the punctuality of Britons, they are impatient and frustrated by its absence at home. As Roy said, people agree to meet you at eight o'clock and then don't turn up till much later.

On the other hand, returnees are sometimes insensitive. They may strain relationships with friends and neighbors by their frequent comparisons of Barbados to England. Some talk too much about England and their experiences there when they should be trying to find common ground with people at home.

For women, returning home can present special problems. Most, like Wendy, held wage-paying jobs while abroad; now at home they have difficulty finding work.[7] And in the villages especially, some returnee women find there is not enough to do; some especially miss shopping. While living abroad they enjoyed browsing and looking for bargains in the large, city department stores. At home, these women have lost a favorite pastime.

For women who come back to Barbados without their grown children, the most serious source of unhappiness is often the separation. Ann Bovell speaks for many women when she confided at the end of one interview, "To tell the truth, I feel real bad me being here and the kids being over there (England)." Another woman's response to being apart from her children has been to work even harder, often rising before dawn to sew uniforms for the hotels, in order to earn enough money to travel each year to visit her four off-spring in Canada, England, and Belgium. The parents hope that the children they raised overseas will someday move to Barbados, but few ever do.

Underlying the difficulties many returnees experience in adjusting is that both they and the society to which they have returned have changed. Migrants often do not realize how much their attitudes have been altered by their experiences abroad until they come home. While in England they only see themselves in opposition to white English society, and they tend to think of themselves and the other Barbadian immigrants they live among as being no different from people back home. Only when they return to Barbados and try to resume relationships with old friends and relatives do they first see the differences. Even island locals concede that migrants become more "broad-minded" and more aware of a larger world during their time away. Migrants return home less convinced that the Barbadian or West Indian way of life is necessarily the only right way. They have seen alternatives that sometimes make more sense.

Meanwhile, Barbados is not the same place the migrants left a decade or two before. Although most welcome the new prosperity, an enormous increase in car ownership has snarled traffic, crime and drug use are up, hotel development for tourists has so inflated land prices on the coast that it is not possible to buy a house near the sea, and young Barbadians are less courteous than they were a generation ago. These changes do not fit the image of Barbados that most migrants have retained from their youth, images that brief vacations at home had not corrected. In short, many migrants are dissatisfied because of the lack of fit between what they expected to find at home and what they now experience.

With the passage of time, however, most dreams and fantasies fade, and the returnees learn to cope with the inefficiency and petty annoyances. Gradually, their expectations about what can be accomplished in a day's work are lowered, and the slow pace of island life is eventually seen as a virtue rather than being a source of frustration. Many also cope by occasionally leaving the island on a charter package to Miami or London. Whatever the reason, a trip abroad can satisfy their appetites for the things they miss in Barbados, whether it be city entertainment, particular cuisines, or shopping. Being abroad again also reminds them of the drawbacks of life in a metropolitan society—the impersonality, not feeling safe on the streets at night, racial prejudice, and the "rat race"—and that enables them to accept island life more easily. The figure of 53 percent who were dissatisfied during their first year at home, cited earlier, drops to 17 percent by their third year at home, and continues to decline over time. In short, returnees do adjust.

EPILOGUE

When I first studied Barbadian migrants in the 1980s, most scholars thought of human migration as a one-dimensional movement with a point of departure and a point of arrival. Most studies focused on the experiences and adjustments of migrants in their new host society; only a few scholars were then interested in the sizable minority of migrants who later returned home. In the 1990s scholars began to use the concept of "transnationalism" to describe the fluid, to and fro movement, and the many-stranded ties that migrants maintained between the island homeland and the overseas metropole. Inexpensive and easy travel and new telecommunications technologies (e.g., Internet, e-mail, and cheap overseas telephone connections) enabled these new transnational migrants to stay in close contact with family and friends and keep abreast of politics, sports, music, and current events at home.

Most of the men and women of the 1950s–1960s mass migration to Britain are now seniors in their 70s and 80s and are no longer very mobile. The Barbadians returning "home" today (2009) are more often second-generation migrants. The offspring of the 1950s–1960s migrants, raised in the UK, have developed racially hybrid identities as "Bajan-Brits." Geographers Robert Potter and Joan Phillips (2006) have extensively studied these returning Bajan Brits and the impacts they have in Barbados. Their reasons for migrating to Barbados are diverse. Some are unsure of their life goals and are coming to Barbados to test the waters, to see if they like living in their parents' homeland. Some come hoping to make a difference, to contribute their skills to a developing society. Some have business interests and are hoping to capitalize on their transnational networks and business connections. Some are looking for a racially less divisive society. Whatever their motives, all have chosen to try to make new lives in an island society rather than the metropolitan centers of their youth (Potter and Conway 2008:226). Typical of other transnationals, they maintain ties with the metropole, often retaining property there, keeping in close touch with extended family members and friends there, and generally adhering to "transnational strategies" that enable them to live in, and between, two worlds.

Their socioeconomic contributions to Barbados may be greater than the returnees of Roy Campbell's generation, suggest Potter and Conway (2008). Although fewer in number, they come back at a younger age—and at an earlier stage in their work careers—and possess more advanced technological skills and better professional training. They have computer skills. In Barbados, their hybridized Britishness distinguishes them as experienced, worldlier, and more readily employable than was the case with Roy Campbell's cohort. And by having a foot in both worlds—as true transnationals—they forge important links between the Caribbean and Europe and North America.

Notes

[1] See, for example, Richardson, *Caribbean Migrants* (1983).

[2] For an ethnographic account (aimed at students) of Barbados and the village setting of this study, see G. Gmelch and S. Gmelch, *The Parish Behind God's Back: The Changing Culture of Rural Barbados* (2001[1997]).

[3] During the 1950s, the doors to Britain were wide open to all immigrants from the Commonwealth, though the British government did try to ensure that passports were not given to people with serious criminal records, old people, or unaccompanied children. Although just about

any Commonwealth citizen could enter, the emigrants were, generally speaking, better educated and more skilled than those who stayed behind (Richardson 1983). This changed in 1982 with the passage of the Commonwealth Immigrants Act, which restricted immigration. The act was the outcome of a campaign that began in the mid-1950s, spearheaded by extreme right-wing political groups and some conservative members of Parliament and widely publicized by the press, to control immigration—in particular, the immigration of colored people. Support for the act came largely from those who believed, first, that immigrants were flooding the labor market and thus taking jobs away from native Britons, and, second, that too many colored immigrants were creating a race problem in Britain.

[4] In the early years of emigration to England, the migrants traveled by ship. Over half the ships were Italian, and, in a curious reversal of migration streams, some of the ships carried Mediterranean emigrants to Venezuela on the outward voyage, and then picked up West Indians bound for Britain on the return crossing. The fare was expensive, and many emigrants sold their possessions and borrowed from relatives to raise the money.

[5] Roy was a star batsman for the Trinity team; in 1972, he averaged more than 80 runs per game, and, by the time he left England, he had become the third highest run producer in the history of the Trinity team.

[6] For examples from other cultures, see Gmelch (1980), "Return Migration," pp. 143–144.

[7] The official unemployment rate in Barbados, which seldom drops below 25 percent, is two to three times the level of unemployment in the host societies.

References

Foner, Nancy. 1978. *Jamaica Farewell: Jamaican Migrants in London*. Berkeley: University of California Press.

Gmelch, George. 1980. Return Migration. *Annual Review of Anthropology*, 9:135–159.

———. 1987. Work, Innovation, and Investment: The Impact of Return Migrants in Barbados. *Human Organization*, 46(2):131–140.

———. 1992. *Double Passage: The Lives of Caribbean Migrants Abroad and Back Home*. Ann Arbor: The University of Michigan Press.

Gmelch, George, and Sharon Gmelch. 2001[1997]. *The Parish Behind God's Back: The Changing Culture of Rural Barbados*. Long Grove, IL: Waveland Press.

Marshall, Dawn 1982. The History of Caribbean Migrations: The Case of the West Indies. *Caribbean Review*, 11(1):6–9, 52.

Midgett, Douglas K. 1975. West Indian Ethnicity in Great Britain. In *Migration and Development: Implications for Ethnic Identity and Political Conflict*, eds. Helen I. Safa and Brian DuToit, pp. 57–81. The Hague and Paris: Mouton Publishers.

Potter, Robert, and Dennis Conway. 2008. The Development Potential of Caribbean Young Return Migrants. In *Global Migration and Development*, eds. T. van Naerssen, E. Spaan, and A. Zoomers, pp. 213–230. New York: Routledge.

Potter, Robert, and Joan Phillips. 2006. Both Black and Symbolically White: The Bajan Brit Return Migrant As Postcolonial Hybrid. *Ethnic and Racial Studies*, 29(5):901–927.

Richardson, Bonham C. 1983. *Caribbean Migrants: Environment and Human Survival in St. Kitts and Nevis*. Knoxville: University of Tennessee Press.

Sutton, Constance, and Susan Makiesky-Barrow. 1975. Migration and West Indian Racial and Political Consciousness. In *Migration and Development: Implications for Ethnic Identity and Political Conflict*, eds. H. I. Safa and B. DuToit, pp. 113–144. The Hague: Mouton.

22

First Nations Migration
The Case of Western Canada

Martin Cooke and Danièle Bélanger

In Canada, over half of all Aboriginal people now live in urban centers. Their migration from reserves and native communities to the city has usually been understood as economically motivated, with return migration to Aboriginal communities resulting primarily from failure to adapt to urban life. In this chapter Martin Cooke and Danièle Bélanger adopt a more holistic "systems" perspective on migration to take into account elements of the political, economic, and social context, as well as individual and institutional links between the reserve and the city.

The urbanization of Canadian Aboriginal people was a subject of rising interest in the 1960s and 1970s, when the increasing number of Aboriginal people living in urban centers and their living conditions in the city came to the attention of academics and the popular press. Some common themes prevailed. Migration to the city was primarily considered to be due to a lack of employment opportunities, poor housing conditions, and social problems related to the severe poverty in many Aboriginal communities. However, once in the city, many lived in conditions that were as bad, or even worse, than those they had left on the reserve. Ethnographies such as *Indians on Skid Row* (Brody 1971) described the lives of Aboriginal people in Canada's cities as impoverished and marginal, characterized by unemployment, poverty, crime, and alcoholism. Aboriginal culture was typically characterized as fundamentally incompatible with urban life in this literature, contributing to a stereotypical view of urban Aboriginal people as "caught between two worlds" (Peters 1996:317–318). If some people returned to their home communities after a time in the city, it was ostensibly because of their inability to adapt to the urban environment.

Source: Adapted from Migration Theories and First Nations Mobility: Towards a Systems Perspective. *Canadian Review of Sociology & Anthropology / Revue Canadienne de Sociologie et Anthropologie* (2006) 43(2):141–164.

According to Peters (1996), studies of the social conditions of urban Aboriginal people have since been subsumed under a more general Canadian literature on urban poverty, in which a lack of human capital and education are seen as the common causes of poverty for both Aboriginal and non-Aboriginal people. Although the previous literature may have overstated the importance of culture in describing the problems facing urban Aboriginal people, culture has since been ignored. Instead, the more recent literature assumes that Aboriginal people are simply one of many socially and economically marginalized groups, including single mothers, recent immigrants, and the disabled, among others.

However, the social and political situation of Canadian Aboriginal peoples is uniquely connected to Canada's colonial history. Relationships with traditional territories and communities are important parts of cultural identity for many Aboriginal people, and historical colonialism has created institutions and legal conditions for Aboriginal people that are unlike those experienced by other Canadians. The patterns of migration are also not as straightforward as is often thought. Although migration to cities remains important, evidence from the Census shows that this is roughly balanced by migration from the city to Aboriginal communities (Norris et al. 2001). Nor are conditions in the city accurately characterized as generally impoverished: despite lower average income and education, a large and growing urban Aboriginal middle class exists in many Canadian cities, as do strong Aboriginal cultural, social, and economic institutions (Newhouse and Peters 2003).

These realities need to be incorporated into our understanding of migration patterns and the motivations of those who move. The following sections present some exploratory data from interviews with people who have moved between First Nations communities[1] and the city of Winnipeg. These data provide direct evidence of the various factors affecting individuals' decisions to move. In this chapter we describe some of the insights garnered from these data, including the importance of personal and kinship links between people living in urban and reserve communities, and the roles of institutions such as Aboriginal organizations in facilitating migration between the two areas. We argue that these links can be incorporated within a systems framework that considers migration between two points to be sustained and reproduced by various types of individual, political, and institutional connections. Developed in the context of international migration and circulation, a systems framework provides a better understanding of the phenomenon of First Nations migration than other approaches do, since it takes into account the historical, economic, and cultural context, as well as individual motivations and personal networks.

MIGRATION BETWEEN FIRST NATIONS AND PRAIRIE CITIES

In-depth interviews were conducted with seventeen Registered Indians[2] who had moved to the city of Winnipeg. Respondents were selected through referrals from members of the Aboriginal community in Winnipeg, including various tribal councils. In order to explore the factors to be considered in migration, respondents were treated as knowledgeable informants who would be able to provide information about the processes of migration in general, as well as their own experiences of migration.

Study participants were selected on the basis of their demographic and socioeconomic characteristics. Given the exploratory nature of these data, it was important that the sample include people of different ages and with a variety of experiences. The sample of seven men and 10 women included people of different educational and employment backgrounds. The sample was limited to Registered Indians because of the differences between the mobility of Registered Indians and other Aboriginal people (Norris et al. 2001). Three informants were living in First Nations reserve communities at the time of the interview. Of those who lived in the city, some had moved within the last five years, while others had lived in the city for 20 years or longer. Some people had moved from communities that are within an hour's drive from Winnipeg, while a few had moved from as far away as 600 km. The sample included people who identified themselves as Anishinaabeg, including Ojibwa and Saulteaux, as well as Cree and Dakota.

The Context of Migration

The political context in which this migration stream operates is shaped by the Indian Act of Canada and the historical relationship between Aboriginal peoples and the Canadian government. Registered Indians and Indian Bands have a unique relationship with the Canadian federal government (the Crown). Indian Bands, through historical treaties, are usually communities connected to "reserves," which are Crown lands set aside for their use. Historically, members of recognized Bands have been "Registered Indians," meaning that they are listed in the *Indian Register* maintained by the Department of Indian Affairs and Northern Development.[3] Registered Indians and reserve communities have a unique tax status, and generally receive social and health services directly from the Canadian government, whereas these are provided to other Aboriginal people and non-Aboriginal Canadians by provincial or territorial governments.

Winnipeg, the provincial capital, is the only major city in Manitoba, although there are several smaller cities in both the north and the south of the province. There is little interprovincial migration among Aboriginal people, at least partly because of the long distances between urban centers in western Canada (Clatworthy 1996). There is a substantial Aboriginal population in the city of Winnipeg, but also a large proportion of Registered Indians living in reserve communities elsewhere in the province. According to the 1996 Census, there were approximately 81,700 Registered Indians living in Manitoba, 57% of whom lived in reserve communities, and 25% of whom lived in the city of Winnipeg. Approximately 24,000 non-Status[4] Aboriginal people also lived in Winnipeg, and 6.8% of the total urban population of 660,000 identified themselves as Aboriginal (Statistics Canada 1998a, 1998b, 1998c).

There are 61 reserve communities in Manitoba, ranging in population from under 200 to more than 2,000 people. Some are close enough to Winnipeg or to a smaller city to allow commuting, while others are remote, with access only by air, water, or ice roads, and are up to 1,100 km from the capital city.

Moving in Search of Opportunities

In general, research participants perceived migration to the city as a move in search of better opportunities, particularly for education and employment not available in reserve communities. In addition, the lack of health services on reserves, including dialysis for diabetes patients or care for other chronic conditions, was an important reason for migration to the city. This was especially the case in more remote communities, where prices were much higher while services and economic opportunities were the scarcest. Some participants indicated that employment in certain communities is often limited to working in local administrative positions or in construction jobs, and it was common for people to feel as though young people had no choice but to leave in search of education and employment. The lack of housing in reserve communities was also mentioned by several interviewees as a key reason for moving to the city, and one that prevented people from moving back to their home communities.

> Yeah. For . . . my community, housing was an issue and it continues to be. Despite the number of houses that have been built in my community, there's still a huge waiting list of two hundred, maybe two hundred people waiting in line for housing there. So, people, they end up getting crowded out of the house they're living in because kids start having kids and stuff like that. . . . Families—they need to move out, so they just come to the city. Jobwise, too, some people find jobs here that they can find work at. Education, maybe. Some people, the welfare system makes it accessible, too. That's another thing. (Steve, counselor, late 40s)

At the same time, people also felt that poor living conditions in the city were a problem, causing many to return home. Informants especially became frustrated by the lack of affordable housing in the city, especially for those without relatives on whom they could rely.

> Well, I think they have to, if they're not helped within their family, if they're new into a city . . . they'll look for a house or an apartment. They'll be . . . taken advantage of. But the landlord gets quite good money for their rundown facilities. Another obstacle would be racism. There is racism out there. (Samuel, administrator, 50–54)

Nearly all of the participants stressed the stark differences between Aboriginal communities and the city. These differences provided an impetus for migration to the city as well as return migration to the reserve. Our interviews indicated that return to reserves was common; approximately half of our sample either had made multiple moves themselves or intended to return. One woman even said, with some hyperbole, "we *all* eventually return." The timing of return or expected return varied, with some moving back after just a few years in the city, and others indicating that return on retirement was desirable and that they themselves intended to do so. Two of these people were building their own homes in First Nation communities. About half, on the other hand, indicated that they would not move back to their original communities and were at home in the city.

One notable difference between life on the reserve and life in the city, according to many participants, was the much faster pace of life in the latter. The desirability of the urban lifestyle was seen differently by different people. Two younger First Nations men, for example, said there was a general desire among young people to experience a more exciting urban lifestyle, one that they were exposed to via television and other media. For others, the slower pace of life in Aboriginal communities was a distinct advantage.

Life in the city was thought to present considerable difficulties for many newcomers. About one-third of the interviewees reported that racism and discrimination in the city often prevented people from getting jobs and securing housing. This was an important factor in many people's decision to return to their home communities. Although discrimination generally encouraged return migration to reserve communities, other factors influenced decisions in both directions, prompting moves back and forth between the reserves and the city. Crime and substance abuse were reasons cited by some for leaving their home communities, but others thought that these problems were greater in the city. Residential segregation of Aboriginal people in particular areas of the city, due in part to a lack of affordable housing, was a concern for some, but so was a lack of housing in reserve communities.

Some First Nations people clearly return to their communities because they provide a better environment in which to raise a family. They believe it is easier to pass on Aboriginal values, culture, and language to children in an Aboriginal community, and the community is an environment in which children can be watched over by many family members and friends. Being able to pursue traditional activities such as hunting and fishing, as well as simply being close to traditional lands, was important to some and was seen as a significant advantage to living in an Aboriginal community. However, at least one-third of our respondents saw themselves as urban people for whom outdoor activities held little attraction. One woman stressed that she was not a "country bumpkin."

The cultural context in which migration takes place also includes what some saw as a cultural propensity for movement. That is, as many Aboriginal peoples in Manitoba had traditionally been migratory; contemporary mobility was merely a continuation of these patterns. Two older respondents, for example, told us that seasonal moves with their families to trap and to pursue other subsistence activities were important early experiences for them. Although it was not clear that this traditional mobility had affected their more recent moves to the city, repeated moves were interpreted by some as in keeping with traditional First Nations culture.

Our interviews generally confirmed the predominance of women in migration flows to the city, and the greater number of men moving back to reserves, as found by other authors (Norris et al. 2001). This may be at least partially due to the availability of unskilled, semi-skilled, and resource-based jobs typically associated with male employment in or near reserve communities. Others have suggested that some women may leave reserves to escape abusive situations. One woman did report moving for this reason and described the resulting necessity of breaking ties with her family and her community.

Not surprisingly, the distance between reserves and cities has an effect on both the likelihood and type of migration. Our interviewees said that if people were able to live in their home communities and commute to work in the city, many would do so as a way to obtain the benefits of both areas. Two of our participants commuted between nearby reserves and the city, and one man lived in the city and commuted over an hour to work in his home community. At least one individual drove several hours from a reserve community to work in the city each day. The additional travel costs associated with migrating long distances, particularly to and from remote communities, were thought to impede migration in either direction. In the words of one young man:

> The communities that aren't accessible by road, they tend to lose their children. They generally don't come back because it's so hard or it's so expensive, so they'll move to a closer reserve. Where I'm from, it's not a problem. It's only a six-hour drive either way. If I want to go home, and come back to the city, no sweat. But when you're closer to the city, an hour away, you're not losing anybody. The mobility's so there. I know young people from the eastern side of Manitoba. There's no roads. It's like eight hundred dollars to fly. They don't go home that often. (Gordon, student, late 20s)

Networks and Links

The presence of family and friends was mentioned by almost all respondents as a very important aspect of life in their home communities, and its absence in the city was seen as a major drawback.

> **Martin:** What do you think are the largest problems that people who move to the city are faced with once they get there?
>
> **Dawn** (artist, late 20s): [long pause] No sense of community—you have to start fresh. . . . That's why a lot of people move back. Because it's . . . a lot of people can't handle living in the city. There's a lot of people back home who have never lived in the city. Or some people who have moved to the city, and tried for a couple of years and then moved back, because they don't like living in the city.
>
> **Martin:** What don't they like?
>
> **Dawn:** Well, there's no . . . I guess a sense of community. Like I was back home this weekend, and there's like a real strong sense of community. It's like a soap opera. If you go back to the reserve, somebody will

give you an update of what's been happening lately. . . . So, when I go home, I get those updates. It's like a real sense of community.

Several people mentioned making visits to relatives in the home community, as well as having people come to visit them in the city. Several, including this man, described the importance of extended family in providing instrumental support, such as help with children, or material support, such as sharing food or accommodations:

> That's the thing about living on the reserve . . . all the support there . . . your extended family, or whatever. . . . Like I have three children, two of them are small. Whenever I have to go anywhere I have to get a babysit-ter or make arrangements, something like that. But when I was out in the country I stayed at my brother's place and he's got a whole bunch of kids. And we just leave . . . you know, we just go and do something and the kids would stay and play with the other kids. As long as somebody would stay, like my brother would say to his oldest son, "you just stay and watch the kids." So, like they depend on each other a lot. I think that that's something that people miss when they move to the city—they miss that extended family, because extended families are very important. (Paul, technician, 35–39)

The decision to move, either to the city or back to a reserve community, is clearly influenced by personal relationships. Many who move to the city know someone who is already there, who will be able to provide information, support, and possibly a place to stay. One woman described moving to a city in another province in order to provide support to her sister who was living there. Another, who had moved to the city and returned, said that she had considered moving to a smaller city because she had relatives there.

As much as kin and family can influence one to choose a destination, so a lack of personal ties can make a move less likely or more difficult. For example, people who needed to move to the city for health reasons were thought to be particularly disadvantaged if they did not have someone in the city to help them get to and from appointments and to navigate the urban environment in general. First Nations students who moved to the city to attend college or university were often faced with a lack of support in the city, and this, combined with the difficulty of adjusting to life in the city, caused some to return home. The absence of continued links to the home community is also important in decisions not to return. Two informants said they would not consider moving back to their communities because they felt they no longer had ties there. Some suggested that it is a lack of community ties that leads many people to make multiple moves between the reserve and the city.

Our interviews also highlighted the importance of Aboriginal organiza-tions in the city for people who had moved to Winnipeg. These organizations included legal and social service agencies as well as the Friendship Centre, which provides information and social support as well as a place to meet and simply be with other Aboriginal people. Some saw the support provided by these urban organizations as a substitute for that normally provided by family and kin in a First Nations community. As one professional woman put it:

> There are no supports . . . no . . . reinforcement of belonging, of being a part of the group. It's an identity. . . . When I have a free evening, and there's bingo at the Friendship Centre, I will go just to be amongst other Indian people. And I don't know anybody, but I'll sit there, and I'll play bingo . . . they're my people. (Emma, health administrator, 40–45)

Aboriginal organizations also form important migration links between Aboriginal communities and the city by employing Aboriginal people in the city. Tribal councils and Aboriginal political organizations have offices in the provincial capital, and respondents confirmed that a certain amount of migration is by people working for these organizations, including frequent return trips to conduct business in reserves and the city.

It was common for people to mention that the lack of housing and employment in their home communities was compounded by what they saw as the political distribution of these resources. Some people had left their communities because they believed that they could not find employment due to nepotism, and others felt that people who were likely to return were those who were able to access Band resources such as housing or employment through relatives in government.

> After that there was a change in government. They elected a new chief and council. The guy I knew who got in as chief didn't like me, so I was out of a job . . . so I had to come back into Winnipeg, and I've lived in Winnipeg, in the North End, ever since. (David, traditional Elder, early 60s)

> It's a big issue. We have communities that have a lot of housing out there, but the thing is they don't look after their housing. And those are the people that get houses every other year, because they're in the family. . . . The people who are not within the ruling party never get a house. (Ron, administrator, early 50s)

THEORETICAL INSIGHTS

As in any migration stream, migration between First Nations and the city of Winnipeg is a complex process, and people undertake moves for a variety of reasons. Our interview data support some of the existing characterizations of migration between reserves and cities. They support the idea that employment is a crucial motivating factor in decisions to migrate. They confirm the influence of geography and remoteness as well as the availability of housing, education, and health services in migration decisions. Perhaps the strongest factor, though, concerned the importance of personal networks and relationships on the decision to migrate and to choose a specific destination. An absence of family and kin in the city was a major problem that led some to return home. For those who did not have continuing relationships with people in their home community, plans to return seemed less likely. The ability to get a job or housing in many communities was reported to depend on these personal networks. For some people in the city, Aboriginal service organizations provide an important source of social support, particularly in the absence of personal networks, as well as a source of employment. These urban Aboriginal institutions can serve as an enduring link between urban and reserve communities.

Since the 1980s, Aboriginal migration in Canada has been considered primarily an economic issue, with people moving in search of work and returning to Aboriginal communities when that work was unavailable. However, our interview research suggests that we must not underestimate the importance of personal and institutional networks in thinking about First Nations migration. In terms of the selectivity of migrants, the presence or absence of networks may ultimately be more important than individual human capital or community characteristics.

SYSTEMS APPROACHES TO MIGRATION

Systems approaches offer a way of bridging macro-level studies of relations between areas, such as the dependency relations between core and hinterland, with the micro-perspectives that consider individual migration decisions. Fawcett provides a typology of the macro-level connections between countries that influence migration. That is, countries may be connected by various state-to-state relationships such as economic dependency and a history of colonialism, as well as by tangible relationships such as trade and financial flows, and regulatory links such as immigration policies (Fawcett 1989). Examples include the continued connections and migration flows between the Netherlands and former colonies in the East Indies, or between the United Kingdom and Barbados. Increasingly, the activities of migrant agencies form important links in these international migration systems, serving as recruiters of migrants and aiding adjustment into the receiving society.

In addition to these long-standing relationships between areas, relationships between individuals are important components in a migration system. Boyd describes the importance of family and personal networks as links between areas in these systems, including kinship and friendship links and individual ties to communities. These links "mediate between individual actors and larger structural forces. They link sending and receiving countries. And they explain the continuation of migration long after the original impetus for migration has ended" (Boyd 1989:661).

Investigating social networks can help our understanding of the selectivity of migration and the existence of return or counterflows. It can also explain migration decisions that are motivated by normative considerations or cultural expectations, such as the expectation to return home to help family members, rather than more instrumental economic considerations, such as the need for employment or education. The inclusion of social networks in a framework to study migration provides a way to move beyond a narrow focus on the motivations of individual actors while still recognizing that migration is the result of individuals making decisions to cope with their lived reality (Gurak and Caces 1992:151).

In the context of migration between First Nations and western Canadian cities, the economic and political context stimulates both temporary and long-term migration to the city. This includes a general lack of employment and educational opportunity in reserve communities, limited housing, and a lack of health care services. Social problems, substance abuse, and crime in both the city and in some reserve communities can lead to migration in either direction. Gender relations, including differences in men's and women's education and employment and women's increased risk of domestic violence, form a crucial part of the social structural context of migration.

At the individual level, migration to the city is greatly facilitated both by the presence of kin and friends and by the presence of Aboriginal service and cultural organizations in the city. Similarly, the continued presence of interpersonal links with home communities, strengthened and maintained through frequent visits and communication with those who remain there, may make return migration more likely for some and also enable access to community resources such as employment or housing. Even for people who have well-established occupational and social ties within the city, the presence of personal links might make retirement in their home communities an attractive option.

The figure on the opposite page shows a tentative schematic of the components of this migration system. Following Kritz and Zlotnik (1992:3), it includes elements of the social, political, economic, demographic, and spatial contexts, as well as some of the important links between the two areas. One of the advantages of a systems approach to migration is that it can identify many of the ways in which migration can be affected by policy, both purposely and inadvertently. Health care policies, the funding of Aboriginal organizations in the city, housing, and labor market policies can all have an impact on the macro factors that provide much of the impetus for migration, as well as affecting the selectivity of migrants. However, it also demonstrates that migration flows can outlive the contextual conditions that initiate them. There is a variety of reasons that people choose to move in either direction, and the presence of continued links between the two areas suggests that, as in international migration systems, internal migration may continue even after aspects of the macro context have changed.

CONCLUSION

In conclusion, whereas previous studies on migration between reserves and urban areas have focused on the characteristics of individuals and communities, the interview data presented here highlight the importance of personal networks as well as institutional links between the two areas in decisions to move between First Nations communities and the city of Winnipeg. These

Political Context

- Indian Act of Canada
- Federal responsibility for services on reserve
- Services and residence on reserves generally only available to Band members

Economic Context

- High unemployment in many communities
- Limited services in many reserve communities, including housing, health care, education
- Poor housing conditions in the city

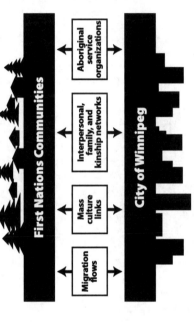

First Nations Communities

Migration flows · Mass culture links · Interpersonal, family, and kinship networks · Aboriginal service organizations

City of Winnipeg

Social/Cultural Context

- Dramatic differences between urban and rural lifestyles
- Social problems such as crime and substance abuse in the city and some communities
- Domestic violence
- Gendered employment opportunities on-reserve and in the city
- Racism and discrimination in employment and housing in the city
- Growing urban Aboriginal middle class

Demographic Context

- 57.6% of Registered Indians in Manitoba live in reserve communities
- 6.8% of Winnipeg population identifies as Aboriginal
- 19,430 Registered Indian Band members live in CMA

Spatial Context

- Winnipeg the major city in the system, along with several smaller cities
- Some communities within commuting distance, some very remote
- Residential segregation within the city

Source: Statistics Canada, 1996 Census Data Cat. Nos. 93F0025XDB96001, 93F0025XDB96001, 93F0025XDB96004, 93F0025XDB96006, 95F0181XDB-4

A Systems Framework for Migration between First Nations Communities and Winnipeg

links, as well as the various contextual dimensions of the migration system, can be incorporated within a systems approach to migration that has been developed in research on other migration streams. By considering the various elements of the migration system, this approach can better incorporate the bidirectional nature of migration between the two areas and the factors that might contribute to its stability or change.

Notes

[1] In the Canadian context, "First Nation" refers to an Aboriginal community, typically associated with a particular treaty agreement and/or reserve lands as defined under the Indian Act of Canada. "First Nations people" generally refers to those who identify themselves as members of groups sometimes known as "North American Indians." First Nations peoples are culturally diverse and are distinct from the other groups identified in the Constitution Act (1982), the Métis and the Inuit.

[2] Roughly half of the Aboriginal population in Canada is registered under the Indian Act of Canada, and these are known legally as "Registered Indians." Most members of Indian Bands or First Nations are Registered Indians.

[3] The rules regarding who can be a Registered Indian and who cannot changed in 1985, allowing communities to set their own rules for Band membership. Bill C-31, An Act to Amend the Indian Act of Canada, also allowed the re-registration of approximately 100,000 people who had lost registration status due to the previous rules, and their children. These included women who lost status because they married non-Registered men, and men and women who lost registration status after receiving university degrees or performing military service (Clatworthy, Hull, and Loughren, 1997; Wherrett, 1996).

[4] Aboriginal people not registered under the Indian Act of Canada. Some non-Status people may be members of a First Nation.

References

Boyd, Monica. 1989. Family and Personal Networks in International Migration: Recent Developments and New Agendas. *International Migration Review,* 23(3):638–670.

Brody, Hugh. 1971. *Indians on Skid Row: The Role of Alcohol in the Adaptive Process of Indian Urban Migrants.* Ottawa: Department of Indian Affairs and Northern Development.

Clatworthy, Stewart J. 1996. *The Migration and Mobility Patterns of Canada's Aboriginal Population.* Ottawa: Canada Mortgage and Housing Corporation, and the Royal Commission on Aboriginal Peoples.

Clatworthy, Stewart J., Jeremy Hull, and Neil Loughren. 1997. Implications of First Nations Demography. Report by Four Directions Consulting Group for the Research and Analysis Directorate, Indian and Northern Affairs. Ottawa: Department of Indian Affairs and Northern Development.

Fawcett, James T. 1989. Networks, Linkages, and Migration Systems. *International Migration Review,* 23(3):671–680.

Gurak, Douglas T., and Fe Caces. 1992. Migration Networks and the Shaping of Migration Systems. In *International Migration Systems: A Global Approach,* eds. Mary Kritz, Lin Lean Lim, and Hania Zlotnick, pp. 150–176. Oxford: Clarendon Press.

Kritz, Mary M., and Hania Zlotnik. 1992. Global Interactions: Migration Systems, Processes, and Policies. In *International Migration Systems: A Global Approach,* eds. Mary Kritz, Lin Lean Lim, and Hania Zlotnick, pp. 1–15. Oxford: Clarendon Press.

Newhouse, David, and Evelyn Peters, eds. 2003. *Not Strangers in these Parts: Urban Aboriginal Peoples.* Ottawa: Policy Research Initiative.

Norris, Mary Jane, Dan Beavon, Eric Guimond, and Martin Cooke. 2001. *Migration and Residential Mobility of Canada's Aboriginal Groups: An Analysis of Census Data.* Ottawa: Indian and Northern Affairs Canada.

Peters, Evelyn J. 1996. Aboriginal Peoples in Urban Areas. In *Visions of the Heart: Contemporary Aboriginal Issues,* eds. David A. Long and Olive Patricia Dickason, pp. 238–333. Toronto: Harcourt Brace.

Statistics Canada. 1998a. Census of Canada, 1996, Table 93F0025XDB96001: Total Population by Aboriginal Identity (7) and Registered Indian Status (3), Showing Indian Band/First Nation Membership (3), for Canada, Provinces, Territories and Census Metropolitan Areas, 1996 Census (20% Sample Data) [machine readable data file]. Ottawa: Statistics Canada. 1998-02-16.

———. 1998b. Census of Canada, 1996, Table 93F0025XDB96004: Registered Indian Population by On/Off Reserve (3) and Sex (3), Showing Age Groups (11), for Canada, Provinces and Territories, 1996 Census (20% Sample Data) [machine readable data file]. Ottawa: Statistics Canada. 1998-02-16.

———. 1998c. Census of Canada, 1996, Table 93F0025XDB96006: Indian Band/First Nation Members by Indian Tribe/Nation (50), Showing On/Off Reserve (3), for Canada, Provinces and Territories, 1996 Census (20% Sample Data) [machine readable data file]. Ottawa: Statistics Canada. 1998-02-16.

Wherrett, Jill. 1996. Briefing Paper: Indian Status and Band Membership Issues BP-410. Library of Parliament: Ottawa.

23

Japanese Brazilian Ethnic Return Migration

Takeyuki (Gaku) Tsuda

In the early 1900s, thousands of Japanese citizens emigrated to Brazil in search of better living conditions and to escape rural poverty at home. After World War II, a second wave of Japanese followed. But by the late 1980s, some of these Brazilian citizens of Japanese descent began returning to Japan as unskilled "foreign workers." In this chapter, Takeyuki Tsuda examines the experiences of the returnees who, although of Japanese descent, were born in Brazil and are culturally Brazilian. They have become Japan's newest ethnic minority. Their socioeconomic marginalization in their ethnic homeland, and their dislike of certain features of contemporary Japanese society, has caused them to strengthen their Brazilian nationalist sentiments while they struggle to make themselves at home in Japan.

Since the late 1980s, Brazilians of Japanese descent have been "return" migrating to Japan as unskilled foreign workers. Japan's immigrant population is currently estimated at over 300,000, and the Japanese Brazilians are now the second largest group of foreigners in Japan. Although they are of Japanese descent, since most of them were born in Brazil and are culturally Brazilian, they have become Japan's newest ethnic minority. Because of their socioeconomic marginalization in their ethnic homeland, the Japanese Brazilians have strengthened their Brazilian nationalist sentiments in response to what they perceive to be the negative aspects of Japanese society. As a result, they assert their cultural differences in Japan by intentionally acting in Brazilian ways in order to ethnically differentiate themselves from majority Japanese. Although they feel alienated from their ethnic homeland, many have become immigrant settlers and are increasingly making themselves at home in Japan.

Source: Written expressly for *Urban Life*.

JAPAN AS A "RECENT" COUNTRY OF IMMIGRATION

International migration has been responsible for creating many of the world's ethnic minority groups. When migrants cross national borders and settle in foreign countries, they become immigrant ethnic minorities that are racially and culturally different from the dominant populace and frequently become targets of discrimination and socioeconomic marginalization. Although many countries have indigenous minorities, most ethnic minorities in the contemporary world are immigrant minorities.

Until the late 1980s, Japan was one of the few advanced industrial countries in the world that had not imported large numbers of unskilled immigrant laborers since World War II to sustain its economic growth. Although the country experienced labor shortages in the late 1960s and early 1970s, government officials decided against admitting unskilled foreign workers partly because they wished to maintain Japan's supposed ethnic homogeneity and instead embarked on a concerted effort to increase labor productivity through mechanization and the utilization of female and elderly workers (see Mori 1997:37–42). At the end of the 1980s, Japan finally succumbed to the pressures of global migration as it faced various labor market and demographic pressures, which forced it to import large numbers of unskilled foreign workers. The rapid expansion of the Japanese economy in the 1980s created a rising demand for unskilled labor that could not be met by the domestic labor supply because of the country's rapidly shrinking and aging populace (Japan has the world's lowest fertility rate), a well-educated and affluent populace unwilling to perform unskilled 3D (dirty, dangerous, and difficult) jobs, inability to further tap previously underutilized sources of labor power (women, elderly, and rural workers), and the limits of further mechanization and offshore production. The result was an acute unskilled labor shortage, especially among small and medium-sized firms, which threatened to cripple the booming economy.

Despite its economic need for immigrant labor, the Japanese government maintained the country's long-standing ban on unskilled foreign workers and imposed tough penalties on those employers and labor brokers who knowingly recruit and hire illegal immigrants when it revised the Immigration Control and Refugee Recognition Act (implemented in 1990). However, the government tacitly created various "side-door" policies that enable the legal importation of large numbers of unskilled foreign workers under visa categories officially intended for other purposes. In addition, because Japan has insisted on a closed-door policy that officially prohibits unskilled immigration despite its strong economic demand for foreign labor, a large number of illegal immigrants have entered the country in response to the large number of relatively high-paying, unskilled jobs (Tsuda and Cornelius 2004).

Although it may seem that Japan made a transition from a former country of emigration to a country of immigration in this manner (Douglass and Roberts 2000:7), the notion that Japan was not an immigration country until recent decades is itself a myth. From 1910 to 1945, when significant numbers of Japanese left the country to colonize Asia and then fight in World War II, 2.1 million Koreans immigrated to Japan—some as forced laborers—to work in Japanese factories, creating a Korean Japanese minority group that continues to suffer from ethnic discrimination and economic marginalization. Thus, the post-1985 influx of foreign workers is just the latest chapter in Japan's immigration history. Japan now has a diverse immigrant population from various countries in East and Southeast Asia, Latin America, and even the Middle East. Although the total number of foreign workers (at close to 1,900,000)[1] is less than 1.5 percent of the country's total population, it represents a sharp increase from the pre-1985 period.

THE RISE OF NIKKEIJIN IMMIGRANT COMMUNITIES

The largest and most prominent of Japan's recent immigrants are the South American *nikkeijin* (the Japanese word for Japanese descendants born and raised outside of Japan), who began "return" migrating to Japan in the late 1980s and currently number close to 390,000. As part of the revised 1990 Immigration Control and Refugee Recognition Act, the Japanese government decided to implement an ethnic preference immigration policy that grants the nikkeijin renewable visas with no activity restrictions as a partial concession to labor-deficient employers who had been clamoring for unskilled foreign workers. Although it was evident that the nikkeijin would be working in Japan's factories, Japanese government officials were able to justify this side-door policy by claiming that the nikkeijin were not unskilled immigrant workers per se, but ancestral returnees who were being invited back to their ethnic homeland to explore their Japanese heritage. In addition, because of a racial ideology in which those of Japanese descent are expected to be culturally Japanese to a certain extent, even if they were born and raised abroad, government policy makers assumed that the nikkeijin would be culturally similar and assimilate smoothly to Japanese society in contrast to racially and culturally different foreigners from East and Southeast Asia (Roth 2002). In this manner, nikkeijin immigrants were viewed as an effective way to deal with the labor shortage without undermining Japan's official ban on unskilled immigrant workers or disrupting Japan's cherished ethnic homogeneity.

Most of the nikkeijin immigrants have been second- and third-generation Japanese Brazilians who began migrating to Japan because of an economic crisis in Brazil in the 1980s. Although they are relatively well educated and mostly of middle class background in Brazil, they still earn five to 10 times their Brazilian salaries in Japan as unskilled factory workers.[2] Because most of the Brazilian nikkeijin migrate with the intention of returning to Brazil in a couple of years, they are called *dekasegi*, the Japanese word for temporary migrant workers. However, many have brought over their families to Japan, and the process of long-term immigrant settlement has already begun (see Tsuda 1999b, Yamanaka 2000). Since the Japanese Brazilians were born and raised in Brazil, they do not speak Japanese very well and have become culturally Brazilianized to various degrees. As a result, despite their Japanese descent, they are treated as foreigners in Japan and have become the country's newest immigrant minority.

The expansion of the Japanese Brazilian immigrant community has been remarkable. Whereas the number of Brazilians registered as foreigners in Japan was only 14,528 in 1989, it rose to 224,299 by 2000 and to 316,967 by 2007. Although the initial immigrants were poorer, as the tremendous economic benefits of migration became clear, more well-to-do Japanese Brazilians began return migrating as well. Transnational labor broker networks were quickly established. These brokers recruit nikkeijin in Brazil, obtain visas for them, finance their travel to Japan, and then provide them with factory jobs, housing, insurance, and social support in Japan. Labor brokers have greatly expanded the migrant flow by reducing the difficulty and risk of migration and enabling those who do not have transnational social connections to Japan (or even funds to buy a plane ticket) to migrate. As a result, a "culture of migration" has developed among Japanese Brazilian communities in Brazil, where migration has become so prevalent and routine that many depend on it for their economic well-being and socioeconomic advancement. Because these sociocultural structures facilitating and sustaining migration have become so firmly entrenched, the volume of migration continues to increase even though its original economic causes have subsided.[3]

Since a majority of Japanese Brazilian immigrants work in small and medium-sized businesses in the manufacturing sector, they tend to be clustered in satellite industrial towns, and only a minority work in the service sector in Japan's large cities. Although they are not residentially segregated, prominent Brazilian immigrant communities have developed in certain industrial cities with an expanding array of ethnic businesses, including Brazilian restaurants, food stores and supermarkets, clothing stores, and even boutiques and discos, as well as nikkeijin churches and other organizations. Large labor brokers are especially active in such communities, providing extensive employment, housing, transportation, and other social services mainly in Portuguese. Local governments in such cities (which benefit economically from foreign workers and are legally obligated to provide them with services) have generally been receptive to the Japanese Brazilians and offer information handbooks and pamphlets, health insurance and emergency medical coverage, consultation services, language classes and translation services, educational programs in local schools with nikkeijin children, and even limited political representation through foreigner advisory councils.

THE JAPANESE ETHNIC RECEPTION OF THE JAPANESE BRAZILIANS

Despite their relatively privileged status in Japan as "ethnic Japanese," the Japanese Brazilians are still subject to notable prejudice and social marginalization as an ethnic minority group. Most of the mainstream Japanese informants I interviewed felt a certain amount of ethnic affinity with the Brazilian nikkeijin because of their Japanese descent and clearly preferred them to foreigners of non-Japanese descent. This sentiment was expressed by a Japanese factory worker in Oizumi as follows:

> Discrimination and disparagement is less toward the Brazilian nikkeijin because they have a Japanese face. This creates a feeling of commonality with them as our brethren. Since we see them as people who were originally Japanese, we feel closer to them than other foreigners. There is much more discrimination toward the Korean Japanese.

There was general consensus among those Japanese I interviewed that prejudice and discrimination toward Korean Japanese is higher because they are not of Japanese descent, even though most of them have been born and raised in Japan and are culturally assimilated.

Despite this general sense of racial and cultural affinity, most of my Japanese informants harbored notable ethnic prejudice toward the Japanese Brazilians, who were often perceived as descendants of originally poor and uneducated Japanese of low social class background who could not survive economically in Japan and thus had to abandon their homeland and emigrate to Brazil. Most of my Japanese informants associated migrant workers with poverty and did not know that the Japanese Brazilians are middle class in Brazil. Japanese Brazilians' current status as unskilled factory workers subjects them to a double social class stigma—they are descendants of those who initially fled to Brazil because they supposedly could not survive in Japan and have now returned to Japan because they could not survive economically in Brazil either.

In addition to this type of social class prejudice, there is also considerable cultural prejudice toward the Japanese Brazilians based on negative evaluations of their "Brazilian" behavior. Because of the Japanese ethnic expectation that those who are racially Japanese will also be culturally similar, virtually all of my Japanese informants mentioned that they were disappointed when they realized how culturally foreign the Brazilian nikkeijin are. The Japanese employees on the assembly line at the factory (which I will call Toyama) where I conducted participant observation generally gave their nikkeijin counterparts rather low marks for their work ethic and ability and saw them as lazy, slow, irresponsible, and careless on the job, which was sometimes attributed to their "Brazilianness." Although Japanese employers generally had favorable impressions of their nikkeijin workers, they sometimes saw them as excessively individualistic, conflictual, and lacking in company loyalty because they frequently quit for higher paying jobs. Outside the factory, Japanese residents complain that the Japanese Brazilians are a disturbance because they make excessive noise in apartments, turn up the volume on their stereos, and party until late at night on weekends. Even in cities with relatively high concentrations of immigrants, where local residents have become used to constantly encountering foreigners in the streets, some still do not like to see nikkeijin walking around in groups, dressed in a strange manner, speaking loudly in Portuguese, and otherwise behaving in ways that seem alien.[4]

In addition to ethnic prejudice, Japanese Brazilian immigrants also experience considerable social marginalization as an ethnic minority in Japan. At Toyama factory, nikkeijin and Japanese workers always remained apart during break and lunch hours, sitting in separate rooms or at different tables and conversing only among themselves. Interethnic interaction was limited to brief smiles or greetings in the morning and short exchanges of a few words or simple questions. Although the Japanese Brazilians often work together with the Japanese on the same factory assembly lines, general conversation between the two groups is kept to a bare minimum and was usually limited to work instructions. Likewise, only a few Brazilian nikkeijin have sustained social relationships with their Japanese coworkers outside the factory, have contact with their Japanese neighbors, or participate in local community activities. As a result, what interaction they have with the Japanese outside the factory is generally limited to clerks and workers at local stores, banks, and municipal offices.

The reasons for the social marginalization of the Japanese Brazilians as an ethnic minority are complex. Because of a narrow Japanese national identity in which "Japaneseness" is defined not only by racial descent but also by complete linguistic and cultural proficiency, the nikkeijin are ethnically excluded in Japan as cultural foreigners despite their Japanese descent. The remarks of one local Japanese resident in Oizumi-town were representative of this general Japanese reaction:

> There's a lot of *iwakan* [sense of incongruity] towards those who have a Japanese face but are culturally Brazilian. If they have a Japanese face, we interpret this to mean they are Japanese, so we initially approach the nikkeijin this way. But then when we find they are culturally different, we say they are *gaijin* [foreigners].

At Toyama factory, the Brazilian nikkeijin were often addressed as *gaijin-san* (Mr. or Mrs. Foreigner), although personal names were often used in more familiar situations. The Japanese Brazilians are also referred to as gaijin outside the workplace, especially when they speak Portuguese in restaurants, stores, and trains. Most Japanese tend to keep their distance from such ethnically unfamiliar foreigners. Although most of the Japanese Brazilians are not phenotypically distinct from the Japanese, they wore different-colored uniforms at the Toyama factory as temporary workers contracted from outside labor broker firms, making them "ethnically visible" and easily subject to social exclusion. Even outside the factory, many of them remain visible as cultural foreigners because of their distinctively different manner of speaking, dressing, gesturing, and even walking.

In addition, since a majority of the nikkeijin immigrants cannot speak Japanese effectively, language is obviously a significant cultural barrier to social interaction. At Toyama factory, many Japanese workers did not even attempt to speak with their nikkeijin coworkers because they were afraid of their inability to communicate. The ethnic marginalization of the Japanese Brazilians on the basis of cultural difference was also motivated by ethnic prejudice (described above). I was told a number of times at Toyama factory about Japanese workers who did not interact with nikkeijin foreigners because of ethnic dislike.

The social segregation of the Japanese Brazilians in Japan is not simply a result of their ethnocultural differences but is also caused by their socioeconomic marginalization as migrant laborers. Most of them are employed in the most peripheral sector of the Japanese labor market, since they are used by Japanese companies as a casual labor force of temporary contract workers who are borrowed from outside labor broker firms. As a result, they do not belong to the companies where they work—where they are considered outsiders on the factory floor and are excluded from Japanese social groups. Because they are constantly transferred by their labor broker from one company to another as a readily disposable workforce, few Japanese workers bother to associate with such itinerant laborers. In addition, they often eat in separate lunchrooms, are not invited to company outings and events with Japanese workers, and are sometimes even segregated in nikkeijin-only work sections.

The Brazilian nikkeijin also respond to their ethnic and social exclusion in Japan by withdrawing into their own social groups in an act of ethnic self-segregation. Most of them do not actively seek out relationships with the Japanese because the Japanese do not seek out relationships with them. Although the Japanese Brazilians are beginning to settle long-term or permanently in Japan (see Tsuda 1999b), many continue to view themselves strictly as sojourners who intend to return to Brazil in a few years after accumulating sufficient savings. As a result, they have little incentive to integrate themselves into Japanese society and establish long-term, meaningful relationships with the Japanese. However, despite their self-perceived temporary status, they have already created extensive and cohesive immigrant communities in various parts of Japan (described above), which enable them to conduct their lives exclusively within their own extensive social and institutional networks without interacting with mainstream Japanese.

FEELING BRAZILIAN IN JAPAN: MIGRANT NATIONALISM AMONG THE NIKKEIJIN

The ambivalent ethnic reception of Japanese Brazilian immigrants by their Japanese hosts is disconcerting to many of them and causes them to strengthen their nationalist affiliation as Brazilians in Japan.[5] This impact of ethnic return migration on the nikkeijin is significant, given the relatively strong "Japanese" ethnic identity they had developed in Brazil. As Brazil's oldest and by far largest Asian minority (population over 1.2 million), the Japanese Brazilians are generally well-regarded by mainstream Brazilians for what are perceived to be their positive "Japanese" cultural attributes, their relatively high socioeconomic and educational status, and their affiliation with the highly respected First World country of Japan. In turn, the Brazilian nikkeijin take pride in their Japanese heritage and identify rather strongly with positive images of Japan and Japanese culture, generally distancing themselves from negative stereotypes of "Brazilians" as lazy, untrustworthy, and less educated. As a result, when they return migrate to Japan, they expect to be ethnically accepted, if not welcomed as Japanese descendants, and think that they will have congenial relationships with the Japanese.

Therefore, when the Japanese Brazilians are ethnically marginalized as culturally different "foreigners" in Japan despite their Japanese descent, they feel disoriented, if not shocked, and are forced to reconsider their ethnic identities. When talking about their migrant experiences, they frequently say, "We are considered Japanese in Brazil, but are seen as foreigners here in Japan." Their previous assumptions of cultural commonality with the Japanese are questioned as they realize that their supposedly "Japanese" cultural attributes, which were sufficient to be considered "Japanese" in Brazil, are woefully insufficient to qualify as Japanese in Japan, or even to be socially accepted. The remarks of one second-generation nikkeijin man were representative of this type of experience:

> We think we are Japanese in Brazil, but in Japan, we find out that we were wrong. If you act differently and don't speak Japanese fluently, the Japanese say you are a Brazilian. To be considered Japanese, it is not sufficient to have a Japanese face and eat with chopsticks. You must think, act, and speak just like the Japanese.

The shift in ethnic identity among the nikkeijin from an initially stronger Japanese consciousness in Brazil to an increased awareness of their Brazilianness is also based on a self-recognition of their Brazilian cultural differences in Japan. For instance, although they had frequently noted their more quiet, restrained, and shyer "Japanese" demeanor in Brazil, they discover in Japan that their manner of walking, dressing, and gesturing is strikingly different from the Japanese. Virtually all of my informants claimed that it is easy to tell the Japanese Brazilians apart from the Japanese on the streets because of such differences. For instance, consider the following statement by Tadashi, a nikkeijin worker at Toyama:

> I can see a [Japanese] Brazilian coming from a mile away with about 90 percent certainty. . . . The Brazilians walk casually with a more carefree gait and glance around at their surroundings and they are dressed casually in T-shirts and jeans. The Japanese are more formally dressed and walk in a more rushed manner. The Brazilians also gesture much more than Japanese and walk around in groups, whereas the Japanese are usually alone.

In this manner, the Brazilian nikkeijin realize that even their body language and mannerisms set them apart from the Japanese, forcing them to redefine themselves as more culturally Brazilian than they had previously acknowledged.

The nationalization of ethnic identity among Japanese Brazilian return migrants is also a response to their negative social experiences in Japan. Partly because of their ethnic alienation from Japanese society, many of them develop negative attitudes about Japanese culture and behavior. They often complain that the Japanese are cold, unreceptive, and impersonal in social relationships and unfriendly people lacking *calor humano* (human warmth) and affection. They also note that the Japanese work all the time and do not have active and fulfilling family and social lives. Nonetheless, a number of them have negative evaluations of the actual ability and work ethic of their Japanese counterparts, claiming that the nikkeijin work harder, better, and more conscientiously. Some Japanese Brazilian women had harsh words for the manner in which women are treated in Japanese society, claiming that they are paid less for the same work, are expected to be submissive at work, and are subject to male patriarchy at home. Other Japanese behaviors singled out for criticism were group conformity, lack of individuality, and submissiveness to authority.

In addition, a majority of nikkeijin immigrants are disappointed by the actual material and living conditions in Japan. Because many of them arrive with rather idealistic images of Japan as the *primeiro mundo* (the First World) of ultra-modern cities, advanced technology and industrial development, and luxurious living standards, they are disappointed when they actually experience the narrow streets, small houses, poorer neighborhoods, and the country's relatively low living standards, and find that Japan is much less developed than they had previously imagined. Some of them were also surprised at the small and dingy factories in which much of the work is still being done manually, in stark contrast to images of highly mechanized and modernized Japanese factories. Other Japanese Brazilians had an antiquated perception of Japanese society based on nostalgic images of traditional Japanese culture, epitomized by ancient Japanese shrines, *samurai*, *kabuki*, and *kimono*. They are disillusioned when they realize how modern Japan is so different from the old, traditional Japan that they had savored from distant Brazil.

As the initially positive images that the Japanese Brazilians had of Japan are replaced by a much less favorable understanding of Japanese society, many of them distance themselves from their previous ethnic identification as "Japanese," and the positive value of Brazilian culture and society suddenly emerges to a much greater extent. The supposedly unaffectionate and workaholic nature of the Japanese makes them appreciate the warmth, friendliness, and openness of the Brazilians as well as their ability to enjoy life. When confronted by the relative low living standards of Japan, a number of Brazilian nikkeijin realize that Brazil is not as underdeveloped as previously thought and that urban living standards in Third World Brazil are sometimes better than First World Japan. At the same time, they also feel a need to defend their country against what they believe are the negative images that prevail in Japan of Brazil as poor, backward, and crime-ridden.[6] Although the Brazilian nikkeijin were frequently critical of Brazilian society back home, they often praise Brazil in Japan, even to an exaggerated extent. One of my informants spoke about this positive reassessment of Brazil in the clearest terms:

> Brazilians always think other countries are much better. The Japanese Brazilians saw Japan in this way too. But now, I realize we were wrong. We didn't know what we had in Brazil. There is no better place than Brazil to live, especially because we were born there and have no cultural problems. The people are better there and so are the conditions of living. I value Brazil much more now.

Therefore, in response to the perceived negative aspects of Japanese society, the Japanese Brazilians experience a greater identification with the Brazilian nation through an increased realization and affirmation of those positive qualities that make them ethnically Brazilian. Some of them even used affect-laden terms such as nationalism and patriotism to express their renewed identification with and appreciation of Brazil. This greater sense of Brazilian national allegiance and pride is also symbolized by the prominent display of the Brazilian flag and national colors in nikkeijin ethnic stores and restaurants (and even on their clothes), although the flag is hardly ever displayed in Brazil.[7] During the 2002 World Cup (held in Japan and Korea), thousands of Japanese Brazilians waving the Brazilian flag and dressed in national colors showed up in stadiums all over Japan to cheer on their national team, causing the American TV broadcasters to wonder why so many "Japanese" were so fervently rooting for the Brazilian team![8]

The negative immigrant experiences of Japanese Brazilians in Japan also depend on their low social class status. Because most nikkeijin are well-educated, middle-class professionals or business owners in Brazil, they experience negative class mobility in Japan when they become unskilled immigrant factory workers who must perform 3D jobs that most Japanese shun and despise. Although most nikkeijin come to Japan psychologically prepared to take on these blue-collar jobs and are willing to exchange the loss of social status for financial gain, many recognize the demeaning nature of their work in Japan as well as suffer feelings of damaged pride and even shame. This is especially hard for those who held high-status professional jobs or positions of authority in Brazil, and who find themselves powerless subordinates in Japan forced to obey orders from less educated, Japanese factory workers. Also, since most Brazilian nikkeijin have no prior experience with manual labor, some have trouble adjusting to the physical rigors and strenuous pace of their factory jobs. Complaints about the mechanical and robotic nature of the work were also frequent among my nikkeijin coworkers at Toyama factory.

Such negative work experiences are compounded by what the Japanese Brazilians claim is ethnic discrimination on the job. Although they report that they are generally treated well by the Japanese, they are sensitive to being victims of exploitation and discrimination because of their subordinate social status, inability to understand Japanese, and belief that they are lowly regarded Brazilian foreigners from a poor Third World country. There was general agreement among my nikkeijin informants that they are given the more difficult jobs and are forced to work harder than the Japanese. For instance, according to a young nikkeijin woman:

> There's lots of easy work in the factory, but the Japanese never give us this work. I hear my supervisors saying, "If the work is hard, give it to the Brazilians." They figure they can give us the hardest and dirtiest work because we are from a different country and are in their land. I feel exploited working at the factory.

Others mention being yelled at on the job, mistreated by supervisors, and blamed for mistakes made on the assembly line and for product defects, as well as other problems that arise in the factory. Other issues frequently mentioned as evidence of "discrimination" against them include being fired before Japanese workers during a recession, receiving lower bonuses and fewer benefits, and not being invited to company outings and trips with Japanese workers.

The extent to which this perceived discrimination is "real" is an open question. Although there are plenty of Japanese workers with prejudices about nikkeijin foreigners, I never observed any mistreatment at the Toyama factory, where the Japanese Brazilians were in fact treated courteously (partly because of management pressure).[9] Based on my observations and interviews, it seemed unlikely that Japanese factory supervisors were intentionally giving nikkeijin workers the most difficult and worst jobs. However, because most nikkeijin do not speak Japanese well, they are frequently assigned jobs that can be explained through movements and gestures, which tend to be more physically strenuous.[10] Japanese Brazilian workers are indeed the first to be laid off and do not enjoy the same employee benefits as most Japanese workers, but this is because they are employed indirectly through outside labor brokers firms as *hi-seishain* (informal temporary workers) and not as regular, permanent *seishain*.[11] In fact, some Japanese workers are surprised to hear the nikkeijin feel discriminated against in the factory. One worker who had befriended a number of nikkeijin coworkers spoke about this as follows:

> I noticed early on that the nikkeijin would frequently use the word *discriminação*. When I checked it up in the dictionary, I was surprised to find it meant *sabetsu* ["discrimination" in Japanese]. I do not think that we discriminate at all against the nikkeijin but treat them favorably. Of course, they are given bad work by the [supervisor] sometimes, but the Japanese experience this too. The Japanese Brazilians call this "discrimination," but it is only their point of view. I guess when such experiences accumulate, they perceive it as discriminatory.

Nonetheless, such negative work experiences among Japanese Brazilian immigrants leave them feeling not only ethnic, but also socioeconomic marginalization, reinforcing their status as Brazilian foreigners who are excluded from Japanese society. This heightens their sense of antagonism against the Japanese, and alienates them from their previous "Japanese" identification, while creating a sense of ethnic solidarity among themselves as Brazilian nationals who share common experiences of occupational degradation and discrimination (see also Linger 2001:18, 313; Roth 2002:5).

THE PERFORMANCE OF A BRAZILIAN NATIONALIST IDENTITY

Although the Japanese Brazilians represent a rather unusual case of migration in that they are return migrating to their ancestral homeland, their experiences of ethnic and social exclusion, cultural difference, and discrimination are shared by many other migrants. Such negative experiences frequently cause migrants to react against the host society by reaffirming and strengthening their feelings of affiliation to their home country. In this manner, the dislocations of migration can produce a form of deterritorialized nationalism where national loyalties are articulated outside the territorial boundaries of the nation-state (see Tsuda 2003: chapter 3).

Ethnic identity however, is not simply a matter of internal self-consciousness but is actively displayed, demonstrated, and enacted in practice. Since the resurgence of Brazilian national sentiment among Japanese Brazilian immigrants is a response to their negative ethnic and socio-occupational experiences in Japan, the behavioral assertion of their Brazilian cultural differences becomes a form of opposition to Japanese society. However, it is also an attempt to resist assimilationist cultural pressures. By behaving in conspicuously "Brazilian" ways in Japan, they demonstrate to the Japanese that, despite their racial appearance, they are not Japanese and cannot be held to Japanese cultural expectations.

A common way by which the nikkeijin display their Brazilianness to the Japanese is through dress, which is among the most frequent emblems used to symbolize ethnic difference and identity. In fact, the ethnic effectiveness of clothes as an identifying marker of Brazilianness has actually increased the demand for distinctive Brazilian clothes in Japan. Of course, some Japanese Brazilians wear Brazilian clothes in Japan purely out of physical comfort or habit, but for others, it is a deliberate ethnic display of cultural difference, if not defiance. The manager of a Brazilian clothing store explained that the clothes she sells have distinctive designs, fashions, and colors that cannot be found in Japanese department stores. Jeans have colorful ornamental features and those for women tend to be tighter around the hips (as the buttocks, not the breasts, are the primary locus of female sexual attention in Brazil). Shirts have strong (even loud) colors and may have mosaic patterns, while T-shirts with the Brazilian flag, national colors, or the country's name prominently displayed are also popular.

The display of Brazilian identities in Japan also involves the use of language and greetings. For instance, Martina, a nikkeijin woman, mentioned that although she speaks Japanese well, whenever she walks into a store, she makes a point of speaking Portuguese loud enough so that the Japanese will notice. "I don't want to be confused as Japanese," she said. "So I always show them I am Brazilian." Likewise, the tendency of some nikkeijin to greet each other loudly and affectionately in public by embracing or kissing is a display of Brazilian behavior completely incongruous with Japanese culture.

Some individuals take their ethnic resistance further by exaggerating their Brazilian behavior in Japan in a rebellious, exhibitionist manner by purposefully acting more Brazilian in Japan than they ever did in Brazil. As one informant observed a bit cynically, "Some of these Brazilian youth have this attitude toward the Japanese: 'Hey, I'm Brazilian and I am going to act Brazilian in Japan. And if you don't like it, screw you.' . . . However, in Brazil, they would never have acted like this and do it only in Japan."

Others engage in much more subdued performances of their Brazilian nationalist identity. This is especially true among the more acculturated nikkeijin, who are more accommodating toward Japanese cultural expectations and feel more pressure to act in accordance with Japanese norms. For such individuals, the assertion of their Brazilianness is much less ostentatious than it is among their peers. They usually introduce themselves as Brazilians or foreigners in order to avoid being mistaken as Japanese and thus free themselves from Japanese cultural expectations. Such concerns are most salient among those nikkeijin who speak fluent Japanese and are the most likely to be mistaken as Japanese, especially because of their unwillingness to overtly display Brazilian behavior. Therefore, they sometimes find subtle ways to differentiate themselves as Brazilians. This includes not only introducing themselves as nikkeijin or Brazilian, but also writing out their Japanese last names in *katakana* (a phonetic alphabet used for foreign names) instead of in Japanese characters. Others use even more personal ethnic symbols. For example, Marcos, a Japanese Brazilian journalist in Japan, wears a goatee as his "little rebellion against the Japanese," an idiosyncratic emblem of his ethnic differences with Japanese men, who he believes do not like facial hair.

The performance of Brazilian nationalist identities in Japan occurs not only in individual behavior but also in collective ritual performances. The most important example is the samba parades that the Japanese Brazilians organize in local communities with high nikkeijin concentrations. Although most of them never participated in samba in Brazil and even scorned it as a lowly Brazilian activity, they find themselves dancing samba for the first time in their lives in Japan, and actually finding it a lot of fun. However, since they have insufficient cultural knowledge of this national Brazilian ritual, their ethnic performance in Japan is spontaneous and unstructured and does not conform to prescribed samba dance forms. Indeed, the samba parade I observed in Oizumi-town was a somewhat random cultural performance that was improvised, haphazard, and casual. The "samba costumes" the Japanese Brazilians wore were randomly chosen and ranged from simple bathing suits, clown outfits, and festival clothes with Brazilian national colors, to T-shirts and shorts. Apparently, few of the nikkeijin knew how to design or construct any real Brazilian samba costumes or had the resources to do so. In addition, most of them did not know how to dance the samba properly, and even fewer had the experience or will to execute it properly. The result was a potpourri of costumes and individuals moving their bodies randomly without any pattern, definition, or precise rhythm that resembles actual Brazilian samba. The only part of the parade that required any explicit cultural knowledge was the singer of the samba theme and the *bateria* (the drum section that beats out the samba rhythm), both of which were composed almost exclusively of non-Japanese–descent Brazilians.

Because of this lack of proper cultural knowledge about samba and the unstructured nature of the costumes and choreography, the nikkeijin samba performance had little in common with samba as it is practiced in Brazil and would have been barely recognizable back home. However, given the Japanese context in which this "samba" was being enacted, it was seen as very "Brazilian" because of its cultural distinctiveness in Japan. In other words, as long as the nikkeijin could find some costume that looked vaguely Brazilian and could shake their bodies in one way or another, the performance remained effective as a collective assertion of their Brazilian nationalist identity. This process of cultural authentication is also unintentionally supported by the presence of attentive Japanese spectators, who showed active interest in the unusual and different festivities of another nation. Since the Japanese have even less knowledge about samba than the Japanese Brazilians, they are unable to provide any cultural critique of the performance as inauthentic. For them, anything that seems culturally different and novel is accepted and appreciated as bona fide Brazilian "samba." Therefore, the implicit collusion between participant and observer in a foreign context validates and authenticates the spontaneously generated and random performance as a true display and assertion of a distinctive Brazilian nationalist culture.

THE FUTURE OF THE
JAPANESE BRAZILIAN COMMUNITY IN JAPAN

Although a good number of the Brazilian nikkeijin migrants remain sojourners and "target earners" who will return in the near future to Brazil, a sizable portion of the immigrant population is settling long-term or permanently in Japan.[12] Many have prolonged their stays in Japan because they find it difficult to save money due to the country's high cost of living. Despite overall improvement in the Brazilian economy since the late 1980s, economic uncertainty in Brazil has remained, making many Japanese Brazilians rather pessimistic about their long-term future back home. In anticipation of a longer stay in Japan, an increasing number of them have brought over their families to Japan, which further encourages settlement by reducing homesickness for Brazil and the insecurity of living alone in a foreign country. Indeed, many nikkeijin have become accustomed to comfortable living in Japan because of the presence of family and friends as well as the development of extensive immigrant ethnic communities. As a result, many of them now desire to live more fulfilling family and social lives in Japan. They have become less willing to endure long working hours and economic austerity, making it even more difficult to save sufficient money to return home. In addition, as their children attend Japanese schools and become increasingly assimilated to Japanese society, not only do their social connections and involvement in the surrounding Japanese community intensify, they become increasingly committed to the host country. Furthermore, a good number of Japanese Brazilians who do return to Brazil have difficulties economically re-establishing themselves back home, which forces them to return to Japan to earn more money, resulting in an increasing amount of circular migration between Brazil and Japan. Because of such migratory patterns, it is apparent that the nikkeijin will remain a permanent ethnic presence in Japan, whether as settlers or repeat sojourners.

As for the future ethnic and socioeconomic status of the nikkeijin immigrant community, it is apparent that Japan's myth of ethnic homogeneity will continue to limit their socioeconomic mobility because of their cultural differences. In addition, the Japanese Brazilians who have resolved to reside long-term or permanently in Japan maintain their Brazilian identity and do not show a significantly greater willingness to assimilate culturally to Japanese society (see also Roth 2002:117). Since they remain dependent on the labor broker system for jobs, they continue to be confined to the informal and marginal sector of the Japanese working class, and few have been given permanent jobs with the possibility of regular promotion. In fact, even the social mobility of more Japanized, bicultural nikkeijin has been restricted thus far to jobs as mini-supervisors in the factory, ethnic liaisons in local company and governmental offices, and owners of small ethnic businesses. They are also likely to face greater employment and institutional discrimination if they attempt to enter mainstream Japanese society by competing with native Japanese for jobs, housing, education, and other social services and opportunities.

The Japanese Brazilians will therefore remain a distinct immigrant minority in Japan that will continue to experience ethnic and socioeconomic exclusion into the foreseeable future. As a result, they have ironically become ethnic minorities in both of the societies in which they have resided. Although they were treated in Brazil as a "Japanese" ethnic minority because of their perceived racial and cultural differences, when they return migrate to their ethnic homeland of Japan, they again become ethnic minorities, this time because they are seen as so culturally "Brazilian." In fact, some Japanese Brazilians remark that they are "a people without a homeland." However, even if Japan does not feel like a homeland for the Japanese Brazilians, this does not prevent many of them from making themselves *at home* in Japan. This is especially true for those who have become immigrant settlers and have become very accustomed to living in the country with their families. As mentioned earlier, the Japanese Brazilians have created very extensive and self-contained Brazilian ethnic communities and cohesive social networks of compatriots in various parts of Japan, enabling them to conduct their lives in ethnically supportive and culturally familiar settings exclusively in Portuguese. Many of them mention how comfortable and well situated they are living in these Brazilian immigrant communities, and feel as if they were still back home in Brazil. By providing a sense of ethnic belonging, as well as social support, such communities alleviate the social alienation and exclusion the Japanese Brazilians experience in Japan. Like so many immigrant groups around the world, they have been able to create a permanent home in an alienating, foreign country.

Notes

[1] This is based on the number of people registered as foreigners in Japan plus those illegal immigrants who have overstayed their visas (who do not register with municipal governments). It excludes the approximately 430,000 Korean Japanese who are born and raised in Japan but are still registered as "foreigners" because they are not granted citizenship and have not naturalized.

[2] See Tsuda 1999b for an analysis of the causes of Japanese Brazilian return migration.

[3] Brazil's economy has improved considerably since the late 1980s and Japan's economy has been in recession. See Tsuda 1999a for a detailed analysis of the causes of Japanese Brazilian return migration.

[4] See Tsuda 2003 (chapter 2) for a more detailed analysis of Japanese ethnic prejudice toward the nikkeijin.

[5] For a more detailed analysis of this subject, see Tsuda 2003 (chapter 3).

[6] The Japanese Brazilians often claim that they are asked ignorant questions by Japanese about Brazil, such as whether the country has electricity, cars, and televisions.

[7] The only exception is during the World Cup, when the Brazilian flag is sold by the thousands and is plastered on literally every store, office, home, car, and T-shirt.

[8] The explanation they finally came up with is that because of the number of Brazilians playing on Japanese teams, Brazilian soccer has quite a following in Japan.

[9] At smaller, less well-managed factories, the treatment of nikkeijin workers can be much worse and they are at times yelled at for mistakes, etc. However, as Japanese workers I interviewed (and even some nikkeijin workers) noted, Japanese workers also get yelled at in these factories.

[10] More technical (and less heavy) work that required extensive explanation in Japanese was never given to Brazilian nikkeijin workers at Toyama.

[11] In fact, *Japanese* seasonal and contract workers who are part of the country's casual labor force (including those at Toyama) are treated the same way—they are the first to be dismissed during a production downturn and do not receive the employment benefits of *seishain*.

[12] See Tsuda 1999b for an analysis of the causes of Japanese Brazilian immigrant settlement in Japan.

References

Douglass, Mike, and Glenda S. Roberts. 2000. Japan in a Global Age of Migration. In *Japan and Global Migration: Foreign Workers and the Advent of a Multicultural Society*, eds. Mike Douglass and Glenda S. Roberts, pp.3–37. London: Routledge.

Linger, Daniel T. 2001. *No One Home: Brazilian Selves Remade in Japan*. Stanford, CA: Stanford University Press.

Mori, Hiromi. 1997. *Immigration Policy and Foreign Workers in Japan*. New York: St. Martin's Press.

Roth, Joshua H. 2002. *Brokered Homeland: Japanese Brazilian Migrants in Japan*. Ithaca: Cornell University Press.

Tsuda, Takeyuki. 1999a. The Motivation to Migrate: The Ethnic and Sociocultural Constitution of the Japanese-Brazilian Return Migration System. *Economic Development and Cultural Change*, 48(1):1–31.

————. 1999b. The Permanence of "Temporary" Migration: The "Structural Embeddedness" of Japanese-Brazilian Migrant Workers in Japan. *Journal of Asian Studies*, 58(3):687–722.

————. 2003. *Strangers in the Ethnic Homeland: Japanese Brazilian Return Migration in Transnational Perspective.* New York: Columbia University Press.

Tsuda, Takeyuki, and Wayne A. Cornelius. 2004. Japan: Government Policy, Immigrant Reality. In *Controlling Immigration: A Global Perspective,* 2nd ed., eds. Wayne Cornelius, Takeyuki Tsuda, Philip Martin, and James Hollifield, pp. 439–476. Stanford, CA: Stanford University Press.

Yamanaka, Keiko. 2000. "I Will Go Home, but When?" Labor Migration and Circular Diaspora Formation by Japanese Brazilians in Japan. In *Japan and Global Migration: Foreign Workers and the Advent of a Multicultural Society,* eds. Mike Douglass and Glenda S. Roberts, pp.123–152. London: Routledge.

24

Cityward Migration in Comparative Perspective

Caroline B. Brettell and Robert V. Kemper

Synthesizing ethnographic material from diverse societies, Caroline Brettell and Robert Kemper outline significant patterns of cityward migration. They examine how migrants use diverse strategies of adaptation and institution-building—connecting individuals, families, and entire ethnic groups—to make cities their own. The authors examine projections for future population movements and discuss the importance of cityward migration for integrating countless urban and rural places into global systems. Ultimately, Brettell and Kemper show that the ethnographic research on cityward migration is leading urban anthropologists away from short-term studies of single populations toward multisited, long-term, and interdisciplinary fieldwork.

Many anthropologists who study migration began their research in rural communities where they observed that, while most residents stay in town all their lives, some of their neighbors leave, never to return; others leave for a time and return; and still others come to town from other communities. This observation led some fieldworkers to follow individuals from communities of origin to their destinations and to pay attention to the links that migrants maintain to their home communities, including return migration and the relationship between migration and local development. Other anthropologists started in cities, where they studied migrant communities and subsequently did fieldwork in the migrants' places of origin, whether within the same country or in another nation. Still others have conducted comparative research on two or more migrant populations in a single urban context or comparative research on a migrant population from one sending country that has settled in different urban places across the globe.

Source: Adapted and updated from the authors' article, "Migration and Cities," pp. 30–38 in Melvin Ember and Carol R. Ember, *Encyclopedia of Urban Cultures*, vol. 1. Danbury, CT: Grolier, 2002.

MIGRATION AND THE GROWTH OF CITIES

More than a century ago, in his famous essay on the "laws" of migration, Ravenstein (1885) noted that natives of towns are less migratory than those from rural areas. This movement of peasants and farmers from the countryside to urban centers in search of better economic opportunity has a deep history, but the demographic impact of migration on the growth of cities has been most pronounced since the nineteenth century. Today, largely as a result of rural–urban migration flows in the underdeveloped and developing world, we can speak of global urbanization.

In the United States, it was international migration, supplemented in the late nineteenth century by the flow of population from farms to cities, which launched this process of urban growth. In 1830, New York City had a population of 200,000; 30 years later, it had reached a million, and by the late 1920s, its population was seven million. However, after the passage of the national origins legislation in 1924, the role of foreign immigrants in the growth of American cities diminished (Muller 1993:114). The aging population of southern and eastern European foreign-born and their children moved from urban ethnic neighborhoods to ethnically mixed suburbs, and inner-city urban economies went into decline.

With the U.S. Immigration Act of 1965 a new cycle began. Since 1970, more than half of the nation's population growth can be attributed to the impact of immigration, both legal and undocumented. More than 80 percent of immigrants have settled in major metropolitan areas, often stimulating a revival of both commerce and housing in inner-city neighborhoods in places like Detroit, Chicago, and Newark. But at the end of the twentieth century in the United States, immigrants were also settling in smaller towns across the United States, drawn there by particular employment opportunities. Another important trend that has been documented is the emergence of the so-called "New South"—in particular, the settlement of high numbers of Latinos in cities such as Nashville, Tennessee, and Charlotte, North Carolina, that have had little prior experience with the foreign-born.

Several U. S. cities—including the traditional entry points of New York, Miami, Los Angeles, and Chicago and the newer entry points such as Atlanta, Dallas-Fort Worth, Phoenix, and Minneapolis-St. Paul—have been labeled "gateway cities," with shared economic characteristics directly linked to high proportions of immigrants (Singer, Hardwick, and Brettell 2008). New York City lost more than 10 percent of its population during the 1970s, and the figure would have been greater had it not been for the approximately 783,000 immigrants who arrived in the city during that decade. Between 1980 and 2010, the city's population surpassed eight million, due in large measure to a continuing influx of immigrants. The result of this high rate of immigration is that the proportion of foreign-born in New York City has doubled from 18 percent to 36 percent since 1970. Comparable figures for San Francisco and Los Angeles rose from 22 to 37 percent and from 15 to 41 percent, respectively. Some cities are dominated by particular ethnic groups—currently, nearly half of the residents of Los Angeles County are Hispanic, primarily of Mexican origin; Dade County in Miami is home to the majority of Cuban immigrants in the United States; most Dominicans and half the Russian immigrants have settled in New York; while Chinese immigrants have concentrated their settlement in San Francisco's Chinatown, as well as in New York City's Lower East Side. In some of these cities of immigration, newcomers have been settling directly in the suburbs, thereby rapidly diversifying areas that had been dominated by the white middle and upper-middle class.

A similar process of increasing ethnic diversity has occurred in European cities. Major urban centers such as London, Paris, Frankfurt, and Berlin have become multicultural metropolises with immigrant populations from all over the world. Marseilles is certainly a gateway city for immigrants from North Africa, who are concentrated there as well as in Paris and Lyon. Some of these cities are among the "global cities" identified by Sassen (1991)—that is, places that manage the foreign investment driving globalization and generate a significant demand for immigrant labor in the service sector. However, even traditional sending nations in Europe, such as Italy and Ireland, have recently seen a rise in in-migration from outside of Europe, especially from Africa, Latin America, and the Middle East. The majority of these newcomers have settled in the capital cities. Finally, some European cities such as Barcelona and Istanbul have witnessed growth as a result of internal migration streams from their own rural regions.

In the developing world, the impact of migration on cities is largely a post–World War II and post-colonial phenomenon. For example, the population of metropolitan Mexico City has increased from 5.3 million in 1960 to more than 21 million in 2010—and it still receives thousands of new migrants each month. The starkest sign of massive rural–urban migration throughout Latin America has been the rapid growth of shantytowns in and around its cities, from Santiago de Chile in the south to Tijuana and Ciudad Juárez in the north. Newcomers build housing with whatever cheap materials they can find in areas that lack basic urban services such as water, electricity, sewers, and roads.

After 1960, Africa replaced Latin America as the most rapidly urbanizing continent. Traditional patterns of rural–rural labor migration gave way to cityward migration as opportunities in urban jobs became more attractive than those in mining and agriculture. For instance, the population of Nairobi, Kenya, expanded from around 350,000 at the time of independence in 1962 to an estimated 3.4 million in 2010, but it still cannot make the top-ten list of Africa's major metropolitan areas. According to the best estimates of the United Nations Human Settlements Programme (UN-HABITAT 2008), the 2010 list is headed by Cairo, Egypt (12.5 million); followed by Lagos, Nigeria (10.6 million); Kinshasa, Congo Democratic Republic (9.1 million); Khartoum, Sudan (5.2 million); Luanda, Angola (4.8 million); Alexandria, Egypt (4.4 million); Abidjan, Côte D'Ivoire (4.2 million); Algiers, Algeria, and

Johannesburg, South Africa (both at 3.6 million); and Addis Ababa, Ethiopia (3.5 million). Throughout Africa, urban growth rates have been so elevated in recent years that, taken as a whole, the continent has become the fastest urbanizing region in the world, wresting this dubious distinction from Latin America, which had held this position from the 1940s through the 1970s.

Similar urban transformations have resulted from rural–urban migration in Asian nations. For example, the total population of Bangladesh almost tripled—from 55 million to over 156 million—between 1961 and 2010, while the population of its capital city (Dhaka) exploded from less than 850,000 to become a megacity with an estimated 14.8 million residents. Even in China, despite strong controls on internal population movements, cities continue to grow at higher rates than the countryside. By 2010, the Beijing urban area reached an estimated 11.7 million residents, but it has been outpaced by Shanghai, with its estimated 15.8 million inhabitants.

One important aspect of these migration flows in less-developed countries is the variations in gender composition. In Africa, the Middle East, and South Asia men predominate among rural–urban migrants; while in Latin America, the Philippines, and Thailand women predominate. The same is true for international migrants. In 2000, Caribbean women in the United States outnumbered men (a sex ratio of 85 males/100 females in 2000), while African men outnumbered African women (a sex ratio of 140 males/100 females). The sex ratio among the Mexican foreign born in 2000 was 118 males/100 females. In both sending and receiving societies, these gender-based population flows often bring changes to both gender roles and gender ideologies.

While some scholars have argued that less developed countries are now "over urbanized," they also recognize that it is difficult for governments to stem complex internal migration flows. Migrants do not always proceed directly from village of origin to their final urban destination. In fact, so-called "step migration" can occur as a component of internal or international migration. For example, some residents of the Mexican town of Tzintzuntzan (located in the state of Michoacán) have moved directly to the national capital, whereas others have made intermediate stays in Morelia, capital city of Michoacán, and then moved on to Mexico City. In recent years, many residents of Mexico City, whose parents or grandparents grew up in rural villages like Tzintzuntzan, have migrated to Los Angeles, Houston, or even Chicago (see Kemper's chapter in this volume). Thus, what happens in urban areas of the developing world—including their capacity to absorb the continuing streams of immigrants—will have an impact on the future growth of gateway and global cities in developed countries.

THEORIZING CITYWARD MIGRATION AS PROCESS

Much of the early work on migration was influenced by social science models that emphasized "push" and "pull" factors of migration; that is, what caused some people to leave their home community and what attracted others to move into that community. These models assumed that migrants and their families make rational economic calculations in response to the large-scale differences in land, labor, and capital between the places where they live and the places to which they migrate. In addition to the lack of jobs that drives people from their communities of origin and the prospects for obtaining work that attract migrants to cities, anthropologists also observed the importance of the "bright lights" in drawing people to cities. As the old folk song concludes, "How you gonna keep 'em down on the farm, after they've seen Paree?" Moreover, fieldworkers discovered that when rural dwellers become more aware of conditions in the larger society, they suffer a greater sense of relative deprivation. In effect, it is not just differential access to jobs, but it is also personal contacts, the flow of information between sending and receiving areas, and other social and cultural factors that stimulate population movement.

Among anthropologists, dissatisfaction with purely economic approaches to cityward migration has resulted in a powerful emphasis on the role of social networks in the migration process. Such networks may link multiple destinations rather than just one sending locale to one receiving area. They become self-perpetuating because "every new migrant reduces the costs of subsequent migration for a set of friends and relatives, and some of these people are thereby induced to migrate, which further expands the set of people with ties abroad" (Massey et al. 1993:449). In particular, the sharing and reciprocity that occur within kinship networks that cross national boundaries can create international families, even to the point where the practice of child fostering can aid migrants in achieving their career goals. Several researchers have identified a practice of transnational motherhood; that is, the "circuits of affection, caring, and financial support that transcend national borders" (Hondagneu-Sotelo and Avila 1997:550; see also Parreñas 2001).

This emphasis on social networks has become closely associated with the concept of transnationalism, a concept that pertains to international migrants and the communities to and from which they flow. Transnationalism is useful for understanding immigrant life and identity when migrants operate within social fields that ignore or blur geographic, political, and cultural borders. In addition, transnationalism offers a way to comprehend population movements in a world where improved modes of transportation and modern telecommunications have shortened the social distance between sending and receiving societies. Immigrants who once felt obligated to become fully incorporated into new societies beyond their homelands now are able to maintain ties to their countries of origin. Hybrid identities are becoming the rule rather than the exception as millions of migrants move through the twenty-first century.

From a transnational perspective, migrants are no longer "uprooted" but rather move freely back and forth across international borders and between different cultures and social systems. These migrants bring change to localized communities not only through significant economic remittances but also through their continuing social connections. Some anthropologists have argued that the transnational arrangements constructed by "ordinary migrants, their families and their friends, have undermined both the political dominance exerted by the state and its cultural authority" (Rouse 1995:358). In such situations, as between Mexico and the U.S. or between Hong Kong and the United Kingdom, dual citizenship emerges as a significant policy question from a transnational perspective. This has important implications for urban civic culture in the developed world.

MIGRANTS IN CITIES

The concepts of social networks and transnationalism also have important implications for the way that migrants settle in cities and adapt to urban life. Networks provide a form of social capital that ultimately yields economic capital. Lomnitz (1977), for example, found that kinship networks were the basic units of production and consumption among rural–urban migrants in Mexico. In his work on undocumented Central Americans in Houston, Rodriguez (1987) found that larger social networks are directly correlated with the social and economic resources that can be mustered for settlement. Other scholars have explored the relationship between labor migration and a gift economy or other forms of mutual assistance that bind an immigrant community together. Through such gifting relationships, migrants can transform persons who are strangers into lifelong friends. As Werbner (1990:332) has said, "Through such exchanges, not only men but whole households and extended families are linked, and exchanges initiated on the shop floor extend into the domestic and inter-domestic domain."

Networks are also the basis for the formation of residential clusters or full-fledged ethnic neighborhoods—that is, closely knit migrant social spaces based on ties of kinship, language, and common heritage. Best known, perhaps, are the inner-city areas that have received successive waves of immigrants: the Lower East Side of New York City, the Kensington Market area of Toronto, Canada, and numerous suburbs in the Los Angeles metropolitan region. Several cities (especially New York, San Francisco, and Vancouver) have well-established Chinatowns, while other American cities have developed new ethnic neighborhoods in the past generation. Miami's "Little Havana" and the New York area's Brighton Beach (known as "Little Odessa" because of its Russian immigrants) are just two examples among many that might be cited. Sometimes these ethnic neighborhoods are both residential and commercial centers, but other times they are strictly commercial hubs. For example, Indian immigrants in New York are residentially dispersed, but the Jackson Heights area of Queens serves as the core of their commercial life and social exchange (Lessinger 1995). By contrast, in the Washington Heights area of New York, where Dominican immigrants both live and work, there are between 1,500 and 2,000 visible Dominican-owned enterprises (Pessar 1995). In Berlin, the Kreuzberg area, otherwise known as "Little Istanbul," is a commercial and residential center for the approximately 200,000 Turkish immigrants in that city, and a place to which they have developed a stronger affiliation than to Germany as a whole (White 1997). In Paris, the inner-city "Goutte d'or" area is dominated by immigrants from North Africa. This pattern of ethnic enclaves can also be observed in developing countries, either informally or through government regulations intended to control where foreigners can reside in metropolitan centers. For example, Jewish populations in the diaspora usually have resided in enclaves near their synagogues, although this also can lead to the creation of ghettos.

A high concentration of businesses owned and operated by people who share the same ethnic background provides the basis for the emergence of entrepreneurial niches (where different ethnic groups dominate particular sectors of the urban economy) or what has been labeled an "enclave economy" (Greve and Salaff 2005). Anthropologists have become interested in the extent to which enclave economies, and the high level of self-employment associated with them, deter or promote immigrant incorporation and social and economic mobility. Certainly, immigrant entrepreneurs have contributed in the last two decades to significant growth in small businesses and to the revival of neighborhood stores across America. Some ethnic entrepreneurs move into markets that have been abandoned by native small businesses, generally in underserved urban areas; for example, Korean enterprises have been established in African American neighborhoods in New York and in African American and Hispanic neighborhoods in Dallas. It is not surprising that ethnic conflicts have occurred in many of these situations. Other urban ethnic businesses may be transnational in nature—travel agencies, money exchange services, real estate firms, telephone services, import stores selling ethnic commodities—and therefore reaffirm linkages with the place of origin.

Ethnic entrepreneurs do not operate in a vacuum from the majority population. Occasionally, the newfound dominance of ethnic immigrants in specific economic niches can result in a backlash from the majority population. For example, along the old Route 66 in Flagstaff, Arizona, so many small motels are now owned by persons from the Indian subcontinent that some motels advertise that they are "American owned and operated" and display the U.S. flag in front of the motel office. Alternatively, ethnic entrepreneurs can bring different groups together in unexpected ways. Every weekend, in cities like Dallas, pickup trucks cruise through elegant neighborhoods in pursuit of "estate sale" bargains that can be resold in "garage sales" and "yard sales" in less-affluent sectors of the city. Such economic exchanges are a significant though untaxed transfer of wealth between long-established upper classes and less-affluent, recently arrived ethnic immigrants.

The emergence of ethnic entrepreneurs is equally characteristic of urban immigrants in European cities, where their impact has similar significance. They are

> revitalizing formerly derelict shopping streets by introducing new products and new marketing strategies . . . , fostering the emergence of new spatial forms of social cohesion . . . , opening trade links between far away areas that were hitherto unconnected . . . , and posing challenges to

the existing regulatory framework through being engaged in informal economic activities. (Kloosterman, Van der Leun, and Rath 1999:252)

Equally important is the participation of immigrants in the informal economy, either because of precarious opportunities for work or the absence of citizenship rights.

Although less numerous, ethnic immigrants also play important economic roles in the cities of developing countries. Among the most successful of such entrepreneurs are the Quechua Indians who travel from highland communities to the city of Otavalo, Ecuador, where they dominate the regional marketplace (Meisch 2002). In cities around the world frequented by foreign tourists, native "ethnics" are present selling crafts, clothes, and comestibles. Usually, the natives hawking their goods have had to leave their communities of origin to enter this tourist trade. Thus, Maya Indians have migrated to Cancún, where they can be found working day and night on the beaches in the tourist sectors (ReCruz 1996). Even more ubiquitous are the Indian women, known locally as "Marías," who sit on the sidewalks in tourist zones in Mexico City, hoping to sell their embroideries or to receive a handout from passing tourists. Few of these urban "Marías" were born in Mexico City; on the contrary, they usually have migrated from distant villages with which they maintain contact through remittances and return visits.

Migrant groups in cities often have voluntary associations (benevolent societies, sports clubs, social clubs, political parties, rotating credit associations) and other institutions (churches, schools, newspapers) that mediate the boundary between their places of origin and their urban context. While early studies (Butterworth 1962; Little 1965) of rural–urban migrants in Africa and Latin America argued that such associations facilitate the process of adaptation, more recent studies of such organizations have witnessed their additional role in fostering social incorporation as well as civic engagement in local, national, and transnational arenas. It is through such organizations and institutions that immigrants establish their presence within the urban landscape, claiming space and making place. Consider Brettell's (2005:255–256) observations about Asian Indians in the Dallas-Fort Worth area:

[They] have established several localities of conviviality and informal community. One is Taj Mahal Imports, a grocery store located at the intersection of Beltline (running East-West) and Highway 75 (running North-South) in an old strip mall known as Richardson Heights. This mall . . . is a place where several other Indian entrepreneurs have opened businesses—including a travel agency, several restaurants, a few clothing stores, and a jewelry store. On Saturdays in particular, this shopping mall is a gathering place. Not only do Indians come to do their weekly food shopping, they stop for conversation at the fast food (*chaat*) counter at the back of the store, or they pick up the latest business cards left by other Indian business owners. Young people who volunteer for various charitable service organizations such as ASHA or "Art of Living" use the Taj as a meeting place where they can plan activities or sell tickets for upcoming events. In other words, a good deal of information sharing and mobilization occurs in the informal space provided by the Taj Mahal.

Other research (Richman 2005; Roth 2002) shows that festivals and other events organized by migrants in cities can also help to claim space, maintain cultural practices, reaffirm differences with other urban residents, and sustain links between migrants and their natal societies within a transnational space. For instance, in some American cities, Hispanics—including those with no direct ties to Mexico—celebrate Cinco de Mayo as a way to affirm "Hispanic" culture in the face of U.S. cultural hegemony. In fact, in cities with substantial Hispanic populations, Cinco de Mayo has become a more important celebration than it is in some communities in Mexico. Every year, celebrations in cities like Los Angeles, San Antonio, Dallas, Houston, and Chicago are broadcast in Mexico to be seen on the evening news programs. Thus, Cinco de Mayo has become a visible sign to immigrants and stay-at-homes alike of the importance of the transnational Mexican community. There are similar examples for other migrant populations. Kurashige (2002) describes the racial and identity politics that are central to the celebration of Nisei Week among Japanese Americans in Los Angeles; Sciorra (1999:330) argues that Italian religious processions in a Brooklyn neighborhood are ways to "retake the streets" and to transmit "a public message of territorial proprietorship and local power"; and Kasinitz and Freidenberg (1987) compare a West Indian American Day Carnival and a Puerto Rican Day parade in New York as manifestations of ethnic pride and civic politics.

THE CITY AS CONTEXT

Anthropologists interested in migrant populations recognize that the city is an important context within which to examine the process of adaptation and institution building among migrant populations. This "city as context" approach assumes that each city constitutes a particular social and economic field shaped as much by history as by present-day local, regional, national, and often global forces (Brettell 2003). As receiving areas for immigrants, cities differ in a number of ways. They differ in the depth of their history in dealing with immigrants and in the degree to which they are dominated by one immigrant group (Cubans in Miami, for example) or are characterized by multiple immigrant groups (more than 100 in Los Angeles). As suggested earlier, they differ in the degree to which they have residentially segregated receiving areas. They may have heterogeneous or homogeneous, segmented or more diverse labor markets. And they can be characterized by a particular urban ethos that shapes both institutional arrangements and attitudes toward immigrants (including the presence or absence of discrimination). Goode and Schneider (1994), for example, describe the "divided" city of Philadelphia where vital ethnic neighborhoods—complete with specialty shops, festivals, ethnic churches, and local associations—exist within an urban center overlaid with tensions between whites and blacks. Elsewhere, Goode (1990) describes two important citywide models of difference that are important to the process of incorporation: one of the city as a pluralistic mosaic composed of different cultures and the other as a place polarized by race, racism, and xenophobia. Indeed, ethnic small businesses are often established and maintained as a strategy pursued by immigrants to cope not only with unemployment but also with racism. The racism that immigrants face in receiving societies has been identified as one of the forces of transnationalism because it promotes a sense of economic and political insecurity. In summary, how immigrants are received in particular cities is an important part of their process of integration and their sense of identity. It has often been argued that ethnic identities are forged across boundaries and hence intensified in urban areas where groups confront one another in the competition for jobs, housing, and political advantage.

FUTURE TRENDS

According to demographers, by 2010 nearly one billion people will have migrated within their own national borders, and tens of millions more will have left their home countries to live temporarily or permanently in other nations. Cityward migration will continue to be a significant issue for the world and surely will continue to capture considerable attention among anthropologists and other social scientists. In response, we will reevaluate our traditional fieldwork strategies as we adapt to a transnational world in which multi-site, long-term, interdisciplinary fieldwork takes its place in our ethnographic toolkit next to the tried and true model of single-site, short-term case studies carried out by solitary researchers.

Our long-standing ethnographic focus on indigenous cityward migrants and ethnic immigrants will no longer be sufficient as a foundation for field research or theory building. Instead of emphasizing population flows *to* cities, anthropologists also will examine suburbanization, metropolitan expansion, and urban–rural migration. The abandonment or transformation through gentrification of older, central urban areas will become an increasingly significant political and economic issue in the U.S. and in other countries. At the same time, new communities will be built and designed specifically for people planning to live for three decades after their retirement. In this transformed urban context, careful studies of the social and cultural features of migration *to* and *from* cities will be needed. And such studies are likely to have more policy relevance than did earlier ethnographic case studies of migrants.

The twenty-first century will be accompanied by vast differences in wealth and power within and among the world's societies, and cities will be the critical arena in which these differences will be experienced. By 2005, more than half of the world's people had become urban residents, although many of them recall that their parents or grandparents lived in distant villages and towns relatively unaffected by the bright lights of the big city. By 2020, the world will have 24 mega-cities (i.e., metropolitan areas with over 10 million inhabitants), all but three located in the developing world. And although much of their growth will be due to the excess of urban fertility over urban mortality, migration will still be a significant feature of national and international affairs. Indeed, as in earlier decades, governments will attempt to control city growth and to force urban residents to migrate to other communities or to participate in building new cities in the hinterlands.

Policy makers often see migration as a *negative* force that creates "needs" to be met and "problems" to be solved. On the other hand, over the past several decades, anthropological research has demonstrated that internal and international migration has provided millions of persons, their families, and their communities of origin and destination with unprecedented opportunities for progress. The entrepreneurial success of immigrant populations is one of the great stories of the twentieth century, and the emergence of a transnational world in which millions of people are connected across national boundaries will be one of that century's most enduring legacies.

References

Brettell, Caroline B. 2003. Bringing the City Back In: Cities as Context for Immigrant Incorporation. In *American Arrivals: Anthropology Engages the New Immigration*, ed. Nancy Foner, pp. 163–195. Santa Fe: School of American Research.

———. 2005. The Spatial, Social, and Political Incorporation of Asian Indian Immigrants in Dallas, Texas. *Urban Anthropology*, 34(2–3):247–280.

Butterworth, Douglas S. 1962. A Study of the Urbanization Process among Mixtec Migrants from Tilantongo in Mexico City. *América Indígena*, 22:257–274.

Goode, Judith. 1990. A Wary Welcome to the Neighborhood: Community Responses to Immigrants. *Urban Anthropology*, 19:125–153

Goode, Judith, and Jo Anne Schneider. 1994. *Reshaping Ethnic and Racial Relations in Philadelphia: Immigrants in a Divided City*. Philadelphia: Temple University Press.

Greve, Arent, and Janet Salaff. 2005. Social Network Approach to Understand the Ethnic Economy: A Theoretical Discourse. *GeoJournal*, 64(1):7–16

Hondagneu-Sotelo, Pierrette, and Ernestine Avila. 1997. "I'm Here but I'm There": The Meanings of Latina Transnational Motherhood. *Gender and Society*, 11: 548–571.

Kasinitz, Philip, and Judith Freidenberg. 1987. The Puerto Rican Parade and West Indian Carnival: Public Celebrations in New York City. In *Caribbean Life in New York City: Sociocultural Dimensions*, ed. Constance Sutton, pp. 327–349. New York: Center for Migration Studies.

Kloosterman, Robert, Joanne Van der Leun, and Jan Rath. 1999. Mixed Embeddedness: (In)formal Economic Activities and Immigrant Businesses in the Netherlands. *International Journal of Urban and Regional Research*, 23(2):252–266.

Kurashige, Lon. 2002. *Japanese American Celebration and Conflict: A History of Ethnic Identity and Festival, 1934–1990*. Berkeley: University of California Press.

Lessinger, Johanna. 1995. *From the Ganges to the Hudson: Indian Immigrants in New York City*. Boston: Allyn and Bacon.

Little, Kenneth. 1965. *West African Urbanization: Voluntary Associations in Social Change*. Cambridge: Cambridge University Press.

Lomnitz, Larissa. 1977. *Networks and Marginality: Life in a Mexican Shantytown.* New York: Academic Press.

Massey, Douglas S., Joaquin Arango, Graeme Hugo, Ali Kouaouci, Adela Pellegrino, and J. Edward Taylor. 1993. Theories of International Migration: A Review and Appraisal. *Population and Development Review,* 19:431–466.

Meisch, Lynn. 2002. *Andean Entrepreneurs: Otavalo Merchants and Musicians in the Global Arena.* Austin: University of Texas Press.

Muller, Thomas. 1993. *Immigrants and the American City.* New York: New York University Press.

Parreñas, Rhacel Salazar. 2001. Mothering from a Distance: Emotions, Gender and Intergenerational Relations in Filipino Transnational Families. *Feminist Studies,* 27(2):361–390.

Pessar, Patricia R. 1995. *A Visa for a Dream: Dominicans in the United States.* Boston: Allyn and Bacon.

Ravenstein, Ernest George. 1885. The Laws of Migration. *Journal of the Statistical Society,* 48:167–227.

ReCruz, Alicia. 1996. *The Two Milpas of Chan Kom: A Study of Socioeconomic and Political Transformations in a Maya Community.* Albany: State University of New York Press.

Richman, Karen E. 2005. *Migration and Vodou.* Gainesville: University Press of Florida.

Rodriguez, Nestor. 1987. Undocumented Central Americans in Houston: Diverse Populations. *International Migration Review,* 21:4–26.

Roth, Joshua Hotaka. 2002. *Brokered Homeland: Japanese Brazilian Migrants in Japan.* Ithaca, NY: Cornell University Press.

Rouse, Roger. 1995. Thinking Through Transnationalism: Notes on the Cultural Politics of Class Relations in the Contemporary United States. *Public Culture,* 7:353–402.

Sassen, Saskia. 1991. *The Global City: New York, London, Tokyo.* Princeton, NJ: Princeton University Press.

Sciorra, Joseph. 1999. "We Go Where the Italians Live": Religious Processions as Ethnic and Territorial Markers in a Multi-ethnic Brooklyn Neighborhood. In *Gods of the City,* ed. Robert A. Orsi, pp. 310–340. Bloomington: Indiana University Press.

Singer, Audrey, Susan W. Hardwick, and Caroline B. Brettell, eds. 2008. *Twenty-First Century Gateways: Immigrant Incorporation in Suburban America.* Washington, DC: Brookings Institution Press.

UN-HABITAT. 2008. State of the World's Cities, 2008/2009: Harmonious Cities. London and Sterling, VA: Earthscan (for and on behalf of the United Nations Human Settlements Programme)

Werbner, Pnina. 1990. *The Migration Process: Capital, Gifts, and Offerings among British Pakistanis.* New York: Berg Publishers.

White, Jenny B. 1997. Belonging to a Place: Turks in Unified Berlin. *City and Society, Annual Review, 1996*:15–28.

PART 5

Globalization and Transnationalism

British sociologist Anthony Giddens defines globalization as "the intensification of worldwide social relations which link distant localities in such a way that local happenings are shaped by events occurring many miles away and vice versa" (1999:64). To some extent, this has been happening since the earliest stages of human societies. Certainly, ancient and medieval societies were affected by trade, migration, and conquest, which extended over thousands of miles. Marco Polo, a Venetian merchant who wrote an account of his travels to the realms of Kublai Khan in the thirteenth century, and Ibn Battuta, a North African Muslim who wrote of his sojourns in India and in Africa south of the Sahara, are just two examples of explorers who participated in an earlier "world system" that extended through much of the Eastern Hemisphere. Since the time of Columbus such processes of "globalization" have accelerated.

Many who write about globalization emphasize political and economic processes, but contact between peoples involves all aspects of life. Diseases, for instance, whether the "Black Death," syphilis, influenza, or AIDS, have spread through the world. Religious ideologies, including varieties of Buddhism, Christianity, Hinduism, and Islam, also have diffused across the continents. Artistic ideas, architectural styles, and musical genres have gone global. Furthermore, in sports, the NBA has increasingly been transformed into an "international" basketball association as it tries to compete with soccer, long the dominant global sport.

Cities have always been involved in trade and migration that go beyond the immediate locality to other places. In Part 4, we considered how people move from countryside to city, from one urban area to another, from urban places to the provinces, or even among small settlements in the countryside. Economic and political developments, often originating in far-off lands, set such migrations in motion and push or pull people into cities. When we view cities in global terms, we focus on how urban life is influenced by distant developments, rather than on what is going on within the city itself. For example, the increased migration of Blacks to northern industrial cities in the United States during the twentieth century depended more on changes in cotton production in the Southeast than on opportunities in the North.

The chapters in Part 5 focus on long-distance, transnational interrelationships within an increasingly global system. Nancy Foner sets the stage for the other chapters by providing a historical perspective on globalization and transnationalism. Focusing on immigration to New York City around 1900 and again in 2000, she argues that we should not lose sight of the continuities between past and present. She also shows how our twenty-first-century global "village" depends on new transportation technologies and instant communications. She highlights the growing importance of dual citizenship, cultural pluralism, religious conflicts, and social diversity as products of modernity, while pointing out the countervailing unity created by the global spread of the Beatles, Coca-Cola, IBM, the Internet, McDonald's, Sony, Toyota, and Wal-Mart.

Following Foner's general orientation to New York, Ann Miles provides a case study of an Ecuadorian migrant who makes his way there, but struggles to sustain his connections with his family back home. Meanwhile, his family fears that he will abandon them for the attractions of America. The migrant's story remains incomplete, and closure is not certain. In a similar manner, Dianna Shandy draws on her field experiences in Ethiopia and the United States to describe the role of remittances in transnational relationships between migrants' and refugees' communities of origin and destination. By following the money, Shandy offers insights on how international population movements are so embedded in complex social relationships that they are not easily broken. Karen Leonard's chapter on Hyderabad, India, and its migrants in the United States demonstrates yet another dimension of transnational migration—the extent to which those who are "left behind" often endure disruptions in their lives as profound as those encountered by their kin who have emigrated.

Part 5, and this volume, comes to a close by looking forward to the possibilities of urban life in the twenty-first century. Walter Zenner serves as our guide to a future in which "rural" and "urban" may cease to be meaningful distinctions and the "old urbanism" promulgated by Louis Wirth gives way to a "new urbanism." Zenner suggests that contemporary China—and we might add India to the mix—provides the critical global example for how global economic participation is linked to internal transformations in the relations between villages, towns, cities, and metropolitan areas in developing countries. Watching China and India—the world's two most populous nation-states—being transformed during our lifetime will not be a spectator sport. Even living on the other side of the globe, we are learning that small tears in the social fabric of these countries can have serious repercussions on North America, Europe, Latin America, Africa, and the Middle East. As a result, we all need to be aware of the lessons learned by urban anthropologists over the past half-century. Only by paying attention to what happens in cities and their hinterlands around the globe can we learn to live together in our own urban places.

References

Giddens, Anthony. 1999. *Runaway World: How Globalization Is Reshaping Our Lives.* New York: Routledge.

Readings in Part 5

25. *Transnationalism, Old and New: New York Immigrants,* by Nancy Foner

26. *From Cuenca, Ecuador, to New York, U.S.A.: Families and Transnational Lives,* by Ann Miles

27. *Global Transactions: Sudanese Refugees Sending Money Home,* by Dianna J. Shandy

28. *Hyderabad: Continuities and Transformations,* by Karen Isaksen Leonard

29. *Beyond Urban and Rural: Communities in the 21st Century,* by Walter P. Zenner

25

Transnationalism, Old and New
New York Immigrants

Nancy Foner

While transnational immigration has been a "hot topic" among anthropologists and other social scientists since the 1990s, Nancy Foner argues in this chapter that it is not a new phenomenon. Examining waves of immigration to New York City, Foner finds that those who arrived during the early years of the twentieth century often maintained connections to their homelands and traveled back and forth as they were able. Even so, changes in technology, communication, and modes of transportation mean that twenty-first-century immigrants have many more options for staying in touch with their communities of origin. In addition, Foner points out that the increasing globalization of business and industry has opened up spaces in which cross-border connections become positive assets for the immigrants and for their places of origin and destination.

Transnationalism is not new, even though it often seems as if it were invented yesterday. Contemporary immigrant New Yorkers are not the first newcomers to live what scholars now call transnational lives. While there are many new dynamics to immigrants' transnational connections and practices today, there are also significant parallels with the past.

When scholars began to write about transnationalism in the 1990s, it was often treated as a contemporary phenomenon; a common assumption was that earlier European immigration could not be described in the transnational terms that apply today. By now, despite general agreement that transnationalism is not completely new, there has not been much exploration of exactly what this means (for a notable exception, see Morawska 2001). Transnationalism refers to the processes by which immigrants "forge and sustain multi-stranded social relations that link together their societies of origin and settlement." In a transnational perspective, contemporary immigrants are seen as

Source: This is a revised and updated version of "What's New About Transnationalism: New York Immigrants Today and at the Turn of the Century," *Diaspora* (Winter 1997) Volume 6: 355–376.

maintaining familial, economic, political, and cultural ties across international borders, in effect making the home and host society a single arena of social action (Basch et al. 1994:7).

This chapter offers a closer look at transnationalism past and present. By narrowing the field of analysis to one context—New York City—and comparing contemporary immigration with one period—the turn of the twentieth century—we can begin to specify the kinds of relationships that immigrants have established and maintained with their home societies in different eras. Many transnational patterns, as it turns out, have a long history—and some of the sources of transnationalism sometimes seen as unique today also operated in the past. At the same time, much is distinctive about transnationalism today, not only because earlier patterns have been intensified or become more common but because new processes and dynamics are involved.

This comparison of transnationalism then and now focuses on the two peak periods in New York City's immigration history. Between 1880 and 1920, over one million immigrants arrived and settled in New York City—so that by 1910, fully 41 percent of all New Yorkers were foreign-born. In studies of this earlier era, the focus is on Eastern European Jews and Italians; they were the vast bulk of the new arrivals at the time and defined what was then thought of as the "new immigration." Today, no two groups predominate in this way, and New York's immigrants now include sizable numbers from a variety of Asian, West Indian, and Latin American nations and European countries as well. For this reason, the discussion of the present draws on material on a larger number of groups. Since the 1960s, millions of immigrants have moved to New York City. By 2006, New York was home to a little over three million immigrants, who represented 37 percent of the city's population.

CONTINUITIES BETWEEN PAST AND PRESENT

Like contemporary immigrants, Russian Jews and Italians in New York at the turn of the twentieth century established and sustained links to their home societies at the same time as they developed ties and connections in their new land. They did so for many of the same reasons that have been advanced to explain transnationalism today. There were relatives left behind and ties of sentiment to home communities and countries. Many immigrants came to America with the notion that they would eventually return. If, as one anthropologist notes, labor-exporting nations now acknowledge "that members of their diaspora communities are resources that should not and need not be lost to the home country" (Pessar 1995:76), this was also true, for example, of the Italian government in the past. Moreover, lack of economic security and full acceptance in America plagued immigrants a century ago, too, and may have fostered their continued involvement in and allegiance to their home societies.

Russian Jews and Italian immigrants in New York's past, like their modern-day counterparts, continued to be engaged with those they left behind.

What social scientists now call "transnational households," with members scattered across borders, were not uncommon a century ago. Most Italian men—from 1870 to 1910 nearly 80 percent of Italian immigrants were men—left behind wives, children, and parents; Jewish men, too, were often pioneers who later sent money to pay for the passage of other family members. Those who came to New York sent letters to relatives and friends in the Old World—and significant amounts of money. Jake, the young Jewish immigrant in Cahan's *Yekl and Other Stories of Yiddish New York*, was following a common pattern when he regularly sent money to his wife in Russia. Whenever he got a letter from his wife, Jake held onto his reply "until he had spare United States money enough to convert to ten rubles, and then he would betake himself to the draft office and have the amount, together with the well-crumpled epistle, forwarded to Poveodye" (1970[1896]:27). Gino Speranza, Secretary of the Society for the Protection of Italian Immigrants in the first decade of the twentieth century, claimed that "it was quite probable that 'Little Italy' in New York contributes more to the tax roll of Italy than some of the poorer provinces in Sicily or Calabria" (1974[1906]:309).

Putting away money in New York to buy land or houses in the home country is another long-term habit among immigrants who intend to return. In the last great wave, Italian immigrants were most likely to invest in projects back home. "He who crosses the ocean can buy a house," was a popular refrain celebrating one goal of emigration (Cinel 1982:71). It was not unusual for Italians in New York to send funds home with instructions about land purchases. An Italian told of his five years of backbreaking construction work in New York. Each day, he recalled, "I dreamed of the land I would one day buy with my savings. Land anywhere else has no value to me" (Wyman 1993:130).

Many did not just dream of going back—they actually did. Nationwide, return migration rates have been actually lower in recent years than they were in the past. In the first two decades of the twentieth century, for every 100 immigrants who entered the country 36 left; between 1971 and 1990, for every 100 immigrants who entered 23 left. Return migration, as anthropologist Nina Glick Schiller observes, should be viewed as part of a broader pattern of transnational connection. Those who have come to America with the notion of going back truly have their "feet in two societies." To organize return, Glick Schiller (1996) argues, necessitates the maintenance of home ties. And plans to return entail a continuing commitment to the norms, values, and aspirations of the home society.

Russian Jews in New York a hundred years ago were unusual for their time in the degree to which they were permanent settlers. Because they left behind political repression and virulent anti-Semitism, the vast majority came to the New World to stay. Even then, there was more return migration than is generally assumed. Between 1880 and 1900, perhaps as many as 15 to 20 percent who came to the United States returned to Europe. Many Russian Jewish migrants just planned to return temporarily in order to visit their old hometowns, although "not a few turned out to be one-way visits." Some had aged relatives whom they longed to see; others sought brides, there being a shortage of Jewish women in America; still others went home merely to show off, to demonstrate that they had somehow made good; and in a few cases immigrants returned home to study or to establish businesses (Sarna 1981).

After 1900, however, events in Russia led immigrants in New York to abandon the notion of return. With revolutionary upheaval and the increasing intensity of pogroms, the return migration rate among Russian Jews fell off, going down to about 5 percent. In the post-1900 period there were also few repeat crossers. Of the total number of Jews who entered the United States between 1899 and 1910, only 2 percent had been in the country before, the lowest rate of any immigrant group in the United States in this period.

Many more Italians came with the expectation of returning home. Italians were the quintessential transnational New Yorkers of their time, as much commuters as many contemporary immigrants. Many were "birds of passage" who went back to their villages seasonally. By the end of the nineteenth century, steamships were bigger, faster and safer than before; tickets for the sixteen- or seventeen-day passage in steerage from Naples to New York cost $15 in 1880 and $25 in 1907 and could be paid for in installments. Overall, between the 1880s and World War I, of every 10 Italians who left for the United States, five returned. Many of these returnees—*ritornati* as the Italians called them—remigrated to the United States. According to reports of the United States Immigration Commission, about 15 percent of all Italian immigrants between 1899 and 1910 had been in the United States before.

If economic insecurity, both at home and abroad, now leads many migrants to hedge their bets by participating in two economies, it was also a factor motivating Italians to travel back and forth across the Atlantic. The work Italian men found in New York's docks and construction sites was physically strenuous and often dangerous: the pay was low and the hours long, and the seasonal nature of the building trades meant that laborers had many weeks without work at all. During economic downturns, work was scarcer and, not surprisingly, Italian rates of return went up during the financial depression of 1894 and the panic years of 1904 and 1907. Many Jews in the late nineteenth century, according to historian Jonathan Sarna, returned to Russia because they could not find decent work in America—due to "the boom-bust cycle, the miserable working conditions, the loneliness, the insecurity" (Sarna 1981:266).

Lack of acceptance in America then, as now, probably contributed to a desire to return. Certainly, it fostered a continued identification with the home country or, in the case of Jews, a sense of belonging to a large diaspora population. Because most current immigrants are people of color, it is argued that modern-day racism is an important underpinning of transnationalism; nonwhite immigrants, denied full acceptance in America, maintain and build home ties to have a place they feel they can call home. Unfortunately, rejection of immigrants on the grounds of race has a long history. At the turn of the twentieth century, the white population was seen as divided into many sharply distinguishable races. In the days before "white ethnics," Italians and Jews were thought of as racially distinct in physiognomy, intelligence, and character.[1] Many Americans recoiled in horror from eastern and southern Europeans who were thought to belong to inferior "mongrel" races that were polluting the country's Anglo-Saxon or Nordic stock. In fact, negative images of Italians partly fastened on their darker appearance; many Americans doubted that Italians were white, calling them "swarthy" or referring, like sociologist E. R. Ross, to "the Italian dusk."

Whether because they felt marginalized and insecure in America or maintained ethnic allegiances for other reasons, Italians and Jews then, like many immigrants today, avidly followed news of and remained actively involved in home-country politics. As the historian Matthew Jacobson puts it in his study of "the diasporic imagination" of Irish, Polish, and Jewish immigrants, the homelands did not lose their centrality in "migrants' ideological geographies." Life in the diaspora, he writes, remained in many ways oriented to the politics of the old center. While the immigrant press was a force for Americanization, equally striking, Jacobson says,

> is the tenacity with which many of these journals positioned their readers within the envisaged "nation" and its worldwide diaspora. . . . In its front-page devotion to Old World news, in its focus upon the ethnic enclave as the locus of U.S. news, in its regular features on the groups' history and literature, in its ethnocentric frame on American affairs, the immigrant journal located the reader in an ideological universe whose very center was Poland, Ireland, or Zion. (1995:2, 62)

New York immigrants have also long been tapped by home-country politicians and political parties as a source of financial support. Today, Caribbean politicians regularly come to New York to campaign and raise money; in the past, Irish nationalist politicians made similar pilgrimages to the city. Irish immigrants, who arrived in large numbers in the mid-1800s, were deeply involved in the Irish nationalist cause in the early decades of the twentieth century. In 1918, the Friends of Irish Freedom sponsored a rally in Madison Square Garden attended by 15,000 people, and street orators for Irish freedom spoke "every night of the week" in Irish neighborhoods around the city. In 1920, Eamon de Valera traveled to New York seeking support for Sinn Fein and an independent Irish Republic, where he raised $10 million for his cause.

Moreover, homeland governments a hundred years ago were involved with their citizens abroad. The enormous exodus to America and the return wave brought a reaction from the Italian government, which, like many immigrant-sending states today, was concerned about the treatment of its dispersed populations—and also saw them as a global resource. The Italian government offered subsidies to a number of organizations in America that provided social services to Italian immigrants and set up an emigration office on Ellis Island to provide the newly arrived with information on employment opportunities in the United States. In 1901, the Italian government passed a

A familiar sight to immigrants old and new.

law empowering the Banco di Napoli to open branches or deputize intermediaries overseas to receive emigrant savings that could be used for Italian development. Beyond wanting to ensure the flow of remittances and savings homeward, Italy tried to retain the loyalty of emigrants overseas as part of its own nation-building project. A 1913 law addressed the citizenship issue: returnees who had taken foreign citizenship could regain Italian citizenship simply by living two years in Italy; their children were considered Italian citizens even if born elsewhere. There was even discussion in Italy of allowing the communities abroad to have political representation in Italy.

TRANSNATIONALISM: WHAT'S NEW

Clearly, transnationalism was alive and well a hundred years ago. But if there are continuities with the past, there is also much that is new. Advances in transportation and communications technologies have made it possible for immigrants to maintain more frequent, immediate, and closer contact with their home societies and have changed the very nature of transnational connections. Today's global economy encourages international business operations; the large number of professional and prosperous immigrants in contemporary America are well-positioned to operate in a transnational field. Dual nationality provisions by homeland governments have, in conjunction with other changes, added new dimensions to and altered the scope and thrust of transnational political involvements. Moreover, greater tolerance for ethnic pluralism and multiculturalism in late twentieth-century America, and changed perspectives of immigration scholars themselves, have put transnational connections in a new, more positive, light.

Transformations in communication channels and transportation systems have made an enormous difference. They have increased the density, multiplicity, and importance of transnational interconnections and made it possible for the first time for immigrants to operate more or less simultaneously in a variety of places. A century ago, the trip back to Italy took about two weeks, and more than a month elapsed between sending a letter home and receiving a reply. Today, immigrants can hop on a plane or make a phone call to check out how things are going at home. As Patricia Pessar (1995:69) observes for New York Dominicans: "It merely requires a walk to the corner newsstand, a flick of the radio or television dial to a Spanish-language station, or the placement of an overseas call" to learn about news in the Dominican Republic.

In the jet plane age, relatively inexpensive air fares mean that immigrants, especially from nearby places in the Caribbean and Central America, can fly home for emergencies (like funerals) or celebrations (like weddings), go back to visit friends and relatives, and sometimes move back and forth, in the manner of commuters, between New York and their home community. Among the immigrant workers I studied a number of years ago in a New York nursing home, some routinely spent their annual vacation in their home community in the Caribbean; others visited every few years. A study of New York's Asian Indians notes that despite the distance and cost, they usually take their families back to visit India every year or two. Inexpensive air travel means that relatives from home also often come to New York to visit. In the warmer months, Lessinger (1995:42) reports, when relatives from India make return visits to the United States, "a family's young men are often assigned to what is laughingly called 'airport duty,' going repeatedly to greet the flights of arriving grandparents, aunts and uncles, cousins and family friends." Thanks to modern communications and air travel, a group of Mexicans in New York involved in raising money to improve their home community's water supply were able to conduct meetings with the *municipio* via conference call and to fly back to the community for the weekend to confer with contractors and authorities when they learned the new tubing had been delivered (Smith 1998).

Now that telephones reach into the far corners of most sending societies—and cell phones are ubiquitous and prepaid phone cards cheap—immigrants can hear about news and people from home right away and participate immediately in family discussions on major decisions. Cristina Szanton Blanc describes how a Filipino couple in New York maintained a key role in childrearing decisions although several of their children remained in Manila. On the phone, they could give advice and orders and respond to day-to-day problems. When their only daughter in Manila had an unfortunate romance, they dispatched a friend visiting the Philippines to investigate the situation. Adela, the mother of the family, had herself been back to visit the Philippines three times in six years (Basch et al. 1994:237). In the Jamaican village studied by Horst (2006), almost everyone she knew had a cell phone in 2004, making it possible to speak on the phone with friends and family in the United States to keep them abreast of the latest news, make requests and ask advice, or simply to receive encouragement, like one 14-year-old who called her mother in New York for reassurance before her examinations. Maxine Margolis offers an illustration of how readily Brazilians call home: "When I was in a home furnishing store in Manhattan and asked the Brazilian owner, a longtime resident of New York City, how to say 'wine rack' in Portuguese, he was disturbed when he could not recall the phrase. As quickly as one might consult a dictionary, he dialed Brazil to ask a friend" (1998:115).

In addition to low-cost phone calls, there are other new types of communication such as faxes, videotapes, e-mail, and videoconferencing. Some Brazilians in New York in the 1990s, Margolis tells us, regularly recorded or videotaped 60- to 90-minute messages to send family and friends back home. Like other immigrant New Yorkers, they could participate vicariously, through videotape, in important family events. Lessinger recounts how Indians in Queens gathered to watch full-length videos of weddings of widely-scattered relatives, able to admire the dress and jewelry of the bride and calculate the value of pictured wedding gifts (see Foner 2000:178). Peggy Levitt (2003:177) describes how migrants in Boston from the Dominican village of Miraflores could visit the Web site, Miraflores.com, to find out the weather back home and view photos of the funeral home, baseball stadium, and health clinic funded by the Miraflores Development Committee. In spring 2004, it became possible for Dominican New Yorkers in Washington Heights to communicate with relatives back home through videoconferencing that then cost between $1 and $3 per minute, depending on the size of the room, time of day, and length of the videoconference.

Modern forms of transportation and communications, in combination with new international forms of economic activity in the new global economy, have meant that more immigrants today are involved in economic endeavors that span national borders. Certainly, it is much easier today than a hundred years ago for immigrants to manage businesses thousands of miles away given, among other things, modern telecommunications, information technologies, and instantaneous money transfers. Sociologists have described how many Dominican entrepreneurs in New York have built a base of property, bank accounts, and business contacts there and then make regular trips to the Dominican Republic to exploit economic opportunities in both places (Portes 1996). A few years after a Dominican man Patricia Pessar (1995) knew bought a garment factory in New York, he expanded his operations by purchasing (with his father and brother) a garment factory in the Dominican Republic's export processing zone. While he and his wife and children continued to live in New York, where he had become a U.S. citizen, he also had built a large house in the Dominican Republic.

Many Asian Indian New Yorkers, encouraged by the Indian government's attempt to capture immigrant capital for development, have invested in profit-making ventures in India, including buying urban real estate and constructing factories, for-profit hospitals, and medical centers. Often, relatives in India provide on-the-spot help in managing the business there. After receiving a graduate degree in engineering in the United States, Dr. Vadivelu founded a factory in New Jersey that makes electrolytic capacitors. He later opened two factories in his home state of Andhra Pradesh, making ceramic capacitors for sale to Indian electronics manufacturers. His father and brothers managed both plants on a daily basis; Dr. Vadivelu traveled back and forth several times a year to check on the factories (Lessinger 1995:91).

The Indian example points to something else that's new about transnationalism today. Compared to the past, a much higher proportion of newcomers today come with advanced education, professional skills, and sometimes substantial amounts of financial capital that facilitate transnational connections—and allow some immigrants to participate, in the manner of modern-day cosmopolitans, in high-level institutions and enterprises here and in their home society. The affluence of Indian New Yorkers, Lessinger argues, makes them one of the most consistently transnational immigrants in behavior and outlook. Indeed, *within* the Asian Indian community, it is the wealthiest and most successful professionals and business people who maintain the closest links with India and for whom "extensive transnationalism is a way of life." They are the ones able to afford many phone calls, to invest in India, to frequently fly home where they mix business with pleasure, and have "a certain influence and standing wherever they go" (Lessinger 1995:88–89). The Chinese "astronauts" who shuttle back and forth by air between Taiwan or Hong Kong and America are typically well-educated and well-off professionals, executives, and entrepreneurs who move easily in financial, scientific, and business worlds around the globe. Pyong Gap Min describes international commuter marriages involving high-level Korean professionals and business executives who have returned to Korea for better jobs while their wives and children remain in New York for educational opportunities. The couples talk on the phone several times a week; the husbands fly to New York two to five times a year, while the wives visit Korea once or twice a year (Min 1998).

When it comes to transnational political involvements, here, too, technological advances play a role. The newest New Yorkers can hop on a plane to vote in national elections in their home countries, as thousands did in a Dominican presidential election in the 1990s, although, since 2004, such trips are unnecessary since migrants can now vote in Dominican presidential elections from polling places in New York City. Politicians from home, in turn, can make quick trips to New York to campaign and raise funds. On one weekend in the 1990s, for example, the opposition leader from St. Vincent, the mayor of Georgetown, Guyana, and the chiefs of state from Antigua and Barbados were all in New York visiting constituents (Basch 2001). Candidates for U.S. electoral positions have been known to return to their country of origin for the same reason. Guillermo Linares, for example, briefly visited the Dominican Republic during his 1991 campaign for New York's City Council, where rallies held in support of his candidacy generated campaign funds and afforded opportunities for photos that were featured in New York newspapers.

Apart from technological advances, there are other new aspects to transnational political practices today. While Russian Jews brought with them a notion of belonging to a broader Jewish diaspora community, they had no interest in being part of the oppressive Russian state they left behind. Italians, coming from a country in the midst of nation-state consolidation, did not arrive with a modern "national identity." Except for a tiny group of political exiles, migrants did not care much about building an Italian state that "would welcome them back, protect them from the need to migrate further, or represent the character and glories of the Italian people" (Gabaccia 1998). Among other groups in the past, like the Irish, migration became part of their continuing struggle for national liberation. What is different now is that immigrants are arriving from sovereign countries, with established nationalist ideologies and institutions, and are a potential basis of support for government projects, policies, and leaders in the homeland. Today, some homeland states are redefining their territories to include emigrants living outside them, owing, it has been argued, to the desire to ensure the continuous flow of remittances, the dynamics of competitive party politics in the home country, and the attempt to gather financial and political support among conationals abroad. In the 1990s, then-president Aristide of Haiti popularized the notion of overseas Haitians as the Tenth Department in a country that is politically divided into nine departments or states, and he set up a Ministry of Haitians Living Abroad within the Haitian Cabinet (Glick Schiller and Fouron 1998). Of enormous importance are the dual nationality provisions that now cover a growing number of New York's immigrants. Although the United States naturalization oath requires renunciation of other citizenships, increasingly U.S. law has "evolved in the direction of increased ambiguity or outright tolerance in favor of dual nationality"—what Michael Jones-Correa calls a "don't ask, don't tell" policy (2001:1021). What is striking is the growing number of states of origin that permit their citizens to retain nationality despite naturalization elsewhere. As of December 1996, seven of the 10 largest immigrant groups in New York City had the right to be dual nationals. Since 1998 legislation in Mexico, Mexican Americans, one of the fastest growing immigrant groups in the city, are allowed to hold Mexican nationality as well as U.S. citizenship.

A powerful economic incentive is involved in the recognition of dual nationality by various sending countries. Above all, there is the desire to ensure the flow of money and business investment homeward. According to the Inter-American Development Bank, migrants in the United States sent back a whopping $31 billion to Latin America and the Caribbean in 2003. In 2000, remittances from abroad comprised more than 10 percent of the gross domestic product of countries such as El Salvador, Haiti, Jamaica, and Nicaragua. Beyond remittances, immigrants trade with their home countries and bring in large quantities of tourist dollars (Levitt and Glick Schiller 2004).

While some scholars and public figures worry about the trend toward dual nationality—political scientist Samuel Huntington (2004) has called people with dual nationality "ampersands" with dubious loyalty to the United States—by and large transnational connections are viewed in a more favorable light today than they were in the past. Early in the twentieth century, return migration inflamed popular opinion. "Immigrants were expected to stay once they arrived," writes historian Walter Nugent. "To leave again implied that the migrant came only for money; was too crass to appreciate America as a noble experiment in democracy; and spurned American good will and helping hands" (1992:159). Another historian notes: "After 1907, there was tremendous hostility . . . toward temporary or return migrants. . . . The inference frequently drawn was that [they] considered the United States good enough to plunder but not to adopt" (Shumsky quoted in Nugent 1992:159).

At the time, a common concern was that the new arrivals were not making serious efforts to become citizens and real Americans. Schools, settlement houses, and progressive reformers put pressure on immigrants to abandon their old-fashioned customs and languages and become "one hundred percent American." A popular guide for immigrant Jews advised that to become American, "forget your past, your customs, and your ideals." The Americanization movement's "melting pot" pageants, inspired by Israel Zangwill's play, depicted strangely attired foreigners stepping into a huge pot and emerging as immaculate, well-dressed, accent-free "American-looking" Americans. Expressions of ethnicity were suffocated in the schools where, in the words of New York City's Superintendent Maxwell, the goal was "to train the immigrant child . . . to become a good American citizen" (Brumberg 1986). Much of the scholarship concerning the earlier immigration emphasized how immigrants were assimilating and becoming American; ties to the home society were often interpreted as "evidence for, or against, Americanization" and, in many accounts, were seen as impeding the assimilation process.

Today, when there is an official commitment to cultural pluralism and cultural diversity, transnational ties are more visible and acceptable—and sometimes even celebrated in public settings. Anti-immigrant sentiment is still very much with us, and immigrant loyalties still often questioned, but rates of return are not, as in the past, a key part of immigration debates. In an era of significant international money flows, and when American corporations have huge operations abroad, there is also less concern that immigrants are looting the United States by sending remittances home. Increasingly today, the message is that there is nothing un-American about expressing one's ethnicity and having a strong ethnic identity. In New York, officials and social service agencies actively promote festivals and events to foster ethnic pride and glorify the city's multiethnic character. Practically every ethnic group has its own festival or parade, the largest being the West Indian American Day parade on Brooklyn's Eastern Parkway, which attracts between one and two million people every Labor Day. Exhibits in local museums and libraries highlight the cultural background of different immigrant groups; special school events feature the foods, music, and costumes of various homelands; and school curricula include material on different ethnic heritages. In the quest for votes, established New York politicians of all stripes recognize the value of visits to immigrant homelands. The Dominican Republic—the ancestral home for more than 600,000 New Yorkers—has become a required stop for aspiring (or sitting) city mayors. In the summer of 2003, Mayor Bloomberg had already visited the Dominican Republic three times since being elected two years before. This kind of campaigning across borders adds further legitimacy to transnational connections.

Scholars are now more interested in transnational ties and see them in a more positive way than in the past. In a transnational perspective, the maintenance of multiple identities and loyalties is seen as a normal feature of immigrant life; ties to the home society complement—rather than necessarily detract from—commitments in this country. At the same time as immigrants buy property, build houses, start businesses, make marriages, and influence political developments in their home societies, they are also shown to be deeply involved in building lives in New York where they buy homes, work on block associations and community boards, join unions, run school boards, and set up businesses. Generally, the literature stresses the way transnational relationships and connections benefit immigrants, enhancing the possibility of survival in places full of uncertainty. In an era when globalization is a major subject of scholarly study—and when international travel is easy and international communications instantaneous and inexpensive—it is perhaps not surprising that migrants' contacts with, and visits to, their home societies have, on the whole, excited little negative comment. "Today," journalist Roger Rosenblatt (1993) writes, "when every major business enterprise is international, when money is international, when instant international experiences are pictured on T.V., more people think of themselves as world citizens. Why should not immigrants do likewise?"

CONCLUSION

Obviously, there is much that is new about transnationalism. Modern technology, the new global economy and culture, and new laws and political arrangements have all combined to produce transnational connections that differ in fundamental ways from those maintained by immigrants a century ago. Once ignored or reviled, transnational ties are now a favorite conference topic and sometimes even celebrated in today's multicultural age. Yet, the novelty of contemporary conditions should not be exaggerated. Immigrants who move from one country to another seldom cut off ties and allegiances to those left behind, and immigrant New Yorkers a century ago were no exception. It may have been harder to maintain contacts across the ocean than it is today, but many immigrants in the last great wave maintained extensive, and intensive, transnational ties.

A comparison of transnationalism then and now raises some additional issues that need to be addressed. If academic observers who studied earlier immigrants were guilty of overlooking transnational ties in the quest to document assimilation, there is now a risk of overemphasizing the centrality of transnationalism and minimizing the extent to which contemporary immigrants "become American" and undergo changes in behavior and outlook in response to circumstances in this country. Indeed, as historian David Hollinger (1995:154) observes, today's immigrants "are more prepared for a measure of assimilation by the worldwide influence of American popular culture; most are more culturally attuned to the United States before they arrive here than were their counterparts a century ago."

Perhaps because studies using a transnational approach are in their infancy, we still know little about how extensive various transnational ties actually are for different groups or the many ways that transnationalism affects immigrants—from their family lives to their political involvements—and the communities in which they live. The new immigration, like the old, to quote Hollinger again, is behaviorally mixed. "It displays a variety of degrees of engagement with the United States and with prior homelands, and it yields some strong assimilationist impulses alongside vivid expressions of diasporic consciousness" (1995:153). In the past, Italian immigrants were more transnational in behavior and outlook than Russian Jews, mainly because Jews came to stay whereas large numbers of Italians were labor migrants who aimed to—and often did—go back home after a spell in New York. Today, as well, rates of participation in transnational activities (or for certain types of transnational activities) are also likely to vary by group—and we need research that explores and explains the differences.

There is also variation in the frequency, depth, and range of transnational ties within national origin groups. Just as better-off Asian Indian immigrants are more consistently transnational than their poorer counterparts, so, too, this may be true in other immigrant groups. Legal status is bound to affect the types and extent of transnational connections maintained. Whether migrants came on their own or with their families also must be considered. There are also sure to be differences in the nature and impact of transnational ties between men and women and between the old, young, and middle-aged. And transnational connections may well lose force with length of stay in America, as suggested by research showing that remittances tend to taper off over time.

What is clear is that the transnational practices of present-day immigrants are very much part of the modern scene and have far-reaching effects for the lives of immigrants as well as for the cities in which they settle. What this chapter has shown is that in trying to understand transnationalism among the latest arrivals it is useful to revisit the past to begin to sort out the continuities as well as contrasts between then and now. As historian David Kennedy has written, "The only way we can know with certainty as we move along time's path that we have come to a genuinely new place is to know something of where we have been" (1996:68). Transnationalism has been with us for a long time, and a comparison with the past allows us to assess just what is new about the patterns and processes involved in transnational ties today.

Note

[1] Historians use phrases like "not-yet-white ethnics" and "in-between peoples" to describe Italians' and Jews' ambiguous racial status, sometimes white, sometimes not (see, for example, Barrett and Roediger 1997 and Jacobson 1995, 1998; as well as Foner 2000 and 2005).

References

Barrett, James, and David Roediger. 1997. In Between Peoples: Race, Nationality, and the New Immigrant Working Class. *Journal of American Ethnic History,* 16:3–44.

Basch, Linda. 2001. Transnational Social Relations and the Politics of National Identity: An Eastern Caribbean Case Study. In *Islands in the City: West Indian Migration to New York*, ed. Nancy Foner, pp. 117–141. Berkeley: University of California Press.

Basch, Linda, Nina Glick Schiller, and Cristina Szanton Blanc. 1994. *Nations Unbound: Transnational Projects, Postcolonial Predicaments and Deterritorialized Nation-States*. Amsterdam: Gordon & Breach.

Brumberg, Stephan. 1986. *Going to America, Going to School: The Jewish Immigrant Public School Encounter in Turn-of-the-Century New York City*. New York: Praeger.

Cahan, Abraham. 1970[1896]. *Yekl and Other Stories of Yiddish New York*. New York: Dover.

Cinel, Dino. 1982. *From Italy to San Francisco: The Immigrant Experience*. Stanford: Stanford, CA University Press.

Foner, Nancy. 2000. *From Ellis Island to JFK: New York Immigrants, Then and Now*. New Haven: Yale University Press.

———. 2005. *In a New Land: A Comparative Perspective on Immigration*. New York: New York University Press.

Gabaccia, Donna. 1998. Italians and Their Diasporas: Cosmopolitans, Exiles, and Workers of the World. Paper presented at the conference States and Diasporas. Casa Italiana, Columbia University, May.

Glick Schiller, Nina. 1996. Who Are Those Guys? A Transnational Reading of the U.S. Immigrant Experience. Paper presented at Social Science Research Council conference, Becoming American/America Becoming: International Migration to the United States, Sanibel Island, Florida.

Glick Schiller, Nina, and Georges Fouron. 1998. Transnational Lives and National Identities: The Identity Politics of Haitian Immigrants. In *Transnationalism From Below*, eds. Michael P. Smith and Luis E. Guarnizo, pp. 130–161. New Brunswick, NJ: Transaction.

Hollinger, David. 1995. *Postethnic America*. New York: Basic Books.

Horst, Heather. 2006. The Blessings and Burdens of Communication: The Cell Phone in Jamaican Transnational Fields. *Global Networks*, 6:143–159.

Huntington, Samuel P. 2004. *Who Are We? The Challenges to America's National Identity*. New York: Simon and Schuster.

Jacobson, Matthew. 1995. *Special Sorrows*. Cambridge, MA: Harvard University Press.

———. 1998. *Whiteness of a Different Color*. Cambridge, MA: Harvard University Press.

Jones-Correa, Michael. 2001. Under Two Flags: Dual Nationality in Latin America and Its Consequences for the United States. *International Migration Review*, 35:997–1029.

Kennedy, David. 1996. Can We Still Afford to Be a Nation of Immigrants? *The Atlantic Monthly* (November):52–68.

Lessinger, Johanna. 1995. *From the Ganges to the Hudson*. Boston: Allyn & Bacon.

Levitt, Peggy. 2003. *The Transnational Villagers*. Berkeley: University of California Press.

Levitt, Peggy, and Nina Glick Schiller. 2004. Conceptualizing Simultaneity: A Transnational Social Field Perspective on Society. *International Migration Review*, 38:1002–1039.

Margolis, Maxine. 1998. *An Invisible Minority: Brazilians in New York City*. Boston: Allyn & Bacon.

Min, Pyong Gap. 1998. *Changes and Conflicts: Korean Immigrant Families in New York*. Boston: Allyn & Bacon.

Morawska, Eva. 2001. Immigrants, Transnationalism, and Ethnicization: A Comparison of This Great Wave and the Last. In *E Pluribus Unum? Contemporary and His-*

torical Perspectives on Immigrant Political Incorporation, eds. Gary Gerstle and John Mollenkopf, pp. 175–212. New York: Russell Sage Foundation.

Nugent, Walter. 1992. *Crossings: The Great Transatlantic Migrations, 1870–1914*. Bloomington: Indiana University Press.

Pessar, Patricia. 1995. *A Visa for a Dream*. Boston: Allyn & Bacon.

Portes, Alejandro. 1996. Global Villagers: The Rise of Transnational Communities. *The American Prospect* (March-April):74–78.

Rosenblatt, Roger. 1993. Sunset, Sunrise. *The New Republic* (December 27):20–23.

Sarna, Jonathan. 1981. The Myth of No Return: Jewish Return Migration to Eastern Europe, 1881–1914. *American Jewish History*, 71:256–268.

Smith, Robert. 1998. Transnational Localities: Community, Technology and the Politics of Membership within the Context of Mexico and U.S. Migration. In *Transnationalism From Below*, eds. Michael Peter Smith and Luis Eduardo Guarnizo, pp. 196–240. New Brunswick, NJ: Transaction.

Speranza, Gino C. 1974 [1906]. Political Representation of Italo-American Colonies in the Italian Parliament. In *The Italians: Social Backgrounds of an American Group*, eds. Francisco Cordasco and Eugene Bucchioni, pp. 309–310. Clifton, NJ: Augustus M. Kelley.

Wyman, Mark. 1993. *Round-Trip America: The Immigrants Return to Europe, 1880–1930*. Ithaca, NY: Cornell University Press.

26

From Cuenca, Ecuador, to New York, U.S.A.
Families and Transnational Lives

Ann Miles

Immigrants are often drawn to U.S. cities by dreams of financial security and a better life, not only for themselves but also for family members back home. Through the story of an Ecuadorian called "Vicente Quitasacas," Ann Miles illustrates the unexpected challenges that immigrants face and the questions of identity with which they struggle. Vicente works long hours at a steady job but strains to pay the debts he owes and so is rarely able to send much-needed money to the family in Ecuador. They, in turn, worry about him and fear that he will become so "American" that he will decide never to return home. For his part, Vicente is no longer sure where "home" is.

Transnational migration, which brings people across national borders to live and work, changes the economies and societies of both the places people leave and the places people go to. But, transnational migration is also about individual actors who make very difficult decisions to move far from home to try to make a "go" of it in another place. I explore here the global and local issues that promote emigration from Ecuador to the United States, focusing on one young man, Vicente Quitasacas (a pseudonym). Vicente is very ambivalent about leaving his home, but all the same, it seemed to him to be the best possible option. During the 1980s, his family moved from a rural town to Cuenca, the third largest city in Ecuador. His parents wished to better educate their children in the hopes that they could get ahead in life. That didn't happen. Vicente's decision to follow thousands of other Ecuadorians to New York is based on his own calculations of his future economic prospects,

Source: Adapted from *From Cuenca to Queens: An Anthropological Story of Transnational Migration* (Austin: University of Texas Press, 2004).

but it also involves understanding and working through the emotional dynamics of desire, fear, anger, sadness, elation, loss, regret, and resignation that occur when families are separated.

Most migrants leave for reasons that are both individual and familial. Moving to the United States signals a shift in social identity and status. U.S. migrants have money and cosmopolitan experiences that make them people of substance—at least among their peers back home. The U.S. is associated with modernity and money, powerful currencies in a country like Ecuador where "tradition" has long been a means for perpetuating social and economic hierarchies. When people are relegated to the margins of society, as the Quitasacas family has been, the seemingly endless opportunities for employment in the U.S. are very alluring. Vicente, the eldest son in the family, left to improve not only his own prospects but also those of his family. He felt a responsibility to help his siblings finish school, to ease his parents' worries about their old age, and to save enough to start a business so that someday he might be able to support a wife and children.

The Quitasacas live in a country that has faced a series of political and economic crises in the past decade that has left the nation politically unstable and economically crippled. Over the years, the buying power of many families has diminished to the point where, when I was doing fieldwork in 1999, the economy was so depressed that families were making difficult choices about what they could eat and still be able to send their kids to school. Strikes and protests rocked the country that year as the government suspended or reduced subsidies for rice, gasoline, and even health care. The Quitasacas also live in a city where access to basic opportunities is closely linked to family name and inherited connections. Because of their rural heritage and "Indian" name, they find themselves near the bottom of the social hierarchy, with few options for making a living. Although a certain hopelessness pervades their lives, they demonstrate a remarkable degree of resiliency. Family members make stinging critiques of the social, political, and economic conditions facing them, yet they also discuss the importance of having personal goals and working toward achieving something meaningful in their lives.

LOCAL AND TRANSNATIONAL CONTEXTS

Cuenca is a mid-size city (having grown from estimates of 180,000 to 300,000 people since 1988), yet it feels like a small town. The city is still most vibrant in its "central historical" district, an area of cobblestone streets, open-air markets, and colonial churches. Although I came to Cuenca to study rural-to-urban migration, I was not there long before I was convinced by local scholars in Cuenca to investigate transnational migration to the U.S. At the time, the rate of emigration from Cuenca was increasing rapidly and was interpreted as a serious social issue. I was intrigued by transnational migration because so many of the rural to urban families I was working with were like the Quitasacas; they already had relatives in New York.

Back in 1989, undocumented transnational migration from Ecuador was a topic not discussed easily or openly with strangers, especially North Americans. More than once I was asked if I was from the CIA or, from those better informed, the INS (Immigration and Naturalization Service). Sometimes during a conversation, my informant would suddenly become frightened, and I imagined that she feared she had said too much. If someone else stumbled on our conversation, we would invariably change the subject. The clandestine nature of so much of the process of transnational migration—from securing loans and purchasing counterfeit visas to living illegally in the United States—produced high levels of reticence and anxiety.

By 1993, everything had changed. Transnational migration was on the tip of every tongue, and everyone wanted to discuss it with me. In the intervening years, more dialogue, more research, and more media attention had become focused on the topic. Indeed, transnational migration had reached such a level of familiarity in the popular consciousness that it could even be lampooned. A local musical group was getting a lot of radio air-time with their song, *Cholo Boy*.[1] Blending musical genres, such as Ecuadorian folk music and New York style rap, the song poked fun at the stereotypes of materialism associated with transnational migration to the U.S. In an ironic twist, one of the band members was an American sociologist who was studying transnational migration. Ecuadorians came to understand that, despite rhetoric to the contrary and a few often-told-tales of failed border crossings, the U.S. government has made little effort to detain or deport Ecuadorians. In fact, like many other undocumented immigrant groups in New York, Ecuadorians move about freely in the city and congregate openly in city parks to celebrate Ecuadorian holidays with music, dancing, and roasted guinea pigs.

At the same time that illegal transnational migration was becoming increasingly common, the state of the Ecuadorian economy was worsening, which further exacerbated the flow of emigrants to the United States and European nations. Because most of this emigration is illegal, it is almost impossible to obtain accurate statistics on the numbers of Ecuadorians living elsewhere. Estimates are that anywhere from 400,000 to one million Ecuadorians are living abroad, mainly in Europe, Canada, Venezuela, and the United States. This constitutes as much as 10 percent of the Ecuadorian population. It is not uncommon to hear educated Ecuadorians call New York City the "third Ecuadorian City" (Astudillo and Cordero 1990). By 1999, when the Ecuadorian economy was in a shambles, the issue of emigration from the country was of acute national interest. Major newspapers from diverse regions of the country contained articles that speculated on the rates of emigration, what it meant for the future of Ecuador, and the conditions suffered by undocumented immigrants abroad.

When I asked members of the Quitasacas family why people were migrating, their first response invariably led to a commentary on the state of the Ecuadorian economy, and their second was an explanation of their perceived status within national and local society. "People like them" are leaving

Ecuador because there are no jobs, no way to make a living. As transnational migrants reshape the social and physical landscape of the city of Cuenca, multiple tensions and contradictions arise. Given the entrenched class system of Cuenca, transnational migrants imagine that their experiences in New York and their newly acquired consumption habits will be able to change their families from being poor to middle class, and themselves from cholos into cosmopolitans. At one time the Quitasacas thought that education would provide the key to the success of their children; now they believe that going to the United States may be only way to "do something" in life.

In the end, though, transnational migration is about much more than making a better living; it involves complex negotiations on the individual, familial, and community levels about what really matters. Among the questions that are openly debated among Ecuadorians are the following: Is a young adult male being a good (or bad) son if he migrates? Can children be raised properly without the presence of a father? Does a migrant offer less or more to his family than a man who doesn't migrate? How does a wife and mother who is thinking of migrating choose between her husband in the U.S. and her children in Ecuador? Does leaving mean that the migrant is giving up on Ecuador, or simply earning investment capital for the future? What does a man do with the money he makes? To whom is the migrant obligated? Whom can he trust? What constitutes a good life? How much money is enough money? What is real and what is only imagined about the migrant experience in the United States? Is the migrant a New Yorker or a Cuencano, an Ecuadorian or a Latino, a *cholo boy* or an *iony*?

CUENCA: THE ATHENS OF ECUADOR

Cuenca likes to call itself the "Athens of Ecuador" because of its temperate climate and its "rich" intellectual, architectural, and artistic history. While Guayaquil is thought of as being a bawdy port town and Quito a busy capital city, Cuenca cherishes its reputation for civility and "old world" (i.e., European) charm. Cuenca's downtown cobblestone streets play havoc with today's trucks and cars, but they are lovingly and painstakingly repaired rather than paved over. However, Cuenca has always been closely linked to the global marketplace, and its rural peasantry has a long history of adapting to changing local, national, and global circumstances. Because landholdings were generally small in this region and of relatively poor quality, the region's rural peasants have always found it necessary to supplement their agricultural income—often through seasonal labor in other areas or industries or through artisan production.

Mainly because of rural-to-urban migration, the city and its surrounding area have grown considerably, and its suburbs now extend deep into the countryside. Drawing rural and urban boundaries is almost impossible. Transnational migrants are sending remittances home to wives and parents who are building new homes on the borderlands of rural and urban—creating a unique kind of Ecuadorian urban sprawl where fancy two-story homes bump up against one-room adobe dwellings. Since the late 1990s, crime (or the perception of it) has increased; many people tell me that they no longer feel safe in Cuenca. Everyone has a story or two, true or not, of someone being robbed at gunpoint coming out of a bank or a courier agency.

Similar to many other places in Ecuador, Cuenca is deeply entrenched in a paternalistic tradition that emphasizes the importance of who you are and who you know. Everything—from registering children at a particular school to getting telephone service—is more easily accomplished through *palanca* (a lever). Members of the upper classes carry surnames that instantly bring respect, and have dense networks of individuals upon whom they can call for assistance. In contrast, those at the bottom of Cuencan society, including rural-to-urban migrants like the Quitasacas family, are relatively bereft of palanca. For poor people in Cuenca, establishing influential networks is elusive. When the Quitasacas family moved to Cuenca in the 1980s, they did so in order for the household head to have a steady job, so that the children would get a good education, and so that the family would eventually reach a comfortable standard of living. While the faltering economy certainly figures in their perceived failure to accomplish these goals, the embedded class structure of Cuencan society contributes to making the family feel impotent in their attempts to get ahead.

Transnational migration is one way of sidestepping the effects of a poor economy as well as the limitations imposed by a rigid social structure that impedes social mobility and relegates those without palanca to the margins. While the relative wealth and consumerism of transnational migrants and their families provides a jarring contrast to the elite image of Cuenca, it also provides a mechanism through which marginalized families can reconstruct their identities. While they indeed may never have the "right" name, skin tone, or social connections, migration offers access to some economic leverage. As migrants continue to leave or return home, send money and establish businesses, especially in these dire economic times, their effects on the economic landscape have a considerable cumulative effect. At a time when the national government and the municipality of Cuenca are literally bankrupt, the buying power of migrants cannot be dismissed. In 1999, while the local newspaper in Cuenca reported a virtual depression in the local and national economy, an extended Quitasacas family member, who has been in New York for 15 years, spent tens of thousands of dollars in Cuenca building a house and buying a new car.

The elites of Cuenca are often threatened by the new wealth of migrants, and they perceive migration only in the most negative terms. To the elites transnational migration is synonymous with crass consumerism and is portrayed as leading to rampant immorality and the destruction of traditional cultural values. They believe that migrants have traded family values and cultural continuity for purely material gain. While the elites use transnational migration to expose American capitalism, a prominent theme in Ecuadorian intellectual critiques of global inequality, migrants and their families are much more ambivalent. In contrast to this elite image, the Quitasacas family clearly values what money can buy, but they also worry about the costs to the family of Vicente's absence.

The other side of the elite interpretation of transnational migration that is often told in local media is the tale of the "failed migrant." These stories do have elements of truth, but in the end, they are parables rather than histories. The general theme of these stories is how a migrant, or his family, suffers immeasurable emotional and financial distress when plans fail to work out. In one scenario, the migrant fails to reach the goal of entering the United States and falls victim to unscrupulous *coyotes* (smugglers) along the way. Left penniless somewhere in Central America, the migrant is forced to borrow even more money from his already indebted relatives. One particularly sinister version of this story describes how the migrant is told before he leaves Cuenca to hide money in various places like toothpaste tubes or pant hems. He is then robbed every step of the way by thieves clearly informed ahead of time where the secret stashes of money are hidden. The toothpaste tubes are all taken in Nicaragua, the pant hems searched in Honduras, and so on until the migrant is left stranded and penniless in Mexico.

VICENTE'S STORY

I first encountered Vicente when doing my initial survey of neighborhoods in Cuenca. He was 14 years old at that time (in 1989)—although his small stature led me to think that he might be only 10. Growing up on the margins of Cuencan society was never easy for Vicente, and, for all of his apparent confidence at home, he was quite shy out on the street. He had no problems hopping onto city buses or going to the corner store, but he would get uncomfortable around those whom he categorized as upper class, or "millionaires." Vicente was acutely aware of how he was judged by those who considered themselves socially superior to him, and it was clearly a source of anxiety for him. He would be plagued by this anxiety throughout his teenage years. By early 1995, at almost 20 years old, he was finishing high school, although he was preoccupied with dreams of New York. By the end of that year, Vicente was living on Staten Island. From 1996 to 2000 we spoke a few times a year on the phone, when he would tell me about his job and his living conditions. He was always cheerful and, at least to me, he minimized any troubles that he was having. I learned more about the difficulties of his adjustment from his mother, when I visited her in Cuenca in 1997, than from Vicente himself.

In 1999, I visited Vicente on Staten Island prior to another trip to Ecuador and got a firsthand view of his life in New York. Vicente appeared to be happy and content with his life. In the summer of 2000, we met again to put his thoughts on tape. In the narrative that follows, Vicente seems sure of himself as a person, even though his life at that time was uncertain. His father might come in the upcoming year; he might not. Vicente was thinking of moving in with friends in Queens, but hadn't really decided yet. Next summer might see him doing landscaping upstate or he could still be working in the restaurant. He might save money, buy land, marry, and move back to Ecuador or he might spend the rest of his life in New York. He was like a river, he said; who knew where he would end up.

> I left Ecuador because other countries offer so much more economically. I left for money, because there is no money to be made in Ecuador like there is in this country. I left to help the family because we are not a family of great resources; we are a family of limited resources. We all leave to help out the family and to look for our futures. This is the goal that everyone has, to be able to do something for yourself and for the future. In our country, they don't let us. The government there, well, each one leaves us poorer than the one before. Therefore, if you want to look for good opportunities you have to leave your own country behind.
>
> There's work in Ecuador but it is really only for the people, well . . . the people who have more resources. They get good jobs. But for the people without those capacities, there is nothing. They just don't even give you a chance if you are not one of them. They don't give you any opportunities. And with the economy the way it is, with prices rising and with the Presidents changing all the time, the government is falling apart. Because of this, the jobs are scarce. They cut people from jobs all over. They might give you work for a month or two months, after that they cut you. It's very hard for a person to find a stable job.
>
> I really didn't have a hard time finding work here because I already knew people here. [My friend] Bolivar found me a job. Of course, for others that arrive here "a la aventura" [on an adventure], it is much more difficult. They have to find an apartment and work. For me it wasn't difficult at all. I took two days of rest and then started work as a busboy in a restaurant.
>
> When I first left I felt really sad. There's a lot to think about. First, you leave the family behind you, and you just don't know what is waiting for you in the other country. Second, you never know if you are going to arrive or not. You have to deal with immigration and you could get sent back; third, the money that you borrow—you worry whether you can pay it back and when. All of these troubles you think about while you are "on the road." This is what you think about when you leave your country. I was lucky, everything went really smoothly. I didn't have to wait long in Quito. The longer you wait there the more money it costs. I'm not sure why sometimes it goes quickly, and other times it doesn't.
>
> It cost $8,000 to come here and then I owed Bolivar another $1,000 in interest. It took about two and a half years to pay him back. And then it's been one thing or another. That's why I've only been able to send a little bit back to the family. It took more than two years to pay the loan and then I had the problems with the car, which was very expensive. Because of all of that, it's really hard to send money back.
>
> The thing that is hardest for me here is the language. I understand some and I want to learn more, but it's really hard for me. If you don't

speak English it's really hard to get a good job. I took English classes a while ago. It was on Saturdays for five hours. Every Saturday I would leave Staten Island for Manhattan where the classes were, and then back again to Staten Island. But I didn't really learn much. The English always stayed behind me on the ferry! I've bought some books that I read and sometimes I read the newspaper too. The words I don't know I look up in the dictionary. I might try to learn three or four words but in the end only one stays with me. I'm always listening, but I don't think I have much of a capacity for English.

The other thing that's hard here is the life, the working all the time. It's hard here to find good paying, stable work. But little by little it gets better. There are some people who have really good jobs. They work their eight hours and they get benefits, social security, medical. I work sometimes 15 hours, and sometimes I get paid very little and I have no benefits, no sick days, nothing. In some jobs you need to have the right papers to work but in restaurants you don't. I have a social security number, but well, it's not really mine.

I think about going back to Ecuador. I think that maybe I wouldn't really like it there now. I think that I may be too used to life here. I could go for a visit of two or three months, but then I would want to come back. I'm really used to the rhythm of life here—I get up, go to work, on my days off I go out here and there doing what I want to do. In Ecuador, well, it's all different. Perhaps one day I'll start a business there, but I really don't know.

I'm not so sure if I'll marry an Ecuadorian. No one knows really. Perhaps tomorrow I'll meet a paisano here or even someone else. There are lots of Cuencan women here. But, you know, the ones that come, well, they really change when they get here. I don't really like how they change. Their characters change and they only care about having a boyfriend who makes a lot of money. It's all about material things.

I don't think that I have really, really changed. I've always been a person who tries not to talk badly of others, who tries to get along with everyone and that hasn't changed. Well, maybe I've changed perhaps in some ways. I don't think that much about Ecuador like some others do. Maybe because I'm out here in Staten Island. Here I am with people from all over. At work it is pure Hispanics, but not ones from Ecuador. They are all from Mexico, Colombia, Guatemala, El Salvador. So, I don't talk about Ecuador as much as the others. I don't call Ecuador like I did before. I used to call every two weeks without fail. Now I'll call maybe once a month or so. You know, it's because time is so short and there's so much to do. On my days off, I go out and before I know it, it's time to go home and the next day I work. But, I still miss a lot of things from Ecuador. Mostly, I miss the family. I miss having my father and mother close by. It's the sentimental things of a person's life that I miss. I think about the girlfriends I had and didn't have [laughs]. But you know, you have to move on and struggle, and with the passage of time you begin to forget. Now I don't think about these things like I did before.

My life here is like that of all young men. I have two days a week off of work to rest, sometime less. The rest of the time I work 15 hours a day.

The days that I work I start at noon so in the morning I get up and go for a walk or a run, I might do some cleaning in the house, listen to some music. And then, I head out for work. I won't get home until one AM or so.

I work in a really big Italian restaurant. It's new, it's only been open about seven months. We can serve something like 150 people. There are three separate dining rooms. It's a very expensive place, it has only the best wines, it has a cigar list, cigarette list, it has a really big bar too. It's a place for people with lots of money. Most of them are Italian. They consume a lot; they spend a lot. The atmosphere is perfect. Most of us who work there started together and we are like a family. Before this one opened, I was in another restaurant and I had lots of problems there. There were lots of fights between the people who worked there. But since we've all started at this new place it's been different. [This new restaurant is owned by the same people as the old one where he worked.] We are the ones who opened this place so we have a special bond. So now it's the ones who start new who have to watch out for us old guys, those of us who opened it.

I like to help people. I try to explain how things work until they get used to it. I never like to yell at them about what they are doing, or tell them what is bad or good. Sometimes they [the other workers] just annoy someone because he is a good worker. I don't like that and I try to stop them. That's just not right to me. When I arrive every day, I say hello to everyone. If someone has done something that I don't like or if they were acting rude, I just say hello and nothing more. So everyone knows if I help someone I am doing it with good intentions, not to cause them trouble.

My feeling is that if you do good things now, later on you will harvest good fruits. If you do bad things, you will also get bad things. So, I try to be helpful to everyone. I think about my family, my brothers and sisters and I think that if I'm a bad person here, if I was someone who said rude things, did bad things, the ones who come after you, well they have to clean up after this. Perhaps I would never pay the price, but the rest who come after me, my brothers and sisters or perhaps even my children are going to pay one day, no? I want to be a good person for me and for them.

The restaurant has to be like a family, we spend so many hours all of us together. Most of my friends are from the restaurant. Some are younger than me and they have more free time and some have families they go home to every night. Sometimes on Fridays, if we've had a good night, we'll go out after work. We go to a bar, have a few drinks, sometimes we play pool. We spend a few hours like this, but we don't do it all the time, maybe just once a month or so. Most of them have wives and kids. There are no Ecuadorians around here [Staten Island], so I see them only occasionally on Sundays. Most of them live in Ossining. Then when we meet, we play volleyball or soccer and drink beer. I have to be careful because I can't drink too much, or the next day I feel bad. Those guys like beer too much. When we get together, we talk a lot about Ecuador. We talk about Cumbe; we recall this girl or that one, the fiestas we went to back when we were there. It's nice to sit around and talk about our memories with "paisanos." Of course with the guys at work it's completely different, we talk about what we are going to do.

The most important thing to have here [in the U.S.] is your health. If you are strong and healthy then you can work. Thank God, I have my health. That's the most important thing, because if you can't work, well, then things are impossible. The way I think about it is if you don't have your health you can't reach any of your other goals.

The person who I miss the most in Ecuador is my girlfriend. She's going to graduate from high school this year and then maybe go to the university. But, you know, as time passes you begin to forget about people. One more year and I don't think I'll be thinking about her anymore. Each year I think about her less and less. In the beginning it was really terrible, but it's not so bad anymore. I miss my friends from my high school. We would always go out every Saturday afternoon and play some sport out in the fresh air. Then we'd go back to someone's house and have a meal with their family. Sundays, too. It's the same where my grandparents live [in Cumbe]. On Saturdays and Sundays we get together, play sports, and eat at a different person's house. I really miss being able to leave on the weekends [and go] to the country where the air is fresh like it is in Ecuador. Here I don't have this; I can't visit the family on the weekends. There my time was free, but here I always have to think about work, either that day or the following day. My time is never free. And, I miss the festivals there, in Cuenca and in Cumbe. I miss the parades and the fireworks, things like that. We would always do things together as a family.

I like to remember back to my childhood. They say that to remember is to relive and that's true. We moved to Cuenca when I was about five. My parents were tailors when we first came to Cuenca, about 20 years or so ago. We lived from the time I was in kindergarten until fourth grade in Cuenca, and then returned to Cumbe for a while, for a year or so. We would still go to school in Cuenca and it was too hard to take transportation to school. So, we moved back to the city. Most of my life I lived in the city. When I was young, we lived in the center of town. This was a neighborhood where I had lots of friends. Every apartment nearby had someone. We moved there when I was 10 years old or so. On Friday afternoons, we would play soccer in the patio, all of us together. Saturday or Sundays we'd all go to a big park in the neighborhood of Miraflores up the hill from where we were renting. I'd go up there with all my friends, we'd go on bicycles. Well, my friends had bicycles anyway, but not all of them. Some had money, some didn't. They'd let me borrow their bikes. We did childish pranks—lit firecrackers, threw airplanes around, things like that. We'd play lots of games, especially soccer, running here and there with the ball. It was a really nice time in my life and one I like to think about. With the other kids in the neighborhood every weekend we'd go to a dance or a party.

Life got more difficult later. When you leave childhood and become a young person, things are more difficult. You leave behind the bicycles, the ball, all the toys, and you start thinking about girls. You start looking for girlfriends, first one and then the other. This was from about 16 years old or so. You spend a lot of time looking in the mirror and think about having the best clothes, best shoes and hair, to make a good impression on the girls. It's a difficult time if you don't have much, if you don't have the means to buy nice clothes and to go out. At school, we stopped talking about games and started talking about parties, about girls and which school they went to. It's all about girls. . . .

My future plans are that I want to do something. First, I need to think about having a home. Here I would need more papers to do something like that, so I am thinking it will be in Ecuador. I was thinking about working this whole next year just to buy something there. After I have this, then maybe I'll go there and look for a wife. And then return here again. But now we will be two. Right now, I'm still young and I know with two of us we'd be able to do more. It wouldn't be just me. It's not my goal to have a child right away. What I mean is, if I marry I don't want to have kids right away. If she likes it, we'll stay here, but if she doesn't like it we can work two or three years more and we can go back there and live a stable life. I'm thinking of starting a business, a clothing boutique or something like that. But, first I want to buy a piece of land. Right now, I've got to pay back the debts I have. Perhaps by next year I'll be able to send everything I earn there so I can buy the land. This is my goal. When I have a bit more I'll go there and see how things are, see if my future is there. If not, well, no one knows.

I have to save money first. I owed money on the other car when it crashed and now this replacement car cost me $3,800. So, right now, with what I owe Bolivar, I have only $200 in the bank, and I can't touch that or they'll close my account. Really, I'm broke. That's what I told the family. I am completely broke. I've had to spend money all over the place, and now I have nothing. I have to have a car because of where I work. Two years ago, I was robbed when I left work. I was in the subway around 12:30 AM with three or four "paisanos" [here he means people from work] in the car with me. They all got out at one stop, leaving me there by myself when three black guys got on. They were boys really. I was sitting there reading a magazine and I didn't think they were going to come after me. I didn't have any money. Well I did, but not that much, $20 or $30. I was the only one in the car so they came up to me and asked for my money and they wouldn't leave me be. I don't know if I thought I was a superman or something but I guess because they were so young, I mean they were big but still just kids 14 or 15 years old, I didn't think they'd do anything. Then they assaulted me. They beat me up pretty bad. They left me with a swollen eye and well, it was awful. At the next stop, the doors opened, but no one came on; they went to another car when they saw these guys beating me up. No one wanted problems I guess.

Luckily, at the next stop when the doors opened, I got out and they stayed on. In the end, they didn't even rob me. My wallet was really well hidden inside my jacket. They beat me up because they thought I didn't have anything. Here, if you don't have money, they beat you up, and if you do have money, they beat you up anyway. You can get beat up for both those things. They said that they were beating me up so that the next time I would carry money. This is life in New York at night. I went into a bar outside the station and asked for some ice and I called a taxi to take me home. After that, I bought a means of transportation. I work really long hours and it's hard to get a bus at that time. It was really serious, they kicked me and both my eyes and ear were really swollen. I couldn't work for awhile.

Here you don't know if people are American-American or if they come from somewhere else. . . . Italy, Austria, who knows? Everyone is mixed up. You don't really know where someone is from and whether they are a true American. But mostly I have had good experiences with Americans. They treat you well for the most part. So, for example, in the grocery store they don't treat you badly if you are a Hispanic. If you need a cart or if you are waiting in the lines they are usually polite and they don't see that you are a Hispanic and treat you badly. But other people, no. Among Hispanics, for example, it's not like that. We don't like each other. I don't know why but we won't help each other. It's almost as though we hate each other. So for example at work if an American gives you a job, he'll help you, he'll explain everything. But Hispanics, they won't. It's the same thing if you are out, the Americans never say anything to you. For example at the beach, if you have the volume on your music up the other Hispanics will come and see if you are drinking and they'll call the police. It's Hispanics that do this to each other. Americans never bother you. I've never really had the opportunity to work with Americans but I encounter them at the beach—everywhere. Americans are fine. Once I got lost out on Long Island, and they explained really well to me which way to go. But, if I stopped to ask a Hispanic, he wouldn't help me that way. It's like the same thing that happens at work. Between us there is no helping.

It's the job of the eldest to take care of things in the house, to take care of the brothers and sisters. You have to see that they are well taken care of, perhaps give them a bottle, change diapers, everything. Sometimes you have to wash their clothes, things like that, whatever you can do to help your mother. Here, they expect more economic help. Especially if you are single, you should help your family. You can send money or things from here, things they need but don't have. I'm always thinking about my siblings and my parents. Sometimes I get sad here, but not as much as I did before. Maybe once a month or so I get really sad, usually when I listen to music from home. It makes me think of the old times. Sometimes if something happens at work, if ugly, coarse words pass between me and someone else, then, I'll come home and I'll feel like . . . well, I'll ask myself why I ever came here. Then I'll make myself sad. But, by the next day, I forget and it all passes. Once in a while I'll remember lots of things. Sometimes I get mad because we are taken advantage of at work. But then again I think—they have the right to take advantage of you, it's just business. If they don't watch their business who will? They have the right to cheat us. But then again I think that I don't deserve to be taken advantage of like that. I'm conscientious, I don't deserve that. But that's the way it is. I go home, somewhat bitter and listen to music and it passes. There's really no one I can tell my problems to, only Bolivar's wife. But even then I don't know her that well and I don't want to tell her too much. She's not my family, you know? Therefore, I don't have too much faith to tell her my problems. I'd rather wait until I see my Uncle Patricio, he's family.

I have known my friend Bolivar since Ecuador and he was a lot like me when he was younger. He was really young when he came to the U.S, and he went right to work. He never had his youth like I did in Ecuador. He never had the time in high school when you see girls and go to parties. He came here very young and worked right away. When he came to Ecuador he was older than us [about 10 years older than Vicente], but I introduced him to my friends and to some girls and he would go to parties with us. He would take us to some of the best clubs in town to dance because he had money, no? He got married really young, at 18 years old or so, and they had kids right away. His wife is only 27 or 28 years old.

The thing that I most worry about is my legal status here. To get legal papers here is the most difficult thing, and it's the thing I most want. If you have legal status, you have many more options to support yourself. Up until now I am like a river—going, going, but I don't know where I'm going to end up. If you have residency you have a place to end up. If you like it here you can stay, you can look for the means to stay. You can look for a good job or even invest in a business. This is the most difficult thing, not having legal status. It causes me a lot of anxiety. They say there is going to be an amnesty, but we'll see. I worry now and then that I'll be picked up by immigration and thrown out. I heard that if you have a driver's license it can save you a little but I don't know. At work sometimes they talk about whether immigration could come one day and catch us all.

But, we'll have to see what happens. Sometimes when you get married, you no longer have the same ideas you had before. You have to take into account the ideas of your wife. You change sometimes. But, actually, I don't think anyone will change me. Mami [his mother] hasn't really changed over the years either. She's still really sentimental and sad. I think that she's sad because of all the things that have happened in her life, all the bad things. But I tell her, "You have to be tough." Because she is like that, she has gotten sick. I try not to get too involved in the problems with relatives and the family. I just like to treat people the same and not carry bad feelings from years past. I want to live for right now—not the past.

Vicente's story is not unique. Far from it. "Making something of oneself" in the U.S. is difficult and it has an emotional cost that must be weighed seriously. Doubly burdened by their ethnicity and their national economy, poor young *Cuencanos* like Vicente yearn for the imagined life they see on television and at the movies and that they hear about from their friends and neighbors living in New York. For young men like Vicente, the identity images presented to him are not really in competition with one another. On the one hand, there is the establishment image of the poor urban man—the one that the elites are striving to perpetuate in Cuenca—as a person who is humble and works hard, although with little reward in this lifetime. Limited in educational opportunities and bereft of palanca, the poor are confined to the margins of the social system, where they are consigned to providing the needed labor and services to the elites. This image tells the poor cholo that he shouldn't even hope for more than he has, a sentiment brought home to me when I read the phrase, *La envidia te mata, cholito* [Envy kills you, little peasant] emblazoned above a driver's head on a crowded city bus. This construction is hardly appealing to a young man whose head is filled with images of fantastic American consumerism. On the other hand, there is the more desirable image of the cosmopolitan transnational migrant who sports the most modern clothing and styles and who has a pocketful of money available to set up a business that could make him financially independent. It may take migrants many years of hard labor to achieve this dream, but this is seen as a small price to pay for the rewards that can be earned.

The family members left behind in Cuenca are the ones most aware of, and worried about, the price that may be paid for the financial success of the migrant. One of the most consistently articulated concerns is the veiled worry that their loved one will, in fact, turn into what they see on television—someone consumed with style and money—someone who has lost track of traditionally important values. As desirable as American consumerism may be, family members also make very accurate and poignant critiques of the impact of American capitalism on the "character" of their relatives. In the beginning, they worry that the migrant will fall victim to loneliness and seek solace in alcohol, drugs, or risky sex. Later, they wonder if the migrant will become taken with his own success and start to look down upon his family in Cuenca. The fear is always present that the migrant will adjust *too* well to American life and shrug off responsibilities to the family back home in Cuenca.

Despite the fears of loved ones, for most migrants life in New York does not involve making radical changes in "character" or behavior, but rather it is a subtle process of adjustment and accommodation—one that takes several years. In the beginning, phone calls are numerous and long, gifts and remittances are regular if not large, and thoughts of returning home discussed often. Over time, this frequently changes. In fact, Vicente admits that, as time goes by and life in New York City becomes "normal," he is losing his strong emotional attachment to Ecuador. Now he can't be sure if he'll ever return there to live.

LIVES AND STORIES

Vicente's migration, while certainly the most extraordinary event in his life, also reverberates significantly in the lives of the family members he has left behind. So, for example, his mother, who unabashedly favors Vicente, is devastated by his absence, and she has never been the same. His father is proud that he was able to "send his son the easy way" and that he didn't face the dangers of taking a shipping boat from Guayaquil and walking across the desert, as so many other Ecuadorians have done. Vicente's brother, who is politically astute, thinks migration is bad for Ecuadorians and that Vicente is allowing himself to be exploited by American capitalism, and his sister, who lost her parent-approved chaperone, is resentful because she is now forbidden to go to school parties and functions. His youngest brother, who was just three years old when Vicente left, knows his brother only from photos, videos, and long-distance phone calls. All of them miss him and question whether, in the long run, leaving Ecuador was the best thing to do. In 2005, Vicente was able to help the family pay for hospital expenses when his youngest sister fell ill, but he grieved alone in New York when she passed away. The longer Vicente stays in New York, the more disappointed his family is in him as they come to realize that the hopes they had for their lives are not going to be realized through Vicente's remittances.

Family relationships were laid bare after Vicente left, as his sudden removal from the home revealed just what roles he played in the family—son, confidante, chaperone, tutor, cultural broker, and beloved, although sometimes resented, older brother. Vicente stopped being someone who was integrated into the everyday and became, for better or worse, the embodiment of the family's dreams, desires, and hopes. His failure to fulfill those dreams weighs heavily upon everyone. Because of Vicente's lack of success, his father had to migrate, his mother is literally worried sick, and his siblings question the strength of familial bonds in the face of both temptations and challenges. The Quitasacas are repositioning the line between irrational hope and reasonable expectations as their imagined vision of Vicente's experiences in the United States (and what that would do for their life in Cuenca) fade in order to make way for reality.

Vicente is less ambivalent, however, about what kind of person he is. While he sometimes questions the strength of his attachment to being a "Hispanic" or an Ecuadorian, and wonders if he remains an obedient son or a helpful brother, he is remarkably sure about who he is as a person. He believes that his basic character, which so concerns his family back home, is very much as it always was. Indeed, he told me that he tries to be a good person and to be conscientious and responsible. He makes few excuses for himself. He knows that he ought to do better when it comes to saving money, but he is proud that, despite the hardships he faces, he never has taken advantage of others.

Vicente's migration reveals the very complex and ambivalent understandings that the Quitasacas have in relation to the systems of stratification in which they operate. The Quitasacas cannot be viewed solely as victims of global economic processes nor, as the elites of their own country would have it, unwitting consumers of global "culture." Yet, their relationship to the cultures of power is not easy to disentangle. They live in a world (both in Ecuador and New York) that consistently marginalizes them and limits their opportunities. However, that does not mean that the Quitasacas passively accept their fate. They have been trying for years to succeed within the system in Cuenca—they have worked hard at low-paying jobs, they have dressed in Western clothing, and they have sent their children to school. But these efforts have made little difference in the face of a shrinking economy. Nor has migration to the U.S. been a magic solution to their circumstances. While they believe that the United States can offer greater economic possibilities, they also know that they are leaving one system of exploitation for another. They understand that Hispanics, especially those who remain undocumented, often are treated like dogs. Still, they hope that the transnational system of exploitation operating in New York will pay much better than the local one in Cuenca. In this sense, they share the popular perception that the United States is a land of abundance and equal opportunity and that poverty is either short lived or self-inflicted. The painful and sometimes debilitating effects of poverty are not caused solely by absolute deprivation but, in circumstances of abundance, by *relative* deprivation, discrimination, and exploitation. The story of the Quitasacas family is more than the story of a single family. It is just one of tens of thousands of such stories of the people of Ecuador, Latin America, and many nations around the world. Of course, like all true stories, this one does not really have an ending. And this is the final irony of doing anthropological fieldwork over the years with families like the Quitasacas, whether in Ecuador or in the United States.

Note

[1] In this region of the country a *cholo* (m) is most often a derogatory comment to insult a male who aspires to be more than he is. It is often said as an insult to rural or Indian men who try to be cosmopolitan but clearly can't really pull it off. In Cuenca, *chola* (f) is a much more positive designation, but it is not without controversy and contradiction (see Weismantel 2001). A *cholo boy* in local humor indicates someone, usually of the popular classes—whether rural or urban—who admires and emulates all things American, especially consumer goods. *Iony* is a more recent term, which, according to Pribilsky (2001), describes returned migrants who have adopted American attitudes and customs. The term iony derives from the New York tourism slogan of the 1980s, "I ♥ New York!"

References

Astudillo, Jaime, and Claudio Cordero. 1990. *Huayrapamushcas en USA*. Quito: Editorial el Conejo.

Pribilsky, Jason. 2001. "Nervios" and Modern Childhood: Migration and Shifting Contexts of Child Life in the Ecuadorian Andes. *Childhood: A Journal of Global Research*, 8(2):251–273.

Weismantel, Mary. 2001. *Cholas and Pistachos: Stories of Race and Sex in the Andes*. Chicago: University of Chicago Press.

27

Global Transactions
Sudanese Refugees Sending Money Home

Dianna J. Shandy

Drawing on fieldwork conducted in both the United States and Ethiopia, Dianna Shandy investigates the role of remittances—money sent by emigrants to family and friends in the home country—in creating connections between urban and rural spaces, and among nations. Shandy focuses on Nuer refugees, originally from the Sudan, but now living in the U.S. She discovers that the prospect of receiving remittances from abroad leads some Nuer to move to Ethiopia's capital city of Addis Ababa, where transferred funds can be more easily received. She also finds that remittances are not merely a transfer of wealth between relative "haves" and "have-nots," but also serve to maintain ties of reciprocity within families separated by warfare and emigration.

The slogan "Reliability you can trust" emblazoned on a yellow map of Africa greeted me as I waited to meet up with Sudanese friends outside the Western Union kiosk in the sprawling, dusty Ethiopian capital of Addis Ababa. Staring at this sign, I was struck by the vital role these ubiquitous money transfer offices play in larger, multistranded transnational processes, interweaving rural, urban, and global.

Remittances, or the sending of money by foreign workers to their home country, are a crucial part of these transnational processes. These remittances are often handled by money transfer offices that shuffle more than US$20 billion each year and play a vital and rapidly expanding role in helping people send money home (Simpson 2004). Western Union (2008), for example, mushroomed in size from 50,000 agent locations in 1998 to more than 320,000 in 2008 and now reports earnings of nearly US$1 billion a year, primarily through helping international migrants move money home (DeParle 2007a). Western Union and other money transfer offices like it serve as store-

Source: Adapted from *Nuer American Passages: Globalizing Sudanese Migration* (Gainesville: University Press of Florida, 2007).

fronts, or localizing venues, for the daily, lived experience of globalization. Therefore, in a world on the move, they offer a unique window into the linkages between refugees in the diaspora and those who remain in Africa. By exploring the impacts of these transfers on both sides of the transaction, it is possible to document remittances as a vital, yet precarious, component of survival for those who remain in Africa, especially for those who are victims of war-induced displacement.

This chapter draws on ethnographic research conducted in the United States since 1996 and more briefly in Ethiopia in 2004 to explore how remittances sent by Sudanese, primarily Nuer, refugees living in the United States to Nuer refugees in Ethiopia served as a catalyst for migration from refugee camps in rural areas to the capital city, Addis Ababa. The chapter argues that these financial flows, while addressing a set of unmet needs, impose a new state of vulnerability on those who left the camps for urban areas.

WHO ARE THE SENDERS?

Nuer are a famous people in anthropology. They were the subject of three books by the well-known late British social anthropologist Sir E. E. Evans-Pritchard (1940, 1951, 1956), who described their pastoralist mode of subsistence, complex segmented kinship system, and religion. Evans-Pritchard conducted research with the Nuer in southern Sudan in the 1930s. Nuer existence revolved around the needs of their cattle, especially the need to move the animals from high to low ground and back again each year. During the dry season, the cattle were herded to lower ground where there was still water and grass. During the rainy season, the lowlands became a swampy lagoon, and the herds had to be moved to higher ground where rain had replenished the range. This transhumant lifestyle and the need to guard cattle against raiders from nearby tribes had shaped Nuer society.

Nuer society has suffered devastating shifts in the decades since Evans-Pritchard conducted his fieldwork. Most significantly, during 1983–2005 the Khartoum government, located in northern Sudan, was engaged in war with southerners, including Nuer, who were seeking self-government. This conflict in the Sudan frequently is attributed to social distinctions based on geography (North–South), ethnicity (Arab–African), and religion (Muslim–Christian). But, as the more-recent and ongoing Darfur crisis in western Sudan has illustrated, these are fluid categories. From a southern perspective, northern Muslim Arabs entered their land in the 1800s looking for ivory and slaves. Northerners were favored under colonial rule, which gave them more power and increased tension with people, such as the Nuer, living in the South. In 2005, a Comprehensive Peace Agreement between southern rebels and the Khartoum government went into effect. As of this writing, it remains unclear whether the peace agreement will endure and, if so, for how long.

The population of Sudan is estimated at 40 million. While it is difficult to develop reliable estimates for war-induced displacement and death, it is calculated that two million people were killed by the North–South war and another four million were displaced within Sudan. Approximately 650,000 took shelter in neighboring countries, including Ethiopia.

Among those who took shelter in neighboring countries, beginning in the early 1990s, some 30,000 or so southern Sudanese were resettled in the United States as refugees. As a refugee population arriving in the United States, most lacked formal schooling beyond the secondary level and have been integrated onto the lowest rungs of the socioeconomic ladder. Many ardently seek educational opportunities and are striving to carve out a place for themselves in the United States that allows them to meet their responsibilities to family in the United States, while addressing the needs of those left behind. While some do manage to return home to visit family left behind, in most cases, responding to the needs of family in Africa involves sending money home. This arrangement means that those who are themselves the least financially stable and most marginalized in U.S. society are shouldering the humanitarian burden for the aftereffects of one of Africa's most devastating civil wars.

Migration scholar Nicholas Van Hear (2003) notes that "one of the most important influences refugees and other migrants can have on their countries of origin is through the remittances they send." It is important to clarify that, in this case, as of that for many other refugee populations fleeing civil conflicts, the impact is not necessarily limited to country of "origin" per se and applies to neighboring countries of asylum where many refugee populations reside. Van Hear goes on to describe the variety of methodological reasons that make it impossible to calculate what percentage of the annual $300 billion (see DeParle 2007b) global flow of migrants' remittances is sent by refugees. These limitations include the patchiness of remittance data, the impossibility of disaggregating refugee remittances from those of other migrants, and the fact that refugees remit to a constellation of countries, not just their country of origin.

While it is impossible to calculate precise amounts with available data, it is possible to describe the ways Sudanese refugees remit using both formal and informal avenues. Formal money transfer channels like Western Union, and its competitors, are used heavily, as are informal avenues. Informal, but not casual, ways to dispatch funds include sending money with acquaintances making the trip back to Africa and utilizing what are termed "alternative remittance systems" (Omer 2004). Until events of September 11, 2001, Somali remittance companies, or *hawala*, provided a regularly used lower-cost alternative to send money from North America to Ethiopia. Interviews with Sudanese in the United States prior to 9/11 elicited a description of a process where people went to the home of a Somali immigrant and gave him money and details about the recipient. The Sudanese counterpart in Ethiopia would go to collect the money from the Somali man's "brother" in Ethiopia. This system made these transactions a few dollars cheaper than Western Union's, particularly for sending smaller sums. Scrutiny of these remittance companies and allegations of money laundering and ties to terrorism have closed some of them, or driven them underground. As a result, even if Sudanese still use hawala, they are no longer eager to disclose this in interviews. The other informal approach is to send funds and goods along with Sudanese who are making the temporary journey back to Africa.

With each of these approaches come advantages and disadvantages. How African customers weigh these options has become big business for remittance companies like Western Union who have their eye on the markets ushered in by the post-Cold War surge in African emigration. Hume (2002), for example, documents that more Africans immigrated to the United States during the 1990s than had come during the previous 180 years. Almost axiomatically, new immigrant groups mean new pathways along which remittances will flow.

IMPACT OF REMITTANCES

With an understanding of who is sending the money and how, we can examine the impact of these funds on the lives of Sudanese recipients in Ethiopia. These remittances do not just sustain people; they broker possibilities for dramatic social change in the form of reconfigured residential patterns, local economies, and power structures. Through this lens, the impact of refugees who are resettled in the United States or in other Western countries is amplified beyond the small numbers of persons who board planes. We will see that remittances from U.S.-based Nuer serve as a catalyst for movements from refugee camps to the capital city in Ethiopia.

Shaping Residential Patterns

More than 35 Western Union offices dot the Addis Ababa landscape, with 188 locations nationwide in Ethiopia. Living in the shadows of these offices are several thousand Sudanese refugees who depend for daily subsistence on the remittances accessed through these offices. To retrieve the resources housed within these kiosk-like structures, all you need is a control number, a "test question" (e.g., your grandfather's name or the town where you were born), and a "relative" abroad. If not a relative, you might hope for a "friend," perhaps a schoolmate or someone you knew from your hometown.

Some Sudanese come to Addis when they receive instructions via telephone from a Sudanese sponsor living abroad that there is money awaiting them in the capital. Even the rumor that a relative might be *thinking* of sending money is enough to prompt people to make the journey from rural areas to the city. The money often is earmarked for educational costs for the individual to complete his (and it is usually a male) secondary or tertiary education at one of the countless "private colleges." Others come to escape danger as in the case of what one woman described as a "security situation" due to a vendetta levied against her family, because a relative was "involved in killing" as a soldier. Many are simply caught in the crossfire of flare-ups between camp refugees and local inhabitants over control of and access to resources. Others come to Addis as prospectors of sorts, hoping to get information to establish a connection with a lost relative or friend abroad. A few come to Addis directly from the Sudan, as in the case of one woman, her husband, their three children, and the woman's sister. In this case, the family sold what cows remained in their herd after the latest assault and made their way on foot westward, traveling many days to cross the border into Ethiopia. They bypassed United Nations High Commissioner for Refugees (UNHCR) camps en route to Addis Ababa, where they hoped to receive remittances from a relative in the United States. This case highlights the limitless reach of globalizing processes, where even the seemingly most isolated regions are tied into a larger system along whose lines cash, information, and even people flow relatively unimpeded, even in the midst of a civil war. Urban areas serve a unique role as an important node in actual and hoped-for flows of resources.

The demographic profile of the Sudanese who arrive in Addis also is revealing. Cash flows facilitated by expanded global networks reshape residential patterns. Gender ratios in the Ethiopian refugee camps are reportedly about half male and half female. This ratio of men to women in Addis shifts to three to one. Therefore, while roughly equal numbers of males and females may leave Sudan for Ethiopia, many more men continue on to the capital city. This gender imbalance is repeated among the first waves of Sudanese arrivals in the United States (see Shandy 2007).

Therefore, money transfer offices act as a sort of siren, beckoning those with little hope and an elevated tolerance for risk to Africa's urban slums. Thus, remittances play a distinctive role in fueling rural to urban migration in Africa, resulting in residency practices that are intimately linked to local economies.

Reconfiguring Local Economies

Destruction of the means of livelihood is one of the principal reasons people become refugees. In Ethiopia, for Sudanese refugees whom I interviewed, daily survival is subsidized by humanitarian agencies if the refugees remain in the refugee camp, where they are provided what most concur are inadequate rations. In refugee parlance, those Sudanese in western Ethiopian camps are being warehoused—left for an extended period in camps with no immediate solution in sight. Those Sudanese I encountered in Addis had rejected the fate of being forgotten by the rest of the world and sought to procure some additional support. Furthermore, when asked why they came to Addis, many said they had feared for their lives while gathering firewood in the areas surrounding the refugee camp. Leaving the camp to gather wood, or for any other reason, was especially perilous in western Ethiopia, where tensions between locals and refugees ran particularly high and even resulted in the gunning down of seven Ethiopian government refugee workers as they drove in their jeep in December 2003 (Lacey 2004).

Hearing that so many people went from the camp to collect wood, I couldn't fathom the insatiable consumption that would necessitate so much wood, envisioning all of western Ethiopia ablaze. It was only later that I understood that people collected firewood not for their own personal use but as a commodity to sell.

Since formal employment is illegal for most refugees in Ethiopia, they must work in the informal economy or rely on remittances. Therefore, given the limited options to earn an income, most Sudanese rely on direct or indirect access to remittances from Nuer living abroad.

Optimally, those who live in Addis receive monthly remittances of US$50 to US$100, while those who remain in the camps tend to get what people called "one-time payments," or an installment of cash to meet a designated need, such as medical care. The monthly infusion of cash is fundamental to the survival of Sudanese in Addis, but it is important to appreciate that these remittances support a way of life that is more complex in Ethiopia than was the simple subsistence in Sudan. I encountered no Sudanese in Ethiopia who could be considered prosperous by Ethiopian standards, with the exception of those U.S. and Australia-based Nuer who had returned on temporary visits to see family or to look for a wife. However, inequities do exist among Ethiopia-based Nuer, and these remittances introduced or, in some cases, reinforced power hierarchies.

Altering Power Structures

The transformation of African societies and ways to access power within them has dominated African Studies literature since the mid-1960s. Colonial infrastructures, wage-labor employment, Christian conversion, formal schooling, and urbanization are documented as key catalysts of significant social transformation (see Bond 1982; Comaroff 1985; Little 1966; Mayer 1961; Schapera 1947; Scudder and Colson 1980). Among the Nuer, one thread of continuity running through their entire documented history is the dominance of cattle in marking social status. In the past decades, educational attainment has been grafted onto this arrangement. In the climate of the Sudanese civil war, cattle-keeping, while still pursued, was risky. Similarly, educational credentials did not guarantee access to employment or, as experienced by Nuer in the diaspora, employment commensurate with educational qualifications (see AbuSharaf 2002; Hutchinson 1996). Within this chaotic and fragmented social order, access to a remitting sponsor abroad has emerged as a marker of status and a promise of human security.

CASH FLOWS IN CONTEXT

For a long time, remittances have served as a lifeline for many in developing countries, including those in Asia, Latin America, the Caribbean, and even Europe. Because the frequency and amount of remittances to Africa have increased only recently, much less is known about them. One of the key factors fueling increases in remittances to Africa is the concomitant increase in emigration from Africa to places like Europe, North America, and Australia. In this section, we will explore the North–South flow of cash within a more-complex set of multistranded and multidirectional transnational flows involving people, goods, and information.

In the case of Sudan, as previously discussed, millions of people were displaced by the war. Of these, several hundred thousand flowed across the border into neighboring countries like Ethiopia, Kenya, Uganda, Congo, and Egypt. And, among the refugees who crossed an international border, approximately 30,000 were selected for resettlement to the United States since the early 1990s. The United Nations and many national governments, including the United States, define a refugee as a person who has a well-founded fear of persecution due to race, religion, nationality, membership in a particular social group, or political opinion, and who has left his or her home country. How the United Nations or national governments apply this definition when they seek to certify individuals as refugees varies.

It is important to appreciate that while refugee status is conferred at the level of the individual, the experiences of Nuer refugees demonstrate the ways in which the actions of individuals were undertaken on behalf of family (or corporate) groups. In one case that I followed in both the United States and in Ethiopia, the family living in Ethiopia pooled all of the blankets they had just been given by the UNHCR and sold them to enable the eldest living son to undertake a perilous journey from the refugee camp in Ethiopia to a camp in Kenya. The camp in Kenya was known to be offering resettlement slots for the United States. Others I interviewed in Ethiopia described a process where "resettlement forms," which enable people to apply to have their case considered by UNHCR, were scarce. When forms did become available, they were distributed on a representational basis—such as one per family—throughout the camp. Families then designated individuals to apply for resettlement. If the individual was selected for resettlement abroad, it was broadly understood that the individual owed a certain debt to his family for having been the one chosen to apply. Flowing from this was the expectation that one way the individual could repay this debt would be through remittances.

Both of these examples illustrate the ways in which refugees living in places like the United States are enmeshed in reciprocal arrangements with those left behind. At one time their family invested in him (usually it was a male); now is his time for repayment. In other words, North–South cash flows, while seemingly asymmetric in terms of who is giving and who is receiving, need to be seen within a larger temporal and spatial context. Those in the diaspora who remit are perhaps obtaining some peace of mind. Yet, they are also maintaining a stake as a member within a complex web of social, political, and economic ties. Beyond repaying debts, Nuer are also investing in their future when they remit to those who remain in Africa.

Knowing the different reasons for and uses of remittances informs us of how rural, urban, and global arenas are inextricably interwoven. The refugee living in upstate New York is bound to his brother living in an African capital city, and they are both linked to still another brother residing in a rural area and maintaining the herd of cattle. Many hold out hope for a lasting peace in the Sudan, and we are in the midst of witnessing the role of remittances in easing the transition back to African society for those who choose to return.

CONCLUSION

In this chapter I have attempted to present an overview of a largely undocumented practice that is difficult, if not impossible, to identify from a macro-level standpoint. This ethnographic view of refugees from southern Sudan sending remittances to their compatriots in Ethiopia highlights the vital nature of these resource flows in sustaining life under very difficult circumstances. More than just sustaining life, however, these remittances alter social life in unexpected and powerful ways through shaping and reshaping residential patterns, local economies, and power structures. Viewed in this way, remittances need to be incorporated in our understanding of factors precipitating rapid social change in Africa.

These remittance processes provide a dynamic view of globalization on the local level and an alternative way of appreciating North–South cash flows. Instead of aid flowing in through the usual cast of governmental and nongovernmental donor agencies, this case has offered possibilities to explore the impact of cash trickling directly into the hands of ordinary people and, perhaps, contributes to a broadening of how we understand globalization as a complex phenomenon socially mediated from below.

Urban areas are central to these multistranded, multidirectional transnational processes, and they are also a nexus that links the rural and the global. The money transfer offices described here play a vital role in this vast interweaving of people, place, and space. Yet, the flows of cash need to be seen within their social context.

Highlighting the roles of resettled Nuer in supporting those left behind provides a window into the complex and dynamic social worlds of people who are assumed to be functioning within a minimalist, survival-based framework. A greater appreciation of the sociocultural factors informing forced migrants' decisions and behavior has significant implications not only for the ways we theorize the human condition but also for the kinds of programmatic responses that are built upon these understandings.

References

AbuSharaf, Rogaia M. 2002. *Wanderings: Sudanese Migrants and Exiles in North America.* Ithaca, NY: Cornell University Press.

Bond, George C. 1982. Education and Social Stratification in North Zambia: The Case of the Uyombe. *Anthropology and Education,* 13:251–268.

Comaroff, Jean. 1985. *Body of Power, Spirit of Resistance: The Culture and History of a South African People.* Chicago: University of Chicago Press.

DeParle, Jason. 2007a. A Western Union Empire Moves Migrant Cash Home. *New York Times* (November 22).

———. 2007b. Migrant Money Flow: A $300 Billion Current. *New York Times* (November 18).

Evans-Pritchard, E. E. 1940. *The Nuer: A Description of the Modes of Livelihood and Political Institutions of a Nilotic People.* Oxford: Clarendon Press.

———. 1951. *Kinship and Marriage Among the Nuer.* Oxford: Clarendon Press.

———. 1956. *Nuer Religion.* Oxford: Clarendon Press.

Hume, Susan. 2002. Contemporary African Migration to the United States: Are We Paying Attention? Paper presented at the Association of American Geographers, Los Angeles.

Hutchinson, Sharon. 1996. *Nuer Dilemmas: Coping with Money, War and the State.* Berkeley: University of California Press.

Lacey, Marc. 2004. A River Washes Away Ethiopia's Tensions, for a Moment. *New York Times* (June 15):A14.

Little, Kenneth. 1966. *West African Urbanization.* Cambridge: Cambridge University Press.

Mayer, Philip. 1961. *Townsmen or Tribesmen.* London: Oxford University Press.

Omer, Abdusalam. 2004. *A Report on Supporting Systems and Procedures for the Effective Regulation and Monitoring of Somali Remittance Companies* (Hawala). Nairobi: UNDP.

Schapera, Isaac. 1947. *Migrant Labour and Tribal Life: A Study of Conditions in the Bechuanaland Protectorate.* London: Oxford University Press.

Scudder, Thayer, and Elizabeth Colson. 1980. *Secondary Education and the Formation of an Elite.* New York: Academic Press.

Shandy, Dianna J. 2007. *Nuer-American Passages: Globalizing Sudanese Migration.* Gainesville: University Press of Florida.

Simpson, Glenn R. 2004. Easy Money: Expanding in an Age of Terror Western Union Faces Scrutiny. *Wall Street Journal* (October 20).

Van Hear, Nicholas. 2003. Refugee Diasporas, Remittances, Development, and Conflict. Migration Policy Institute. http://www.migrationinformation.org/Feature/display.cfm?id=125 (accessed 4/21/09).

Western Union. 2008. http://www.westernunion.com/WUCOMWEB/staticMid.do?pagename=HomePage&method=load&countryCode=US&languageCode=en (accessed 9/23/08).

28

Hyderabad
Continuities and Transformations

Karen Isaksen Leonard

Her curiosity aroused by a celebration in Los Angeles of the 400th anniversary of the Indian city Hyderabad, Karen Isaksen Leonard began to explore Hyderabadi emigration to the United States and other countries. She describes the changes and disruptions that came to Hyderabad beginning with Indian independence from Britain in 1947, including the division of Hyderabad State and the imposition of an unfamiliar "official" language. The pace of change has only increased as Hyderabadis become more active participants in the global economy and leave home—often permanently—to pursue educational and work opportunities. Through her analysis, Leonard demonstrates that those who have been "left behind" can suffer the same feelings of disruption and loss as do those who have departed.

This study began in 1990 in Los Angeles, when a notice in California's Indian ethnic newspaper, *India-West,* caught my eye: the Hyderabad Deccan Association of California was celebrating Hyderabad city's 400th anniversary. I attended that celebration at a local community center along with 1,000 Hyderabadis—I had had no idea there were that many Hyderabadis in the Los Angeles area. The evening of festive Hyderabadi food, Urdu speeches and poetry, and gorgeous Hyderabadi fashions made me long to return to my roots in Indian and Hyderabadi history after almost a decade of working on other topics, and I resolved to study Hyderabadis abroad to see why they were leaving their homeland and relocating elsewhere. I realized the members of my social network in Hyderabad would be good resources, as their children were among those emigrating.

When I first worked in Hyderabad in the 1960s, people from there rarely moved out. Hyderabadis used to fend off non-*mulkis* (noncountrymen, foreigners, or outsiders), people coming from Madras and North India. They

Source: Adapted from the author's book, *Locating Home: India's Hyderabadis Abroad.* (Stanford: Stanford University Press, 2007).

themselves seldom left Hyderabad even for a short time, and when they did, people wept at the railway station; a daughter married off to Lucknow seemed to be going far, far away. By 1990, however, it was clear that many people from Hyderabad lived in the United States. People in their 50s still were not coming to this country, but their children were moving abroad for education, work, and, all too often, from a parent's point of view, settlement. I had not really noticed these movements, nor had I thought of them as a collective phenomenon until the Los Angeles Hyderabadi celebration brought them home to me very dramatically.

ORIENTATIONS

Hyderabad city and the former Hyderabad State are my starting points for an exploration of migration, settlement, and social memories. A major historical theme in Hyderabadi history has been the relationship between indigenous people and immigrants, natives and newcomers. The definitions and occupants of these categories have changed over time. In the Deccan, that broad plateau in southern central India, the medieval terms were *Dakhni* (native) and *afaqi* (non-native), and more recently, mulkis (countrymen) and non-mulkis. The native-newcomer theme has shaped all of India's history:

> The Indian identity all through its recorded history has been shaped by the interaction of myriad immigrating cultures which readapted and integrated themselves with the new milieu without losing their respective individualities so that the end product was a colorful social mosaic rather than a dull homogenized mass. (Banga 1991:xv)

Furthermore, as the native-newcomer theme suggests, people have moved about for centuries in South Asia, leaving old homelands and finding new ones. Like other South Asians, Hyderabadis attach as much, if not more, importance to the relationship between humans as an aspect of belonging and attachment than to fixed places, such as an ancestral village or a "native place" (Srivastava 2005). The native-newcomer theme has obvious relevance not only to Hyderabadi and Indian history but also to contemporary world patterns of migration and modern notions of citizenship.

Hyderabad is the name of both a city and a state that has undergone dramatic political transitions in India's recent history. In 1948, Hyderabad State became part of independent India, and in 1956, as part of the reorganization of state boundaries along linguistic lines, it was divided among three new states. The city, formerly the capital of Hyderabad State, became the capital of the new Telugu-speaking state of Andhra Pradesh, producing major reorientations of language and culture. Hyderabad city was India's fifth largest city at the turn of the twenty-first century.

"Hyderabadi," or a person from Hyderabad, was an identity that linked one closely to the princely state on India's Deccan plateau ruled by the Nizam of Hyderabad. This involved citizenship not so much in the modern sense of participation in political decision making as in the sense of having a claim on the state for one's livelihood. Mulki became a legal category with preference for state jobs in the late nineteenth century, and a process was established for non-mulkis to become mulkis. Being a mulki also implied closeness and loyalty to Hyderabad State. People's working definitions of mulki differ: some restrict membership in the mulki category to those resident in the Deccan by the mid-eighteenth century (consolidation of the Nizam's rule), whereas others include immigrants to Hyderabad up to the late nineteenth century but bar those coming in after that. Some think that people could become mulki Hyderabadis well into the twentieth century.

Hyderabadis were not only citizens of Hyderabad State but they also shared in and helped to constitute Hyderabadi culture, producing a sense of community particularly strong for members of the ruling elite. Hyderabadi culture was often termed Mughlai because its feudal overtones and elaborate courtesies derived from the Persian-based court culture of the Mughal empire in Delhi. The first Nizam came to the Deccan as provincial governor for the Mughals in the early eighteenth century and only gradually established his independence. The Nizam's ruling class incorporated Marathi-, Telugu-, and Kannada-speaking nobles, officials, and local elites as well as Persian-, Urdu-, and Hindi-speakers who accompanied him from northern India. The nobility, the Mughlai bureaucracy, and the military included adherents of all religions, although Muslims were the majority of the urban, ruling elite, and Hindus formed the bulk of the rural peasantry.

Char Minar (4 minarets), the heart of the old city and symbol of Hyderabad. [Courtesy of Christopher Butt, New York City]

Hyderabadis experienced traumatic changes after 1948 as India imposed a new regime. Some Hyderabadis migrated to the new state of Pakistan, created along with India in 1947, but Indian rule in Hyderabad meant such major readjustments that it was almost as though those who stayed had moved to a new place. Some Hyderabadis found the American civil war novel, *Gone with the Wind,* evocative of the trauma. They likened old Hyderabad to the American South, some of them with nostalgic approval, others with disapproval.

These changes in the homeland in the decades after 1948 strongly influenced emigrants and the ways they reoriented themselves to their new settings. Most obviously, the state of origin has changed: the former Hyderabad State became Andhra Pradesh, with very different boundaries and constituent languages. Or was the real homeland Hyderabad city, standing more or less on its own all along? In fact, both the continued existence and the historical nature of this homeland, Hyderabad, whether city or state, proved to be matters of controversy. Most self-identified Hyderabadis abroad were first-generation migrants over the age of 50 who claimed some connection with the old Hyderabad State or its urban Mughlai culture, and many such people thought that their Hyderabad no longer existed.

Second, the meaning of "Hyderabadi" clearly changed, as people connected themselves to redefined state borders and cultures. Mulki status carried legal privileges in the old Hyderabad State and was always contested, and mulki status was still proudly claimed by many older emigrants. But political events sent some longtime Hyderabadis abroad and brought many newcomers from coastal Andhra into the city, producing people claiming to be Hyderabadis who may not have known the word *mulki.* The traditional greeting in Hyderabad was *adab* (respects), a nonreligious salutation uttered as one raised his or her right hand to the forehead, bowing slightly. Now many people say either *salam aleikum* or *namaste,* greetings many associate with Islam or Hinduism, respectively.

LATE TWENTIETH-CENTURY LIFE IN HYDERABAD CITY

After the first years of dramatic readjustment, we come to the recent past. The urban landscape has altered greatly over the last few decades. Those great hierarchies of language, class, and gender that marked the Nizam's kingdom have largely disappeared. One can no longer see the grand sweep of the cement roads, which were regularly washed and cleared for the passing of the Nizam and the great nobles. Also gone are the purdah cars and taxis parked before shops and schools, the purdah curtains held by servants as women and girls went from conveyance to entryway, and other aspects of gendered lives in the palaces and courtyards. Telugu has replaced Urdu in schools and vies with it on the streets.

The late-twentieth-century city was almost wholly changed in physical as well as cultural character, making it hard for longtime Hyderabadis to sustain their civic pride. A limerick best evokes the pain of rapid urbanization, of growing from three-quarters of a million people in 1940 to more than 6 million in the greater metropolitan area in 2001, according to the Indian Census Bureau.

> In Hyderabad's traffic, the fumes
> engulf you in clouds as you zooms,
> Your temper will seethe,
> It's so hard to breathe,
> No wonder this town's full of tombs.

The most famous tombs, the Qutb Shahi, go back some 400 years and bring us to a final limerick. This one highlights the dramatic ruptures in the city's history made obvious by largely abortive attempts to celebrate Hyderabad's 400th birthday in the city itself (it also highlights the diasporic dimension).

> In London, L.A., Jeddah, and Kuwait,
> They've celebrated Hyderabad's anniversary fete.
> But here in A.P.,
> Not even a tea,
> Come on, politicians, let's set a date!

Why such delays in the celebration, why such controversy? Lingering memories of the Police Action of 1948 and the Linguistic States Reorganization of 1956 marked contemporary politics at the end of the twentieth century, but the political boundaries have proved less significant than clashes of cultural orientation, clashes of the new and old languages of power and structures of feeling. The population of Hyderabad city is still heavily Muslim, particularly in the old city, and Urdu still has a hold on the city as a whole. Telugu regional culture and British Indian culture both threaten the Mughlai Persian and Urdu culture that ruled there for so long. The Andhra peasant castes dominate the political arenas of city and state, causing the decline of specific communities and the rise of others. Telugu-speakers, however, had looked south and east, to Madras city and coastal Andhra towns like Rajahmundry, and the abrupt reorientation to Hyderabad remains to be consolidated.

The meaning of the city to its inhabitants depends very much on which inhabitants one is talking about: there is no shared vision, no real urban community comparable to earlier times. The Andhra politicians certainly are trying to assert control over Hyderabad, but they have not quite succeeded in vanquishing the city's strongly marked Indo-Muslim character.

The imposition of the Nizam's capital city on formerly British Telugu-speaking coastal Andhra is still being worked out. Hyderabad, especially the old city, appears to the Andhras much as Indian towns allegedly appeared to Englishmen, above all else "disorderly." Yet to old Hyderabadis it is the Andhras who appear disorderly, uncivilized, and barefoot; it is they who make the city dirty, crowded, and chaotic. The evolving sets of natives and newcomers have very different senses of architecture, decoration, and color, and the renaming of streets and localities emphasizes the disjunctions. Language is very much a matter of contention in the modern city, with Urdu still the language of the street in many localities. Some members of the old elite refuse to hire workers who cannot follow their directions in Urdu, and old Hyderabadi families make do with servants who do not know the old culture, cannot cook the old dishes, and cannot greet or serve guests properly.

From the 1950s to the turn of the twenty-first century, Hyderabad has been incorporated into greater India's developing urban culture, sharing trends evident elsewhere in the nation. In the 1960s, fancy gas stations with extensive grounds suddenly appeared to serve the new and privileged class of car and scooter owners; in the 1970s, palatial movie houses accommodated new audiences for India's expanding cinema industry. In the 1980s, family restaurants were opened, and the city's exclusive clubs added family entertainments. In the early 1990s came the flashy pubs, following the fashion in Bangalore. Now, former palaces transformed into marriage halls in the 1980s, bedecked with lights and with already-existing purdah arrangements, are being supplanted by banquet halls in modern hotels and huge new Telugu-style marriage halls with rooms common to both men and women. Osmania University is still there, with its striking Indo-Saracenic architecture, but the new federal University of Hyderabad has been built at some distance from the city, demonstrating the reach of the Indian nation-state centered in Delhi.

Some who live in the city are trying to bridge the historical ruptures and build a contemporary history together, and part of that effort is mutual education, through books, films, and symposia. Only in the last few years has the 1948 Police Action been discussed, chiefly through the preparation and showing of a national television (Doodarshan) special one-hour documentary on the last days of the Nizam's state. Historians of Hyderabad, both mulki and non-mulki in origin, are writing books at least partly intended to deepen the newcomers' appreciation of the city's past.

Citizens of diverse backgrounds work together to ameliorate the urban conditions that make everyday life in the city stressful. Water is available at certain hours only, so it is stored by the rich in tanks on roofs but stored by the poor in pots. New apartments and condos present impressive facades and interiors, but the lifts cannot work when the electricity is off and water often cannot make it to the upper floors, so small boys find employment carrying water to the top floors, much as the water carriers of old provided water to the great palaces. Despite the best efforts at improvement of urban services and city beautification, cooperation breaks down when it comes to the old city, largely Muslim in population and increasingly deserted by the upwardly mobile. The official attitude toward the old city seems to be one of indifference and neglect, and the political will to remedy this seems lacking.

Always a destination for migrants from both inside and outside South Asia, Hindus from the subcontinent, Persians from Iran, Turks and Uzbeks from Central Asia, and smaller increments of Arabs, Africans, Anglo-Indians, Frenchmen, Sikhs, and Parsis, Hyderabad's boast was that those who came settled there and seldom ventured out. Now the flow of migrants is reversed. People from the city and former state of Hyderabad have migrated abroad in some numbers since the late 1940s and especially since the late 1960s, when push factors gave way to pull ones as Western democracies changed their immigration and citizenship policies and the Persian Gulf states began offering employment opportunities. Hyderabad is now the center of a dynamic modern Telugu culture, one that will receive attention from other researchers in the future as the transformations underway gain still more momentum.

REORIENTATIONS

Two sisters, Miriam Bilgrami and Khadija Mehdi, talked to me in a Banjara Hills home in Hyderabad; most of their grandchildren were in the United States and Canada. One sister said:

> All my children are abroad, all my grandchildren are abroad; we didn't want it this way, we could never think it would be like this. But providence. . . . My eldest sister is in Lucknow; she married there, and my mother was so upset, sending her all that way out of Hyderabad. But look at us.

The other sister reported that all her grandchildren dislike India and hate to come to it. She has visited them in Los Angeles, but she tells them, "India is my home; you must respect it, you must visit me here." A third grandmother, Pushpa Umapathi, talked unhappily about her visits to Texas, where her daughter and son-in-law had just bought a house although "of course they are planning to return to Hyderabad." There, her granddaughter anxiously asked her not to wear a sari when walking her to school. When I asked if her grandchildren identified as Hyderabadi in any way, she burst out: "Hyderabadi? They're not even Indian."

Life for the residents of Hyderabad city has changed in ways that go far beyond new architecture and road names, rising population density, and new administrative and street languages. The changes after the Police Action in 1948 and the creation of Andhra Pradesh in 1956 were overwhelming enough, as Hyderabadis struggled to find places in independent India and the new Telugu-speaking state. Families moved from the old city to the new, and young men took up new careers. More women began to work and have careers. Globalization, however, has meant another level of change altogether.

Since the 1960s, Hyderabadis have participated in an increasingly global economy and society. Almost every family has members overseas. For aging parents, once-welcomed opportunities abroad for their children have led to painful and possibly permanent separations. Family histories rooted in Hyderabad and India have been swept aside and replaced by new narratives grounded in new places. Family members try hard to see continuities or relinquish the past. As the grandmothers' laments above indicate, it was those left behind in Hyderabad who had the greatest difficulty adjusting to the expanded and reoriented family networks.

Houses and Households

The lives of people in Hyderabad were affected by the diaspora in many ways. Property in Hyderabad was thought to be a magnet pulling the emigrants back, and family after family mentioned ancestral property or investment in new property as performing this function. But properties, especially homes, had altered in form and function because of the diaspora. Gracious, old-fashioned residences, large enough for joint family living, were being torn down and new flats constructed, with the parents in one flat and another one or two flats left vacant for the children's holiday visits. Aging couples with no children or servants left to assist them were moving to apartments in multistory buildings, only to find that they could not properly receive their visitors or see them out as the old etiquette demanded.

Having their families stretched across national boundaries produced stress among family members in Hyderabad. Parents with one or more sons still in Hyderabad were most content. The parents with sons settled abroad and daughters married to men working in the Gulf faced difficult decisions, torn between going to reside with their sons (the more culturally acceptable option) or staying alone in Hyderabad near their daughters (whose husbands would more likely return to Hyderabad). Patterns of visiting abroad reflected gender differences, as mothers could and did stay longer with their children while fathers could not stay long or preferred to be back in Hyderabad. Parents who wanted to join their children abroad could be held up by litigation or property settlements in Hyderabad. Sometimes "property settlement" was a euphemism, as they really were waiting for an elderly parent or relative to die so that inheritances could be settled. Since households in the countries overseas and in Hyderabad itself were more likely to be nuclear, visiting parents could be a strain on a young couple abroad, particularly if the marriage had not been parentally arranged and one partner was "not from the community." As marriages became more a matter of private individual decisions, the choices could reflect commitments to old Hyderabadi culture or to the new settings, challenging and reorienting other family members.

Daily life in Hyderabad involved changes in eating and dining habits. New foods were being introduced directly by family members from abroad. (In 1981, before this was common, my daughter and I were startled to be served "vegetarian burritos" in a traditional Gujarati banking family's home by a daughter-in-law visiting from California.) Dinner times were shifted to accommodate TV programs from abroad that could be discussed with relatives settled there. Certain days and times were reserved for taking overseas phone calls: people declined invitations or arrived late because Dolly was calling from Canada, Syed from Melbourne, or Shanta from London at a preset time.

People in Hyderabad became resources for those abroad who called on them for information or performance of family services. While I was staying at the Gir home, the brother of Lalitha's brother's wife called from Toronto and asked who had authored a particular *ghazal* (musical rendition of a Persian or Urdu poem); he and his wife wanted to present it in a *mushaira* (gathering featuring ghazals). The Girs told him to call back in 15 minutes and telephoned a local poet (Rasheed Ali Khan) for the answer in the meantime. Connections between classmates could be drawn on as well. One man went abroad, after his mother had supported his education for years, and, heading an academic department in Canada, he never came back. When his mother was dying, he called on an old classmate to help. She made hospital arrangements and paid for them and then, after the woman's death, transported the body in her car from the hospital to the cremation grounds and lit the fire. Later, her friend came back, sold the family property, and returned to Canada.

Remembering and Forgetting

Political changes in Hyderabad, combined with economic and social changes brought by India's development and globalization, have altered the opportunity structure for successive generations of families based in Hyderabad. Most family histories started with memories of government service with the Qutb Shahis, Mughals, British, and Nizams. Western-style educators, engineers, and doctors pioneered modern livelihoods not dependent on the state, although in old Hyderabad these professionals were often part of the ruling elite or close to it. Those who worked for political and social change in mid-twentieth-century Hyderabad, like those in India's nationalist movement, were often lawyers (more commonly called pleaders, *vakils,* and advocates). Some district-based Hyderabadis gained political power after 1948, especially before 1956, and a few Hyderabadi administrators and politicians rose to the all-India level. Women joined modern professions, particularly as educators and doctors, and they too began to study and work abroad. Still newer professions, in computer science, physics, chemistry, academics, and business, attracted young emigrants. Changing occupational structures in Hyderabad and the world have reoriented families.

Language changes in Hyderabad and abroad strongly influenced what was remembered and what was forgotten. People bemoaned the fact that their own children and especially their grandchildren could no longer speak Urdu (or Telugu or Marathi or Kannada), much less read and write it. In Hyderabad itself, knowledge of Urdu was declining, and of course, the change dated from the Police Action. Lalitha Gir, a student at Nizam College during the transition years (1948–1952), had intended to take Urdu with Agha Hyder Hasan, a famed teacher whose ancestors served the Mughal court. During those years, Ali Yavar Jung, Hyderabadi vice-chancellor of Osmania, presided over Nizam College's changeover to Hindi as the new mandatory language. To encourage Hyderabadis to take Hindi and Sanskrit, students taking those languages got 50 percent to 60 percent marks despite poor learning, Lalitha charged. In a Muslim family noted for educational achievements, Khadija Mehdi had to choose Urdu or Sanskrit for her son's second Public School language during her husband's absence, and she chose Urdu. Her husband returned and disapproved: "The children now have to learn Hindi, so Sanskrit would have been better." Even among working-class families in the old city, where Urdu remained the home and street language, Urdu was declining. Those who went to the Middle East were opting for English-medium schools for their children, whether they were the Indian Embassy schools in the Gulf or the private schools in Hyderabad newly accessible to them. Major shifts in linguistic competence opened up new vistas but also erased entire worlds of poetry, jokes, and performance traditions.

Despite the many changes, the older generations clung to the old friendships, the crosscutting networks that anchored them in Hyderabad city and state. One heard stories. Orthodox Muslim women brought whiskey to Hindu friends who appreciated it. Muslims called Hindu friends in the wee hours of the morning, saying they had to get up and come for a wedding ritual that could not be performed without them. Hindus loyal to their Muslim servants in the old city during times of communal riots and curfews braved the police to take them food and water. People called on each other or phoned each other on the holidays still mutually observed—Id, Diwali, New Year's Day, and the birthdays of family members. Such stories made little sense to the children of Hyderabadi immigrants in Pakistan or elsewhere and will probably be forgotten. The children's own memories, being constituted in new settings abroad as they entered schools, made friends, and met others in their neighborhoods and workplaces, were orienting them to quite different worlds.

References

Banga, Indu, ed.1991. *The City in Indian History: Urban Demography, Society, and Politics.* New Delhi: Manohar.

Srivastava, Sanjay. 2005. Ghummakkads, a Woman's Place, and the LTC-walas: Towards a Critical History of "Home," "Belonging," and "Attachment." *Contributions to Indian Sociology,* 39(3):375–405.

29

Beyond Urban and Rural Communities in the 21st Century

Walter P. Zenner

As the number of people engaged in agriculture around the globe decreases and as telecommunications are found throughout the world, the old distinction between what is "rural" and what is "urban" has become much less relevant. In fact, in some ways urbanism is everywhere today. Using examples from the United States, Walter Zenner explores what this distinction meant in the recent past and what it may mean today.

Until recently, it was convenient to classify communities as either urban or rural. Urban communities were generally seen as having large concentrations of people, the vast majority of whom were engaged in nonagricultural occupations. Relationships within cities were seen as impersonal and transitory in character. By contrast, the old conception of rural communities encompassed scattered homesteads and villages, the residents of which were isolated and semi-literate cultivators and nomads. Their relationships were seen as primarily face-to-face contacts over long periods of time. This is the world which provided the framework for Louis Wirth's concept of "Urbanism as a Way of Life." Even in the 1930s, when Wirth wrote his essay, people lived in a world where large numbers of people still cultivated the land.

The human population of the world changed during the twentieth century from one that was predominantly rural to one that was predominantly urban. Our twenty-first century world is a very different place from what our grandparents and great-grandparents knew. Today the number of people involved in agriculture is diminishing throughout the world, including Africa, the Middle East, Latin America, and Asia. Commerce can be accomplished everywhere. Urban markets and locations are no longer needed. The move-

Source: Written expressly for *Urban Life*.

ment of retailing, which in the middle of the nineteenth century spread through peddlers in rural areas, was succeeded by catalog sales through companies like Sears, Roebuck and Company and the ability of rural folk to travel by car to the shopping districts of nearby towns. This was followed by the growth of shopping centers and malls that provided ample free parking for shoppers from far and wide. Now it is possible to shop on the Internet without setting foot in a store or even seeing and handling the merchandise. Much of what was once special about the city is now found virtually everywhere. People far from the major metropolitan areas can obtain clothing, furniture, and other goods in the current fashion. Similarly, a wide variety of entertainment is available outside of urban theaters, facilitated through electronic media. Thus, the old distinctions between remote, isolated, rural agricultural communities and urban industrial centers are no more.

As Wirth noted more than 70 years ago, in the city people are divided by occupation and degrees of wealth. Individuals with many different ethnic origins and holding very different religious beliefs mingle on a daily basis. Urban settlements often have high population densities. In countries like the United States, where land is relatively cheap, an alternative to crowded cities is suburban sprawl. These demographic trends, combined with modern technology, have given rise to contemporary societies throughout the world that exemplify what Nels Anderson (1962) saw as the characteristics of industrial urban society.

1. A high degree of specialization in labor and mass production of goods and services has taken place. As we all know, one must be trained to perform the necessary tasks of modern life. Most of us need a college education, graduate degrees, and other training to accomplish these tasks.

2. There is almost total commitment to mechanical (as opposed to animal) power, both in work and nonwork situations. For example, when we make meals we no longer chop wood for fuel or go to the well for water. We are more likely to use an electric coffee maker than we are to boil water and pour it over coffee that we have ground by hand. Similarly, people are as likely to brush their teeth with an electric appliance as with a toothbrush.

3. Individuals are increasingly detached from traditional controls, such as gossip or the watchful eyes of relatives and neighbors. People are more and more transient. Fewer people than in the past live their lives in the same place where they and their parents were born. Their feelings of obligation and loyalty are not as firm as in past generations. People are more dependent on secondary institutions, such as corporate and government bureaucracies and the Internet.

4. High mobility in daily movements, changes of jobs and residences, and changes in social status mark contemporary life.

5. There is continuous change in the human-made elements of the environment, including structural renewal and technological innovation. We take

change for granted, whether in new fashions in clothing, cars, or restaurant food, or with regard to new technology.

6. The individual and the group are completely subordinated to mechanical time, and the increasing control by clock time over appointments and coordination of movements is apparent. "Mechanical" means that we use mechanisms, such as clocks, rather than less exact instruments like observation of the sun or the ringing of church bells. People must arrive at work, school, and many leisure activities at specified times, marked in minutes.

7. There is considerable anonymity, which is related to transiency. We need outside verification to prove who we are, whether it is a driver's license, credit card, Social Security number, PIN number, or a photo identification card.

8. Thus, there is increasing commitment to records and conformity to their use in verification of attendance, actions, contracts, and pledges. There is, in fact, a constant conflict between the desire for freedom from constant surveillance and the need to keep control over people.

Anderson's article delineating these characteristics appeared in 1962, before the invention and global distribution of the personal computer, and these characteristics have become even more marked with our growing dependence on electronic communications. With improvements in telecommunications, mass media, and the ease of transportation, fewer and fewer places in the world are isolated. More and more people from large urban areas in the United States are moving into widely scattered, less-settled areas, where they can watch the same television shows, make cell phone calls, and connect on the Internet with people all over the world.

We find that these processes, including *homogenization, urbanization,* and *globalization,* are happening even in seemingly remote wilderness areas. One such place is the Queen Charlotte Islands off the northwest coast of North America. The people who live on these islands have participated in the world economy since the nineteenth century. Their first involvement was through the fur trade. Later, they engaged in such activities as commercial fishing, logging, and mining. While they bought many of their necessities with cash, like other rural people they did not have direct daily contact with people from cities. Now, as their traditional industries decline, they look to tourism for employment. Tourism involves them even more directly with other people in the world. They are connected to their guests from the outside by computers and faxes in a way they did not know before.[1]

CONTINGENT RURAL-URBAN DIFFERENCES

Even though people in most places are not as isolated as they once were, location remains important in differentiating communities. While a distinction between agricultural/pastoral rural communities and industrial urban centers is no longer as sharp as it once was, we continue to sense differences between the rural and the urban. Such differences are *contingent*, that is, temporary or applicable to a particular setting and not universal to all places and times.

Size matters. In a small community, daily interactions may still be fairly personal. After a while you may know everyone who walks down the main street or who has breakfast in a particular café. The experiences of a former student of mine, who we'll call Michael, illustrate this. When he was 10, his family had moved from Brooklyn to a small town in Upstate New York. In this place, Michael was startled to discover that people knew who he was before he even enrolled in school. He is still uncomfortable with the fact that, in this place—only 30 miles from a city of about 90,000—his neighbors know so much about his personal life.

Like Michael, most people identify a place as rural or urban for historical and biographical reasons. People from New York City, like Michael, view a small upstate community, even one that is essentially a suburb of a medium-sized city, as if it were a peasant village, while they view themselves as urban sophisticates. As Susan Keefe (1994) noted in a study of urbanism in Appalachia, people whose families have resided in Appalachia for a long time see themselves as rural and tied to the land, while viewing others who have moved into the region as "urban outsiders," who always will be a different breed of people. In addition to loving the beauty of their land, Appalachian "natives" also remember who lived where and associate these places with particular family members and neighbors. Even though the region was only 52 percent rural in 1980, when Keefe began her study, large numbers of both natives and recent residents were still engaged in agricultural pursuits. Natives, however, try to keep a small plot of land to use for gardening whether they live in rural or urban areas. The attachment to the land on the part of outsiders, especially middle and upper income part-time residents, is more abstract. They see the place as one of beauty to be preserved. The differences between the two sometimes lead to paradoxes. For instance, the "natives," who tend to be working class, support the building of super-highways through this "rural landscape," because roads lead them to jobs and speed the delivery of supplies from the outside. The "newcomers" are more likely to oppose such roads, which they see as spoiling the "pristine landscape" of their new homes (Keefe, 1994). With their "rural state of mind" the natives do not want to live in an artificial theme park; rather, they want involvement in the national economy.

People in Appalachia and other parts of the United States may link their identity to symbols of their image of the rural way of life. This includes such elements as a particular way of speaking, defending one's honor, gun ownership and hunting, and adherence to certain religious traditions and churches, such as the Southern Baptist church and Pentecostalism. Dennis Covington, a journalist, wrote a book (1996) about a sect that sought to verify individual salvation through the handling of rattlesnakes. This religious tradition has generally been identified with Appalachia. To urban elites who live outside the region, this is a sign of Appalachia's "primitive" and exotic nature. Covington, whose family originated in the region, felt that he was able to identify with the "snake handlers" because he shared their rural roots. Increasingly, Southern rurality is not an agricultural way of life, but an ethnic heritage based on shared memories.

THE PASSING OF THE OLD "URBANISM"

Many places in the United States today are not urban in the sense that there is a distinct city as opposed to the countryside. This is in contrast to the model of the *preindustrial city* (Sjoberg 1960), which was characteristically a walled settlement containing the main institutions of government, religion, crafts production, and trade. It was a large, dense, diverse settlement surrounded by small villages or homesteads. Its most notable structures were churches or other large houses of worship, palaces, courts of law, and the market. Today we can still see evidence of such preindustrial cities in places like York in central England, Carcassonne in southern France, or Timbuktu in Mali.

By the nineteenth-century city walls had lost their original power, as factories grew on the city outskirts and avenues of stores replaced the traditional market area. Still, the city was sharply marked from the countryside. By then, however, new residential areas began to surround the city. In some countries these were for the workers, whereas elsewhere these were designed for the affluent middle class and for the wealthy. Nevertheless, one could still perceive a difference between urban and rural. While city life was seen by many as marked by impersonality and lawlessness, most people who lived in the city did have families, networks of friends, and a communal life. While they did encounter many strangers on a daily basis, they also knew their way around the city and maintained wide contacts with people whom they knew. In any case, the boundary between the city and the countryside was clearly demarcated by both official boundaries and the decrease in population density.

This is no longer the case in the United States, even though population density does decrease the farther one is from the central city. As one gets farther from the New York City metropolitan area and closer to Upstate New York, housing becomes more and more dispersed and densities are much lower. Yet, even in such "ex-urban" areas, most people are no longer employed in agriculture. Rather, most locally employed people work in the service sector. Other residents commute to New York City and, increasingly, people are able to work as employees or as providers of services for corporations and yet never go to the office. Computers, fax machines, and cell phones have facilitated learning and working at a distance. Retirement communities, resorts, and second homes for people who live in metropolitan areas are found in many of these ex-urban places, which are served by local businesses. Such ex-urban areas are only "rural" by comparison with cities and suburbs, but do not resemble rural peasant villages of the past.

Meanwhile, the old central cities are also changing the services they provide. In the 1930s and 1940s, when Wirth was writing, central cities were truly the centers of activity. The "downtown" area of a city, even a small city, was crowded with people all day and well into the evening. The main department stores where people bought clothing, furniture, and hardware were located there. The offices of lawyers and doctors were also downtown. People came into these areas by trolley, bus, or car. Train stations were the major hubs for transportation, and were always busy. Large cities like New York, Chicago, or Boston had more than one train station, and cabs took people from one station to the other—as they still do in London and Paris.

I grew up in the Lakeview area of Chicago, a neighborhood now called "Wrigleyville." While my parents bought food at grocery stores, butcher shops, and supermarkets in our neighborhood, for clothing and major items we shopped elsewhere, either in other neighborhoods about a mile away or downtown, which was six miles away. We usually went to downtown Chicago via trolley, bus, or elevated train. Going downtown was a major outing, which we did once a month or so, and involved much planning. My mother would look for clothing for my sister and me (and so we were dragged along). As a special treat we would eat in a downtown restaurant and maybe take in a first-run movie in a downtown theater. At that time, the first run of a film could be found only in a downtown theater. After a few weeks, the movie would then be shown in the neighborhood theaters at lower prices, as part of a double feature.

Such active downtown business districts continued into the 1960s. By the mid-1970s, the downtowns of many American cities had become deserted at night and the streets were not crowded during the day either. Businesses of all types were abandoning central cities throughout America. For instance, in Chicago much of the shopping that used to be done in what was called "the Loop" on State Street moved to North Michigan Avenue, which became known as the "Magnificent Mile." But more significant were the new suburban shopping malls, which offered a wide range of products in one convenient location. Moreover, the specialty stores that marked the old downtown are no more. Most of the retailers found in the central cities are branches of large chains that also have stores in the suburbs. Today what most distinguishes central-city shopping districts is that one must pay a premium price for one of the scarce parking spaces.

Yet, central cities continue to have attractions. Lawyers, for example, often prefer to be downtown, in part because of the proximity of law courts, but also to be near other lawyers. Large firms of architects, accountants, and other professionals can also be found downtown. In some cases, older buildings in some downtown areas have been converted to new purposes in order to draw people back into the city. The old stock market (Bourse) in Philadelphia and the Quincy Market in Boston, for example, have been transformed into shopping malls. Some seaports and railroad stations have attracted aquariums and have become tourist attractions. In many ways, these places are more attractive now than they were half a century ago when central cities flourished.

Just as rurality has become entwined in memory and personal identity, so has urbanism. My student Michael's memory of Brooklyn exemplifies this. He is not alone. Many people, especially natives of New York or Chicago now living elsewhere in a suburb or a smaller city, wax nostalgic about their former lives in the "big city." They contrast the sterile landscape of their present residences with the city's variety and excitement. They recall that, even if you had no other plans on a weekend, you could always go to a museum or wander downtown. Older urban neighborhoods that have been generally derided as rundown slums or ghettos are now sometimes remembered as "urban villages" where people knew what was going on during the day on their street. The autonomy of city kids playing stickball, ledgeball,[2] or touch football on the sidewalk or the streets stands in sharp contrast with Little League baseball parks, soccer fields, or hockey rinks so prevalent in the suburbs.

CROSS-NATIONAL NOTES

Most of this discussion of the transcendence of the old urban-rural distinction has been grounded in examples from the United States. While the blurring of rural-urban differences is occurring throughout the world, communities are drawn into what we might call the "global web of relationships" in diverse ways. One example is China, where the pace of urbanization and industrialization picked up speed in the 1970s and has continued unabated. Millions of rural people have moved into urban centers throughout the country, although the government has tried to prevent many of them from permanently settling in the cities. Many former Chinese peasants work in the cities, despite their illegal status and their inability to get good housing and education for their children. Occupations in historically agricultural villages have changed rapidly, as fewer people engage in farming and more have found jobs in nonagricultural, export-oriented industries. The inhabitants of these peasant communities and the Chinese government continue to distinguish these communities as "cities," "towns," or "villages." Yet, the ways of life found in such various localities are becoming more and more alike (Guldin 1996). Although the process of industrial urbanization in China got underway later than in North America, it too has resulted in that country's transformation far beyond the old distinctions of "urban" and "rural."

Notes

[1] This situation was described by Matthew Rogers, an ethnographer doing research in the Queen Charlotte Islands of British Columbia. The radical changes that have occurred in communications during the past 40 years are also described by Edward Bruner (1999).

[2] Stickball, the variant on baseball played in the streets of New York City, is better known than its Chicago counterpart, ledgeball. Ledgeball was played by throwing a tennis ball or rubber ball at a ledge or step. Sometimes it was played like baseball with running to bases, but there was no pitcher or catcher, only fielders. Sometimes, the zones were considered to be the equivalents of bases. Two or more players could play at a time.

Acknowledgments

I want to thank George Gmelch, Jessica Henry, and Hannah Gaw for their comments on an earlier draft of this chapter.

References

Anderson, Nels. 1962. The Urban Way of Life. *International Journal of Comparative Sociology*, 3:175–188.

Bruner, Edward M. 1999. Return to Sumatra: 1957, 1999. *American Ethnologist*, 26:461–477.

Covington, Dennis. 1996. *Salvation on Sand Mountain: Snake Handling and Redemption in the Southern Appalachians.* New York: Viking.

Guldin, Gregory Eliyu. 1996. *Desakotas* and Beyond: Urbanization in Southern China. *Ethnology*, 35:265–283.

Keefe, Susan Emley. 1994. Urbanism Reconsidered: A Southern Appalachian Perspective. *City & Society, Annual Review*, ed. Constance P. deRoche, pp. 20–34. Washington, DC: American Anthropological Association.

Sjoberg, Gideon. 1960. *The Preindustrial City.* Glencoe, IL: The Free Press.

About the Authors

Julie Adkins is a PhD candidate in cultural anthropology at Southern Methodist University, where she has served as adjunct faculty in the Department of Anthropology and the Perkins School of Theology. Her dissertation research focused on homelessness in the city of Dallas, and, in particular, the city's response. She co-edited *Bridging the Gaps: Faith-Based Organizations, Neoliberalism, and Development in Latin America and the Caribbean* (2009) and *Not by Faith Alone: Social Services, Social Justice, and Faith-Based Organizations in the United States* (2010). Her research interests include the U.S. and Latin America, poverty and homelessness, faith-based organizations, and tourism.

Danièle Bélanger is the Canada Research Chair in Population, Gender and Development, and Associate Professor at the University of Western Ontario, London, Canada. Her current research is on migration within Asia, particularly temporary labor migration and marriage-based migration from Southeast Asia to East Asia. Her previous research focused on family and gender issues in Vietnam. She is co-editor of the recently published volume *Reconfiguring Families in Contemporary Vietnam* (2009).

Theodore C. Bestor is Professor of Social Anthropology and Japanese Studies and Chair of the Department of Anthropology at Harvard University. He has written extensively on life and culture in Tokyo. His most recent book, *Tsukiji: The Fish Market at the Center of the World* (2004), an ethnography of the world's largest wholesale market for fresh and frozen seafood, followed his earlier works on Japan: *Doing Fieldwork in Japan* (2003), and *Neighborhood Tokyo* (1989). Bestor's next book, tentatively titled *Global Sushi*, will examine the global fishing industry, the popular culture of sushi, and the environmental crisis of overfishing. He has served as President of the Society for East Asian Anthropology and the Society for Urban Anthropology.

Philippe Bourgois is the Richard Perry University Professor of Anthropology and Family and Community Medicine at the University of Pennsylvania.

He is the author of numerous publications, including the C. Wright Mills and Margaret Mead award-winning *In Search of Respect: Selling Crack in El Barrio* (1995). His studies of ethnic relations in Central America led to a book entitled *Ethnicity at Work: Divided Labor on a Central American Banana Plantation* (1989) and his concern with global violence resulted in *Violence in War and Peace* (2002). In 2009 he co-authored *Righteous Dopefiend*, a photo-ethnography that documents a community of homeless heroin injectors and crack smokers in San Francisco.

Caroline B. Brettell is Dedman Family Distinguished Professor in the Department of Anthropology and University Distinguished Professor at Southern Methodist University. She has written extensively on problems of international migration, and on Portuguese emigration in particular. Her most recent books include the co-edited volumes *Citizenship, Immigration and Belonging: Immigrants in Europe and the United States* (2008) and *Twenty-first Century Gateways: Immigrant Incorporation in Suburban America* (2008). She has served as President of the Society for the Anthropology of Europe and the Society for Comparative Study of Society and History.

Melissa L. Caldwell is Associate Professor of Anthropology at the University of California, Santa Cruz. Her book *Not by Bread Alone: Social Support in the New Russia* (2004) explores the social networks mobilized by the elderly Russians who attend a soup kitchen program in Moscow and the African and North American volunteers who serve them food. Her forthcoming book, *Living Organically on Russia's Dacha Frontier*, documents Russians' love of their summer cottages and gardens and how recent changes in cottage and garden reflect broader sociopolitical changes in Russia. She is also co-editor of *The Cultural Politics of Food and Eating* (2005) and editor of *Food and Everyday Life in the Postsocialist World* (2009).

Martin Cooke is Assistant Professor in the Departments of Sociology and Health Studies and Gerontology at the University of Waterloo. His research interests are in social policy and the life course and the social demography of Aboriginal populations. Recent research projects examine the labor market experiences of older workers and the dynamics of social assistance receipt. He is also the principal investigator of a study of the health and social conditions of Aboriginal Peoples across the life course funded by the Social Sciences and Humanities Research Council of Canada.

Nancy Foner is Distinguished Professor of Sociology at Hunter College and the Graduate Center of the City University of New York. She is the author or editor of more than a dozen books, including *From Ellis Island to JFK: New York's Two Great Waves of Immigration* (2000) and *In a New Land: A Comparative View of Immigration* (2005). Her latest book, *Across Generations: Immigrant Families in America* (2009), is a collection of ethnographic essays focusing on intergenerational relations. She has chaired the International Migration Section of the American Sociological Association and has served as President of the

Society for the Anthropology of Work and the Society for Urban, National, and Transnational/Global Anthropology.

George M. Foster (1913–2006) carried out field research in Mexico, Spain, Latin America, and South Asia during a career spanning more than six decades. He authored and edited more than 20 well-known books, including *Anthropologists in Cities* (1974), *Applied Anthropology* (1969), *Empire's Children: The People of Tzintzuntzan* (1948), *Long-Term Field Research in Social Anthropology* (1979), *Medical Anthropology* (1978), and *Tzintzuntzan: Mexican Peasants in a Changing World* (1967). Foster served as President of the American Anthropological Association, was elected to the National Academy of Sciences, and received the Bronislaw Malinowski Award from the Society for Applied Anthropology.

Nell Gabiam received her PhD in Anthropology in 2008 from the University of California, Berkeley. Her dissertation research centered on the relationship between identity, development, and human rights within the context of a UNRWA (United Nations Relief and Works Agency for Palestine Refugees in the Near East) sponsored development project in two Palestinian refugee camps in northern Syria. In 2009–2010, she held a postdoctoral fellowship at the Center for the Study of Race, Culture and Politics at the University of Chicago. Her future research will focus on sub-Saharan-African migration to the Middle East.

George Gmelch is Professor of Anthropology at the University of San Francisco and Roger Thayer Stone Professor of Anthropology at Union College. He has studied Irish and English Travellers; return migrants in Ireland, Newfoundland and Barbados; commercial fishermen; Alaska natives; Caribbean villagers and tourism workers; and American professional baseball players. He is the author of 10 books, many scholarly articles, and has written widely for general audiences, including the *New York Times,* the *Washington Post, Psychology Today, Society,* and *Natural History.* He is currently doing research on tourism in California's Napa Valley.

Sharon Bohn Gmelch is Professor of Anthropology at the University of San Francisco and at Union College in upstate New York. She has published seven books, including *Tinkers and Travellers,* which won Ireland's Book of the Year Award in 1976; *Nan: The Life of an Irish Travelling Woman* (1986/1991), a finalist for the Margaret Mead Award; *The Tlingit Encounter with Photography* (2008); and, an edited volume on *Tourists and Tourism* (2004; second edition, 2010). Her interests include visual anthropology, gender, ethnicity, and tourism.

Judith Goode is Professor of Anthropology at Temple University. She has done urban ethnographic research in Medellín and Bogotá, Colombia, and in Philadelphia. Her projects focus on work and class as well as immigration, ethnic group formation, and intergroup relations. She is co-editor of *The New Poverty Studies: The Ethnography of Power, Politics, and Impoverished People in the United States* (2002). She is a former President of the Society for Urban Anthropology.

William Jankowiak is Professor of Anthropology at the University of Nevada, Las Vegas. His research and teaching interests include ethnographic studies of contemporary Chinese society, especially Mongolian culture, as well as human universals such as love and family bonds. His publications include *Sex, Death and Hierarchy in a Chinese City* (1993), *Urban Mongols: Ethnicity in Communist China* (1994), *Romantic Passion: The Universal Experience?* (1995), *Drugs, Trade and Colonial Expansion* (2003), and *Intimacies: Sex and Love Across Cultures* (2008).

Robert V. Kemper is Professor of Anthropology at Southern Methodist University. His research interests include migration and urbanization, community development, tourism, Mexico, and the United States. His numerous publications include *Anthropologists in Cities* (1974), *Migration and Adaptation: Tzintzuntzan Peasants in Mexico City* (1977), *Migration Across Frontiers: Mexico and the United States* (1979), and *Chronicling Cultures: Long-Term Field Research in Anthropology* (2002). He has served as President of the Society for Latin American Anthropology and the Society for Urban Anthropology, as well as editor of *Human Organization*, Editor for Social-Cultural Anthropology of the *American Anthropologist*, and Associate Editor for *Urban Anthropology*.

William Leggett is Assistant Professor of Anthropology at Middle Tennessee State University. He has published in the journals *Identities* and the *Anthropology of Work Review*, as well as in the edited volumes *Ethnic Landscapes in an Urban World* (2007) and *Ruminations on Violence* (2007). His fieldwork focuses on transnational corporations throughout Southeast Asia, with special attention to the negotiation of identity and the role of the social imagination within spaces of transnational encounter. Currently he is conducting research with new immigrant populations in the American South.

Karen Isaksen Leonard is a historian and anthropologist at the University of California, Irvine. She has done research on the social history and anthropology of India and on Punjabi Mexican Americans, South Asian Americans, and Muslim Americans. She recently published a book on the construction of identity in the diaspora by emigrants entitled *Locating Home: India's Hyderabadis Abroad* (2007/2008). Her book, *Muslims in the United States: The State of Research* (2003), is an extended bibliographic essay relating Muslim Americans to the changing religious, social, and political landscape in America. Leonard's other books include: *Social History of an Indian Caste: The Kayasths of Hyderabad* (1978), *Making Ethnic Choices: California's Punjabi Mexican Americans* (1992), and *South Asian Americans* (1997).

Oscar Lewis (1914–1970) did research in Canada among the Blackfoot Indians and in India. He is best known for his in-depth study of the Mexican village of Tepoztlán and for his use of life histories in studying the poor in Mexico, the United States, and Cuba. He worked for the U.S. Department of Agriculture as a social scientist and was a key figure in starting the Department of Anthropology at the University of Illinois, where he taught from

1948 until his death. The last 20 years of his life were focused on urban studies. Oscar Lewis published many successful books, the most controversial being those in which he presented his "culture of poverty" concept, especially *Five Families: Mexican Case Studies in the Culture of Poverty* (1959) and *La Vida: A Puerto Rican Family in the Culture of Poverty—San Juan and New York* (1966).

Setha Low is Professor of Environmental Psychology, Geography, Anthropology, and Women's Studies, and Director of the Public Space Research Group at The Graduate Center, City University of New York. Her current research is on the impact of private governance on New York City co-op residents. Her most recent books include: *Politics of Public Space, Rethinking Urban Parks: Public Space and Cultural Diversity* (2005), *Behind the Gates: Life, Security and the Pursuit of Happiness in Fortress America* (2004), *The Anthropology of Space and Place: Locating Culture* (2003), *On the Plaza: The Politics of Public Space and Culture* (2000), and *Theorizing the City: The New Urban Anthropology Reader* (1999). She has served as President of the Society for Urban Anthropology and the American Anthropological Association.

Sally Engle Merry is Professor of Anthropology and Director of the Law and Society Program at New York University. Her work explores the role of law in urban life in the United States, in the colonizing process, and in contemporary transnationalism. She is currently doing a comparative, transnational study of human rights and gender. Her recent books are *Colonizing Hawai'i: The Cultural Power of Law* (2000), which received the 2001 J. Willard Hurst Prize from the Law and Society Association, *Human Rights and Gender Violence: Translating International Law into Local Justice* (2006), *The Practice of Human Rights: Tracking Law between the Local and the Global* (2007), and *Gender Violence: A Cultural Perspective* (2008). She is a former President of the Law and Society Association and the Association for Political and Legal Anthropology. In 2007 she received the Kalven Prize of the Law and Society Association, awarded to recognize a significant body of scholarship in the field.

Ann Miles is Professor of Anthropology and Gender and Women's Studies at Western Michigan University in Kalamazoo, Michigan. Her research in southern Ecuador over the past 20 years has focused on migration, families, and social change, as well as the commodification of medicine and healing. She is the author of *From Cuenca to Queens: An Anthropological Story of Transnational Migration* (2004) and co-editor of *Women and Economic Change: Andean Perspectives* (1997). In 1998, her article in *Medical Anthropology Quarterly* entitled "Science, Nature and Tradition: The Mass-Marketing of Natural Medicines in Ecuador" won the Steven J. Polgar Prize given by the Society for Medical Anthropology.

Derek Pardue is Assistant Professor in the Department of Anthropology and International and Area Studies at Washington University in St. Louis, where he researches hip-hop, popular culture, cities, and violence in Latin America and Portuguese-speaking nations of the world. He is the author of *Ideologies of Marginality in Brazilian Hip Hop* (2008) and editor of *Ruminations on Violence* (2007).

Dianna J. Shandy is Associate Professor and Chair of the Department of Anthropology at Macalester College in Saint Paul, Minnesota. She teaches a broad spectrum of courses on anthropology, Africa, refugees, human rights and humanitarian response, and transnational migration. She is the author/coauthor of three books: *Nuer-American Passages: Globalizing Sudanese Migration* (2007), *The Cultural Experience: Ethnography in Complex Society* (2nd ed., 2005), and *Glass Ceilings and 100-Hour Couples: What the Opt-Out Phenomenon Can Teach Us About Work and Family* (2010).

Takeyuki (Gaku) Tsuda is Associate Professor of Anthropology in the School of Human Evolution and Social Change at Arizona State University. His primary academic interests include international migration, diasporas, ethnic minorities, ethnic and national identity, transnationalism and globalization, the Americas, and contemporary Japan. His numerous publications include *Strangers in the Ethnic Homeland: Japanese Brazilian Return Migration in Transnational Perspective* (2003), *Controlling Immigration: A Global Perspective* (2nd ed., 2004), *Local Citizenship in Recent Countries of Immigration: Japan in Comparative Perspective* (2006), *Ethnic Identity: Problems and Prospects for the Twenty-first Century* (2006), and *Diasporic Homecomings: Ethnic Return Migration in Comparative Perspective* (2009).

Jay Sokolovsky is Professor and Chair of the Department of Anthropology, Interdisciplinary Social Sciences and Criminology at the University of South Florida, St. Petersburg. His specialties include urban anthropology, anthropology of aging, rural development in Mexico, and video documentation. The third edition of Dr. Sokolovsky's award-winning book, *The Cultural Context of Aging*, was published in 2009. His research has been done in a Mexican peasant village; New York's inner city; Tampa, Florida; the new town of Columbia, Maryland; and in urban neighborhoods in Croatia and England. His latest ethnographic video, *Urban Garden: Fighting for Life and Beauty*, documents the community garden movement in New York City.

James Diego Vigil is Professor in the Department of Criminology, Law and Society, University of California, Irvine. His specializations are urban research, poverty, culture change, socialization and education, and Mexico and U.S. Southwest ethnohistory. His books include *From Indians to Chicanos: The Dynamics of Mexican American Culture* (1980; 2nd ed., 1998), *Personas Mexicanas: Chicano High Schoolers in a Changing Los Angeles* (1997), *Barrio Gangs: Street Life and Identity in Southern California* (1988), *A Rainbow of Gangs: A Cross-Cultural Study of Street Youth in Los Angeles* (2002), and *Gang Redux: A Balanced Anti-Gang Strategy* (2010). He has served as President of the Association of Latina/Latino Anthropologists.

Louis Wirth (1897–1952) was born in Germany. Until his death he was Professor of Sociology at the University of Chicago and a leading figure in the so-called "Chicago School" of urban-ecological sociology. He was interested in social theory, the social ecology of human communities, the sociology of knowledge, and the application of sociology to public policy. In addition to his work on urbanism, he focused attention on the role of thought and ideology in social life and on minority problems. His book *The Ghetto* (1928), a study of the Jewish immigrant community in Chicago, is considered a classic contribution to understanding American urban life. His major ideas are presented in *Louis Wirth on Cities and Social Life* (1964).

Jeffrey Witsoe is currently Visiting Assistant Professor of Anthropology at Union College. He previously held the positions of Visiting Scholar and Senior Research Coordinator at the Center for the Advanced Study of India at the University of Pennsylvania. He holds a PhD from Cambridge University and an MA from the University of Chicago. He is currently engaged in a project studying the relationship between migration, caste empowerment, and the rural economy in India. In the future, he is planning a research project in Iran that will examine the differential impacts of the Islamic Revolution on local life within different communities.

Walter P. Zenner (1933–2003) was born in Germany. He spent the majority of his professional life in the Department of Anthropology at the State University of New York at Albany, where he taught from 1966 until his retirement in 2002. He was the author of *Minorities in the Middle: A Cross-Cultural Analysis* (1991), *Persistence and Flexibility: Anthropological Perspectives on the American Jewish Experience* (1988), and *A Global Community: The Jews from Aleppo, Syria* (1999). He served as President of the Society for Urban Anthropology.